WISCONSIN'S BEST
BEER GUIDE

A Travel Companion
FOURTH EDITION

by Kevin Revolinski

Fountaindale Public Library
Bolingbrook, IL
(630) 759-2102

THUNDER BAY
PRESS

West Branch, Michigan

Wisconsin's Best Beer Guide, 4th edition
by Kevin Revolinski

Thunder Bay Press
West Branch, Michigan 48661
www.thunderbaypressmichigan.com

First edition June 2010
Second edition November 2012
Third edition September 2015
Fourth edition August 2018

19   18   17   16   15   1   2   3   4   5

ISBN: 978-1-933272-65-8

Photographs by Preamtip Satasuk except where credited.
Cover photography by Kevin Revolinski.
Original book and cover design by Julie Taylor.
Fourth Edition cover design by Greg Kretovic of 7NineDesign.

Printed in the United States of America

Note: Prices, special offers, hours, availability, etc. listed in this guide are subject to change.

For Grandpa Louie

He told me this joke once and I said I'd put it in the next edition of this book...

Two guys sitting at the bar. One guy sips his beer and makes a face. "I think there's something in my beer." His buddy tells him, "Well, why don't you send it to a lab to be tested." So he does. About a week later he gets a letter. "What's it say?" asks his friend. "Says here I should rest that horse for two weeks and it should be fine."

TABLE OF CONTENTS

Table of Contents

Table of Contents

PREFACE

In 2006 I wrote my first version of this book finding a brewing scene that included just over 60 breweries. By the first edition of the newly titled *Wisconsin's Best Beer Guide* in 2010, there were over 70. For the second edition we rolled up over 90, and over 130 for the third. This time around we have just shy of 200 brewing places to visit, and just over a dozen came out of that last edition. The numbers of craft beer bars, growler fills/liquor stores, and restaurants with a couple dozen craft beers on draft have increased as well, making the "Stumbling Distance" suggestions for each brewery richer and more difficult to choose.

The Wisconsin reputation for beer is well known. In September 2011 when the *Today Show* came to Green Bay to broadcast live from Lambeau Field on the opening day of NFL football, I was invited on to line up a few samples for Al Roker at 8 AM. Beer for breakfast? Sure, why not? And a bit of cheese and bratwurst on the side that day.

More and more people aren't interested in just drinking any old thing. There is an increased expectation of quality and a call to support your local businesses. More and more, the average beer drinker is taking a good long look at the local beers. Craft beer perhaps still intimidates some drinkers who aren't accustomed to a few of the bolder styles or who have gotten used to the "lawnmower" beers of summer. There is no question that people's palates are getting more sophisticated. Just note the most popular beers listed for each of the breweries. Back in 2006 it was strictly the pilsners or whatever had "Light" tacked on at the end of the beer name. That's not the case anymore, and even as we've perhaps gotten over the hops-heavy trend of IPAs, many establishments have found their Scotch ales, stouts, and Belgian-style brews taking the lead. Barrel-aging has become expected for at least special occasion releases, and sours are getting a surprising amount of attention.

Yes, a few breweries went under or changed hands since the last edition, but Wisconsin still has a net gain of over 70, and there are more to come. Here's a tip of the hat to the ones who closed their doors or changed their sign.

Brady's Brewhouse
Brenner Brewing Co.
Chatterhouse Brewery
Common Man Brewing
Fixture Brewing Co.
Granite City Brewery
Gray's Tied House
Horny Goat Hideaway
Mines Creek Brewery
RockPere Brewing

Silver Creek Brewing Co.
Sweet Mullets Brewery
Woodman Brewery
Came and went between editions:
Benjamin Beer Company
Bent Kettle
Leatherheads

I put a few breweries in this edition that weren't quite open when we went to print but would be a month or three after that. I wanted to make sure this book would be up-to-date for as long as possible after its release. Just be sure to phone first or check a website if you're making a long pils-grimage. This is a static guidebook (until the next edition) and changes can happen overnight.

Drive safely and don't drive at all when you've had too much. The mission here is to have fun exploring while trying new brews and revisiting favorites. Go enjoy the great brews Wisconsin has to offer and stop at a few other cool places along the way. Lift a pint and let the pils-grimage begin!

DRINK WISCONSINBLY

Wisconsin: It's not just a state, it's a lifestyle—a mindset—and it's a drinking style. Richard Lorbach of Waukesha came up with this perfect expression, and he's been selling t-shirts ever since. Sure, it starts with a t-shirt, but pretty soon you know you want to collect the pint glass, shot glass, mug, flask, can cooler, bottle openers, magnets, and then for the advanced level of Wisconsin love, perhaps the Drink Wisconsinbly neon sign. Tailgate Wisconsinbly and Fish Wisconsinbly are also options as is a pink breast cancer-themed Fight Wisconsinbly shirt. So get out there and show everyone how you drink. And if all this wasn't enough, you can now have Wisco beer, food and cocktails at the award-winning Drink Wisconsinbly Pub (135 East National Ave, Milwaukee, 414-930-0929, drinkwi.pub)

INTRODUCTION

We live in "God's Country" with water from when the earth was pure, when glaciers melted and left artesian wells that would create the foundation of a land of lagers, an empire of ales, where Schlitz made Milwaukee famous, Pabst got blue ribbons, and Miller called its beer "champagne" and put its name on that time when we just needed a good brewsky. (It's Miller time!) Even our baseball team is the Brewers. This is a Beer State where *kraeusening* is tantamount to breathing and a brewed beverage is something akin to a fine French wine or Scotch whiskey. We are only considered Cheeseheads because Beerheads seemed inappropriate for prime-time television—what with the kids watching and all—and frankly the cheese wedge was simply easier to balance than a beer mug when they designed the hats—not to mention spillage.

At one time before the Dark Ages of 1919 to 1933 (Prohibition), Wisconsin had a brewer at practically every crossroads with farmers doing their own little operations and bigger bottle works setting up in town. You couldn't swing a cat without hitting one. When consumption of our veritable holy water became a mortal and legal sin, many were the breweries that went beer belly up. The larger ones survived, a few got by on root beer and soda (Pabst survived with cheese), and for this we can lift a pint. Miller, Pabst, Schlitz, G. Heileman, Blatz—the list of Hall of Famers is long in Wisconsin, but we live in a new golden age. Since the late 1980s, we have witnessed a rise in the number of local breweries. Places that love beer for beer's sake. Places that aren't necessarily looking to send a keg to a tavern in Hoboken, New Jersey, or a million cases to a liquor store in L.A. Point Beer always claimed, "When you're out of Point, you're out of town." Nowadays, they might be getting a little more distance on shipping, but they have a good… er… point: many of Wisconsin's beers are personal, and unless you take your glass outside the screen door behind the bar, you won't find some of these brews beyond a good dart toss from the tap handle. Many of us Wisconsinites are fortunate to have someone looking out for us with a handcrafted lager or ale. Who in this state should not have their own personal hometown beer? (My condolences to those who don't, but don't worry—this book can help you adopt.) Designate a driver (or pack your sleeping bag in the trunk), turn the page, and set off on a *pils*-grimage to the breweries of Wisconsin.

BUT I DON'T LIKE BEER

You'll hear it time and time again when you ask a brewer—pro or homebrewer—why they got into brewing. Many of them will tell you they were dissatisfied with what was on the market back before the advent of the modern craft beer revolution. Maybe they took a trip to Germany. Maybe they were inspired by another homebrewer. But in the end, regardless of that original motivation, it becomes a passion for quality beer. I have to admit it took me a long time to come to beer. If you had offered me a beer in college, I would likely have gone the choosy beggar path and asked if you had any vodka or rum instead. I really didn't even like beer. I can already hear the collective gasp of horror, but let me explain: beer was social lubricant, something you sipped at with friends at a cookout, bought for the cute woman at the other end of the bar, or beer-bonged on occasion. I didn't like the taste so much and—oh the humanity—often didn't even finish them. I killed many a houseplant at parties and have gotten hordes of bees drunk at picnics with the remains of a bottle of Something-or-Other Light.

But consider this: what better person to send around on a beer discovery journey than the person who knew absolutely nothing? I'd be learning from scratch and whatever I found would be useful for a beginning beer drinker or at least commiserating confirmation for the connoisseur. And since Wisconsin is my home state, there was more than a little pride involved as well, like I might be introducing my family to friends or fellow travelers.

It wasn't until craft beer that I became a Born Again Beer Drinker. Beer experts already know, and commercial beer drinkers might be leery of the fact, that outside of the mass-produced impersonal brews, beers are as different as people. They have tremendous character, and the people who dedicate their lives to brewing are characters as well. Traveling to visit a brewery—what I like to call a *pils*-grimage—is as much about appreciating the subtleties and variations of beer as it is about taking a peek into local communities and beer's place in them. Part of what makes Wisconsin great, and what makes brewing great, is that even the little guy can get in on the action. All respects to the giants of the mass-market beer industry, but how cool is it to walk into a local place and see the brewmaster standing at the bar sharing suds with the guy next door?

This book is a compilation of all the places that brew their own beer commercially in Wisconsin. That means from the megabrewer MillerCoors all the way down to the little nanobrewery Amery Ale Works in Amery. The list changed often as pubs closed and others pounced on the used equipment and opened up elsewhere. Since the first book *The Wisconsin Beer Guide: A Travel Companion* in 2007, through these three editions of *Wisconsin's Best Beer Guide*, the numbers have been growing faster and faster, and those falling to the wayside are fewer and fewer. We are now about to tip 200.

Using the very latest cutting edge state-of-the-art rocket-science-level technology, I established the locations of all of the breweries in the state. OK, actually it was a Sharpie and a free Wisconsin highway map paid for with tax dollars and available at www.travelwisconsin.com or 800-432-8747. I sat down with the list and divided the state into six zones. Each of those zones is listed in the Where's the Beer At? section and shows the brewtowns alphabetically. If you already know the name of the brewery you are seeking, look for it in the cross referenced lists at the beginning of Where's the Beer At? The center brewery of each zone is generally no more than an hour's drive from any of the surrounding breweries in that same zone. Make sense? Worked for me!

And do I still hate beer? Not on your life! Just characterless beer maybe. I am a convert. I gained about ten pounds from my research the first time around and chose to write *60 Hikes Madison* right after that to wear it off. You may notice *Best Easy Day Hikes Milwaukee* appeared on the market at the same time

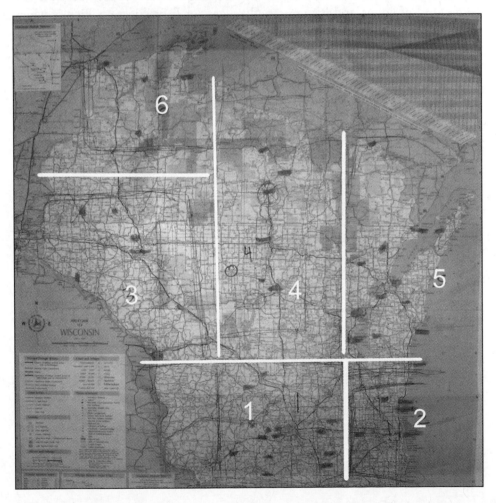

the second book was released. And this one? Well, let's just say I need to write another hiking book. I call it the guidebook-writing weight-control program. Results may vary.

WHAT IS BEER?

Beer is produced by fermenting some sort of starch product. In many cases this is barley, wheat, oats, or rye, but even corn, rice, potatoes, and certain starchy roots in Africa have been used. In parts of Latin America, corn is chewed, spit out, and left to ferment and become a sort of corn beer called *chicha*. I've tried it... *before* my traveling companion told me about the chewing process. We are no longer on speaking terms. Don't expect MillerCoors to be rolling it out in mass quantities very soon. And since you don't hear anyone advertising "brewed from the finest Senegalese cassava roots" you can guess barley is still the primary grain of choice. (If you've tasted some of those commercial non-Wisconsin beers though, you've gotta wonder.) There's no distilling for beer—that would make it some kind of liquor, and it's not strictly sugars or fruit juices—which is where your wine comes from.

The History of Beer

MANNA FROM HEAVEN

Yes, beer is pure brewed right here in "God's country" (Wisconsin, or so claimed G. Heileman's Old Style Beer), but it wasn't always so. Egyptians loved it long before; Sumerians wrote down recipes for it on stone tablets, and you can imagine the drunken bar brawls over at the Viking lodge. Beer dates way back beyond 5000 BC, which is before *writing* even. (I think Ernest Hemingway, F. Scott Fitzgerald, and many other writers have also put the one before the other.)

The word itself comes to us by way of Middle English *ber*, from Old English *bEor* which goes to show you just how difficult life must have been without spellchecker. The English version surely comes from *bior* which was Old High German which became Old Low German by the end of a serious night of drinking.

BEER IN WISCONSIN

In 1998, I traveled to Czech Republic to see a bit of the land my forefathers left behind for the sake of Wisconsin. I landed in Frankfurt, Germany, (cheaper flight!) and with a rental car drove to Prague. Remember the movie *Stripes* with Bill Murray? His character said this about getting into Czechoslovakia: "It's like going into Wisconsin—you drive in, you drive out." Well, it is. In fact, as I bundled up in a jacket and faced an unseasonably cold June in Plzen, this is pretty much what struck me. My great-grandparents had packed up all they had into small trunks or had a big garage sale perhaps, left behind everyone they knew on this earth—friends, family, perhaps a few creditors—spent much of their remaining money on ocean liner tickets, braved the long and sometimes dangerous Atlantic crossing, had their names misspelled at Ellis Island* and went overland halfway across a continent to settle in the same damn place they left behind. Seriously. Change the highway signs to English and set up some road construction detours and I may as well have been driving down County Trunk C outside of Stevens Point. But these immigrants' absurd notions of improving their lots worked to our benefit: conditions were perfect here for making the same great German, Belgian, Czech, etc. beers of Northern Europe—and so they did.

---

* 'Hey Bucko?'—one of the family surnames had an unfortunate pronunciation with the English spelling so we had to add the 'h' after the 'c' (Buchko) to get everyone to pronounce it right, otherwise anyone addressing us felt they were potentially getting a little surly. Fuggetabout 'Lajcak,' many of us just let people say it as they will.

The brewing equation in Wisconsin goes like this:
Immigrants
+
cold (frozen tundra)
+
water (unfrozen tundra)
+
grain (that flat sort of boring part near my hometown)
+
happy hour
=
beer!

Or even more simply:
Cold thirsty immigrant farmers = beer.

BEER TERRITORY

How serious were the European settlers about beer? Consider this: Wisconsin became a state in 1848. 1856 was the first kindergarten. The first brewery? 1835 in Mineral Point founded by John Phillips. The Welsh, coming to work in the lead mines, really started things off. Milwaukee's first brewery was Milwaukee Brewery (never would have thought of *that* name), founded in 1840. Despite our reputation for lagers, this brewery was doing English-style ales and porters. The name changed to Lake Brewery (interestingly we have Lakefront and Milwaukee Brewing Co. again these days), but the locals knew it by the surname of one of the founders: Owens' Brewery. The competition in town led Milwaukee to be the great brew city that it is. They had almost *fifty* breweries only twenty years later. And of course the state itself also blossomed with breweries. Most of this was due to the massive German immigration. *Prosit!* (A German toast to your health. Sometimes also *prost!*)

PROHIBITION

Just before the ratification of the 18th Amendment in 1919, people were as bitter as an IPA on mega-hops about the Germans, what with the World War and all, and of course it was the German-Americans running most of the breweries in Wisconsin! So we had some beer hate on the brew. A: Americans hate Germans. B: Germans make beer. C: Americans hate… now wait a minute! Why can't we all just get along? But the Prohibitionists had been on the boil already since the middle of the nineteenth century for religious and social motivations.

So the fat lady was singing you might say, but not in Wisconsin. Thirty-two states already had Prohibition in their state constitutions—Wisconsin was one of sixteen that did not.

In 1917 Congress passed a resolution to shut down sales, transportation, and production of all forms of alcohol. States signed off on it and the amendment went into effect on July 1, 1919. If you were looking for loopholes, the Volstead Act in October defined alcoholic beverages as containing over one-half percent of alcohol. So do the math here. At best, you'd need about NINE BEERS to drink the equivalent amount of alcohol as a normal picnic beer! Even the most ambitious drinkers weren't going to be getting a buzz.

Beer was one of the top industries in the state and it had just been banned.

The best way to make something attractive? Prohibit it. This also goes a long way to making it profitable on the black market. Stories of Al Capone and bootleggers and the mob in Chicago are widely known. But Wisconsin played the backyard to this story. Capone had his hangouts in the Northwoods, and there were old escape tunnels he allegedly employed below Shipwrecked Brewpub in Door County. Something as crazy as outlawing beer was doomed to fail, and when Prohibition was repealed by the Twenty-first Amendment in 1933, there was much celebration. Miller sent a case to President Roosevelt. Many communities such as Cross Plains even had parades (see Esser's Cross Plains Brewing).

Not long after, the University of Wisconsin-Madison decided to serve beer on campus. This just seems normal to a Wisconsinite, but apparently there are a lot of colleges that still do not. What's *that* all about? Wisconsin even has a university named for beer: UW-Stout. OK, that's just coincidence actually, but I like the idea.

SO I MARRIED AN AXE-PROHIBITIONIST: CARRIE A. NATION

Imagine a six-foot, 175-pound teetotaler woman with an axe and an attitude. And you thought *your* marriage was rough. Once married to an alcoholic, Carrie A. Nation went on a rage against alcohol in the 1890s and until her death in 1911. Often joined by a chorus of hymn-singing women, she is known for marching into taverns and busting up the place with a hatchet. A resident of then dry-state Kansas, she wandered up to Wisconsin on occasion to lecture us. If you find yourself passing through Fond du Lac sometime (Zone 5), stop by J.D. Finnagan's Tavern and you'll find the "Historic Schmidt Sample Room, Scene Of The Famous Carrie Nation Hatchet Swinging Episode, July 18, 1902" where she smashed up a bottle of whiskey offered as a peace gesture by someone she was arguing with. The fighting words? "Every German in Wisconsin should be blown up with dynamite." Now *that's* harsh.

PHOTOGRAPHS COURTESY OF ESSER'S CROSS PLAINS BREWERY

BEER COMMERCIALS

Advertising wasn't a big deal right away. Who needed an ad to know where the brewery was across the street? As breweries got bigger and started shipping over distances (Milwaukee's population in the nineteenth century was too small to drink all the beer, and so they shipped to Chicago), there was a rise in beer propaganda. It started with newspapers, of course, and then on into the radio age. When the beloved radio show Amos 'n' Andy went to TV in 1951, Milwaukee's Blatz Beer was the sponsor.

Thanks to all the advertising, the names of Wisconsin's old beers are widely known. Think of Schlitz, "the beer that made Milwaukee famous." Laverne and Shirley worked at the fictional Milwaukee equivalent "Schotz" brewery.

"Schlemiel! Schlimazel! Hasenpfeffer* Incorporated!" Old Style was "pure brewed in God's country" with waters from when the earth was pure (over in La Crosse at G. Heileman Brewing). Pabst Blue Ribbon: "PBR me ASAP." Old Milwaukee which "tastes as great as its name" boasted in their ads, "It doesn't get any better than this." Always an ad with some guys fishing in Alaska or eating crawdads in the bayou or whatever and the voiceover about New Orleans or someplace and Milwaukee being a thousand miles apart and it didn't make any difference to these guys who knew good beer. I wasn't really convinced that people would go so far out of their way for an Old Mil until I saw it appeared to be the import of choice in Panama when I lived there in 2003! "Welcome to Miller Time" "when it's time to relax, one beer stands clear" (the champagne of beers). And of course the "Tastes great, less filling" debates of Miller Lite. My favorite Lite commercial was the one with Bob Uecker, voice of the Milwaukee Brewers baseball team, being moved from his seat by an usher to the worst bleacher seat—"I must be in front row!" Classic.

Well, despite surviving the dry years on soda or near beer (or in the case of Pabst, cheese!), most of the breweries hit hard times by the late 60s, and some even crawled into the 70s before giving up the ghost. Rhinelander, Marshfield, Oshkosh, Rahr Green Bay, Potosi, Fauerbach—all these breweries bit the dust. One of the survival strategies of the big guys was to buy up the labels of the sinking ships and thus acquire the loyalists who went with them. So, for example, places like Point continued to brew Chief Oshkosh, and for years Joseph Huber Brewing (now Minhas Craft Brewery) produced Rhinelander and Augsburger.

A handful of the giants made it a bit further through the troubled times. Schlitz, once America's largest brewer, made it to the 80s (still at number three in size) when Stroh's of Detroit bought them out. G. Heileman did some label buying (they bought Blatz in 1969) and then was passed around itself in the late 80s and early 90s until it was bought by Pabst in 1999. When all Heileman's breweries were shut down, City Brewery took over the original La Crosse facilities and kept the previous brewmaster. Now City Brewery does a pretty sizeable business with contract brews. They even repainted the famous World's Largest Six Pack grain silos. Pabst closed in Milwaukee in 1996 and the last of its breweries shut its doors in 2001. The offices moved to Texas, Chicago, then California, but now they have a small brewery in the old church within their former brewing complex in Milwaukee! They own the labels for a variety of old Wisconsin beers including Old Style, Special Export, Old Milwaukee, and Schlitz, but those they contract brew, some of them at Miller.

Who's left standing after all this? It's hard to say and depends on one's definition. Miller, of course, remains but has been bought and merged a couple times and is now MillerCoors in the United States. Point Brewery still lives, and though Leinenkugel was bought by Miller, they still operate independently and

---

* Hasenpfeffer is a traditional German stew made from marinated rabbit.

retain their classic integrity. Gray Brewing in Janesville is an old timer as well, but Prohibition switched them to a successful line of sodas, and it wasn't until the 90s that they started producing beer again.

Even as a few old-school brewers lay there bleeding, a few fresh upstarts were putting down roots and starting a trend that continues to grow and gives this book a reason for being. Randy Sprecher was working at Pabst when the blade of downsizing swept through. With a bit of inspiration, a modest sum of capital, and a whole lot of used equipment, Sprecher founded a "microbrewery" in 1985, the first in the state since Prohibition. Of the original small breweries to start up in the 80s, Capital Brewery (1986) and Lakefront (1987) are still up and running, and continuing to grow in popularity.

The history of Wisconsin brewing continues as we speak, with new brewpubs opening every year and a few unfortunates falling by the wayside. But you can play your part in making history: support your local brewers!

WHEN FARM BREWERIES WERE KING

One of the most overlooked breweries in your typical history of brewing is the farm brewery. OK, perhaps you get the image of Old Farmer Braun brewing up a batch of bad brewsky in the kitchen sink, but such is certainly not the case. On farms all across the state, from the 1830s to the 1860s, the good stuff was being made. These brewers—primarily German immigrants—knew their craft. Wisconsin had just become a state in 1848, and a revolution in the same year over in Germany was driving some people to seek a better life. And what's a better life without beer, pray tell?

Location was key. To brew, farmers needed a property with an artesian well, and since they were all lager brewers, they needed a freezable water source—such as a stream that could be dammed—for the ice needed to keep the beer below 55 degrees while it fermented and was lagered (though most brewing was simply done in the winter when air conditioning was already amply provided).

Don't compare the farm breweries to sly moonshiners or bootleggers; these were legitimate businesses and tax records for many of them still exist. The German brewers adhered to Reinheitsgebot, the strict German Purity Law. Doing it all yourself, from the crops to the stein, was by no means a simple job. The farmers grew all their ingredients—hops and barley—and then needed to malt the grain. This part of the process took up about three-quarters of the facility. The actual brewing, in fact, took a much smaller portion of the space and labor. It was done typically in open top, iron brew kettles over an open wood flame. Imagine sweating over a smoky fire and then crossing the yard through a Wisconsin subzero winter to get to the 45-degree beer cellar. Lager was called Summer Beer, and if the temperature was too high in the cellars either the fermentation would blow up the kegs or the beer itself would spoil. Ice blocks and straw, however, could last long into the summer. Ever wonder why your grandparents referred to the freezer portion of your refrigerator as the ice box? The same method was at work on a smaller scale in homes.

By the end of the 1870s, most farm brewers were already out of business. Better transportation and the discovery of pasteurization meant that city brewers could ship beer farther without spoilage. Some of them had chemists on staff. Advertising made a contribution as well. And then, of course, there was just plain competitive big-business strategies—the big city guys could come into town and court the saloons by offering whatever the saloons needed—new set of tables? Chairs? Maybe a new roof? Plus they could just drop prices to drive off the local competition. Then dairy farming went big and farmers saw better money (the cities didn't do so well raising milk herds).

Few are the remains of the farm breweries today; most of the structures have been worked into other more modern buildings or simply dismantled completely. These were pretty big operations in little townships and in rural sites (and the locations of remains are often still out in the country). Roman arches that mark old lagering cellars can still be found here and there. Most were never recorded in history books, so it takes an expert to identify them. Wayne Kroll of Fort Atkinson is one such person dedicated to the preservation of the record and has spent a lot of time searching them out. To date he has confirmed 150, but there are surely more. Wayne estimates there were once 25–30 farm breweries in the average county, one in nearly every township. Production was probably 100 to 300 barrels per year.

Some of the city breweries started as farm operations. Fred Miller was initially rural, though he bought some of his ingredients so was not quite a true farm brewery. And yes, nowadays Dave's Brew Farm operates in a wind-powered barn, and Sand Creek was founded in a farm shed, but these modern brewers aren't farm breweries in the strictest sense either.

Want to know more? Check out Wisconsin's Frontier Farm Breweries by Wayne Kroll, self-published. Order it from the Wisconsin Historical Society in Madison or Wayne Kroll himself at W3016 Green Isle Drive, Fort Atkinson, WI 53538, kroll@centurytel.net.

HOPS

Pioneers in Wisconsin found their new home to be an agricultural haven, and in the middle of the nineteenth century many farmers had success growing wheat. After that market peaked for them and prices dropped, many moved on to dairy farming which contributed to a great cheese industry and our future reputation as cheeseheads. Others found another crop that was in high demand locally and paying big prices: hops.

The first hops in Wisconsin were planted at what is now Wollersheim Winery near Prairie du Sac. Prior to the Civil War, much of the nation's hops were being grown in the east, but problems with a destructive pest, the hop louse, took their toll. Wisconsin, um, "hopped on the bandwagon," and by the end of the 1860s the crop had grown to over fifty times its yield at the beginning of that decade. Sauk County led the state and was one of the top growing regions in the United States. Much of the hops got on the rails in Kilbourn City and was shipped to other parts of the country. (Kilbourn City became Wisconsin Dells.)

A blight, however, in 1882 put the smackdown on Wisconsin hops. That, combined with dropping hop prices, was the end of hoppy times, and the industry eventually found itself backed into a corner of sorts in the Washington State region.

A hop shortage in 2008 had brewers extremely concerned about where they could get hops in a timely manner and without breaking open piggy banks to afford them. The hops availability has gotten better, but the scare has inspired more and more Wisconsin growers to look at growing them. Brewers, however, have committed to buy what the farmers grow. Hops are a sensitive plant, and the risks—from pests to rainfall to blight—are numerous. But hops, I mean, *hopes* are high that this is a return to the heyday of Wisconsin hops.

THE DIVINE PROCESS

Water + Malt + Hops + Yeast

The first step in brewing beer is *MASHING*, and for this you need a malted grain, such as barley, and it needs to be coarsely ground. In Wisconsin we are fortunate to have our very own source of malt in Chilton (see Briess later in the book and check out the malting process). The brewer will add hot water to the malt to get the natural enzymes in the grain to start converting the starches into the sugars necessary for fermentation. Think of your bowl of sugared breakfast cereal growing soggy and then making the milk sweet. It's kind of like that, only different.

The next step is *SPARGING* when water ("from when the earth was pure") is flushed through the mash to get a sweet liquid we call *WORT*, which in all caps looks like a great alternative radio station we have in our capital, Madison. See? I told you we're all about beer here. The wort is filtered to remove the barley husks and spent grain, and then sent to the brew kettle.

Wort then needs to be boiled to kill off any unwanted microcritters and to get rid of some of the excess water. This generally goes on for about an hour and a half. It is at this stage that any other flavoring ingredients are generally added, including hops.

Once this is all done, the fermentation is ready to begin. A brewer once told me, "People don't make beer, yeast does." Yes, yeast is the magical little element that monks referred to as "God is Good" when they were making their liquid bread in the monasteries. If you wanted to grab a brewsky in the Middle Ages (and believe me you didn't want to drink the water), the best place to stop was the local monastery. The monks made beer, the travelers spent money, the church got along. Everyone happy. How the church ended up with Bingo instead of beer we may never know. Bummer.

Yeast eats sugars like the little fat boy in *Willie Wonka and the Chocolate Factory*, and as we all know from a long afternoon of drinking and stuffing our faces, what goes in must come out. As Kurt Vonnegut once put it and as unpleasant as it may seem, beer is yeast excrement: alcohol and a little bit of gas. Reminds me of a night of Keystone Light, actually.

ALES VS. LAGERS

There are two basic kinds of beer: ales and lagers. It's all about yeast's preferences. Some yeasts like it on top; some prefer to be on bottom. Up until now, yeasts have not been more creative in their brewing positions, but we can always fantasize.

Ale yeasts like it on top and will ferment at higher temperatures (60–70 °F) and so are quicker finishers (1–3 weeks) than lagers. Usually ales are sweeter and have a fuller body, which really starts to take this sexual allusion to extremes.

Lagers, on the other hand, use yeasts that settle in at the bottom to do their work and prefer cooler temps of about 40–55 °F. They take 1–3 months to ferment and condition. Lagers tend to be lighter, crisper and drier than ales and are the most common beers, often easier to get along with for the average drinker and they don't mind if you leave the seat up. (In fact, you may as well, you'll be coming back a few times before the night is done.) For lager we can thank the Bavarians who—when they found that cold temperatures could control runaway wild yeasts in the warm summer ale batches—moved them to the Alps. The name lager comes from the German "to store."

Wisconsin, being the frozen tundra that it is in the wintertime, was ideal for this type of beer, and we have the German immigrant population to credit for getting things started here. Cold water, winter, and great farmland, so now we count Germantown, Berlin, *New* Berlin, Freistadt, and Kohler among our communities. And Czechs as well. Did you know there are two Pilsens in Wisconsin? My grandfather, in fact, was a Pilsner and made a point of supporting pilsners quite well over the years.

Ale is the first real beer that was made and it was sort of a mutation of another alcoholic drink called *mead*. This was made with fermented honey. Remember the mead halls when you read *Beowulf* in high school? OK, I didn't read it either, but the Cliffs Notes mentioned it some. This is the sweet and potent concoction that put the happy in the Vikings as they pillaged and plundered. Someone added a bit of hops, and later some malt, and the hybrid *brackett* evolved. You can still find both of these here in Wisconsin (see White Winter Winery in Iron River) along with the ales and lagers. We don't discriminate like that. Equal opportunity drinkers we are.

THESE ARE NOT YOUR MALTED MILKBALLS

Malting is a process of taking a grain, such as barley or wheat, getting it to start germinating, and then drying it quickly to cut off that process. I like to call this *germinus interruptus*, but then I like to make a lot of words up, so take that with a grain of barley.

So the malting process is 1: get grain (seeds) wet; 2: let it get started; 3: roast it in a kiln until dried. And here's where the specialty malts come in. You can roast the malted grains to different shades, a bit like coffee beans, and you can even smoke the stuff for a real twist on flavor (check out Rauchbier).

Why is barley the most common grain? It has a high amount of those enzymes for beer. So although corn, wheat, rye, and even rice can be used, you'll see that barley is the king of the malts. If you have gluten troubles, this is bad news because barley has it, but fear not—Wisconsin to the rescue. Check out Madison's ALT Brew, a certified all gluten-free brewery, and Lakefront Brewery's gluten-free brew made with yet another grain called sorghum.

I know you're wondering, because I was too: What about malted milk balls? There *is* a connection, in fact. William Horlick of Racine, Wisconsin, sought to create a food for infants that was both nutritious and easy to digest. He mixed wheat extract and malted barley with powdered milk to form malted milk. Walgreen's Drugstores almost immediately started selling malted milkshakes, and *Voila!* another great Wisconsin idea entered the world.

WHAT'S HOPPENIN', HOP STUFF?

So why the hops? It's a plant for cryin' out loud; do you really want *salad* in your beer?? Actually, without refrigeration beer didn't keep all too well. The medieval monks discovered that hops had preservative properties. The sun never set on the British Empire which meant it never set on the beer either. So the Brits hopped the ale hard to get it all the way to India and thus India Pale Ale was born. (No, the color is not really pale, but compare it to a porter or a stout, and the name makes sense.)

Plus the bitterness of hops balanced the sweetness of the malt. And while they use hops to bring that bitterness, a "hoppy" beer isn't the same as saying a "bitter" beer.

The point in the process when you put the hops in makes all the difference, and generally it goes in the boil. Boil it an hour and it's bitter; half an hour and it's less bitter with a touch of the flavor and aroma; toward the end of the boil and you lose the bitter and end up with just the aroma and flavor, making it highly "drinkable." (You will hear people describing beer as very "drinkable," and it would seem to me that this was a given. Apparently not.) There is another way to get the hoppiness you want. Dry hopping—which sounds a lot like what some of yous kids was doin' in the backseat of the car—is actually adding the hops after the wort has cooled, say, in the fermenter, or more commonly in the keg.

But let me tell you this, when I first sipped a beer I only stared blankly at brewers when they asked me, "Now, do ya taste the hops in this one?" How was I to know? I mean, if someone from Papua New Guinea says, "Do you get that little hint of grub worm in that beer?" I really have nothing to go on. Before touring or on your brew tour, if you aren't already hops-wise, ask someone if you can have a whiff of some. I did, and suddenly the heavens parted and Divine Knowledge was to me thus imparted. I could then identify that aroma more accurately, and I have to confess I'm still not sure I taste it in those mass market beers.

THERE'S SOMETHING FUNNY IN MY BEER

So you know about the German Purity Law and the limits on what goes into a beer, but obviously there is a whole range of stuff out there that thumbs its nose at boundaries. Some of this is a good thing, some of it not so much. These beyond-the-basics ingredients are called *adjuncts*.

Let's talk about the type of adjunct that ought to make you suspicious and will elicit a curse or look of horror from a beer snob. In this sense an adjunct is a source of starch used to beef up the sugars available for fermentation. It is an ingredient, commonly rice or corn, used to cut costs by being a substitute for the more expensive barley. Pale lagers on the mass market production line commonly do this. It doesn't affect the flavor and often cuts back on the body and mouth feel of the brew, which is why if you drink a mass market beer and then compare it to the same style (but *without* adjuncts) from a craft brewer you will taste a significant difference.

You may hear beer snobs use the word adjunct when ripping on the mass produced non-handcrafted brews, but there are other ingredients which are also adjuncts that we can't knock so much.

Wheat, rye, corn, wild rice, oats, sorghum, honey—many are the options

WHAT ARE IBUs?

Compounds in hops are what bring bitterness to your beer. IBU stands for International Bittering Units and gives beer drinkers something else to say about how bitter a beer is besides "really really" or "very very very" or "just a bit." Brewers use a spectrophotometer which measures how light passes through or reflects off a solution and thus determine the chemistry of their beer. This system offers an objective scientific accounting of a beer's bitterness, which, of course, is harder to otherwise pin down with our subjective tongues. The higher the number, the greater the actual bitterness. However, this number may not always predict your own experience of the beer. A beer with a lot of malt and a higher IBU of 60, for example, might not taste to you as bitter as a pint of bitters made with less malt and rated at 30 IBU. There is a limit to how much of the bittering compounds are actually soluble, so one cannot simply add hops infinitely and go screaming toward 100s of IBUs. (Heaven knows, because someone would have done it by now!) Plus, there's a limit to how much your tongue can even perceive. Debate goes on about what those limits are but pretty much after about 110 IBUs you are likely near the limit.

that don't just serve to save a buck or two on the batch ingredients but rather bring something to the beer. Maybe a longer lasting head, a silkier mouth feel, or a sweeter taste. And in the case of a wheat beer, can one really call wheat an adjunct? Most would say no. Word dicers will say yes. Whatever.

Fruits and spices are also friendly adjuncts. Think of cherry, orange, or pumpkin flavors in certain brews, or spices such as coriander in Belgian wit beers, ginger, nutmeg, or even cayenne pepper like Valkyrie Brewing's Hot Chocolate Stout or the Great Dane's Tri-Pepper Pils. Brewers can add chocolate, milk sugar, or even coffee as in the case of Lakefront's Fuel Café Stout or Stone Cellar's Caffeinator Doppelbock. I had mint in a stout from South Shore. Furthermore's Knot Stock is black pepper in an IPA. By German Purity Law, of course, this is a big no-no, but there's nothing wrong with pushing the envelope a bit for some new tastes. It's not cutting corners, but rather creating new avenues.

Are you gluten-sensitive? Well, bummer for you, beer has that. But an alternative grain called sorghum does not, and Lakefront is making beer with it, and ALT Brew in Madison makes nothing but gluten-free beers. Adjunct? I'd say not. Point Brewery took a Specialty Ale gold at the 1991 Great American Beer Festival for its Spud Premier Beer—made with the starch from Wisconsin potatoes!

GREEN BEER

It may sound like I'm talking about St. Patrick's Day, but this is about local brewers doing their part to work toward a cleaner, energy-efficient future while keeping us well stocked in suds. One of the first brewers to go "green" was Central Waters Brewing Company. They have solar panels heating water, providing power, and saving them money. The system pays for itself in roughly seven years and the savings over the lifetime of it are enormous. Dave's BrewFarm has some wind and solar power going as well, and the Grumpy Troll in Mt. Horeb installed solar panels at the beginning of 2010. Milwaukee Brewing Co. used vegetable oil from the Milwaukee Ale House to heat their boiler thus reducing fuel consumption, repurposing the old oil, and reducing bad exhaust gases.

Having a grain silo eliminates the need for hundreds of bags of malt. Heat exchangers recapture the heat of cooling wort. Cooling water can be used to clean the tanks. In fact, New Glarus Brewery's expanded brewhouse uses the heat from a previous brew by pumping the wort into another tank and bringing in the next.

Using recycled equipment is another method of minimizing a brewery's impact on the environment. So many have used old dairy equipment in the past, but many more have purchased another brewer's systems. (Although industry growth now supports a lot of locally manufactured brewing equipment.)

Keeping the ingredients local is another great contributor to Wisconsin's economy that also cuts down on the energy required to bring grains in from far away. Capital Brewery made a buzz when they worked with growers on

Washington Island to get the wheat for their Island Wheat beer several years back. It was a shot in the arm for a struggling industry, and other brewers around the state—Lakefront Brewery and South Shore Brewery to name a couple—followed suit. South Shore now grows all its own grain. The recent hops shortages have inspired more growers to invest in hops production and cooperatives.

Not only are more and more brewers using local ingredients, but many more are also recycling the spent grain, sending it out to area farmers as feed for farm animals. As Bo Belanger of South Shore says, "Essentially we're paying the farmer to grow his own feed. I just borrow it for a moment for the sugars."

The latest trend has been in packaging: the aluminum can. Milwaukee Brewing Co. still does bottles but has greatly increased their use of cans. The lighter weight saves energy and money on shipping/transportation, and aluminum doesn't let the beer-spoiling light in like glass. Plus it's easier to recycle.

And let's not forget, if you are drinking at your local brewpub, there's a bottle or can that was never needed. Pack a growler for carry-out purposes!

SOUR ALES

Throw out what you think you know about keeping your brewing equipment all squeaky clean so as not to spoil a brew. Yes, that is extremely important for brewing typical beers, but it's a rule that gets a little bending when making a sour ale. This is not a beer gone wrong but an a beer purposely soured, and has become quite popular in the US.

REINHEITSGEBOT!

Gezundtheit! Actually, it's not a Bavarian sneezing; it's the German Purity Law. Want to know how serious the Germans were about beer? By *law* dating back to 1516, beer had to be made using only these three ingredients: barley, hops, and water. (The law later added yeast to the ingredient list once Louis Pasteur explained to the world the role of the little sugar-eating microorganisms in the process.) But this meant you wheat or rye or oat lovers were out of luck. Barbarians! Bootleggers! Outcasts! Why so harsh on the alternative grains? Because these grains were necessary for breads and these were times of famines and the like. Fortunately, times got better and we have the wide variety of ales and lagers that we see today. Nevertheless, the Germans came to Wisconsin quite serious about beer (see Farm Breweries). In the end, the law was used more to control competitors and corner a market—so much for its pure intentions.

There's more to beer quality than a list of ingredients anyway; it's the *purity* of those ingredients that makes all the difference. It's also the time, patience, and care of the brewer that lifts the brew to a higher level. Am I talking about craft brewing here? I most certainly am!

"Sour" is a descriptor not an official single style. Most commonly associated with Belgium (lambics or Flanders red ales), sour ales are intentionally allowed to go "bad." And by bad, we mean good. Wild yeasts and/or bacteria are purposely introduced to the beer to give it a sour or tart acidity.

Fruit can be added for a secondary fermentation, but many sours use bacteria such as Lactobacillus or Pediococcus, or a special yeast, such as "Brett" (Brettanomyces), which occurs in nature on fruit skins. Brewing such a beer can be challenging in that by introducing these wilder elements into the brewhouse, a brewer increases the risk of infecting other beers that aren't intended to be soured. When done well, this is a unique beer experience, another alternative for those who claim they don't like any kind of beer, and maybe a crossover for those wine drinkers. Some sour styles need time to age and develop in a barrel, months or even years, thus giving us complex flavors as in a Flanders red or oud bruin. Others are "kettle sours," such as Berliner Weisse or Gose, which are soured in the brew kettle by adding lactic acid bacteria culture and allowing it to ferment a bit before continuing with the normal brewing process and going straight to cans to be drunk. The flavor imparted is sharp like unsweetened lemonade or plain yogurt.

TASTING YOUR BEER

Back in the days of youth I suppose savoring the taste of your beer meant you belched after pouring it down your throat. Since you have evolved to drinking craft beers, you may take a bit more time to savor it. Here are a few pointers for savoring the stuff:

Sniff it for aromas. Remember your nose works with your tongue to make you taste things. Kids plug their noses to eat liver for a reason! Get a bit of that beer in your sniffer before you sip by swirling it around in your glass to raise that aroma like you would with wine.

OK, now sip it. Swirl it a bit around on your tongue. Gargling is generally frowned upon, however. Is it watery or does it have a bit of body to it? Squish it against the roof of your mouth with your tongue to appreciate the "mouth feel."

Swallow! Wine tasters can spit it out during a tasting but beer has a finish that you can only get at the back of the tongue where the taste receptors for bitterness are. The most graceful option is to swallow. (Remember what I said about gargling!)

Everyone's tastes are different, of course, and some may prefer a bitter IPA to a sweet Belgian tripel, but the test of a good beer is that bittersweet balance. Now if you want to be good at this tasting business, you need to practice. I know, I know, oh the humanity of it all! But you can suffer all this drinking if it really matters to you. Repeat the process with various craft brews and you will start to see how different all the beers are. Is this one too bitter? Too malty? Is the hops aroma strong, fair to middlin', barely noticeable? Hints of chocolate? Coffee? Caramel? Is it citrusy? Creamy? Crisp? Even smoky? (See "rauch beer" in the glossary.)

Is that *butterscotch* I'm tasting?!?

Shouldn't be! Beware of diacetyl! This natural byproduct of yeast is actually used in artificial butter flavoring. At low levels diacetyl gives a slippery mouth feel to the brew. A bit more and the buttery flavor starts to appear. Brewers need to leave the yeast a couple days or so after the end of fermentation and it will reabsorb the flavor-spoiling agent. The warmer temp of ale brewing makes this happen faster.

Here's something that will sound crazy: a good beer will even taste good when it has gone warm in your glass. (Some will even taste better!) Now try THAT with your crappy picnic beer!

BARRELS OF FUN

Remember pull tops*, those little throwaway raindrop-shaped openers from beer cans that you used to cut your foot on at the beach? Prior to the pull tops and the modern apparatus that thankfully stays attached, some cans needed an opener like you'd use for a tin can of condensed milk. Thus some great collectibles in the beer can world are the first pull-top cans which boasted No Opener Needed (Pabst was one). There were also cone-tops, cans that opened like a bottle with a cap and had heads like the Tin Man. But before all this, and before the advent of the aluminum kegs, there were wooden barrels. The cooper—the guy who built and tended them—was almost as important as the brewer. He had to choose the right wood and get a tight fit in a world without duct tape and crazy glue. Imagine! Gone, you might say, are *those* days. But not so! Many of the craft brewers still age some of their beers in wood. Especially popular are the recycled bourbon barrels which give that whiskey aroma to the beer, but now rum, rye, wine and even tequila barrels are being used. Look for a barrel-aged brew at your local brewery and see what all the buzz is about.

---

*   Point Brewery was the last brewery to use pull tabs.

BEER ENGINES AND NITRO

On your exploration of the brewpubs you may find a beer engine. No, I'm not talking about an alternative motor for your car that runs on brewsky. The beer engine looks suspiciously like a tap handle, but not exactly. Normally, beer is under pressure from carbon dioxide—or air you pumped into the keg at a party—which pushes your pint out at the tap. Now this can affect your beer, of course.

Air will eventually skunkify it (which is why pubs aren't using it; at a party you will probably finish the keg in one go, so it doesn't matter anyway), and too much CO2 increases the carbonation of the brew, sometimes beyond what is desirable. There are a couple of tricks that can avoid all this.

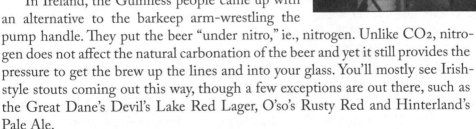

The beer engine is one. It is a piston-operated pump that literally pulls the beer up from the barrel or holding tanks. So when it looks like the barkeep is out at the water pump in an old western, he or she is actually using a beer engine. When you use this, the beer gets a cascading foam going in the glass (very cool and hypnotic, really) and a meringue-like head. Look for the tap with the long curved swan-neck spout that delivers the beer right against the bottom of the glass to make that special effect.

In Ireland, the Guinness people came up with an alternative to the barkeep arm-wrestling the pump handle. They put the beer "under nitro," ie., nitrogen. Unlike CO2, nitrogen does not affect the natural carbonation of the beer and yet it still provides the pressure to get the brew up the lines and into your glass. You'll mostly see Irish-style stouts coming out this way, though a few exceptions are out there, such as the Great Dane's Devil's Lake Red Lager, O'so's Rusty Red and Hinterland's Pale Ale.

PRESERVING YOUR BEER

You probably know enough to cool your beer before you drink it, but remember that many craft brews are not pasteurized. Yes, hops are a natural preservative, but let's face it, we are not sailing round the Cape of Good Hope to India eating hardtack and hoping for the best for the ale. This is fine beer, like fine wine, and deserves some tender loving care.

If during your brewery travels you pick up a (carefully pre-cleaned) growler, put that thing on ice! If you don't refrigerate unpasteurized beer, you are getting it at less than its best and perhaps eventually at its worst. Basically, anything above 75 degrees may begin to produce some off flavors. Excepting bottle-conditioned live yeast beers, beers degrade over time; they get old. Hoppy beers show the deterioration even faster. The higher the temperature, the faster that process goes. (A beer in a hot room for a week will taste perhaps twice as old as one kept at normal room temperature.) If you are picking up brew on a longer road trip, take a cooler along or bring it inside to your hotel room. The longer you leave good beer exposed to light and heat, the more likely the taste will deteriorate until you have the infamous beer of Pepé Le Pew.

That said, beer is not milk, so don't freak out if the temperature is a little high for a short while or if it is being re-cooled a few times. The hot trunk coming back from the liquor store? Not a big deal. A week in the trunk on vacation in July? Don't do it.

BREW YOUR OWN

OK, I know what you're thinking: if so many of these brewmasters started in their basements, why can't I? Well, truth is, you can!

Check your local homebrew shop to get what you need. A basic single-stage brew kit includes a 6.5 gallon plastic bucket with a lid and fermentation lock, a siphoning tube, bottle brush, handheld bottle capper and caps, and hopefully, instructions. You then need a recipe pack and about 50 returnable-style bottles (not twist-offs). (Grolsch bottles with the ceramic stopper also work great; you only need to buy new rubber rings for the seal.) The kit starts around $50.

A two-stage kit throws in a hydrometer, thermometer and a 5-gallon glass "carboy" where the brew from the bucket goes to complete fermentation. Now you can watch it like an aquarium. Don't put any fish in it though.

Ingredient kits have all you need for a certain recipe. Simple light ales might start around $25 while an IPA with oak chips can get up around $50. Each makes about 50 bottles of beer. In many cases you are using malt extracts thus skipping the grinding of grain in the wort-making process. As you go deeper into the art you will likely want to do this yourself as well.

If your future brewpub patrons are really slow drinkers or Mormons, this basic kit will do you fine. That said, the pros are by no means always using the state-of-the-art equipment either. Remember Egyptians and Sumerians were already making beer over 5000 years ago and they didn't even have toilet paper yet. Um… my point is, big brewers might have the funds to get the fancy copper brew kettles made in Bavaria and a microbiology lab, while others, like the guys at Central Waters at least got their start with used equipment that had other original purposes. Old dairy tanks are popular. And Appleton Beer Factory actually welded their own tanks. Talk about hardcore.

Before you get all excited about naming your beers and what the sign on the pub is going to look like, consider Lake Louie Brewing founder Tom Porter's thoughts on the challenges of starting a brewery.

ON STARTING A BREWERY

If you want to start a brewery, use somebody else's money. Because you can go big to start, big enough to make it a profitable minimum, and then if it goes belly up you just tell them, "Sorry, guys, I did the best I could!" I'm on the hook for it, win or lose. It *does* give you tremendous impetus to not fail. There's no doubt about it. "Hey, you gotta make good beer." That's a given. There's nobody out there making really crummy beer anymore, they all went belly up and we all bought their used equipment. It's a given that the beer is pretty darn good. Yeah, there are different interpretations of style, but it's really all about costs. I could be in the muffler business, or I could be in the hub cap business; I could be making paper clips for chrissakes, as long as the paper clip quality is as good as everybody else's, it doesn't matter. The reality is you better be darn good on cost control and you better know business, and I didn't. I was an engineer. Engineers sit way in back of a great big company. Someone else goes and sells it, someone else decides if there is profit in it. By the time the paper ever gets to your desk, it's a done deal. I went from the engineering business to having to do the business, the books, the capital decisions, the sales... *inventory* control. All those things: debt amortization, accounting... ggarrggh, accounting? Man! I never went to accounting classes. I got out of those thinking they were like the plague to me. "A credit is a debit until it's paid?!?" *What?!?*

My accounting system that started out when I started this brewery is I had a bucket of money. And every time I get some more I put it in the bucket. And when I need it, I take it out of the bucket. When the bucket's empty I got to stop taking money out until I get some more to put in. Well, that system still works here, but there's a WHOLE—SERIES—OF BUCKETS now! There's literally *dozens* of buckets. It gets hard to remember which one do I put it into and which one do I take it out of. And sometimes you don't notice one's empty. So business and accounting—that's really been my learning curve. I went from going "What's a balance sheet?" to a profit and loss statement, and now I work off cash flow statements and sometimes I split them up. I want to know where the push and pull is of my cash flow, because that's really what makes a good businessman. And I'm learning this because I HAVE to. And it has had NOTHING to do with making good beer. The good beer part is a given. You've gotta have it. If you don't have it, don't even think about it. But having that is not enough. I have a lot of people here coming through the door on tours and such saying, "I'm thinking of starting a brewpub. Gees, I make really good homebrew." And I say, "That's a really good first step." But the second through fortieth steps are... how are your plumbing skills? How're your carpentry skills? Can you pour concrete? Can you weld? And then can you balance a balance sheet every thirty days?

Tom Porter, founder/brewmaster *Lake Louie Brewing*

BARLEY'S ANGELS

Few things are more irritating than the notion that women somehow don't like beer. Testament to the nonsense of that idea is an organization called Barley's Angels (barleysangels.org). An international network of local chapters—100 chapters in 7 countries—Barley's Angels unites women around the world who appreciate good beer. They host events, both for fun and education, such as beer and food/chocolate pairings or cooking with beer discussions, and they organize beer outings. Bringing women together over beers is their mission as is helping breweries, beer bars, and restaurants grow their beer-wise female client base. Join a chapter or start one if there's not one near you. Follow them on Twitter @ barleysangelsor and Facebook.com/barleysangels.org. There are two chapters currently in Wisconsin:

Barley's Angels – Milwaukee
Email: barleysangelsmke@gmail.com
Info: https://www.facebook.com/barleysangelsMKE
Meeting schedule: Monthly
Meeting location: Roving

Barley's Angels – Lakeshore Chapter
Email: BarleysAngelsLakeshore@gmail.com
Info: https://www.facebook.com/MoJoSheboygan
Meeting schedule: Monthly
Meeting location: MoJo, 1235 Pennsylvania Avenue, Sheboygan WI 53081

SOME FOOD WITH YOUR BEER

PAIRING AND PALATES with Lucy Saunders

Think about your taste buds and what you savor: the five elements of taste—salty, sweet, bitter, sour and savory umami—are foremost. Pour a glass of beer and ponder its possible pairings.

But start with sniff, not a sip. In tasting beer, often aromatics can suggest herbs, spices or other ingredients that might make a bridge for a potential food pairing.

Hops can be piney and resinous—which suggests rosemary or juniper berries. Citrusy hops meld well with tropical flavors such as mango or lemons and limes.

Witbiers brewed with coriander and orange zest bring out the best in seafood and many salads. Malty, bready notes suggest caramelized flavors and meld well with rind-washed cheeses. Peppery, high ABV brews will extend the heat of chiles and spicy foods. Yeasty dark ales balance the acidity in dark chocolate.

Since everyone's palate and threshold of sensitivity differs, know how to approach a pairing.

I interviewed Chef Jonathan Zearfoss, a professor at the Culinary Institute of America, about pairing tips. "The standard approach to flavors is to complement, contrast, or create a third new flavor through the synergy of flavor," he says.

For example, Zearfoss read a menu description of a rauchbier that suggested pairing it with smoked foods. "I had the rauchbier with a lentil salad made with smoked bacon and a vinaigrette. On my palate, the acidity of the vinegar cut through the smoke. But my friend, who was eating a pasta with cream sauce, found that the smoky taste coated her palate and became cloying."

"The taste memory is composed of the synergy between the drink and the food," says Zearfoss, "and that's especially true with beer since it has a definite aftertaste." Texture elements in beer—carbonation, residual yeast—also contribute to flavor.

When tasting a beer that's new to you, try sampling both bottled and draft versions of the same beer. Fresh beer tastes best, and be sure you know what the brewer wanted the beer to taste like.

There's a delightful weaving of the experience of drinking beer: your sensations, your palate and overall enjoyment. With literally hundreds of beer styles from which to choose, allow experimentation and sampling beyond your usual preferences. It's an adventure you can enjoy in Wisconsin. Cheers!

© 2018 Lucy Saunders

Lucy Saunders is the author of five cookbooks and has written about craft beer and food for more than 20 years. One of my favorites of her books is Grilling With Beer *and her most recent is* Dinner In the Beer Garden. *For more tips on beer and food pairing, plus free recipes, follow her @ lucybeercook*

MAP YOUR CAPS

I confess: I was a collector of many things as a child. Beer cans (of course), stamps, coins, rocks, baseball cards (and basketball, football and Star Wars), and much more, including bottle caps. Laugh all you want, but now collecting bottle caps is a thing, thanks to a couple of engineers in Madison, Wisconsin.

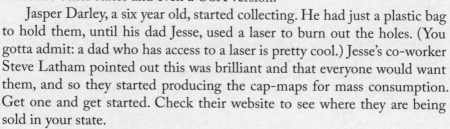

These cool wooden cutouts of the State of Wisconsin are riddled with holes perfectly sized so you can wedge the cap off your Wisconsin beer to record it for posterity. There are other states and even a USA version.

Jasper Darley, a six year old, started collecting. He had just a plastic bag to hold them, until his dad Jesse, used a laser to burn out the holes. (You gotta admit: a dad who has access to a laser is pretty cool.) Jesse's co-worker Steve Latham pointed out this was brilliant and that everyone would want them, and so they started producing the cap-maps for mass consumption. Get one and get started. Check their website to see where they are being sold in your state.

beercapmaps.com

Facebook.com/beercapmaps

LOUIS PASTEUR CHANGED BEER FOREVER

Well, and milk too, I suppose. But really, which one is more important? Louis demonstrated that there wasn't any sort of magic mumbo jumbo going on in the brewing process and that, actually, fermentation was brought about by microorganisms (that'd be the yeast). Prior to this the theory was spontaneous generation, that things just happened, but he figured out it was airborne yeasts that got into the brew kettles. The alcohol, of course, comes as a byproduct as the little buggers went about eating the sugar. (Author Kurt Vonnegut once described alcohol as "yeast excrement," but that's kind of a gross thought, so let's forget it.)

It wasn't just yeast getting in there—there were other little critters messing up things and making people sick or simply skunking up the beer. Solution? Pasteurize it. (Notice the name is from Louis. I'm just pointing it out in case you are four or five beers in on that case you bought already.) Pasteurization was heating the liquid (milk, beer, etc.) and killing off the nasty bits that would eventually spoil the beverage (or worst case, such as with milk, make the drinker quite sick!).

CANS VS. BOTTLES

Because you couldn't spend your entire life at the saloon—though many have tried—we developed methods of taking some brew home with us. Growlers and the like worked fine but didn't last long. Bottling was the best method back in the late 19th century. But canning beer was in the works, at least in research, even before Prohibition. But that dark space between the 18th and 21st Amendments put cans on hold. Beer reacts with steel, so to prevent that American Can Co. developed a can liner. G. Krueger Brewing of New Jersey became the first to use the "Keglined" cans in 1935, and from that point forward, cans grew to take over the market. Continental Can Co. gave us the "cone top" that same year, a can with a tapered top capped like a bottle. Milwaukee brewer Jos. Schlitz Brewing is allegedly the first brewery to use them (though some argue La Crosse's G. Heileman Brewing beat them to it). Rice Lake Brewing of Wisconsin was the last.

But most cans were flat-topped cylinders. Initially, one needed a pointed can opener (a "church key") to puncture the top to get at the beer. Then the pull tab arrived, invented by Ermal Fraze in 1959, and this was big news. You can still find old Pabst steel cans touting "No opener needed!" A prized can for collectors. After a couple decades of cutting our feet on those tabs at the beach, the Sta-Tab came into favor—the little lever we still use today that stays with the can—unless you are collecting them for the Ronald McDonald House. As the craft brewing age came upon us, bottles became the favored packaging. Beer tastes better from glass, we said. The bottles are sexier, we believed. In a bar brawl one couldn't break a can and cut someone.

Pragmatism, however, has brought back the cans—both in 12- and 16-oz sizes—and it all makes good sense. No returns or deposits. Easy to recycle. Easier to stack and thus easier to ship and store. Lighter, quicker to cool, and not so fragile like glass. Plus, it keeps the beer-damaging light out completely. We still may think it tastes different, but that's why you should always pour your beer into the proper glassware anyway.

WHERE'S THE BEER AT?

(INTRO TO THE LISTINGS)

The listings for all the commercial brewers in Wisconsin are divided here into the six zones I mentioned before. Each section has a map of that portion of the state with the brewtowns marked. Within each zone the communities are listed in alphabetical order with the brewpubs and breweries below the town heading. Watch for a few extra non-brewing but brewing-related attractions and other interesting bits you can read during your journey.

HOW TO USE THE LISTINGS:

OK, this isn't rocket science but let's go over a brief summary of the finer points of the listings.

Brewmaster or Head Brewer: So you know who to ask brewing questions.

Number of Beers: This may indicate the number of different brews in a year and/or the number of beers on tap.

Staple Beers: Always on tap, flagships, year-round beers.

Rotating Beers: Like roulette only with beer, the beers that may come and go, often seasonal brews, series beers, or in some cases one-offs that are listed here only to show the breadth of their brewing styles. Mention of casks, barrel-aging or other specialties might be here as well.

Best Time to Go: Be aware that opening hours, happy hours, or trivia nights, etc. here listed may change, especially seasonally. Best to call or check websites or Facebook pages to be sure.

Samples and **Tours**: Prices (and tour times) may change from what you see here.

Got food? Brewery taprooms may get approval to serve food, though many probably still don't. In that case, most are likely "food friendly," meaning you can order delivery or bring your own grub into the taproom. **Brewpubs** by legal definition serve food and may offer a full bar and other breweries' beers.

Directions: For those without a GPS, these written directions should indicate the nearest major highway and specific driving directions and distances. Sometimes bus and metro lines/stops are also shown in italics, as are nearby trails and paths for cyclists.

Special Offer: *This is NOT a guarantee. The brewer reserves the right to rescind this offer at any time and for any reason.* This is something the management of the place you're visiting suggested they'd give to a patron who comes in and gets **this book** signed on the signature line of that particular brewer in the back of the book. This is a **one-time bonus** and the signature cancels it out. You must have a complete book, and photocopies or print-outs don't count. I didn't charge them and they didn't charge me; it's out of the goodness of their hearts, so take it as such and don't get all goofy on them if the keychain turns out to be a bumper sticker or supplies have run out or the bartender that night didn't get the memo about how the offer works. And if they are offering a discount on a beer, it is assumed that it is the brewer's own beer, not Bud Light or some such stuff or that fancy import you've been wishing would go on special. Legal drinking age still applies, of course. Not all brewers are participating, and that will be noted on each brewer's page.

Stumbling Distance: Two or three cool things near the brewery that are very local, very beery, very Wisconsin, or just plain cool. Some may be more of a short car ride away. If you really *are* stumbling, get a designated driver for those.

And that's about it, the rest should be self-explanatory. Enjoy the ride! Last one all the way through the breweries is a rotten egg. Or a skunk beer.

LISTINGS BY BREWER

LISTINGS BY BREWTOWN

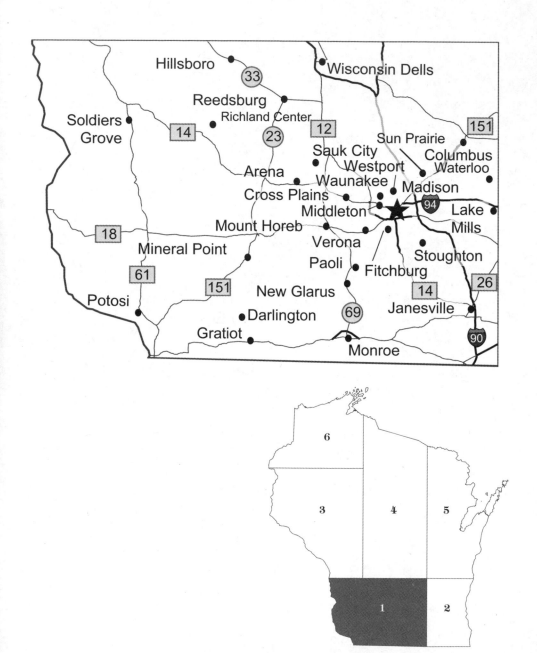

ZONE 1

Arena: Lake Louie Brewing
Columbus: Cercis Brewing Company
Cross Plains: Esser's Cross Plains
    Brewery
Darlington: City Service Brewing
Fitchburg: Great Dane Brewpub
Gratiot: Pecatonica Brewing Co.
Hillsboro: Hillsboro Brewing Co.
Janesville: Gray Brewing Co.
Janesville: Rock County Brewing Co.
Lake Mills: Sunshine Brewing Co.
Lake Mills: Tyranena Brewing Co.
Madison: Ale Asylum
Madison: ALT Brew
Madison: Delta Beer
Madison: Funk Factory Geurzeria
Madison: Giant Jones Brewing Co.
Madison: Great Dane Brewpub
Madison: Great Dane
      Brewpub—Hilldale
Madison: Karben4 Brewing
Madison: Lucky's 1313 Brewing
Madison: Next Door Brewing Co.
Madison: One Barrel Brewing
Madison: Rockhound Brewing Co.
Madison: Vintage Brewing Company
Madison: Union Corners Brewery
Madison: Working Draft Beer
Middleton: Capital Brewery
Mineral Point: Brewery Creek
    Brewpub

Monroe: Bullquarian Brewhouse
Monroe: Minhas Craft Brewery
Mount Horeb: Grumpy Troll Brew
    Pub
New Glarus: New Glarus Brewing Co.
Paoli: The Hop Garden Tap Room
Potosi: Potosi Brewing Co.
Reedsburg: Corner Pub
Richland Center: Mel's Micro
    Brewing & Pubbery
Sauk City: Vintage Brewing Sauk
    Prairie
Soldiers Grove: Driftless Brewing Co.
Stoughton: Viking Brew Pub
Sun Prairie: Full Mile Beer Co. &
    Kitchen
Verona: Boulder Brew Pub
Verona: Hop Haus Brewing Co.
Verona: Wisconsin Brewing Co.
Waterloo: Hubbleton Brewing Co.
Waunakee: The Lone Girl Brewpub
Waunakee: Octopi Brewing Co.
    (Untitled Art Brewing)
Westport: Parched Eagle Brewpub
Wisconsin Dells: Port Huron
    Brewing Co.
Wisconsin Dells: Wisconsin Dells
    Brewing Co.
    (Moosejaw Pizza)

LAKE LOUIE BREWING

7556 Pine Road • Arena, WI 53503 • 608-753-2675
lakelouie.com
Founded: 2000   **Brewmaster:** Tom Porter
Annual Production: 6,000 bbls   **Number of Beers:** 13–15

Staple Beers:

- » BUNNY GREEN TOE IPA
- » PILSNER
- » POPULATION 834 PALE ALE
- » TOMMY'S PORTER (Lager)
- » WARPED SPEED SCOTCH ALE

Rotating Beers:

- » BROTHER TIM'S BELGIAN STYLE TRIPEL
- » CHICKEN DANCE DOUBLE RYE IPA
- » DESSERT ISLAND PASSION FRUIT IPA
- » LOUIE'S RESERVE SCOTCH ALE
- » MAPLE SURPLE (brown ale w/maple syrup)
- » MILK STOUT
- » OKTOBERFEST
- » PRARIE MOON FARMHOUSE BELGIAN STYLE ALE
- » SKULL CHUCKER IPA

Most Popular Brew: Warped Speed Scotch Ale

Brewmaster's Fave: "The next one we haven't made yet."

Tours? On Saturdays, check the Facebook page. Tours are free, include samples, and fill fast. Kids will be given an espresso and a free kitten. Allegedly.

Where can you buy it? Lake Louie beer can be found state-wide in bottled six-packs (four-packs for specialty brews) and as tap accounts in various bars.

Special Offer: Not participating. Tours and samples are already free!

Directions: From US Hwy 14 go north on Oak Street in Arena. Turn left where it ends and becomes Elizabeth St/ Pine Dr. Follow this until it too takes a right angle turn to the right. Just about 1000 feet past this on the right you will see the Porter mail box and the driveway to the brewery.

The Beer Buzz: Another engineer gone brewing, founder/owner Tom Porter quit his job, cashed in the 401K, and made his garage into a brewery. "I figured I'd fail, but fail small and recover." Not so much. He brewed it all himself, produced about 200 gallons every two weeks, and then did all the deliveries as well. And it caught on. Tom used to get his parents in to pack boxes sometimes. They once had a waiting list for wannabe customers. Limited releases would sell out in less than two days, and it wasn't uncommon to see serious fans following the delivery truck on release dates. They no longer have to deliver their own beer, and a brewery expansion has helped them keep ahead of demand—just barely. It's popular stuff.

Tom bought the original brewing system from a microbrewery that gave up its ghost in Eugene, Oregon. It took four semi-trucks to get it to Wisconsin. The brewery is on twenty acres Tom got from his uncle. The name comes from the pond there where he and some friends used to go skinny dipping when they were in high school. Uncle Louie would come and chase them out of his "lake."

Big Lebowski scholars will know the significance of Bunny Green Toe. Pop 834 is the new name for Arena Premium Pale Ale. Louie's Reserve, for those in the know, is Liquid Reefer as it was dubbed when Tom tried the first batch out on the locals. They changed the name so as not to antagonize the ATF, what with them brewing in the middle of the woods and all. Many great beers have come and gone here, and what you see this year may change next. One notable heavy hitter was the Russian Imperial Stout, Mr. Mephisto, named for a classic Madison late-night TV horror-movie host. If you get nostalgic pining for that brew to come back, head to Weary Traveler Freehouse in Madison. That Dark Traveler beer they have on tap? Yeah, that's an unfiltered version of Mr. Mephisto.

Facebook.com/LakeLouie   Twitter LakeLouieBeers   Instagram LakeLouieBrewing

Want to do what Tom did? Read his "On Starting a Brewery" in the History of Beer section.

Stumbling Distance: Get your cheese curd fix at *Arena Cheese* (arenacheese.com, 300 US Hwy 14, 608-753-2501), the place with the big mouse out front. There's a window into the production area so you can watch.

CERCIS BREWING CO.

140 N Dickason Blvd • Columbus, WI 53925 • 920-350-0500
cercisbrewing.com
Opened: April 2018   **Head Brewer:** Randy Sunde
Annual Production: 450 barrels
Number of Beers: 12 on tap (3 seasonals and some guests)

Staple Beers:
- » LIGHT CREAM ALE OR KOLSCH
- » PALE ALE
- » IPA
- » AMBER OR ESB
- » PORTER, STOUT OR SCOTCH ALE
- » SEASONALS

Tours? Yes, by chance or by appointment.

Samples? Yes, sample flights.

Best Time to Go: Open Mon & Wed-Thu 4-9pm, Fri-Sat 3-11pm, Sun 11-4pm. Closed Tue. **Where can you buy it?** Here on tap and in growlers to go.

Got food? Yes, artisan pizzas and appetizers to start, and when the kitchen gets up and running, upscale pub fare. Full bar.

Special Offer: Half price on your first pint of house beer when you get your book signed.

Directions: From US-151 take Exit 118 and go southeast toward Columbus on WI-16/ James St. Continue 1 mile then turn left onto Dickason Blvd. and the brewery is on the right.

The Beer Buzz: The name should be familiar… if you're a botanist or landscaper maybe. Cercis canadensis is the genus and species name of a strain of the redbud tree that only grows in the area. In fact, Columbus is Redbud City USA. The building here dates back to 1920 when this was Redbud Lanes bowling alley. Unfortunately, Redbud Brewery once existed and so they didn't want to run into any trademark issues and chose to use the genus name, Cercis. All the remained of the bowling alley is the hardwood floor and a strip of corrugated metal where the ball return once was.

Kurt and Keith Benzine, their brother-in-law Randy Sunde and Tyler Walker, a former alderman in Columbus, bring a combined 100 years of homebrewing experience, and had long talked about the idea of opening a brewery. When Hydro Street Brewing closed in Columbus back in 2015, the partners starting making offers to the city to buy Hydro Street's equipment. The process took months and in February 2017 they bought this building and took a long time to build out what you see. They found a boiler for their brewing system in an old bowling alley in Oshkosh. (Jeff Fogle of Appleton Beer Factory lent a hand connecting the steam system of the brewery.) The 1938 tiger maple bar is also restored from a bowling alley as are 20 feet of lane wood for a bar rail that sets the brewhouse apart from the space. While Randy is in charge of the brews, the beer here is a bit of a collaborative effort.

Free WiFi. Mug Club.

Facebook.com/cercisbrewing and Twitter @CercisBrewing

Stumbling Distance: Columbus has a lot of antique shops, including Columbus Antique Mall & Museum (239 Whitney St, 920-623-1992, columbusantiquemall.com). Visit *Sassy Cow Creamery Store* (4192 Bristol Rd, Columbus, 608-837-7766, sassycowcreamery.com) for an ice-cream cone (29 flavors) or take some home. Looking for good cheese? Watch for *Schultz's Cheese Haus* (schultzscheese.com, N6312 Hwy 151, Beaver Dam, 920-885-3734) on your way to Columbus, selling Wisconsin's finest since 1962.

ESSER'S CROSS PLAINS BREWERY

2109 Hickory Street • Cross Plains, WI 53528 • 608-798-3911
essersbest.com
Founded: 1863   **Brewer**: Sand Creek Brewery
Number of beers: 4

Staple Beers:
- » CROSS PLAINS SPECIAL (lighter pilsner)
- » ESSER'S BEST (hearty lager, caramel color)
- » Golden Blonde Ale (English pale ale)
- » ANNIVERSARY ALE (amber ale)

Tours? By appointment only.

Samples: Yes

Best time to go: Not during Badger football home game days!

Where can you buy it? In area stores and bars throughout Wisconsin.

Got food? Go to Main Street for restaurants.

Special Offer: Bring your book for a signature and get a free sample and an Esser's Best patch.

Directions: Come into Cross Plains on US Hwy 14 (Main Street) and turn north on Hickory Street and they're right there on your left.

The Beer Buzz: George Esser came all the way from Cologne, Germany, in 1852 and started brewing beer for us in 1863, beating out his buddy Heinrich Leinenkugel to get a brewery started in Cross Plains. Esser's Best was brewed until 1910 when the Essers gave up brewing in favor of being a distributor. Six generations later, the family has taken the recipe from George's German diary and is producing the original with the help of the Sand Creek Brewery. The "brewery" has a collection of cool odds and ends from the old-school brewing days as well as an old hack (horse-drawn carriage) that they pull out for special events. Cross Plains threw one helluva parade in '33 when Prohibition ended and the Essers were part of the 75 year anniversary in 2008. They threw another big party and parade in 2013 to celebrate 80 years of legal beer. This is one of the oldest family businesses in the USA with the 5th and 6th generations running the show now. Great stories here, and Wayne and Larry love to chat it up, but be sure to make an appointment.

Facebook.com/EssersBest

Twitter @EssersBest

Stumbling Distance: Check out *Coach's Club* (1200 Main St, 608-413-0400) which uses Esser's Best to beer batter some fish for an excellent Friday night fish fry. *Main Street Lanes* (1721 Main St., 608-798-4900) offers great burgers and sandwiches. Nearby Black Earth Creek offers some world class trout fishing. The Table Bluff and Cross Plains Segments of *The Ice Age National Scenic Trail* (iceagetrail.org, 2110 Main St, 800-227-0046) is just outside of town and the Ice Age Trail Alliance's office is in Cross Plains. Pack some beer for the hike! (See my book *60 Hikes Within 60 Miles of Madison!*)

CITY SERVICE BREWING CO.

404 Main St. • Darlington, WI 53530 • 608-482-1930
cityservicebrewing.wixsite.com/cityservicebrewing
Opened: June 1, 2017   **Head Brewer**: Dick Tuescher
Annual Production: 50 barrels   **Number of beers**: 12 on tap (with a few guest beers)

Staple Beers:

- » ALTERNATOR (GERMAN ALT)
- » 1ST GEAR APA
- » RED LINE IRISH RED
- » ROAD TRIP (ENGLISH MILD)

Rotating Beers:

- » Centennial Blonde IPA
- » ...plus flavored malt beverages and more to come

Most Popular Brew: 1st Gear APA

Brewmaster's Fave: Red Line Irish Red

Tours? Yes, by chance or by appointment.

Samples: Yes, 4- and 6-cylinder sample flights.

Best time to go: Tasting Room is open Thu 4-9pm, Fri 4-10pm, Sat 12-10pm, Sun 1-6pm. Coffee Shop: Tue-Friday 7am-11am, Sat 8am-Noon. Come in June for the Darlington Canoe Festival (darlingtoncanoefest.com), not just for paddlers.

Where can you buy it? Here on tap and in growlers to go.

Got food? Some snacks, cheese & sausage plates, but also food-friendly, bring your own. Housemade sodas.

Special Offer: A free flight of house brews when you get your book signed.

Directions: State highways 81 and 23 meet in downtown Darlington and the brewery is right at the intersection where the meet and go north together.

Cyclists: Cheese Country Trail passes 2 blocks west of the brewery

The Beer Buzz: Ted and Angie Thuli bought and fabulously refurbished this painted white-brick service station on a downtown corner. Ted actually worked here in high school. Ted is from a family of cheesemakers (see their Thuli Family Creamery, also part of a reclaimed service station) and is part-owner of Darlington Dairy Supply. They converted the shop front to a coffee and baked goods joint which opens in the mornings, and invited longtime friend and homebrewer Dick Tuescher to brew in the back room and serve over the front counter as a taproom in evenings. Built from the building's old ductwork, the bar top is actually set upon a '62 Lincoln Continental cut in half lengthwise and folded into a right angle. When they turn on the headlights, it's a real sight to behold – as is the entire place. From top to bottom it is filled with antique items and signage from the automotive industry and more. A stop sign makes a good tabletop. The taps come out of oil cans mounted on the wall with gears, pistons, and wrenches for tap handles. A '38 German NSU motorcycle on the wall was reclaimed from a lake bottom after 56 years and comes with a story framed on the wall.

Live music on weekends, especially in summer. A beer patio is out front around the pump island.

Free WiFi. Facebook.com/cityservicebrewing

Stumbling Distance: Darlington has a beautiful old-school downtown. Look for the giant shark that is *Thuli Family Creamery* (112 W Ann St, 608-482-0215), a "creamery on wheels" that produces several cheese, yogurt, and more. *Annie's Bar & Grill* (300 Washington St, 608-776-3773) has a good fish fry. *Paddlers* will enjoy the stretch of the *Pecatonica River* north of town. **Hotels:** *Super 8* (201 Christensen Dr, 608-776-8830) and *River View Lodge* (245 W Harriet St, 608-482-2172) in town, but *Brewery Creek Brewpub & Inn* (in this book) is 15 minutes north in Mineral Point.

The Great Dane Pub and Brewery

2980 Cahill Main • Fitchburg, WI 53711 • 608-442-9000
greatdanepub.com
Founded: 2002   **Brewmaster:** Rob LoBreglio   **Head Brewer:** Craig Karels
Annual Production: 1,400 bbls   **Number of Beers:** 12 taps

Staple Beers:
» Crop Circle Wheat
» Imperial IPA
» Jon Stoner's Oatmeal Stout
» Landmark Lite Lager
» Old Glory American Pale Ale
» Stone of Scone Scotch Ale
» Verruckte Stadt German Pils

Rotating Beers:
» Amber Lager *(summer)*
» Bock
» Doppelbock *(winter)*
» Foxy Brown
» Fruit Milkshake IPAs
» Maibock *(spring)*
» Oktoberfest

Most Popular Brew: Crop Circle Wheat

Brewmaster's Fave: Peck's Pilsner

Tours? By chance or appointment but always welcomed.

Samples? Yes, a sip to decide, dontcha know, or sampler platters of four beers for about $6.50 (add 2 more for $2.50).

Best Time to Go: Happy hour is 4–6 weekdays and offers beer discounts.

Where can you buy it? On-site growlers, pub kegs, and half barrels (with 24-hour notice), but see their other locations near Hilldale Mall (also a brewpub), an east side location, and the original downtown Madison location. The Duck Blind at Madison Mallards Northwoods-League baseball games is fueled by 4 specially brewed Great Dane beers. For something farther afield, find the Dane in Wausau, WI. 100+ tap accounts around the state and now some cans in distribution.

Got food? Yes, a full menu of soups, salads, burgers, and entrees. The bratburger (created on a dare) is an original with bacon on a pretzel bun. Beer, brat, and cheese soup is Wisconsin in a bowl. Beer bread is standard, fish and chips available, and a load of other great dishes. Friday night pilsner-battered fish fry!

Special Offer: A free 10-oz beer!

Directions: From the Beltline Hwy 12/14/18/151, go south just over 1 mile on Fish Hatchery Road and the brewpub is in the complex to the right, across from the fish hatchery.

The Beer Buzz: You can change the scenery, but the beer remains the same. With a few beers unique to this location, this Dane is a nice option for those who don't want to go all the way downtown for their great beer. In the upper level of a strip mall across from the Fish Hatchery on Fish Hatchery Road just south of Madison, this place draws more of the after-work crowd and families on the weekends.

Inside you'll find dark hardwood floors around a horseshoe-shaped bar in a high-ceiling room with a large projection screen TV. (Packer and Badger games!) To the right along the wall under glass is the brewhouse on both the first floor and mezzanine, and copper brew kettles greet you by the door. The rooftop terrace is partly canopied in case of summer sprinkles and has a bar of its own. The mezzanine with four pool tables and shuffleboard rests over a quieter dining area with spacious booths and windows looking out over the parking lot toward the greenery of the Fish Hatchery across the road. When Brewer Pat Keller retired, Brewer Craig took over. Craig started in the kitchen in the downtown location in 1996. He worked his way up into the brewhouse and spent some time at all three brewing locations in Madison.

From the parking lot out front you will see the sign on the pub upstairs, but look to the left (if you're facing it) for the white grain silo and a black arrow to find the outdoor stairs up the hill to get in. There is an access road behind the mall and ramp parking if you want to avoid the steps. Smoking is allowed out on the patio.

Free WiFi. Facebook.com/greatdanefitchburg and Twitter @ greatdanepub

Stumbling Distance: *Liliana's* (www.lilianasrestaurant.com, 2951 Triverton Pike, 608-442-4444) is a New Orleans-themed fine-dining restaurant with a stellar wine list, all of which are available by the glass. *The Thirsty Goat* (3040 Cahill Main, 608-422-5500, thirstygoatbrew.com) has some good draft beers, BBQ, and plenty of TVs.

Pecotonica Brewing Co.

Taphouse Address: 136 E Main St • Warren, IL(!) • 815-745-1069
pecatonicabeer.com
Opened: 2014   **Head Brewer:** Tim Quinn
Annual Production: 1,000 barrels (40 bbls here)
Number of Beers: 12 on tap with guest beers

Staple Beers:

- » Alphorn Ale
- » Muskelager
- » Nightfall Lager
- » Pecatonica IPA
- » Quinn's Amber Lager

Rotating Beers:

- » Oktoberfest

Most Popular Brew: Muskelager

Brewmaster's Fave: Irish Red

Tours? Maybe by chance or by appointment.

Samples: Yes, flights of four 4-oz. pours and a pint of your choice for $8.

Best Time to Go: Open seasonally on Thu (6-close) and year round Fri 4-close, Sat noon-close, Sun 2-close. Live music on Saturdays.

Where can you buy it? Here on tap and in growlers to go.

Got food? Yes, maybe Chex mix and popcorn, but food friendly too.

Special Offer: Buy your first pint and get the second for half off when you get the book signed.

Directions: From the intersection of WI-11 and WI-78 in Gratiot, head south on WI-78 for 7.5 miles, and the taphouse is on the left.

The Beer Buzz: Named for the winding river through Wisconsin into Illinois, this brewery also starts in Wisconsin and ends up south of the border. Their official home is 5875 Main Street Suite A in Gratiot, but the tap house is just inside Illinois in Warren. Don't panic. While I never really encourage going outside the lines in a Wisconsin book, it made sense for the brewery. So consider this like a Wisconsin embassy, and as long as you're there within the property, you're in Wisconsin.

Brothers Tim and Tom Quinn (and silent partner A.C.) started distribution before they opened a visitable location, being careful to create a following and start making money rather than go directly into debt from day one. Potosi contract brews and bottles the large quantities for them, but the beer on tap is brewed here.

The building is an old Woolworth's with exposed brick walls and a décor of canoes and old outboard motors, mounted fish and duck decoys with some beer signs and other breweriana. They also have what is alleged to be Al Capone's poker table in the party room upstairs where you'll also find the brewhouse. Fermentation takes place on the ground floor before sending the beer to the basement to serving tanks. Oktoberfest is well received and is typically available year round now. The brothers' five-acre hop farm provides the hops for in-house brews.

Free WiFi. ATM onsite. Mug Club. Facebook.com/ PecatonicaBeerCompany

Stumbling Distance: Next door is *Wally's Pizzeria* (122 E. Main St, 815-745-3555). Getting here can be a great little Beer & Cheese route if you stop in Shullsburg, WI: Award-winning *Roelli Cheese Haus* (15982 WI-11, Shullsburg, 608-965-3779, roellicheese.com) is 15 minutes away, while *Shullsburg Cheese Store* (210 W Water St, Shullsburg, 888-331-1193) is in 6 miles from there.

HILLSBORO BREWING CO.

Brewpub: 815 Water Ave
Brewery Taproom: 206 E Madison St. • Hillsboro, WI 54634 • 608-489-7486
hillsborobrewingcompany.com

Founded: February 2012   **Brewers**: David Dietz and Snapper Verbsky
Annual Production: 750 barrels   **Number of Beers**: 14 taps, 12 of them house beers

Staple Beers:

- » BIG JIM BOURBON BROWN
- » BOHEMIAN CLUB
- » HILLSBORO PALE ALE
- » IRISH AS FECK (RED ALE)

- » JOE BEER (porter)
- » LEAPING LEMUR CREAM ALE
- » SNAPPY IPA

Rotating Beers:

- » BIG HEFE
- » KICKAPOO OIL (BLACK LAGER)
- » OKTOBERFEST

- » SAP (brewed with 100% maple sap in place of water)

Most Popular Brew: Joe Beer

Brewmaster's Fave: Hillsboro Pale Ale

Tours? Yes, by chance or by appointment.

Samples: Yes, flight of 4 five-oz pours for about $6.

Best Time to Go: Brewpub is open Tue–Sun 11AM–10PM. Closed Sundays from Nov 15–Apr 15. Brewery tap room: "Mug Club" Mondays 4:30pm-

8:30pm. Watch website or call for weekend taproom hours at the brewery once it opens.

Where can you buy it? Here on tap and to go in growlers, fine bars and restaurants around West Central Wisconsin, and soon in the taproom at the separate brewery down the street.

Got food? Yes, a full pub menu with salads, appetizers, sandwiches, and square pizza on a housemade crust (GF available). Friday night fish tacos are a big hit. Text GOTJOE to 36000 for daily lunch specials

Special Offer: Your first Hillsboro beer is free when you get your book signed.

Directions: State Highways 33, 80, and 82 come into downtown Hillsboro from either direction and become Water Ave. Look for the brewpub at the corner of Water and Mill St. The brewery will be a couple blocks east at 260 E. Madison St.

The Beer Buzz: Snapper and Kim Verbsky operate this popular brewpub in Hillsboro, and you can expect to be surrounded mostly by locals. Snapper's family has been local for 5 generations. He turned down a college wrestling opportunity to stay in Hillsboro and go into business with his father Joe, a carpenter. Thus you can see where the restoration talent came from. Joe was a homebrewer, and for a full year he worked on a beer recipe to get it just how he wanted it. He had always thought of having a brewery, and when he perfected that beer in 2012, he was ecstatic. Sadly, just days later, Joe died in a car accident. It was a devastating loss, but Snapper keeps his father's memory and beer alive in that Joe Beer you're drinking.

Snapper has a talent for restoring old buildings, and the brewpub was one of them. Back in 1906 it was a general store, but over the years it served a variety of purposes, including a shoe store. You can still see the old sign here on the wall as well as the old wood floor, tongue-in-groove ceiling, and brick walls. The concrete top bar has old shed siding on it as does the front of the building. The brewery name is a historical one as you can see from the old Hillsboro Brewery's beer cases and photos. There's plenty of room at the bar, as well as tall tables and booths. Two TVs pipe in sports.

When Snapper started brewing for the public, he headed over to Corner Pub in Reedsburg where brewer/owner Pete shared his equipment with him. As the demand grew, Snapper knew he needed his own set up. In 2015 he remodeled a tavern down the street at 1001 Water Ave. to make a brewery for a new 10-barrel system. Because demand is still growing, the brewery will be moving again to 206 E Madison St. This historic 26,000 sq. ft. building was originally a creamery built in 1914. It will house the brewery, tap room, two lage event spaces (late 2018-2019), and a gift shop. The hours for the taproom there may be limited, but check with the bar or website. *Trivia note:* the last four digits of the phone number spell PIVO, Czech for beer.

Free WiFi. Facebook.com/hillsborobrewingcompany

Twitter @HillsboroBrewCo

Stumbling Distance: *The Cheese Store & More* (186 Madison St, 608-489-2651) has Wisconsin cheese, ice cream, and a lunch menu. If you need a place to crash, a good option is *Hotel Hillsboro* (1235 Water Ave, 608-433-2807, hotelhillsboro.com). This is the Driftless Area, the land untouched by the last glaciers, so the driving around here can be quite scenic. *Wildcat Mountain State Park* (E 13660 WI-33, Ontario, WI, 608-337-4775, dnr.wi.gov) is an excellent place to camp and the *Kickapoo River* zigzagging past it is popular with paddlers (see my book *Paddling Wisconsin*).

GRAY BREWING CO.

2424 W Court Street • Janesville, WI 53548 • 608-754-5150
graybrewing.com
Founded: 1856   **Brewmaster**: Fred Gray
Annual Production: 3,500 bbls   **Number of Beers**: 9

Beers:

- » BITTER SHENANIGANS IPA (draft only)
- » BULLY PORTER
- » BUSTED KNUCKLE IRISH-STYLE ALE
- » HONEY ALE
- » OATMEAL STOUT
- » RATHSKELLER AMBER ALE (draft only)
- » ROCK HARD RED (malternative)
- » TAP JOCKEY (fruit beer)
- » WISCO WHEAT

Most Popular Brew: Busted Knuckle or Oatmeal

Brewmaster's Fave: Oatmeal Stout

Tours? Yes, $5 Regular Owners Brewery Tour is 3pm second Sat of every month. VIP tour is $20 and adds unlimited samples until 4pm and a souvenir glass. Groups of 12+ can book a tour on other Saturdays. Call or email events@graybrewing.com.

Samples? Yes.

Best Time to Go: Tasting room is open only Fri 4:30-9pm and Sat 2-7pm. Growler Hour is Sat 2-3pm before the tours.

Where can you buy it? Available in 6-pack bottles in Wisconsin, Illinois, and Pennsylvania. Busted Knuckle sells in 4-packs of 16oz. cans.

Got food? No.

Special Offer: Not participating at this time.

Directions: From I-90 take WI-26 (Exit 171) and turn southwest on Milton Ave/WI-26. Drive 2.9

miles and take the slight right on Centerway, continuing another mile. Turn right on Court St and go 1 mile and the brewery is on the right.

The Beer Buzz: Founded by Irish immigrant Joshua Gray in 1856, this was the first all-ale brewery in Wisconsin, and Fred is the fifth generation of the Gray family to operate it. Only 15% of the production is actually beer, the rest is some very popular sodas—especially the root beer. Soda is what carried the brewery through Prohibition and the Grays stuck with it until the plant was burnt down by arson in 1992. When they decided to press on, it was with the plan of their forefathers: beer and soda. The malt beverage is the raspberry-flavored Rock Hard Red. The lobby has a nice collection of breweriana and there's a gift shop.

Facebook.com/GrayBrewingCo

Stumbling Distance: *Barkley's Burgers, Brews & Dawgs* (2710 W Court St, 608-563-4481, barkleysbbd.com) is a dog-themed bar & grill with fish fry and local beers. They have a small dog park. Hikers check out the *Devil's Staircase segment* of the *Ice Age National Scenic Trail* (iceagetrail.org), which passes through town. (See my book *60 Hikes Within 60 Miles of Madison*)

Rock County Brewing Co.

10 North Parker Drive • Janesville, WI 53545 • 608-531-8120
RockCounty.beer
Opened: 2016
Annual Production: 200-250 barrels   **Number of Beers:** 8–10 on tap

Beers:
> »   A few staples and many many rotating brews

Tours? By chance or by appointment.

Samples: Yes

Best Time to Go: Open Thu 4–9PM, Fri 4—10pm, Sat 11am–10PM, Sun 10:30am—6pm.

Where can you buy it? Here on tap and in growlers/howlers to go.

Got food? No, but food friendly and possible food trucks.

Special Offer: A free sample of Rock County beer.

Directions: US 51 follows Parker Dr a bit through town. On the east side of the Rock River Bridge (US 51) at Centerway and Parker, go south on Parker to the corner of Milwaukee St and the brewery is on the left.

The Beer Buzz: When his employer downsized and he lost his job, founder/brewer John Rocco turned to beer. In order to continue homebrewing during leaner times, he started buying and selling brew supplies in 2009. By 2012, he opened Farmhouse Brewing Supply (3000 Milton Ave, Ste 109, 608-305-HOPS, FarmhouseBrewingSupply.com). John and two of his three partners, Andrew Walker and Ed Sundstedt, brew as a team. A fourth, Antoni Canzian, still lives in Pennsylvania.

Located in a restored 1900 Carriage Factory building, the brewery has a 3-bbl system on a budget—cobbled together from old dairy equipment and new brite tanks. They brew so many different beers that naming them just isn't feasible. With few exceptions beers are named by style and coded with the date they were brewed to distinguish them from previous versions of that recipe. A Year/Month number format takes a beer brewed in June of 2018, for example, and adds 1806 at the end.

Free WiFi.   Facebook.com/rockcountybrewing and Twitter @RockCountyBeer Instagram @RockCountyBrewing

Stumbling Distance: *Frankie's Supper Club* (12 S Main St, 608-352-7411) is your place for nicer dining (plus fish fry) though it is not a supper club in the traditional sense. *Lark* (60 S. Main St, 608-563-1801, larkjanesville.com) serves New American cuisine with seasonal ingredients and craft cocktails.

SUNSHINE BREWING CO.

121 S Main St • Lake Mills, WI 53551
sbc.beer

Opening: Fall 2018   **Head Brewer:** Lane Smith
Annual Production: 100 barrels   **Number of Beers:** 6-8 on tap

Staple Beers:

» TRIPEL 8   » TURN IT UP IMPERIAL IPA

Rotating Beers:

» Belgian-Style Imperial Brown   » Saison

» Porter   » Witbier

Most Popular Brew: Turn It Up

Brewmaster's Fave: Tripel 8

Tours? Yes, by chance or by appointment. It's a small place.

Samples: Yes, sample flights.

Best Time to Go: Open Thu-Sat. Check Facebook for times.

Where can you buy it? Here on tap and in bombers to go. Some draft accounts and bomber distribution in the area and as far as Trixie's in Madison.

Got food? No, but food friendly.

Special Offer: A free pint when you get your book signed.

Directions: From I-94, take Exit 259 and head south on WI-89/Main St for 0.9 mile and the brewery is on the right just before Rock Creek. *Cyclists:* This is 1 mile north of the *Glacial Drumlin State Trail* where it crosses Main St.

The Beer Buzz: Husband and wife team Lane and Sherry Smith incorporated this nanobrewery in 2016, but the project took time to come to fruition. They had planned to name it Houblon, the French word for hops. Much of the French around here, however, doesn't extend beyond fries or dressing, so they found something easier to pronounce. The Smiths moved here from notable beer city San Diego, and in pursuit of this project, Lane took the craft brewing certification course at Madison College (taught by Madison Beer Brain Joe Walts of Ale Asylum).

Lane started contract brewing at Madison's defunct House of Brews to get the beer to market before they started working on a taproom and brewhouse. This building sat vacant for decades, but its 16-inch-thick Cream City brick walls once protected ice harvested from the lake for Knickerbocker Ice Co. It overlooks Mill Pond to the west, convenient for beer and a sunset. Lane operates a two-barrel system visible in the taproom. Sherry is an artist so expect local art on the walls. Lane has a thing for Belgian style beers as do his yeast strains.

Facebook.com/sunshinebrewingcompany and

Twitter/Instagram @sunshinebrewco

Stumbling Distance: *Lewis Station Winery* (217 N Main St, 920-648-5481, lewisstationwinery.

com) is a boutique winery with samplings and a patio with live music. *The Grist Bar & Table* (103 S Main St, 920-945-2122, thegristlm.com) has great entrees, burgers, salads, and small plates (including curds) and a nicely curated list of 12 drafts and many bottled craft beers. *Crawfish Junction* (W6376 Co Rd A, Johnson Creek, 920-648-3550, crawfishjunction.com) a Cajun place in nearby Johnson Creek actually was voted best fish fry in Madison in the past. *James J Chocolate Shop* (80 Enterprise Dr, 920-648-3334, jamesjchocolateshop.com) has local handcrafted heaven. **Hotel:** *Fargo Mansion Inn* (406 Mulberry St, 920-648-3654, fargomansion.com) or *Sweet Autumn Inn* (1019 S Main St, 920-648-8244, sweetautumninn.com).

TYRANENA BREWING CO.

1025 Owen Street • Lake Mills, WI 53551 • 920-648-8699
tyranena.com
Founded: November 1998   **Brewmaster**: Rob Larson
Annual Production: 4,500 bbls
Number of Beers: 6 year-round, 6 seasonal, a variety of specialties

Staple Beers:
  » BITTER WOMAN IPA
  » CHIEF BLACKHAWK PORTER
  » HEADLESS MAN AMBER ALT
  » ROCKY'S REVENGE (bourbon-barrel aged brown ale)
  » STONE TEPEE PALE ALE
  » THREE BEACHES HONEY BLONDE

Seasonal & Specialty Beers:
  » DOWN 'N DIRTY CHOCOLATE OATMEAL STOUT
  » FARGO BROTHERS HEFEWEIZEN
  » GEMUETLICHKEIT OKTOBERFEST
  » PAINTED LADIES PUMPKIN SPICE ALE
  » SCURVY IPA WITH ORANGE PEEL
  » SHEEP SHAGGER SCOTCH ALE

"Brewers Gone Wild!" is a series of limited batches of "big, bold or ballsy beers." Past brews include: Who's Your Daddy? Bourbon Barrel-Aged Imperial Porter, Bitter Woman from Hell Extra IPA, Carnal Knowledge Double Oatmeal Stout, Fatal Attraction Imperial Black IPA, Spank Me Baby! Barley Wine-Style Ale, The Devil Made Me Do It! Imperial Oatmeal Coffee Porter.

Most Popular Brew: Bitter Woman IPA

Brewmaster's Fave: Bitter Woman IPA

Tours? Yes, free tours *most* Saturdays at 2 and 3:30PM, but check the website for exact dates/times.

Samples? No, but you can buy some in the tasting room. Occasionally there is a fun beer only available on tap here.

Best Time to Go: Off season hours for the tasting room are usually Wed–Thu 4:30–10PM, Fri 3–11PM, Sat 12PM–11PM, Sun 12PM–8PM. In summer, they usually open Mon–Tue 4:30–10PM, but check to be sure. Live music every Saturday and in summer on Fridays as well.

Where can you buy it? Here on tap and to go in growlers, and distributed in bottles all over Wisconsin and in goodly portions of Minnesota, Indiana, and the Greater Chicago area.

Got food? No, but you can carry-in or have it delivered from area restaurants. (No outside beverages though!)

Special Offer: Not participating

Directions: From the 259 Exit on I-94 head south towards Lake Mills and take the first left (east) at Tyranena Park Road (Cty Hwy V). The first right after Cty Hwy A is Owen St.

The Beer Buzz: What does Brewmaster Rob love about this job? "At the end of the day, sitting down to a beer that I brewed." When Rob left his previous job, he had to sign a 5-year non-compete agreement which essentially meant he was bound for a career change. Life's little curveball worked to the benefit of the rest of us because Rob decided to open this brewery. It takes its name from a Native American name for the nearby lake. Settlers came up with the inventive moniker Rock Lake for the rocks along the shore and Lake Mills for the town's grist mill. For a while in the 1870s, the town tried out the name Tyranena but it was soon changed back, perhaps for spelling difficulties. Rob's favorite legend of the origin of the name is that it was given to the Ho Chunk tribe by a "foreign tribe" that had lived there before them. Could it have been the same pyramidal mound-building tribe of Aztalan down the road? Who knows?

The tasting room is decorated with historical photos of Lake Mills and offers glassware, apparel, and samples for purchase. There's a beer garden in summer and even a gas grill that patrons can use.

Facebook.com/tyranena and Twitter @ tyranena

Stumbling Distance: *Aztalan Inn* (920-648-3206, W6630 Hwy B at Cty Hwy Q) is a local favorite for Friday fish fries. *Hering's Sand Bar* (920-648-3227, 345 Sandy Beach Rd) is only open in the summer but also offers the fish fry as well as cheese curds, with outdoor seating and a view of the sunset. Locally loved and arguably dangerous are the "sliders," yummy greasy burgers at the *American Legion Post 67 Hamburger Stand* (133 N Main St, only in summer—locals freeze them for winter). Rinse the arteries with some Tyranena products afterward*. First Saturday in October is the *Tyranena Oktoberfest Bike Ride* at the brewery, with food, live music, and… well, you know—beer.

---

*   Not actual medical advice, consult a heart specialist and don't sue me.

ALE ASYLUM

2002 Pankratz Street • Madison, WI 53704 • 608-663-3926
aleasylum.com
Founded: May 2006   **Brewmaster**: Dean Coffey
Annual Production: 20,000 bbls and rising
Number of Beers: up to 20 on tap; more in distribution

Staple Beers:

- » AMBERGEDDON AMBER ALE
- » BEDLAM! (IPA)
- » DEMENTO (Session Pale Ale)
- » HOPALICIOUS (American Pale Ale)
- » MADTOWN NUTBROWN ALE
- » 12 OZ. CURL (PILSNER)
- » VELVETEEN HABIT IPA
- » UNSHADOWED (German Hefeweizen)

Rotating Beers:

- » BEDLAM! (Belgian-style Dubbel)
- » B2D2 IPA
- » CONTORTER PORTER
- » DIABLO BELGA (Belgian-style Dubbel)
- » DR. VENUUM IPA
- » GODDAMBERGEDDON IMPERIAL AMBER
- » HIGH COUP IPA
- » HU$H MONEY IPA
- » NAPALM BUNNY DOUBLE IPA
- » OFF SWITCH DOUBLE IPA
- » OKTILLION OKTOBERFEST
- » PLUSH CRUSH SESSION PALE ALE
- » SATISFACTION JACKSIN (Double IPA)
- » TEARS OF MY ENEMIES

Taproom Only:

- » BALLISTIC IPA
- » BIG SLICK STOUT
- » GOLD DIGGER BLONDE ALE
- » KINK (BELGIAN-STYLE ABBEY)
- » MERCY (BELGIAN-STYLE GRAND CRU)
- » PANTHEON (IMPERIAL BROWN ALE)
- » STICKY MCDOOGLE (SCOTCH ALE)
- » TRIPEL NOVA (BELGIAN-STYLE TRIPEL)
- » ...PLUS ONE-OFFS, SPAWN SERIES TEST BATCHES, BARREL-AGED BEERS

Most Popular Brew: Hopalicious

Brewmaster's Fave: "I can't choose one of my children above the others. That'd be rude!"

Tours? They offer six on-the-hour tours every Sunday between 12:00–5:00. This 30–45 minute trip around the brewery is $5 (cash only) and includes a free pint of your choice plus a special sampling.

Samples? Yes, sips to help decide and sampler flights.

Best Time to Go: Friday nights are busiest. Open Mon–Thu 11AM–midnight; Fri–Sat 11AM–2:30PM, Sun 11AM–10PM. Happy hour M-Th 3-6pm. All day Tue. Watch for Ferment Dissent, their fall heavy-beer fest with rare barrel-aged beers and live music.

Where can you buy it? On tap here and in growlers, six-packs, twelve packs (bottles and cans) and cases to go. Six-packs, twelve-packs (bottles and cans), cases and kegs are available from Wisconsin, Minnesota, and Illinois craft-beer retailers. On tap and in bottles in many Wisconsin bars.

Got food? Excellent seasonally changing menu and nothing deep-fried with the exception of a great Friday fish fry featuring cod and a weekly changing 2nd option (blue gill, perch, walleye, shrimp). Sandwiches, salads, soups, and some veggie options.

Special Offer: A free beer during your signature visit.

Directions: From Hwy 151/East Washington Ave, take First Street north a block to where it ends at Packers Avenue. Go right here and follow it to International Lane, the road to the airport. You'll see the brewery on the corner on your right, but you'll need to go down International to the next right (Anderson St) to get to Pankratz, your next right.

The Beer Buzz: Located just west of Dane County Regional Airport (Truax Field/

MSN) is one of Madison's hottest contributors to the art of brewing. On how he started homebrewing, Brewmaster Dean offers this about his college days: "I was too poor to buy good beer and too proud to drink cheap beer." So he took matters into his own brew kit. He made a name for himself during his ten years at the now defunct Angelic Brewpub, and when he broke out on his own Dean was without limits. "Some places have strict rules about what remains on tap. I just want to play." *Fermented In Sanity* is the motto here. The name Ale Asylum acknowledges this as a refuge to pursue the art of beer. All beers are unfiltered and unpasteurized and are strictly grain, hops, yeast, and water.

From the get-go Ale Asylum was a hit and growth came rapidly. Hopalicious and Madtown Nutbrown have become staples at area bars. In August 2012 they completed construction of this 45,000 square-foot production brewery, and their annual production capacity jumped from their current 11,000 barrels/year to a maximum capacity of 50,000 barrels/year. To ensure they wouldn't have to move again, the brewery is designed to expand an additional 85,000 square feet. More seasonals make it to distribution now, changing every year. The list of taproom only beers is now long and some may come back in a future calendar. Their previous digs in an old industrial office space (now *Karben4 Brewing*) was too cramped for their growing business and had to be manipulated to be a brewery; this place is specifically designed for it, straight out of the brain of Dean Coffey.

The taproom area has a long stainless steel bar, tall tables, and high ceilings, and a mezzanine level with a smaller bar and lounge furniture (via steps in back near the restrooms). A separate dining area has booths and tables. A large patio area and a rooftop deck are outside.

Free WiFi. ATM onsite. Facebook.com/aleasylum

Twitter @Ale_Asylum, Instagram @Ale_Asylum

Stumbling Distance: Just north on Packers Ave is *Smoky Jon's Championship BBQ* (smokyjons. com, 2310 Packers Ave, 608-249-7427, smokyjons.com), an award-winning carry-out or casual sit-down joint. The other direction out on East Washington will take you to *The Malt House* (2609 E Washington Ave, 608-204-6258, malthousetavern.com). One of Madison's finest beer and whiskey bars, it is owned by a beer judge. *Bear & Bottle* (601 N Sherman Ave, 608-630-8800, bearandbottlewi. com) is a cool restaurant/bar dividing the beer menu between California and Wisconsin. *Karben4 Brewing* and *ALT Brew* are 5 minutes east on the other side of the airport. This lies within Madison's Beermuda Triangle.

Beermuda Triangle Madison

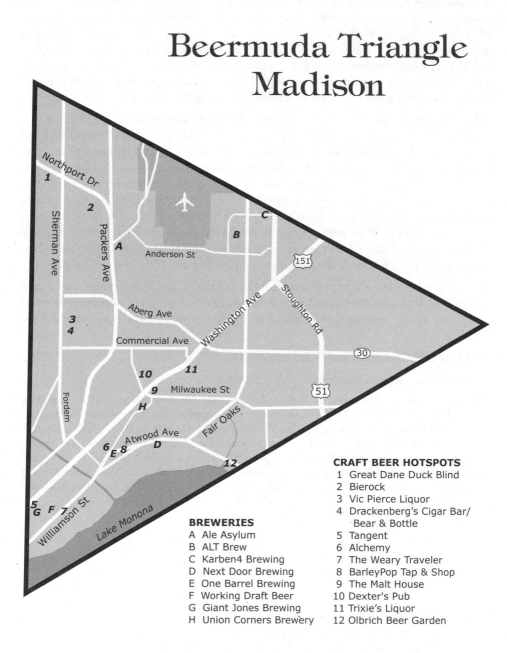

BREWERIES
A Ale Asylum
B ALT Brew
C Karben4 Brewing
D Next Door Brewing
E One Barrel Brewing
F Working Draft Beer
G Giant Jones Brewing
H Union Corners Brewery

CRAFT BEER HOTSPOTS
1 Great Dane Duck Blind
2 Bierock
3 Vic Pierce Liquor
4 Drackenberg's Cigar Bar/
   Bear & Bottle
5 Tangent
6 Alchemy
7 The Weary Traveler
8 BarleyPop Tap & Shop
9 The Malt House
10 Dexter's Pub
11 Trixie's Liquor
12 Olbrich Beer Garden

THE BEERMUDA TRIANGLE: MADISON

Call it synchronicity. Sometimes great things congregate together and there's no explaining why. For a community under 250,000 people, Madison and the surrounding area have a nice variety of breweries and craft beer bars, and the standard for restaurants has even changed remarkably over the year. There is a notable clustering of beervanic bliss on the east side that forms what many of us are calling the Beermuda Triangle. And much like its punny namesake, once you go in you may not ever come out again.

Breweries located in the triangle are *Ale Asylum*, *ALT Brew*, *Giant Jones Brewing*, *Karben4*, *Next Door*, *One Barrel Brewing*, *Union Corners Brewery* *and Working Draft Beer*.

Craft Beer Bars are as follows:

Alchemy Cafe
1980 Atwood Ave, 608-204-7644, alchemycafe.net
Excellent gastropub food with a well-curated tap list.

Bierock Craft Beer
2911 N Sherman Ave, bierockmadison.com
Serving great beers – 24 on tap – and Plains State pastries called bierocks.

Dexter's Pub
301 North St, 608-244-3535, dexterspubmadison.com
Top-notch fish fry, garlic chili fries to die for/from, 24 on tap and frequent tap takeovers.

Bear & Bottle
601 N Sherman Ave, 608-630-8800, bearandbottlewi.com
A Cali meets Wisco eatery with drafts from both states.

BarleyPop Tap & Shop
2045 Atwood Ave, 608-888-1698
A 40-tap craft beer bar and bottle sales in the Atwood 'hood.

Glass Nickel Pizza Co
2916 Atwood Ave, 608-245-0880, glassnickelpizza.com
Often voted the best pie in town, the Nickel's great tap lineup is often overlooked.

Madison Mallards at Warner Park
2920 N Sherman, 608-246-4277, mallardsbaseball.com
Several beer stations, including the all you can drink/eat Duck Blind.

The Malt House
2609 East Washington Ave, 608-204-6258, malthousetavern.com
Best selection of beer in town, owned and operated by a beer judge and four-time president of Madison Homebrewer's and Taster's Guild.

Mickey's Tavern
1524 Williamson St, 608-251-9964
A Madison classic with great bar food, a notable brunch, and several great taps.

Tex Tubb's Taco Palace
2009 Atwood Ave, 608-242-1800, textubbstacos.com
Popular for Tex-Mex, this restaurant has a good craft beer list and often hosts releases and events.

Tip Top Tavern
601 North St, 608-241-5515, thetiptoptavern.com
Recently redone with a nicer menu, the tavern also serves craft beer.

Trixie's Liquor/Growlers To Go-Go
2929 East Washington Ave, 608-442-5347, trixiesliquor.com
An excellent selection and knowledgeable staff, plus 16 drafts for growler fills.

Vic Pierce Liquor
609 North Sherman Ave, 608-244-4147
The north side's best bet for craft beer to go.

ALT BREW

1808 Wright Street • Madison, WI 53704 • 608-352-3373
altbrew.com
Founded: 2012 (Brewery opened 2015)   **Brewmaster**: Trevor Easton
Annual Production: 300 barrels   **Number of Beers**: 16+ Certified Gluten-Free

Staple Beers:

- » COPPERHEAD COPPER ALE
- » HOLLYWOOD NIGHTS BLONDE IPA
- » KICKBACK KÖLSCH
- » RUSTIC BADGER FARMHOUSE ALE

Rotating Beers:

- » BELGIAN TRIPEL
- » BLACKWATER SCOTCH ALE
- » CAMPFIRE COFFEE MILK STOUT
- » CI-BORG 49 APPLE ALE
- » 1808 ROBUST PORTER
- » HEADLESS IMPERIAL PUMPKIN ALE
- » MACHÉRIE CHERRY PORTER
- » PICNIC SHANDY
- » RAVENSWOOD IMPERIAL BROWN
- » SOLSTICE SAISON
- » VELVET MIDNIGHT BOURBON-BARREL AGED IMPERIAL BROWN
- » ...plus other seasonals

Most Popular Brew: Hollywood Nights

Samples: Yes, sample flights available.

Brewmaster's Fave: On a hot summer day? Rustic Badger. Hanging with friends? Hollywood Nights.

Best Time to Go: Open Tue-Fri 3-9pm, Sat 11am-9pm, Sun 11am-5pm. Closed Monday.

Where can you buy it? Here on tap and to go in growlers. A few local draft accounts and in stores in bombers throughout Madison. Find their beer on a map on their website.

Got food? Yes, light menu of hummus, chips & salsa, olives, cheese and charcuterie plates, plus pizzas.

Tours? Yes, scheduled Saturday afternoons.

Special Offer: A buy your first pint of Alt Brew, get one free during your signature visit.

Directions: From Stoughton Rd/US 51 just north of Washington Ave, head north one block to Anderson St. Turn left, and take the next right on Wright St. Pass Madison College and turn into the lot of the next long building on the left. You will find the brewery here.

The Beer Buzz: Necessity is the mother of fermentation. Trevor started as a homebrewer in college, and after he got married, his wife Maureen was diagnosed with celiac disease. Beer would make her sick. He couldn't brew at home either, because it would contaminate their kitchen. So he became determined to make gluten-free homebrew. The first six months he says were really bad, but he started to work things out with these alternative grains and it started to improve. After two years, they realized that if they hosted a party, they'd actually move through their own beer faster than anything else. People seemed to like it a lot. As public knowledge about celiac has grown, so has the demand for gluten-free products, and they saw this as a unique business opportunity. They were living in Chicago at the time, but both were originally East Siders in Madison. They put together a business plan, moved back to Madison, and met with Page Buchanan at House of Brews. Page tried the beer and recommended Trevor brew there. Trevor and Maureen got legal approvals as Greenview Brewing in 2013 and

took over a space at House of Brews. Though this was technically an alternating proprietorship, the equipment was exclusive to avoid contamination. In 2014, they had beer on the market.

All their ingredients, and thus the beers, are Certified Gluten-Free not gluten-removed. Trevor uses sorghum, rice, millet, honey, teff, and buckwheat, and works with a couple of gluten-free malters. Great care needs to be taken to avoid contact with malted barley or wheat or rye. They adopted the name Greenview, the name of their street when they were in Chicago, but changed the brand name to ALT Brew. The new name fit as Trevor uses the alt bier style as a base for a clean, well-balanced beer, and alt also suggests their alternative ingredients. The couple opened a simple taproom and brewery in fall of 2015 with the same one-barrel system they had been using at House of Brews. The large taproom space features a bar and tables, shuffleboard, and a room dedicated to pinball machines. Sidewalk seating in season. Board games on hand.

Free WiFi. Facebook/altbrew and Twitter/Instagram @ AltBrew

Stumbling Distance: This location is just off the bike path near Madison College (MATC) and block and a half from *Karben4 Brewing*. *Ale Asylum* is minutes away on the west side of the airport. This is inside Madison's Beermuda Triangle. Try some alternative food: the award-winning Venezuelan eatery *La Taguara* (3502 E Washington Ave, 608-721-9100, lataguara-madison.com) lets you order online for dine-in or carryout.

PHOTOS COURTESY OF ALT BREW

DELTA BEER LAB

167 E. Badger Rd. • Madison, WI 53713
delta.beer

Opening: Late 2018 **Head Brewer:** Tim "Pio" Piotrowski
Annual Production: 1,400 barrels **Number of Beers:** 12 on tap

Staple Beers:
- » Golden Ale
- » IPA

- » Porter

Rotating Beers:
- » Barleywine (Silver Medal at GABF 2017)
- » Bock
- » Oktoberfest

- » Witbier
- » (seasonals, sours, fruit beers, adjuncts, barrel-aging, house sodas, root beer)

Brewmaster's Fave: Belgian Witbier

Tours? Yes, by chance or by appointment.

Samples: Yes, sample flights.

Best Time to Go: Open Mon-Thu 4-9pm. Fri 4-11pm, Sat 11am-11pm, Sun 11am-9pm.

Where can you buy it? Here on tap and six-pack cans to go.

Got food? Yes, there's a commissary kitchen for vendors who serve from what appears to be a built-in food truck. Vendors rotate.

Special Offer: Not participating at this time.

Directions: Get off the Beltline/US-12/18 at Exit 262 for Rimrock Road. Go south of the Beltline one block on Rimrock and turn right (west) on Badger Rd. Continue about 0.1 mile and take the driveway on the left that passes along a series of businesses in an office park building. The brewery is more than halfway to the back.

Cyclists: One mile west of Capital City Trail if you take Nob Hill Rd west and turn right on Badger Rd.

The Beer Buzz: For such a young guy, Brewer/Founder Pio has sure been around a lot, and much of it on foot: in 2017, before settling in Madison he trekked the Appalachian Trail 2,189.8 miles from Georgia to Maine in 146 days. The hike of a lifetime marked a break from his days brewing for others and his plan to open his own.

Born and raised in Stevens Point, Pio homebrewed through college. He worked as a YMCA Camp Director in California but then studied in the American Brewers Guild diploma program doing his apprentice work at Oskar Blues Brewery in Colorado. He also worked as an assistant brewer in three Rock Bottom brewpubs out there, learning from three head brewers with very different philosophies and styles, "a great foundational experience," he says. Rock Bottom promoted him to head brewer in their Minneapolis location. Blue Plate Restaurant Co. picked him up from there to head a new brewing project in Minneapolis, The Freehouse. In three years, Freehouse became the largest brewpub by volume in the state of Minnesota. (Which is saying something in a state that includes powerhouses Fitger's and Town Hall.)

Pio has long focused on traditional styles but brought in a brewer with right-brain thinking to create a sort of yin and yang environment. They brew on a 10-barrel system from Wisconsin's own Quality Tank Solutions. The taproom shows lab elements in the interior design, and long community tables. Delta is the symbol for change. On the product side, this is a lab changing simple ingredients into a variety of great beers. But Pio also has a great passion for social change and tolerance; the brewery is involved in a variety of local groups focused on activism and social justice. The brewery aims to pay a living wage and as such is rejecting the tipping model of sustaining employees in favor of living wages and revenue sharing.

Expect darts, shuffleboard, bags, and board games, and a patio in back. Parking is in the lot out front.

Free WiFi. Facebook.com/deltabeerlab

Stumbling Distance: If you're attending an event at the *Alliant Energy Center* (1919 Alliant Energy Center Way, 608-267-3976), this is your pre-/post-event brewery. To the southeast of here are some nice parks with walking trails, especially *Capital Springs Recreation Area* (3113 Lake Farm Rd) and *Lake Farm Park. Capital Springs Disc Golf Course* (3398 Lake Farm Rd) is also near.

Funk Factory Geuzeria

1602 Gilson St. • Madison, WI 53715
funkfactorygeuzeria.com
Founded: 2015   **Blender:** Levi Funk
Annual Production: 220 barrels/season

Lambic-style Beers:
- » Door Kriek (sour cherries from Door County)
- » The Fox And The Grapes (with Foch grapes)
- » Framrood (with raspberries)

Other Beers:
- » Cervino (Beer/Wine Hybrid)
- » Cherry Meertz
- » Meertz
- » sour saisons

Samples: Yes, build your own flight of 6 oz. pours.

Best Time to Go: Open Thu-Fri 3-10pm, Sat 11am-12am, Sun 11am-7pm. Watch for expanded summer hours.

Where can you buy it? Here on tap and in bottles to go. You can find limited bottles in the Madison area.

Got food? Yes, small plates of meat/cheese/bread/pickles and popcorn or nuts. But it's food friendly and food trucks show up on summer weekends.

Tours? By chance or by appointment.

Special Offer: A free 6 oz. sampler when you get your book signed.

The Beer Buzz: This is where the wild things are. Lambic, a style generally associated with Belgium, is a beer made from spontaneous fermentation—in other words, wild yeasts and bacteria native to the place they are brewed. They are aged in wood barrels where they pick up their most significant microorganisms. Of the 80 or so little critters

in there, the most important are the yeasts Saccharomyces cerevisiae, Saccharomyces pastorianus and Brettanomyces bruxellensis. Lambic is a sour beer with a varying tartness, and the style has been catching on in the US. Brewers may add fruit (fruited lambic), as is the case in a kriek (sour cherry) lambic. Not a surprise in a state known for its Door County cherries. Another style of beer, known as geuze, is created when two lambics are blended. An older lambic—aged 2–3 years—and a "young" lambic that is only about a year old.

This is the funk that Levi Funk (actual name) has going on here, and people are eager to get their hands on a bottle. Previously he drove to O'so Brewing to collaborate and left the barrels in their large space. In 2014, however, he found a warehouse on Madison's south side that had sat empty, slowly decaying for 30 years. With the help of his wife Amanda, a talented remodeling designer, they turned a dismal place into a brighter one that now is home to pyramids of barrels. He got his wort from O'so Brewing, but now is on his own and uses various brewers' wort and blends his geuze which is eventually sold in corked and caged 750 ml bottles. 2018 saw the first annual release of the geuze blend.

Spelled either geuze or gueuze, the pronunciation is varied and elusive. Belgians have more than one language in the region, so that accounts for some of the differences. I've heard just plain gooz here in the States, but it sounds to me more like geh-ooz, with the two syllables themselves blending nicely like two lambics. In documentaries from Belgium in Flemish (Belgian Dutch), it sounds more like GH(y) ER-zuh, with the tricky-sounding Dutch g. Good luck with that. Just point at the bottle.

And if you think these beers are uncommon, check out meerts (rhymes with 'hertz). To our knowledge, this is the only US brewer/blender making this lower ABV relative to lambic, and one of perhaps a handful worldwide. It was traditionally made from the second runnings of lambic and served with only a few months of aging and is perhaps more approachable, a gateway sour beer. With less aging, Levi gets more meerts faster to keep customers satisfied as they wait for the longer-aged beers. He acquired three 1,000-gallon foeders (previously for cognac) to produce his meertz, and has some fruited varieties (cherry, kiwi melon, apricot, etc.) as well.

Free WiFi. Facebook/funkfactorygeuzeria and Twitter @ FFGeuzeria

Stumbling Distance: Some great soul-food fried chicken, philly steak, catfish, and wings at *Naty's Fast Food* (1616 Beld St, 608-709-6745). Maybe the best Mexican in town at *Taqueria Guadalajara* (1033 S Park St, 608-250-1824, lataqueriaguadalajara.com).

GIANT JONES BREWING CO.

931 E. Main St. • Madison, WI 53703 • 608-620-5172
giantjones.com
Opened: 2018   **Head Brewer:** Eric Jones
Annual Production: 1,000 barrels   **Number of Beers:** 6 on tap

Staple Beers:
» CYCLOPS DOUBLE IPA

Rotating Beers:
» ANTIGONUS BELGIAN STRONG (summer)
» BENANDONNER SCOTCH ALE (Celtic God of Combat, one of the Giants who made Giants Causeway) (fall)
» BLUE OX AMERICAN BARLEYWINE (spring)
» CAELUS IMPERIAL STOUT (fall-winter) (Uranus)
» IDRIS ENGLISH BARLEYWINE (winter)
» POSEIDON IMPERIAL PORTER (spring-summer)
» SATURN WEIZENBOCK (fall-winter)
» JUPITER LIGHT WEIZENBOCK (spring-summer)

Most Popular Brew: Cyclops Double IPA

Brewmaster's Fave: Antigonus (Erika) and The One I'm Drinking (Eric)

Tours? Yes, by chance or by appointment.

Samples: Yes, sample flights of four 5-oz pours for about $6. 2-oz. sample pours for $1.

Best Time to Go: Open Thu-Sat 4-10pm.

Where can you buy it? Here on tap in 8-oz. to 10-oz. pours and in 750ml bottles to go. Are draft accounts and self-distributed bottles.

Got food? No, but food friendly.

Special Offer: Half off a single Giant Jones glass when you get your book signed.

Directions: From US-151/East Washington, 9 block NE of the Capitol, turn south on Brearly St. Drive one block and it is at the corner of Brearly and Main in the same building at Old Sugar Distillery. Cyclists: A half block north on Brearly off the Capital City Trail.

The Beer Buzz: "Basically we're a barleywine brewery," says Brewer Eric. Think boutique brewery like boutique winery. Everything certified organic, big beers in big bottles. They aren't kidding when they say

Giant – all beers are north of 8% abv – and beer names are often those of giants from mythology and lore. Benandonner is the Celtic god of combat, one of the giants that made Giants Causeway. Caelus is the Roman counterpart to the Greek Uranus, which was less attractive as a beer name.

Appleton native Eric Jones is a homebrewer, Cicerone, and Grand Master beer judge, so it may come as a surprise that early on he didn't really like beer. (Sounds a bit like this author.) Then 3 Floyds Brewing's Alpha King turned him on to craft. His father had been homebrewing since 1982, and so Eric followed suit. His mother grew up in Madison, and Eric ended up at UW-Madison. Erika, a Berkeley graduate, came to UW for grad school in 2009. They had been trying to open a brewery ever since. This was their 3rd formal attempt. Third time's a charm. They are East Side residents, having bought a house here in 2014 when Old Sugar Distillery next door was still new. They loved that space and wanted something similar when the time came. In 2016, they started looking, and in 2017 settled on this location in the same building, originally a Greyhound bus station and repair garage. Note the large glass garage door that opens in nice weather. High ceilings show open rafters and the brewhouse stands behind a railing. The front door is actually on Brearly St, not Main. Parking is on the street. This not a tipping establishment, says Eric – everyone gets paid fair wages.

Free WiFi. Facebook.com/GiantJonesBeer and Twitter @GiantJonesBeer Instagram @ GiantJonesBrewing

Stumbling Distance: In the same building is *Old Sugar Distillery* (608-260-0812, oldsugardistillery.com). Just over a block away on East Washington are *Bos Meadery* (849 E Washington Ave, 608-628-3792, bosmeadery.com) and *MadisonTap* (829 E Washington Ave, 608-478-0188, madisontap.com) which has a nice assortment of craft beers and live music in their courtyard in season. Add another block to get to *High Noon Saloon* (701 E Washington Ave, 608-268-1122, high-noon.com), one of Madison's best music venues (also has craft beer). *Tangent Kitchen & Taproom* (803 E Washington Ave) features great food and original beers brewed for them by *Vintage Brewing* from both the Madison and Sauk City locations. Live music venue *The Sylvee* (25 S. Livingston St, thesylvee.com) is in the same building.

BEER JELLY FOR YOUR BEER BELLY

Some call her Chef K, others The Pickle Lady, but to me Kimberly Clark Anderson is the Beer Jelly Lady. She's already doing quite well online and at markets with her unique pickles and preserves—including Mexican sour gherkins, Moroccan-spiced pickled asparagus, pickled Brussels sprouts, blueberry balsamic jam, strawberry lavender, red currant with cardamom. Plus Gussie Mary pickled asparagus and carrots cut for cocktails. And her Chili Hot Chow Chow may be the next Sriracha sauce. But then she had a genius idea: beer jelly.

She was prepping for Fermentation Fest (fermentationfest.com) one October and did a tasting with a brewer to learn a bit about pairing. She had maybe one too many, and when she got home she thought, "I can make jelly out of anything, why not beer?" Great on crackers, toast, and a variety of other combos. "Not all beer works, but put great beer in, get great jelly out." Flavors include Smoked Porter, Oatmeal Stout, Scotch Ale, APA, Oktoberfest, Cherry beer, Tangerine IPA, and Bourbon barrel aged beers. Available in 4-oz jars. Find it: chefkclark.com

BEER GALORE: STATE STREET

State Street connects the Capitol with the University of Wisconsin. Primarily a pedestrian zone (buses, bikes, and delivery are allowed), it is the heart of downtown. Overture Center for the Arts (overturecenter.org) is here with two main performance halls, art museums and rooftop dining, and across the street is The Orpheum for concerts. Restaurants, bars, shops, and sidewalk cafes run the length. And it is also a canyon of craft beer. Highlights from the Capitol to the university's lakeside include:

Cooper's Tavern (20 W Mifflin St, 608-256-1600, thecooperstavern.com) just on the Capitol Square, has a nice selection of craft beers with some Belgians.

Freiburg Gastropub (107 State St, 608-204-2755, freiburgmadison.com) is a German-themed restaurant with many imported German beers on tap.

Cask & Ale (212 State St, 608-467-9450, caskandalemadison.com) has a nice selection of craft beers with 300 whiskeys.

Mr. Brew's Taphouse (305 W Johnson St, 608-819-6841, mrbrewstaphouse.com) keeps 72 on tap.

HopCat (222 W Gorham St, 608-807-1361, hopcat.com/Madison), the Grand Rapids-based beer bar, has a whopping 130 beers on tap, plus food and a rooftop terrace.

Paul's Club (204 State St, 608-257-5250, facebook.com/PaulsClub), a Madison classic, a bar with a fake tree in the middle, is now a newer bar with a fake tree—plus a 24-tap lineup.

The Side Door Grill (240 W Gilman St, 608-310-4800, thesidedoorgrill.com), a best-kept-secret, (personal fave), a 40-tap bar with excellent pub food.

Vintage Brewing's sister restaurant (529 University Ave, 608-250-0700, vintagemadison.com) serves their beers and more just off State Street.

State Street Brats (603 State St, 608-255-5544, statestreetbrats.com) not huge on craft, but the brat scene, sports TV, and patio deserve a nod.

UW Memorial Union (800 Langdon St, 608-265-3000, union.wisc.edu), home of the **Rathskeller** and the lakeside **Terrace**, is the very heart of the community and ideal in the summer. Watch the sunset and hear free live music while drinking an impressive assortment of Wisconsin and other craft beers by the glass or in pitchers on the shores of Lake Mendota. You no longer need to be a Union member to purchase beer. In winter, the music continues but indoors in what could be a German beer hall. Also served are outdoor grilled food (burgers, brats), fired-oven pizzas, and the famous Babcock ice cream. Out-of-staters should at least taste Blue Moon, a very Wisconsin ice cream flavor.

The Great Dane Pub and Brewery

123 E Doty Street • Madison, WI 53703 • 608-284-0000
greatdanepub.com
Founded: November 1994
Brewmaster: Rob LoBreglio   **Head Brewer:** Michael Fay
Annual Production: 2,700 bbls   **Number of Beers**: 17 on tap plus a couple casks

Staple Beers:

- Black Earth Porter
- Crop Circle Wheat Ale
- Devil's Lake Red Lager (on nitro)
- Emerald Isle Stout
- Landmark Lite
- Old Glory APA
- Peck's Pilsner
- Stone of Scone Scotch Ale
- Verrückte Stadt German Pils

Rotating Beers:

- Barleywine
- Furious River IPA
- John Jacob Jingle Heimer Schmidt Dunkel-Doppel-Hefe-Weizenbock (ask them to say it for you really fast)
- A couple Belgian Brews throughout the year
- Fruit Beers in summer
- Always 1–2 Gravity Casks
- Irish Ale around St. Patty's
- Oktoberfest
- Spiced Holiday Ale
- *... and loads of others*

Most Popular Brew: Crop Circle Wheat

Brewmaster's Fave: Verrückte Stadt German Pils

Tours? By appointment only.

Samples? Yes, a sip to decide, dontcha know, or sampler platters of four beers for about $6.50 (add 2 more for $2.50).

Best Time to Go: Happy hour 4–6 pm Mon–Fri plus free popcorn. When the university is in session, the place hops on weekends (and even when it's not). Sunday brunch is nice too.

Where can you buy it? On-site growlers and Crowlers (fill-on-demand 32-oz cans), pub kegs, and half barrels (with 24-hour notice), but see their other locations at Hilldale and in Fitchburg (also brewpubs), and the Great Dane East Side location. The Duck Blind at Madison Mallards Northwoods-League baseball games is fueled by four specially brewed Great Dane beers. For something farther afield, find the Dane in Wausau, WI. 100+ tap accounts and cans in distribution throughout the state.

Got food? Yes, and it's very popular for lunch and dinner. Full menu of soups, salads, burgers, entrees and more. The bratburger (created on a dare) is an original with bacon on a

pretzel bun. Beer, brat and cheese soup is Wisconsin in a bowl. Beer bread is standard, fish and chips available, and a load of other great dishes. Friday night pilsner-battered fish fry!

Special Offer: A 10-oz beer and all the coasters you can eat.

Directions: Head for the Capitol and follow the Capitol Loop (two streets out from the Capitol) along Doty Street where it meets King and Webster St. The Dane is on the corner. Street parking is metered until 6 PM or park in the ramp on the opposite end of the same block.

The Beer Buzz: The Great Dane has been around long enough to be a landmark in itself just off the Capitol Square in Madison, but its home is also the former Fess Hotel, built in the 1850s with an addition in 1883 and remodeled in 1901. The opening of the Dane by college buddies Rob LoBreglio and Eliot Butler saw some more remodeling in 1994, and it is now a lively joint with music, a pool hall, and three bars. You'll spot the big neon Brewpub sign as you come up the hill. The Rathskeller (the basement bar) was once a stable for horses and keeps the original stone walls. Outside dining is a seasonal bonus in the beer garden where hops climb the bricks on the backside of the building. There are also some tales of spirits of the nonalcohol kind, perhaps former guests of the Fess.

All the character of the historic building and the awesome menu aside, the beer is the crowning centerpiece of this place. On the way to the restrooms downstairs, you can pass the tanks where this magical stuff works its way up to the bars through a tangling system of tap lines referred to as The Matrix. The Red Lager is run through a Guinness tap (under nitrogen) which gives it that cascading foam head which can hypnotize you to drink more beer. This is brewmaster Rob LoBreglio's pride and joy. Expect innovative ideas from this bunch, always with an insistence on quality. The Dane now also sells Eliot Butler's Scotch Ale jerky as well as beer soap. "It'll get you clean but not necessarily sober."

Free WiFi. Facebook.com/greatdanedowntown and Twitter @ GreatDanePub

Trivia note: Right across the street is a sign marking the site of Madison's first public house: Peck's Cabin.

Stumbling Distance: *The Old Fashioned* (www.theoldfashioned.com, 23 N Pinckney St, 608-310-4545), highly recommended, offers an all-Wisconsin menu and 52 taps of Wisconsin beers plus a truckload in bottles. The menu is 100% Wisconsin style, with beer-cheese soup, brats, the state cocktail, and the best curds in town. The *Wisconsin State Capitol* (www.wisconsin.gov, 608-266-0382) is one block from here and a definite must-see with daily free tours and a 6th floor observation deck and museum. The square itself hosts a variety of events throughout the year, but especially a Saturday morning *Farmers' Market* (exclusively local produce, cheese, meats, and other products) and Wednesday evening *Concerts on the Square* or *Jazz at 5* in summer. Down the hill from the Dane are *Come Back In* (508 E Wilson St, 608-258-8619) and *Essen Haus* (514 E Wilson, 608-255-4674), connected at the hip: one is quite tavern with 24 craft taps plus bottles, the other is quite German, with German tap beers, glass boots, and often a polka band. Free peanuts and popcorn at both. *Bos Meadery* (849 E Washington Ave, 608-628-3792, bosmeadery.com) has a tasting room serving their meads and offering tours. *Old Sugar Distillery* (931 E Main St, 608-260-0812, oldsugardistillery.com) produces craft rum, ouzo, whiskey and honey liqueur and serves cocktails in their tasting room Thu–Sat with a limited snack/appetizer menu. Free tastes and tours. Working Draft Beer and Giant Jones Brewing are near.

BREW & VIEW

Beer pairs well with a lot of things, not the least of which is film. **The Majestic Theatre** in Madison (around the corner from *The Great Dane Pub and Brewery*) is typically a live music venue but also hosts DJs and theme parties. The theme here (besides beer) is cinematic gems. The Brew and View tradition started with the classic *The Big Lebowski*, which makes a return from time to time. Other classics? *Office Space, Dazed and Confused, This is Spinal Tap*—you get the idea. Watch for these events! 115 King St. | majesticmadison.com | 608-255-0901

MADISON'S BIERGARTEN AT OLBRICH PARK

Situated along the shore of Lake Monona in Olbrich Park this hotly debated public beer space finally came to fruition in 2017. Bring your own food if you like, but they do serve Nürnburg-style bratwursts, soft pretzels, and fresh cheese curds. Family friendly for sure and the Olbrich Botanical Gardens are across the way. Open daily in season around 4pm, and at noon on Sat-Sun, with last call at 9pm. Six on tap plus a cider. 3527 Atwood Ave | olbrichbiergarten.com | 608-237-3548

THE GREAT DANE PUB AND BREWERY (HILLDALE)

357 Price Place • Madison, WI 53705 (Hilldale Mall on Midvale Blvd.)
608-661-9400
greatdanepub.com
Founded: 2006
Brewmaster: Rob LoBreglio   **Head Brewer**: Nate Zukas
Annual Production: 3,000 bbls   **Number of Beers**: 15 on tap, 1 cider, 2 beer engines

Staple Beers:

- » Black Earth Porter
- » Crop Circle Wheat
- » Emerald Isle Stout
- » Imperial IPA
- » Landmark Lite Lager

- » Old Glory American Pale Ale
- » Peck's Pilsner
- » Stone of Scone Scotch Ale
- » Verruckte Stadt German Pils

Rotating Beers:

- » Barleywine
- » Bock
- » Doppelbock (winter)
- » JOHN JACOB JINGLE HEIMER

SCHMIDT DUNKEL-DOPPEL-HEFE-WEIZENBOCK (ask them to say it for you really fast)

- » Maibock (spring)

- » Mudluscious Imperial Stout
- » Oktoberfest
- » Oranje Crush Saison
- » Pine Marten Red Ale

- » Siam Strong Pale Ale
- » Tangerine Dream (dry-hopped doppel-hefe-weizenbock)

Most Popular Brew: Imperial IPA

Brewer's Fave: "Impossible to pick one."

Tours? By chance or appointment but always welcomed.

Samples? Yes, a sip to decide, dontcha know, or sampler platters of four beers for about $6.50 (add 2 more for $2.50).

Best Time to Go: Happy hour is 4–6PM and offers beer discounts. Watch for Bockfest in Jan/Feb before Fat Tuesday. A fest for charity featuring the largest gathering of bock beers in the world. The Dane contributes around 16 and 10 other brewers come with some as well.

Where can you buy it? On-site growlersand Crowlers, pub kegs, and half barrels (with 24-hour notice), but see their other locations in Fitchburg (also a brewpub), an east side location, and the original downtown brewpub. The Duck Blind at Madison Mallards Northwoods-League baseball games is fueled by 4 specially brewed Great Dane beers. All beer for the ballpark is produced here and a bit extra shores up production in Fitchburg as well. For something farther afield, find the Dane in Wausau, WI. 100+ tap accounts and cans distributed throughout the state.

Got food? Yes, a full menu of soups, salads, burgers, and entrees. The bratburger (created on a dare) is an original with bacon on a pretzel bun. Beer, brat and cheese soup is Wisconsin in a bowl. Beer bread is standard, fish and chips available, and a load of other great dishes, including a delicious Thai curry (a version of *khao soi*). Friday night pilsner-battered fish fry!

Special Offer: A free 10-oz beer!

Directions: From the Beltline Highway (12/14/18/151) go north on Midvale Blvd until just before University Avenue and turn left at Heather Crest (or come south one long block south of University Avenue and turn right). The Dane is on the left corner at the next cross street right before the Hilldale Mall building.

The Beer Buzz: This brewpub was a challenge to an outdated brewing law in Wisconsin that didn't allow a brewer producing over 4,000 barrels each year to have more than two brewing locations. When the Hilldale location opened its doors in 2006 it could not serve its own brews and for a while got by on featuring other Wisconsin beers. When the law finally

changed in 2007, the expected varieties of Dane brews started flowing. Brewer Eric took over here, leaving Michael in charge at the downtown location. Nate was assistant brewer for 3 years before taking the lead in 2012.

Abundant table seating for diners is complemented by booths in the bar area as well as tall tables and a long narrow bar-table with stools down the middle of the room in front of the bar itself. The near west side location has been a huge success, and an expansion in 2009 opened up more seating including a mezzanine section and added room for pool tables, shuffleboard and foosball. Lots of big TVs pipe in sports from around the world. The Dane equation for its multiple locations can be expressed thus: similar enough that you can count on all of them for good beer and good times, different enough that you want to visit them all. Parking is on the street or in a nearby free ramp. The stout's name mud-luscious comes from a puddle-wonderful poem by e.e. cummings i think.

Stumbling Distance: Nearby are fabulous eateries: *Café Porta Alba* (cafeportaalba.com, 608-441-0202) with some true Italian wood-fired oven pizza, sushi at *Sushi Muramoto* (muramoto.biz, 608-441-1090), and the tequila bar and southwestern restaurant *Pasqual's* (pasquals.net, 608-663-8226). Right down the row in front of Hilldale Mall. Inside the mall complex is the new *Café Hollander*, a Madison version of Milwaukee's well known Europub with a long list of Belgian beers.

BASEBALL AND A BEEYAH HEEYAH! (A BEER HERE!)

It's our national pastime, the perfect way to enjoy a summer afternoon—nostalgic, exciting, and as American as apple pie and American Idol. Beer, I mean. And it goes great with baseball, too. Wisconsin's professional baseball team is of course the Milwaukee Brewers (brewers.mlb.com) and they play in Miller Park. That's as beery as it gets. Don't be surprised to see some Wisconsin craft beers there as well. New Glarus Brewing's Spotted Cow is a given, plus local brewers such as Lakefront and Milwaukee Brewing Co., plus Leinie's and Point.

Part of the Summer Collegiate Baseball's Northwoods League, the Madison Mallards (mallardsbaseball.com) at Warner Park on North Sherman Ave offer games that are a lot of fun but don't pinch the wallet so much as the majors do. The ballpark has several beer stands with Wisconsin and other craft beers in the lineup. The Duck Blind, a great beer garden serviced by The Great Dane, provides all you can eat and drink in the Duck Blind and nearly 20 beers are on tap including Great Dane brews and others.

Up in Appleton, Fox River Brewing provides Snaketail Ale for the Wisconsin Timber Rattlers, a Class A minor league team of the Midwest League affiliated with the Milwaukee Brewers, and Dock Spiders Pale Ale for the Dock Spiders in Fond du Lac. Be careful as you pass the next cup down the bleacher row. Nobody likes a spiller.

KARBEN4 BREWING

3698 Kinsman Blvd • Madison, WI 53704 • 608-241-4812
karben4.com
Founded: September 2012 **Brewmaster:** Ryan Koga
Annual Production: 12,000 barrels **Number of Beers:** up to 10 on tap (40+ per year)

Staple Beers:

- » BLOCK PARTY AMBER ALE
- » DRAGON FRUIT IPA
- » FANTASY FACTORY IPA
- » LADY LUCK IRISH RED
- » UNDERCOVER SESSION ALE

Rotating Beers:

- » CHAMPAGNE TORTOISE ENGLISH MILD
- » DEEP WINTER COFFEE STOUT
- » DIET STARTS TOMORROW (DST) (chocolate oatmeal stout)
- » IDIOT FARM DOUBLE IPA
- » MARTIAN SUNRISE RED IPA
- » NIGHTCALL SMOKED PORTER
- » SILK SCORPION BLACK IPA
- » TOKYO SAUNA PALE ALE
- » plus other monthly seasonals, one-offs and various barrel-aged and sour beers

Most Popular Brew: Fantasy Factory

Brewmaster's Fave: Depends on his mood.

Tours? Yes, free tours at 3PM on Saturdays.

Samples: Yes, 5oz pours for $2-$3 each

Best Time to Go: Open daily 11am-10pm, Sun 10am-8pm. Watch Facebook for beer release parties. Tap It Tuesday, a firkin 1st Tuesday of the month, and Brewers Series beers off the one-barrel pilot-system release on the 3rd Thursday.

Where can you buy it? On tap here and in growlers to go. Distributed in 6-pack bottles and draft accounts throughout Wisconsin, and adding cans in 2018.

Got food? Yes, a list of "Boards" with cheese and sausage, chips and dip sorts of things, plus soups, sandwiches, salads and flatbreads. Sunday brunch has its own menu 10am–2pm. Most of the food is locally sourced, much from Fischer Family Farm. There is a full bar.

Special Offer: Buy your first Karben4 pour, get one free during your signature visit.

Directions: Take US Hwy 151 on Madison's east side (E Washington Ave) and turn north on Hwy 51/Stoughton Rd. At the cross street Kinsman where there's a McDonald's on the right, go left and it is the first driveway on the right. *Karben4 is also on the #6 bus line.*

The Beer Buzz: Nature abhors a vacuum, they say. As soon as Ale Asylum moved out of this place to their new big brewery, Karben4 moved right in, even keeping some of the previous brewers' equipment. Ryan went to school for pre-med so has a background in biology, chemistry, and psychology. But life took a malty turn when he moved to

Montana for a grad program in sports medicine. Another guy in his program was a brewer and needed some bottling help, and Ryan took on the job for rent money. He wasn't into beer, didn't homebrew, but when he popped open an oatmeal stout on the line, he had his A-ha! moment and was hooked. "All beer experiences should be like this," he says. He finished school and picked up more responsibilities at the brewery and was soon co-brewer. Then the other guy left.

What's the best part about brewing? "The people you meet in the tap room." He met his wife at the brewery in Montana, as well as his best friend, doctor, mechanic... "You get to meet a lot of cool people." Yes, beer brings us together. Originally from Appleton, he made the move back to Wisconsin at just the right time to take over the old Ale Asylum digs. Growth and success came pretty fast.

Geeks Brewing Co. was the original name idea. Ryan has the passion of a beer geek

and believes the name ought to reflect that, thus the sci-fi sounding name. In terms of brewing style, he loves the varieties of malt out there. While he's fine with a hoppy brew (and his Fantasy Factory is killing it with 70% of their distribution), he really likes looking at beer from the malt angle. He also likes to do a lot of research into a beer style and reads the culinary and cultural history of a place to influence his recipes.

The taproom has polished concrete floors, high industrial ceilings, and a gray interior contrasted by some very colorful paintings—each one inspired by each beer—by artist Tom Kowalke. A long bar bends around the kitchen and various tables and tall tables fill the room. Three 70-inch TVs that come on for the Packers/Badgers and other big events. A nice outdoor patio/beer garden is under a trellis. Plus their darts, music playing, and plenty of merchandise behind the bar. Parking in front is limited but go all the way around back for more and walk in through the beer garden door.

Free WiFi. ATM onsite.Facebook.com/Karben4

Twitter @ Karben4 Instagram @Karben4Brewing

Stumbling Distance: *Dexter's* (www.dexterspubmadison.com, 301 North St, 608-244-3535) is a stellar neighborhood bar and grill with superb burgers, unbelievable garlic-chili fries and loads more, plus a rotating menu of top-notch microbrews. Dexter's lies at one corner of the *Beermuda Triangle* (see One Barrel Brewing's Stumbling Distance). *Ale Asylum* is 5 minutes west on the other side of the airport.

Lucky's 1313 Brew Pub

1313 Regent St • Madison, WI 53715 • 608-250-8989
luckys1313.com
Opened: 2015   **Head Brewer:** Keith Symonds
Number of Beers: 24 on tap, some guest beers

Staple Beers:

- » Midnight Wheat
- » Happy-Go-Luccky Pale Ale
- » Horseshoe Stout
- » Madtown Hops IPA
- » Greenbush Golden Ale

Tours? Yes, by chance or by appointment.

Samples: Yes, sample flights available.

Best Time to Go: Open Mon-Thu 11am-2am, Fri-Sat 11am-2:30am, Sun 11am-2am. Free darts on Sundays.

Where can you buy it? Here on tap and in growlers to go.

Got food? Yes, a full menu of bar food, including pizzas, burgers, wings, and Friday fish fry. Daily soups, salads, and a full bar and cocktail menu.

Special Offer: Not participating.

Directions: US-151 through Madison follows John Nolen Drive for a bit along Lake Monona. Where US-151 turns off John Nolen onto North Shore Drive, follow it west and through a couple curves before it turns into Regent St. The brewery is in a big brick building on the left. *A 7-minute walk to Camp Randall, about 15 minutes to the Kohl Center.*

The Beer Buzz: Horseshoes abound, but the best luck here is to be so close to Camp Randall during Badger football season. In the 1920s and 30s this was Meier's Garage, owners of a Yellow Truck franchise that General Motors would pick up and rebrand GMC. The family started a bus service that eventually became Badger Bus, and here is where those buses were serviced. From 1969 to 2015 it was home to Foreign Car Specialists. A remodeling transformed the old brick building into a giant sports bar and brewpub with 14 TVs, long communal

tables, tall tables, and a large horseshoe-shaped bar. The industrial look is preserved with high exposed-rafter ceilings and a concrete floor. Glass doors to the brewhouse show Beer Church above them. Garage doors open to the street and the back to air it out and accommodate crowds during Badger game days. A whole second section, as big as the main, doubles capacity during special events. That side has its own bar as well. Brewer

Keith originally started up Next Door Brewing, and went on to do brewery consulting work before landing here in late 2017.

Free WiFi. ATM onsite. Facebook.com/Luckys1313

Twitter @LuckysBrewPub Instagram @Luckys1313_Madison

Stumbling Distance: A breakfast institution, *Mickies Dairy Bar* (1511 Monroe St, 608-256-9476) offers breakfast scramblers that would hold you down in a gale and malteds served along with that last extra bit in the metal cup. *Greenbush Bakery* (1305 Regent St, 608-257-1151, greenbushbakery.com) has the best donuts and serves them late-night (or early morning?). Continue west and follow Monroe St to find true Napoletana-style at *Pizza Brutta* (1805 Monroe St, 608-257-2120, pizzabrutta.com) and Madison's finest Belgian beer bar and eatery *Brasserie V* (1923 Monroe St, 608-255-8500, brasseriev.com). 26 taps, 300+ bottles, frites and more. **Hotel:** *HotelRED* (1501 Monroe St, 608-819-8228, hotelred.com)

NEXT DOOR BREWING CO.

2439 Atwood Ave • Madison, WI 53704 • 608-729-3683
nextdoorbrewing.com
Founded: January 2013   **Head Brewer:** Dave Hansen
Annual Production: 200 barrels (plus 1,000 bbls contract brewing)
Number of Beers: 11 on tap; 30 beers per year

Staple Beers:

- » BUBBLER BLONDE
- » DARTH PORTER
- » KALEIDOSPOKE PALE ALE
- » IRON BRIGADE STOUT
- » LUMINOUS IPA
- » ROCKET'S RED

Rotating Beers:

- » HYPERBOLIC DOUBLE IPA
- » IMPERIAL RYE STOUT
- » JETPACK TURTLE IPA
- » MUTHA PUCKA (sour blonde with pineapple)
- » PLUMPTUOUS SCOTCH ALE
- » WHEAT FORK HEFEWEIZEN
- » …mostly ales, sours such as Berliner Weisse, some fruit infusions and oak/barrel aging, and occasional firkins

Most Popular Brew: Kaleidospoke Pale Ale

Samples: Yes, a full flight of 11 sampler beers for $20.

Brewer's Fave: Darth Porter

Best Time to Go: Mon 4–10PM, Tue 11AM–10PM, Wed–Thu 11AM–11PM, Fri–Sat 11–12AM, Sun 11AM–9PM (Sunday brunch specials 11AM–3PM). Happy hour runs Mon 4–9, Tue–Thu 4–7PM, and Fri 3–6PM, with different specials each night.

Where can you buy it? Here on tap in pints and half-pints and to go in growlers, and occasional limited 22-oz bombers onsite and six-pack 12-oz bottles (twelve-pack cans of Bubbler) in Madison, Milwaukee and Fox River Valley markets.

Got food? Yes, a menu of sliders, croquettes, small plates (including curds and poutine), soups/salads, and burgers/sandwiches. Friday fish fry.

Tours? Yes, by chance or by appointment.

Special Offer: A free half pint of Next Door beer during your signature visit.

Directions: Follow Williamson Street east and it becomes Eastwood, then Atwood. The brewery is on the right. (From East Washington, head south on 1st St and take a left on Eastwood.)

Cyclists: not far off the Capital City Trail

The Beer Buzz: Set in a former appliance repair shop, Next Door Brewing happened when Keith Symonds, a Wisconsin native with a mission to start a brewpub, found Aric Dieter and Pepper Stebbins, who had the same ambition. They built out this neighborhood location and for a while Keith did the brewing before moving on to other projects. A couple talented brewers have passed through here, and yet another, Dave Hansen, a UC-Davis master brewer grad, took up the reins late in 2017. An East Side Madison native, his background is actually in music (see David of Titletown Brewing as well), percussion to be exact. Dave oversaw the Big Eddy line of beers at Leinenkugel's 10th Street Brewery in Milwaukee before returning to his hometown as a head brewer. They run a three-barrel electric brew system and have 36 barrels of fermentation capacity. They are also doing some contract brewing (with Potosi Brewing) in addition to the beer made onsite, to keep up with the demands of distribution.

The dining area offers tables, half-booths and big communal tables (made from wood salvaged from the old Point Brewery malt silos). The bar area has an L-shaped bar and some tall tables, and a counter along the wall looking through glass into the brewery. A few TVs come out during major sporting events and there are some board games on hand. A lot alongside the building offers a bit of off-street parking.

Free WiFi. Facebook/NextDoorBrewing and Twitter @ NextDoorBrewing

Stumbling Distance: *Stalzy's Deli* (2701 Atwood Ave, 608-249-7806, stalzysdeli.com) is right across the street and does great sandwiches. *Bunky's Café* (2425 Atwood Ave, 608-204-7004, bunkyscafe. net) is a longtime favorite with Mediterranean/Italian fare. *Harmony Bar & Grill* (2201 Atwood Ave, 608-249-4333, harmonybarandgrill.com) is a real tavern with good grub (especially their pizza) and a short but decent tap list.

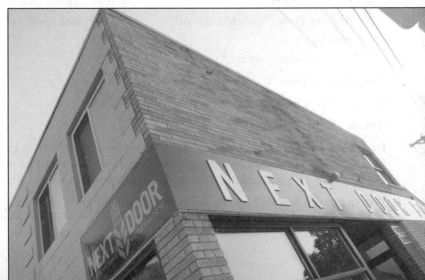

ONE BARREL BREWING

2001 Atwood Ave. • Madison, WI 53704 • 608-630-9286
onebarrelbrewing.com
Founded: July 2012   **Brewmaster:** Matt Gerdts
Annual Production: 4,200 bbls   **Number of Beers:** 12 on tap

Staple Beers:

- » BANJO CAT BLACK IPA
- » COMMUTER KÖLSCH
- » FANNY PACK IPA
- » PENGUIN PALE ALE

Rotating Beers:

- » BREAKFAST BEER IMPERIAL COFFEE STOUT
- » EMPEROR PENGUIN IMPERIAL IPA
- » HOP CITY IPA
- » INTENTIONALLY LEFT BLANK
- IMPERIAL IPA
- » WILLIE SCOTCH ALE
- » Sour beers, barrel-aged beers and many other come-and-go brews

Most Popular Brew: Commuter Kölsch

Brewmaster's Fave: Fanny Pack IPA

Tours? Yes, randomly and if you ask politely, but the tour can be done from your bar stool.

Samples? Yes, flights of four 5-oz pours for about $10.

Best Time to Go: Open Mon–Wed 4–11PM, Thu 4PM–1AM, Fri 2:00PM–1AM, Sat 12PM–1AM, Sun 12PM–9PM. Thursday is Bike Night when you can get your first beer for $1 if you come on bike (just show your helmet).

Where can you buy it? Here on tap and to go in growlers, plus on draft around Madison. Six- and four-pack bottles at select locations statewide.

Got food? Yes, various pre-made foods from local vendors, Wisco picnic (cheese curds and summer sausage), Fraboni's pizzas, and Batch Bakehouse soft pretzels, for example. Or just carry in—it's OK!

Special Offer: A hug or the best high five you'll ever get, plus $1 off your first One Barrel beer when you get your book signed!

Directions: From East Washington Ave (US Highway 151) go south on S. 2nd Street and then go right on Winnebago Street a half block to where it intersects Atwood Avenue. It's right there at this intersection on the corner, known as Schenk's Corners.

Cyclists: not far off the beer-connecting Capital City Trail

The Beer Buzz: As might be apparent in the name, this little brewery brews the hard way at the taproom: one barrel (two half-barrels, 31 gallons, see the index if you're measure-curious) at a time. (Larger batches for distribution are brewed offsite.) Peter Gentry was born and raised in this neighborhood, Schenk's Corners, as was his father. This is as local as you get. Gentry thought he was buying his father a brewing kit back in 2004 when he picked one up from the Wine and Hop Shop in Madison. But it turned out Peter loved it more. He brewed for friends at first but won the Grumpy Troll brewing challenge in

2008. From there he went on to a national competition and in 2010 his #2 Strong Ale got honorable mention in the US Beer Tasting Championship. He quit his day job in 2011 to plan this brewery, which opened not long after. They also have a sour program in the basement, so you can expect a monthly release that will go fast.

Set in an old brick building that was once a cooper's shop (barrel maker, how appropriate!) and then a grocer's in the early 1900s, the brewpub has hardwood floors and exposed brick walls. Track lighting is left over from its previous occupation as an art gallery. The brew system is glassed in at the back of the bar. They brew 4 or 5 one-barrel batches per week, so you can expect something new every time you stop in. They've got board games, a jackalope on the wall, and a large-screen TV, which is only unveiled for special games.

Brewer Matt worked at now defunct Brew & Grow on Willy Street, and spent some time brewing at Next Door Brewing. A longtime homebrewer, he has a degree in soil sciences with chemistry and biology.

Free WiFi. Facebook.com/OneBarrelBrewing

Twitter and Instagram @OneBarrelBrewCo

Stumbling Distance: This is Schenk's Corners, the heart of one of Madison's old neighborhoods, and there are a number of places to eat around here. *Tex Tubb's Taco Palace* (608-242-1800, tex-tubbstacos.com) is next door and serves Tex-Mex and hosts the occasional beer event. Great tap lists await at *Alchemy Café* (across the intersection, 608-204-7644, alchemycafe.net), *Dexter's Pub & Grill* (301 North St, 608-244-3535, dexterspubmadison.com), and *The Malt House* (2609 E Washington Ave, 608-204-6258, malthousetavern.com). The *Barrymore Theatre* is also a stone's throw down Atwood Ave offering great live music of local, national, and international acclaim. *Next Door Brewing* is minutes away east on Atwood Ave.

One Barrel also touches on the *Beermuda Triangle* (see Beermuda Triangle text box).

ROCKHOUND BREWING CO.

444 South Park Street • Madison, WI 53715 • 608-285-9023
rockhoundbrewing.com
Opening Date: January, 2016   **Brewmaster**: Nate Warnke
Annual Production: 500 barrels   **Number of Beers**: up to 16 on tap (some guests)

Staple Beers:

- » BALANCED ROCK RYE
- » GRANDPA'S LAGER
- » GRINDER COFFEE PORTER

- » ICE SHANTY BOCK
- » MOSQUITO BITE IPA
- » OUTCROP OATMEAL PALE ALE

Rotating Beers:

- » GLOWING EMBERS (brandy-barrel-aged smoked hop ale)
- » MIDNIGHT HARVEST (Belgian-style multi-grain ale)
- » PLOWSHARE FARMHOUSE ALE

- » SHOT ROCK SCOTCH ALE
- » TUMBLED BOULDERS (WHISKEY-BARREL-AGED RYE IPA)
- » WIND KNOT BLACK LAGER
- » ...plus some barrel aging.

Most Popular Brew: Too soon to tell.

Samples: Yes, flights of 4 and 6 available.

Brewmaster's Fave: Balanced Rock Rye

Best Time to Go: Open Sun, Tue–Thu 11AM–11PM, Fri–Sat 11AM–1AM. Closed Mondays. Happy hour runs weekdays 3-6pm, but is extra happy on Thirsty Thursdays. Check the website to be sure.

Where can you buy it? Here on tap and to go in growlers.

Got food? Yes, a full menu of upscale pub food (risotto, salmon BLT), including appetizers (duck nachos, poutine, curds, hummus), soups and salads, sandwiches and more. Friday fish fry and a full bar.

Tours? Yes, by chance or by appointment.

Special Offer: Buy your first pint of Rockhound beer, get 1 free during your signature visit.

Directions: US 151 passes right through Madison on several connecting streets. From where West Washington meets Park Street, go one block south on Park St and it is on the corner of Park and Drake in a multi-story building with retail at street level.

The Beer Buzz: Rockhound is an old-fashioned term for a geologist or rock collector, which is owner/brewer Nate Warnke's academic training: a geology degree. What does one do with such a degree? Make beer, of course.

Nate got into homebrewing ten years before opening this place because his wife Tracy wanted to try it. They took it on as a hobby, and she found she preferred to be the taste tester, a role she takes quite seriously. Under pressure from Tracy, Nate decided to go pro late in 2013, but it took about two years to bring his brewpub to fruition.

He lives in this neighborhood, so already had a preference for this location, plus it has the benefit of being close to downtown and on a major street that brings a lot of traffic in and out each day. Park Street has been an "under-served" neighborhood and he sees good things coming here. When a new building with street-level retail started going up on Lane Bakery's former site, he knew this was the place. When asked how he'd describe his brewing philosophy, he thought a moment and replied, "Balanced." Nothing super hoppy or super malty. Glowing Embers took Best Beer at Isthmus Beer & Cheese Fest in 2018.

He has 4,000 square feet, half of which is the restaurant with booths, tables, and a 23-seat u-shaped bar. Windows let in a lot of light, and the lone TV comes on for specific sporting events. He operates a 5-barrel system in the next room. Parking is on the street.

Free WiFi. Mug Club. Facebook/rockhoundbrewing

Twitter @ rockhoundbrew

Instagram @ rockhoundbrewing

Stumbling Distance: *Henry Vilas Zoo* (702 S Randall Ave, 608-258-9490, vilaszoo.org) is free and nearby, as is the 1,260-acre, trail-filled *UW Arboretum* (608) 263-7888, arboretum.wisc.edu) along Lake Wingra. *Taqueria Guadalajara* (1033 S Park St, 608-250-1824, lataqueriaguadalajara.com) serves the best Mexican in town. *The Mason Lounge* (416 S Park St, 608-255-7777) is a very laid back, neighborhood bar with 15+ craft beers on draft served in Mason jars. *Greenbush Bar* (914 Regent St, 608-257-2874, greenbushbar.net) is a city classic with old-school thin-crust Sicilian pizza in a basement location with craft beer and Christmas lights.

VINTAGE BREWING CO.

674 S Whitney Way • Madison, WI 53711 • 608-204-2739
vintagebrewingco.com
Founded: December 2009   **Director of Brewing Operations**: Scott Manning
Annual Production: 2,000 bbls   **Number of Beers**: 18–25 house beers on tap

Staple Beers:
- » DEDICATION ABBEY DUBBEL
- » MCLOVIN IRISH RED ALE
- » MOSASAUR IPA
- » SCAREDY CAT OATMEAL STOUT
- » SISTER GOLDEN KÖLSCH
- » WEISS NIX WEISSBIER
- » WOODSHED OAKED IPA

Rotating Beers:
- » ABDOMINABLE SNOWMAN COFFEE BLONDE ALE
- » BETTER OFF RED HOPPED-UP AMERICAN RED ALE
- » BOCKS O-CHOCOLATES CHOCOLATE DOPPELBOCK
- » CITRA ZEN PALE ALE
- » DIAMOND STAR HALO (SOUR ALE)
- » GOTTER OTTER BRITISH STRONG PALE ALE
- » MACH SCHNELL! PILSNER
- » MAXIMILIAN STOUT IMPERIAL STOUT
- » ROCHAMBEAU BELGO PALE ALE
- » RYE HAVOC RED RYE IPA
- » SCHWARZFAHREN SCHWARZBIER
- » TIPPY TOBOGGAN ROGGEN BOCK
- » TREPIDATION...BELGIAN ABBEY
- » ... 80+ more collaborations, one-offs, rare styles, barrel-aged and sour ales

Most Popular Brew: Woodshed Oaked IPA.

Brewmaster's Faves: Rochambeau, Maltiplicity, and Palindrome.

Tours? Free, but by advance appointment only.

Samples? Yes, a complimentary "skosh," to try before you buy, or full 5-oz tasters ranging from $2-4 each, or available in flights.

Best Time to Go: Open for lunch and dinner daily 11AM–close. Monday Happy Hour: discounted select VBC pints! "Thirsty Thursday" VBC and guest draft beer discounts. In season, the patio opens up for dining and drinking in the sun.

Where can you buy it? Served here or at sister pubs *Vintage Spirits & Grill*, 529 University Ave, Madison, and and *Vintage Brewing Sauk Prairie*, 600 Water St, Sauk City, plus on tap at finer bars/restaurants in Madison, Milwaukee and Racine areas.

Got food? The menu offers made-to-order, from-scratch dishes and the chef favors local ingredients with modern twists. They offer their own fine beers but also an assortment of other great brews making this a great foodie and, um, beery? destination.

Special Offer: A half-price Crowler or growler fill (up to 2) of Vintage beer when you get your book signed.

Directions: From Hwy 12-14 (the Beltline) take the Whitney Way exit heading north. Cross Odana Road (the traffic lights one block away from the highway overpass) and take the next left into the parking lot of the Whitney Square strip mall. Vintage is in a stand-alone building in the lot.

The Beer Buzz: *Vintage Spirits and Grill* already had good success over on University Avenue with its retro style and convivial spirit. So when JT Whitney's Brewpub closed its doors in 2009 and this location remained vacant, the family-based partnership at Vintage decided it was time not just to serve great beer but to brew it as well. Vintage aims for some class without snobbery combining a plush lounge atmosphere with some old-school brewery décor.

Brewer Scott was born and raised in Wisconsin and graduated from the University of Wisconsin-Madison. From 1997 on, his professional brewing took him out west to places in AZ, CA and NV. His brother Bryan and cousin Trent had been secretly plotting a brewpub for years with the aim of luring Scott back to the Beer State. The nefarious plan worked and Scott has happily become his own boss and brewmaster for their family business. The beers and food have earned distinction, and the business just keeps growing. *Vintage Brewery Sauk Prairie* opened in 2018, a larger capacity brewpub right on the Wisconsin River up in Sauk City. In addition to Vintage's two locations in Madison, Vintage's co-owners also opened *Tangent Kitchen & Taproom* in Madison's *Beermuda Triangle* for a more avant garde menu and some original brews from the two Vintage breweries.

Stumbling Distance: Do mini-golf, a year-round driving range, a par 3, a climbing wall, or batting cages interest you at all? Go across the highway from here to *Vitense Golfland* (www.vitense.com, 5501 Schroeder Road, 608-271-1411). *Geeks Mania* (6502 Odana Rd, 608-316-1644, geeksmania.com) is an all-you-can-play vintage arcade game and pinball heaven. Just south of Madison off Hwy 151 is *Bavaria Sausage* (www.bavariasausage.com, 6317 Nesbitt Rd, 800-733-6695) which sells a wide variety of German and other sausages (a lot of it made in-house) and much more. Fresh cheese curds are delivered here on Thursday afternoons and Friday mornings.

Union Corners Brewery

2438 Winnebago Ave. • Madison, WI 53704   Phone: NONE YET
unioncornersbrewery.com
Opened: Fall 2018   **Head Brewer:** John Puchalski
Annual Production: up to 700 barrels
Number of Beers: 24 on tap, plus 8 ciders, hard sodas, guest beers

Staple Beers:
- » Belgian Single
- » Black Pepper Rye Pale Ale
- » Brown IPA
- » Oated Amber
- » Roasted Porter

Rotating Beers:
- » Lichtenhainer Smoked Sour
- » Oktoberfest
- » Hefeweizen
- » Morel Mushroom Nut
- Brown Ale
- » Seasonal Sours With Lactobacillus
- » Various barrel-aged brews

Brewmaster's Fave: Belgian Single or APA

Tours? Yes, by chance or by appointment, but watch for classes.

Samples: Yes, sample flights of four or more 5-oz pours.

Best Time to Go: Open Mon-Fri 11am-midnight, Sat-Sun 9am-midnight.

Where can you buy it? Here on tap and in growlers to go.

Got food? Yes, full kitchen. Hand food tacos, sliders, sandwiches and such, no need for utensils. Special menus for latenight and weekend brunch.

Special Offer: Buy 1 beer, get one free OR buy two tasters, get two free when you get your book signed.

Directions: From US-151/East Washington Ave, turn east on Milwaukee St, go one block and turn right, and the brewery is on the right at street level at the end of the block. Be aware of the back-in angled parking on the street; the City will ticket you if you don't!

The Beer Buzz: John Puchalski used to run Brew and Grow on Willy Street, but he got into homebrewing long before that in college when friends invited him along. The hook was set and he started reading, eventually reading more books about brewing than he'd read in college altogether. He went back to study at Siebel Institute before starting at Brew and Grow, where he eventually ended up running the place. Then Eric walked in.

Eric Peterson spent over 20 years in the medical equipment industry before he got sick of it. In 2006 he was in Boston and discovered a brew-on-premise establishment with a wall of ingredients and a menu of 150+ recipes that allowed for tweaks. Great idea, he thought. He became a regular there and brought home loads of delicious, unique beers and it got him thinking. For 12 years he fermented the idea until he ran into John at Brew and Grow. They crunched the numbers and now there's beer in your glass.

Eventually they hope to open similar locations around Wisconsin. John liked the educational aspect of B&G. Union Corners offers brewing seminars where the brewer – amateur or pro – comes to the brewery, selects one of eight basic recipes, goes through a short questionnaire on how they want to customize their batch, and then attends a lecture where they get to brew their batch with John. A nominal fee pays for the experience and you can also buy some of your batch to take home. But your name and face remain on the beer if it ends up on tap (and if you choose). About 20-25 people join each seminar.

They run a 4-bbl brewhouse, limited in size due to the parking garage underneath and consequent floor-strength limitations. They have no liquor license but expect a few brews with a cocktail soul to them, incorporating barrel-aging. Bloody Mary blonde, Mint Julep Imperial Blonde (brown sugar and honey, mint aged in bbn barrels), etc. There are board games on hand, plus TVs for gamers (E-sports) and occasional sports. The digital menu shows the popularity of beers on tap.

Union Corners is not a bit of worker-labor history as one might expect. Rather this was where the trains stopped for arriving Union Army recruits, where they'd have their last drink at the tavern there before walking to Camp Randall.

Free WiFi. Mug Club. On Facebook.com/UnionCornersBrewery and Instagram @ UnionCornersBrewery

Stumbling Distance: Union Corners is inside Madison's Beermuda Triangle. *The Malt House* (2609 E Washington Ave, 608-204-6258, malthousetavern.com), the fantastic craft beer and whiskey bar is a short block from here. *One Barrel Brewery* is the other direction on Winnebago.

Working Draft Brewing Co.

1129 E Wilson St • Madison, WI 53703 • 608-709-5600
workingdraftbeer.com
Opened: March 2018   **Head Brewer**: Clint Lohman
Annual Production: 600 barrels
Number of Beers: 116 on tap (1 gluten-free from Alt Brew)

Beers:

- » West Coast IPAs
- » German Lagers
- » Local Poet Pilsner
- » Oatmeal Stout
- » Pulp Culture Hazy IPA

Most Popular Brew: Pulp Culture Hazy IPA

Brewmaster's Fave: He's a pilsner nerd.

Tours? Yes, by chance or by appointment.

Samples: Yes, sample flights of four 4-oz pours for about $10.

Best Time to Go: Open Mon-Thu 3-10pm, Fri-Sat 11am-11pm, Sun 11am-9pm. Watch for live acoustic performances.

Where can you buy it? Here on tap and in Crowlers to go.

Got food? Yes, fast casual eats from Fox Heritage Farms (Dan Fox of Heritage Tavern). Pulled pork, spent-grain pretzels, etc. Special craft soda from Madison's Macha Tea Co.

Special Offer: A free pint of house beer when you get your book signed.

Directions: From US-151/East Washington Ave. turn southeast on Ingersoll St. and continue two blocks, crossing Central Park to turn left on Wilson St. The brewery is on your right. *Cyclists:* The brief on-street segment of the *Capital City State Trail* is right in front of the brewery.

The Beer Buzz: Ben Feifarek worked at Madison's esteemed Wine & Hop Shop for several years before taking over ownership in 2012. Ryan Browne came on in 2011 and they eventually started kicking around the idea of starting a brewery. J Bowen joined the project as owner and partner and connected them to Jeff Glazer, Madison attorney and expert in brewery legal consulting (and one of the co-founders of Madison Craft Beer Week) who encouraged them to apply to the Law & Entrepreneurship Clinic at the University of Wisconsin Law School. Under Jeff's supervision, law students guided Ryan, Ben and J through the legal labyrinth, saving them countless hours and dollars. They followed this with a successful application to the Business & Entrepreneurship Clinic. They had the plan, the permits, and the place. But despite being experienced homebrewers, they wanted a head brewer.

Brewer Clint always had a love of cooking and making things, and while working in manufacturing he'd drive past Ale Asylum every day on the way to work, thinking brewing would be the perfect mix. He started to homebrew with a friend, already knowing he wanted to go pro. He got hired by Page Buchanan at House of Brews and despite first being assigned menial tasks, stuck with it for a year, moving into brewing. Page referred him to Scott Manning at Vintage, and he added another two years to his experience. Wisconsin Brewing tapped him for part-time work which turned into 3.5 years of brewing with Kirby Nelson. A series of fortunate events. Kirby would eventually officiate Clint's wedding. Clint knew Ryan through the brew supply shop and serendipitously contacted him about brewing just hours after the intended brewer for the new brewery fell through.

The brewery name aligns with Ryan's background, which is creative writing. Brewing, like writing, is a process, and any piece will go through several iterations in that process. So it is with the beers here. One version of a brew may have its malt bill changed, or the hops swapped, and patrons may have the opportunity to taste those differences side by side. No word on whether there is a definitive final draft here, but you get the point. (The pun on "draft" is a bonus.) Clint brews on a 7-barrel system made by Sprinkman in Waukesha, while a 1-barrel pilot system allows the brewers, the staff, and even area homebrewers to play with small batches.

The brewery and taproom occupy a stylishly redesigned industrial space in the back third of the building previously occupied by RP's Pasta. Local artist Jenie Gao created the 200 square foot mural facing the bar, and the brewery has artist residencies planned in conjunction with Art & Literature Lab on Winnebago St.

Accordion glass doors open to the outdoor patio. A lounge and fireplace occupy one corner. When you're lining up beers and knocking them down at the bar, understand that the counter and table tops are familiar with that routine: they are reclaimed bowling lanes and pin decks from Village Lanes in Monona. Background music or occasional acoustic acts, along with board games and Crokinole (Canadian shuffleboard?) entertain. Parking is in the lot or free along the street.

Free WiFi. Facebook.com/workingdraftbeer

Twitter/Instagram @workingdraftbeer

Stumbling Distance: *State Line Distillery* (1413 Northern Ct, 608-571-4271, statelinedistillery.

com) has a cocktail lounge at its nearby headquarters. *Weary Traveler Freehouse* (1201 Williamson St, 608-442-6207, wearytravelerfreehouse.com) has excellent food (Bad Breath Burger is legend) and a good bar with craft beers, including their own Dark Traveler Limited, a Russian Imperial Stout from Lake Louie Brewing (an unfiltered version of the highly coveted Mr. Mephisto's). In addition to its namesake, *Madison Sourdough Co.* (916 Williamson St, 608-442-8009, madison-sourdough.com) offers pastries, breakfast, lunch and some bottled craft beers.

THE WINE AND HOP SHOP

Dave Mitchell opened a brewing and winemaking supply shop in Madison in 1972, six years before President Jimmy Carter signed Bill 1337 making home-brewing legal. It is said that the malt extract they sold for "baking purposes" had beer recipes on the underside of the lids. Wine making and beer brewing culture in Madison begins with Mitchell. Even Wollersheim Winery worked with him. The first shop opened on E. Mifflin St. in downtown Madison, WI, and moved a few years later to State Street. In 1998 it moved to a location on Monroe St until 2015, moving just a few doors down. In 2012, Dave passed the torch to long-time employee Ben Feifarek, who, with partners, eventually opened *Working Draft Brewing* in 2018. The Wine & Hop Shop remains an inspiration, resource, and supplier of homebrewers and future pros. (1919 Monroe St, Madison, 608-257-0099, wineandhop.com)

CAPITAL BREWERY

7734 Terrace Ave • Middleton, WI 53562 • 608-836-7100
capitalbrewery.com
Opened: April 17, 1986   **Brewmaster:** Ashley Kinart-Short
Annual Production: 20,000 bbls   **Number of Beers**: 24+ annually

Staple Beers:

- » MUNICH DARK
- » MUTINY IPA
- » PILSNER

- » SUPPER CLUB (Classic lager)
- » WISCONSIN AMBER

Rotating Beers:

- » LAKE HOUSE (May-Jul)
- » MAIBOCK (Feb-Apr)

- » OKTOBERFEST (Aug–Oct)
- » WINTER SKÅL (Nov–Jan)

Limited:

- » AUTUMNAL FIRE
- » BLONDE DOPPELBOCK
- » DARK DOPPELBOCK

- » FISHIN' IN THE DARK
- »

Most Popular Brew: Wisconsin Amber (but Supper Club commands the beer garden).

Tours? Yes. Tuesdays, Fridays, Saturdays and Sundays—check the website for the current schedule. Reservations recommended. $7 includes the tour, 4 samples or 1 pint of their beer, and a pint glass to take home. Private tours available.

Samples? Yes, flights are available, ask for the Tasting Tour of 6 samplers.

Best Time to Go: The Bier Garten is open from May to October (weather willing) Tue–Thu 4–9PM, Fri 3–10PM, Sat 12–9PM, Sun 12–5PM with live music on Fridays. Check online for shorter winter hours. Bundle up for *Bockfest* in the Bier Garten the last Saturday of February, when the brewery releases their Maibock and Blonde Doppelbock. When the Bier Garten otherwise closes for winter, head inside for the Bier Stube to keep on drinking. Watch also Burgers & Brews at the end of May, and Block Party at the end of summer/early fall.

Where can you buy it? Here on tap and in growlers to go. Six-pack bottles and 6- and 12-pack cans for most annual and seasonal beers. Their distribution is all over Wisconsin with a growing presence in Minnesota, Iowa, and Illinois, and Tavour.com in WA can ship to even more.

Got food? No, but food vendors come on Tue, Thu, and Fri evenings in season.

Special Offer: $1 off your first pint of Capital beer when you get your book signed.

Directions: Best way to get here is from the West Beltline (Hwy 12/14 on the west side of Madison metro area). Take Exit 252, go east on Greenway Blvd to a three-way stop and go left (north) on High Point Rd just three blocks to Terrace Ave and the brewery is there on the corner.

The Beer Buzz: Capital is one of the elder statesmen of Wisconsin's breweries and for a long time it was known mostly as a lager specialist. In recent years, they have produced a line-up that expands convincingly into ales as well.

Brewer Ashley was an assistant beer manager at The Old Fashioned, the popular Madison restaurant with the finest all-Wisconsin beer list around. She has an International Brewing Diploma from the Siebel Institute of Technology at the Doemens Academy in Munch, Germany, and served as assistant brewer for two years before taking over the lead here. (She is one of three female head brewers in the state—see also Wisconsin Dells Brewing and Thirsty Pagan Brewpub).

The brewhouse holds two 1955 Huppman copper kettles. Be sure to see the trophy case sagging from the wall near the gift shop to appreciate how many awards these brews have won. Check out their website for flavor profiles of their beers. A 7-barrel pilot system gives the brewery the chance to play with a few more limited or one-off beers, and their tap room doubled in size in 2018. In the summer, the Bier Garten has dozens of picnic tables and a stage for live music. It is quite popular with the after-work crowd, and now has a waterproof tent at the center.

Free WiFi. ATM onsite. Facebook.com/CapBrew, Twitter @ capbrew and Instagram @ capitalbrewery

Stumbling Distance: Just a short walk away is *The Village Green* (7508 Hubbard Ave, 608-831-9962) a homey restaurant featuring one of Madison area's best Friday fish fries. Try the grilled summer sausage and Capital on tap. Several modern places offer upscale pub food and well-chosen tap lists, such as *The Freehouse Pub* (1902 Parmenter St, 608-831-5000) and *Craftsman Table & Tap* (6712 Frank Lloyd Wright Ave, 608-836-3988). *Longtable Beer Café* (7545 Hubbard Ave, 608-841-2337, longtablebeercafe.com) is seriously popular for the food and craft beer list and communal tables. *World of Beer* (8225 Greenway Blvd, 608-833-5400, worldofbeer.com) has a huge craft selection. *The Club Tavern* (1915 Branch St, 608-836-3773) has been around over 100 years. Live music, volleyball, great food. The Moose Burger is my fave. Look for crazily cheap beer the first day in the year that the temperature goes over 70. Make a reservation with *Betty Lou Cruises* (bettyloucruises.com, 608-246-3138) to eat Ian's Pizza and drink Capital on Lake Monona.

BREWERY CREEK BREWPUB

23 Commerce Street • Mineral Point, WI 53565 • 608-987-3298
brewerycreek.com
Founded: June 1998   **Brewmaster**: Jeffrey Donaghue
Annual Production: 500 bbls
Number of Beers: 16 taps with guest beers and ciders; 4-8 house beers

Possible Beers:

» ALTBIER	» LONDON PORTER
» AMBER ALE	» PALE ALE
» CREAM ALE	» SCHWARZBIER
» GOLDEN ALE	» ...basically one light, one dark and a
» HEFEWEIZEN	couple in between

Most Popular Brew: Whatever's lightest

Brewmaster's Fave: The most recent. "Imagine you had gallons of beer in your home. It wouldn't take long for you to look forward to the next one."

Tours? By appointment or by chance if he is not busy.

Samples? Yes.

Best Time to Go: Hours are seasonal so double check. Summer Jun–Oct 23 11:30–8 PM Tue–Thu, until 8:30 Fri–Sat, and til 3 PM on Sun. Closed Mondays. In winter only open Thu–Sat hours, but odds are you will have the place to yourself. This is not a late-night place because that would disturb the B&B guests upstairs. Come for a pleasant afternoon or early evening.

Where can you buy it? Here on tap in 12- and 16-oz pours and in growlers to go.

Got food? Definitely! Very homemade meals (the owners live on site). A veggie burger with a reputation all the way back to Madison. Belgian fries, homemade sauces and desserts, and a Friday fish fry (cod). Burgers are made with hormone-free beef. Don't miss the Brewery burger! Housemade root beer as well.

Special Offer: Not participating.

Directions: From US-151 take the Exit 40 to WI-23(Business 151). Turn left on WI-23, drive 1.7 miles and WI-23 turns left on Commerce St. Stay on this street for 0.8 mile and the brewpub is on the left.

Cyclists: This is just off the Cheese Country Trail.

The Beer Buzz: The first commercial brewery was built here by John Phillips in 1835 on Brewery Creek just behind the modern brewpub. Mineral Point had two more breweries thereafter: Garden City, until Prohibition came, and Terrill's Brewery. The latter was renamed "Tornado Brewery" after it was destroyed by one in 1878. It changed names once again, and ended its brewing days as Mineral Springs Brewery in the 60s. You can still see the old building on Shake Rag Street. Brewmaster Jeffrey has been a homebrewer since 1967, and when he and his wife decided they needed a change, they moved here from Minneapolis and found an 1854 warehouse with no heating, wiring, insulation or even interior walls. It was no small feat to turn this place into the charming restaurant, brewery, and guesthouse we see today. If you plan to stay the night in one of the brewpub's guest rooms (recommended), be sure to call for a reservation, but they don't take dinner reservations.

Stumbling Distance: *Mineral Point* (www.mineralpoint.com) is loaded with art galleries, and *"Gallery Nights,"* when the stores stay open a bit later, might be a good time to come to town. *Hook's Cheese Co.* (320 Commerce St, 608-987-3259, hookscheese.com) is only open weekdays until 2PM but is world famous. Get your bleu cheese, cheddar and curds on your way through. If they are closed try the convenience store across the street—they carry Hook's products. History buffs will enjoy *Pendarvis* (www.wisconsinhistory.org/pendarvis, 608-987-2122) a Cornish miners' colony with guides in costume. Not a history buff? Visit the brewpub for a few pints first. Also, see Biking for Beer in the back of the book. *Bob's Bitchin' BBQ* (167 N Iowa St, Dodgeville, 608-930-2227, bobsbitchinbbq.com) is just down the highway in Dodgeville and has people driving hours for their BBQ. The tap list doesn't disappoint either.

BULLQUARIAN BREWHOUSE

1128 17th Ave. • Monroe, WI 53566 • 608-426-6720
Facebook.com/Bullquarianbrewhouse
Opened: May 20, 2017   **Head Brewer:** Ethan Kister
Annual Production: 175 barrels   **Number of Beers:** 10 on tap

Staple Beers:
» ERV'S DARK
» HIBBY'S WIT

» …plus something light and something sour

Rotating Beers:
» Anything he feels like!

Most Popular Brew: Hibby's Wit

Brewmaster's Fave: Bull's Bruin Sour Ale

Tours? Yes, by chance or by appointment.

Samples: Yes, sample flights of 5-oz pours for $1.50-$2 each.

Best Time to Go: Open Mon-Wed-Fri 3:30-9pm, Sat 11am-9pm, Sun 11am-4pm.

Where can you buy it? Here on tap and in bombers and growlers to go. Will exchange his growler for yours for a growler fill.

Got food? Bring your own if you like, but they've also got Emil's Pizza (from Watertown, WI), garlic-cheese bread, soft pretzels, Zuber's landjaegers, plus pickled eggs, pork hocks, and polish sausage. Free popcorn.

Special Offer: A free pint of house beer when you get your book signed.

Directions: Numbers avenues run N-S, streets E-W. 17th Ave is one way north, so get to the main square and go south on 16th Ave, turn left (east) on 12th St, and drive one block and you'll see the brewhouse on the left on the corner of 12th St and 17th Ave.

The Beer Buzz: It may appear as a corner coffee shop, but then you'll notice the eclectic tap handles behind the bar, which include a hand-powered drill, meat cleaver, and a giraffe. They've become so central to the brewery that they appear on beer labels and t-shirts. For years this was a flower shop, so conveniently for Ethan he already had floor drains in the space where he keeps his two-barrel system. Ethan had been homebrewing for 20 years while he worked as a mechanical designer at a pump company. He finally tired of the commute and took his brews public. In his first 9 months, Ethan brewed 28 different beers so don't expect to see too many repeats beyond the couple listed above. Bull's Bruin Sour Ale is made with local yogurt and aged in oak barrels.

The brewery name combines the zodiac signs of Ethan (Taurus, the Bull) and his wife Michelle (Aquarius, the sign of water). Both figure prominently in the decorations. Live music is common, often originals, often bluegrass, and watch for Beer Bingo. Board games and cribbage are on hand.

An interesting note: Ethan figures 60% of his customers are women, dispelling any myths of beer being a guy thing.

Free WiFi. Mug Club. Facebook.com/BullquarianBrewhouse

Stumbling Distance: *Zuber's Sausage Kitchen* (905 19th St, 608-329-6500, ZubersMeats.com) makes a variety of Swiss landjaegers (snackable sausage sticks). Founded in 1931, *Baumgartner's Cheese Store & Tavern* (1023 16th Ave, 608-325-6157), on the historic central square, is Wisconsin's oldest cheese store and a must-see. They serve local beer with their sandwiches. You are definitely in Wisconsin. This is one of the only places you will ever find a limburger and onion sandwich. Feeling bold and invincible? Just ask for a sample of the stuff. There are those who love it. *Turner Hall* (1217 17th Ave, 608-325-3461, turnerhallofmonroe.org) is a 1938 Swiss Emmental-style chalet, and represents the strong Swiss heritage of the town. Pop in for some local and traditional food in a real rathskeller and Bullquarian brews on tap. Check out *Minhas Craft Brewery* and its Stumbling Distance items as well. **Hotel:** *Victorian Garden B&B* (1720 16th St, 608-328-1720, victoriangardenbedbreakfast.com) is six blocks away.

Minhas Craft Brewery

1208 14th (Brewery) Ave • Monroe, WI 53566 • 608-325-3191
minhasbrewery.com
Founded: 1845/2006   **Brewmaster**: Jim Beyer
Annual Production: 300,000+ bbls   **Number of Beers**: 25 plus contract brews

Staple Beers:

- » 1845 Pils
- » Axehead Malt Liquor
- » Boxer Apple Ale
- » Boxer Gluten Free Beer
- » Boxer Ice
- » Boxer Lager
- » Boxer Light
- » Clear Creek Ice
- » Huber Bock
- » Huber Premium
- » Mountain Crest
- » Swiss Amber

Lazy Mutt Beers:

- » Lazy Mutt Double IPA
- » Lazy Mutt Farmhouse Ale
- » Lazy Mutt So Cal IPA
- » Lazy Mutt Traditional IPA

Lazy Mutt Seasonals:

- » Alcoholic Ginger Beer
- » Chocolate Cherry
- » Gluten Free Beer
- » Hazelnut Dark
- » Hefeweizen
- » Oktoberfest
- » Pumpkin Ale
- » Shandy
- » Wet Hopped IPA
- » Winter Bock
- » …plus several contract brews.

Most Popular Brew: Boxer Lager

Brewmaster's Fave: Huber Bock

Tours? Tours run 45–60 minutes and are offered Mon at 11AM, Tues–Thu at 1PM, Fri 1PM and 3PM, Sat 11AM, 1PM, 3PM, and Sun 1PM and 3PM. Make a reservation for large groups (12 or more). The price is $12 per person for ages 12 and up and includes a gift pack containing 4 bottles of beer, 1 Blumers Soda and a branded sampler glass. Call 1-800-BEER-205 to reserve a tour.

Samples? Yes! (and Blumers sodas too. Blueberry Cream is my favorite!)

Best Time to Go: See tour times.

Where can you buy it? Minhas products are in 16 states as far east as New York, as far west as Nevada, and north into Canada, with the core market being the Midwest.

Special Offer: A free pint glass when you get your book signed.

Directions: If you are coming from the west on Hwy 11 take West 8th Street heading east (right) until 14th Ave then go right (south). From the east take Hwy 59 (6th Street) west to 15th Ave, turn left (south) to 12th St then hop a block right (west) to 14th Ave and take a left (south) to the brewery a block away. Coming in on 81 you will hit 8th

Street and follow the rest of the Hwy 11-from-west directions. Hwy 69 will hit 6th St—from there use the from-the-east directions. It's not as bad is it sounds; Monroe is a nice grid and streets are numbered: Streets run east-west, Avenues north-south. If lost, come on, men, the ladies won't mind if you stop for directions for a change.

The Beer Buzz: This is the oldest continuously running brewery in Wisconsin (older even than the state itself!) and the second oldest in the US. As of 2014 it is the tenth largest brewery in the nation based on beer sales volume. One of my first beer memories was a dusty case of Huber Beer empties which sat in our root cellar for much of the 1970s when I was a child. There's a fifty-cent deposit we can never get back! This is that case's birthplace. The brewery switched hands a few times and was known as The Blumer Brewery (now the name of the gourmet sodas produced here) when Bavarian-born Joseph Huber began working here in 1923. The company survived Prohibition with a non-alcoholic beer, Golden Glow, and in the end Huber organized an employee stock buyout which saved the brewery. In 1947, the brewery took his name. In 1960, it started producing Berghoff for a restaurant of the same name in Chicago. Former Pabst executives bought the company from Fred Huber in 1985, and some bad corporate shenanigans led to the near closing of the brewery and the Augsburger label being sold off to Stroh's (Stevens Point Brewery has since picked it up and we can drink it once again). Fred Huber bought the brewery back and with the help of the success of Berghoff beers and some other contract brewing the brewery stayed alive. In 2006, Huber was bought by Canadian entrepreneur Ravinder Minhas and took on its new name. The beer continues to flow and Lazy Mutt, Boxer, and Huber Bock are the flagship brews. Huber Bock still wins awards.

Stumbling Distance: Green County is cheese country. The local welcome center is also the *National Historic Cheesemaking Museum* (2108 6th Ave, 608-325-4636, nationalhistoriccheesemakingcenter.org), worth seeing and more area info is on hand. *Chalet Cheese Cooperative* (N4858 Cty Rd N, 608-325-4343) does tours for 4 or more people and sells cheese on site. *Alp and Dell Cheese* (657 Second St, 608-328-3355, alpanddellcheese.com) is a great cheese outlet and corporate home to *Roth Kase USA* (emmirothusa.com). See also *Bullquarian Brewhouse* and its Stumbling Distance.

THE GRUMPY TROLL BREW PUB

105 South Second Street • Mount Horeb, WI 53572 • 608-437-2739
thegrumpytroll.com
Founded: 2000   **Brewmaster**: Mark Knoebl
Annual Production: 600+ bbls   **Number of Beers**: up to 12 on tap

Staple Beers:

- » CAPTAIN FRED AMERICAN LAGER (named after Captain Pabst)
- » ERIK THE RED
- » HOPPA LOPPA IPA
- » MAGGIE IMPERIAL IPA
- » SPETSNAZ STOUT
- » TRAILSIDE WHEAT

Rotating Beers: (30+)

- » A&J IIPA
- » AMNESIA BALTIC PORTER
- » DRAGON SHIP WIT
- » GRUMPY CRIK PALE ALE
- » KELLER BRAU
- » LIBERTY POLE PALE ALE
- » MONK (Belgian golden strong)
- » NORSKI NUT BROWN
- » NORWEGIAN WOOD
- » OL' EAGLE'S SUMMER PORTER
- » SUNFLOWER FARMHOUSE ALE
- » TROLL'S GOLD LAGER
- » TROLLFEST
- » WEE CURLY SCOTTISH ALE

Most Popular Brew: Captain Fred, Hoppa Loppa IPA, and Maggie Imperial IPA

Brewmaster's Fave: Hoppa Loppa IPA

Tours? No.

Samples: Four-ounce samplers are $1.50 each, or get all 12 on a tray.

Best Time To Go: Open daily at 11AM. Happy hours run from 4–6PM Sun–Wed and Thu 4–close when pints and 11-oz pours are discounted. Badgers and Packers games are always a blast.

Where can you buy it? Only here on tap and in growlers to go and several bottled in 22-oz bombers.

Got food? Yes, in the pub, full lunch and dinner menus. Burgers with local beef, cheese curds and bar fare, but also plenty of great soups, sandwiches, salads, dinner entrees and daily specials. All-day Friday fish fry and Saturday night prime rib. Check out the beer related items: beer-battered fish, Erik the Red Brats, and beer cheese soup! *Their pizzeria (608-437-2741)* on the second floor is a big hit and open Mon–Thu 4–9PM, Fri 4–10PM, Sat 11–10PM, Sun 11–8PM. They also brew their own root beer.

Special Offer: A free 11-oz glass of house beer when you get your book signed.

Directions: Take Business Hwy 18/151 through downtown to 2nd Street. Go south at the stop light and it is at one block down on the left (east) side of 2nd St.

The Beer Buzz: Hard to imagine what makes this troll grumpy with such fine beer on hand. Originally a creamery when it was built in 1916, the building is said to be haunted. The pub name comes from this little town's Scandinavian-inherited obsession with trolls, and you will see plenty of troll-related stuff around town.

Grumpy's Brewer Mark is a long time local award-winning commercial and home brewer with over 25 years of experience. He is a graduate of Siebel Institute of Technology and has worked closely with some of Wisconsin's finest brewers, including New Glarus Brewing and Sand Creek Brewing. They are also active in the brewing community, and you will find them at many beer festivals that occur throughout the Midwest.

Since 2006, the Grumpy Troll has been steadily winning awards for their beers: from prestigious international, national and regional contests including the World Beer Cup, United States Beer Tasting Championship and Beverage Tasters Institute. Check out the walls in the main bar area to see the accolades, including their latest World Beer Cup Silver Award from 2016 for Spetsnaz Stout.

In 2010, the Grumpy Troll made the leap to serving some "green" beer. No, it's not a St Patty's thing. I mean solar panels on the roof generate the electricity for the brewpub. Pick up some Grumpy Troll paraphernalia, including handmade ceramic mugs and Grumpy wear. In season, enjoy some outdoor dining and drinking in the beer garden. All beer is produced onsite in that brewhouse you can see behind the glass.

Free WiFi. Facebook.com/grumpytrollbrew and Twitter/ Instagram @ GrumpyTrollBrew

Stumbling Distance: *Tyrol Basin* (www.tyrolbasin.com, 608-437-4135) is a collection of short runs for skiers and snowboarders just down the road. Just a bit farther west on Highway 151 is *Blue Mound State Park* (4350 Mounds Park Rd., Blue Mounds, 608-437-5711) with a couple of scenic overlook towers, swimming and wading pools, and miles of hiking (or skiing) and mountain biking. Take a one-hour tour of the geological wonder that is *Cave of the Mounds* (2975 Cave of the Mounds Rd, Blue Mounds, 608-437-3038 caveofthemounds.com). Check out Mt. Horeb Summer Frolic in early June or the Art Fair in July. The *Thirsty Troll Brew Fest* is held every September at Grundahl Park.

PHOTO COURTESY THE GRUMPY TROLL

NEW GLARUS BREWING CO.

Hilltop Brewery, 2400 State Hwy 69 • New Glarus, WI 53574
608-527-5850
newglarusbrewing.com
Founded: June 1993   **Brewmaster**: Dan Carey
Annual Production: 223,000 bbls
Number of Beers: 6 on tap at the brewery; 6 year round, 3–5 seasonals, 2–3 Thumbprint beers each year

Staple Beers:
- » MOON MAN
- » RASPBERRY TART
- » SCREAM IPA
- » SPOTTED COW
- » TWO WOMEN
- » WISCONSIN BELGIAN RED

Rotating Beers:

- » Back Forty Bock
- » Black Top
- » Cabin Fever Honey Bock
- » Crack'd Wheat
- » Dancing Man Wheat
- » Enigma
- » Fat Squirrel
- » Oud Bruin
- » Road Slush Oatmeal Stout
- » Serendipity
- » Staghorn Octoberfest
- » Stone Soup
- » Totally Naked

…but this list itself rotates each year! So many beers: Uff-da Bock, Hop Hearty Ale (IPA), Hometown Blonde Pilsner, Norsky (maibock), Solstice (hefeweizen), Coffee Stout, Snowshoe Ale (copper ale), Yokel (unfiltered lager), Copper Kettle (dunkelweiss), Apple Ale, the list can and does go on! Watch for R&D beers and the "Thumbprint" series (see below in The Beer Buzz). Check the website for current beers.

Most Popular Brew: Spotted Cow

Brewmaster's Fave: "I don't have a favorite beer. That's like asking a parent which is his favorite child! Secondly, beer is a food and I never limit myself to one food. I enjoy everything from an American Style Lager (like our Totally Naked) to a sour brown ale (like ours) and everything in between. When I travel, I NEVER drink beer from the big brewers. Fresh, locally brewed beer is the way to go! One must be willing to experiment."

Tours? Yes, a free self-guided audio tour with handheld coded listening devices is available daily from 10–4 at the Hilltop Brewery. The original Riverside facility is closed to the public. However, "hard-hat tours," which include visits to both the Hilltop and Riverside breweries, are still available on Fridays at 1:00 PM for $30 and require reservations. These are led by a brewery ambassador and end with a beer and cheese tasting. They book up long in advance! These tour times may expand, so check the website.

Samples? Tastings cost $8, which gets you three 6-oz pours and a souvenir glass. Or you can order a pint for $8 (refills are $5.50) and you keep the glass.

Best Time to Go: Open daily from 10am-5pm (12-5pm on Sundays).

Where can you buy it? On tap here in the Courtyard and Tasting Room. Distributed in 6-packs and cases in bottles and cans, (4-packs for Thumbprint series), and 750 ml bottles — *only in Wisconsin*. Packaged sales on site in the Beer Depot, including bottles, cases, and barrels. Spotted Cow is pretty popular on tap throughout the state as well. Single bottles of R&D (Randy and Dan) beers are available on occasion only at the brewery, and watch for special release dates when folks line up here to wait.

Got food? No, but there are packaged Wisconsin cheeses in the gift shop. You can bring in your own food in the outdoor courtyard only.

Special Offer: A free tasting when you get your book signed.

Directions: Head south of New Glarus on Highway 69 and watch for the entry on the left. You will see the brewhouse up on the hill but the road goes east first and then comes up the backside of the hill to give you that going-through-the-country-to-visit-a-farmhouse feel. (Intentional!) The Riverside facility (*not open to the public*) is at the north end of town where Highway 69 meets County Highway W. **Cyclists:** See *Sugar River State Trail*.

The Beer Buzz: There are, of course, brewers with multiple brewery locations, but this one has two in the same little Wisconsin town. Deborah Carey is the first woman to be the original founder of a brewery in the US. She is a native of our dear state of Wisconsin and an entrepreneur extraordinaire. Add her husband Dan, a superb brewmaster, and there really is no way they could have failed. Dan did his apprenticeship in Bavaria, studied at the Seibel Institute in Chicago, and earned the Master Brewer diploma from the Institute of Brewing in London. His beer and their brewery have awards all over the place. Dan used to install brewery equipment and several of the Wisconsin microbrewers have a story or two about him. His work at Anheuser-Busch pushed him to do his own thing, and we can all be thankful that Deborah made that possible. The original "Riverside" facility is a story itself with its 1962 vintage Huppmann brewery rescued from oblivion in Selb, Germany, purchased for a ridiculously low price, and hauled halfway round the world to find its new home in a Swiss town in a beer state.

In June 2009, the Careys opened their $20 million expanded brewing facility on a hilltop at the south end of town. This is now where the big work goes on but the Riverside brewery still does smaller specialty batches and all of the sour beers, which Dan has been making since the 80s. Herein is a very large coolship, a wide, shallow open tank where hot wort strains down from the copper brew tanks and cools. Steam from this condenses on the natural timber ceiling and drips back in. The wort rests for 3–4 days with open windows which allow the wild yeasts to lend their touch to the sour brews.

Expansion continues at the Hilltop. The Careys value their employees and have made

HORSING AROUND

In season, the New Glarus Brewery delivers beer the old fashioned way: by horse and wagon. At 1PM on Fridays, you'll hear hooves clopping on pavement as two beautiful big draft horses trot up with some New Glarus delivery staff riding behind them. They follow a route through town, delivering some fresh cases before heading back to the brewery.

brewery improvements that ease the demands of some of the physical work. After all, the employees own the brewery. The hospitality center underwent more design upgrades in 2012 and a look of historic ruins graces the hilltop in and around the outdoor Courtyard, which features a clocktower with musical bells, a fountain, and old brewhouse controls turned into a rinse station for your glass. From the courtyard, stone, ruins and picnic tables are scattered about the hill, offering many places to enjoy a beer with a view.

Spotted Cow has become a Wisconsin standard, found at even the least craft-inclined taverns in the middle of nowhere. Check out Dan's "Thumbprint" series of small, very limited (and typically one-off) batches of beers that he is let loose on. Smoked Rye Bock, Sour Brown Ale, Cherry Stout are some of the past creations. Look for the bottles with the red foil tops. These may never repeat, so if you miss one of these adventurous brews, you may be sorry! The R&D (Randy and Dan) beers are only available at the brewery. (Randy Thiel is the Laboratory Manager.)

Stumbling Distance: New Glarus (www.swisstown.com) has a strong Swiss heritage and you can see it in the style of the buildings and the abundance of fondue. For the best Swiss dining, try either *Glarner Stube* (518 1st St, 608-527-2216, glarnerstube.com) or *New Glarus Hotel Restaurant* (www.newglarushotel.com, 100 6ᵗʰ Ave, 800-727-9477) for fondue and much more. *Puempel's Olde Tavern* (www.puempels.com, 18 6th Ave, 608-527-2045) is an old (1893) classic tavern with folk art murals and the original back bar and ice box. New Glarus beer is on tap! Stop in at *Ruef's Meat Market* (538 1st St, 608-527-2554, ruefsmeatmarket.com) either for some great meats to carry home (wieners, bratwurst, and other sausages) or Landjaeger a sort of Swiss jerky to nibble on immediately. *Edelweiss Cheese Shop* (529 First St, 608-636-2155, edelweisscheeseshop.com) features the award-winning creations of Bruce Workman plus a fine selection of other great cheeses and single bottles of craft beer.

The Hop Garden Tap Room

6818 Canal Street • Paoli, WI 53508
Hop Yard: N8668 County Road D • Belleville, WI 53508
608-516-9649
thehopgarden.net
Opened: April 2015   **Brewers:** Rich Joseph
Annual Production: 350 barrels   **Number of Beers:** 6 taps (3 guest taps)

Beers:

- » Black Hops
- » Farmstead Ale
- » Harvest Moon
- » Nuggetopia IPA
- » Sunset Amber
- » Paoli Gold Ale
- » Rising Sun Wheat

Most Popular Brew: Nuggetopia IPA

Samples: Yes, four 5-oz for $6

Brewer's Fave: Paoli Gold and Nuggetopia IPA.

Best Time to Go: Closed Mondays. Summer hours: Tue-Wed 4-8pm, Thu-Fri 1-8pm, Sat 11am-8pm, Sun 11am-6pm. Frequent live music. Check for shortened seasonal hours on the website in winter.

Where can you buy it? Here on tap by the pint and pitchers, and in growlers, bombers to go. The bombers are distributed to major groceries and liquor stores in the Madison area and parts of southern Wisconsin. Paoli Gold and Nuggetopia sell in six-packs in grocery and liquor stores in southern and western Wisconsin.

Got food? A few snacks for sale. Food friendly. Carry in from Paoli Bread & Brat Haus or have Sugar River Pizza delivered.

Tours? Nothing here to tour, but you can visit the hop farm in nearby Belleville.

Special Offer: $1 off your first pint of Hop Garden beer during your signature visit (as well as anyone in your group at the time)!

Directions: Coming into Paoli on WI 69 from the north/west, turn left on Paoli Rd. From County Road PB from Verona, turn right on Paoli Rd. When you come to the center of Paoli at Range Road, go north. Go right at the next street (Canal St) and the road runs 100 feet right into the parking area of the taproom.

The Beer Buzz: Rich has been growing hops since 2009. He started on his father-in-law's property near Oconomowoc, which is now a 2-acre hop garden. He started looking for a farm closer to where they live in Belleville, and found exactly what he was hoping for.

By 2013 he was selling hops to the Wisconsin Hops Exchange and working with a lot of brewers statewide. He was looking for other business opportunities, and a few brewers suggested he jump from his homebrew habit to commercial brewing. He developed some recipes and took them to Page Buchanan at House of Brews in Madison and worked out a contract brewing arrangement. In January 2015, bombers of Hop Garden brews became available.

Rich wanted to open a taproom at the farm, but zoning restrictions prevented it. Paoli was nearby and it gets a lot of traffic for the art scene and its place in a popular rural bicyclist area. In the center of town is an old mill from the early 1800s which has been remodeled, and at the time the back space was open. So he signed a lease and created the little taproom with an upstairs room for events as well. The doors open up to some seating right outside. His Beer Garden is the entire adjacent green space and as long as there isn't a wedding in progress, you can go all the way to the banks of the Sugar River where it cuts through Paoli. Part of a canal still remains, where the mill used to draw water from the river, send it through the turbine, and dump it back to the river. A big turbine remains in the basement but isn't viewable to the public at this time. Rich aims to create a farm to glass experience, and this is a family operation, with everyone lending a hand at the hop farm or the taproom.

Free WiFi. Mug Club. Facebook/thehopgardenwi and Twitter @ wihops

Pronunciation guide: Paoli = Pay-OH-lie

Visiting the hop farm: You can drive by the hop farm 10 miles south of the taproom (N8668 County Rd D, Belleville, 608-516-9649) just to have a look. Tours and open house dates are scheduled in August, so watch the website for specific dates. Harvest is the first part of September (done by machine), but there are also pick your own hops events.

Stumbling Distance: *Paoli Bread & Brat Haus* (608-845-8087, paolibreadandbrathaus.com) occupies the front of the building and serves soups, sandwiches (brisket, pulled pork, tilapia, brat, etc.), bakery and desserts even here in the taproom until about 4–5PM. *Sugar River Pizza* (1019 River St # 5, Belleville, 608-424-6777, sugarriverpizza.com) delivers. *Paoli Cheese* (6890 Paoli Rd, Paoli, 608-845-7031, paolicheese.com) right in front of the old mill building on the main street has quite an assortment to take home or to the taproom.

POTOSI BREWING COMPANY

209 South Main St • Potosi, WI 53820 • 608-763-4002
potosibrewery.com
Founded: First in 1852, again in 2008   **Brewmaster**: Steve McCoy
Annual Production: 15,000 bbls   **Number of Beers**: 24 on tap, 20–25 per year

Staple Beers:

- » GOOD OLD POTOSI BEER
- » POTOSI CZECH-STYLE PILSNER
- » POTOSI CAVE ALE
- » POTOSI LIGHT LAGER
- » SNAKE HOLLOW IPA
- » (also Potosi Root Beer)

Rotating Beers:

- » FIDDLER OATMEAL STOUT
- » GANDY DANCER PORTER
- » HOLIDAY BEER
- » HOPSMITH IMPERIAL IPA
- » ICE BREAKER (barrel-aged Baltic Porter)
- » INNER SANCTUM BRANDY BARREL-AGED BELGIAN QUAD
- » OKTOBERFEST
- » POTOSI SLUGGER (barrel-aged Oatmeal Stout)
- » RHINE RIVER BLOOD ORANGE
- SAISON
- » RIVERSIDE RADLER
- » SHOT TOWER ESPRESSO STOUT
- » ST. THOMAS BELGIAN ABBEY
- » STINGY JACK PUMPKIN ALE
- » STEAMBOAT SHANDY
- » SUNLIT SESSION IPA
- » TANGERINE IPA
- » TENNYWEISEN HEFEWEIZEN
- » WEE STEIN WIT (Belgian)
- » Various limited editions, barrel-aged beers and sours on the way

Brewmaster's Fave: Snake Hollow IPA

Tours? Yes, check website for tour times on Saturday and Sunday afternoons or to request a tour for 8 people or more of the brewery and/or museum. All-inclusive Potosi Brewery tours with Potosi pint glass and beer samples are $12. ABA National Brewery Museum is here too: open Mon-Sat 10:30am-9pm, Sun 10:30am-8pm (closed Mon-Tue in winter) with a $5 entry fee for self-guided tours ($3 for seniors, free for kids). (Brewery tours include a year long pass to the Museum & Library!)

Samples? Yes, a flight of six 5-oz beers.

Best Time to Go: The restaurant is open daily (in season) from 11am-9pm, museums from 10:30am-9pm Mon-Sat 10:30am-8pm Sun, but check hours in the off season; Mon-Tue they may be closed. Look for live music May-Sep on Friday, Saturday or Sunday in the beer garden. Fall colors around here are awesome, especially on the Great River Road.

Where can you buy it? Here on tap and in growlers and bottles to go, and it is distributed statewide and in parts of IL and IA with eyes on MN.

Got food? Yes, great brewpub fare such as burgers, cheese curds, steaks, chicken. Check out the beer cheese soup with Cave Ale, smoked Wisconsin Gouda, and roasted red peppers, and the Friday fish fry and Saturday night prime rib.

Special Offer: A free pint of their beer when you get your book signed.

Directions: Come into Potosi on Hwy 133 from the west or east. Coming from the east the brewery is on the right side of the road to the west side of Potosi across from the giant cone-top beer can. Hard to miss. If coming from Platteville consider taking County Rd O which is more direct but curvy and scenic.

The Beer Buzz: Potosi is home to the world's largest cone-top beer can. The town also has the longest Main Street in the world and it goes right past the old 1852 brewery building which is home to the ABA National Brewery Museum. But what's a brewery museum without beer? Steve Zuidema of the former Front Street Brewery in Davenport, Iowa, started the brewing again at Potosi, then Steve Buszka (formerly Bell's, O'so) took over. Finally, Steve McCoy took the reins in 2013. (Third Steve is a charm?) Steve McCoy has long been a craft beer fan and homebrewer. He studied biology at UW- La Crosse and went into food and beverage work after graduation. He spent time as lab tech in dairy, then worked at City Brewery in the lab for a year and in production brewing for 5 years before landing here.

In the beginning, Potosi brought back versions of the traditional Potosi brews—Good Old Potosi, for one—but now the lineup includes a wide assortment of ales and some lagers. Potosi Brewery also makes its own root beer with Wisconsin honey, so if beer is not your thing, there's something else to sample on a brewery tour.

In making beer, the quality is, of course, in the ingredients, and the first matter is the water. Many of the breweries of old were built around or on top of artesian wells and natural springs. Potosi is no exception. The water still rushes out of the ground into the old brewery pond behind the beer garden. The flow is so overwhelming that years ago it would get into the brewhouse and collect in puddles on the floor. Remodeling included an overflow pipe which diverts some of the spring water, and you can see it rushing beneath a piece of plate glass in the brewpub floor. Potosians Gary David, his son Tyler, and his father Marvin—three generations of woodworkers—created the beautiful handcrafted bar. The tables around the room are made with the cypress of the old fermentation tanks. As the brewery ad once asked, "Have you had your Good Old Potosi today?"

In April 2015 they opened a 24,000 sq ft production brewery, with a 40-barrel brewhouse, 120-bbl fermenters, and bottling and canning lines, plus a large barrel-aging cooler. They are still using the old system at the brewpub where they make many specialty beers (Helles Bock, Schwarzbier, White IPA, Rye Saison, etc.) typically only available over the bar. They've also started a Belgian sour program using the old lagering caves you see when you walk in the front doors of the old brewery.

The Potosi Foundation, run by a board of elected volunteers, is the sole owner of the brewery, and is actually a 501(c)(3), making this the nation's first not-for-profit brewery. All profits go to charity.

Free Wifi. Facebook.com/PotosiBrewery Twitter/Instagram @PotosiBrewingCo

Stumbling Distance: Hardly much of a stumble, but right inside the same structure is the *National Brewery Museum, Transportation Museum* and the *Great River Road Interpretive Center*. For a roadside attraction, check out the *Dickeyville Grotto* (www.dickeyvillegrotto.com, 305 W Main St, Dickeyville, 608-568-3119) a collection of shrines both religious and patriotic built by

a priest in the 1920s using stone, mortar and all sorts of eye catching little objects. Watch Potosi for the annual Catfish Festival in August, the Potosi Brewfest the 4th Saturday of August, and the Potosi Bicycle Tour in September. *Whispering Bluff Winery* (196 S Main St, 608-763-2468, facebook.com/whisperingbluffswinery) is right across the street. **Hotels:** *Potosi Inn* (102 N Main St, 608-763-2269, potosiinn.com) and *Pine Point Lodge* (219 S Main St, 608-763-2767, pinepointlodgepotosi.com) will do nicely.

Head up the Great River Road to La Crosse for more beer. It's a two-hour drive but worth taking your time for the scenery.

THE GREAT RIVER ROAD

A National Scenic Byway, it runs parallel along the Mississippi River offering a pretty incredible slice of American life and natural views to wear out your camera. Wisconsin's portion stretches 250 miles and passes through 33 towns. It also comes with a free downloadable audio tour (wigrr.com). Much of the land along the route is protected natural areas and the bluffs are beautiful from above and below. Birdwatchers love this area as it is a flyway for migratory species and eagle sightings are basically a given. Local produce, cheese, family restaurants and taverns, B&Bs, wineries and more lie along this route. Boat tours, camping and paddling opportunities (see my book *Paddling Wisconsin*) are also abundant. Check the Wisconsin Great River Road website (wigrr.com, 800-658-9424) for maps, podcasts and more to plan your journey, and visit the Great River Road Interpretive Center at the Potosi Brewery/National Brewery Museum.

TAKE THE PRIDE OF CASSVILLE CAR FERRY

From May through October, cross the Mississippi, from the Great River Road at Cassville to the Iowa Great River Road at Millville. The service dates back to 1833. (608-725-5180, cassville.org/ferry.html)

THE NATIONAL BREWERY MUSEUM™

Like any good Wisconsin boy, I collected beer cans when I was young. It was a veritable rite of passage to acquire all the Schmidt cans with their varying pictures, and a must for any collection was the Pabst Blue Ribbon beer can with the dawn-of-the-pull-tab message, "No Opener Needed." You were a hero in my neighborhood if you found one of the old bottle-can hybrids first introduced to the market by Milwaukee's Jos. Schlitz Brewing known as a cone-top. Potosi Wisconsin offers the opportunity to see the World's Largest Cone-top, in fact, but more importantly Potosi is also home to the National Brewery Museum.

The Potosi Brewery opened in 1852 and made a long run until 1972. The brewery that once produced Good Old Potosi lay in ruins and by the 1990s trees were growing through the roof, but locals had a plan to revive some of the town's heritage. What if they restored the old brewery and started brewing again. Better yet, what if that restored building was a tourist attraction?

Just so happens that the American Breweriana Association wanted a museum location to display the amazing collections of their members. Breweriana—collectible beer memorabilia and not a bad name for your first-born daughter I might add—ranges from cans and tap handles to beer signs and rare lithographs. Where would such a brewing tribute make its home? Milwaukee? Nope. St. Louis? No way. How about Potosi, Wisconsin, population 711?

How did that happen? Well, Potosi threw their bid in and the ABA made the rounds in 2004 to hear the proposals and see the sites. Remember the forest through the roof of the old brewery? It seemed as if their chances were slim indeed, but after the ABA members sneaked a peek at the building, the next day they said Yes. The reason for that was the brand-spanking new firehouse. They believed that if little Potosi could provide such a facility for their volunteer fire department and rescue squad, they could redo the brewery.

What's to see here? A vintage Pabst lithograph print worth $15,000. Rare character steins from the 1920s and 30s—even some of Mickey Mouse and Donald Duck—tap handles, serving trays, clocks, calendars, posters and even oil paintings fill the rooms. Watch vintage beer commercials and documentaries about the brewing process on a few video monitors. Another room holds a research library with information on nearly all of the American breweries that ever existed. On the ground floor is a transportation museum and an interactive interpretive center for Wisconsin's segment of the Great River Road Scenic Byway (a really lovely roadtrip all by itself with local beer both here and up in La Crosse). An old lagering cave is viewable behind a glass wall, and a gift shop offers all sorts of Wisconsin paraphernalia and a selection of locally produced cheeses, wines, syrup, honey, and beer.

I highly recommend a visit, and when you are done, have a meal and a Potosi beer in the brewpub!

Entry to the Great River Road Interpretive Center and Transportation Museum is free. The brewery museum charges $5 (free for 17 and under, $3 for 60+). (potosibrewery.com, 608-763-4002, 209 S. Main St., Potosi)

Directions: Potosi is located on the edge of the Mississippi River in the southwestern corner of Wisconsin on the Great River Road Scenic Byway (wigreatriverroad.org). Come into Potosi on Hwy 133 from the west or east. Coming from the east the museum is on the right side of the road to the west side of Potosi across from the giant cone-top beer can.

Double your fun and visit Potosi during its annual catfish festival, the second full weekend in August, when more than 2,300 pounds of fish are fried.

CORNER PUB

100 Main Street • Reedsburg, WI 53959 • 608-524-8989
Email: Facebook.com/cornerpubbrews/
Founded: 1996   **Brewmaster:** Pete Peterson
Annual Production: up to 100 bbls   **Number of Beers:** 10 on tap

Possible Beers:

» APA
» BOCK (winter)
» BOURBON SCOTCH ALE
» BROWN ALE
» CREAM ALE
» DRY STOUT (St. Pat's sometimes)
» KÖLSCH

» MILK STOUT
» OKTOBERFEST (fall)
» PORTER
» RED DOT IPA
» SAISON
» SMOKED PORTER
» WEISS (summer)

Most Popular Brew: Porter or Red Dot IPA

Brewmaster's Fave: Red Dot IPA

Tours? Not really. By chance.

Samples? No.

Best Time to Go: Open Mon 10:30am-2pm, Tue-Thu 10:30am-10pm, Fri-Sat 10:30am-11pm, Sun 12-6pm. Hours subject to change! Double check on Facebook page. Live music is common. Butterfest (reedsburgbutterfest.org) in June recognizes Reedsburg as one of the world's largest producers. Come for the awesome Fermentation Fest (fermentationfest.com) A Live Culture Covergence in October, featuring 60+ classes led by chefs, artists, bakers, chocolatiers, and fermentation experts.

Where can you buy it? Here on tap or in growlers to go.

Got food? Good hearty pub fare, fresh burgers, deep-fried local curds, and fish fry every Wednesday and Friday.

Special Offer: Not participating.

Directions: Hwys 33 and 23 run right through town as Main St. Corner Pub is on the corner (oddly enough) at the first block of E Main St.

The Beer Buzz: This little two-barrel brewhouse is what microbrewing is all about—local beer, handcrafted, nothing glitzy or overdone. A small-town humility and a product worth some pride. Pete started homebrewing with a buddy of his in 1995 and moved it into his EndeHouse Brewery and Restaurant in 1996. In 2002, Pete brought his brewing into the current location. He enjoys the modest production, and this is as unpretentious a place as you'll find. Local pastries and muffins are for sale by the door. Sports banners hang from the ceiling, and four TVs pipe in the important games. Live music is hosted occasionally on a small stage. The popcorn at the bar is free and comes with the caveat: "Can't always guarantee freshness." Food's good, people are friendly, and the beer is quite fine as well. In 2008 some regional flooding swamped the brewhouse, and for a while the equipment was out on the sidewalk and beer was on hold. They got through it. Check

out the mural on the side of the building dedicated to the history of hops growing in the area. If you like a little smokiness to your beer, do not miss Pete's Smoked Porter—one of my personal favorites.

Stumbling Distance: Just a couple blocks away is the start of the state's "400" bike trail which connects up to the *Elroy–Sparta Trail*. Check out the Beer, Boats and Bikes section for a pedaling-for-beer idea. Reedsburg is famous for its antiques shops, and there are several in town. *Wisconsin Dells* is not far down the road and *Devil's Lake State Park* is definitely not to be missed with its rocky outcroppings from where the glacier stopped in the last Ice Age (see also the *Ice Age National Scenic Trail* there). Fall colors are great here. Over 60 varieties of cheese—including fresh curds—are waiting to be eaten twelve minutes northwest of Reedsburg at award-winning *Carr Valley Cheese Co.* in nearby LaValle (www.carrvalleycheese.com, S3797 Cty Hwy G, LaValle, 608-986-2781).

FERMENTATION FEST

Art, food, ideas and the people who love them gather at Fermentation Fest. It's not just beer, but all things fermented—pickles, wine, sauerkraut, sourdough, cheese, soy sauce—are celebrated and discussed here. Put on by the *Wormfarm Institute* (wormfarminstitute.org) and scheduled across two weekends in October, the fest offers classes, seminars, tastings, products for sale, and entertainment. Additionally, art is on the scene: the DTour is a 50-mile self-guided route (drivable or bikable) "through scenic working lands" to see temporary art installations, Roadside Culture Stands, Pasture Performances, and more. fermentationfest.com

Mel's Micro Brewing & Pubbery

21733 US-14 • Richland Center, WI 53581 • 608-647-1116
melsmicro.com

Opened: 2016   **Head Brewer:** Ross "Mel" Nelson
Annual Production: 12 barrels   **Number of Beers:** 2-5 on tap, plus guests

Staple Beers:

» Wolfhound Irish Stout

Rotating Beers:

» Amber Ale

» Brown Ale

» IPA

Most Popular Brew: Wolfhound

Brewmaster's Fave: Changes with seasons

Tours? Not really.

Samples: Some day.

Best Time to Go: Open Tue-Sun 11am-close, Mon 4pm-close. Happy hour Mon-Fri 4-6pm.

Where can you buy it? Here on tap and in growlers to go.

Got food? Yes, tavern/grill food. Possibly random free fresh popcorn.

Special Offer: During your signature visit, 10% off Mel's merchandise, including his glass growlers with a fill.

Directions: US-14 passes through town. Heading north it takes a turn west follows 6th St. Continue west 2.5 miles and Mel's is on the south side of the highway.

The Beer Buzz: Ross Melven Nelson is Mel here. He grew up in Richland Center, went to school at UW-Madison, and then spent 10 years in computers and 5 more as an engineer at the iron foundry here in town. He enjoyed homebrewing as a hobby, and when he found no satisfaction in engineering, he left the foundry. They closed a month later, so clearly they couldn't make a go of it without him. Now he is brewer/owner/manager/bartender/cook/janitor of his own place just north of town on Highway 14. Built in the 1960s as a convenience store, the building quickly turned tavern and when Mel took it over, he added a small brew system. He has since upgraded to a 1-barrel system. The meandering concrete bar may be the longest I've seen in a Wisconsin tavern.

Mel's got darts, a jukebox, 3 pool tables, 4 TVs for sports, an outdoor sand volleyball pit and small patio out front. Free WiFi. ATM onsite. On Facebook.

Stumbling Distance: Richland Center is the birthplace of Frank Lloyd Wright and his *A.D. German Warehouse* (300 S Church St, 608-647-2808) downtown is on the FLW Trail. **Pine River Paddle & Tube** (608-475-2199) can put you on the Pine River north or south of the city, for varying length trips. OK for beginners. *Oakwood Fruit Farm* (31128 Apple Ridge Rd, 608-585-2701, oakwoodfruitfarm.com) has 20+ apple varieties and opens for the season in August. *Weggy Winery* is 15 minutes south (30940 Oak Ridge Dr, Muscoda, 608-647-6600, weggywinery.com).

VINTAGE BREWING SAUK PRAIRIE

600 Water St • Sauk City, WI 53583 • 608-370-8200
vintagebrewingcompany.com
Opened: January 2018
Director of Brewing Operations: Scott Manning   **Head Brewer:** Page Buchanan
Annual Production: 3,000 barrels
Number of Beers: 40 on tap, including nitro, casks, guest beers/ciders
Staple Beers:

- » DEDICATION ABBEY DUBBEL
- » MCLOVIN IRISH RED ALE
- » MOSASAUR IPA
- » SCAREDY CAT OATMEAL STOUT
- » SISTER GOLDEN KÖLSCH
- » WEISS NIX WEISSBIER
- » WOODSHED OAKED IPAW

Rotating Beers:

- » ABDOMINABLE SNOWMAN COFFEE BLONDE ALE
- » BETTER OFF RED HOPPED-UP AMERICAN RED ALE
- » BOCKS O-CHOCOLATES CHOCOLATE DOPPELBOCK
- » CITRA ZEN PALE ALE
- » DIAMOND STAR HALO (sour ale)
- » GOTTER OTTER BRITISH STRONG PALE ALE
- » MACH SCHNELL! PILSNER
- » MAXIMILIAN STOUT IMPERIAL STOUT
- » ROCHAMBEAU BELGO PALE ALE
- » RYE HAVOC RED RYE IPA
- » SCHWARZFAHREN SCHWARZBIER
- » TIPPY TOBOGGAN ROGGEN BOCK
- » TREPIDATION...BELGIAN ABBEY
- » ...plus Woodshed Ales, collaborations, one-offs, rare styles, barrel-aged and sour ales

Most Popular Brew: Weiss Nix

Brewmaster's Fave: Rye Wine or Diamond Star Halo

Tours? Yes, scheduled on weekends. Check website.

Samples: Yes, sample flights of four 5-oz pours.

Best Time to Go: Open Mon-Sat 11am-last call, Sun 9am-9pm. Happy hour Mon-Fri 4-7pm.

Where can you buy it? Here on tap and in Crowlers, growlers, bombers and 5- and 15.5-gallon kegs to go.

Got food? Yes, a full menu and full bar.

Special Offer: A half-price Crowler or growler fill (up to 2) of Vintage beer when you get your book signed.

Directions: Coming into Sauk City on US-12, take WI-78 north 0.2 mile and the brewery is on the right (riverside). Cyclists: Keep your eye on the paved Great Sauk State Trail which currently runs past the brewery on the river side and is planned to connect to Devil's Lake State Park.

The Beer Buzz: Previously, Vintage had brought Woodshed Ale House to Sauk City, but then stepped it up when they closed it and built this brick beauty of a brewpub overlooking the Wisconsin River in Sauk Prairie, the sort of compromise name of conjoined towns Sauk City and Prairie du Sac. Similar to the layout in Madison, the brewpub space offers a large separate bar area with a four-sided island bar, but even more dining space, including a mezzanine floor of it for overflow seating or special private events. There the similarity ends. Add a 30-barrel brewhouse and 90-bbl fermenters rising up from the basement as high as the dining room. Add the outdoor patio with a 10-tap bar in back, and the roomy deck on the side of the building offering views of eagles diving for fish, and you've got quite the destination brewpub going here. Page Buchanan, who made a name for himself with his House of Brews in Madison, took on the head brewer position, a perfect fit.

A big aquarium greets you at the entrance and a host seats diners. Six TVs around the space pipe in special games. Second-floor event space can accommodate groups up to 300 people, so weddings are already booking up.

In addition to Vintage's two locations in Madison, Vintage's co-owners also opened *Tangent Kitchen & Taproom* in Madison's *Beermuda Triangle* for a more avant garde menu and some original brews from the two Vintage breweries.

Free WiFi. ATM onsite. Mug Club. Facebook.com/vbcsaukprairie and Instagram @vintagebrewingco

Stumbling Distance: *Wollersheim Winery & Distillery* (7876 Wisconsin 188, Sauk City, 608-643-6515) offers tours and tastings. *Green Acres* (7470 WI-78, Sauk City, 608-643-2305) is a classic supper club for steaks and fish fry. Canoe the Wisconsin from here with *Sauk Prairie Canoe Rental/ WI River Outings* (7554 US-12, Sauk City, 608-375-5300). This area teems with eagles in winter – come for *Bald Eagle Watching Days* in January.

Driftless Brewing Co.

102 Sunbeam Blvd. W • Soldiers Grove, WI 54655 • 608-624-5577
driftlessbrewing.com
Founded: 2013 (Taproom open Fall 2018)   **Head Brewer**: Chris Balistreri
Annual Production: 120 barrels but expanding
Number of Beers: 10–12 on tap (with guests)

Staple Beers:
  » Dirt (Brown Ale)
  » The Local Buzz (Golden Honey Ale)
  » Kick-Axe (Pale Ale)
  » Cultivation Series (IPA)

Rotating Beers:
  » Seasonal Saisons and Lagers
  » Various Belgian style ales and IPAs
  » Some barrel-aged beers

Most Popular Brew: Depends on the venue; each has a niche.

Brewmaster's Fave: Seasonals, barrel-aged brews and lots of IPAs.

Tours? By appointment only.

Samples: Yes.

Best Time to Go: Thu-Fri 1-5pm, but expanded hours starting Fall 2018 - best to check the Facebook page or call for hours.

Where can you buy it? Here on tap and in 22-oz bombers and growlers to go, and distributed here in the Driftless Area: bombers at Viroqua Food Co-op, Kex Food Co-op in Gays Mills, and on tap at Old Oak Inn and Country Gardens in Soldiers Grove, Kickapoo Creekside in Readstown, and Dave's Pizza, The Rooted Spoon, The American Legion, and Driftless Cage in Viroqua.

Got food? Only some snacks, but they're food-friendly, so you can also order locally off menus onsite or bring your own.

Special Offer: Buy your first beer in the taproom and get one free beer of equal value when you get your book signed.

Directions: US 61 runs north-south through town. At the southern end of town look for Driftless Brewing Company on the west side of the Highway across from the Mobile station. Turn in here and park. The brewery has the tall white-paneled peaked passive solar roof.

The Beer Buzz: This project had been kicking around in Chris' mind since the late 80s. He'd go to keg parties, pay the cover, and still bring his own beer (Augsburger or some imports). He followed the craft beer movement closely in its early years and fired up his first brew kettle in 1988. In 2011 Chris took the Master Brewers Association of America's brewing course at UW-Madison.

Chris and co-founder Michael Varnes-Epstein started brewing in a dairy barn in Excelsior, Wisconsin, in the middle of the middle of nowhere. Being deeply connected to the land and the area, they took on the name given to this corner of the state, the Driftless Area. They were licensed and ready to go in January 2013, brewing a 20-gallon batch and hand-bottling it to be sold at the Viroqua Co-op. They delivered 10 cases on a Friday and by Monday they got a call: We need more! Six months later they needed to expand and relocated to Soldiers Grove, where they were joined by Cynthia Olmstead and Scott Noe to help with all aspects of the expansion and running the brewery.

Soldier Grove itself had relocated back in 1981 when it was washed away from its original site by a flooding Kickapoo River. The new town became the first "solar village" with buildings all over town built with passive solar. The brewery is located in the former grocery store, which had been empty for eight years, and you can see the oddly towering peaked roof made to absorb heat even in winter. They bought it in March 2014 and sold their first deliveries on the fourth of July that year.

In Spring 2018 they began expanding to a 15-barrel brewhouse and this should be up and running in late fall of 2018. By this time the 70-seat taproom should also be open. From the beginning, Driftless Brewing has focused on using local and regional Wisconsin ingredients, and they work directly with companies, co-ops, and farmers. The staff harvest locally-grown fruits and other ingredients themselves. This place offers a laid-back local sort of vibe set amid the beauty and abundance of the Driftless Area.

Free WiFi. Facebook.com/DriftlessBrewingCompany

Stumbling Distance: *The Old Oak Inn Bed & Breakfast* (500 Church St, 608-624-5217, theoldoakinn.net) is an impressive Victorian home, a perfect place to stay during your visit to the area. It also has a great Friday fish fry and other specially scheduled public dining. See *Roadtripping the Driftless Area.*

One hour to the breweries of La Crosse and Onalaska from here.

ROADTRIPPING THE DRIFTLESS AREA

The Driftless Area is that southwestern corner of Wisconsin that shows deep river valleys and no glacial debris or "drift" thanks to having been spared the grinding of the glaciers in the last glacial period of the Ice Age (125,000–12,000 years ago). Consequently, there are no lakes but lots of hills and winding roads, making it generally a very scenic place to do a road trip. Fall colors are a given but also watch for various festivals. Here's just a short list of events and local products you should check out if you've come all the way to **Driftless Brewing** in Soldiers Grove:

Gays Mills Folk Festival (gaysmillsfolkfest.org) is Mothers' Day weekend in May.

Soldier Grove Dairy Days (soldiersgrove.com) is a June festival.

Driftless Area Art Festival (driftlessareaartfestival.com) is in Soldiers Grove the third weekend in September, gathering a vast area of regional artists.

Gays Mills Apple Festival (gaysmills.org) is the last full weekend in September.

The Kickapoo River runs through the area on its famously serpentine course to the Wisconsin River, and offers some great paddling, typically farther up-river between Ontario (40 min from Soldiers Grove) and La Farge (25 min) through the *Kickapoo Valley Reserve*. (See my book *Paddling Wisconsin*)

The Driftless Angler (106 S Main St, Viroqua, 608-637-8779, driftlessangler. com) supplies and guides fly-fishers and has lodging options.

Mt. Sterling Co-op Creamery (505 Diagonal St, Mt Sterling, 608-734-3151, buymtsterlinggoatcheese.com, Mon–Fri 8AM–4PM) is the local goat cheese producer and gets raves (and awards).

Westby Cooperative Creamery (401 S Main St, Westby, 800-492-9282, westbycreamery.com)

Organic Valley (507 W Main St, La Farge, 608-625-2602, organicvalley.coop) produces some very fine dairy products and more, and operates a retail store Mon–Sat in La Farge.

Wisco Pop (1201 N Main St, Viroqua, 608-638-7632, wiscopopsoda.com) is the local soda pop made in Viroqua and distributed in the area and as far as Madison.

Kickapoo Coffee (608-637-2022, kickapoocoffee.com) is a Viroqua coffee roaster whose beans are available wholesale and served at select coffee shops.

For an abundance of information about Wisconsin's Driftless Area, go to driftless-wisconsin.com

Viking Brew Pub

211 East Main Street • Stoughton, WI 53589 • 608-719-5041
vikingbrewpub.com

Founded: 2014   **Brewmaster**: David Worth
Annual Production: 200+ barrels   **Number of Beers**: 12 taps (one or two guest beers)

Staple Beers:

» Midnite Sun Cream Ale
» Nordic Blonde

» Soot in My Eye (Black Rye IPA)

Rotating Beers: (examples)

» Great Heathen Wit
» Sigurd Scotch Ale
» Uff Da Tripel

» Valhalla's Delight (chocolate peanut butter porter)

Most Popular Brew: Nordic Blonde.

Samples: Yes, 4-oz pours for about $1.50 or Log Flight of 4 for $6

Best Time to Go: Open Mon, Wed–Thu 4–10pm, Sat 11am–12am, Sun 12–8pm. Closed Tuesdays.

Where can you buy it? On tap here and in growlers and bomber cans to go.

Got food? Yes, Scandinavian dishes, pub fare with appetizers, burger baskets, soups and salads, and a Friday fish fry (cod, perch, salmon, shrimp, and walleye). Norwegian meatballs on Sat, and daily specials.

Tours? Yes, on request.

Special Offer: $1 off your first Viking beer during your signature visit.

Directions: US 51 passes right through downtown as Main St. 3 blocks east of the bridge over the river and on the south side of the street at the corner of Forrest St.

The Beer Buzz: If you were looking for a smoke-breathing Viking dragon ship—and who isn't?—this is the place to go. It's pretty much the first thing you see when you walk in: a magnificent oak bow with a dragon's head nearly up to the ceiling, blowing smoke on demand. Owners Vik ("Vike" not "Vick") and Lori Malling opened this brewpub in 2014 in the remodeled 19th-century

Stoughton State Bank building and started as a beer bar with some contract brewing at Madison's House of Brews. By summer of 2015, they brought the brewing in-house. The 3.5-barrel brewhouse is visible from the bar, and they keep a pilot system in the basement to play with. Vik used to fly tanker aircraft for the Air Force, from Vietnam through the Gulf War and Kosovo, a career spanning 34 years. Vik developed the staple beer recipes but handed off brewing responsibilities to Brewer David who has been homebrewing since forever and has a satchel of awards for his efforts.

Vik and his father-in-law Duane Brickson used to go on regular pils-grimage outings to nearby breweries. Duane off-handedly remarked that some day Stoughton would have one and they wouldn't have to drive so far. Inspired by the simple model of Madison's One Barrel Brewing, Duane, a talented master carpenter, sat down and drew up some plans for what they might build

for various possible locations in Stoughton. What you see before you was hand built (and the dragon head was hand carved) by his son Mitchell, partly using century-old wood reclaimed from an old silo at Stevens Point Brewery. Smoke blows when the Packers or Badgers score. Metal worker Aaron Howard designed the Viking logo—or rather his 1993 sophomore year metal shop project was adopted by Vik and Lori. Aaron, now with a blacksmith shop in Madison, was happy to sell it knowing it would have a good home.

The bar area shows a lot of natural logs and wood, and along with the two-sided bar, offers booths and tables. Five TVs pipe in sports and the "upper" room (a couple steps up next door) even has a few couches ideal for a group during a big game. Best Things Wisconsin named the pub among the ten best theme bars in the state.

Free WiFi. ATM onsite. Mug Club. Find them on Facebook. Twitter/Instagram @ VikingBrewPub

Stumbling Distance: The gloriously remodeled *Stoughton Opera House* (381 E. Main St, 608-877-4400, stoughtonoperahouse.com) brings in some top-talent performers throughout the year. *Big Sky Restaurant* (176 E Main St, 608-205-6278) across the street has some high-class, outstanding gourmet food people come from out of town for. *Fahrenheit 364* (364 East Main St, 608-205-2763) is known for their cocktails. In summer, watch for *Gazebo Musikk* on Thursday nights, free concerts in Stoughton Rotary Park (401 E Main St, facebook.com/gazebomusikk).

FULL MILE BEER CO. & KITCHEN

132 Market St. • Sun Prairie, WI 53590
fullmilebeercompany.com
Projected to Open: August 2018   **Head Brewer:** TBA
Annual Production: 600-700 barrels
Number of Beers: 12-14 on tap, plus guest cider

Staple and Rotating Beers:

TBD*

Most Popular Brew: Too soon to tell!

Brewmaster's Fave: TBD

Tours? Yes, check website.

Samples: Yes, sample flights of four 5-oz pours.

Best Time to Go: Open Tue-Sun for lunch and dinner. Check website.

Where can you buy it? Here on tap and in crowlers and growlers to go.

Got food? Yes, a full kitchen serving elevated pub fare. Expect a fish fry, curds, and brick-oven pizzas. Locally sourced as much as possible. Full bar, heavy on the whiskeys.

Special Offer: A free pint of house beer and another for your companion when you get this book signed.

Directions: From US151, take Exit 101 and follow Main St east for 2 miles. Turn right (south) on Market St, go two blocks, and the brewpub is on the corner on your right.

The Beer Buzz: Nathan Kinderman and C.J. Hall were childhood friends in Oregon, WI. They kept in touch over the years and in about 2008 they had one of those crazy plan-making conversations fueled by beer. But over time it kept coming up and in 2014, CJ, a longtime homebrewer, quit his job and told Nathan, who had a background in restaurants and bars, "Let's do this." They made a deal to be part of a local developer's new construction, occupying the lower level of a building on a previously empty lot downtown, and a plan to open a brewpub with equal attention to the beer and the food.

They purchased a 10-barrel system from QTS in Marshfield which is visible through big windows. The outdoor patio holds 60 people. Games, such as cribbage, are on hand, and TVs come on for game day. Live music is expected several times per month.

Free WiFi. Mug Club. Facebook.com/fullmilebeerco

Stumbling Distance: *Eddie's Alehouse* (238 E Main St, 608-825-1515, eddiesalehouse.com) has dozens of craft beers on draft. *Chicken Lips* (5508 County Hwy N #3, 608-837-6721) has amazing sauced and dry-rub wings. Best pizza in town, with creative toppings and hand-crafted Italian-style crust awaits as *Salvatore's Pizza* (121 E Main St, 608-318-1761 salvatorestomatopies.com). *Beans 'n Cream* (345 Cannery Square, 608-837-7737, beansncreamcoffeehouse.com) is a great community coffee shop. *Cannery Wine & Spirits* (240 E Main St, 608-318-0595, cannerywineandspirits.com) hosts tastings, offers 400+ beers, and sells brewing supplies. Watch for Sun Prairie's *Sweet Corn Festival* (facebook.com/sweetcornfestsunprairiewi) out at Angell Park every August.

Boulder Brew Pub

950 Kimball Lane • Verona, WI 53593 • 608-845-3323
boulderbrewpub.com
Opened: April 2018   **Brewmaster:** Kara Hulce
Number of Beers: 24 taps with guest beers

Beers:

- Classic Styles
- IPAs
- Kettle Sours and Fruited Beers
- 60 Schilling Scotch Ale
- …plus seasonals

Brewmaster's Fave: Kettle sours

Tours? Yes, on request and by appointment, plus watch for classes and tastings.

Samples? Yes, sample flights available.

Best Time to Go: Open Sun-Thu 11am-9pm, Fri-Sat 11am-10pm. Happy hour Mon-Fri 3-6pm. Great for Wisconsin sporting events.

Where can you buy it? On tap or growlers of house beer to go.

Got food? Yes, a full menu and full bar. Burgers, wood-fired oven pizzas, wraps, plus some beer-pairing items.

Special Offer: A free pint of house beer when you get your book signed!

Directions: The brewpub/eatery is located just off of Hwy 151 at Verona. From Exit 79 take Old PB toward town and turn left onto Whalen Rd. It's across from the BP gas station.

The Beer Buzz: In February 2018, Jon Novick, a longtime customer of Gray's Tied House, bought the brewpub and made it his own. The 450-seat restaurant remains a big draw for its food and now features a much wider and varying assortment of house beers. The 7-barrel system is visible from outside and from the bar. Two outdoor patios make up the beer garden which has portable heaters and a bonfire pit to extend the Wisconsin dine-outside season a bit. Expect acoustic guitar music inside and a fireplace lounge. A private bar upstairs makes this a good place for parties, and the thirteen large-screen TVs bring in crowds on game days.

Brewer Kara hails from Niagara, Wisconsin. She has a degree in Chemistry, and pursued her master at University of Wisconsin, studying in the fermentation program in the Food Science department. Prior to going to grad school she worked in the lab at Death's Door Distillery and spent many years homebrewing. She's done research with a genetics group on lager yeast, which until 2011 had been known to be a long-ago hybrid of an ale yeast and an unknown strain. In 2011, Chris Hittinger at UW figured out this mystery yeast was Saccharomyces eubayanus, which has since been found in nature in Sheboygan, Patagonia, and East Asia. Her studies had her brewing with it for research and to determine how the pre-hybrid strain performed. This "new" old yeast may have a future in brewing.

Free WiFi. On Facebook. Instagram @boulderbrewpub

Stumbling Distance: Choco-holics won't want to skip *Candinas Chocolatier* (www.candinas.com, 2435 Old PB, Verona, 800-845-1554, Mon–Sat 10–5) where Swiss-trained Markus Candinas makes divine assortments that have been nationally recognized. Just farther up the road toward Madison is *Bavaria Sausage Inc.* (www.bavariasausage.com, 6317 Nesbitt Rd, Fitchburg 53719, 608-271-1295, Mon–Fri 8–5, Sat 8–1) which makes a whole variety of outstanding sausages and sells over 100 different cheeses, including fresh cheese curds. From Hwy 151 just south of Madison turn west on Cty Hwy PD and a quick left onto Nesbitt Road heading south. See this brewpub in the Biking for Beer section at the back of the book as well.

Hop Haus Brewing Co.

231 South Main St. • Verona, WI 53593 • 608-497-3165
hophausbrewing.com
Opened: June 24, 2015   **Brewmaster:** Phil Hoechst
Annual Production: 250 barrels   **Number of Beers:** up to 12 on tap

Staple Beers:
- » El Andy IPA
- » Magic Dragon Double IPA
- » Plaid Panther Scotch Ale
- » Super Big Time IPA
- » Sweet Sunglasses Blonde Ale
- » Wildcat Amber Ale
- » Yardwork Crushable IPA (Session IPA)

Rotating Beers:
- » Crispin Original
- » Fat Eddie Milk Stout
- » Flowers and Fog American Stout
- » Hidden Stash IPA
- » Jean-Claud Van Dubbel
- » Peace Train Pale Ale
- » Polka Dot Rainbow Belgian Tripel

Most Popular Brew: Hidden Stash IPA

Brewmaster's Fave: IPAs

Tours? Yes, check the website for the future schedule or call for an appointment.

Samples: Yes, five 5-oz pours for about $9.

Best Time to Go: Open Mon–Thu 4–10PM, Fri 3–11PM, Sat 12–11PM, Sun 12–8PM. Double check on the website.

Where can you buy it? Here on tap and in growlers to go. Distributed throughout southern Wisconsin - east to Milwaukee, north to Wisconsin Dells, west to Platteville and south to the state line. In bottles: Plaid Panther Scotch Ale, Magic Dragon Double IPA & El Andy IPA, two canned varieties: Sweet Sunglasses Blonde Ale & Yardwork Crushable IPA (session IPA).

Got food? Yes, popcorn, cheese plates, fried staples (cheese curds, chicken tenders, french fries), pizza and soft pretzels. Check the website for food pop-ups and food carts. Also, food friendly.

Special Offer: $1 off your first pint of house beer during your signature visit.

Directions: US 18/151 runs south of Verona. Whether you take Exit 81 from the east nearer Madison or Exit 76 coming from the west, it will put you on Verona Ave which passes right through town. Take it to Main St/County Road M and turn south.

The Beer Buzz: Owners Phil and Sara Hoechst opened this little brewery in downtown Verona. Looking for German beer? Well, Phil was *born* in Germany. Granted, he grew up here in Verona. He came to Wisconsin as a child when his father took a job at University of Wisconsin. Both Phil and Sara graduated from UW, but moved to Denver where Phil took up homebrewing. They had their first son and moved back to Verona to raise a family. They decided to open a brewery and developed a 5-year plan in 2012, which turned out to be a 2.5-year plan. When they started looking for a space, this former Cousin's Subs/Chocolate Shoppe ice cream parlor opened up and suddenly everything just fell into place.

Phil runs a 3-barrel system you can see through the windows of the taproom and his brewing gravitates toward IPAs and Belgians. Along with the staple beers, expect frequent one-offs. Large storefront windows let in a lot of light, and the bar and one wall incorporate reclaimed barn wood. A mix of regular and tall tables spread throughout the room and there are three TVs, some board games, and live music. The amber ale is named for Verona's high school team mascot. Parking is off-street.

Free WiFi. Facebook.com/HopHausBrewingCompany and Twitter/Instagram @ Hophausbrewing

Stumbling Distance: The brewery is right off the *Military Ridge State Trail* if you are a cyclist (trail pass required). See the Biking For Beer section of the book. *Tuvalu Coffeehouse & Gallery* (300 S Main St #101, 608-845-6800, tuvalucoffeehouse.com) also offers live music in the evenings. *AJ's Pizzeria* (300 S Main St, 608-497-1303, ajsverona.com) delivers to the taproom.

WISCONSIN BREWING CO.

1079 American Way • Verona, WI 53593 • 608-848-1079
wisconsinbrewingcompany.com
Founded: November 1, 2013   **Brewmaster**: Kirby Nelson
Annual Production: 20,000 bbls
Number of Beers: 12 on tap here; 4 year round plus seasonals/limited releases

Staple Beers:

- » BADGER CLUB (amber lager)
- » YANKEE BUZZARD (American IPA)
- » CHOCOLATE LAB (porter)
- » RED ARROW (APA)
- » WISCONSIN VACATION (pilsner)

Rotating Beers:

- » BETRAY ALE, DRY-HOPPED MAIBOCK
- » BOURBONIFIED DEPTH CHARGE, BA SCOTCH ALE
- » CUPID'S ENVY, BARREL-AGED ESPRESSO PORTER
- » DARK SOMETHING, DARK ALE
- » DEPTH CHARGE, SCOTCH ALE
- » PATRON SAINT, OKTOBERFEST
- » PORTER JOE, COFFEE-INFUSED PORTER
- » RE: FRESH, RADLER
- » SUNSET BRUISE, HAZY IPA
- » S'WHEAT CAROLINE, AMERICAN WHEAT ALE
- » WISKATOR, DOPPELBOCK
- » ZENITH, SAISON

Most Popular Brew: Badger Club

Brewmaster's Fave: Cupid's Envy

Tours? Yes, free tours. Visit the website to view availability and sign up.

Samples? Yes, flights of 5-oz pours: 4 for $6.50 or 12 for $16.50.

Best Time to Go: Taproom open Tue–Thu 3-9pm, Fri 3-10pm, Sat 11am-10pm, Sun 12-7pm. Closed Mondays. Extended hours in summer. Free live music in the Backyard every Friday night, May through September. Check website for hours and calendar of special events.

Where can you buy it? Here on tap and in growlers, 6-packs, 12-packs, cases, and limited edition bombers to go. Distributed throughout Wisconsin.

Got food? Only some snacks for purchase, but it is food-friendly and local menus are on hand for delivery. Friday Night Backyard Concerts feature a brat stand (May-Sep).

Special Offer: A free pint of their beer when you get your book signed.

Directions: From US-151 take exit 79 and go south on County Highway PB. Turn left on American Way and the brewery is on your right here in Verona Technology Park.

The Beer Buzz: Wisconsin Brewing Company isn't just a name; it's the philosophy upon which the brewery was built. The German-engineered brewhouse was built in Hudson, WI. The water and fermentation tanks are made in Elroy, WI. The pumps are made in Middleton, WI. The fiberglass decking comes from Milwaukee. And so on. Anything that couldn't be sourced from Wisconsin is American-made, including the apparel and merchandise in the gift shop. A stainless steel map of Wisconsin in the taproom shows many of the companies that had a hand in building the brewery.

Brewmaster Kirby Nelson, truly one of the founding fathers of craft beer in Wisconsin, brings more than three decades of experience to bear here, and has won perhaps a couple hundred awards throughout his career. Wisconsin Brewing's 24,000 square-foot facility, with its orange silos, sits on five acres of land on the southern edge of Verona. The 80-barrel brewhouse is visible through two walls of windows in the taproom. A gift shop opens off to the side. The expansive Backyard is a patio and lawn space with its own bar and abundant seating with picnic tables, a fire pit, and Adirondack chairs (many cut in the shape of Wisconsin) overlooking an idyllic nine-acre pond. Thirsty hikers are going to like this: the *Ice Age National Scenic Trail* passes right by the brewery. The brewery allows leashed dogs both out here and in the taproom, which is convenient if you've just taken your four-legged friend to the popular nearby dog park at Prairie Moraine (1970 County Highway PB).

Beer drinkers can also participate in the Forward Tapping program, which allows guests to sample pilot brews fresh out of R&D and give feedback on the experimental beer. Beer styles range from classic, old-world recipes to new, innovative creations. Forward Tappings take place the third Thursday of every month, and are always free. Additionally, Wisconsin Brewing releases limited edition beers that are only available at the brewery, such as Cupid's Envy and Wiskator.

Wisconsin Brewing also collaborates with Campus Craft Brewery, which is a part of the College of Agriculture and Life Sciences at the University of Wisconsin-Madison.

This landmark collaboration launched four brands in its first four years: Inaugural Red,

S'Wheat Caroline, Red Arrow, and Re: Fresh.

Free WiFi. Facebook.com/wisconsinbrewingcompany Twitter/Instagram @WisBrewingCo

Stumbling Distance: The Verona Segment of the *Ice Age Trail* starts at the Ice Age Junction site off County Highway PD, heads south through *Badger Prairie County Park*, passes under East Verona Avenue and ends in *Prairie Moraine County (Dog) Park* not far from the brewery. (Find this hike in detail in *60 Hikes Within 60 Miles of Madison*.) Also, the *Military Ridge Trail* isn't far away for bikers (See Biking for Beer in the back of the book). Choco-holics must visit *Candinas Chocolatier* (2435 Old PB, 800-845-1554, candinas.com) where Swiss-trained Markus Candinas makes divine assortments that have been nationally recognized. *Sugar River Pizza Co.* (957 Liberty Dr, 608-497-1800, sugarriverpizza.com) has creative pies and craft beers. *4 Sisters Tapas* (958 Liberty Dr, 608-497-3004, 4sistersverona.com) is another delicious choice. Back toward Madison *Bavaria Sausage* (6317 Nesbitt Rd, Fitchburg, 608-845-6691, bavariansausage.com) offers great German-style products, and not just sausages either.

Hubbleton Brewing Co.

W10445 Hubbleton Rd. • Waterloo, WI 53594 • 920-253-7141
Facebook.com/HubbletonBrewingCo
Opened: July 2017 **Head Brewer/Janitor:** Dan Schey
Annual Production: 500 barrels **Number of Beers:** 5 on tap

Staple Beers:
 » Cattail Pale Ale
 » Crawfish River Porter
 » Crooked Judge IPA

Rotating Beers:
 » Fred the Moose Double IPA
 » Huntsman's Breakfast Chocolate Coffee Stout
 » ...expect new beers monthly

Most Popular Brew: Crawfish River Porter and Huntsman's Breakfast

Brewmaster's Fave: Crawfish River Porter

Tours? Yes, of the brewery and possibly the hop yards in season.

Samples: Yes, free samples.

Best Time to Go: Open Fri 5-8pm, Sat 1-5pm, but considering extended seasonal hours/days so check the website.

Where can you buy it? Here on tap and in six-pack bottles and cases, and growlers to go. Self-distributed in a handful of area bars and shops. Check their Facebook page.

Got food? Bar snacks. Food friendly.

Special Offer: A free pint of beer when you get your book signed.

Directions: From I-94 take Exit 259 and head north on WI-89 fo 1.8 miles, then turn right on County Road G. Stay on G for about 8 miles (even as it joins and departs WI-19) until you reach Hubbleton Road. Turn right, drive 0.6 mile and its on the left (south) side of the road.

The Beer Buzz: A while back, Dan Schey got the idea that he should grow some grapes and maybe start a vineyard. So starting with 200 vines he did that for a couple years. Then he realized, Meh. Not really a wine guy. So he left it at that and they have maybe enough for some family wine. A couple years after that he decided maybe hops was more his thing. After two years he had 3200 plants and 8 different varieties on 3 acres. Some other growers were doing the same, and in 2011 while drinking beer together in Dan's basement, they all decided to found the Wisconsin Hop Exchange. Dan sat as president for a couple years while growing hops and working a full-time job as head of maintenance at HammerHead Trenchless Equipment.

In 2016, when his son Mike was still living at home, Dan came to him and said, "I wanna talk to you about something." Mike grew wary. "Usually that means you forgot to pay a bill or they found something they shouldn't have." As Mike tells it, "He said, 'You know how I grumbled about starting a brewery? Yeah, I'm gonna do it.'" Dan had been homebrewing since 1994 and they had their own hops, so why not? They put together a floor plan to turn the pole shed out back into a brewery, then got a production license and started brewing on a three-barrel system. Initial reactions to the brews were quite favorable, but Dan continued to tinker with recipes until Mike sat him down and showed him on paper that in three months he could be making more than his old job. In March 2018, Dan decided to brew full-time. Mike also quit work and took up the sales and marketing of the brewery.

This is a Mom and Pop sort of operation. The small taproom is more a corner of the brewery, a small collection of bar stools and a short bar by the windows and the door. It's often standing room only and in season folks head outside. Dan and Lori Schey have about 40 acres, 3 of them hop yards. The mowed area around the house is a sort of free-range beer garden in summer when hours and days are likely to expand beyond the current two-day/seven-hours per week. Expect horseshoe pits and perhaps a grill for personal use and some planned walking trails.

The unincorporated Hubbleton is a mile or so from the front door. Beer names are tied to local culture: Crooked Judge is named for Levi Hubble an 1848 circuit court judge whose duty was to collect land tax. Not all of that made it to state coffers. The State impeached him for his sticky fingers. The Crawfish River runs nearby. Fred the Moose is a white elephant gift from Dan's mother. The two-foot statuette made the rounds for 15 years before ending up on the bar counter. Fred had found a home. They named the beer after him so no family member could re-gift him again. The beer labels were designed by Graphic Artist Emma Bohorfoush (emmafran.com).

Free WiFi. Facebook.com/HubbletonBrewingCo

Stumbling Distance: Cajun eatery *Crawfish Junction* (W6376 CR A, Johnson Creek, 920-648-3550, crawfishjunction.com) has Hubbleton on tap and does a legendary fish fry. *Buckeez Saloon* (W7135 State Hwy 19, Hubbleton, 920-253-9753) does Friday fish fry and Saturday prime rib. *Lyon's Irish Pub* (201 E Main St, Watertown, 920-262-6336, lyons-irish-pub.com) has good bar food, sandwiches, pizzas in a quiet place.

The Lone Girl Brewpub

114 E. Main St. • Waunakee, WI • 608-850-7175
thelonegirl.com
Opened: June 2016   **Head Brewer:** John Russell
Annual Production: 1000 barrels   **Number of Beers:** 10-12 on tap, plus guest cider

Staple Beers:

- » Ham the Astrochimp IIPA
- » Off the Rails IPA
- » Speal Easy Lite
- » Sweet Baby Stout (on)

Rotating Beers:

- » Double Trubbel Pumpkin Spice
- » Porter
- » Problem Child Stout (in J. Henry Bourbon barrels)
- » Summer Lovin' Mango Wheat
- » Towhead Belgian Blonde
- » (some barrel aging)

Most Popular Brew: Off the Rails IPA

Brewmaster's Fave: Quadnado Belgian Quad

Tours? Yes, by chance of by appointment.

Samples: Yes, flights of $2 samplers.

Best Time to Go: Open daily 11am-close, but closed for lunch on Monday. Happy hour is 3-5 Tue-Fri.

Where can you buy it? Here on tap and in bombers and growlers to go. Some draft accounts around town.

Got food? Yes, a notably good full restaurant menu that includes a Friday fish fry, curds, and items ranging from jumbo pretzels to marsala ravioli. They work beer into many of the recipes. A full bar with cocktails and beer floats incorporating local Calliope ice cream.

Special Offer: A free magnet with book signature.

Directions: WI-19 and WI-113 enter Waunakee from the west and east, respectively, and become Main St. The brewpub is just to the east of the train tracks on the south side of the road.

The Beer Buzz: With almost 7,000 square feet, this brewpub, co-owned by Kevin and Kerry Abercrombie and Paul and Tammi Kozlowski, sits at the heart of Waunakee. Brews, with a few exceptions, are mostly sessionable, and in the first two years, over 20 styles have hit the taps. Beer names honor their children, Brewer John's daughter is the sweet baby of the stout, but the terrible two's inspired Problem Child. Between the two families they have six boys, but the brewpub is named Avary, the lone daughter in the Abercrombie family. (Double Trubbel comes from her twin brothers.)

A Kansas native, Brewer John had 12 years of homebrewing under his belt when he took this job, but it's not his only work. He holds a PhD and part of his research at the UW focuses on the glands that allow you to swallow, an important matter for Parkinson's sufferers. The brewpub is built on Main Street near the railroad tracks through Waunakee. The tanks are visible from the street. The restaurant/taproom features concrete floors and reclaimed wood, with tables and large booths for seating. Five TVs plus projection screens (with more on the roof) make it nice for sports as well. The rooftop deck has room for 150, and features a full bar and a gas fire pit, and hosts live music in season. It's a family-friendly space with even some toys on the roof patio and events such as an annual Santa brunch.

Free WiFi. Facebook.com/lonegirlbrewing and Twitter @lonegirlbrewing

Stumbling Distance: *Drumlin Ridge Winery* (6000 River Rd, 608-849-9463, drumlinridgewinery.com) does tours and tastings. Watch for summer concerts Live from the Park (facebook.com/LiveFromThePark) at Village Park.

OCTOPI BREWING (UNTITLED ART BREWING)

1131 Uniek Dr • Waunakee, WI 53597 • 608-620-4705
octopibrewing.com
Founded: 2015
Annual Production: 20,000 barrels (3,500 bbls for own brands)
Number of Beers: 14 taps (some guest brews), 2 nitro taps, and a beer engine for a weekly cask beer

Staple Beers:
- » DACHS BREWING ('badger' in German)
- » OCTOPI BREWING
- » UNTITLED ART

Most Popular Brews: NE IPAs, adjunct stouts, fruited sours

Samples: Yes, sips for choosing and flights for sampling.

Best Time to Go: Open Tue-Fri 4-10pm, Sat 2-10pm, Sun 12-7pm. Happy hour Tue-Fri 4-6pm.

Where can you buy it? Here on tap and in Crowlers, cans, bottles, and growlers to go. Statewide distribution in bottles, cans, and draft accounts.

Got food? They have their own food truck with a seasonal menu.

Tours? No.

Special Offer: Buy your first Octopi tap beer, get one free when you get your book signed.

Directions: From WI 19/113 on Waunakee's east side, go south on Hogan Rd. Turn right on Uniek Dr and the brewery is on your left.

The Beer Buzz: Founder Isaac Showaki is originally from Mexico and spent many years working on the business side of things with big breweries in Latin America. Outside work he had a hankering for craft beer, and when he moved to New York, he'd frequently visit his local bodega and pick up 6 or 7 new craft beers to try each time. Not enough. He rounded up investors and moved to Chicago to open the first Latin-American craft brewery in the US: Five Rabbit Cervecería. He hired Randy Mosier (author of *The Brewers Companion*) to create some recipes for

him, and then he had them contract brewed. He quickly found he couldn't get the quality or quantity that he wanted for his brand. In one 18-month period, he needed to work with 8 different contract breweries. He decided if he ever opened another brewery, it'd be a contract brewery and he'd do it right. He left Five Rabbit in 2014, and here we are.

A lot of young breweries lack the resources or capacity to grow, and Octopi aimed to be a one-stop solution for small breweries or startups. Before opening, they had sold out their capacity for their first year. He chose Wisconsin because of the abundance of ingredients in the area, and Waunakee because of all the places he visited, this city asked, "What can we do to bring you here?" They were impressively supportive. Two of their own brands are Dachs Brewing, which delivers Wisconsin Premium Lager, and Untitled Art, brewing a variety of creative beers that come and go.

The 50-barrel Esau & Hueber brewhouse is German-made and fully automated to minimize the risk of human error. A GEA Westfalia centrifuge cuts down on fermentation times. A 30-head filler German bottling line is also onsite kicking out 150 bottles per minute. The 70-person taproom has windows into brewery operations. The bar, tables, and cold storage room are built with reclaimed wood from Chicago—Navy Pier, to be exact. There's a TV and projection screen for special events, a pool table, and board games, plus a beer garden outside for seasonable weather.

Free WiFi. ATM onsite. Facebook.com/OctopiBrew and Twitter/Instagram @ octopibrew

Facebook.com/untitledartbeer

Stumbling Distance: *Doughboy's Pizza* (246 N Century Ave, 608-850-4960) has thin and hand-tossed pies and delivers. *Lucky's Bar and Grille* (1008 Quinn Dr, 608-850-5825, luckysbarandgrille. com) has good bar food, 24 beers on tap, and 33 TVs for the Packers and much more. *The Lone Girl Brewing* is minutes away.

Parched Eagle Brewpub

5440 Willow Rd. Suite 112 • Westport, WI 53597 • 608-204-9192
parchedeagle.com
Founded: 2015   **Head Brewer**: Jim Goronson
Annual Production: 150 barrels   **Number of Beers**: 5–6 on tap; plus a couple guests

Staple Beers:

- » Crane Ale APA
- » Hop-Bearer American IPA
- » Janethan Robust Porter
- » Parched Eagle Golden Ale
- » Verily Belgian Trappist Dubbel

Rotating Beers:

- » Alferd (black rye imperial saison)
- » Brookie's Sour Brown (Flanders brown ale)
- » Decemberfest (Munich dunkel)
- » Dreamland (witbier)
- » Durok (saison)
- » Grainne's Special Bitter (ESB)
- » Harpy (American strong ale)
- » Homie (American barleywine)
- » Maniac (Baltic porter)
- » Oktoberfest
- » Pegboy Pils (German pilsner)
- » Señor Smoke (Scotch ale)
- » Stella (Belgian dark strong ale)
- » Sweetness (imperial sweet stout)
- » Utopian Imperial IPA
- » The Weakling (Belgian tripel)

Most Popular Brew: Hop Bearers

Brewmaster's Fave: Hop Bearer

Tours? Yes, by chance.

Samples: Yes, sample flights of four 5-oz pours for about $6. An extra $1 for five.

Best Time to Go: Open Wed–Thu 3–11pm, Fri 3pm–12am, Sat 2pm–12am, Sun 2pm–8pm. Closed Mon–Tue.

Where can you buy it? Here on tap and in growlers to go. See also Parched Eagle Taproom in Madison (below).

Got food? Yes, a few sandwiches plus Bavarian pretzels and cheese and sausage platters.

Special Offer: $2 off your first pint of Parched Eagle beer when you get your book signed.

Directions: County Road M comes directly here from Middleton. Out of Madison, take WI 113/Northport Dr north, cross the Yahara River, and turn left at the lights on CR M. Watch for a turn lane through the grassy median and turn left on Willow Road. Pass the gas station there and turn right into a parking lot across the front of a strip of shops. The brewery is about in the middle.

The Beer Buzz: Even some people in Madison aren't going to know Westport by name, but it is a community on the north side of Lake Mendota near where the Yahara River enters the lake. Addresses may read Waunakee, but this is indeed Westport, and while the little community may not get proper respect, it does have a proper brewpub.

President and Head Brewer Jim was 29 when his parents gave him a Mr. Beer kit back in 1995. He loved craft beer already and here was an economical method of acquiring it. Encouraged by House of Brew's Page Buchanan, Jim went all grain and was soon hell bent on opening a brewpub. He attended Siebel Institute's World Brewing Academy and is a certified beer judge. Page continued to advise and encourage him until Jim finally partnered up with Tom Christie, another craft beer fan and mead maker, to open this brewpub. The name came up when Jim previously thought to open this in Sauk Prairie, a place famous for eagle watching. The name stuck, out of pure awesomeness.

The taproom features a short bar with some crazy cool metal tap handles (eagle talons clutching a crystal marble), some tall tables, and a second room with more tables. A parking lot is right out front along this line of shops with some outdoor seating on a patio between the sidewalk and the lot. Alternatively, drink this beer in Madison: *Parched Eagle Taproom* (1444 E Washington Ave, 608-204-9192) is open all days but Monday, serving its own and others' beers.

Free WiFi. Mug Club. Facebook/parchedeagle and Twitter @ Parchedeagle

Stumbling Distance: Next door is some good Greek food and a full bar at *Athens Grill* (5420 Willow Rd, Waunakee, 608-220-3340, athensgyros.com). *Mariner's Inn* (5339 Lighthouse Bay Dr, Madison, 608-246-3120, marinersmadison.com) inside the nearby marina to the east has been around since 1966 for some old-fashioned supper club dining.

PORT HURON BREWING CO.

805 Business Park Road • Wisconsin Dells, WI 53965 • 608-253-0340
porthuronbeer.com

Founded: 2011   **Brewmaster:** Tanner Brethorst
Annual Production: 650 bbls   **Number of Beers:** 10 on tap; 7 in distribution

Staple Beers:

- » ALT BIER
- » HEFEWEIZEN
- » HONEY BLONDE
- » PORTER
- » TWELVE BOTTOM IPA

Rotating Beers:

- » CZECH PILSNER
- » KÖLSCH
- » OATMEAL STOUT
- » OKTOBERFEST
- » RADLER
- » SCOTCH ALE
- » SMOKED MAIBOCK

Most Popular Brew: Honey Blonde

Brewmaster's Fave: "The one in my hand! I like 'em all!"

Tours? Yes, scheduled on Fri and Sat. Call or check the website for times.

Samples: Yes, 4–6 beers in a flight for about $4–6

Best Time to Go: Taproom is open Wed-Sun, but call or check website for up-to-date times. Check out the seasonal beer garden!

Where can you buy it? Growlers, six-packs, and by the pint at the taproom. Bottled six-packs and draft accounts can be found in an increasing circle around The Dells, plus Madison, Milwaukee, La Crosse, and SW Wisconsin.

Got food? Free popcorn and pretzels. Also food friendly.

Special Offer: A free pint with your book signature.

Directions: From the center of the Dells take Broadway/Hwy 13 heading east. Where 13 heads north at a junction with Hwys 16 and 23, you continue straight east on Hwy 23 (still Broadway) and watch on your right for where Broadway breaks away from 23. Follow it and the next left is Business Park Road. The brewery is on your left.

The Beer Buzz: This is the first brewery in Columbia County since 1958! It starts with a running club. Tanner's father used to have a running and beer club. First the running, then drink a different Wisconsin beer every time. They eventually lost interest in the running part. Meanwhile, Tanner got a homebrew kit in college, and it compelled him to get a summer job at Tyranena Brewing in Lake Mills. "I was a sponge that summer, soaking up knowledge." He finished an Ag Business Management degree at UW-Madison and six months later he was at the Siebel Institute for the full course which included

some time hitting breweries in Germany and Belgium. A week after completion, he landed a job at *Lake Louie Brewing*. The guy that used to be chased down the highway in the Lake Louie truck by people looking for limited release beers? That was him.

He then spent 3 years at Capital Brewery when his family decided it was time for an intervention. They came to him and suggested he open his own brewery. "It had been a running joke before," he says. Something talked about after a few beers. His father and uncles were dead serious and said if he drew up a solid plan, they would get behind it. Two years later he turned an ink plant in a Wisconsin Dells industrial park into a spacious brewery. Sit in the taproom and you look right into the brewery. Look for the awesome Flux Capacitor (you know? *Back to the Future?*) among the equipment; it's signed by Huey Lewis. The woodwork at the bar was done by his uncle. In fact, the brewery name itself is a reflection of a family ethic. His grandfather's 1917 Port Huron steam tractor still runs and is still in the family. As his grandfather once said, "There are two things you should never rush: a good story and quality built beer." Tanner also brews 10-gallon batches on a pilot system for taproom only. The taproom has one TV for Packers/Badgers/Brewers, music playing in the background, and board games and cribbage. Live music is getting more common, and a beer garden was added in 2016. Phoebe, his daughter, has been going to the brewery since she was 3 days old. When she was 2 and starting to talk, she looked into a bucket in the brewhouse and asked, "What's that?" "Beer bubbles," Tanner told her. For a while after that whenever they headed out to the brewery it was "We're gonna go to beer bubbles." Yes. And so should you.

Free WiFi. Facebook.com/PortHuron

Stumbling Distance: *Showboat Saloon* (showboatsaloon.com, 24 Broadway, 608-253-2628) has food, drinks, live entertainment, and Tanner's beers on tap. In fact, Broadway is the main drag in the Dells, a place to find a lot shops and restaurants and some historical buildings. Almost next door is *The Sand Bar* (130 Washington Ave, 608-253-3073) with fish fry and great tacos. Try *Ravina Bay Bar & Grill* (ravinabay.com, 231 E Durkee St, Lake Delton, 608-253-0433) overlooking Lake Delton if you're looking for a good old Friday fish fry. If you're a paddler, pick up my book *Paddling Wisconsin* and get on the Wisconsin River near here.

WISCONSIN DELLS BREWING CO.

110 Wisconsin Dells Parkway South • Wisconsin Dells, WI 53965
(Moosejaw Pizza & Dells Brewing Co.)
608-254-1122
dellsmoosejaw.com
Founded: 2002   **Brewmaster**: Jamie Baertsch
Annual Production: 1,400 bbls   **Number of Beers**: 25 annually, 10 on tap

Staple Beers:

- » APPLE ALE (year round only in distribution otherwise seasonal)
- » DELLS CLASSIC (Kölsch)
- » HAZEL'S NUT HOUSE ALE
- » HONEY ALE (brewed with pure Wisconsin honey)
- » KILBOURN HOP ALE
- » RELAXIN' RASPBERRY ALE
- » RUSTIC RED ALE
- » SCONNIE ALE
- » SCONNIE LIGHT

Rotating Beers:

- » APPLE ALE
- » BEARD FEST
- » BLONDE BOCK
- » DELLS PILSNER
- » RED IPA
- » STAND ROCK BOCK
- » STRAWBERRY BITCH

Most Popular Brew: Hazel's Nut House Ale and Relaxin' Raspberry

Brewmaster's Fave: Beard Fest, Dells Pilsner, Blonde Bock

Tours? Yes, by appointment or by chance.

Samples: Yes, about $11 for 6, $15 for 10 (5-oz pours)

Best Time to Go: Open daily 11AM–12AM, but restaurant closes 10:30PM Sun–Thu, 11PM Fri–Sat. Watch for the Dells on Tap beer fest featuring 35+ brewers along with live entertainment the 3rd weekend in October.

Where can you buy it? On tap here and in growlers, cans, and bottles to go. Distribution of 6-pack bottles (4-packs for seasonals), mixed 12-packs, 16-oz cans in 4-packs, 12-oz cans in 12-packs, and craft sodas in 12-oz bottles in 4-packs or mixed 12-packs is mostly within a 20-mile radius of the Dells, but some product makes it as far south as Madison and even Beloit.

Got food? Oh yeah, their specialty is in their name! (Look for the giant moose sprawled on the roofs of their delivery cars.) They also have Beer Bread (Honey Ale) and Beer & Cheese soup (Honey Ale). Fantastic Friday Fish Fry. Check the website for printable coupons.

Special Offer: Not participating.

Directions: From I-90/94 take Exit 89 (Hwy 23) and go east and it will be on your right. Or from I-90/94 take Exit 92 (Wisconsin Dells Parkway) and head north and it will be on your left.

The Beer Buzz: This is not your typical tavern, and just walking in the front door ought to make you stop and simply take it in a bit. Designed like a giant backwoods lodge, the three-story, three-bar restaurant seats 500 and is laden with more game mounts than Hemingway could have shaken an elephant rifle at, including giant moose heads and chandeliers fashioned out of antlers. The name comes from Moosejaw, Canada, where,

during Prohibition, Al Capone and his gang of "hooch" runners used tunnels to bring booze into the US. If the decor isn't enough to please your eye, the gleaming 15-barrel copper-clad brewhouse upstairs should be.

Jamie Baertsch was the first female head brewer in Wisconsin and remains one of the few (but growing number of) female head brewers in the state (see also Earth Rider in Superior, Capital Brewing in Middleton, Bobtown Brewhouse in Roberts, Boulder Brew Pub in Verona, Brews on the Rock on Washington Island) and she's been around a good while now. It was her college professor in biotech who suggested she look into brewing beer. She is whipping out the suds and making a killer APA—actually a WPA, Wisconsin pale ale (Kilbourn) made with locally grown hops! This is a pretty large-scale operation for a brewpub, and Jamie keeps the copper tanks polished and purring. Two of her favorite beers were named after her two favorite people (her kids). The brewery started distributing in bottles in January 2014 and added cans in May 2014.

Stumbling Distance: 12 miles south of the Dells toward Baraboo is *The Barn* (WI-123 Trunk, Baraboo, 608-356-2161), one of the best selections of craft beer in the area and a great place to eat. It's inside a repurposed barn. *Wisconsin Dells* is the center of Wisconsin tourism and combines resort town with natural wonder. *Noah's Ark America's Largest Waterpark* (www.noahsarkwaterpark. com, 608-254-6351) and a whole assortment of water park attractions are huge in summer, and many hotels have *indoor* water parks that rival the outdoor brethren. *Original Wisconsin Ducks* (www.wisconsinducktours.com, 608-254-8751) uses reborn WWII amphibious craft to run tours of the river and its awesome landscape. Odd museums, souvenir shops, shows, parks, restaurants, and casinos—the Dells can fill its own guidebook. Grab a beer at *Moosejaw* while you decide where to start stumbling.

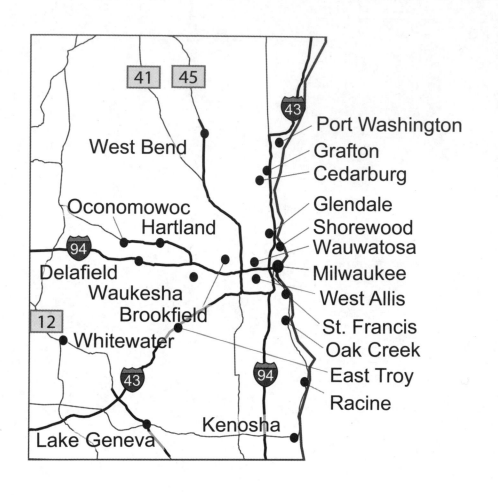

ZONE 2

Brookfield: Biloba Brewing Co.
Cedarburg: The Fermentorium Brewery
    & Tasting Room
Cedarburg: Rebellion Brewing Co.
Delafield: Delafield Brewhaus
Delafield: Water Street Brewery: Lake
    Country
East Troy: East Troy Brewing Co.
Glendale: Bavarian Bierhaus
Glendale: Sprecher Brewing Co.
Grafton: Water Street Brewery: Grafton
Hartland: Melms Brewing Co.
Kenosha: Public Craft Brewery
Kenosha: R'Noggin Brewery
Kenosha: Rustic Road Brewing Co.
Lake Geneva: Geneva Lake Brewing
    Co.
Milwaukee: Black Husky Brewing Co.
Milwaukee: Broken Bat Brewing Co.
Milwaukee: City Lights Brewing Co.
Milwaukee: Company Brewing
Milwaukee: Component Brewing Co.
Milwaukee: D14 Brewery (District 14
    Brewery)
Milwaukee: Dead Bird Brewing Co.
Milwaukee: Eagle Park Brewing Co.
Milwaukee: 1840 Brewing Co.
Milwaukee: Enlightened Brewing Co.
Milwaukee (Greendale): Explorium
    Brew Pub
Milwaukee: Gathering Place Brewing
    Co.
Milwaukee: Good City Brewing Co.
Milwaukee: Good City Brewing
    Taproom (downtown)

Milwaukee: Lakefront Brewery
Milwaukee: Miller Brewing Co.
Milwaukee: Milwaukee Ale House
Milwaukee: Milwaukee Brewing
    /2nd Street Brewery
Milwaukee: Milwaukee Brewing
    Co./9th Street Brewery
Milwaukee: MobCraft Beer
Milwaukee: New Barons Brewing
    Cooperative
Milwaukee: Pabst Milwaukee Brewing Co.
Milwaukee: Rock Bottom Restaurant
    and Brewery
Milwaukee: Tenth Street Brewery
Milwaukee: Third Space Brewing Co.
Milwaukee: Urban Harvest Brewing Co.
Milwaukee: Vennture Brew Co
Milwaukee: Water Street Brewery
Oak Creek: Water Street Brewery
Oconomowoc: Brewfinity Brewing Co.
Port Washington: Inventors Brewing Co.
Racine: Littleport Brewing Co.
Racine: Racine Brewing Co.
St. Francis: St. Francis Brewery and
    Restaurant
Waukesha: Raised Grain Brewing Co.
Wauwatosa: Big Head Brewing Co.
Wauwatosa: Fermentorium Barrel
    House
Wauwatosa: Stock House Brewing Co.
West Allis: Westallion Brewing Co.
West Bend: Riverside Brewery and
    Restaurant
Whitewater: 841 Brewhouse
Whitewater: Second Salem Brewing Co.

BILOBA BREWING CO.

290 N. Brookfield Rd. • Brookfield, WI 53045 • 262-309-5820
bilobabrewing.com
Opened: April 2014   **Brewers**: Gordon Lane and Kristen Lane
Annual Production: 200 barrels   **Number of Beers**: 10 on tap

Possible Beers:

- » BIERE DE MARS
- » BILOBA BLANC
- » BITTER BITCH IPA
- » DARK SIDE
- » DUNKEL
- » HEFEWEIZEN
- » GOLDEN ALE

- » RYE OF THE WORT
- » SAISON ON OAK
- » SCOTTISH ALE
- » SECTION 25
- » SMOKIN' GRAMMA
- » plus some barrel aging

Tours? Yes.

Samples: Yes, flights of all ten beers on a numbered platter.

Best Time to Go: Open Thu 5–9:30PM, Fri 5–10:30PM, Sat 1–6PM.

Where can you buy it? Here on tap in pints and half pints, and in growlers and some 22-oz bombers to go.

Got food? Not really, just water and sodas, and some Bavarian pretzels from Milwaukee Pretzel Co. Occasionally, caterers are here and food trucks on most Friday nights. Otherwise it is food friendly, bring your own.

Special Offer: Not participating.

Directions: Take Brookfield Rd (south 1.2 miles from Capitol Dr or north 2.6 miles from Bluemound Rd) and the brewery is on the east side of the road.

The Beer Buzz: This is a family affair, with Gordon and Jean Lane and their two daughters working together. Kristen and her father do the brewing. Her sister Kathryn Glomski runs the tasting room. Gordon has another pretty important connection to beer: before retiring he was president of Briess Malt in Chilton, provider of specialty grains since forever to much of the brewing industry here in Wisconsin and beyond.

They repurposed dairy equipment for some of the brewing, use an energy-efficient gas heater for the wort, and collected used furniture for the taproom. Spent grain, of course, goes to a local farmer. Their eco-minded approach got them recognition from Wisconsin Sustainable Business Council's Green Masters Program.

This is a community taproom, and likely busy with locals coming to relax and chat. A few board games are on hand and there may be some background music. Photos of mug club members are on the wall. Clipboards hold the day's beer menu.

Free WiFi. Mug Club. Find them on Facebook, Twitter @ BilobaBrewing and Instagram @ bilobabrewing

Stumbling Distance: *Cafe Manna* (3815 N Brookfield Rd, 262-790-2340, cafemanna.com) serves vegetarian fare with local beer. Carnivores might prefer casual atmosphere and upscale food at *Mr. B's—A Bartolotta Steakhouse* (18380 W Capitol Dr, 262-790-7005, mrbssteakhouse.com). It's a wine place, not beer.

THE FERMENTORIUM BREWERY & TASTING ROOM

7481 Hwy 60 • Cedarburg, WI 53012 • 262-421-8593

thefermentorium.com

Opened: March 17, 2016   **Head Brewer:** Kristopher Volkman
Annual Production: 1,00 barrels   **Number of Beers:** 24 on tap (4 guests)

Staple Beers:

- » COVERED BRIDGE (Golden Ale)
- » JUICE PACKETS (Unfiltered IPA)
- » NEVER A FROWN (Brown Ale)
- » SAFE PASSAGE (American Porter)

Rotating Beers:

- » DIVINE SANCTUARY (Belgian Tripel)
- » OKTOBERFEST
- » OPERATION: NIGHTHAWK (Imperial Stout)
- » STONE HEARTH (Dunkelweizen)
- » SWEATER WEATHER (Imperial Milk Stout)
- » UNDERWATER PANTHER (Double IPA)
- » WHISPERING SCYTHE (strong ale with rye)
- » ...plus so many more and some barrel aging

Most Popular Brew: Juice Packets

Brewmaster's Fave: Juice Packets

Tours? No.

Samples: Yes, sample flights of six 4-oz pours.

Best Time to Go: Open Mon-Fri 4-10pm, Fri-Sat 11:30am-10pm, Sun 11:30am-6pm. Happy hour is Mon-Fri until 6pm. Watch for Downdogs and Drafts (yoga, the fee includes a couple beers).

Where can you buy it? Here on tap and in howlers and growlers to go. Statewide on draft or in four-pack 16oz. cans.

Got food? Just bar pizzas and hot dogs, but otherwise food friendly if you bring your own.

Special Offer: Buy your first house beer, get one free when you get your book signed.

Directions: Highway 60 goes right through Cedarburg and this is on the west side of town. From I-43 take Exit 92 and head west on Highway 60 for 1.9 miles and the brewery is on the left (south) side of the road.

The Beer Buzz: Juice Packets made a great first impression from this brewery occupying a former pet supply building at the edge of town. Founder Kristopher Volkman and the Fermentorium team all started as homebrewers. Beers are listed above the bar on a board with some amazing chalk art by staff. Lots of styles and brews come through here, including Traditional Series, Brewer's Reserve Series, Hop Wheel Series, Pilot Series, and Barrel Series. In 2018 they were already expanding production and opened another taproom in Wautwatosa ('Tosa).

The taproom has a collection of tables and some lounge furniture and there's plenty of space at the bar. A projection TV for special games, hamerschlagen and a couple of tabletop arcade games. Lots of local art on the walls for sale. The small pilot system is the founder's homebrew system. Watch for new brew Thursdays.

Free WiFi. Mug Club. Facebook.com/TheFermentorium

Instagram and Twitter @TheFermentorium

Stumbling Distance: *Cedar Crest Ice Cream* (7269 Hwy. 60, 800-877-8341, cedarcresticecream. com) corporate office is next door, but there's a retail store here too. In 2018, the brewery announced plans to open *The Fermentorium Barrel House* and sour-beer barrel-aging facility in Wauwatosa at 6933 W. North Ave.

REBELLION BREWING CO.

N57 W6172 Portland Rd. • Cedarburg, WI 53012
rebellionbrewingusa.com
Founded: 2018   **Brewers:** Dale Georgeff and Rod Otto
Annual Production: 800+ bbls   **Number of Beers:** 15 on tap

Staple Beers:

- » AMBER
- » DINGALING LIGHT LAGER

- » ROD'S SPICY BANANA

Rotating Beers:

- » BOCK
- » HONEY WEISS
- » IPAs
- » OKTOBERFEST

- » PUMPKIN BEER
- » SESSION ALES
- » STOUTS

Most Popular Brew: Dingaling

Brewmaster's Fave: Amber

Tours? Not exactly. All the brewing facilities are visible, but if someone's around, they'll chat about brewing.

Samples? Yes, sample flights available.

Best Time to Go: Closed on Mondays and Tuesdays. Open Tue–Fri 3-10pm, Sat-Sun 10am-10pm. In summer it is nice to sit alongside the river and watch the ducks.

Where can you buy it? Here on tap or in growlers to go, and plans for distribution.

Got food? Yes, some snacks to start. They make their own root beer and "the best hot pickles in the state." Food trucks on weekends. Food friendly and local menus are on hand.

Special Offer: A free beer when you get your book signed.

Directions: From I-43 take Exit 89 (Pioneer Rd). Go west to Washington Ave and take that north to Columbia Rd and go right (east). The first right before the bridge is Portland Rd and the Landmark Building.

Cyclists: The Ozaukee Interurban Trail passes 1 block north of here.

The Beer Buzz: Cedarburg is only twenty minutes north of Milwaukee. Rebellion Brewing is in the basement of the Landmark Building on the corner of Portland and Columbia Roads in the historic downtown. In the mid-1800s, German and Irish immigrants built five dams and mills on Cedar Creek, and this one, built in 1855, was a flour mill. The pub entrance is around back down along the river where you will find some great outdoor seating. Inside you will pass the remnants of the water-powered mill and enter through a large wooden door. This place has the air of an old lagering cellar with its wood ceiling and the brick and stone walls. There are old photos on the wall, flags, drunk history, 3 TVs for mostly sports, and a pre-Prohibition vibe. The 15-barrel brewhouse is there for all to see, cordoned off from the rest of the bar.

In 2004 this opened as Silver Creek Brewing, but in 2018, as the previous owner looked to retire, Dale Georgeff and Rod Otto jumped in to take over. Both from Cedarburg, Rod and Dale brewed together over 20 years in their garages, ultimately building a double garage in Dale's backyard, The Bite Me Bar. While they kept many of the Silver Creek brew recipes, they began adding their own and are aiming to expand production.

Occasional live music. Free WiFi.

Stumbling Distance: As an alternative to the grains, try the grapes at *Cedar Creek Winery* (N70 W6340 Bridge Rd, 800-827-8020, cedarcreekwinery.com). Housed in an 1860s woolen mill, the winery offers a 45-minute tour. *North 48 Bar* (W62N599 Washington Ave, 262-421-8723) is a great up-nort' kind of bar with good beer and cocktails.

DELAFIELD BREWHAUS

3832 Hillside Drive • Delafield, WI 53018 • 262-646-7821
delafieldbrewhaus.com
Founded: May 1999   **Brewmaster**: John Harrison
Annual Production: 900 bbls   **Number of Beers**: 8–10 on tap, 12–15 per year

Staple Beers:

- » DELAFIELD AMBER
- » DOCKSIDE ALE (Kölsch)
- » NAGA-WICKED PALE ALE
- » PEWAUKEE PORTER
- » SOMMERZEIT HEFE WEIZEN

Rotating Beers:

- » 8 MALT STOUT
- » BELGIAN QUAD
- » BELGIAN GRAND CRU
- » BENGAL BAY IPA (all Citra hops)
- » CHOCOLATE MALTED MILK STOUT
- » EINHORN BOCK (gold medal in WBC)
- » FRUHLINGZEIT MAIBOCK (spring; gold medal in WBC)
- » Fruit beers (year-round, different fruit ales: mango, raspberry, blueberry)
- » HOP HARVEST IPA (with Cascade hops grown in the beer garden)
- » IMPERIAL IPA
- » MILLENNIUM BELGIAN-STYLE
- » TRIPEL
- » OATS AND BARLEY OATMEAL STOUT
- » OKTOBERFEST (fall)
- » PILSNER (summer)
- » RADLERS (summer)
- » WHISKEY BARREL-AGED BEERS (BARLEYWINE, RUSSIAN IMPERIAL STOUT and OKAUCHEE SCOTCHIE during holiday season)

Most Popular Brew: Delafield Amber then IPA

Brewmaster's Fave: Oktoberfest, Maibock, and Pilsner! Depends on the season.

Tours? Yes.

Samples? Yes, about $7.50 for six 4-oz samples (or you can sample them all).

Best Time to Go: Happy hour is Monday, Wednesday, Friday 3–6PM. Live music on Saturday nights and a great Sunday breakfast buffet. Oktoberfest is on tap in September.

Where can you buy it? Here on tap and in growlers to go, plus ⅙, ¼ and ½ barrels. Half-liter bottles of staple beers for sale on site and in local liquor stores.

Got food? Yes, a full menu! John makes his own Beer-B-Q sauce and mustard, and you can buy bottles of it to take home. Fish fry on Fridays is Amber-battered, ribs come with the special Beer-B-Q sauce, and lunch and dinner have expansive menus. (If you have a party of 30 or more you can set up a beer dinner!)

Special Offer: A pint of John's beer or root beer.

Directions: If you take Exit 287 for Hwy 83 and go south there will be three traffic light-controlled intersections. The first is re-entry to 94, the second is Wal-Mart, and the third is Hillside Drive. Take it left (east) and follow it to the pub.

The Beer Buzz: Before brewing professionally, John was a homebrewer in the 1980's and worked first in masonry and then as a branch manager for an outfit that sold fire safety equipment. "What's the best way to ruin a hobby?" he asks rhetorically. "If you don't love beer, how can you be in this business?" Originally, he founded Wisconsin Brewing Co. (not the new one in Verona) out of Wauwautosa in 1995, but when they were flooded out in '99—yet left high and dry by the insurance company—he opened this place overlooking I-94. He has total creative freedom and has put it to good use: he's made over 90 different beers since they opened! In 1999 Harrison won an award for Millennium Tripel at the World Beer Championship, for Barley Wine at the GABF, and a huge trophy with Rhinelander beer labels all over it from the Master Brewers Association. Recent WBC awards included a silver for Hop Harvest IPA in 2014, as well as multiple golds for his Einhorn bock, maibock and Strawberry Ale.

The first thing you see as you walk in under the high ceiling is the brewhouse which rises up behind a low wall like some kind of pipe organ, and John can be seen composing his brews out here in the open. He designed the brewing facility first and then built the building around it. "Brewery in your face" he calls it and shuns the idea of tanks behind glass somewhere over behind the kitchen next to the bathroom. A private collector with some investment in the brewhaus displays his outstanding collection of breweriana along the walls. The basement is a banquet room that can hold up to 200 and a mezzanine has even more seating and another bar. The two front corners of the bar are closed off into private booths inside of giant wooden lagering barrels from Milwaukee's Dunck Tank Works from the late 1800s. Another old tank has been fashioned into a wood-fired oven for the pizzas. In addition to the variety of beers, he makes root beer. His IPAs are so popular, he had to purchase another fermenter and two more serving tanks to keep up with demand.

Stumbling Distance: *I.d.* (415 Genesee St. #1, 262-646-1620, iddelafield.com) offers a creative eclectic menu of shared plates with a focus on local ingredients, plus craft cocktails and a well curated beer list with 16 on tap. *Lapham Peak* (laphampeakfriends.org, W329N846 Hwy C), part of the Kettle Moraine State Forest, is a great place for hiking or mountain biking, and it also has lighted cross country ski trails. A 45-foot observation tower gives the highest view in the county of this unique topography left behind by the glaciers of the last Ice Age and the *Ice Age National Scenic Trail* actually passes through the park. (See my books *Best Hikes Near Milwaukee* or *Hiking Wisconsin*)

WATER STREET LAKE COUNTRY BREWERY

3191 Golf Road • Delafield, WI 53018 • 262-646-7878
waterstreetbrewery.com
Founded: 2000   **Brewmaster**: George Bluvas III
Annual Production: 800 bbls   **Number of Beers**: 8–9 on tap

Staple Beers:

- » BAVARIAN WEISS
- » HONEY LAGER LIGHT
- » OLD WORLD OKTOBERFEST
- » PUNCH YOU IN THE EYE PA
- » RASPBERRY WEISS
- » VICTORY AMBER

Rotating Beers:

- » BELGIAN WIT
- » BLACK IPA
- » BLACK LAGER (Schwarzbier)
- » DOPPELBOCK
- » IMPERIAL STOUT
- » IRISH STOUT
- » RAUCHBIER
- » SAISON
- » … and many more!

Most Popular Brew: Honey Lager Light/Old World Oktoberfest

Brewmaster's Fave: Pale Ale

Tours? Yes, but by appointment.

Samples? Yes, $8 gets you seven to nine 4-oz beers.

Best Time to Go: Summer offers outside seating next to a man-made pond in a strip mall parking lot. Lunch and dinner are busy! Best after 7PM if you just want a beer.

Where can you buy it? Growlers and tap accounts at sister restaurants: Louise's, Trinity, Harp, Black Rose, Solo Pizza—all in Milwaukee, and at Water Street Grafton and Oak Creek.

Got food? A full menu. Scotch eggs, beer-marinated Usinger bratwurst are total Wisconsin, the rest ranges from sandwiches to pasta, steak and seafood.

Special Offer: Not participating.

Directions: From I-94 take Exit 287 and go north on Hwy 83 to Golf Road. Take this to the right (east) and follow the gentle S-curve and you will see the brewpub on your left behind a small pond.

The Beer Buzz: Escape from the nearby shopping to a breweriana-laden brewpub. The copper brewhouse gleams behind glass and beer fans can marvel at a vast collection of cans and tap handles as well as signs from the regional breweries of the past. Wood beams rise overhead to a central skylight above the bar. Brewmaster George does quadruple duty here and in the downtown Milwaukee location and others in Grafton and Oak Creek.

The building, a bit like a German hunting lodge or beer hall, was previously a different restaurant that couldn't make a go of it. Water Street knew they would have better luck and so with little alteration to the structure crammed in a brew system. (Not a microbrewery, but a microscopic brewery, says George).

Stumbling Distance: Looking for something frosty? You're in a good neighborhood. *Le Duc Frozen Custard Drive* (240 Summit Ave, Wales, WI, 262-968-2894) does it up the old-fashioned way in a 70's style outlet in Wales two miles away. Or if you want it Italian, get over to Waukesha's *Divino Gelato Café* (www.divinogelatocafe.com, 227 W Main St, Waukesha, 262-446-9490) for authentic ice cream Italiano and specialty drinks and soups. *Pewaukee Lake* is popular for swimmers. *Delafield Brewhaus* is right across the freeway.

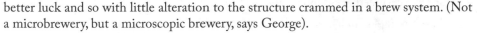

OLD SCHOOL BREWING
AT OLD WORLD WISCONSIN

For years the 600-acre living museum that is Old World Wisconsin has shown us what life was like for the early settlers, with hands-on activities, staff members in period dress, 10 working farmsteads, and opportunities to try historic crafts and skills. Now you can see how brewers used to make beer before the industrial breweries took over. In partnership with the Museum of Beer and Brewing, brewers use techniques and equipment from the 1800s (think boiling over an open wood fire) and heirloom hops and barley grown onsite to brew the beer. Visit the Life on the Farms Picnic Area to try watch the process and have a sample of the results along with German pretzels (plus root beer). Check the website calendar for select Saturdays from June to October. Additionally, each date will offer a different Wisconsin brewer's beers for sale. The brewing process lasts from 10am-3pm.

The Wisconsin Historical Society at Old World Wisconsin

S103 W37890 Hwy 67, Eagle, WI

262-594-6300

oldworldwisconsin.org

EAST TROY BREWING CO.

2905 Main St. • East Troy, WI 53120
etbrew.com
Opened: August 2018   **Head Brewer:** Ryan Hammerel
Annual Production: 500-800 barrels
Number of Beers: 24 taps include 2 wines and guest beers

Beers:

- » CHERRY WHEAT
- » IPAs
- » PALE ALES
- » PILSNER
- » PORTERS
- » STOUTS

Seasonal Beers:

- » BOCKS
- » OKTOBERFEST
- » … plus barrel-aged beers

Tours? Yes, scheduled or by appointment.

Samples: Yes, flights of 4-6 three-oz. pours.

Best Time to Go: Open daily in summer 11am-11pm, Fri-Sat 11am-12am. Winter hours (after Labor Day until April) might be shorter, and closed on Tue. Sunday of Memorial Day Weekend is East Troy Brewfest.

Where can you buy it? Here on tap and in growlers to go, plus some local self-distribution as far as Milwaukee.

Got food? Yes, a full kitchen, pizza oven, soft pretzels, some spent grain gets into a few menu items. Local mead is served as gluten-free beverage option.

Special Offer: A free pint of house beer when you get your book signed.

Directions: From I-43 take Exit 38, then go west on WI-20/North St for 1 mile. Turn left (south) on Division St and continue 0.5 mile. At the traffic circle, take the first exit onto Main St and the brewery is at the corner on the left.

The Beer Buzz: Owners Ann and Ted Zess grew up here in East Troy and in addition to having their own engineering company, they've served on the school board and Chamber of Commerce. When Ann and Ted travel, they go to brewpubs, and when they first attended Milwaukee's Firkin Fest, they decided to start East Troy Brewfest. The fest took place in the town square where they half-joked with people about an old bank building there. 'See that? That's gonna be a brewpub someday.' That someday came when the space became available, and now East Troy has its first brewery ever. Brewer Ryan, a longtime homebrewer, brewed at Delafield Brewhaus before moving here to get things started starting off with a 10-barrel brewhouse and a pilot system. He brews a wide range of beers, some sessionable, other big, and all unfiltered, and primarily using Briess malts from Chilton, WI and Tenacious Badger Hops from Wisconsin Rapids.

The old vault and door are still in place, and antique safety deposit boxes were brought in for brew club as a membership perk. There's an enclosed patio behind large utility doors and an outdoor area with a firepit (dog friendly). An inside lounge area has couches and a fireplace near the brew tanks. Bar area offers high-top tables and the bar resembles the old teller area. Entertainment includes board games, a big screen projection TV, and a stage for live music. The brewery focuses on using locally sourced ingredients, composting, and cutting down on waste. A retail area includes swag and local products from Hometown Sausage Kitchen and Hill Valley Dairy (curds!).

Free WiFi. Brew Club. Facebook.com/ETBrew and Instagram @EastTroyBrewery

Stumbling Distance: East Troy is perhaps most famous for its outdoor concert venue, *Alpine Valley* (2699 Cty Rd D, alpinevalleymusictheatre.org). *East Troy Railroad Museum* (2002 Church St, 262-642-3263, easttroyrr.org) operates a restored train on the old interurban line, often hosting events or dinners onboard, or just for the 10-mile ride between this depot and another near The Elegant Farmer in Mukwonago. *Hometown Sausage Kitchen* (W1184 Co Rd L, 262-642-3264, hometownsausagekitchen.com) has award-winning artisan sausage and smoked meats. *The Hive Taproom* (W2463 County Rd ES, mead) serves its own local-honey mead, plus kombucha and sodas. **Hotel:** *Pickwick Inn B&B* (2966 Union St, 262-642-5529, pickwickinn.com) an author-themed Victorian walking distance from your beer.

BAVARIAN BIERHAUS

700 W. Lexington Blvd. • Glendale, WI 53217 • 414-236-7000
thebavarianbierhaus.com
Opened: April 2016   **Head Brewer:** Nate Bahr
Annual Production: 800 barrels   **Number of Beers:** 10 on tap

Staple Beers:
- » HERR DUNKEL
- » HAUS HEFEWEIZEN
- » PREMIUM HELLES LAGER

Rotating Beers:
- » BELSNICKEL DOPPELBOCK
- » MAIBOCK
- » NIGHT MARAUDER RYE IPL
- » KING OF PRUSSIA BALTIC PORTER
- » OKTOBERFEST
- » OPACITY OATMEAL STOUT
- » ORNERY BREWER IPA
- » SMOKED AMBER LAGER

Most Popular Brew: Hefeweizen or Dunkel

Brewmaster's Fave: Dunkel or Helles

Tours? Yes, free half-hour tours on Fridays.

Samples: Yes, sample flights of four 6-oz pours for about $11.

Best Time to Go: Closed Monday. Open Tue-Thu 4-10pm, Fri-Sat 11am-12am. Happy hour runs 4-6pm

Where can you buy it? Here on tap in liters, half liters and 14oz. tulip glasses, and in growlers to go.

Got food? Yes, Bavarian classics from schnitzel to sauerbraten, pretzels and beer cheese, and Wisconsin fare, beer-battered walleye, pierogies, brats and Friday fish fry.

Special Offer: $1 off your first half-liter haus beer when you get your book signed.

Directions: *Heading north on I-43* from Milwaukee, take Exit 78 for Silver Spring Rd. Turn right (south) on Port Washington Rd, and take the next right on Lexington Blvd. Continue 0.2 mile and the bierhaus is on your right. *From the north on I-43*, also take Exit 78. Turn left (east) on Silver Springs Rd, then the first right on Port Washington, and drive 0.3 mile to turn right on Lexington Blvd.

The Beer Buzz: "There's something to be said for a clean, refined German beer," says Brewer Nate. Formerly Bavarian Inn, which closed in 2006 after a run of almost 70 years, the new manifestation of a real Bavarian beer hall is even better than before: it brews its own truly German-style beers. Bavarian Soccer Club operates the surrounding fields and as the property stood empty for so many years, some soccer parents decided they wanted to save it. Back in the 1930s, German clubs leased land to Port Washington Road, so the influence has long been there. A popular Oktoberfest and Highland Games are held in these fields.

A tall blue grain silo with a beer mug on top lights up at night in the parking lot in front a an Old World looking building. The main hall features long communal tables lined up under a peaked wooden ceiling, and a full bar stands before the brewing system. A long mural of Munich covers one wall and a projection screen shows soccer matches. The King Room is a full bar area with fireplace named for King Gambrinus, a patron saint of beer.

Brewer Nate was homebrewing when he got in at Lakefront Brewery where he spent 2.5 years gaining valuable experience. Lakefront is noted for its lagers, and that's where Nate fell in love with them. With the exception of a couple pale ales, he is brewing German styles on the 15-barrel system.

The brewpub features occasional live music, and you can expect soccer or World Cup on the projection TV. Bavarian Bierhaus has a free app that gets you discounts and possibly free beer when you download it.

Free WiFi. Mug Club. ATM onsite. Facebook.com/bavbierhaus and Twitter @ BavBierhaus

Stumbling Distance: *Kopp's Frozen Custard* (5373 N Port Washington Rd, 414-961-3288) is legend for burgers and custard. *Sprecher Brewing* is three minutes south of here as is a decent **Hotel:** *Holiday Inn Milwaukee Riverfront* (4700 N Port Washington Rd, 414-962-6040, himilwaukee.com)

Sprecher Brewing Co.

701 West Glendale Avenue • Glendale, WI 53209 • 414-964-2739
sprecherbrewery.com
Founded: 1985   **Brewmaster:** Randy Sprecher
Annual Production: 12,000 bbls
Number of Beers: 20 beers/10 sodas on tap; 20+ beers (plus 2 ciders, 1 Perry, 6 hard products)

Staple Beers:

- » Abbey Triple
- » Black Bavarian
- » Hefe Weiss
- » India Pale Ale
- » Special Amber

Chameleon Beers:

- » Firelight
- » Hop On Top
- » Ryediculous
- » Witty
- » Also: Hard Root Beer, Hard Ginger Beer, Hard Apple Pie

Rotating Beers:

- » Dopple Bock
- » Generation Porter (with Dutch cocoa and raspberry)
- » Imperial Stout
- » Irish Stout
- » Mai Bock
- » Oktoberfest
- » Pilsner
- » Touch Of Blue (Blueberry Lambic)
- » Wee Heavy Scotch Ale
- » Winter Lager (Munich Bock)

Series Beers:

- » Whole Cone Series: Citra Bomb, Magnum PA
- » Belgian Progression Series: Enkel, Dubbel, Tripel, Quad

Watch for bourbon-barrel-aged brews and Limited Releases

Most Popular Brew: Special Amber, Black Bavarian

Brewmaster's Fave: Mai Bock

Tours? Yes, but online reservations are highly recommended (414-964-2739) as some tours fill up fast. The tour is kid friendly (they make sodas too) and prices are $8 adults, $5 under 21. Tours start weekdays at 3; Sat and Sun from noon to 4:20. Friday, Saturdays and Sundays have *Reserve Tastings* for $20 which bring out the premier and limited edition brews and pair them with artisanal cheeses. Check the website for tour additions and updates.

Samples? Yes, four beer samples and a commemorative tasting glass (21+); unlimited soda for all ages.

Best Time to Go: Anytime is good. Tours are not required. Stop in for a beer, a glass of wine or cocktails. Food available. Watch for special events.

Where can you buy it? Here on tap and bottled, of course, and in area taverns, stores, and restaurants. Distribution is heaviest regionally. The beer sells as far east as Massachusetts, as far west as California and south to Florida. Much of the Midwest especially around Wisconsin has it too. Throughout the summer, look for the Sprecher tap firetrucks in Milwaukee County Parks, aka the Traveling Beer Gardens. Sprecher can also be found at its Walkers Point taproom at 706 S. 5th St.

Got food? Yes, pizza, large soft pretzels, sausage, cheese curds & more.

Special Offer: A Sprecher trinket of some sort.

Directions: Just off of I-43 heading north from Milwaukee, one street south of the 77A exit.

The Beer Buzz: After returning from military service in Germany, Randy Sprecher could not find (or afford) the kind of flavorful beer he enjoyed in Augsburg. Frustrated, he decided to build his own brewery and worked toward that goal. After completing a special studies program in fermentation science at UC-Davis, Sprecher became a brewing supervisor at Pabst Brewing Company in Milwaukee in the early 1980s. When Pabst downsized, he established Sprecher brewery—the first craft brewery in Milwaukee since Prohibition—in 1985, with $40,000 in capital, a gas-fired brew kettle and repurposed used equipment. Randy Sprecher first brewed Black Bavarian in 1969, and as a signature beer, it has earned accolades from beer critics in *Men's Journal*, *Beer Advocate Magazine* and the *Washington Times*. Most recently Black Bavarian won the 2014 World Beer Cup Gold Medal (Schwarzbier), and I must say it's my favorite Sprecher brew. Among other notable awards, Sprecher Brewery won the 2004 GABF Small Brewery of the Year and Small Brewery Brewmaster of the Year. In the last few years, Sprecher introduced some low-alcohol "hard" products, starting with a hard version of their famous root beer, followed by Hard Ginger Beer and Hard Apple Pie.

As a company Sprecher believes it is important to have a positive effect on the local economy and has been dedicated to using locally produced ingredients as much as possible—cherries from Door County, cranberries from the area, ginseng from around Wausau, honey from Germantown.

The tour reveals some Bavarian murals in the bottling room and the tasting room is designed to look like a bier garten. Up to 20 beers and 9 sodas are on tap to sample. Stop in the gift shop on your way out. Sprecher is active on social media—follow them and you'll know about upcoming events and beer releases. Don't forget about their whole other line up with **Chameleon** beers (which are also on tap in the tasting room).

Stumbling Distance: Just a block away is the best butter burger you will ever have at *Solly's* (414-332-8808, 4629 N Port Washington Rd), a family-run joint since 1936. Homemade pie and a fish fry. (Say, that rhymes.) Celebs know about it too, and there is a plate for regular customer and long-time voice of Milwaukee Brewers baseball, Bob Uecker. Sprecher sodas are on tap. Less than 10 minutes east is *Draft and Vessel* (4417 N Oakland Ave, 414-533-5599, draftandvessel.com), offering 16 rotating taps for sampling, drinking, or growler filling. Various snacks and large bottles also for sale.

CHAMELEON BREWING

If you're searching for this new Wisconsin brewery, the trail will lead you right to the front doors of Sprecher. Brewed by the same folks who do your Black Bavarian, Chameleon is sort of set apart from the other Sprecher products, intended to appeal to another market, a younger one and drinkers who prefer lighter session beers. These are less traditionally European than the Sprecher line and aiming to stand out as simply Wisconsin craft ales. Chameleon beers are created and brewed by Sprecher's brewmaster, and they're high-quality, winning awards at Los Angeles International Commercial Beer Competition—Gold for Hop on Top, Bronze for Ryediculous IPA—and a Gold for Witty from the Beverage Tasting Institute. (chameleonbrewing.com)

SPRECHER AND BEER GARDENS

Each summer the Milwaukee County Park System operates Sprecher's two Traveling Beer Gardens™. Throughout the summer the Traveling Beer Gardens™ stop in different parks for 12 days where they serve Sprecher beers, sodas and hard products from renovated fire trucks. Light snacks and pizzas are available from a concessions trailer; Sprecher's Restaurant & Pub serves Usinger's brats as well. Opening day at each stop, beer and soda are free while they last. Schedules for times and locations are at sprecherbrewery.com or the park system's website (county. milwaukee.gov/Parks/BeerGardens).

Photograph Courtesy Of Anne Sprecher

WATER STREET GRAFTON BREWERY

2615 Washington Street • Grafton, WI 53024 • 262-375-1402
waterstreetbrewery.com
Founded: 2010　**Brewmaster:** George Bluvas III
Annual Production: 800 bbls　**Number of Beers:** 8–9 on tap

Staple Beers:

- » BAVARIAN WEISS
- » HONEY LAGER LIGHT
- » OLD WORLD OKTOBERFEST
- » PUNCH YOU IN THE EYE PA
- » RASPBERRY WEISS
- » VICTORY AMBER

Rotating Beers:

- » BELGIAN WIT
- » BLACK IPA
- » BLACK LAGER (Schwarzbier)
- » DOPPELBOCK
- » IMPERIAL STOUT
- » IRISH STOUT
- » RAUCHBIER
- » SAISON
- » … and many more!

Most Popular Brew: Honey Lager Light/Oktoberfest

Brewmaster's Fave: Pale Ale

Tours? Yes, but by appointment.

Samples? Yes, $8 gets you seven to nine 4-oz beers.

Best Time to Go: Open daily at 11AM and popular for weekend brunches 10AM to 3PM.

Where can you buy it? Growlers on site and tap accounts at sister restaurants: Louise's, Trinity, Harp, Black Rose, Solo Pizza—all in Milwaukee, and the original Milwaukee location, and Water Street in Delafield and Oak Creek.

Got food? A full menu. Scotch eggs, beer-marinated Usinger bratwurst are total Wisconsin, the rest ranges from sandwiches to pasta, steak and seafood.

Special Offer: Not participating.

Directions: From the intersection of I-43 and Hwy 60 (Washington St), go east on Hwy 60 just a matter of feet and take the first street south which is still Washington St. The brewery will be on your right.

The Beer Buzz: Water Street, one of the oldest brewpubs in Milwaukee expanded first to Delafield and now north to Grafton with this third location (and a fourth in Oak Creek). The beers remain the same as Brewmaster George does quadruple duty here and in the Delafield, Oak Creek and downtown Milwaukee locations.

The restaurant, like the others, has breweriana on the walls. The main dining area is lined with booths and a high wood ceiling rises up past the surrounding mezzanine and its copper fermentation tanks. The large u-shaped bar sticks out from an impressive wood back bar. Like in Delafield this is a small brew system tucked inside. There is additional seating in another room. Outside you'll see wood siding that looks quite old school and the rising grain tank on the roof.

Stumbling Distance: *Milwaukee Ale-House* (ale-house.com, 1208 13th Ave, 262-375-2337) also has an outlet here in Grafton, and although they are not actually brewing there, you can get all the same Milwaukee Brewing Co. beers. If you are looking for some local foods and other products to take home, check out *Slow Pokes Local Food* (slowpokeslocalfood.com, 1229 12th Ave, 262-375-5522) for meats, cheeses, fermented foods, gluten-free items, and so much more.

MELMS BREWING CO.

418 Merton Ave. • Hartland, WI 53029 • 262-361-4946
melmsbrewery.com
Opened: March 17, 2018   **Head Brewer:** Brandon Van Epps
Annual Production: 180 barrels   **Number of Beers:** 7-12 on tap

Staple Beers:
- » HOOTENANNY FARMHOUSE ALE
- » LAKE COUNTRY IPA
- » PALE ALE
- » REFLECTION IMPERIAL PORTER
- » RHAPSODY BOHEMIAN PILSNER
- » WOODSHED IMPERIAL AMBER

Rotating Beers:
- » BLARNEY STONE STOUT (St. Patrick's Day release)
- » MALTY IPA FOR WINTER
- » OATMEAL STOUT
- » OKTOBERFEST
- » WEISS

Most Popular Brew: Woodshed

Brewmaster's Fave: Depends on the day

Tours? Not really, but always willing to chat about brewing.

Samples: Yes, sample flights of five 4-oz pours for about $10.

Best Time to Go: Open Thu-Fri 6-10pm, Sat 4-11pm, Sun 1-6pm. But watch for expanding hours!

Where can you buy it? Here on tap and in growlers to go. Will fill yours! Packaging in the works.

Got food? You can order *Falbo's* pizza from next door (with their app) and they'll deliver to the taproom. Food friendly, bring your own.

Special Offer: $1 off your first house beer when you get your book signed.

Directions: From WI-16 take Exit 183 and turn north on Merton Ave. It's in the strip mall on the right. If you are coming from the west, get off at Exit 182, turn left (north) on North Ave and a quick right on Hartbrook Dr. Continue 0.6 mile and turn left on Merton and it's on the right.

The Beer Buzz: In this great renaissance of local beer, sometimes the original breweries too are reborn. In 1854, Franz Neukirch and his son-in-law Charles T. Melms founded Menomonee Brewery in Walker's Point in Milwaukee. It would eventually be renamed

C.T. Melms Brewery. In six years it would become Milwaukee's largest brewery. But Melms died in 1869 and Phillip Best & Co. bought the brewery (as Best would go on to become the largest brewery in the country, and eventually become Pabst). Almost a century and a half later, Melms' great-great-great-great-nephew Bob Stack decided to bring back the family business.

Melms collaborates with Brewfinity in Oconomowoc in an alternating proprietorship on the larger batch beers and brews smaller experimental and one-off beers on a pilot system onsite. The taproom has board games, giant Jenga, bags, and is a family friendly environment. Big screen TVs for the games.

Free WiFi. Facebook.com/MelmsBrewery and Twitter @MelmsBrewery

Stumbling Distance: *Pink Mocha Café* is in the same building open until 4pm, but good for brunch. *Palmer's Steakhouse* (122 E Capitol Dr, 262-369-3939, palmerssteakhouse.com) for your supper clubbin' needs. Less than 20 minutes north is *Holy Hill* (1525 Carmel Rd, Hubertus, holyhill.com) a basilica and national shrine to Mary, with a steeple you can climb for a view all the way to Milwaukee. Excellent in fall. Crossing the property there is a segment of the *Ice Age National Scenic Trail* (iceagetrail.org) which also passes the brewery 0.5 mile to the west. (see my book *Best Hikes Near Milwaukee*)

Public Craft Brewing Co.

716 58th Street • Kenosha, WI 53140 • 262-652-2739
publiccraftbrewing.com
Founded: August 2012   **Brewmaster:** Matt Geary
Annual Production: 500 bbls   **Number of Beers:** 8–9 on tap; 18+ beers annually

Staple Beers:
- » BITS & PIECES (Mosiac IPA)
- » BONE DRY (Irish Stout Nitro)
- » GETAWAY WIT (Belgian witbier)
- » K-TOWN BROWN ALE

Rotating Beers:
- » BRAIN BASTER ENGLISH BITTER
- » HANDLE BAR BLONDE
- » HEADLESS SCOTTSMAN (pumpkin Scotch ale)
- » HOT CHOCOLATE (chili chocolate stout)
- » GINGERBREAD MONK (Belgian dubbel w/ginger)
- » NO FRONT PORCHES (smoked imperial red)
- » SUMMER SESSION IPA
- » SWEET COLLEEN'S IRISH RED
- » THE TOBER (festival ale)
- » UP ALL NIGHT (coffee milk stout)
- » WEISS CITY (Berliner weiss)
- » Various special beers, one-offs such as LUCKY SPILE MAPLE BOCK
- » A firkin every Friday

Most Popular Brew: Bits & Pieces

Brewmaster's Fave: Bone Dry Irish Stout

Tours? Informal and by chance.

Samples: Yes, usually flights of 8 plus root beer for about $15 (fewer beers possible).

Best Time to Go: Open Tue-Thu 3:30–9pm, Fri 3:30pm-12am, Sat 12pm-12am, Sun 12-6pm. Closed Monday.

Where can you buy it? Here on tap and in growlers, bombers, and 16-oz cans to go. On tap and in stores throughout Kenosha, Racine, Walworth, and Milwaukee Counties.

Got food? Pretzels and cheese, popcorn. Food friendly. Menus onsite, possible food trucks outside, check Facebook.

Special Offer: A free pint of Matt's beer when you get your book signed.

Directions: From I-94 take Exit 342 and head east on 52nd St/Hwy 158 until Hwy 32/Sheridan Rd. Go right (south) six blocks and take a left on 58th St. The brewery is on the left in the next block.

The Beer Buzz: Built in the 1910s, this bowstring truss-roofed brick building was an auto shop (they found the old pits when digging the drains for the brewery) and spent some time as a grocery store before it was divided in half intended to be two smaller businesses. Brewer Matt didn't aim for this to be a bar. This is really a brewery. While there is a tap room, it's really a production facility. No TVs, no food. Basically, it's a place to come in, sample, and chat a bit.

Matt Geary has been homebrewing since college. When he felt general discontent with his career, that hobby started looking tempting. Everyone says "We should open a bar!" So Matt went to Siebel in Chicago for a beer course. Then he did a feasibility study and decided it would work. "'Holy cow!' I thought, 'I'm really doing this.'" Matt plans to brew British styles tending toward the mild beers which he feels are a little underrepresented.

Matt likes the social aspect of beer, and finds it encourages good discourse. The idea behind Public was that it was for everyone. Get people a place to come together and talk and learn from each other and let the beer be at the hub of it, the common thread. The brewery also has what Matt calls The Public Library, a collection of resources on brewing that homebrewers are free to stop in and peruse. The brewery takes part in The Big Read (neabigread.org), a National Endowment for the Arts initiative each year by brewing a special beer. They did Old Poe Old Ale, a cask-conditioned ale (like cask of amontillado, get it?) in 2013, No Front Porches Smoked Imperial Red Ale for Farenheit 451 in 2014, and were working on something for To Kill a Mockingbird.

There are no TVs here; just come and hang out, have conversations. Handle Bar Blonde features a tap handle made from a bike handle attached to a bike bell that rings with the pour.

Free WiFi. Facebook.com/deservingpublic and Twitter/Instagram @ PublicBrewing

Stumbling Distance: If you are looking for

a Kenosha institution, don't miss *Frank's Diner* (508 58th St, 262-657-1017, franksdinerkenosha. com) open for classic food from the wee hours to the wee hours. *Ashling on the Lough* (125 56th St, 262-653-0500, ashlingonthelough.com) is an Irish pub/restaurant with a good UK beer selection and some of Public's brews as well. The two most important attractions out on the interstate are *The Brat Stop* (262-857-2011, bratstop.com) and *Mars Cheese Castle* (262-859-2244, marscheese.com), your best source for Wisconsin cheeses and a large selection of beer, among other things.

R' Noggin Brewing Co.

6521 120th Ave. • Kenosha, WI 53142 • 262-960-1298
rnogginbrewing.com
Opened: September, 2016 **Head Brewer:** Jeff and Kevin Bridleman
Annual Production: 325 barrels **Number of Beers:** 5 on tap

Beers:

» Carpet Creature Cream Ale (Always On)
» Clown Casket Red Double IPA
» Demonoggin NE IPA
» Hare Hollow Double IPA
» You're Killing Me S'mores Milk Stout
» IPAs And Sours In Summer, One Sour On At All Times,
» New England IPA, Reds, Stout

And Porter, Some Barrel Aging,
» Russian Imperial Stout, Mango Habanero Blonde Ale In Tequila Barrels
» Dreamsicle Ipa (Orange Cream), Space Monkey Sucker Punch Sour New England IPA
» … rotating every two weeks, 52 different beers in first 18 months

Most Popular Brew: Carpet Creature Cream Ale or You're Killing Me S'mores

Brewmaster's Fave: Hare Hollow DIPA (Jeff), Citrus Asylum DIPA (Kevin)

Tours? Yes, but everything is out in the open.

Samples: Yes, sample flights of three, four, or five 4-oz pours for about $6/$8/$10.

Best Time to Go: Open Wed 5:30-9pm, Thu 3:30-9pm, Fri 3:30-10pm, Sat 12-9pm, Sun 12-6pm. Closed Mon & Tue.

Where can you buy it? Here on tap and in growlers to go, and a tap account next door at Rivals Sports Bar.

Got food? Milwaukee Pretzels and Wells Bros. Pizzas. Occasional food trucks and always food friendly, bring it or order delivery.

Special Offer: $1 off your first pint of beer when you get your book signed.

Directions: From I-94/41 take Exit 342 and turn east on WI-158. Take the very next right on Frontage Rd/120th Ave. Drive 0.9 mile south and the brewery is on the left.

The Beer Buzz: Three brothers. Brother Chris got a homebrew kit in 2007, but brothers Jeff and Kevin, who went along with him to Northern Brewer to pick out a beer style ended up coming home with kits themselves and ended up getting serious. Batch two was on to real grain. Then monthly batches, then graduation parties, and then a wedding. Those who drank their beers were enablers: "you should open your own place!"

Three years later, Jeff, an architect by day, contacted some real estate brokers he knew. The winning location was on the Frontage Road behind some trees at the end of a gravel driveway. Jeff lived nearby and didn't even know it was here. Of the 7 acres, 2.5 are buildable, while the rest is soggy lowlands. Previously, the owner of a trucking company used this building as a repair shop, thus the mammoth two-story garage doors. For 10 years it stood empty until Jeff and Kevin decided to fill it with beer. "We went from our garage to a bigger garage" says Jeff. The name R'Noggin came from their brewing philosophy: Whatever comes out of our heads is what we're brewing. The logo is a skull with a bow tie and a top hat, with two cards in the hat band: the 2 and the 7 of hops. Two guys brewing seven days a week. It's also the worst starting hand in poker.

The brew system is behind the bar (no seating at the bar). The taproom has picnic tables with higher than average tops so it's a bit like sitting at a bar. A creepy clown in the mezzanine, a Halloween decoration from Jeff's house, overlooks the taproom where you'll also find the clown casket. When weather gets better in May, you may find parking lot parties, bands and food trucks. They host a kick-off party for Kenosha Craft Beer Week first weekend of May.

Entertainment includes board games, cribbage, cornhole, a couple TVs, and an arcade game console with 100 classic games. Euchre and cribbage leagues run at various times, and outside they play Skulls and Femurs (wood blocks) or *Kubb*, an alleged Viking game.

Growler Club. Facebook.com/RNogginBrewing and Twitter @rnoggin_brew Instagram @rnogginbrewing

Trivia note: a 4-oz pour in the UK is a *noggin*.

Stumbling Distance: *Uncle Mike's* (6611 120th Ave, 262-857-2392, mikelikesbeer.com) has 99 different beers on draft or in bottles. *Rivals Sports Pub & Grille* (6325 120th Ave, 262-909-1086, rivalskenosha.com) is right next door and serves R'Noggin beer. *Mars Cheese Castle* (2800 W Frontage Rd, 855-352-6277, marscheese.com) is just north on I-94, a sort of Wisconsin Embassy of sorts, and definitely unmissable.

RUSTIC ROAD BREWING CO.

5706 Sixth Ave. • Kenosha, WI 53140 • 262-320-7623
rusticbrewing.com
Founded: June 22, 2012   **Brewmaster:** Greg York
Annual Production: 300 bbls   **Number of Beers:** 14 on tap

Staple Beers:

- » HAZELNUT HARVEST AMERICAN   AMBER ALE
- » SINGLE TRACK IPA

Rotating Beers:

- » ACCOMMODATION AMBER
- » BELGIAN TRIPEL
- » CABIN UP NORTH DOUBLE CHOCOLATE MILK STOUT
- » CERVEZA DE MAYO
- » OKTOBIER
- » QUEEN BEE BELGIAN STRONG ALE

- » RUSTIC SAISON
- » SOUTHPORT WHEAT BAVARIAN STYLE
- » SPRINGSBACK! MAIBOCK
- » …a new beer each month plus a White Buffalo beer series, quarterly seasonals and occasional lagers.

Most Popular Brew: Hazelnut Harvest Ale

Brewmaster's Fave: Belgian Tripel and Queen Bee

Tours? Yes, but you can see everything from the door. It's a nickel tour. (Actually it's free, so you've saved a nickel. Bonus!) Watch for brewing classes; come in as an individual or a group and participate in the brewing of a batch from start to finish.

Samples: Yes, sample flights of available.

Best Time to Go: Open Wed-Thu 4-10pm, Fri 4pm-1am, Sat 11am-1am, Sun noon-6pm. Happy Hour Mon-Fri. Live music on most Saturday nights, America's Pub Quiz on Fridays.

Where can you buy it? Here on tap or in growlers to go, plus draft accounts in Kenosha, Racine, and Walworth Counties. Packaged cans of Hazelnut Harvest and Single Track IPA in local stores as well as Wisconsin Dells and the Appleton/Oshkosh markets.

Got food? Pizzas and pretzels only but with a full commercial kitchen planned to open in 2018.

Special Offer: A free bumper sticker when you get your book signed.

The Beer Buzz: The idea started like many: one too many homebrews one night. Greg said, "One day when I retire, I will open a brewery." At that moment of beer talking, the idea was a big thing. It'll have a movie theatre, pool tables, a bowling alley… But unlike most of our similarly big ideas, Greg's became reality. In 2009, he had heard "one too many stories of a 35-year old crossing a finish line and dying," and he began contemplating how life doesn't always wait around for you. While he had to scale down the Big Idea—sorry, no bowling alley, folks—it became the Serious Idea.

In 1999 during his last year of college, Greg went in for halfsies on a brew kit with of buddy of his and started homebrewing (dormbrewing?). The first batch was great. In the second, the thermometer shattered in the brew kettle and they had to dump it. At the end of the year, Greg bought out the other half of the kit. Then he began to read everything he could and started going to conferences. The brew passion evolved and continued to grow. In 2010 he took Best In Category at the Wisconsin State Fair with a Summer Saison.

When he was ready, he put together a scaled-down vision of something manageable, something small and more artisanal. "There was once a brewery on every block, providing for the locals, and they'd come down with their bucket each day." The brewery is a repurposed office building that had been empty. He worked with the landlord to take an eyesore and make it a fabulous little place in the heart of the south downtown, next to the performing arts center. It has a coffee house sort of vibe. The name Rustic Road comes from the legislated preservation program begun in 1973 to save Wisconsin's scenic country roads.

In the summer of 2017, Greg added a business partner and made the leap to purchase a building in downtown Kenosha to renovate instead of continuing to rent in the small location. Together they have expanded distribution outside of the taproom in addition to adding a full service restaurant and adding to the capacity of the brewery. No bowling alley (yet) though.

It's a cool space with lots of room to grow in the future including some outdoor seating. Beers change often and the brew crew does a few special brews such as a donut beer for Mike's Chicken & Donuts (a cream ale with vanilla) and a collaboration with Public Brewing on a

brew for Kenosha's Craft Beer Week in May. Rustic Road was selected to brew a special beer for The Northwoods Baseball League called Five Tool Ale.

Rustic Road's Maibock was originally named Helles Yeah. You may recognize that as Leinenkugel's trademarked name for their Munich Helles Lager. In these days of increasing legal bickering over trademarks, it is interesting to note that Greg produced his Helles Yeah first. When Leinenkugel's came up with the name and saw it had already been used, Dick Leinenkugel himself came down to ask Greg's permission. Class act.

Free WiFi. Mug club. Facebook.com/rusticroadbrewery Twitter @RusticBrewing Instagram @rusticroadbrewing

Trivia note: Kenosha's first brewery, Muntzenberger Brewing, opened in 1847, a year before Wisconsin's statehood.

Stumbling Distance: *Captain Mike's Beer and Burger Bar* (mikelikesbeer.com, 5118 6th Ave, 262-658-2278) shouldn't be missed, a crazy-big beer list. *Wine Knot Bar & Bistro* (wine-knot.com, 5611 6th Ave, 262-653-9580) is a great restaurant across the street. And do check out the Kenosha Harbor Park and the Market—great for walking around. Sister establishment *Mike's Donuts & Chicken* (707 56th St, A., 262-764-9520)—or is it Chicken & Donuts?—is not to be missed. You can carry out to the breweries.

GENEVA LAKE BREWING CO.

750 Veterans Parkway, Suite 107 • Lake Geneva, WI 53147 • 262-248-2539
(Watch Facebook for possible new taproom address in the future)
genevalakebrewingcompany.com
Founded: February 1, 2012   **Head Brewer: Pat** McIntosh
Annual Production: 1,000 bbls   **Number of Beers:** 12 on tap; 8 per year

Staple Beers:

» BLACK POINT OATMEAL STOUT (22-oz bombers)
» BOATHOUSE BLONDE
» CEDAR POINT AMBER ALE

» IMPLOSION DOUBLE IPA
» NO WAKE IPA
» WEEKENDER WHEAT (22-oz bombers)

Rotating Beers:

» IMPERIAL CHERRY STOUT (December)
» OKTOBERFEST (September)
» WHITE RIVER PALE ALE (summer)

Most Popular Brew: No Wake IPA

Brewer's Fave: Implosion Double IPA

Tours? By appointment or by chance, and a shuttle from the new taproom to the brewery is planned.

Samples: Yes, three and six 5-oz pours.

Best Time to Go: The taproom is open Mon 11AM–3PM, Wed–Thu 3–7PM, Fri–Sat 11AM–8PM, Sun 11AM–3PM. Closed Tuesdays. Check the site for expanded hours.

Where can you buy it? Here on tap and to go in Crowlers and growlers, cans and bombers. Distributed in the local area. Cedar Point, Boathouse Blonde, and No Wake are in 12-oz cans, while Oatmeal Stout, Weekender Wheat, Implosion, and Imperial Cherry Stout sell in 22-oz bombers.

Got food? No. Food friendly and menus onsite for delivery.

Special Offer: A pint glass when you get your book signed.

Directions: From Hwy 120 outside Lake Geneva, take Exit 330A and head west toward town (still Hwy 120 South) and follow it again when it turns left on Edwards Blvd. Just over a half mile turn left onto E Townline Rd and left again onto the next street, Veteran's Parkway. It's in the two U-shaped buildings on your left.

The Beer Buzz: Pat McIntosh spent 28 years working the corporate end of the manufacturing industry, and when he retired early he was looking for a big change. His son Jonathan gave him a very good idea. You see, Lake Geneva is a tourist mecca (thus the Weekender Wheat name) and draws good traffic from Chicago. As Jonathan noted, most touristy areas have at least one craft brewery or brewpub, but Lake Geneva had none.

Pat and Jonathan had started homebrewing back in 2005 or so. It's a big leap from your basement to a production brewery, but they were up to the challenge. They both took some coursework, and Jonathan enrolled in the Siebel Institute in Chicago. With guidance from brewing consultant Tim Lenahan of Brew to Win, they got their first two recipes perfected, and then developed two more as they opened their facility in an industrial condo in town. The taproom soon followed. Pat took over the brewing by himself and recently pulled back on wide distribution to focus more on serving it over the bar. In summer 2018 he will open a new taproom in downtown Lake Geneva so visits to the actual brewery will only be during scheduled tours.

Geneva Lake is actually the second largest lake in Wisconsin, with 21 miles of shoreline and a widest point of 2.6 miles.

Facebook.com/GLBrewCo and Twitter @ GenevaLakeBrew

Stumbling Distance: The lake is the main attraction, of course. A hiking trail follows the shoreline for 20+ miles (see my book *Best Hikes Near Milwaukee*). Pick up delicious local sausages/meats from *Lake Geneva Country Meats* (5907 WI-50, 262-248-3339, lakegenevacountrymeats.com). *Champs Sports Bar & Grill* (747 West Main St, 262-248-6008) is the biggest beer seller in town (Geneva Lake is on tap) and a perfect place to gather for the big games. *University of Chicago's Yerkes Observatory* (astro.uchicago.edu/yerkes, 373 W Geneva St, Williams Bay, 262-245-5555) is open every Saturday for free tours. *Chuck's Lakeshore Inn* (352 Lake St, Fontana, 262-275-3222) at the other end of the lake sits right on the water for some casual bar fare and good drinks.

MILWAUKEE

Wisconsin's largest city was once the nation's (and world's) largest manufacturing zone. It is the birthplace of Harley Davidson, the home of Happy Days, Laverne & Shirley, and That 70s Show, and the site of Summerfest, the world's largest outdoor music festival. An influx of German immigrants in the nineteenth century brought with them the one thing Milwaukee is most associated with: beer.

This is the original Brew City—Beer Town, U.S.A. By the late 1860s, Germans were associated with the 48 or so breweries already up and running. The very first was Milwaukee Brewery—known locally as Owens' Brewery—which was built by three Welshmen in 1840 and brewed ales not lagers.

Many brewing giants emerged from the competition. What began as Empire Brewery in 1844 and then Best & Company became Pabst Brewing Co. in 1889, going on to win the blue ribbon associated with its flagship beer. Valentine Blatz opened his brewery in 1851. Originally founded as a tavern brewery in 1849, the brewery of the beer that "made Milwaukee famous" would become Joseph Schlitz Brewery in 1858, two years after its former bookkeeper bought the works from the founder's widow and then married her. At one time Schlitz was the largest brewery in the world. Frederick Miller bought the Planck Road Brewery (founded by Phillip Best's brother Charles) in 1855, and the massive operation that is there today still brews.

While Miller Brewing (MillerCoors) still produces millions of barrels each year, Pabst closed the brewery in 1996 and contract-brewed Schlitz, Blatz, and other classic brands. That changed in 2017 when they opened a small brewery again near their old site. Thanks to the birth of craft breweries in the 1980s, Milwaukee's brewing tradition is alive and well—and growing every year. In addition to the many breweries beyond this page, you will also find beer-related attractions that you should consider on any *pilsgrimage* to the Great Brew City. Museums, restaurants, revived or repurposed old buildings, and more. Have a look; Milwaukee is going to take some time if you really want to explore it well. A fantastic explosion of breweries in the last few years truly makes this Brew City once again.

BLACK HUSKY BREWING CO.

909 E. Locust St. • Milwaukee, WI 53212 • 414-509-8855
blackhuskybrewing.com
Founded: March 2010   **Brewmaster:** Tim Eichinger
Annual Production: 700 barrels   **Number of Beers:** 12 on tap

Staple Beers:
- » THE ORIGINAL BLACK HUSKY PALE ALE
- » DECK DOG SUMMER ALE
- » OIHF (Oustanding In His Field, robust milk stout)
- » SPROOSE DOUBLE IPA (with spruce)

Rotating Beers:
- » BIG BUCK BROWN
- » DOGFATHER PALE ALE
- » HARVEL THE MARVEL
- » JODLERKÖNIG OKTOBERFEST
- » SCHUTZENGEL WHITE IPA
- » VAIN PALE ALE
- » … plus frequent one-offs/experimental beers

Beware of the Dog Series:
- » HAROLD THE RED IMPERIAL RED
- » HEADBUTTER BARLEYWINE
- » HOWLER IMPERIAL PALE ALE
- » SMOKE MONSTER
- » SPARKLY EYES (Imperial Sproose)
- » ST. NIKKILAUS SPICED CHRISTMAS ALE
- » THREE SCRUTINEERS TRIPEL
- » TWELVE DOG IMPERIAL STOUT

Most Popular Brew: Sproose Joose.

Brewmaster's Fave: "Hard to say. Depends on the time of year. Sproose Joose, I suppose."

Tours? Yes, Saturdays, check Facebook. $10 gets you two samples and a pint glass. Untapped Tours visits here too.

Samples: Yes, four pours for about $15.

Best Time to Go: Open Mon-Thu 3-9pm, Fri 3-10pm, Sat 12-10pm, Sun 12-5pm. Beware winter hours: closed Mon-Tue.

Where can you buy it? Here on tap and to go in growlers, and in stores and on draft in the Madison and Milwaukee areas.

Got food? Nope, but food friendly and local menus on hand.

Special Offer: A Laurel and Hardy handshake.

The Beer Buzz: Tim and his wife Toni figured they'd never retire anyway so may as well find something they could do indefinitely. "Find something you love doing, something you really believe in so that it doesn't feel like work." He thought about volunteering at another brewery, but then thought, "Why? So I can learn to clean?" There is a lot to learn, and starting on your own, they felt it was better to just dive right in, as a nanobrewery. "Risks are smaller, and we're poor. We can't afford to borrow $500,000!" The learning curve was steep, but they went from 28 barrels to 200 in a year. They bottled over 20,000 bottles by hand one year. Their first kettles were made out of half barrels with the tops cut off.

Fast forward to 2016. From a cabin in the woods, Tim and Toni picked up and moved operations to this great corner spot in Milwaukee's Riverwest neighborhood. Formerly an auto repair shop, the brick building holds a large brewhouse and taproom. The bar area has some lounge seating and a TV. The bar shows rough-hewn logs, a nod to their Northwoods origins. See photos behind the bar of the namesake, Howler, their beloved black husky. Board games, cribbage and Jenga are on hand. Outside is a fenced in area occupying the corner of the block and functioning as a beer garden and stoves come out to extend the season.

Free WiFi. On Facebook. Twitter @BlackHuskyBrews

Stumbling Distance: *Klinger's East* (920 E Locust St, 414-263-2424) is well known for its fish fry. *Café Corazon* (3129 N Bremen St, 414-810-3941, corazonmilwaukee.com) does good Mexican with local ingredients and, of course, margaritas. *Dino's Riverwest* (808 E Chambers St, 414-562-9171, dinosriverwest.com) is 3rd generation family Italian. Three blocks southwest to *Company Brewing*.

Broken Bat Brewing Co.

231 E. Buffalo St. • Milwaukee, WI 53202 • 414-316-9197
brokenbatbrewery.com
Opened: 2017   **Head Brewer:** Dan McElwee
Annual Production: < 1,000 barrels   **Number of Beers:** 8 on tap

Staple Beer:
  » Straight Chedd (Apricot Pale Ale)

Rotating Beers:
  » Climb The Wall Farmhouse Ale
  » Corre Corre Mexican Lager
  » Crooked Number Coffee Stout
  » Double Play Double IPA
  » Frozen Rope Wheat
  » Golden Sombrero American Pilsner
  » High & Tight Single IPA
  » Mint Condition Porter
  » Mr. Octoberfest
  » 755 The King Imperial Stout
  » Spin It Double IPA
  » Ugly Finder IPA
  » …plus some stouts, pilsners, and barrel-aging.

Most Popular Brew: Straight Chedd

Brewmaster's Fave: Double Play Double IPA

Tours? No. (You can see it all from the bar.)

Samples: Yes, The Cycle, a flight four 6-oz pours for about $14.

Best Time to Go: Open Thu 4-10pm, Fri 3-11pm, Sat 12-11pm, Sun 12-6pm. Occasional live music.

Where can you buy it? Here on tap and in growlers to go, with a few local draft accounts.

Got food? No, just some gourmet popcorn, but also food friendly.

Special Offer: A free pint of house beer when you get your book signed.

Directions: Follow Water St south past Milwaukee Public Market, south of I-794 into the Historical Third Ward. Turn left (east) on Buffalo St and the brewery is in the basement of the building on the right.

The Beer Buzz: This subterranean baseball-themed brewery is down some stairs beyond a baseball bat door handle inside the 1896 Fred Vogel Jr. Building in the Historic Third Ward. Originally occupied by a shoe company, the old building, like much of the Third Ward, has found new life, and in this case, new beer.

Milwaukee natives Dan McElwee and Tim Pauly are a couple of nerds: one for beer, one for baseball, two great things that go great together. They came up with the concept to combine them in a brewery, and when it turned out that their friend who owned this building suddenly had a vacant space in the lower level, they went to bat.

Walls are Cream City brick and the floor is polished concrete. There's room for a dozen at the bar, and the rest of the space features tall tables, and a separate bar facing the open brewhouse. The awesome metal tap handles were designed by Mark Mario, an artist friend of the founders. Six TVs pipe in the ballgames and other sporting events, and a dart board and board games are on hand. The taproom is dog friendly with treats and water bowls for all canine visitors. Parking is metered on the streets.

Free WiFi. Facebook.com/BrokenBatBrewingCompany and Twitter/Instagram @ BrokenBatBrew

Stumbling Distance: The Historic Third Ward is a reclaimed collection of old brick buildings that now feature a variety of great bars and restaurants, among other things. *Milwaukee Ale House* is half a block away. *The Wicked Hop* (345 N Broadway, 414-223-0345, thewickedhop.com) has a notable selection of local and imports. Huge selection of beer and rooftop patio at Euro-style *Café Benelux* (346 N Broadway, 414-501-2500, cafebenelux.com).

City Lights Brewing Co.

2210 W Mt Vernon Ave • Milwaukee, WI 53233 • 414-436-1011
citylightsbrewing.com
Opened: February 2017   **Head Brewer:** Jimmy Gohsman
Number of Beers: 16 on tap

Signature Beers:
- » Amber Ale
- » Coconut Porter
- » IPA
- » Mosaic Pale Ale

Draft/Specialty Beers:
- » Brown Ale
- » Coffee Stout
- » Double IPA
- » Irish Red Ale
- » Session IPA
- » Vienna Lager

Most Popular Brew: Coconut Porter

Tours? Yes, Fri 5 and 7pm, Sat 2, 4, and 6pm. Advance tickets available on website. $10 includes a pint glass and a free beer.

Samples: Yes, sample flights of four 5-oz pours for about $10-12.

Best Time to Go: Open Tue-Thu 4-10pm, Fri-Sat 12-12,Sun 12-6pm. Closed Mondays except during Brewers home games. They run a shuttle to Miller Park; tokens available with the purchase of a beer on game day.

Where can you buy it? Here on tap and in growlers to go, and distributed in six-pack cans throughout Wisconsin, Illinois and Minnesota.

Got food? Yes, pub fare and a Friday fish fry.

Special Offer: Not participating at this time.

Directions: *Five minutes from Miller Park!* From I-94 through Milwaukee, take Exit 309B and head south on 25th St for 500 feet. Turn left (east) on Mt. Vernon Ave and the brewery is 0.2 mile along on the left. Drive 0.2 mile and the brewery is on your left.

The Beer Buzz: This was originally Milwaukee Gas Light Company's West Side Water Works. Here coal was turned to coal gas, the fuel for city street lights and in homes. The company commissioned Milwaukee architect Alexander Eschweiler, known for his pagoda-like gas station designs for Wadham's Oil & Grease Co., to design the facility.

Built in 1902, it used Carnegie steel and Tiffany hand-glazed brickwork.

The brewery started as a family business, 4 Brothers Blended Beer Co. But to make the leap to something bigger they brought in other partners, experts in their fields, and rebranded. City Lights Brewing took over two buildings in 2016: The brewery and taproom occupy the old Power House, while the lab and packaging area lie in the Condenser House. You can see the handsome green-roofed brick buildings from the interstate and a tower holds a lighted City Lights Brewing Co. sign.

Brewer Jimmy got into craft beer during his time in Colorado. Homebrewing followed and then he took the leap to pro, completing the American Brewers Guild Intensive Brewing Science & Engineering program in Middlebury, Vermont. The venerable Dr. David Ryder (Stella Artois, Siebel Institute, MillerCoors) joined the brewery as Chief Innovation Officer in 2016.

The taproom is an industrial space and the old time clock is still there with time cards for a monthly hour-accumulation challenge. The brewhouse is on display through windows behind the bar. The beer garden allows leashed dogs. Watch for live music and special events. Plenty of parking in the lot outside.

Free WiFi. Facebook.com/citylightsbrewing and Twitter @CityLightsBeer Instagram @ citylightsbrewing

Stumbling Distance: *Miller Park* for a Brewers game. *Sobelman's Pub & Grill* (1900 W St Paul Ave, 414) 931-1919, sobelmanspubandgrill.com) for the burgers and Bloodys. *Mitchell Park Conservatory*, best known as *The Domes* (524 S Layton Blvd, 414-257-5611, milwauke-edomes.org) are three fascinating botanical gardens under glass. *Milwaukee Four Seasons Skate Park* (200 N 25th St, 414-933-7275, 4seasonssk8park.com) is right next door to the brewery if you have teenagers along or want to relive the glory of your boarding days.

MILWAUKEE NIGHTLIFE & DRINK CULTURE INFO

For an always-changing nightlife guide and articles pertinent to the Milwaukee bar scene and drink culture in general, look for a copy of the free magazine *Milwaukee Alcoholmanac* (alcoholmanac.com). About 70 pages of articles, photos and ads about drink and food and drink in Brew City. A new issue comes out every two months. Facebook.com/Alcoholmanac

BAR ON THE RUN

Way back in the day, **Potosi Brewing** (Zone 1) used to have a bar on wheels to take around to special events. Here in Milwaukee they've put a new twist on that idea. Get on board the Pedal Tavern for the most unusual pub crawl. The mobile tavern has room for 16 (10 seats have pedals) and is often booked for groups. Choose from some pre-made routes or put together your own. Individuals can join as well during specified times for about $25 for a 2 or 2.5-hour ride. The tavern does not actually serve alcohol but gets you Happy Hour prices at each of the many pubs and breweries you will hit. The **Historic Third Ward** and **Walker's Point** are popular touring areas and home to several breweries (pedaltavern.com, 414-409-8022).

PHOTOGRAPH COURTESY OF POTOSI BREWING CO.

COMPANY BREWING

735 E Center Street • Milwaukee, WI 53212 • 414-930-0909
companybrewing.com
Founded: 2015　　**Brewmaster**: George Bregar
Annual Production: 250 bbls
Number of Beers: 32 taps (14 for beer, including guest beer, mead, cider, kombucha, nitro coffee, others for cocktails)

Possible Beers:

- » BOUNCE HOUSE (session wheat)
- » GREEN GALLERY NE IPA
- » HIGHLOW (American pale ale)
- » HOP-SIDED IPA
- » LUNCHPAUZE SAISON
- » NIGHT RYE'D (rye porter)
- » OAKY DOKE (white oak red ale)
- » POMP AND PAMPLEMOUSSE (grapefruit IPA)
- » POOR FARM PILS (in cans)
- » ... plus many others including session pale ales, saisons, belgian styles

Most Popular Brew: Pomp and Pamplemousse

Brewmaster's Fave: Lunchpauze Saison

Tours? Yes, by appointment or by chance.

Samples? Yes, 8-oz pours called "cuppers"

Best Time to Go: Open Tue–Sun 4-close (kitchen 4–10PM, brunch Sun 10AM–2PM). Closed Mondays. "Tappy Hour" runs weekdays from 4–6PM.

Where can you buy it? Here on tap in cuppers and pints and in howlers and growlers to go. Poor Farm Pils is available in six-pack cans.

Got food? The menu, served 5–10 daily (and brunch on Sat–Sun from 10AM), includes appetizers (Scotch olives, Wisconsin pretzel, mushroom/walnut pate, etc.), vegetarian/vegan, fish and meat entrees but also burgers and sammiches, and a mix of Wisconsin, pub, and healthy. Wisco Pop.

Special Offer: Get Tappy Hour pricing during your book signature visit.

The Beer Buzz: George Bregar, a homebrewer and former director of coffee for Colectivo is a resident of the neighborhood and had long wanted to open a brewpub here. Conveniently, one was already occupying the space. When Stonefly Brewing (and Onopa Brewing Co. before that) closed, Company moved in. He did a complete makeover of the place, bringing in maple flooring from ReStore which has become maple wall covering. The bar once resided in the Schlitz Brewery tasting room. Everything they serve is on tap: the beer, wine, soda, even cocktails, thus happy hour here is referred to as Tappy Hour. George operates a 7-barrel system to keep those beer taps busy, and he doesn't want to lock himself into any particular beer or style.

Company Brewing's tagline is "Quality Nourishment," which extends to the food and the beer and their mission to foster good *company*—as in companionship and community not the corporation sort. This is, first and foremost, a neighborhood brewpub. Live music is common. Parking is on the street.

Free WiFi. Facebook.com/CompanyBrewing Twitter @CompanyBrewing

Stumbling Distance: *Fuel Café* (fuelcafe.com, 818 E Center St, 414-374-3835) is a popular coffeehouse with sandwiches just down the street in this funky eclectic neighborhood. (They also contribute one of their brews to one of Lakefront Brewery's brews.) *Nessun Dorma* (2778 N Weil St, 414-264-8466) is a personal favorite, serving gourmet sandwiches and wine, with a nice beer selection of Belgians and microbrews. *Centro Café* (centrocaferiverwest.com, 808 E Center St, 414-455-3751) serves some really nice and reasonably priced Italian right across the street. *Milwaukee Beer Bistro* (2730 N Humboldt Blvd, 414-562-5540, milwaukeebeerbistro.com) has 13 taps and 50+ bottled/canned beers, plus a lunch, dinner, and brunch menu that is predominantly beer-infused. Three blocks northeast to *Black Husky Brewing*.

THE MUSEUM OF BEER AND BREWING

Really, how is it that Milwaukee does not have a museum dedicated to beer yet? These things take time, but rest assured some people are on it. The Museum of Beer and Brewing is dedicated to preserving and displaying the proud history of beer and brewing throughout the world and especially North America. At present this museum is mostly virtual, but that does not mean you have no place to go. The museum may one day have a permanent site, but in the meantime this society organizes events (even beer and cheese pairings) and exhibits in the Milwaukee area. Check their website for what's coming up, virtual exhibits, a gift store, and some really interesting articles related to brewing history (brewingmuseum.org).

MILWAUKEE'S BEER GARDENS

Milwaukee is a bit of a German town, isn't it? Summer in Germany means beer gardens, so it's no surprise that Milwaukee follows suit. Milwaukee County Parks host various bier gartens.

Rules are you can bring your own food and non-alcoholic beverages but there is no outside alcohol and you can't bring a grill. Often there is live music and the event is quite family friendly and typically pet friendly as well. Glassware for your beer requires a refundable deposit; you are not allowed to take them home or purchase them except where indicated.

Estabrook Park Beer Garden
The Landing at Hoyt Park
South Shore Terrace Beer Garden (2900 South Shore Drive) home of Miller 1855 Bar
Whitnall Park (on Root River Parkway, 5879 S 92nd St, Franklin)
Humboldt Park Beer Garden (operated with St Francis Brewing Co.)
Milwaukee County Parks Traveling Beer Garden™ as the name suggests, has no permanent home. It sets up in several locations throughout the city during a 16-week summer schedule that includes many different parks. *Sprecher Brewing* and Sprecher Restaurant & Pub collaborate to provide the beer, sodas, hard sodas, and German food, and seating and polka playing follows with them.

(county.milwaukee.gov/Parks/BeerGardens)

EVERY PICTURE TELLS A (BREWERY) STORY

Milwaukee photographer Paul Bialas has a thing for historical breweries. His large, hard-cover books are collections of black and white shots of the Milwaukee area breweries that in some instances have fallen into ruins or been repurposed. The photos are fascinating looks at these old structures as works of art, and his first two—Schlitz, Brewing Art and Pabst, An Excavation of Art—are tributes to the past. His latest work, however, combines shots of old structures with the new ones when he takes on the city's largest brewery in Miller, Inside the High Life. Each book goes beyond the images and includes CDs containing 70 minutes of interviews and anecdotes from former employees. Find out more about Paul and his work, and order his books at lakecountryphoto.com. Contact him at pjbialas@yahoo.com.

PHOTOS COURTESY OF PAUL BIALAS

Component Brewing Co.

2018 S 1st St. • Milwaukee, WI 53207 • 414-979-1088
componentbrewing.com
Opened: June 2018　　**Head Brewer:** Jonathan Kowalske
Annual Production: 200 barrels　　**Number of Beers:** 10 on tap

Possible Beers:

- » ESB
- » India Pale Lager
- » IPAs
- » Kettle-Sours
- » Pilsner
- » Stout

Brewmaster's Fave: IPA

Tours? No.

Samples: Yes, flights available.

Best Time to Go: Open Thu-Sun to start. Check website or Facebook to be sure.

Where can you buy it? Here on tap and in growlers and 16-oz fill-on-demand cans to go.

Got food? No, but food friendly.

Special Offer: Half off your 1st beer when you get your book signed.

Directions: From I-94/43 south of Milwaukee, take Exit 312B for Becher St. Go east on Becher St (toward the lake) for 0.3 mile and the brewery is in the large brick building on the left. Turn left onto 1st St to enter the parking lot. (You can also come south from downtown on Water St which becomes 1st St before hitting Becher St.) In the corner along the side of the building facing 1st St, find the stairs up to the second floor.

The Beer Buzz: Nature abhors a vacuum. So when *Eagle Park Brewing* vacated their original space at Lincoln Warehouse in Bay View, naturally another brewery had to rush in and fill it. Jonathan Kowalske had his beer epiphany in 2013 when a friend brought a homebrew to a party and he was surprised it could taste so good. Soon after, on a stop at *O'so Brewing*, he slipped next door into their homebrew supply shop and found a simple homebrew bucket kit on sale. He bought it, tried it out, and the hobby went crazy as he started brewing all the time, "probably more often than my wife would like." He brought his brews to a Christmas gathering a few years back, bringing his two cousins DJ and Steve Kowalske into homebrewing. *Eagle Park* was one of Jonathan's favorite breweries in the area, close to his home, and when their former space and equipment became available, the three partners made a quick decision and jumped on it. They lean toward a hop heavy brewing style, with a few IPAs on at any given time, but you can expext at least a couple lines dedicated to lagers at all times.

Free WiFi. Facebook.com/ComponentBrewing and Twitter/Instagram @ComponentBeer

Stumbling Distance: *Enlightened Brewing* is in the same warehouse on street level. Look for the cash-only *Tacos El Charrito* food truck (178 W Becher St, 414-210-8277, facebook.com/LoncherasElCharrito) near the warehouse.

D14 BREWERY & PUB

2273 S Howell Ave • Milwaukee, WI 53207 • 414-744-0399
d14beer.com
Opened: September 2014   **Brewmaster**: Matt McCulloch
Annual Production: 200 barrels   **Number of Beers**: 10 on tap, plus occasional firkins

Staple Beers:
>   » BELGIAN, AMERICAN AND ENGLISH   » Rarely ever repeats a brew
      STYLES   »
>   » Sours and barrel aging as well

Most Popular Brew: Whatever's new

Brewer's Fave: "The beer I haven't had yet"

Tours? Not really, but bar stool tour/chat if he's available.

Samples: Yes, flights of 4 five-oz pours for $2–3 per glass.

Best Time to Go: Open Tue–Thu 3PM–12AM, Fri 3PM–2AM, Sat 12PM–2AM, Sun 12PM–12AM. Closed on Mondays. Happy hour runs Tue-Fri 3–7PM. Live music on occasion.

Where can you buy it? Here on tap and in growlers to go. Limited growlers depending on supply.

Got food? Fresh made pizzas and some snacks. Also food spreads on special occasions.

Special Offer: One half-price flight of 4 beers during your signature visit.

Directions: Follow Kinnickinnic Ave (WI 32) south into Bay View and Howell splits in a V to the right. The brewery is there on the right at the split before the corner at Lincoln Ave.

The Beer Buzz: Matt started homebrewing in 2005 and was soon doing it every weekend. His father, a teacher, was a smart investor and left him some good money when he passed away. Matt looked for a way to invest it and that weekend habit gave him an idea. He didn't want to try to compete with the larger distribution breweries. One day he stopped in at Public in Kenosha and it clicked: he could do this in a corner bar space. He chose Bay View as it was up and coming, and the 20s–40s art and music loving demographic here is strong. The 1890s building, once an IGA in the '30s, needed some major renovation including bringing it up to fire code. He did all the woodwork himself, and it includes 9 varieties of hardwood. The bar top and back bar are made of basswood, the tables are of cherry. There are coat/purse hooks and outlets under the bar. The windows looking in on the brewhouse are actually old convenience store cooler doors. The boys and girls bathroom doors came from a 1922 Beloit grade school. The kayak frame you see is the last father-son project they worked on together. Matt credits his father for the financial and physical skills he needed to pull this whole thing off. The brewery name derives from the 14th District of the City of Milwaukee, which encompasses this neighborhood, Bay View.

Matt brews one or two new beers each week and in his first 180 batches, 140 of them were unique brews, never done before, likely never to brewed again. Current beers are posted on a chalkboard behind the bar. Local art adorns the walls and there's a dartboard. There are TVs, but they only come on for special events such as a Packers game. Parking is on the street.

ATM onsite. Facebook.com/d14beer and Twitter @ District14MKE

Stumbling Distance: *Goodkind* (2457 S Wentworth Ave, 414-763-4706, goodkindbayview.com) has a nice farm to fork menu with large and small plates, an impressive tap list of 20 carefully chosen beers plus specialty bottles. *Sugar Maple* (441 E Lincoln Ave, 414-481-2393, mysugarmaple.com) has a dive bar environment and 60 craft tap selections. *Café Centraal* (2306 S Kinnickinnic Ave, 414-755-0378, cafecentraal.com) is a Euro café with related food and Belgian beers. *Burnhearts* (2599 S Logan Ave, 414-294-0490, burnhearts.tumblr.com) has 24 choice taps, a cask, great cocktails, and a crap ton of bottles/cans. *Odd Duck* (2352 S Kinnickinnic Ave, 414-763-5881, oddduckrestaurant.com) does superb, creative, shareable small plates and creative cocktails. *Guanajuato Mexican* (2317 S Howell Ave) gets raves. The oddly-houred *1840 Brewing Co.* is on the other side of the block, a couple minutes' walk.

BAY VIEW

    Established as a company town in 1868 for Milwaukee Iron Company, Bay View first lured immigrants from steel town Sheffield, UK, but Poles, Germans, Italians, Irish, and others came soon after, making this one of the most ethnically diverse communities in the area. Bay View had a few years as an independent village before Milwaukee annexed it in 1887. Workers' rights activism was strong here, and on May 5, 1886 during a 14,000-person strike and demonstration to fight for an 8-hour work day, seven people, including a 13-year-old, were shot dead by National Guardsmen. See State Historical Markers at Zillman Park (#372) on Kinnickinnic and at Superior St/Russell Ave. (#275). Today Bay View has become a great destination for local dining and craft beer and cocktails, especially along Kinnickinnic Ave. Two Bay View breweries so far: *1840 Brewing* and *D14 Brewery* while St. Francis is to the south and the breweries of 3rd Ward/Walker's Point are to the north (*MobCraft, Urban Harvest, Sprecher, Milwaukee Ale House, Broken Bat*)

DEAD BIRD BREWING CO.

1730 N 5th St. • Milwaukee, WI 53212
deadbirdbrewing.com
Founded: 2015   **Opening:** Summer 2018   **Head Brewer:** Nick Kocis
Annual Production: 240 barrels
Number of Beers: 12 on tap (2 sodas, 1 guest beer, 1 guest cider)

Staple Beers:

- » PAMPLEMOUSSE APA
- » WINNIPEG RUN (German Amber Lager)

Rotating Beers:

- » DEVIL MONKEY (Imperial NE IPA)
- » MUSCLEMAN (10% abv 100 IBU west-coast-style IPA)
- » TOTTENVOGEL (Dead Bird) Oktoberfest
- » IN SPRING (with Argentinian Torrantes)
- » STRUMPET (tart Montmorency cherry Imperial Stout - Nov)
- » WINE THIEF (Napa Valley Savignon Blanc grape must Imperial Belgian Wit)
- » Plus many one-offs, pilsner, saison, Belgian Pale,
- » Beer cocktails on tap

Most Popular Brew: Pamplemousse

Brewmaster's Fave: Muscleman

Tours? Yes, by chance or by appointment.

Samples: Yes, 2-oz pours.

Best Time to Go: Open Mon-Thu 3-10pm, Fri 3-12am, Sat 12pn-12am, Sun 12-6pm, always accommodating Packers game. Indoor bocce ball league nights. Retro arcade game, live music and vinyl nights.

Where can you buy it? Here on tap and in growlers or Crowlers to go. Imperial beers in 22-oz. bombers. Ponplmouse and Wine Thief in cans in the Greater Madison and Milwaukee area.

Got food? Yes, small plates, appetizers and a wine list. High-octane barley-based beer used as a base in Bloody Marys and other cocktails.

Special Offer: A free pint when you get your book signed.

Directions: Take 6th St north from WI-145/Fond Du Lac (Exit 73A from I-43) or 8th St (which becomes 6th St) south (Exit 73B from I-43). Where 6th St meets Walnut St turn east and take the second left (north) on 5th St, and the brewery is on the right.

The Beer Buzz: While the doors opened here in 2018, Nick Kocis and Jeremy Hach founded Dead Bird in spring of 2015 while Nick was working at now defunct House of Brews in Madison. House of Brews, under the ownership of Page Buchanan, did a lot of contract brewing, and as Nick puts it, "My company was paying Page to pay me to manufacture my own beer." Their first release was Pamplemousse, an American Pale Ale with ruby red grapefruit zest, and it was very well received. First beers hit the shelves in November 2015. By summer of 2017 their bombers were coming out of MobCraft Brewing and they were gearing up to open their own place.

Jeremy and Nick went to Middleton High School together, and at UW-Platteville, they homebrewed together, thinking it'd be cheaper (it wasn't). Nick's background is in microbiology and biochemistry, relevant to brewing, while Jeremy's Masters thesis was about managing the build-out of an electric 1-bbl system. He and Jeremy built a "Frankenbrew" 1.5-barrel electric system to start with while keeping an eye on bigger stuff once they get going here. In house they'll be wood-aging and brewing sours while initially continuing to contract brew for the distribution. Stop in and try some "Outstanding Beer by Upstanding Gentlemen."

Free WiFi. Mug Club. Facebook.com/DeadBirdBrewingCo and Twitter/Instagram @ DeadBirdBrewing

Stumbling Distance: This is 3 minutes west of *Lakefront Brewery. The Brown Bottle* (221 W Galena St, 414-539-6450, brownbottlemke.com) is a tavern with a good fish fry and nice beer selection. Great American food (burgers and such, but creative a bit) including a lot of vegan fare at *Mi Casa Su Casa* (1835 N M.L.K. Drive, 414-488-9916).

EAGLE PARK BREWING CO.

823 E. Hamilton Ave. • Milwaukee, WI 53202 • 414-585-0123
eagleparkbrewing.com
Opened: January 28, 2017   **Head Brewer:** Jackson Borgardt
Annual Production: 2,000 barrels   **Number of Beers:** 12 on tap

Staple Beers:
- » HUEY LEWIS AND THE BOOZE
- » IMMORTAL SOUL
- » LOOP STATION
- » SET LIST

Rotating Beers:
- » a variety one-offs – over 50 per year!

Most Popular Brew: Immortal Soul or Set List

Tours? Yes, tours on Saturdays. Check the website.

Samples: Yes, sample flights of three 7-oz pours for about $10.

Best Time to Go: Open Tue-Thu 4-10pm, Fri 3-12am, Sat 11am-12am, Sun 11am-6pm.

Where can you buy it? Here on tap and in Crowlers to go. Draft accounts and 12oz. can six-packs throughout Greater Milwaukee.

Got food? Yes, a full menu of familiar Wisconsin fare influenced by International cuisine. Free popcorn.

Special Offer: Buy your first pint get one free when you get your book signed.

Directions: From I-43 take Exit 74 and head east on McKinley Ave for 1.8 miles. Turn left on Water St and stay on it 1.2 miles and then turn right on Hamilton St. The brewery is on the right.

The Beer Buzz: Garage band or garage brewer? Such was the choice of brothers Max and Jackson Borgardt who loved both but ultimately chose to start a brewery with Jake Schinker. They started in the Lincoln Warehouse with so many other small businesses and when defunct Like Minds Brewing vacated this property, they pounced on it. The 1920s Cream City brick building was originally a garage – they found the old oil stains when they ripped up the floor. Local lore has it that Al Capone kept cars here as well. The brewery has a full kitchen and when they moved in they added a full menu to their offerings. The taproom is a bright space thanks to three massive skylights. Great patio space outside and an adjoining parking lot.

Free WiFi. Frequent Flyer Club. Facebook.com/EPbeer and Twitter @EagleParkBeer Instagram @EagleParkBrewing

Stumbling Distance: *Birch + Butcher* (459 E Pleasant St, 414-323-7372, birchandbutcher.com) features an onsite butcher and wood-fired hearth for Midwestern cuisine. *Red Lion Pub* (1850 N Water St, 414-431-9009, redlion-pubmke.com) is a very British experience with ales, a full menu that includes latenight grub, and a Friday night fish fry (that's fish and chips to a Brit). *Lakefront Brewery* is across the Milwaukee River, a six-minute walk. The famed bumper sticker "I Closed Wolski's" appears round the world now – about 20,000 more each year – and here's your chance to check that off your bucket list: *Wolski's Tavern*, an historic tavern with pool, darts, free popcorn and, obviously, beer. 3 blocks from Eagle Park Brewing: 1836 N Pulaski St, 414-276-8130, wolskis.com.

CRUIZIN' FOR SOME BOOZIN'

Check out listings in the back of the book for a way to float your way around to some breweries here in Milwaukee!

1840 Brewing Co.

342 E. Ward St. • Milwaukee, WI 53207 • 414-236-4056
1840brewing.com
Opened: August 2017   **Brewmaster:** Kyle Vetter

Beers:

- » Biere De Garde Bruin
- » The Cashmere Sweater IPA (double dry-hopped hazy IPA)
- » Neon Knights Imperial English Porter
- » Sumerian Origin Wheat Ale

Tours? Only by private appointment. $20/person (5 minimum) for an hour-long talk and tasting.

Samples: No.

Best Time to Go: This is complicated. The place officially opens to the public one Saturday per month (2nd Sat of each month, for now) or Thu-Sun that weekend for VIP members. Read below!

Where can you buy it? Here in 500ml and 750ml cork and capped bottles. 95% of the beer is sold during those 4 days each month.

Got food? No, but food friendly.

Special Offer: Not participating at this time

Directions: Follow Kinnickinnic Ave (WI 32) south into Milwaukee's Bay View neighborhood, crossing the Kinnickinnic River. At Zilman Park, turn right on Ward St. and the brewery is on the right at mid-block.

The Beer Buzz: If you want to be special be exclusive. At the time of writing, this unusual brewing project opens its doors to the public only one day per month. VIP members may have three days in addition to that one. The line goes down the street and round the corner that Saturday. Exceptions might be beer dinners, holidays and other special events, but members, of which there are over 120, have the advantage of getting first dibs on new beer releases.

Kyle has his wort made by brewing partners offsite (*Explorium, Third Space, Eagle Park, Fermentorium, Enlightened*, have all participated) and then he brings it here in food-grade totes to start fermentation. He brews some IPAs and clean stouts and porters, but most brews call for alternative wild yeasts, often souring bacteria, and then 90% are not just aged in barrels but also fermented in them. Afterwards he may make multiple blends. While lambic brewers are his inspiration, he points out these are American beers. In his first six months, he made 17 different beers – all of them go into corked/capped bottles of 500 or 750ml.

Kyle is from Mequon, WI but spent 15 years in Colorado. He started with homebrew in 2003 but took a job with Ska Brewing the next year. After college he came back to Wisconsin for a spell and sold real estate, but the beer called and he was back in Colorado in no time, at Aspen Brewing, where he worked his way up to lead brewer and barrel manager. When he was ready, he and Stephanie Vetter opened 1840. It's set in a deep, narrow industrial building with exposed ceiling and concrete floors, with a tasting area with a few tables and concrete bar up front near the only windows, and then a large space full of barrels extending to a small brewing area in back. Local art for sale on the walls, and a few board games for folks who stay and open their bottles.

Free WiFi. Membership Club. Facebook.com/1840brewing and Twitter @1840brewingco Instagram @1840brewing

Stumbling Distance: *D14 Brewery* is a block south of here. *C-viche* (2165 S Kinnickinnic Ave, 414-800-7329, c-viche.com) serves nice Latin fare and cocktails around the corner. Italian fans will love *Santino's Little Italy* (352 E Stewart St, 414-897-7367, santinoslittleitaly.com) with pastas and Neapolitan-style pies.

ENLIGHTENED BREWING CO.

2018 S 1st St. • Milwaukee, WI 53207 • 414-364-6225
enlightenedbeer.com
Opened: February 2, 2015   **Director of Operations:** James Larson
Head Brewer: Mike Guten
Annual Production: 250 barrels   **Number of Beers:** 8 on tap

Staple Beers:
- » A PRIORI (APA)
- » CREAM CITY BRIX (cream ale)
- » KETTLE LOGIC (amber)
- » PROTOTYPICAL PORTER

Rotating Beers:
- » BENEVOLENT BREW (IPA)
- » THE DAILY STIPEND (American pale wheat)
- » THE HUMAN CONDITION (saison)
- » SUSTAINED THOUGHT (stout)
- » TE IPSUM (APA)
- » New beers every month!

Most Popular Brew: Cream City Brix

Brewmaster's Fave: Cream City Brix, a "brewer's beer," says James.

Tours? No.

Samples: Yes, flights of four 150ml pours in beakers for about $12.

Best Time to Go: Open Wed 4-10pm, Thu 4-11pm, Fri-Sat 3pm-12am, Sun 1-6pm. Happy hour Wed-Fri 4-6pm. Closed Mon-Tue.

Where can you buy it? Here on tap and in growlers and howlers/Boston rounds to go, plus some draft accounts around Bay View and the rest of Milwaukee.

Got food? Just some New Zealand Hand Pies (meat pies) by Drift (food truck) but food friendly – bring your own. They have several recommended eateries that will deliver via Grub Hub & Forward Bicycle Courier.

Special Offer: $1 off your first house beer when you get your book signed.

Directions: From I-94/43 south of Milwaukee, take Exit 312B for Becher St. Go east on Becher St (toward the lake) for 0.3 mile and the brewery is in the large brick building on the left. Turn left onto 1st St to enter the parking lot. (You can also come south from downtown on Water St which becomes 1st St before hitting Becher St.)

The Beer Buzz: On the northern edge of Milwaukee's southside Bay View neighborhood stands Lincoln Warehouse, a former facility for the A&P grocery chain in the 1920s; this space here was loading docks: flour in and bread out. Now it's still grains in and liquid bread out.

Beer brings people together, even when they may otherwise disagree. Co-owner James Larson had a drinking group, the Enlightened Imbibers, who enjoyed having enlightened and enlightening conversations about diverse and often "off limits" topics at someplace that served good beer. James started homebrewing and shared with the group, until the urge to brew went beyond the circle.

James studied brewing and distilling at Heriot-Watt University in Scotland and then took a job brewing at Bells Brewing in Kalamazoo. When they first opened, James helped out behind the bar, naturally, but that got them in a bit of hot water as one cannot be a partner and a bartender. You can't be a member of more than one tier in the three-tier brewer-distributor-retailer kingdom. (For more head-scratching stories like this see *The Brewing Projekt* in Eau Claire.)

Enlightened previously operated on the second floor in a 500-square-foot space with a half-barrel system, what they called "homebrewing on steroids," but moved here in July 2016 to the loading dock area for more brewing space, and added a 3.5-barrel system. The taproom itself can still get a little tight considering their popularity. High industrial ceiling and windows to match, a portrait of Lincoln, and the shell of an antique radio from back when such a thing was a piece of furniture. A short simple bar and some high-top tables and a long rough-cut wood communal table. Beyond the tasting area is the

brewing space stretching away in a very industrial fashion. Cribbage is on hand. Watch for frequent limited releases. Dog and kid friendly – if they're on leashes.

Free WiFi. Facebook.com/EnlightenedBrewing and Twitter/Instagram @EnlightenedBeer

Stumbling Distance: *Component Brewing* is upstairs in the same warehouse. *Transfer Pizza* (101 W Mitchell St, 414-763-0438, transfermke.com) has 40+ pies, plus wine, beer, and live music. *Lincoln Warehouse* has been an incubator, if not home, to a number of great small businesses. (*Eagle Park Brewing* got its start here.) No need to leave the building for: *Twisted Path Distillery* (next door, 414-405-8900, twistedpathdistillery.com), *Melt Chocolates* (between dock doors #6 and #7, experiencemelt.com, watch for beer/chocolate pairings) and gluten-free *Mor Bakery & Café* (morfoodsmke.com).

BREWERY INCUBATOR: THE CRAFTER SPACE

Founder John Graham was in Colorado on a work trip and had a whole Sunday free before a late flight out. He went to a brewery where a guy at the taproom gave him a list of other places to hit that day. As he made this pilsgrimage through town, he realized what an amazing beer culture they had. Why don't we have this in Milwaukee? he thought. Milwaukee had a history of beer barons and giant breweries, but until very recently, the craft beer scene seemed too small for its size and reputation. In 2014 he founded The Crafter Space which offers a 10-week **Barley to Barrel** program to get aspiring brewers what they need to get started, scale up recipes, build a brand, investigate real estate, sort through legalities, and more. Greg of Copper State Brewing, Chad of Brewfinity, New Barons Brewing Cooperative, Sabbatical Brewing, Component Brewing, and others who are still working at other breweries awaiting their future, have all taken advantage of this knowledge. Everyone has different skills and needs and these annual classes brings brewery hopefuls together in groups of 12 as they work to further build Milwaukee's awesome beer culture.

Participants brew three batches in the program in teams at a partner brewery. Enlightened Company and Milwaukee Ale House are the current partners, but the organization hopes to find its own space for a brewery and classroom. Watch for it!

thecrafterspace.com

barleytobarrel.com

THE EXPLORIUM BREW PUB

5300 S. 76th St. Unit 1450A • Greendale, WI 53129 • 414-423-1365
exploriumbrew.com

Opened: January 25, 2017   **Head Brewer:** Kyle Ciske
Annual Production: 700 barrels   **Number of Beers:** 24 on tap

Staple Beers:
- » CAPTAIN KIDD'S LOST IPA
- » DOC RAE SCOTTISH ALE
- » HUMBOLDT'S HOMELAND HEFEWEIZEN
- » LIVINGSTONE'S PORTER
- » PATAGONIAN HITCHHIKER LAGER
- » SHACKLETON'S ENDURANCE BARLEYWINE
- » SUTTER'S SECRET GOLDEN ALE
- » THREE SAINTS BAY IMPERIAL STOUT

Rotating Beers:
- » AMELIA'S APA
- » CROCUS LAGER
- » MANGO HEFEWEIZEN
- » SAISON DE FLORISCONSIN
- » SCHWARZBIER
- » …plus many other styles and some barrel aging

Most Popular Brew: Doc Rae Scottish Ale

Brewmaster's Fave: Doc Rae Scottish Ale

Tours? Yes, typically Fri-Sun at 1 and 3pm. $10 tour includes a pint and glass.

Samples: Yes, 4-oz pours of anything for $2-2.50.

Best Time to Go: Open 11am-10pm daily, until midnight Fri-Sat. Cask beers tapped every Thursday at 4pm. Happy hour Sun-Fri 3-6pm

Where can you buy it? Here on tap and in crowlers, bombers and 750ml bottles. Will fill stainless steel growlers. Draft accounts as far as Appleton but mostly Milwaukee area.

Got food? Yes, full restaurant menu with house pizzas, flatbreads, sandwiches, soups and salads, entrees, appetizers, a kids' menu. A souped up beer cheese soup, cheese curds, various dishes with beer worked into them and a full bar with barrel-aged cocktails.

Special Offer: A free pint of house beer when you get your book signed.

Directions: Heading west on I-43/I-894 head south 1 mile on 76th St and Southridge Mall is on your left. (If heading east on I-43/I-894, take Exit 7, go south 0.2 mile on 60th, turn right on Layton and go 1 mile to turn left (south) on 76th.) When you enter the mall area, turn right and watch for Explorium's sign on the side of the mall near the southwestern entrance.

The Beer Buzz: Mike and Joan Roble co-own this adventurous brewpub. Mike's mother and father opened The Brew Shack, a brew supply store, in Tampa, Florida and then Tampa Bay Brewing Co. two years later. Mike, a building designer and civil engineer, helped. In 2014 he quit his job and moved to Florida to help open their production brewery and restaurant. (Tampa is Cigar City, and this explains the cigar sales and the cigar friendly patio at Explorium.) His wife Joan, who has a degree in physics and a background in aerospace engineering, helped with the training manual for the Tampa business, and they brought their enthusiasm and a plan back to Wisconsin where they opened a 10-barrel brewhouse and restaurant in Southridge Mall.

Why a mall? you might ask. Because of their philosophy: "We want to reach out to non-craft-beer drinkers and bring them into the fold." This mission also accounts for some of the light, approachable beers on the menu. "Explore. Taste. Discover" it reads along one wall of the restaurant. Note the names of famous explorers in the beer names. Brewer Kyle is a Siebel Institute grad and previously brewed at Silver Creek Brewery in Cedarburg.

There is a bar area and a dining side and the mugs of club members line the ceiling. The whole space has a kid-friendly, family-restaurant atmosphere. Board games, giant Jenga, and cornhole entertain and the outdoor patio has a fire pit and a bar with all the taps. Live music is on stage here in season. This is a mall, so there's plenty of parking.

Free WiFi. Mug Club counts 200+ members. Facebook.com/ExploriumBrew and Twitter/Instagram @ExploriumBrew

Stumbling Distance: In Greendale the classic local bar is *Ray and Dot's* (6351 W. Grange Ave., 414-421-1960, rayandots.com) a hole-in-the-wall tavern dating back to 1957 and attached to the VFW hall. Pool, darts, cheap drinks. *The Hale House* (10539 W Forest Home Ave, Hales Corners, 414-377-9392, hale-house.com) has a good fish fry and craft beer.

Gathering Place Brewing Co.

811 E. Vienna Ave. • Miwaukee, WI 53212 • 414-364-6328
gatheringplacebrewing.com
Opened: August 19, 2017   **Head Brewer:** Corey Blodgett
Annual Production: 750-1,100 barrels   **Number of Beers:** 12 on tap

Staple Beers:
- » Friendly Debate IPA
- » Spirited Debate IPA
- » Ryed Of The Valkyries (dark rye lager)
- » Stor Bjørn IPA (big bear)
- » Treffpunkt Kölsch

Rotating Beers:
- » Biere De Garde
- » Heated Debate IIPA
- » Hopfen Dampf (Bavarian farmhouse)
- » Murdered By Crows (coffee rye stout)
- » Radler

Most Popular Brew: Spirited Debate IPA

Brewmaster's Fave: Trefpunkt Kölsch

Tours? Yes, Sat and Sun for $10, reservable online, with 25% saved for walk-ins.

Samples: Yes, sample flights of five.

Best Time to Go: Wed-Fri 3-10pm, Sat 12-10pm, Sun 12-6pm.

Where can you buy it? Here on tap in full and half pours, and in growlers to go, with quarterly special releases in 750 ml bottles. A few area draft accounts.

Got food? No, but it is food friendly and food trucks often park outside on Saturdays. Menus from local places are on hand and soda pop is served.

Special Offer: Buy one flight, get one free with book signature.

Directions: From I-43 take Exit 76A and head east on Capitol Dr/WI-190 for about 1.2 miles. Turn right (south) on Fratney St and in one block it runs right into Vienna and the brick building the brewery shares space in. Turn left on Vienna and park on the street.

Cyclists: the Oak Leaf Trail passes within 3 blocks of here.

The Beer Buzz: Founder Joe Yeado started brewing on his stovetop in 2007 but within a few years had won 35 awards, including wins at the Sam Adams homebrewing competition in 2013 and 2014. At the time he lived in Washington, D.C. and shifted his focus to the business of brewing. He fell in love with beer culture in Germany, where the brewery functioned as a sort of living room for locals. Thus when he moved back to Milwaukee, where he had gone to college, he chose Riverwest, an area with a strong neighborhood identity. The name Milwaukee itself is from a Potawatomie word (*minwaking*) for "gathering place by the waters," and his kölsch is named for "gathering place" in German. As a community partner, the brewery gives 1% of its sales to different non-profits in the city. This is also a Community Supported Brewery (CSB) with 75+ members who get a growler per month and first tastes of new releases.

Knowing how tricky it is to run a business and be head brewer at the same time, Joe

hired Brewer Corey, a UW-M graduate who bought his first homebrew kit at a brew supply on Chambers St., where Lakefront Brewery later opened for the first time. Corey brewed professionally in Portland and Seattle for 15 years, his most recent gig being lead innovation brewer at Widmer Brothers. He brewed 18 different beers in his first six months here and you can expect a lot of seasonals and one-offs. Variety is important here and they take styles and put their own touch on them. For example, the Stor Bjørn is a Norwegian Farmhouse IPA.

You'll pass through arched steel beams from an Army Quonset hut arranged like the rib cage of a mighty beast as you enter this reclaimed space in a 1949 Frigidaire factory. The room has high ceilings and polished concrete floors with a collection of tall tables, and the interior design is impressively done by their neighbor Flux Design. The brewhouse is open to the room set aside by a low railing. The L-shaped bartop was a basketball court in a previous life, and plaques with beers on tap dangle from chains behind it.

Board games are on hand and free WiFi. Facebook/ and Twitter @

Stumbling Distance: Check out *Riverwest Filling Station* (701 E Keefe Ave, 414-906-9000, the-filling-station.com), a beer-centric restaurant that fills growlers and a great place to watch the Packers game. In season, *Estebrook Beer Garden* (4600 Estabrook Pkwy, 414-226-2728, estabrook-beergarden.com) is just north of here, overlooking the Milwaukee River inside Estebrook Park, while *Hubbard Park Beer Garden* (3565 N Morris Blvd, 414-332-4207, hubbardparkbeergarden.com) lies due east. *Cyclists:* The paved *Oak Leaf Trail* passes through the Milwaukee River parks corridor east of here. Get off at Capitol Dr, head west across the river about 1300 feet, and take Fratney south a block.

MILWAUKEE PRETZELS

Soft pretzels, the fresh variety of the Bavarian-style beer buddy, made right here at **Milwaukee Pretzel Co.** You'll see them on the menu in many Wisconsin brewpubs, tasting rooms, bars and restaurants, and their bakery is not far from *Gathering Place Brewing* at 3950 N. Holton St. in Milwaukee (414-759-3127, milwaukeepretzel.com). **The bakery does not take walk-ins or give tours**, so do not stop in unannounced. But if your destination does not serve their product: 1) suggest they consider it, and/or 2) order some online or leave a message in advance (at least the day before) and select "pick up at bakery."

Good City Brewing Co.

2108 N. Farwell Ave. • Milwaukee, WI 53202 • 414-539-4173
goodcitybrewing.com
Opened: June 2016   **Brewmaster:** Andy Jones
Annual Production: 2,500 barrels
Number of Beers: up to 12-16 on tap, including cask ales

Staple Beers:
- » Motto (Mosaic pale ale)
- » Pils
- » Reward (double IPA)
- » Risk (IPA)

Seasonal Beers:
- » Dr J (NE IPA)
- » Film Fest Lager (Märzen)
- » Velocity (IPA)

Rotating Draft Beers:
- » BFG (barleywine)
- » Density (Imperial stout)
- » Detail (porter)
- » En Fleur (saison)
- » Lord Lyon (Scotch ale)
- » Stadt (smoked lager)
- » Strahl (hefeweizen)
- » ...to name a few, plus barrel-aged beers

Most Popular Brew: Motto

Brewmaster's Fave: Proud of his Pilsner

Tours? Yes, scheduled on Saturdays at 1 and 2pm, first come, first served. $10 includes a full pour and commemorative glass.

Samples: Yes, 5-oz pours for $2.50-4 each.

Best Time to Go: Open Mon-Sat 11am-12am, Sun 11am-10pm.

Where can you buy it? Here on tap and in Crowlers, growlers and bombers to go. Distributed in cans in the Milwaukee and Madison areas and a bit in the Fox Valley and Door County.

Got food? Yes, an eclectic and seasonal menu of snacks, salads, pub food, entrée plates and cheese boards. Plus a brunch menu, desserts, kids' menu items, and beer cocktails.

Special Offer: Not participating at this time.

Directions: From I-43 take Exit 73B for North Ave. (Go left-north on 7th St from the end of that exit if you are coming from the south. If coming from the north, you merge on 8th St and turn left-east on North Ave.) Drive east toward the lake 1.8 miles on North Ave, then take a sharp right on Farwell. Not quite two blocks farther, the brewery is on the left. Farwell is one-way heading south; if coming from downtown, take parallel Prospect Ave up to North Ave, turn left, and go left again on Farwell.

Cyclists: This is steps from a segment of the Oak Leaf Trail.

The Beer Buzz: As perhaps you figured from the name, the founders of this brewery love Milwaukee. All three of them made a decision to settle here and make great beer.

Andy Jones got his start at the venerable Goose Island in Chicago before taking the plant manager position at the also venerable *Lakefront Brewing*. Dan Katt and David Dupee met when David was still in grad school back in 2009, and they became close beer buddies. The meeting of these three founders, however, didn't happen until 2015 when they found each other in Portland, OR during a craft brewers conference. Wheels were set in motion and by the next year it was game on. No sooner had they converted the old Crank Daddy bike shop space into a production brewery and taproom than they started expanding, with a full restaurant, event space and a rooftop patio, plus increases in production to keep up with popular demand. The brick building stands at the corner of Farwell and Windsor Place, with glass utility doors that open in front in season. A long L-shaped bar faces some tables and several longer communal tall tables.

Their motto, Seek the Good is further expressed in a monthly Saturday morning volunteering outing that invites the public to help out a local non-profit. If you miss that, you can still Drink for Good: a special night is set aside for a chose non-profit and while owners guest bartend, all tips go to the cause.

Free WiFi. Mug Club. Facebook.com/GoodCityBrewing and Twitter/Instagram @ GoodCityBrewing

Stumbling Distance: *Comet Café* (1947 N Farwell Ave, 414-273-7677, thecometcafe.com) is a neighborhood staple and city institution, serving comfort food, coffee, cocktails and craft beers. Veggie, vegan, GF grub as well. *Von Trier* (2235 N Farwell Ave, 414-272-1775, vontriers.com) is a very cool German-style bar with 32 draft beers and triple digit bottled varieties. Watch for the enormous *Good City Taproom* (with food menu) in the entertainment block on Juneau Ave across from the Milwaukee Bucks area downtown. Spring 2019!

GOOD CITY BREWING TAPROOM

333 W. Juneau Ave. • Milwaukee, WI 53203
goodcitybrewing.com
Opening: Early 2019   **Brewmaster:** Andy Jones
Number of Beers: up to 24 on tap

Staple Beers:
- » MOTTO (Mosaic pale ale)
- » PILS
- » REWARD (double IPA)
- » RISK (IPA)

Rotating Draft Beers:
- » SOUR BEERS
- » VARIOUS ONE-OFFS, SPECIAL BREWS

Tours? Yes, in planning.

Samples: Yes.

Best Time to Go: Open daily. Check website for specific times

Where can you buy it? Here on tap mostly, but their flagship beers are distributed in cans in and around Milwaukee, Madison, Fox River Valley and Door County.

Got food? Yes, a full kitchen serves the 1st floor and a second kitchen serves their event space upstairs.

Directions: From I-43 take Exit 73A for WI-145 East and head east on Fond Du Lac Ave/WI-145. Continue straight as it becomes McKinley Ave. Turn right on Old World 3rd St, drive one block and turn right on Juneau and Good City is on the left.

The Beer Buzz: This is *Good City Brewing's* second location, situated across the street from the Milwaukee Bucks' arena. In efforts to create an entertainment zone next to the arena, the Bucks organization reached out to Good City, offering a place to open a taproom downtown. At the time of writing it was still in planning but hopes are it is open by February 2019. Good City has their sour program here, and a pilot system which they can create small batches of specialty beers on. The flagships and other beers from their production brewery are also available.

Free WiFi. Facebook.com/GoodCityBrewing and Twitter/Instagram @ GoodCityBrewing

Stumbling Distance: Head up the hill into the old Pabst Brewery campus and you've got *Pabst Milwaukee* brewing in the old church, Milwaukee Brewing Co. in their *9th Street Brewery*, *Brewhouse Inn & Suites*, and *Best Place*, the gift shop/tour/event space inside the former hospitality center and offices. Around the corner heading south on Old World 3rd St is a collection of great spots including *Mader's, Milwaukee Brat House, Old German Beer Hall, Uber Tap Room, Wisconsin Cheese Mart, Usinger's Famous Sausage*. Welcome to Milwaukee!

LAKEFRONT BREWERY

1872 N. Commerce St. • Milwaukee, WI 53212 • 414-372-8800
lakefrontbrewery.com
Founded: 1987   **Brewmaster:** Marc "Luther" Paul
Annual Production: 44,000 bbls
Number of Beers: 10 year-round, 11 seasonals, and various limited releases

Staple Beers:

- » EAST SIDE DARK
- » EAZY TEAZY (green tea infused)
- » EXTENDED PLAY IPA
- » FIXED GEAR
- » FUEL CAFÉ COFFEE STOUT (organic)
- » IPA
- » LAKEFRONT PILS (formerly KILSCH

- PILSNER)
- » NEW GRIST GLUTEN-FREE PILSNER (organic)
- » NEW GRIST GINGER-STYLE GLUTEN-FREE ALE (organic)
- » RIVERWEST STEIN

Rotating Beers:

- » Bridge Burner Strong Ale
- » Cherry Lager, Spiced Winter Lager, Pumpkin Lager
- » Imperial Pumpkin
- » Maibock
- » Oktoberfest
- » Organica
- » *My Turn Series, Single Hop Series, Double IPA Series*, plus barrel-aged beers

Most Popular Brew: Riverwest Stein (in Milwaukee), IPA (out of state), New Grist (in Canada)

Brewmaster's Fave: Bridge Burner

Tours? Daily, but hours vary according to day and season. Check the website! You can (should) buy tickets in advance online. Seriously, this is one of the best tours in the Midwest—Bob Freimuth was awarded best brewery guide in Milwaukee, and *Maxim* and *Tripadvisor* rate the tour as tops. Bob drinks with the guests. OK, they *all* drink with the guests. I'm partial to Brother Jim's tours. Tour price includes a souvenir pint glass, four 6-oz pours. ALSO, after your tour receive a dated "Beer On Us" coupon, good for a free Lakefront beer at several places listed on the back before a certain hour that day. If tours sold out on Saturdays, you can still get a mini-tour with samples. **Homebrewers take note:** a 90-minute technical tour with pairings is on Sundays at 11AM for about $35. The brewery also runs Beer Academy Classes.

Samples? Before, during, and after the tour.

Best Time to Go: Fridays for a Fish Fry, but any old time is nice. There's a dock for boats (kayaks?) in the summer.

Where can you buy it? Bottles and draft throughout Wisconsin. Riverwest and Eazy Teazy come in cans.

Nationwide in 37 states, a bit in Canada, and even Japan if you know where to look. (I do!) On tap at Miller Park!

Got food? Yes, serving classic Wisconsin fare daily. On Friday evenings from 4–9PM enjoy a fish fry with live polka band!

Special Offer: A Lakefront Brewery bumper sticker.

Directions: From I-43 take Exit 73A for WI-145 East and head east on Fond Du Lac Ave/WI-145. Stay straight and Fond Du Lac becomes McKinley, the Knapp. At Water St turn left and continue to Pleasant St. Turn left, cross the bridge and turn right on Commerce St. The brewery is on the right on the river just before the Holton Street Bridge.

The Beer Buzz: Russ and Jim Klisch come from a long line of brewery history. Yes, their grandfather drove the street sweeper for Schlitz back in the 30s. This microbrewery, situated just under the Holton Street Viaduct, occupies the former coal-fire power plant that once gave the juice to Milwaukee's first light rail. Now the Klisch's make some juice of their own here in this historic neighborhood at the foot of Brewer's Hill. Lakefront was the first U.S. brewery brewing under its own label to be certified organic. Organic is a catchy title—and important quality—for modern times, but as Russ points out, old school brewing was organic already at a time when industrial farms and widespread chemical use didn't exist. New Grist has gained notoriety as a gluten-free beer (no wheat or barley) using sorghum and rice for grains, and the Fuel Café Stout uses Milwaukee's roasted Alterra coffee from the cool and quirky local coffeehouse from which the beer takes its name. Watch for the My Turn series, a different brew every time. Everyone in the brewery is part of your beer. These are made from start to finish by someone other than Luther. Dan the Tax/Compliance Manager made a Baltic Porter and won bronze in 2012 at the World Beer Cup.

For the total Wisconsin experience, don't miss the Lakefront Palm Garden's Friday Fish Fry complete with live polka band.

ATM onsite and a gift shop. Facebook.com/lakefront and /lakefrontbrewerybeerhall Twitter @Lakefront or @LFBbeerhall Instagram @LakefrontBrewery

Stumbling Distance: You can see the old breweries—Schlitz, Pabst and Blatz—from atop Brewer's Hill. *Eagle Park Brewery* is across the river, a six-minute walk. You can cross the river on the Holton St Marsupial Bridge—a walkway/bike path hung under the viaduct—and get to Brady Street where you will find a whole slew of great bars including *The Nomad Pub, The Hi Hat, The BBC, Hooligan's, The Palm and Roman Coin. Di Moda* (1758 N Water St, 414-331-0020, dimodapizza. com) is a wood-fired pizza joint with year-round outdoor seating. Weekend brunch is highly regarded. Check out *The Wicked Hop* (thewickedhop.com, 345 N Broadway, 414-223-0345) in the Historic Third Ward—they exclusively serve Lakefront's Poison Arrow IPA. Lakefront also brews Motor Oil for the Motor Bar & Restaurant at the *Harley Davidson Museum* (harley-davidson.com, 400 W Canal St).

PABST MANSION: LIFE AS A BEER BARON

Frederick Pabst brought us a Blue Ribbon beer back in 19th century. German immigrant Jacob Best, Sr. opened Empire Brewery in 1844 (four years before Wisconsin became a state) which his son Phillip took over and renamed Best & Co. and then Phillip Best & Co. and it became the largest brewery in the country. Pabst, a steamship captain, married Phillip's daughter Maria and invested in the brewery as well. Phillip died in 1869, and Pabst became president of the brewing company in 1872 before changing the name to his own in 1889. The blue ribbon was an award from competition but it wasn't until 1899 that the beer itself became known as Pabst Blue Ribbon Beer. Over a million barrels were being brewed before the turn of the century.

A beer baron of Pabst's caliber desired some serious digs, and this Flemish Renaissance Revival mansion is a real beauty. Completed in 1892, the mansion was wired for electricity and had a state-of-the-art heating system. The good captain filled it with great artwork and spared no expense on the interiors. Pabst died in 1904, however, and his wife two years later. From 1908 to 1975 the Archdiocese of Milwaukee occupied the home, but it was sold once again. This time someone had plans for something much more beautiful and magnificent, a true tribute to the times… er, a parking ramp? Seriously?

Fortunately for all of us, Milwaukee entrepreneur John Conlin stepped in and held the house until Wisconsin Heritages, Inc. could round up the dough to keep it from the wrecking ball. It has been no small expense to save this tremendous piece of Milwaukee's history, and restorations on the mansion continue. Much of it has been completed; however, this has been a painstaking

process especially as some of the skills that went into making it are no longer readily available.

A tour of this mansion is a must on any brew visit to Milwaukee, and you can either guide yourself or join a guided tour on the hour. Reservations are required for the latter. Behind the Scenes and Private Tours are also available for about double the normal price. No photos allowed.

Open Mon–Sat 10 AM–4 PM and Sun 12–4 PM. Closed Wednesdays mid-January through February, and Easter. Special hours and prices during the holiday season. Wheelchair accessible and parking. Admission is $12 for adults ($13 from mid-Nov to mid-Jan).

2000 West Wisconsin Avenue • Milwaukee, WI 53233

pabstmansion.com | 414-931-0808

HISTORICAL ATTRACTION: BEST PLACE IN MILWAUKEE!

It's not just bragging. "Best" is a big beer name in Milwaukee. Before Pabst Brewing became Pabst Brewing, it was actually the brewery of Jacob Best Sr. who founded it in 1844 (before Wisconsin became a state). Best's son Phillip and Phillip's son-in-law, the venerable Captain Frederick Pabst, made a huge success of it, and Pabst eventually took it over and gave the brewery his name. The brewery closed in 1996 but you can still find Pabst Blue Ribbon (PBR) in bars as far away as Nepal (seriously) and in 2017 Pabst came back and opened a microbrewery in the former church up the street from here. PBR is the beer of choice of hipsters everywhere. And you can have one at the end of this tour in the brewery's Blue Ribbon Hall. Be sure to get your picture taken with Captain Pabst in the courtyard. The tour takes you through the story of Pabst, starting in Blue Ribbon Hall, moving on to the restored Great Hall and the captain's office, and ending in the Sternewirt, the guest hall.

Several Wisconsin beers are on tap in the beer hall and guest hall. Tours cost about $10 and last an hour. You can book on the website, but walk-up tours are on Sunday, Monday, Wednesday & Thursday at 12, 1:30, 3 and 4:30 Friday & Saturday at 11, 12, 1 & 2. Private and group tours are available year round and can be scheduled most days. Be aware that weddings here are popular (over 100 per year!) and can occasionally affect the tour schedule.

Best Place's gift shop doesn't just sell t-shirt, caps, and other Best Place paraphernalia; it also has an assortment of rare and collectible Pabst items from the old brewery itself as well as a number of others. This is super for collectors of breweriana. Best Place at the Historic Pabst Brewery, the former Pabst Corporate Offices and Visitor's Center is a Certified Historic Structure on the National Register of Historic Places. And there is much more going on out here. Milwaukee Brewing Co. opened a second brewery in the old distribution center, Brewhouse Inn & Suites occupies the former brewhouse, and a Pabst brewery occupies the old church up the street.

Directions: To get there from I-43 (if heading north) take the exit for WI-145. Keep right at the fork following signs for WI-145/McKinley Ave and merge onto WI-145. At N 6th Street go right and take the first right onto W Juneau Ave. Turn slightly right onto Winnebago for a half a block. Turn left at N 8th Street. Take the first right onto W Juneau Ave. If you're coming from the north though, take exit 72E for Highland Ave/11th St. Turn left at W Highland Ave. Turn left on N 8th St and take the first left onto W Juneau Ave. Or just type the address into your GPS maybe. Whew.

Best Place at the Historic Pabst Brewery

Open daily from 11:30am (10:30am Fri-Sat) but closed Tuesdays

901 W. Juneau Avenue | Milwaukee, WI 53233

bestplacemilwaukee.com | 414-223-4709

Combine a tour here with a visit to the Pabst Mansion for a discounted price! Call 414-779-1663.

Miller Brewing Co. (MillerCoors)

4251 W State Street • Milwaukee, WI 53208 • 414-931-2337
millercoors.com or shopmillerbrewing.com
Founded: 1855
Annual Production: 7.4 million bbls here; 60.5 million worldwide

Staple Beers brewed here:

» Miller Genuine Draft
» Miller High Life
» Miller Lite
» Leinenkugel's Summer Shandy and seasonals

» Blue Moon Belgian White and seasonals

Most Popular Brew: Miller Lite

Tours? ? Free One-hour tours of the historic Miller Caves and plant operations. Open Mon–Sat Labor Day through Memorial Day. Open Mon-Sun Memorial Day through Labor Day. Visit themillerbrewerytour.com or call 414-931-BEER for daily updates. Visit Facebook.com/millerbrewerytour. Closed select holidays.

Samples? Three beer samples at the end of the tour.

Best Time to Go: Monday–Friday. Saturday can be busy and reservations are unavailable at this time.

Where can you buy it? Where *can't* you buy it? World famous!

Got food? Pretzels available with beer samples after your tour.

Special Offer: The girl in the Moon Gift Shop, located at 4251 W. State Street, will offer 10% off any one item of your choice. Offer excludes sale or clearance merchandise. Please mention promo code: Beer Guide.

Directions: From I-94 west take Hwy 41 north to the State Street/Vliet Street exit. Turn right (south) on 46th Street, then left (east) on State Street. Go a half block east

on State and the Visitor Center is on your right (south).

The Beer Buzz: Frederick J. Miller settled in Milwaukee in 1855 with a special brewer's yeast and an ambition to brew "confoundedly good beers." The story begins when Miller emigrated from Germany to Milwaukee and bought Plank Road Brewery (built by Charles Best). The beer was immediately popular, and he was soon selling well beyond Milwaukee. You can still see a brewhouse he built on State Street with "F. Miller" and "1886" visible at the top. The brewery was passed to his sons in 1888 and they built the Miller Inn, the Refrigeration building, and the Stables. The oldest part of the Milwaukee Brewery is the storage caves, built in the 1850s by the Best brothers and later expanded by Frederick Miller to keep beer cold through the sometimes-hot Wisconsin summers; they are still on the tour route today.

Beer drinkers had their first taste of High Life on December 30, 1903, and soon it picked up the moniker "Champagne of Bottled Beer." (Later shortened to Champagne of Beers after 1967.) The brewery survived Prohibition through real estate investments and by making near beer, soda, and malt syrup, and modernized as soon as Prohibition was repealed. After World War II, Frederick C. Miller, a grandson of the founder, worked to make it the fifth largest American brewery. Miller died after a plane crash in 1954 (see the Caves photo), and the presidency of the brewery left the Miller family for the first time. Philip Morris bought it in 1970. Miller Lite was introduced in 1975, starting a whole new trend toward light beers which—along with a series of popular "Great taste … less filling" celebrity ads—helped make Miller the second largest brewer in the United States. In 1988 Miller acquired Jacob Leinenkugel Brewing of Chippewa Falls, Wisconsin, and a fifth generation of Leinenkugels continues to run the brewery. In 2002, Miller Brewing was bought by South African Breweries and became part of SAB Miller, one of the largest brewers in the world. Today, as part of MillerCoors, a Molson Coors Company, Miller Brewing is one of Wisconsin's largest employers, with about 1,400 employees and a payroll of nearly $175 million. The company continues to utilize its heritage, as to this day, Miller beers are brewed with the same yeast strain Frederick carried with him from Germany.

Legend Has It: The iconic Miller High Life Girl in the Moon—one of the oldest advertising symbols in the U.S.—dates to 1907, when it was trademarked by Miller ad director A.C. Paul. The story is Paul was hunting alone in northern Wisconsin and became lost in the woods, spent the night there, and had a vision of a woman perched on the moon.

Despite many stories and myths, the model for the Miller Girl in the Moon is unknown. Stories claim that she was a granddaughter of Miller founder Frederick J. Miller, and different Miller family branches claim that their grandmother or great-grandmother was the model.

Facebook.com/millerbrewerytour

Stumbling Distance: Head over to *Miller Park* to watch the Milwaukee Brewers play some ball. During the holidays, take a drive down to the Plank Road Brewery to see the awesome light show set to music. You may have seen something similar in one of their commercials. For a killer bar burger, you can't miss *Sobelman's Pub & Grill* (milwaukeesbestburgers.com, 1900 W Saint Paul Ave, 414-931-1919).

MILLER PHOTOGRAPHS COURTESY OF PAUL BIALAS.

MILLER CAVES

Built by Charles Best, these caves are all that remains of the original Plank Road Brewery, which Miller founder Frederick J. Miller took over in 1855. The 44-inch thick walls are made of brick and limestone, and the caves made a great cool place for fermentation, aging, and storing beer. Ice blocks cut from frozen lakes and hauled by horses kept them cool in winter and sawdust and hay insulated them in summer. The caves went back 600 feet and could hold as many as 12,000 barrels. Brewery president Frederick C. Miller created a tour program in 1952 and made a caves museum. The gas lighting was replaced by electricity and the displays were added. The museum officially opened in October 1953, and Milwaukee's famous pianist Liberace was part of the dedication ceremony.

The photo, taken on December 17, 1954, is of one of the famous "Cave Dinners" and shows Frederick C. Miller having lunch with other members of the Wisconsin State Brewers Association. Later that same day Miller was fatally injured in a plane crash at Mitchell Field in Milwaukee. Also killed were his son Frederick C. Miller, Jr. and the two pilots, Joseph and Paul Laird. That was the last cave dinner until a fundraiser for the Museum of Beer and Brewing revived the tradition.

PHOTOGRAPH COURTESY OF MILLER BREWING

MILWAUKEE ALE HOUSE

233 N Water Street • Milwaukee 53202 • 414-276-2337
ale-house.com
Founded: 1997 **Brewmaster**: David Richard
Annual Production: 1,400 bbls
Number of Beers: 12 on tap, at least 3 rotating styles all the time

Staple Beers:

- » BOOYAH APRICOT SAISON
- » HOP FREAK DOUBLE IPA
- » HOP HAPPY IPA
- » LOUIE'S DEMISE AMBER ALE
- » MKE IPA
- » O-GII IMPERIAL WIT
- » OUTBOARD CREAM ALE

- » POLISH MOON MILK STOUT
- » PULL CHAIN PALE ALE (APA)
- » SHEEPSHEAD STOUT
- » SNAKE OIL STOUT (Russian Imperial Stout w/espresso on nitro)
- » BREWER'S DAY OFF SERIES

Rotating Beers: (see The Beer Buzz)

Most Popular Brew: Louie's Demise Ale

Brewmaster's Fave: Snake Oil

Tours? By chance or by appointment.

Samples? Yes, flights of four or six 5-oz samples.

Best Time to Go: Open daily at 11AM. Happy hour specials Mon-Fri (and another on Thu night from 9-close!), trivia night on Wednesday, Karaoke on Thursday, live music often on Fri-Sat at 9:30pm.

Where can you buy it? Crowlers and growlers at the bar plus six-packs in cans and bottles throughout Wisconsin, Chicago, and the Twin Cities. Plus various draft accounts. See Crate Club at their 2nd Street Brewery.

Got food? Yes, a handcrafted, fresh menu with suggested beer pairings. A classic Wisconsin Fish Fry is featured on Fridays.

Special Offer: $2 off your first MKE Brewing beer or sample flight during your signature visit.

The Beer Buzz: Welcome to the Historic Third Ward of downtown Milwaukee. Once a warehouse and manufacturing district, the Third Ward is now a thriving arts and entertainment neighborhood of renovated brick and timber buildings. This particular structure dates from the late 1880s when it was a saddlery; the old beer wagons used to come here to service horses and repair wagons. Jak Pak Co. bought the building in the 1940s, and it became the first manufacturer to mass-produce hula hoops. By the mid-70s, the building was empty, and so it sat until someone had an idea.

Jim McCabe, an electrical engineer by trade, saw the potential of the old district and felt the city needed a local brew and entertainment venue. The Milwaukee Ale House became one of the first to move into the neighborhood just as the idea of reviving it took off. The City's Riverwalk runs directly behind the brewpub, so there's outside seating and a few boat slips as well. Schooners actually used to dock here to get fitted for sails before sailing back into Lake Michigan. The beer names have good stories—ask your bartender. The beer here has been so successful that the same group of beer nuts running the show at this location opened a second, larger brewery over on

2nd Street: Milwaukee Brewing Co. and a third even larger brewery in the old Pabst distribution building (see separate listings). Live music is common, and the bar has a couple of pours coming from beer engines.

Not only is this Milwaukee Brewing Co.'s birthplace, but it is also the testing grounds for any new or experimental beers. Test batches, seasonals, and cask-conditioned brews come and go, and a number of guest taps are curated by the brewers as well. Brewer's Day Off Series features two unique draft-only beers each month.

Free Wifi. Facebook.com/milwalehouse and Twitter @ alehouse

Stumbling Distance: Six blocks from here on the shore of Lake Michigan Santiago Calatrava's architectural masterpiece, the *Quadracci Pavilion* at the *Milwaukee Art Museum* (mam.org, 414-224-3200). The museum has a sizeable collection including many works by Wisconsin-born Georgia O'Keeffe. Even if art doesn't do it for you, do not miss the Quadracci opening and closing its "sails" at 10, 12, and closing time. The world's largest music festival is the 11-day *Summerfest* also on the water's edge right next to the museum. The event features eleven stages with the best music in a variety of genres—just a 5-block walk from here. The pub sponsors several charitable events throughout the year including *Louie's Last Regatta* for Children's Hospital of Wisconsin and *Mid-Winter Brew Fest* for the MACC Fund usually in February. Check out *The Wicked Hop* (the-wickedhop.com, 345 N Broadway, 414-223-0345) for some fine beer selections and the *Milwaukee Public Market* (milwaukeepublicmarket.org, 400 N Water St) for an assortment of local vendors selling eats, deli items and cheese, candies, wines, beers, even fresh seafood.

MILWAUKEE BREWING COMPANY 2ND STREET BREWERY

613 South 2nd Street • Milwaukee, WI 53204 • 414-226-2337
mkebrewing.com
Founded: 2007   **Brewmaster**: Kurt Mayes
Annual Production: 15,000 bbls   **Number of Beers**: 12 on tap

Staple Beers:
  » HOP FREAK TEA-INFUSED DOUBLE IPA
  » HOP HAPPY IPA
  » LOUIE'S DEMISE AMBER ALE
  » MKE IPA
  » O-GII IMPERIAL WIT
  » OUTBOARD CREAM ALE

Rotating Beers:

Seasonal "Timed Release" series:
  » CITRUS HAPPY GRAPEFRUIT IPA
  » OKTOBERFEST
  » POLISH MOON MILK STOUT
  » WEEKEND @ LOUIE'S (with Rishi's Organic Blueberry Rooibus and Hibiscus teas)

Destination Local (750ml bottles):
- » GIN-BARREL-AGED O-GII
- » GRAND MADAME BARLEYWINE
- » LOUIE'S CHERRY BOUNCE
- » LOUIE'S RESURRECTION (4-pack bottles)
- » RECOMBOBULATION
- » WALK OFF TRIPEL

Most Popular Brew: : Louie's Demise Ale and MKE IPA

Brewmaster's Fave: O-Gii

Tours? Yes, $10 gets you the tour, a pint glass, a free beer token for elsewhere and beer samples. Tours are scheduled (see website) on Fridays and Saturdays plus there's a 5–7PM Open House on Saturdays with casual samplings. Check the website for schedule and make reservations, however, walk-ins are also welcome.

Samples? Yes, can't have a tour without samples.

Best Time to Go: Other than stopping by to buy beer to go, the public visits are limited to the tour times. For a taproom experience, check their second location at 1128 N. 9th St.

Where can you buy it? There's beer to go here Mon-Thu 4-6pm, Fri 3-8pm, and Sat 12—7pm. Distributed throughout Wisconsin, the Chicagoland area, the Twin Cities and Fargo. Crate Club: members come in once a month, fill a reusable $5 crate with 20 bottles of beer for about $15.

Got food? Nope.

Special Offer: A highly prized trinket when you get your book signed.

The Beer Buzz: Just a few blocks south of sister brewhouse Milwaukee Ale House, this brewing facility opened in 2007 to meet a higher demand for the three staple beers heading to market in cans and bottles. Equipment includes an in-house lab from Pabst, grain handling equipment from a caffeine plant in Milwaukee, and water tanks from Texas. Ain't it funny how beer just brings things together? Housed in what used to be a produce company, the facility offered the brewers an opportunity to bottle a boatload of beer and go far beyond Metro Milwaukee.

The beer names typically have some kind of story. For Booyah, you'd need to head to the Green Bay area where Walloon immigrant culture brought this throw-everything-in sort of soup. Polish Moon, however, is right down the block at the former Allen-Bradley building: a lighted, four-face clocktower that's bigger than Big Ben. Overlooking what was once the Polish neighborhood, the clock shone down on workers on their way to their jobs in the wee hours.

The brewers are concerned about being environmentally friendly. The cans are actually more efficient and less wasteful than glass bottles. In 2013, the brewery was accepted into the Wisconsin DNR's Green Tier Program because of their sustainable practices. By the way, the MKE you see on the packaging is the airport code for Milwaukee's airport, General Mitchell International Airport. In 2018 they opened a second, larger brewery on the old Pabst Brewery campus, and it includes a proper tasting room.

Facebook.com/milwaukeebrewing and Twitter @ MKEbrewco

Stumbling Distance: For an incredible locally-sourced dinner, make reservations for *Braise* (braiselocalfood.com, 1101 S. 2nd St, 414-212-8843) which practices Restaurant Supported Agriculture, and serves gourmet dishes from a menu that constantly changes based on what's available. Get fresh cheese curds across the street at *Clock Shadow Creamery* (clockshadowcreamery. com, 138 W Bruce, 414-273-9711) and fresh ice cream at *Purple Door* (purpledooricecream.com, 138 W Bruce, 414-231-3979) in the same room!

MILWAUKEE BREWING CO.
9TH STREET BREWERY

1128 N. 9th St. • Milwaukee, WI 53204 • 414-226-2337
mkebrewing.com
Founded: 2007   **Brewmaster:** Kurt Mayes
Annual Production: 20,000 barrels   **Number of Beers:** 20 on tap

Staple Beers:

- » HOP FREAK TEA-INFUSED DOUBLE IPA
- » HOP HAPPY IPA
- » LOUIE'S DEMISE AMBER ALE
- » MKE IPA
- » O-GII IMPERIAL WIT
- » OUTBOARD CREAM ALE

Rotating Beers:

Seasonal "Timed Release" series:

- » CITRUS HAPPY GRAPEFRUIT IPA
- » OKTOBERFEST
- » POLISH MOON MILK STOUT
- » WEEKEND @ LOUIE'S (With Rishi's Organic Blueberry Rooibus And Hibiscus Teas)

Destination Local (750ml bottles):

- » GIN-BARREL-AGED O-GII
- » GRAND MADAME BARLEYWINE
- » LOUIE'S CHERRY BOUNCE
- » LOUIE'S RESURRECTION (4-pack bottles)
- » RECOMBOBULATION
- » WALK OFF TRIPEL

Most Popular Brew: Louie's Demise Ale and MKE IPA

Brewmaster's Fave: O-Gii

Tours? Yes, $12 gets you the tour, a pint glass, a free beer token for elsewhere and beer samples. Tours are scheduled (see website) on Fridays, Saturdays and Sundays plus there's a 5–7PM Open House on Saturdays with casual samplings. Check the website for schedule and make reservations, however, walk-ins are also welcome.

Samples? Sample flights available.

Best Time to Go: Taproom is open daily. Check the website. Likely 4-10pm on weekdays and longer on weekends.

Where can you buy it? Here on tap and in Crowlers and growlers to go, as well as bottles and cans. Distributed throughout Wisconsin, the Chicagoland area, and the Twin Cities. See Crate Club at their 2nd Street Brewery.

Got food? Yes, by fall of 2018 expect a full menu for lunch and dinner.

Special Offer: A highly prized trinket when you get your book signed.

The Beer Buzz: Formerly known as Building 42 on the campus of Milwaukee's famous Pabst Brewing Co., this was Pabst's distribution center and the last building they built. Your PBR passed through here for 20 years before Pabst shut down its operations in 1996. It remained empty until Milwaukee Brewing Co. came in to create their second brewery, and what a brewery it is. There's a harmony to this story: Milwaukee Brewing Co. got some equipment out of the old Pabst brewery back when they first started.

MKE Brewing had been running out of space at their 2nd Street Brewery and they needed something expanded that could handle the industrial side of things while being accessible for the public. For tours and the public experience, 2nd Street was not ideal. Problem solved! This brewery has history, a classic look, and the brewery-on-the-hill vantage point with a view of Milwaukee's skyline. Being a couple blocks from the arena for the Milwaukee Bucks doesn't hurt either. The industrial side of the brewery is more purposely laid out and designed in Wisconsin. Along with the increased production space is a proper taproom up front. Says brewery founder Jim McCabe, "It's the reverse mullet: party in the front, business in the back." Expect unique offerings in the tasting room, and check out the rooftop experience with its own bar overlooking downtown.

Brewer Kurt has a culinary background and moved up through the ranks at the brewery before taking lead when longtime brewmaster Bert Morton moved on. All the Herb-In Legend beers have Milwaukee's own Rishi Tea worked into the recipes.

Free WIFI. Facebook.com/milwaukeebrewing and Twitter @ MKEbrewco

Stumbling Distance: Also within the former Pabst campus you can find *Brewhouse Inn & Suites*, *Pabst Milwaukee Brewery & Taproom*, *Best Place*, and *Jackson's Blue Ribbon Pub*. This is walkable from the arena for the Milwaukee Bucks, as well as *Mader's* and *Milwaukee Brats* on Old World 3rd Ave.

GATEWAY TO WISCONSIN I

From late April/early May through October, the *Lake Express* (lake-express.com, 866-914-1010), a comfortable, high-speed passenger and car ferry, makes two (three from July to September) round-trip crossings of Lake Michigan between Muskegon, Michigan and Milwaukee. The trip takes 2.5 hours and comes into Milwaukee just south of where the Summerfest grounds are. Take the I-794 overpass heading south and the first exit (Exit 3) takes you down to the port area.

PABST REPURPOSED:
BREWHOUSE INN & SUITES

What could be a better beer experience than to go to Milwaukee for all the brewery visits and then spend the night in an historic brewery? For years after 1996, the massive brick buildings of the old Pabst Brewery stood vacant, a sad reminder of the decline of Milwaukee's brewing in the late 20th century. But forget that—we are in the new Golden Age of Beer here in the Brew City with so many fine brewers and more breweries in planning. Development projects amid the old Pabst site have brought us the very cool Best Place in the former hospitality center and offices, another Milwaukee Brewing Co. brewery, and even an actual Pabst brewery. At the heart of the old brewery campus, where the big Pabst sign still crosses high over the street, you can stay the night in the former brew house.

The $19 million redevelopment of the late 1800s buildings brought Milwaukee a uniquely beerstoric hotel property. Called the **Brewhouse Inn & Suites**, the 90-room hotel offers studios as well as one- and two-bedroom accommodations for extended stays. You can still see the original copper brew kettles all polished up like they were still in operation. A large, stained-glass window featuring a picture of the legendary beer icon King Gambrinus has also been preserved. Winding staircases, a mezzanine-area skylight, and some beer themes in six of the suites create an atmosphere one wouldn't have imagined. Three of the suites have balcony views of downtown. An outdoor patio offers gas grills and terrace seating. Also within the complex is **Jackson's Blue Ribbon Pub** (1203 N 10th St, 414-276-7271, jacksonsbrp.com) which serves American bistro fare and keeps a long tap list of great beers.

The **Pabst Brewery** has been given a second life. Book a stay here for your next pils-grimage to Milwaukee!

1215 N. 10th Street, Milwaukee | 414-810-3350 | brewhousesuites.com

MobCraft Beer

505 South 5th Street • Milwaukee, WI 53204 • 414-488-2019
mobcraftbeer.com
Founded: 2013 (Taproom 2016) **Brewmaster**: Andrew Gierczak
Annual Production: 2,600 barrels **Number of Beers**: 24 on tap; 90+ beers per year

Staple Beers:
- » Ahopalypse Hazy IPA
- » Batshit Crazy (coffee brown ale)
- » Low Phunk Sour Ale
- » Oddball Kölsch
- » Vanilla Wafer Porter

Past Winner Beers:
- » Aunt Hazel (bourbon-barrel-aged hazelnut milk stout)
- » Dudeism White Russian Stout
- » Wisconsin Old Fashioned
- » Amber (brandy-barrel-aged with cherries and orange)

Monthly crowd-sourced batches, and a new sour beer every other month

Most Popular Brew: Batshit Crazy and the monthly crowd-sourced brew.

Samples: Yes, taste until you find what you like. Sample flights available.

Best Time to Go: Open Mon-Thu 3-10pm, Fri 3pm-12am, Sat 12-12, Sun 12-10pm.

Where can you buy it? Growlers, cans, bombers, kegs to go. Distribution throughout Wisconsin and select places in IL and MI, plus they can ship to 36 states.

Got food? Pizza and soft pretzels.

Tours? Yes, on Fridays around 5:45 and Saturdays at 3 and 4:30. $12 gets you a 45-min tour and two pints to drink. Book on website.

Special Offer: A free pint of MobCraft beer during your signature visit.

Directions: From I-43 heading south take Exit 311 for National Ave and go east (toward the lake) on Mineral St and turn left on 5th St. The brewery is on the left just before the big roundabout. From downtown, 6th St takes you south to this roundabout; get out of the circle at 5th St and the brewery is right there at the corner.

The Beer Buzz: What if you could suggest some crazy beer ideas and someone would make it? This is how MobCraft first got everyone's attention: Crowd-sourcing brews. Brewer Andrew studied fermentation science at University of Wisconsin-Madison, and has brewed for Leinie's and made ethanol at an ethanol plant. His twin brother Tony went to college with co-founders Henry Schwartz and Giotto Troia and taught them how to homebrew. Andrew came over to help often, and they decided to look at the possibilities of opening a brewpub. For a bunch of young guys, that idea looked awful expensive, so they went back to the drawing board. How could they get something going without a lot of investment, and how could they do something different? Crowd sourcing. Followers on the web and in social media would propose some often wacky beer ideas, the public would vote, and MobCraft would come up with a recipe for the winning suggestion. This caught on fast. They brewed under an alternating proprietorship arrangement with Madison's now defunct House of Brews and started filling draft accounts and selling bombers. They added cans in the summer of 2015, but their space at HOB was getting cramped. They settled on this Milwaukee location (leaving Madisonians heartbroken) and brought in a 30-barrel brewhouse from Quality Tank Solutions (manufactured in Marshfield, WI). A separate 2,000 sq ft room houses oak barrels and foeders for their sour beer production.

This old brick and cinder block building originally housed a metal manufacturing outfit but had functioned as an indoor parking lot for the last several years. The 2,000 sq ft taproom has a bar of reclaimed wood, a stage for live music, windows into the brewhouse and the sour room, and three garage doors that open to outside seating in seasonable weather. Parking is on the street.

Don't go thinking all their beers are suited to adventurous palates. Even the crazy concoctions may be more subtle than you expect, and that Oddball Kölsch is as approachable as anything. To the amusement of Packers fans, MobCraft collaborated with Green Bay's Badger State Brewing to produce Dubbel Czech, a double blonde that plays on Quarterback Aaron Rodgers' discount double-check State Farm insurance commercials.

Free WiFi. Facebook.com/MobCraftBeer and Twitter/Instagram @ MobCraftBeer

Stumbling Distance: *Conejito's Place* (539 W Virginia St, 414-278-9106, conejitos-place.com) is right behind them, serving cheap and popular Mexican fare on paper plates. *The Iron Horse Hotel* (500 W Florida St, 888-543-4766, theironhorsehotel.com) is an awesome biker-themed boutique hotel with a great patio bar, totally walkable. *Great Lakes Distillery* (616 W Virginia St, 414-431-8683, greatlakesdistillery.com) makes small-batch gin, whiskey, rum, vodka, absinthe and more, and does tours, tastings and events. Open daily. *Sprecher Brewing's* taproom is 2 blocks south on 5th and *Urban Harvest Brewing* is 5.

SPRECHER WALKER'S POINT TAPROOM

706 S. 5th St., Milwaukee, WI 53204
414-964-2739
sprecherbrewing.com
Open Thu-Fri 4-10pm, Sat 12-10pm, Sun 12-5pm

When Brenner's Brewing closed these doors, *Sprecher Brewing*, Milwaukee's first craft brewery, came in to fill the space. While their Glendale brewery is definitely worth a visit and features a tasting room and tour, this second taproom puts them right in the mix with the vibrant Third Ward/Walker's Point/Bay View craft beer scene. There are 24 on tap, and one can get flights, including Flight of the Griffin – all 24. Expect pub games, cribbage, and beers served in yards and half-yards. *Urban Harvest Brewing* is 3 blocks south on 5th, *MobCraft Beer* is 2 blocks north, and *Mikwaukee Brewing's 2nd Street Brewery* is 4 blocks east. You could call this area Little Mexico: within a 1–3 block radius lie some of the city's best Mexican eateries: *Conejito's Place, Botanas, La Casa de Alberto* and *Cielito Lindo.*

New Barons Brewing Cooperative

Milwaukee, WI
newbaronsbrewing.com
Head Brewer: John Degroote　　**Annual Production:** 90 barrels

Beers:

- » Beglian Tripel, IPAs, Porter, Wit
- » Styles are all over the style map

Brewmaster's Fave: Pecan Porter

Where can you buy it? Kegs only for now. Monthly happy hour (2nd Thursday of the month) at one of the places that carries their beer. Also at regional beer fests. Consistently on tap at *Enlightened Brewing*.

The Beer Buzz: Does it seem like everyone is opening a brewery these days? Now you can own one too. With a hat-tip to the Beer Barons of yesteryear, this brewery is set up as a co-op allowing members literally own a piece of the brewery. President and Head Brewer John Degroote homebrewed since before he could legally drink, and while he wanted to join the ranks of the exploding craft beer movement in Milwaukee, he wanted to be different. This is the first brewery cooperative in Wisconsin. At the time of writing, they had not yet found a brick-and-mortar location, so they've been brewing on the equipment over at Enlightened Brewing as an alternating proprietorship. As they build up production they look forward to having a permanent home.

Beer is a good catalyst for getting a conversation started and member/owners are finding their beer is an asset. NBBC brought a couple kegs to a chiropractor member's office to bring in people and help him get clients. Four members of a local band bought stock and the coop brought beer to a bar they were playing at to increase exposure to help the get future gigs. Learn more about membership at their website. Facebook.com/newbarons-brewing @Instagram @newbaronsbrewcoop

Pabst Milwaukee Brewery & Taproom

1037 W. Juneau Ave. • Milwaukee, WI 53233　•　414-908-0025
pabstmkebrewery.com
Opened: 2017　　**Head Brewer:** John Kimes
Annual Production: up to 4,000 barrels　　**Number of Beers:** 13 on tap

Staple Beers:

- » Pabst Andeker
- » Pabst Blue Ribbon

Rotating Beers:

- » Beach Snap Sour
- » Cream City Oatmeal Stout
- » Little Toe Wheat
- » Nor'eastie Boys IPA
- » Special Edition Eisbock
- » ...and many more

Most Popular Brew: Pabst Andeker

Tours? Yes, Sat-Sun from 1-3pm, $10 per person.

Samples: Yes, sample flights of four 4-oz pours for about $10, or eight for $16.

Best Time to Go: Open Thu-Fri 4-11pm, Sat 12-11pm, Sun 12-5pm. Watch for the Pabst Street Festival, an anniversary party every May.

Where can you buy it? Here on tap and in growlers to go.

Got food? Only during special events.

Special Offer: A free sample flight when you get your book signed.

Directions: From I-43 take Exit 73A and head east on WI-145/Fond Du Lac Ave. At the next intersection, turn right on 6th St. Drive 0.2 mile and turn right (west) on Highland Ave. Count three blocks on your right and turn right on 10th St. At the end of the block turn left and you can see the church on your left at the end of the block. Street parking with meters.

The Beer Buzz: In July of 2015 it was announced that Pabst, the legendary Milwaukee brewery that closed in 1996, was coming back to Milwaukee. While the brewery shut its doors, Pabst had continued as a corporation, buying up labels of beers—many of them old favorites such as Schlitz, etc.—and keeping them on the shelves in your local liquor store. All of this was done through contract brewing with other companies. As the corporate offices moved around a bit—Texas, Chicago, California—impassioned fans in Milwaukee wanted that beer back in Brew Town. (Oddly enough, the Miller Brewery here in Milwaukee was, in fact, brewing Pabst here and still is.)

Then the news broke. Pabst had purchased the 1873 First German Methodist Church that still stands within the former brewery complex. In fact, this is the second time Pabst has bought this property. In 1895 they acquired and repurposed it to serve as an employee restaurant and lounge (the Forst Keller), which became best known for its Friday fish fry. Naturally.

The abandoned brewhouse has already been repurposed as a hotel, Brewhouse Inn & Suites, and the hospitality center and corporate offices are now open to the public as Best Place, a gift shop, event hall, bar, and fascinating tour. While they don't brew the iconic Pabst Blue Ribbon (though it's served), the production here aims to be more modern and even experimental.

The first floor functions as a brewery and tasting room. Right through the center of the church beneath the high ceilings runs an open horseshoe bar and the windows spill their light on either side. Head up to the choir loft for a nice view of it. A beer garden behind the church features a wall with signatures of former brewery workers. Over 10 years ago, as the entire Brewery Complex stood vacant and decaying, no one could have imagined the impressive rebirth here plus the return of Pabst.

Free WiFi. Facebook.com/PabstBrewery and Twitter/Instagram @PabstBrewery

Stumbling Distance: You have *Brewhouse Inn & Suites* and *Jackson Blue Ribbon Pub* across the street, and *Best Place* and *Milwaukee Brewing Co.* one block over. Down the hill is the arena for the Milwaukee Bucks where you can also find *Good City Brewing's* 2nd taproom. It's not quite 10 blocks to two notable German-style restaurants: *Mader's* (414-271-3377, madersrestaurant.com) and *Milwaukee Brat House* (414-273-8709, milwaukeebrathouse.com) in the 1000 block of Old World 3rd St just north of Pere Marquette Park on this side of the river.

ROCK BOTTOM RESTAURANT & BREWERY

740 N Plankinton Avenue • Milwaukee, WI 53203 • 414-276-3030
rockbottom.com/milwaukee
Founded: March 1997   **Brewmaster**: David Bass
Annual Production: 1,100 bbls   **Number of Beers**: 11 on tap, 40 per year

Staple Beers:
- » HEARTLAND WHEAT (a rotating wheat line)
- » HOP BOMB IPA
- » MAD HATTER KÖLSCH

- » NAUGHTY SCOT SCOTCH ALE
- » RACCOON RED
- » SPECIALTY DARK (rotation, anything brown or darker)

Rotating Beers:
- » ALT
- » BALTIC PORTER

- » BELGIAN DUBBEL AND TRIPEL
- » BOCK
- » DARK LAGER
- » DUNKELWEIZEN
- » IMPERIAL STOUT
- » MAIBOCK
- » OCTOBERFEST
- » PALE ALES
- » PILSNER
- » PORTER
- » Cask-conditioned ales and many more

Most Popular Brew: Naughty Scot
Brewmaster's Fave: Pilsner

Tours? Yes, ask your server. Groups should make appointments. Saturdays are best, especially in summer.

Samples? Yes, six 4-oz beers for about $6.

Best Time to Go: Open from 11 AM. Summer opens the great patio on the river with an outdoor bar. Happy hour runs Mon–Fri 3–6.

Where can you buy it? Here on tap and to go in growlers.

Got food? Yes, a full pub menu and some menu items are paired with particular beers.

Special Offer: Free sampler when you get your book signed.

The Beer Buzz: Rock Bottom originated in Denver, Colorado, and after twenty-plus years now runs a total of 28 other locations including this one in an old bank building on the river in downtown Milwaukee. Despite being part of a larger chain, the brewpub does brew on premises and mills its own grain. The main floor offers a full menu restaurant and a bar that backs up against the brewhouse under glass. You can still see the old vault downstairs where there is another bar with a more casual bar atmosphere. The best place to hang—at least in nice weather—is outside on the terrace. An outside bar serves you as you watch the river go by.

Listen for the hostess answering the phone: "Hello, you've hit Rock Bottom." The name comes from the original brewpub which was on the ground floor of the Prudential building in Denver. Remember the insurance ads? "Get a piece of the rock." Am I dating myself here?

David started like many as a homebrewer. It's one thing to brew in your basement, but quite another to nail a gold medal at the Great American Beer Festival as he did with 106 Pilsner in 2009. Rock Bottom is located one block off of Plankington and Wells, and reachable by boat/kayak on the Milwaukee River. Become a Rock Rewards member (membership is free) and receive great deals, email news, and invitations to special events.

Stumbling Distance: This is close to the new arena of the Milwaukee Bucks. You are also a block or two from *Riverside* and *Pabst* theaters. This is a good place to head after a concert or performance. Actually, you're really not far from anything here. *Water Street Brewery* is close, as is *Milwaukee Ale House*. Or *Shops of Grand Avenue* mall (home to *Brew City MKE*, the Milwaukee Beer Museum & Bar). Or the *Milwaukee Public Museum* or *Milwaukee Performing Arts Center* or… well, you get the picture. In summer, check out the live music of *River Rhythms* on Wednesdays in Pierre Marquette Park three blocks north. *Cathedral Square Jazz in the Park* is every Thursday and three blocks east. Right across the river is a commemorative *statue of the Fonz* from the classic TV show Happy Days (set in Milwaukee). The famous *Safe House* (779 N Front St, 414-2712-007, safe-house.com), a spy-themed bar, is also near the Fonz. Be sure to find out the password.

BREW CITY MKE
MILWAUKEE BEER MUSEUM & BEER BAR

Drinking at the museum? A popular temporary exhibit at the Milwaukee County Historical Society became permanent when Brew City MKE opened in a former Appleby's at the entrance to the Shops of Grand Avenue. The little museum is also a bar–and doesn't that sound very Wisconsiny?—with 8 Wisconsin beers are on tap and a couple dozen in bottles and cans. The museum "seeks to promote a greater appreciation of Milwaukee County's Brewing History and Heritage, in the hope that a better understanding opens the issues and challenges Milwaukee County faces today."

Admission is about $10 ($7 for ages 13-20) which includes a beer or soda, and also gets you into the actual Milwaukee County Historical Society Museum (910 N Old World 3rd St, 414-273-8288, milwaukeehistory.net)

Brew City MKE, 275 W. Wisconsin Ave. (at 3rd St & Wisconsin Ave)
414-897-8765 • brewcitymilwaukee.com • (closed Mon-Tue)

10TH STREET BREWERY

1515 North 10th Street • Milwaukee, WI 53205
leinie.com
Founded: 1996   **Brewmaster:** Dan Pierson
Annual Production: 45,000+ barrels (estimate)   **Number of Beers:** varies

Tours? Not open to the public!

Special Offer: Not participating.

The Beer Buzz: Not everyone knows this brewery is even here. Passing by on Interstate 43 one could easily mistake the big Leinie's banner as a mere billboard. But this is the 10th Street Brewery, or the "Tiny Leinie" if you prefer. It's not actually so tiny when you consider the 45,000 barrels it produces each year. Built in 1986, G. Heileman's Brewing used it to produce Blatz beer, one of the old brands it had purchased. Leinenkugel's Chippewa Falls brewery needed help keeping up with demand, so in 1996 they purchased this place and started brewing here as well.

Third Space Brewing Co.

1505 W St Paul Ave • Milwaukee, WI 53233 • 414-909-2337
thirdspacebrewing.com
Opened: September 2016   **Head Brewer:** Kevin Wright
Annual Production: 2,000+ barrels   **Number of Beers:** 8-10 on tap

Staple Beers:
- » Acres Edge Toasted Oatmeal Stout
- » Happy Place Midwest Pale Ale
- » That's Gold Kölsch
- » Unite The Clans Scottish Ale
- » Upward Spiral IPA

Rotating Beers:
- » Java Blanca Coffee Cream Ale
- » (Coffee Beer series, kettle sours, and some barrel aging)

Most Popular Brew: Happy Place

Brewmaster's Fave: Happy Place

Tours? Yes, on Saturdays at 1 and 3pm. $10 for 30-minute tour includes two beers and a glass. Check website.

Samples: Yes, sample flights of four 5-oz pours for about $12.

Best Time to Go: Closed Mon-Tue. Open Wed-Thu 4-9pm, Fri 2-10pm, Sat 12-10pm, Sun 12-5pm. Brewmaster's Toast is 5:45 on Fridays.

Where can you buy it? Here on tap and in growlers and bombers to go. Distributed in six-pack 12oz. and four-pack 16oz. cans in Greater Milwaukee as well as draft accounts.

Got food? Clock Shadow cheese curds, Mike Pretzel Co. pretzels, and often food trucks. Screamin' Sicilian Pizza Co. and Urban Pie Co. Also food friendly.

Special Offer: Buy 1 house beer, get 1 free when you get your book signed.

Directions: From I-94 heading east, take Exit 310A, turn right on 13th St, and right again at the next corner, St. Paul Ave. Heading west on I-94 from the giant interchange, take Exit 309B, turn left on 25th, and again left on St. Paul Ave. and go 0.6 mile to find the brewery on your right.

The Beer Buzz: You can't miss the building with its charcoal gray paint and a long bright green arrow that leads you around back to the entrance. The former loading dock there is a beer garden in season. The building, with its terracotta bricks, dates back to the 1920s and was used as a factory by an 1880s-founded metal-stamping company. For 30 years, however, it stood abandoned until beer found it. Stand at the bar or take a tall table. Another low bar separates the taproom area from the brewhouse, making beer a spectator sport for patrons.

Brewer Kevin is a Milwaukee Eastsider who attended UC-Davis's brewing program in 2009. After graduation, he worked in Southern California for about six years before he decided to move home. There were opportunities but he wanted to get into a startup brewery. An old buddy Andy Gehl was looking for a career change and they partnered up to create this. The brewery has its own canning line. The coffee beers use brews from Stone Creek Coffee down the street. Games include giant Jenga and cornhole. Canine-friendly with dog bowls at the door.

Free WiFi. Facebook.com/thirdspacebrewing and Twitter @ThirdSpaceBrews Instagram @ThirdSpaceBrewing

Stumbling Distance: *Sobelman's* (1900 W St Paul Ave, 414-931-1919, sobelmanspubandgrill. com) is renowned for their burgers and Bloody Marys. *The Harley Davidson Museum* (400 W Canal St, 877-436-8738) is fantastic even if you are not into motorcycles. *Stone Creek Coffee's* Factory Café (422 N 5th St, 414-431-2157, stonecreekcoffee.com) is the flagship location and offers free factory tours on Sundays at noon.

URBAN HARVEST BREWING CO.

1024 South 5th Street • Milwaukee, WI 53204 • 414-249-4074
urbanharvestbrewing.com
Opening: November, 2015   **Brewmaster**: Steve Pribek
Annual Production: 100–150 barrels   **Number of Beers**: up to 16 taps

Staple Beers:
» 414 GOLDEN ALE
» ACH YA DER HEY-FE WEIZEN
» BLACK PUPPY PALE ALE
» CORKSCREW IPA
» ESPRESSO AMBER
» H.C. IPA
» LUPY (Cascade IPA)
» NOOKIE NOOKIE (pale ale)
» OLD TOWNE AMBER
» RADAR DE STOUT

Seasonal Beers:
» BLOOD ORANGE WHEAT
» CASCADE IPA
» DOUBLE CORKSCREW IPA
» IMPERIAL BLOOD ORANGE WHEAT
» LEMONY WICKET SUMMER WHEAT
» MAPLE BROWN
» OKTOBERFEST
» PRIBOCK
» WEIZENBOCK
» WHO THE HELLES ALICE?

Specialty Beers:
» BIG RING BOURBON RED
» BOURBON BROWN
» IMPERIAL CHOCOLATE WHISKEY
   STOUT
» WHISKEY PORTER
» WHISKEY SCOTCH

Most Popular Brew: Black Puppy Pale Ale

Brewmaster's Fave: Double Corkscrew and Bourbon Red

Tours? Yes, first-come, first-served at 3pm on 2nd and 4th Saturday of the month.

Samples: Yes, sample flights of four for about $8.

Best Time to Go: Open Wed–Thu 4–9PM, Fri–Sat 2–10PM. Happy hour Wed-Thu, 4-6PM. Live comedy Fri-Sat nights. This is a stop on Milwaukee Food Tours.

Where can you buy it? Here on tap and to go in growlers.

Got food? No, but free popcorn and food friendly, and area menus available. Occasionally food trucks park outside.

Special Offer: First pint of house beer free when you get your book signed.

Directions: From I-43 heading south take Exit 311 for National Ave and go east (toward the lake) on Mineral St and turn right on 5th St. The brewery is on the left. From downtown, 6th St takes you south to this roundabout; get out of the circle at 5th St and continue 5 blocks south and the brewery is on the left.

The Beer Buzz: You may have seen Brewer Steve around at some Milwaukee area beer festivals serving his beer. In 2013 he brewed under the name Mill Street Bierhaus, and it looked like at any moment they were going to open a brick and mortar place for us to visit. The plans were frustrated by a series of sites and leases falling through, sometimes even at the last minute, and to further complicate things, Mill Street Brewery in Toronto wasn't too keen on their name. That's all water under the Water Street Bridge. Steve is back with a new brewery name and sweet location near a couple other breweries. "Things happen for a reason," he says. He found a nondescript place in Walker's Point on Craigslist, got in touch with the landlord, signed a lease, and was suddenly moving forward again, no hassles.

Steve has been brewing since 1999. He always had the brewery idea in mind (no restaurant), but knowing the brewpub was the thing to do at the time, he didn't pursue it. Then Greg York of *Rustic Road Brewing* did a presentation for the Milwaukee Beer Barons and put the nano-brewery idea in his head. Greg told him if one doesn't do it now, it's not going to happen. The nano concept is to go in with lower costs and do unique batches in smaller amounts to get yourself up and running before taking on big ideas. Expect numerous creative and unique seasonals and limited releases.

This is a three-story Cream City brick building with wood floors, previously occupied by a theater company. It came with a 54-seat theater, which is back in use: every Friday and Saturday hosts live comedy by MojoDojoComedy.com. Get tickets, they sell out! The 4,000 sq ft on the first floor is divided between brewing space and a taproom with the original wood floors, a bar and tables. Some music plays in the background and a couple TVs may show sports. The room has a nice laid-back neighborhood pub feel to it. Rather than a typical tap system, they use 2 chest freezers (keezers) with a wood collar for the taps. Windows along the front let in a lot of light. His 2-barrel system is visible on the first floor, and the fermentation vessels and a walk-in cooler are in the basement. Sidewalk seating has space for about 30 and that area is dog friendly.

Free WiFi. Mug Club. Facebook/Urban-Harvest-Brewing-Company

Stumbling Distance: *Crazy Water* (839 S 2nd St, 414-645-2606, crazywaterrestaurant.com) is an upscale fusion sort of bistro set in an old tavern. *Botanas* (816 S 5th St, 414-672-3755, botanas-restaurant.com) serves casual Mexican fare. *Sprecher Brewing* is 3 blocks north and *MobCraft Beer* is 5. *Drink Wisconsinbly* (135 E National Ave, 414-930-0929, drinkwi.pub) was rated best new bar in 2017, best pub 2018, and as you expect serves Wisconsin only beers and food. Fish fry battered with Lakefront's Eastside Dark, curds, brandy Old Fashioneds served from a bubbler. You know the drill. Distinguished Riverwest coffee shop *Fuel Café* (630 S 5th St, 414-847-9580, fuelcafe.com) opened a Walker's Point location, same great coffee, cocktails, WI draft beers (super happy hour 3-6!) and delicious food menu with all-day breakfast.

VENNTURE BREW CO

5519 W. North Ave. • Milwaukee, WI 53208 • 414-856-4321
vennturebrewco.com
Opening: Summer 2018   **Brewers:** Simon McConico and Rob Gustafson
Annual Production: 500 barrels
Number of Beers: 10 on tap and 4 cold brew coffees on tap

Brewers' Fave Styles: Simon: farmhouse sours | Rob: clean, crisp pilsner or IPAs

Tours? Yes, by chance or by appointment.

Samples: Yes, sample flights of three 5-oz pours for about $5.

Best Time to Go: Open daily, all day with the coffee shop, 5am-10pm. Beer can be served from 9am.

Where can you buy it? Here on tap and in growlers to go.

Got food? Yes, pastries and such with the coffee, but the restaurant next door *Tusk* has pub grub and small plates to bring over to the taproom/café. Food friendly, bring your own.

Special Offer: A free house beer or flight when you get your book signed.

Directions: From I-41 take Exit 42A for North Ave and drive 3.6 miles east and the brewery is on the right. From I-94 take WI-175 north for 1.8 miles and turn left (west) on Lisbon Ave. Turn left again in 500 feet on North Ave, drive 0.5 mile and the brewery is on the left.

The Beer Buzz: Coffee + Beer + Community: much like in a Venn diagram, this is the shared data set, thus the double N in their name. The three founders, Jake Rohde, Simon McConico, and Rob Gustafson, used to take what they called "BeerVenture" trips together, which is where the idea for a brewery/coffee roaster/café/taproom started to take form. When looking for a space, the location – in their neighborhood – was the most important factor. They all live within about three minutes of the brewery/coffee roaster. Jake is the coffee guy, while Simon and Rob do the other sort of brewing.

Their 5-barrel system makes batches just big enough to linger a while, but small enough to keep a steady changing of the beer menu. Other than initial plans to have a light Saison table beer and Berliner Weisse, the beer will be "all over the place on style." Expect them to lean toward lighter, sessionable beers, but there are no limits, and a barrel-aged coffee stout is not out of the question. And coffee working its way into a number of brews is just a given.

Originally this was a hardware store and took some serious work to refashion into a nice community café and taproom. Two big garage doors open in season and allow a bit of sidewalk seating. The single TV comes on only for limited sporting games, otherwise this has the conviviality of a pub as well as the personal space of a coffee shop, and three owners – all with leanings toward creativity and arts – are active in all aspects within and around Vennture.

Free WiFi. Facebook.com/VenntureBrewCo and Twitter/Instagram @VenntureBrewCo

Stumbling Distance: *The Fermentorium Barrel House* (6933 W North Ave, thefermentorium.com) the second location for the Cedarburg brewery, is right down the street as is *Stock House Brewing*. *McBob's Pub & Grill* (4919 W North Ave, 414) 871-5050, mcbobs.com) is an old neighborhood standby with fried fish and the best corned beef in Milwaukee.

CREAM PUFFS AND CRAFT BEER

The **Wisconsin State Fair** is perhaps best known for its Original Cream Puff, which has been served there since 1924. The number eaten each year is creeping up on a half million. This being Wisconsin, of course, we have to bring beer into this mix. **The Micro** is an open-air pavilion serving an assortment of beers from Wisconsin breweries. Beer education events, pairings, some cheese and sausage plates, and even a keg killer t-shirt giveaway for those who finish a barrel are part of the fun. Flight School is a separate bar within, serving beer flights of select beers/styles. The Micro even has its own app and FB page (Facebook.com/themicrofair). The state fair runs 11 days in early August.

(640 S 84th St, West Allis, 800-884-FAIR, wistatefair.com)

WATER STREET BREWERY

1101 N Water Street • Milwaukee, WI 53202 • 414-272-1195
waterstreetbrewery.com
Founded: 1987   **Brewmaster**: George Bluvas III
Annual Production: 600 bbls   **Number of Beers**: 8–9 on tap

Staple Beers:

- » BAVARIAN WEISS
- » HONEY LAGER LIGHT
- » OLD WORLD OKTOBERFEST
- » PUNCH YOU IN THE EYE PA
- » RASPBERRY WEISS
- » VICTORY AMBER

Rotating Beers:

- » BELGIAN WIT
- » BLACK IPA
- » BLACK LAGER (Schwarzbier)
- » DOPPELBOCK
- » IMPERIAL STOUT
- » IRISH STOUT
- » RAUCHBIER
- » SAISON
- » … and many more!

Most Popular Brew: Honey Lager Light/ Oktoberfest

Brewmaster's Fave: Pale Ale

Tours? Yes, but by appointment.

Samples? Yes, $8 gets you seven to nine 4-oz beers.

Best Time to Go: This place hops a bit more at night and is popular with the twenty-something and university crowd. It gets busy around lunch and dinner.

Where can you buy it? Growlers and tap accounts at sister restaurants: Louise's, Trinity, Harp, Black Rose, Solo Pizza—all in Milwaukee, plus the Water Street locations in Delafield, Oak Creek and Grafton.

Got food? A full menu. Scotch eggs, beer-marinated Usinger bratwurst are total Wisconsin, the rest ranges from sandwiches to pasta, steak and seafood. A little upscale.

Special Offer: Not participating.

The Beer Buzz: Owner R.C. Schmidt wanted to start something that paid a little homage to his German heritage. That'd be beer, of course, and when he opened Water Street there weren't any brewpubs in the state and less than 50 in the whole country. The building itself dates to 1890 and is one of the first commercial structures in the city to have electricity. It had served various purposes over the years—grocery store, floral warehouse, apartments. When it was renovated, efforts were made to keep the stamped tin ceiling and Cream City brick. The project was one of the first in a renaissance of a rundown neighborhood that is now quite trendy. The dining is great and the ambience classy but social—don't expect pool tables or live music. The breweriana collection here is amazing and the Schlitz reverse-glass corner sign is a true rarity. The collection includes 6,000 cans on display, tap handles, coasters, serving trays and neon signs and can be seen at all three brewpub locations.

George started brewing when he was 17 years old because "the government wouldn't let me buy it, but I could get ingredients." A friend first showed him how to make wine out of apple juice. Later he worked under great brewmasters at Lakefront and Water Street (where he started working in 1999). Now he does quadruple duty here and at Water Street Lake Country out in Delafield as well as Water Street in Grafton and Oak Creek.

Stumbling Distance: *Uber Tap Room and Cheese Bar* (1048 N 3rd St, 414-272-3544, ubertaproom. com)—the name says it all—36 on tap and paired with that other thing Wisconsin is famous for. *Milwaukee Public Museum* (www.mpm.edu, 800 W Wells St, 414-278-2728) is in walking distance from here and home to an IMAX theatre. *The Pabst Theater* (www.pabsttheater.org, 144 E Wells St, 800-511-1552) is just a great place to see a concert and also just down the street. After a show, the crowd often comes to Water Street. The 1883 *Historic Turner Restaurant* (1034 N. 4th St, 414-276-4844) offers more great dining in a historical setting. This is one of the best Friday fish fries in town and Water Street beer is on tap. Looking for other brewpubs nearby? Check out the Milwaukee Trolley.

WATER STREET OAK CREEK BREWERY

140 West Town Square Way • Oak Creek, WI 53154 • 414-301-5290
waterstreetbrewery.com
Opened: 2015   **Brewmaster:** George Bluvas III
Annual Production: 800 bbls   **Number of Beers:** 8–9 on tap

Staple Beers:

- » BAVARIAN WEISS
- » HONEY LAGER LIGHT
- » OLD WORLD OKTOBERFEST

- » PUNCH YOU IN THE EYE PA
- » RASPBERRY WEISS
- » VICTORY AMBER

Rotating Beers:

- » BELGIAN WIT
- » BLACK IPA
- » BLACK LAGER (Schwarzbier)
- » DOPPELBOCK
- » IMPERIAL STOUT

- » IRISH STOUT
- » RAUCHBIER
- » SAISON
- » ... and many more!

Most Popular Brew: Honey Lager Light/Oktoberfest

Brewmaster's Fave: Pale Ale

Tours? Yes, but by appointment.

Samples? Yes, $8 gets you seven to nine 4-oz beers.

Best Time to Go: Open daily at 11AM and popular for weekend brunches 10AM to 3PM.

Where can you buy it? Growlers on site and tap accounts at sister restaurants: Louise's, Trinity, Harp, Black Rose, Solo Pizza—all in Milwaukee, and Water Street Lake Country in Delafield and Water Street's Grafton location.

Got food? A full menu. Scotch eggs, beer-marinated Usinger bratwurst are total Wisconsin, the rest ranges from sandwiches to pasta, steak and seafood.

Special Offer: Not participating.

Directions: From I-94 take Exit 322 and go east on WI 100/Ryan Rd for 1.6 miles. Turn left on Shepard Ave, go 0.6 mile, and turn left on Centennial Dr. After 0.2 mile, turn right on Village Green Ct and left on Town Square Ct.

The Beer Buzz: Water Street, one of the oldest brewpubs in Milwaukee expanded first to Delafield, then to Grafton with a third location, and now here in Oak Creek. The beers remain the same as Brewmaster George does quadruple duty here and in the other locations.

The restaurant, like the other Water Street locations, has breweriana on the walls, but a huge collection in this case. The main dining area offers booth and table seating. Like in Delafield and Grafton, there is a small brew system tucked inside. There is additional seating in another room.

BREWFINITY BREWING CO.

N58W39800 Industrial Road, Ste D • Oconomowoc, WI 53066 • 262-456-2843
brewfinitybrewing.com
Founded: March 2018   **Brewmaster:** Chad Ostram
Annual Production: 400 bbls   **Number of Beers:** 16 on tap, 20-24 throughout the year

Staple Beers:

- » 80S LOVE CHILD IPA
- » JORGE JALAPEÑO ALE
- » SKI SLIDE VIENNA LAGER
- » RUNTIME RED

Rotating Beers:

- » BOCK
- » OKTOBERFEST
- » WHEAT
- » … plus several one-offs

Most Popular Brew: Jorge Jalapeño Ale

Brewmaster's Fave: Vienna Lager

Tours? Yes, by chance or by appointment.

Samples: Yes, a flight of six 5-oz beers for about $14

Best Time to Go: Closed Monday and Tuesday. Open Wed–Thu 4–10pm, Fri 4–11pm, Sat 12–11pm, Sun 12–7pm.

Where can you buy it? Here on tap and in growlers and howlers to go, and a few draft accounts in the area.

Got food? Yes, bar pizzas, edamame, soft pretzels, and select sandwiches.

Special Offer: A free pint of house beer when you get your book signed.

Directions: Coming into Oconomowoc from the west side on Highway 16, take a right (south) on Division Street into an industrial park. Go left on Industrial Road and the brewery is on your left.

The Beer Buzz: Originally this was Sweet Mullets Brewery, the creation of longtime brewer Mark Duchow. Mark left in 2015 and a partnership made a go of it for a couple years. Chad Ostram and Eric Zunke are homebrewer friends who've been brewing for over 20 years. Chad always figured he'd start a brewery someday when he retired. When Sweet Mullets came up for sale as a turnkey operation, he couldn't pass up the opportunity. They took over in 2016 and rebranded in 2018 as Brewfinity Brewing Co. They changed it from a brewpub to a brewery, and while they kept the rustic industrial style taproom with a bar and tall tables, they beefed up the equipment on the brewing side to increase capacity.

Chad and Eric focus on more traditional styles. In the taproom watch for trivia on Wednesdays, and monthly bingo. Pass the time drinking beer and watching videos on CHIVE TV, playing board games and cribbage. Free WiFi. Facebook.com/Brewfinity

Stumbling Distance: Many people talk up what a great community theater Oconomowoc has. Check out *Theatre on Main's* website for a schedule of events and get some tickets for before/after a brewpub visit. (theatreonmain.org, 25 S Main St, 262-560-0564). *The Crafty Cow* (153 E Wisconsin Ave, 262-354-8070, craftycowwi.com) is a local craft beer bar with a pub menu. For a great selection of craft beers, stop in at *Sonoma Cellars* (1290 Summit Ave, 262-567-7500, sonomacellars.com). Their original location is in Delavan (1807 East Geneva St, Delavan, 262-740-2200), not far from *Geneva Lake Brewing*. The website offers a blog with reviews and new arrivals.

INVENTORS BREWPUB

435 N. Lake St. • Port Washington, WI 53074 • 262-284-4690
inventorsbrewpub.com
Opened: 2018   **Head Brewer:** Adam Draeger
Annual Production: 100 barrels   **Number of Beers:** 12 on tap

Staple Beers:

- » BEACH ROCK ESB
- » EDISON IPA
- » PW GOLDEN (P-DUB)
- » SEVEN HILLS PALE ALE
- » SS PORTER

Rotating Beers:

- » FLUGHOSEN BERLINER WEISSE (Flight Pants)
- » BIG REAPER WEE HEAVY
- » OZAUKEE WHEAT (HEFEWEIZEN)
- » WITBIER VON BRAUN

Most Popular Brew: PW Golden

Brewmaster's Fave: TLZ (Tender Loving Zombie, an Adam-Draeger-style beer)

Tours? Yes, Friday evenings or by chance or by appointment.

Samples: Yes, Wright Flights, four 4-oz pours in a biplane for about $8-10.

Best Time to Go: Open Wed-Sun 11am-close, Mon-Tue 4pm-close.

Where can you buy it? Here on tap, but no growlers.

Got food? Yes, counter service for tacos, fish fry, curds, poutine, burgers and even a kids' menu.

Special Offer: Not participating at this time.

Directions: From I-43 take Exit 100 and head south toward Port Washington on WI-32 for 1.4 miles. Turn left on Jackson St, go 0.2 mile, and turn left on Lake St. The brewery is 500 feet farther, on the left in an American Legion hall.

Cyclists: The Ozaukee Interurban Trail passes right behind the brewery.

The Beer Buzz: If this looks like an American Legion hall with a grain silo, it's because it is. Brewer/founder Adam rents the space from them, so veteran photos and memorabilia still adorn the place. For 70 years the Legion has owned this building, but the story of the site goes back to 1847 when Lakeside Brewery was founded here. The proximity to lake water and a hill behind it for lagering caves made the location ideal. In 1905, it became Port Washington Brewery, surviving until Prohibition (and perhaps a bit *during* Prohibition as they apparently got caught. After the Dark Age it reopened; from 1933 to 1947 it was Old Port Brewing, and this hall, the former bottle-washing house, is the last standing structure. They brewed Old Port Premo, "the beer that made Milwaukee furious." And in 2018, "everything old is new again."

Adam and his wife Erin met at UW-Platteville and studied to become engineering physicists (a fancy title that basically means they are qualified for both electrical and mechanical engineering work) and that background contributes to the Inventors name (and beer names often incorporate that theme). Jobs took them to Iowa for a few years and when the economy tanked, Erin suggested they move to Colorado. Adam studied at Siebel Institute and World Brewing Academy in Munich and then worked in Denver

at Yak and Yeti Brewpub and Colorado Plus Brewpub, during which time he won multiple awards for his beers. When they decided to move back to Wisconsin, they looked for a location on the water without a community brewery. Port Washington fit the bill. Adam sunk some money in another location but it wasn't working out. But the city really wanted him to stay – the mayor and city planner both called and told him the American Legion was seeking a tenant.

Friends call him Captn Adam; he built a 16-foot cedar wood boat and has the beard, so he just adopted the nickname. The bar top is covered with pennies and the wood is from his grandfather's turn-of-the-century barn. The bar area is separate from a larger central hall that has a 16-foot common table, barrel-stave chandeliers, and some lounge seating. For entertainment board games, cribbage, a jukebox, cornhole and a projection screen for televised games. Some seating outside in summer where you can enjoy the view: the brewery faces a park and Lake Michigan beyond. (There's a playground there if you have kids along.)

Free WiFi. ATM onsite. A rewards punch card for 20 styles; after completion you are etched on the wall of fame and invited to join Mug Club. Facebook.com/inventorsbrewpub and Twitter @Inventors_Brew Instagram @InventorsBrewpub

Stumbling Distance: With somewhere between 900-1000 different beers (18 taps), *Sir James Pub* (316 N Franklin St, 262-284-6856, sirjamespub.com) may be the most impressive beer bar in the state. Unpretentious and awesome. *Twisted Willow* (308 N Franklin St, 262-268-7600, twistedwillowrestaurant.com) downtown serves local-ingredient dishes in 19th century house. Venture up the hill to tour *Port Washington Lighthouse* (311 Johnson St, 262-284-7240, portwashingtonhistoricalsociety.org). Watch for the *Upper Lake Park Beer Garden* on the bluff across the street in summer and the band shell hosts concerts.

LITTLEPORT BREWING CO.

214 Third St. • Racine, WI 53403 • 262-633-8239
littleport-brewing.com
Opened: August 2018   **Head Brewer:** Mark Flynn
Annual Production: 500 barrels   **Number of Beers:** up to 24 on tap

Staple Beers:

- » CREAM CITY ALE
- » FLYNNIAN'S RAINBOW RED ALE
- » GRANDMA LATKA'S LAGER
- » GUTBUSTER STRONG SCOTCH ALE
- » I94 SPITFIRE IPA

- » KNAPP'S KÖLSCH
- » LITTLEPORT PALE ALE
- » TUG PALMER PORTER
- » WIGLEY WELSH PALE ALE

Rotating Beers:

- » BELGIAN CHOCOLATE STOUT
- » BELGIAN CHOCOLATE RASPBERRY STOUT
- » LEMONGRASS WIT

- » MILK STOUT
- » MY OWN LITTLE HELLES
- » NOROLA SAHTI

Brewmaster's Fave: Gutbuster

Tours? Yes, by chance or by appointment.

Samples: Yes, sample flights of 5 or 8 available.

Best Time to Go: Open Mon-Thu 11am-8pm, 11am-10pm Fri-Sat, Sun 11am-5pm.

Where can you buy it? Here on tap and in growlers to go, and local draft accounts and cans in some stores.

Got food? No, but food friendly.

Special Offer: A free three-sample flight when you get your book signed.

Directions: From I-94 take Exit 329 and follow County Rd K 5.2 miles to a traffic circle, and bypass it in the right lane to stay on Northwestern Ave, which becomes State St, for 4.7 miles. Cross the Root River and turn right on Wisconsin and the brewery is there on your left.

The Beer Buzz: Owners Mark and Christine Flynn had long planned to open a brewery in Racine. In 1998, they bought the 5-story grain mill across the street, which has been in business over 100 years. Brewers used to buy grain there and malt it themselves. In the same building they opened Hop To It, a homebrewing supply store, and started the local club Belle City Brewers & Vintners. Mark had many years of homebrewing and awards behind him when the couple decided to open the brewery in the old brick building across the street. Renovations kept the old beams but added a U-shaped bar and a 10-barrel brewhouse out in the open behind a rail, and reinforced the former hayloft as a second floor. No music or very low music – the aim here is you can have a conversation. The TV is for Packers games only.

Brewing and science geeks take note: this may be the first *cavitation* brewing system used in the US for the full brewing process (not just hops additions). The Italian-made brew kettle uses pressure changes to create and then collapse tiny bubbles in the wort. The process does not require milling the grain, sparging or even boiling, and the energy used is greatly decreased. Brewer Mark expects that it will reduce each batch's ingredients by a third, and brew time by half. The rest of the equipment was built by QTS in Wisconsin. In addition to the brews here on tap, he makes exclusive beers for local establishments.

The brewery name is doubly significant. Back when Racine was first put on the map, intentions were to make this a major port on a Great Lake. They could have used some fire alarms, however: several devastating fires set them back and in one case only a single building – the D.P. Wigley building across the street – was left standing, thanks perhaps to a metal roof. In the end the big port turned out to be a little one. Christine's father Melvin was born in Littleport, Iowa. Whereas the little port on Lake Michigan had trouble with fire, the Iowa town had water issues, as in too much of it. Frequent flooding was so bad that after a May 1999 flood nearly took it off the map, the government said no more aid and folks packed up and moved.

Free WiFi. Mug Club. Facebook.com/LittleportBrew and Twitter @ Instagram @

Stumbling Distance: Once a tied house for Pabst, *Ivanhoe's* (231 Main St, 262-637-4730, theivanhoepub.com) is an Irish tavern with pub food. *Pepi's Pub & Grill* (618 6th St, 262-633-6111, pepispubngrill.com) is part sports bar and has a great craft beer list. *ReefPoint Marina Brew House* (2 Christopher Columbus Causeway, 262-898-7333, reefpointbrewhouse.com) for good food, fish fry and a lake view. *Joey's West* (9825 Kraut Rd, Franksville, 262-456-0105) has an acclaimed Friday fish fry so you might have a long wait. *Olde Madrid* (418 6th St, 262-619-0940, oldemadrid.com) serves great tapas, paella, sangria and all things Spanish.

RACINE BREWING CO.

303 Main St. • Racine, WI 53403 • 262-631-0670
racinebrewingcompany.com
Opened: March 3, 2018   **Head Brewer:** Andy Molina
Annual Production: 200 barrel   **Number of Beers:** 6 on tap, plus sodas

Beers:

- » BARBIE ANN'S BLONDE ALE
- » ENCHANTED FOREST IPA
- » HULA CHASER COCONUT PORTER
- » LAKEHOUSE CREAM ALE
- » MOLLY MALONE IRISH RED ALE
- » VILLAGE PILLAGE STOUT
- » ZIP SLED CREAM ALE
- » (always rotating and bringing back whatever people demand)

Most Popular Brew: Hula Chaser Coconut Porter

Brewmaster's Fave: Village Pillage Stout

Tours? Yes, 2nd and 4th Saturday of the month.

Samples: Yes, sample flights of four or six 5-oz pours for about $6 and $9. Plus soda/beer flight combo options.

Best Time to Go: Open Wed-Thu 3-9pm, Fri 3-11p, Sat 12-11pm, Sun 12-6pm. Closed Mon-Tue.

Where can you buy it? Here on tap and in growlers to go.

Got food? DeRango's Pizzas (local), hot pretzels, chips, beer floats, house draft sodas Spruce Beer, Root Beer, Raspberry, Orange, Lemon-Lime. Also food friendly, bring your own or order in.

Special Offer: Buy your first pint of house beer, get the second one free when you get your book signed.

Directions: Take WI-32 right through Racine where it becomes Main St. The brewery is at the corner of Main and 3rd St on the east side of the street.

The Beer Buzz: Andy and Angie Molina were born and raised here in Racine (but got married by Elvis in Vegas) and both homebrewed. Their first brewery tour together was at Tyranena Brewing when they thought, 'Yes, this is awesome and we want to do it.' They entered Belle City Brew Fest (brewfestracine.com): Angie's IPA took 2nd place while

Andy's ran out fast. Angie won a private tour and night's stay from Wisconsin Brewing Co., but the real winner was Racine which eventually ended up with a new brewery. Andy had 17 years in at InSinkErator, and Angie had 20 years of pre-school experience. This was something totally new and they still had kids at home. Andy, a machine operator, a set-up kind of guy, and Angie, with admin background and good with 'bossing,' made a perfect team. As she put it to him: "Why not do what you love?" (His reply: "Cuz fishing doesn't pay?")

This building previously held two stores, one side candles and scented oils, and the other an old-time photography studio with costumes and backdrops. They opened the space up and that small studio became an indoor beer garden. While digging drains Andy pulled up Cream City brick from Racine's first courthouse, which had been knocked down and buried in concrete in the basement.

Andy saw an ad for a 4-bbl fermenter and went to buy it, but the seller also had a six-unit half-barrel brew-on-premise system. All six are linked together and he sends his wort into them and puts additions in each. Barbie Ann is named for Angie's mother, and their most popular beer is made with freshly toasted organic coconut. The taproom has a short bar and some cafeteria tables, and there are a couple TVs, board games, cribbage, plus occasional live music, comedy shows, karaoke, or game nights.

Free WiFi. On Facebook and Twitter @racinebrewingco

Stumbling Distance: Once a larger franchise, *Kewpee Sandwich Shop* (520 Wisconsin Ave, 262-634-9601) has old-school fresh fast-food hamburgers and fantastic malts/shakes. Sit at the diner counter or take it to the brewery. *Salute Italian Restaurant* (314 Main St, 262-633-9117) serves pizza and pasta for reasonable prices. You can't leave Racine without a kringle, and one of the best is *O & H Danish Bakery* (5910 Washington Ave, 800-709-4009, ohdanishbakery.com). Architecture fans: the *Frank Lloyd Wright Trail* begins here with the S.C. Johnson Buildings and Wingspread. Follow the highway signs from here through Milwaukee, Madison and on to Taliesin near Spring Green. *North Beach* has been rated #1 in the state and they do serve beer there.

St. Francis Brewery & Restaurant

3825 South Kinnickinnic Ave • St Francis, WI 53235 • 414-744-4448
stfrancisbrewery.com
Founded: 2009   **Brewmaster**: Matt Hoffman
Annual Production: 450 bbls   **Number of Beers**:15 on tap

Staple Beers:

- » Envy – IPA
- » Greed – Session IPA
- » Lust – Weissbier
- » Sloth – Brown Ale
- » Wrath – Amber Ale

- » Kitzinger Kölsch
- » (also hand-crafted sodas including 49 Maples Root Beer, Cherry, Orange Cream, Vanilla Caramel and Cherry Cola)

Rotating Beers:

- » Gluttony – Rotating Seasonal
- » Pride – Rotating Seasonal

- » Monthly cask-conditioned ales

Tours? By appointment, $5 includes two samples.

Samples? Yes, a sample platter of 6 beers goes for $8.

Best Time to Go: Open Mon–Thu 11AM–10PM, Fri–Sat 11AM–11PM, Sun 10AM–9PM.

Where can you buy it? On tap here and in growlers to go. St. Francis in partnership with Miwaukee County Parks operates a Craft Beer Garden (Wisconsin beers only) in summers at Humboldt Park.

Got food? Yes, a full pub menu with sandwiches, soups, and salads. Fridays host fish fries and all-u-can-eat Sunday brunch. Beer is worked into a couple of dishes including the ale-braised beef, stout BBQ sauce on some ribs, and the classic beer cheese soup.

Special Offer: $2 off your first pint of house beer when you get your book signed.

Directions: Take I-794 to Howard Ave and go east toward the lake just a short distance to Kinnickinnic Ave and you can see the pub on your left.

The Beer Buzz: You can't miss this place at the corner of a busy intersection: a grain silo stands in the middle of its outdoor seating area. The 7200 sq-foot-building has a long bar, plenty of dining (and banquet) space and that breezy terrace in the sun. Parking is off street and easy. Regulars can join a mug club for discounts and special offers. St. Francis is a nice little community just south of Milwaukee and this is its first brewery.

The brewery updated their beer menu to the Seven Deadly Sins theme in 2013. Brewer Matt joined the brewery in 2017 and has brewed with Avery Brewing in Colorado and 3 Sheeps Brewing and Lakefront Brewery in Wisconsin. In partnership with Milwaukee County Parks, the brewery operates a cash-only summer beer garden in Humboldt Park (ATM onsite).

Facebook.com/SaintFrancisBrewery Twitter/Instagram @StFrancisBrew

Stumbling Distance: Just north of here on Kinnickinnic (or K K as locals call it) are two of the best beer bars in the Milwaukee area: *Roman's Pub* (romanspub.com, 3475 S Kinnickinnic Ave, Milwaukee, 414-481-3396) and *Sugar Maple* (mysugarmaple.com, 441 E Lincoln Ave, Milwaukee, 414-481-2393).

RAISED GRAIN BREWING CO.

(old) 2244 W. Bluemound Rd. Suite E
(new) 1725 Dolphin Dr. Suite B • Waukesha, WI 53186
262-505-5942
raisedgrainbrewing.com

Opened: September 2015   **Head Brewers:** Dr. Scott Kelley and Dr. Jimmy Gosset
Annual Production: 1,200 barrels   **Number of Beers:** 13 on tap

Staple Beers:
- » BLACK WALNUT IMPERIAL STOUT
- » GUITAR CITY GOLD LAGER
- » NAKED THREESOME IPA
- » PARADOCS RED IIPA

Most Popular Brew: Naked Threesome IPA

Brewmaster's Fave: Paradocs & Black Walnut

Tours? Yes, one-hour tours on Sat 3 & 4pm for about $10 includes samples, a beer and a glass. Sign up online.

Samples: Yes, flights of four 5-oz pours for about $10 with pretzel bites.

Best Time to Go: Open Tue 4-9pm, Wed-Thu 4-10pm, Fri 3pm-12am, Sat 12pm-12am, Sun 11:30am-6:30pm. Watch for Beer Yoga.

Where can you buy it? Here on tap and in growlers, howlers, and bombers to go. Also in cans and on draft in many places throughout Milwaukee and Waukesha Counties. Watch for their pop-up beer garden in summer, and they may be on tap at Miller Park.

Got food? Yes, a full kitchen with in-house smoked meats, brick oven pizzas and BBQ, sharable plates and appetizers. (Food truck at the old location.)

Special Offer: Not participating at this time.

The Beer Buzz: The story of this brewery lies in that beer name: Paradocs. Two home-brewers, who happened to be doctors, brewed together for 8 years before finding two more business partners and getting serious about their (brewing) operations. Within a year of opening, they got Gold at Great American Beer Fest for Paradocs. In 2018 they moved up from their 7-barrel system to a 20-barrel in an industrial space at 1725 Dolphin Dr. five times as large as their original digs at 2244 W. Bluemound Rd. Suite E. The production brewery is already brewing but the taproom remains at the original location **until late 2018/early 2019. Check the website to confirm!**

The taproom features board games, cribbage, giant Jenga, cornhole and some TVs for games, especially the Badgers (all partners are UW grads). Watch for their Naked Hop Series beers. In summer, drink at one of their Pop-Up Beer Gardens: on Thursday, Friday and Saturday afternoon/evenings Raised Grain sets up in varying parks throughout Waukesha and Washington Counties, serving 5 beers for your picnic. (Waukesha parks have daily entry fees but they may give you a beer token for your trouble.) Follow the location on their website or Facebook.

Free WiFi. Brewmaster's Circle (like Mug Club). Facebook.com/raisedgrainbrewing and Twitter @raisedgrain Instagram @raisedgrainbrewingco

Stumbling Distance: Waukesha was the home of guitar legend **Les Paul** and the *Waukesha County Museum* has an exhibit dedicated to him (101 W Main St, 262-521-2859, waukeshacountymuseum.org). *Jimmy's Grotto* (314 E Main St, 262-542-1500, jimmysgrotto.com) serves pizza and more but is known for their "deep-fried pizza," what they call Ponza Rotta.

BIG HEAD BREWING CO.

6204 West State Street • Wauwatosa, WI 53213 • 414-257-9782
bigheadbrewingco.com
Opened: September 2013   **Head Brewer**: Jason Raines
Annual Production: 300 barrels   **Number of Beers**: 7 on tap

Staple Beers:

- » BLONDE
- » FIREFLY IPA
- » SMaSH (single malt, single hop)

Rotating Beers:

- » BELGIAN DARK
- » DORTMUNDER
- » HEFE
- » IRISH STOUT
- » OKTOBERFEST
- » RASPBERRY CREAM ALE
- » ... and other specialty, experimental and seasonal brews

Most Popular Brew:IPA

Tours? Yes, by chance or by appointment.

Samples: Yes, flights of seven 4-oz pours for about $10.

Best Time to Go: Open Wed–Fri 4–10PM, Sat 1–11PM. Happy hour runs 4–6PM Wed–Fri. Closed on Sun–Tue.

Where can you buy it? Here on tap and in growlers to go.

Got food? Free popcorn. Snacks and jerky, frozen pizzas. Food friendly, so carry in what you want.

Special Offer: $1 off your first Big Head beer when you get your book signed.

Directions: From I-94, take Exit 307A toward 68th/70th St. Turn north on 68th St and go 1.1 miles. Turn right on State St and go 0.4 mile. Turn left on 62nd St and the brewery is in the brick building on your left, despite what the street address might suggest about State St.

The Beer Buzz: Andrew Dillard, whose self-proclaimed oversized noggin this brewery was named for, founded this place with homebrewing partners Pat Modl and Pat Fisher in 2013 in hopes of making diabetic-friendly beer. However, Andrew's day job transferred him, and that never happened, and Pat Fisher owns it now. Brewer Jason has a Masters in Food Science with an emphasis on Fermentation.

Wauwatosa's first brewery, Big Head is located in a 5,000 sq ft cinder block construction warehouse. Inside the front door is a taproom with a small bar—actually a small counter hanging from chains. A chalkboard on the wall lists the brews on tap. A couple coolers bear pictures of The Fonz and Richie from *Happy Days* on the doors: Real Cool and Cool. Mismatched tables and chairs are arranged about the room, and the tap room spreads through a garage door into the next room where you can find the brewhouse and the restrooms. For your drinking entertainment, they have shuffleboard, darts, pinball, cornhole, and even beer pong. There's an old piano, and they host live music most Wednesdays and Fridays.

Free WiFi. Growler Club. Find them on Facebook and Twitter @ bigheadbrewery

Stumbling Distance: Go west on State Street into the heart of Wauwatosa ('Tosa, as the locals say) and you'll pass *Leff's Lucky Town*, (7208 W State St, 414-258-9886) for burgers, beer and sports TV; *Café Hollander* (7677 W State St, 414-475-6771) for Euro gastropub fare, a big beer list heavy on Belgian imports; *Café Bavaria* (7700 Harwood Ave, 414-271-7700) for German cuisine and beer, and several other eateries in between. Best liquor store in town is *The Malt Shoppe* (813 N. Mayfair Rd, 414-585-0321, maltshoppetosa.com) with Certified Cicerone Beer Servers, a huge selection of beers, and 30 taps for growler fills.

THE FERMENTORIUM BARREL HOUSE

6933 W. North Ave. • Wauwatosa, WI 53213
thefermentorium.com
Opened: 2018   **Head Brewer:** Kristopher Volkman
Number of Beers: 24 on tap

Beers:
- »   Assorted Sour Styles
- »   ...Plus beers from their Cedarburg brewery

Tours? No.

Samples: Yes, sample flights of four 5-oz pours for about $6.

Best Time to Go: Open Wed-Thu 4-11pm, Fri-Sat 11am-11pm, Sun 11am-pm. Check website to be sure.

Where can you buy it? Here on tap and in growlers to go. Statewide distribution of Cedarburg beers.

Got food? No, but food friendly.

Special Offer: Buy your first house beer, get one free when you get your book signed.

Directions: I-41 (Exit 42A) to the west and I-43 (Exit 73B) to the east both intersect North Ave. While others may prefer taking WI-175 north from I-94 (Exit 308C), going left (west) on Lloyd St, and turning right (north) on 70th St to North Ave. where the brewery is on the right hand corner.

The Beer Buzz: The Fermentorium opened in 2016 in Cedarburg and quickly made a name for itself. Early in 2018 they announced they'd open a taproom and barrel house in Wauwatosa. Now part of a growing beer corridor here where east Wauwatosa ('Tosa) meets Milwaukee, the barrel house focuses on their sour beer program. Other beers from their production brewery, of course, are on tap, but keeping sour production separate from "normal" beers is a good idea to avoid contamination. They have two 30-bbl foeders and a stock of barrels in a 3,000-square-foot facility, The tasting room features a long bar and mixed seating.

Free WiFi. Facebook.com/TheFermentorium and Twitter/Instagram @The Fermentorium

Stumbling Distance: *Cranky's* (6901 W North Ave, 414-258-5282, crankyals.com) is breakfast and donuts or pizza and fish fry, depending on what side of noon you go there. *Stock House Brewing* is two blocks west of here, and Milwaukee's *Vennture Brew Co* is a mile to the east. Head to Cedarburg (Zone 2) to see the original Fermentorium!

A GALLERY OF GROWLERS

Ray's Growler Gallery & Wine Bar (8930 W North Ave, Milwaukee, 414-258-9521, raysgrowlergallery.com) is part of Ray's Liquor, an excellent place to find your favorite craft beers and more. The store is open all week, but the tasting room upstairs opens Wed–Sun and offers tap takeovers, educational events, and, of course, growler fills during its more limited hours. "Every single beer that we tap into at Ray's Growler Gallery will either be a beer made exclusively for the Gallery, a rare brewery-only release, or a special selection that will not be available anywhere in bottle." Convinced yet? They also serve by the glass.

Stock House Brewing Co.

7208 W. North Ave. • Wauwatosa, WI 53213
mark@stockhousebrewing.com
stockhousebrewing.com

Opened: Memorial Day, 2018   **Head Brewer:** Mark Henry Mahoney
Annual Production: 250-300 barrels   **Number of Beers:** 6-8 on tap

Beers:

» Always changing!

Brewmaster's Fave: A big bold stout

Tours? More like beer education classes.

Samples: Yes, sample flights available.

Best Time to Go: Open Thu-Sun, check online for hours.

Where can you buy it? Here on tap and in Crowlers and growlers to go, plus some draft accounts in the North Ave neighborhood.

Got food? No, but food friendly. Order from nearby restaurants.

Special Offer: Buy your first house beer get the second one free when you get your book signed.

Directions: I-41 (Exit 42A) to the west and I-43 (Exit 73B) to the east both intersect North Ave. While others may prefer taking WI-175 north from I-94 (Exit 308C), going left (west) on Lloyd St, and turning right (north) on 72nd St to North Ave. where the brewery is on the north side of the street.

The Beer Buzz: Brewers used to lager beers in stock houses and from that practice this neighborhood brewery takes its name. Co-founder and brewer Mark Mahoney works with a 1.5-barrel system, so batches come and go quickly, and the philosophy here is

"Never make the same beer twice." Expect something like an amber or cream ale and a Guinness-like stout to often be among the offerings, Mark's homage to classic styles, but then quite a bit of room for play.

Brewer Mark has lived in this neighborhood since 2006 and considers it the hottest spot in Milwaukee, with a many a new restaurant popping up and very supportive residents. When he saw the For Rent sign in the window of this 1908 building in the heart of 'Tosa (Wauwatosa), he was thrilled. He got his first homebrew kit in 2006 and not long after that he found himself working for Goose Island (pre-merger), followed by some time brewing for Tyranena Brewing and Furthermore Beer (now part of the Sand Creek lineup). Mark met business partner Paul Hepp through Paul's business *Fun Beer Tours Milwaukee* (see "Beer, Boats, Buses and Bikes"). Also part of the team are Chris Berryman, who handles marketing, and Shane Grulke, who grows nearly all of their hops in three locations, including one south of the old Pabst Farms in Oconomowoc.

The taproom has a bar with about a dozen seats and a collection of high-top and normal tables. Two TVs and a projection screen provide Packers, Brewers, Bucks and Badgers coverage, and board games and cribbage are on hand. There's a patio out back, which is dog-friendly and offers high-top tables and cornhole.

Free WiFi. Secret Society (like a Mug Club). Facebook.com/StockHouseTosa

Stumbling Distance: The *Fermentorium Barrel House* (6933 W North Ave, thefermentorium.com) the second location for the Cedarburg brewery, is right down the street as is the beer & coffee combo *Vennture Brewing*. *Ono Kine Grindz* (7215 W North Ave, 414-778-0727) for all dishes Hawaiian, from poké and ramen to pulled pork and Kona coffee. *Cosmo's Café* (7203 W North, 414-257-2005, osmoscafewauwatosa.com) has the best gyros. *North Avenue Grill* (7225 W North Ave, 414-453-7225, northavegrill.com) does great diner food and serves beer/wine. All three of these deliver to the taproom.

WESTALLION BREWING CO.

1825 S. 72nd St. • West Allis, WI 53214 • 414-578-7998
westallionbrewing.com
Opened: April 2, 2017   **Head Brewer:** Erik Dorfner
Annual Production: 700-1,000 barrels   **Number of Beers:** 7-11 beers on tap

Staple Beers:
- » GENERALE SCOTTISH ALE
- » LILLEHAMMER GOLD HEFEWEIZEN
- » PEANUT BUTTER PORTER
- » WESTERN DAYS VIENNA LAGER

Rotating Beers:
- » BELGIAN DUBBEL
- » CHOCOLATE MINT STOUT
- » CINNAMON ROLL BROWN ALE
- » DRUNKLE DUNKEL
- » GRAPEFRUIT IPA

Most Popular Brew: Peanut Butter Porter or Scottish Ale

Brewmaster's Fave: Scottish Ale

Tours? Scheduled on website. $10 for an hour tour with lots of sampling.

Samples: Yes, build your own sample flights.

Best Time to Go: Open Wed 5-10PM, Thu-Fri 4-10PM, Sat 12-10PM, Sun 12-6PM.

Where can you buy it? Here on tap and in growlers to go, and a few West Allis draft accounts.

Got food? No, but food friendly, plus some pretzels maybe on hand and local menus for delivery.

Special Offer: Buy one house beer, get one free with book signature.

Directions: From I-94, take Exit 307A and turn south on 70th St. Drive 1.2 miles, turn right on National Ave, and continue 0.1 mile. Turn left at the 2nd cross street, 72nd St. Continue 0.2 mile and the brewery is on the right.

The Beer Buzz: "We bought the walls and floor," says Erik, who, with his wife Kim, co-founded this brewery along the railroad tracks in West Allis. The rest of the moldy, abandoned structure had collapsed. The name comes from the local shortened form of the town, 'Stallis, which makes the residents 'Stallions. Erik grew up here and the opening date is also the founding of the city. West Allis was home to manufacturer Allis-Chalmers in 1901, and today this city is a factory town in transition. The community and the mayor (in the painting on the wall) have been very supportive of this brewery project. You'll find a very local, laid-back neighborhood vibe.

Erik majored in History, writing papers about beer, which apparently paid off. One night Kim told Erik he should quit his job and go work at Lakefront Brewery. He passed it off as the beer talking, but she repeated the idea the next day. He started there unloading trucks, worked his way into the brewhouse, and just kept going – a homebrewer's dream. Kim, who handles everything besides the brewing, was the event coordinator at Best Place, the former Pabst hospitality center in Milwaukee where Erik also guided tours (worth visiting!).

The simple concrete-floored taproom has a small bar and a collection of tables and picnic tables. On the back wall is a big black stallion and a photo of West Allis native son Liberace. Beyond the beer, shuffleboard, board games, and a single TV entertain, and live music is often scheduled.

Free WiFi. ATM onsite. Facebook.com/Westallionbrewing

Stumbling Distance: *West Allis Cheese & Sausage Shop* (6832 W Becher St, 414-543-4230, wacheese-gifts.com) has exactly what it says there. Good stuff! *Alphonso's The Original* (1119 S 108th St, 414-755-0341, alphonsostheoriginal.com) serves up great pizza. *The Drunk Uncle* (1902 S 68th St, 414-727-5855) has Westallion on tap and a good selection of other reasonably priced craft beers.

RIVERSIDE BREWERY & RESTAURANT

255 S Main Street • West Bend, WI 53095 • 262-334-2739
riversidebreweryandrestaurant.com
Founded: October 2005   **Brewmaster**: Scott Bartell
Annual Production: 240 bbls   **Number of Beers**: 8 on tap, 27 or so per year

Staple Beers:
- » BENT RIVER BERRY WEISS
- » DIZZY BLONDE WEISS
- » MAIN STREET AMBER ALE

Rotating Beers: *(2 or 3 Brewer's Choices)*
- » BEE HOME SOON HONEY ALE
- » BROKEN OAK ABBEY DUBBEL ALE
- » CLEV'S AGED OLD WORLD OKTOBERFEST
- » FEELIN' LUCKY IRISH STOUT
- » IMPERIAL PALE ALE
- » IRON TRAIL PALE ALE
- » LUNA NEGRA ESPRESSO STOUT
- » MUGGLES' FUGGLES ESB
- » RASPBERRY FRUIT WEISS
- » SCATHING WIT

Most Popular Brew: Main Street Amber Ale

Brewmaster's Fave: "I will not pick a favorite from among my children."

Tours? Yes, available some Fridays, best by appointment. Call the brewery!

Samples? Yes, seven 4-oz mugs for about $8.95.

Best Time to Go: Open Mon-Thu 11am-9pm, Fri-Sat 11am-12am, Sun 11am-8pm. Happy hour is weekdays 3-5pm, Friday night fish fry. In warm weather, go for the outside seating. Live music in the bar on Saturday nights. Be sure to join the Mug Club for some good deals.

Where can you buy it? Only here on tap or in growlers to go.

Got food? Yes, a wide selection in fact. Beer-battered cheese curds and mushrooms, beer cheese soup, excellent ribs, steaks, seafood, top-notch sandwiches, and the fish fry offers cod, walleye, lake perch, and shrimp.

Special Offer: A free pint when you get your book signed.

Directions: Follow Hwy 33 through town to the west side of the river and take Main St south through a traffic circle. Riverside will be down the street on your left past the Walnut St intersection.

The Beer Buzz: The brewpub is just south of the quaint downtown and its collection of historic buildings and shops in a Cream City brick building on the river. This used to be a vacuum cleaner store but has since been totally remodeled in a sort of 1920s décor with breweriana and photos of pre-Prohibition scenes on the walls. (The place received a local award for interior design.) Outdoor dining has two options: the sidewalk along the street and the terrace along the river. Owner Wayne Kainz was the manager of another restaurant, and when he and his wife, Dana, decided to open their own place, the downtown association brought him the brewpub idea. Riverside Brewery and Restaurant has that hometown restaurant appeal, and quality food served with great beer is never a bad thing. It's a good place to meet up with friends or family and has a touch of class.

Stumbling Distance: The downtown is a nice collection of little shops in historic buildings and walking distance from the pub. If walking's your thing, the path along the river is nice enough and features a series of sculptures, and the Ice Age Trail runs right to town (iceagetrail.org – see my book *Best Hikes Near Milwaukee*). *Dublin's* (110 Wisconsin Ave, 262-338-1195, dublinswi.com) occupies an old Victorian house, serves fine food and has 40 fine beers on tap. The *Museum of Wisconsin Art* (205 Veterans Ave, 262-334-9638, wisconsinart.org) showcases Wisconsin artists only with permanent and temporary exhibitions. Are you ready for a Wisconsin-style safari? *Shalom Wildlife Sanctuary* (1901 Shalom Drive, 262-338-1310, shalomwildlife.com) gives a two-hour guided wagon ride through 100 acres full of bison, elk and deer. Shalom Dr is five miles north of town off Hwy 144. Be sure to call for a reservation

841 Brewhouse

841 East Milwaukee Street • Whitewater, WI 53190 • 262-473-8000
841brewhouse.net
Founded: 2015   **Head Brewer**: Mark Strelow
Annual Production: 200 bbls **Number of Beers**: 20 taps; 6 house beers, plus guest taps

Staple Beers:

- » Amber Lager
- » Oatmeal Stout
- » Session IPA

- » Midnight Porter
- » Warhawk Wheat Ale

Rotating Beers:

- » Golden Pilsner
- » Oktoberfest
- » Rye Ale

- » Summer Weiss
- » Winter Porter

Most Popular Brew: Amber Lager

Brewer's Fave: Warhawk Wheat

Tours? No, but you might meet the brewer by chance.

Samples? Yes, five 3-oz glasses for about $6.

Best Time to Go: Open Mon-Sat 10:30am-12am, Sun 9am-12am. Kitchen closes at 9pm (8pm on Monday).

Where can you buy it? Here on tap and in growlers to go.

Got food? Yes, a full bar and full menu, including a Friday fish fry (cod, walleye) and prime rib on Fri/Sat. Here's something unusual: hand-dipped, battered *Colby* cheese curds (not cheddar).

Special Offer: Your first pint of 841 Beer for $2 during your signature visit.

Directions: Business Hwy 12 is Milwaukee St. If you come in on Hwy 59 from the north or south, it passes the pub on Milwaukee as well.

The Beer Buzz: On the east side of town, this supper club draws 'em in for the food as well as the microbrews. Since 1972, there has been a restaurant on this site. Randy Cruse got a brew kit for Christmas and ended up bringing craft beer to Whitewater at his restaurant Randy's Funhunters, and in 2015, he passed the torch. Randy sold the business to Jim Burns who has long had success with Ray's Family Restaurant over in Edgerton.

His son Lucas Burns manages here. They remodeled the interior but have kept the beer on. Randy guided Mark in the beginning before passing the reins to him as head brewer.

The restaurant is a bit brighter and more modern than before. A long wood bar meets you

as you walk in. Booths and tables are off in the dining room, and there's outside seating as well. The brewhouse is visible through windows in the back corner. Nine TVs spread throughout make this a good place to catch a game.

Free WiFi. ATM onsite. Facebook.com/841Brewhouse

Stumbling Distance: Nightlife in Whitewater is downtown where the college-aged patrons hang out. *Casual Joe's* (319 W James St, 262-458-4751, casualjoes.com) has great local BBQ from the chef behind the fine dining restaurant *The Black Sheep*. The town is also the southern end of the *Kettle Moraine Scenic Drive*. Starting at Cty H/Hwy 12, a 115-mile stretch meanders north through the natural beauty left behind by the glaciers of the last Ice Age. *Whitewater Lake* is popular with boaters. *Frosty's Frozen Custard* (535 E Milwaukee St, 262-473-2320) is just down the road and offers some great frozen delights.

Second Salem Brewing Co.

111 W Whitewater St • Whitewater, WI 53190 • 262-473-2920
secondsalem.com
Opened: 2014   **Head Brewer**: Christ Christon
Annual Production: 300 barrels   **Number of Beers**: 12 on tap

Staple Beers:
- » The Beast Of Bray Road Amber Ale
- » Black Mass Stout
- » Bone Orchard IPA
- » Old Main Golden Ale (OMG)
- » Second Salem Porter
- » Witchtower Pale Ale

Rotating Beers:
- » Christmas Spiced Ale
- » Full Sleeve Iba
- » The Reaper (American Pale
- Wheat)
- » Wild Man Of La Grange Hefeweizen

Most Popular Brew: The Beast of Bray Road Amber Ale

Brewer's Fave: Oktoberfest

Tours? By chance or by appointment.

Samples: Yes, flights available, $2-3 per pour.

Best Time to Go: Open Mon–Fri 11am-close, Sat–Sun 10am-close. Happy hour Mon–Fri 3-6pm.

Where can you buy it? Here on tap and to go in growlers and cans, plus cans in distribution in Madison and Milwaukee areas.

Got food? Yes, a full menu with appetizers, soup/salad, sandwiches/burgers, and a few entrees. Watch for daily specials and a Friday fish fry that includes walleye.

Special Offer: Buy your first house beer, get the second one free during your signature visit.

Directions: From US 12 crossing south of Whitewater, go north on Janesville St 0.8 mile, and turn right on Whitewater St. Go 0.5 mile and it is on the right.

The Beer Buzz: Second Salem is an old nickname for Whitewater. As you look at all the beer names and imagery you get the impression this might be a Halloween theme, but the truth is Whitewater earned that nickname for a rich local folklore that involves everything from ghosts and witches to werewolves. Bone Orchard IPA is named for the three cemeteries in town.

Speaking of history, this building dates back to the nineteenth century, its past lives including time as a blacksmith's, leather shoe factory, Model T assembly line, and a furniture store. Brewer Christ's father ran a restaurant up front, but in 2010, Christ took over and converted the back section to a craft beer bar called Lakefront Pub. His goal was to add brewing one day. He and Thayer Coburn talked about the idea but were missing something critical: a brewer. A year later, Karl Brown, a history professor with some brewing experience, took a teaching job at University of Wisconsin-Whitewater and became the last piece of the puzzle. They put a one-barrel system up front and soon started serving house beers. Brewer Karl got the ball rolling and left it to Christ who in

turn brought in a couple of assistant brewers to help him keep up with demand. A bit of contract brewing at House of Brews in Madison soon became necessary, and now they are in the hopes of expanding their system.

The taproom moved up front where there are tall and regular tables and a long bar, plus a couple of TVs. You can also shoot pool or play darts. Midway back in the building is a lounge space with couches. That former backroom bar opens for overflow, and there's a patio behind the building overlooking the lake beyond the railroad tracks. A painting of Nicholas Klinger's Brewery, an 1864 brewing company that would become Whitewater Brewery in the early 1900s, hangs on the wall in back. That brewery closed in 1942. Posters on the walls and their corresponding beer labels offer some very cool artwork designed by graphic artist Sarah Hedlund. See their new logo a they move into distribution a bit.

Free WiFi. ATM onsite. Facebook/SecondSalemBrewing and Twitter @ secondsalem

Stumbling Distance: *The Sweet Spot* (226 W Whitewater St, 262-473-5080, sweetspotwhitewater. com) serves baked goods, breakfast and lunch items and has two locations: this coffee shop and the bakehouse (1185 W Main Street). *The Black Sheep* (210 W Whitewater St, 262-458-4751, EatAtBlackSheep.com) offers farm-to-table fine dining.

ZONE 3

Altoona: Modicum Brewing Co.
Amery: Amery Ale Works
Black River Falls: Sand Creek Brewing Co.
Bloomer: Bloomer Brewing Co.
Chippewa Falls: Brewster Bros. Brewing Co.
Chippewa Falls: Jacob Leinenkugel Brewing Co.
Cornell: MoonRidge Brew Pub
Dallas: Valkyrie Brewing Co.
Durand: Durand Brewing Co.
Eau Claire: The Brewing Projekt
Eau Claire: K Point Brewing
Eau Claire: Lazy Monk Brewery
Hudson: Hop & Barrel Brewing
Hudson: Pitchfork Brewing
La Crosse: City Brewery
La Crosse: Pearl Street Brewery
La Crosse: 608 Brewing Co.
La Crosse: Turtle Stack Brewery
Menomonie: Lucette Brewing Co.
Menomonie: brewery nønic
Menomonie: Zymurgy Brewing Co.
New Richmond: Barley John's Brewing
Onalaska: Skeleton Crew Brew
Onalaska: Two Beagles Brewpub
Osseo: Northwoods Brewpub
River Falls: Rush River Brewing Co.
River Falls: Swinging Bridge Brewing Co.
Roberts: Bobtown Brewhouse
St. Croix Falls: Trap Rock Brewing Co.
Somerset: Oliphant Brewing Co.
Whitehall: FFATS Brewing Co.
Wilson: Dave's BrewFarm

MODICUM BREWING CO.

3732 Spooner Ave. • Altoona, WI 54720 • 715-895-8585
modicumbrewing.com
Opened: July 7, 2017   **Head Brewer:** Eric Rykal
Annual Production: 250 barrels   **Number of Beers:** 12 on tap

Beers:

- » ARCHETYPE
- » DIVINE DRAMEDY (with Belgian Candi sugar)
- » GIBBERISH
- » GIMMICK (changing hops)
- » THE HEAVENS

- » IDIOM
- » LITTLE RUCKUS
- » MODICUM ORIGINAL
- » ORIGINAL GRAND CRU
- » PEEL
- » STRAWBOSS

Seasonal Beers:

- » EXCLAMATION!

- » TERRA (self-harvested wet hops)

Most Popular Brew: Modicum Original

Brewmaster's Fave: Changes by the day

Tours? Yes, by chance or by appointment.

Samples: Yes, 5-oz pours for about $2 each.

Best Time to Go: Open Wed-Thu 3-10pm, Fri 2pm-12am, Sat 12pm-12am, Sun 12pm-8pm.

Where can you buy it? Here on tap and in bombers and growlers to go.

Got food? Snacks such as popcorn, pretzels, beef sticks, curds, and roasted nuts. But also food friendly if you got your own.

Special Offer: A free 5-oz. pour of house beer when you get your book signed.

Directions: From Business US-53 through Eau Claire, go east on Highland Ave (it becomes Spooner Ave) for 0.1 mile and the brewery is on the left (north) side of the street in a small strip of shops.

The Beer Buzz: Modicum is a small amount of a good thing. Such is the mission of this little neighborhood brewery just outside Eau Claire in the town of Altoona. Eric Rykal's new brewing career direction and Mike Blodgett's retirement gig. Eric approached his father-in-law Mike, a builder by trade, with the idea of a brewery, and Mike suggested he take on a partner. As luck would have it, Mike was available. They found this spot in Altoona, in a small strip of shops. Once a bank – you can still see the vault – the building's most recent purpose was a church. The black walnut and white oak used here is from Mike's own property.

Eric was a homebrewer who wanted to step it up. Volunteered a year at Lucette Brewing and got hired, working there for five years before join-ing The Brewing Projekt as head brewer. Eric prefers creative brews and doesn't want to be pigeonholed by a style, yet still always seeks balance. They grow hops at home which make it into special brews such as the seasonal Terra. In a few years they hope *all* hops will be their own. The taproom has an industrial ceiling and cement floors with tall tables and bar seating. The brew system stands beyond a short wall facing the bar. Board games and cribbage are on hand, and an event room in back also has a TV for the big games. A bit of outdoor seating in season.

Dog friendly. Free WiFi. Facebook.com/modicumbrewing

Stumbling Distance: *Bug Eyed Betty's* (1920 S Hastings Way, Eau Claire, 715-514-2505) does good pub food. When's the last time you went bowling? *Wagner's Lanes* (2159 Brackett Ave, Eau Claire, 715-833-6700, wagnerslanes.com) also has good food and drink. Mexican and margaritas at *Cancun Bar & Grill* (2120 Highland Ave, Eau Claire, 715-552-8011, cancunmexicangrillwi. com).

AMERY ALE WORKS

588 115th St • Amery, WI 54001 • 715-268-5226
ameryaleworks.com

Opened: 2017   **Head Brewer:** Jenna Johnson
Annual Production: <100 barrels   **Number of Beers:** 1 on tap*, plus 10 guest beers/
ciders

Staple Beers:
  » BAR(N) BREW

Tours? Not really, but maybe by chance.

Samples: Yes, sample flights of four 4-oz pours for about $6.

Best Time to Go: Open Thu 4-9pm, Fri 11am-10pm, Sat 11am-10pm, Sun 11am-4pm. Food served until 9pm on Thu-Sat evenings. Thursday is trivia night.

Where can you buy it? Here on tap only, but no growlers initially.

Got food? Yes, a seasonally changing, locally sourced menu that may include pretzel with beer cheese dip, barnboards (meat and cheese tray served with crackers and fruit), flatbreads, paninis, salads, grilled cheese, hot dogs, desserts. Pizza night on Thursday.

Special Offer: A free house beer when you get your book signed.

Directions: Amery is 25 minutes southeast of St. Croix Falls. From US-8 head south 6.3 miles on WI-46. Turn right (west) on Deronda St/County F, go 1.7 miles, and turn left on 115th. Continue 0.7 mile and the bar(n) is on your left.

Cyclists: 1 mile from the Stower Seven Lakes State Trail running 14 miles from Amery to Dresser. Heading east of Amery is Cattail State Trail, 18 miles to Almena!

The Beer Buzz: Jenna Johnson purchased an old barn in the small town of Amery back in 2014, working nights and weekends for almost 3 years to transform what had been an antique shop into what she thought would become a venue for barn weddings. But it became much more than that. Jenna came from outside the community, but this is Wisconsin, and she was met with great community support both in the building process and the consumption. Beer brings people together. The bar(n) officially opened in 2017 as a beer and wine only joint on select weekends until Jenna acquired her kitchen permit, and began rolling out a menu and hiring a team to help her. By summer 2017, she had 12 employees and was open Thu-Sun as a restaurant and bar. In fall that year she got her brewery permit, and in December Amery Ale Works joined the ranks of Wisconsin brewers. Wonder Woman Jenna still works her full-time job but is here nights and weekends brewing beer, managing the bar(n), coordinating events, and managing HR, accounting, and marketing. And, of course, sitting down for a beer with her customers.

This is a small system and Bar(n) Beer will be a constantly changing brew. Others may take over the guest taps as the brewery grows. This project is a 100% woman-owned company. A great local vibe in a cool space.

*for now!

Free WiFi. On Facebook and Twitter @ameryaleworks

Stumbling Distance: For a meticulously locally sourced seasonal menu, check *Farm Table* (110 Keller Ave N, 715-268-4500, farmtablefoundation.org). *D.D. Kennedy Environmental Area* (1459 Kennedy Mill Ave, 715-485-9294) is great for snowshoeing or cross county skiing (they even have lighted ski trails). *Kayak the Apple River* near Somerset (1998 93rd St, Somerset, 715-338-4078, appleriverkayak.com). Hit the *Ice Age National Scenic Trail* from its western terminus in *Interstate State Park* (1275 WI-35, St Croix Falls, 715-483-3747). Good camping/paddling there also.

SAND CREEK BREWING CO.

320 Pierce Street • Black River Falls, WI 54615 • 715-284-7553
sandcreekbrewing.com
Founded: 1999   **Brewmaster**: Todd Krueger
Annual Production: 9,000+ bbls   **Number of Beers**: 14–16 each year

Staple Beers:

- » APA (hand-drawn tattoo on label by local tattoo artist Jimmy Fingers)
- » BADGER PORTER
- » ENGLISH-STYLE SPECIAL ALE
- » OSCAR'S CHOCOLATE OATMEAL STOUT
- » SAND CREEK HARD LEMONADE
- » WILD RIDE IPA
- » WOODY'S EASY ALE (low hop, low abv session ale)
- » HARD LEMONADES, CRANBERRY, POMEGRANATE, LIME, CHERRY

Rotating Beers:

- » BLACK CURRANT ALE
- » CRANBERRY SPECIAL ALE (fall)
- » DOUBLE OSCAR'S OATMEAL STOUT (also on nitro)
- » FRANK'S DOUBLE IPA
- » GROOVY BREW (Kölsch, summer)
- » ODERBOLZ BOCK
- » OKTOBERFEST (a.k.a. BLACK RIVER RED)
- » RYE DOPPELBOCK

Most Popular Brew: Oscar's Chocolate Oatmeal Stout

Brewmaster's Fave: Depends on season/mood/hangover (or Oscar's).

Tours? Yes, Thu 5-10pm, Fri 3-10pm, Sat noon-10pm.

Samples? Yes, free sips and sample trays for about $11 with eight 5-ounce beers and a special reserve beer.

Best Time to Go: Taproom hours Thu 5-10pm, Fri 3-10pm, Sat noon-10pm (subject to change). Taproom is also open Mon–Fri 8am-5pm for growler fills or bottle sales only. *Karner Blue Butterfly Festival* in July, when 500 people tour the brewery that day or *Sand Creek Brewery Oktoberfest*, the first Saturday in October right down the road at the fairgrounds with crafts and music all day and night. Watch for live music events.

Where can you buy it? Pints here plus growlers, bottles, cases, pub kegs, sixth- and half-barrels. Throughout Wisconsin, parts of Minnesota, Iowa and Illinois (mostly Chicago area).

Got food? No, but on Friday nights you can bring in something in. Food trucks come in once a month (whenever there's live music) and local restaurants deliver.

Special Offer: A free pint and a hearty handshake and/or pat on the back.

The Beer Buzz: The brewing force is strong in this one! Beer has been happening here since 1856 when Ulrich Oderbolz opened his brewery on this very same site. It was sold and renamed Badgerland Brewery but went beer belly up in 1920. (Yep, Prohibition!) Then all hell broke loose here: turkeys, land mines, Coca Cola, and finally just storage, until 1996 when Jim and Dave Hellman remodeled the brick building and started Pioneer Brewing Co. In 1998, they acquired Wisconsin Brewing Co. from Wauwatosa and moved those brews to Black River Falls. Meanwhile, out on a farm near Downing, WI, Cory Schroeder and Jim Wiesender turned a farm shed into a brewery (talk about retro) and a semi-trailer into a beer cooler. Pudding tanks for mash kettles? If the tank fits… Thus was born Sand Creek Brewing Co., and in 2004 they bought Pioneer and left the farm. Original Pioneer Brewmaster Todd stayed on with the new owners and the lagers and ales kept flowing. They also have a history of contract brewing beers and have been responsible for helping start up Fulton and Lake Monster in Minneapolis, Half Acre in Chicago, Fargo Brewing in North Dakota, and Door County Brewing to name a few. In 2000, Sand Creek took two golds at the World Beer Cup (Oscar's and Black River Red)—the first microbrewery to do it and followed up with another gold in 2002 for Oderbolz Bock. The tasting room feels like you are hanging with the neighbor guy at a bar he put in his basement—except this neighbor also happens to have a half dozen or so great homemade beers on tap. A bigger taproom is in planning and might happen in 2019.

Infinity Beverages in Eau Claire (infinity-beverages.com) takes Double Oscar's and Rye Doppelbock and distills them and ages them in whiskey barrels to make two varieties of Beerskey.

Stumbling Distance: *Rozario's* (42 N 1st St, 715-284-0006) near Main St is the best pizza in town and has beer on tap. Get your fresh cheese curds at *Mocha Mouse* (themochamouse.com, 715-284-2541, 500 Oasis Rd, Hwy 54 exit 116 by the orange moose) and sample any of the cheeses or have breakfast, lunch or a cup of Joe or some ice cream. Visit the **Black River Chamber of Commerce** (blackrivercountry.net, 800-404-4008) for current ATV- and snowmobile-trail conditions along with scuba diving (no, seriously), paddling (see my book *Paddling Wisconsin*) and biking info. *Re-Pete's Saloon & Grill* (300 Gebhardt Rd, 715-284-3322, repetessaloonandgrill.com) will get you a Friday fish fry, a Saturday prime rib, and several Sand Creek taps.

BLOOMER BREWING CO.

1526 Martin Road • Bloomer, WI 54724 • 715-271-3967
bloomerbrewingco.com
Founded: 2012   **Head Brewer**: Dan Stolt
Annual Production: 120 barrels   **Number of Beers**: 6 on tap

Staple Beers:

- » BLOOMER BEER
- » BLOOMER TOWN BROWN
- » BUCKINGHAM ALE
- » COW BELL CREAM ALE

- » DUNCAN SPRING IPA
- » STOLTY'S A-HORIZON STOUT
- » WEATHERED BRICK

Rotating Beers:

- » BACK PORCH
- » HOG BREATH SMOKEY MAPLE BACOM BROWN ALE

- » OKTOBERFEST
- » WINTER BOCK

Most Popular Brew: Buckingham Ale

Brewer's Fave: Duncan Spring IPA

Tours? Yes, by chance or appointment.

Samples: Yes, four 5-oz pours for about $5

Best Time to Go: Open Wed-Thu 5-10pm, Fri 4-10pm, Sat 1-8pm. Call or see website.

Where can you buy it? Here on tap and to go in growlers and bottles, and maybe a couple local draft accounts. Bottles distributed in area stores.

Got food? Only free popcorn, but food friendly. **Firewoods Traveling Pizzeria** (firewoodspizzeria.com) and other food trucks park outside some days in season.

Special Offer: Your first 12-oz house beer is free during your signature visit.

Directions: From US 53, take the exit for WI 40 and head east into Bloomer for 0.8 mile. Turn right on Main St, then left on 17th Ave and continue 0.3 mile. Turn left on Martin Rd and the brewery is on the right in the back of an industrial building set back far from the street. Follow the signs on either side of the building to get to the brewery. (ADA-entry to the left.)

The Beer Buzz: Bloomer Brewing is located in the former Bloomer Brewing building from 1874. Down in the basement is an old lagering cave built into the hillside. Brewer/founder Dan went to Fort Lauderdale to visit his eldest son who took him to a Brew on Premise with 120 recipes to make a batch together. That started him on the brewery idea and his wife Cindy thought he was nuts. She's reassessed his sanity since he opened this place and gets a steady stream of locals and travelers. Dan's actually been renting this space since 1985 when he set up his own septic and excavation business here, and he's been fixing up the space. (The stout's name, A-Horizon, is a digging term referring to the dark top soil layer.)

Dan has the local polka station on while he's brewing. Gets him in the mood. He started with 40–80 gallon batches but may be going bigger soon. All his brews have 5% corn

in them for lighter flavor and drinkability. His spent grain goes to a local farmer.

The taproom shows some breweriana and eclectic curios, and a couple of other rooms have more collectibles. A room with a pool table has a few dozen hunting trophies mounted on all the walls. A small stage occupies a corner of the taproom for occasional live music.

Mug Club with smart copper cups. ATM onsite. Facebook/ bloomer-Brewing-Co

Stumbling Distance: Next door right on the street is *The Next Place Bar & Grill* (1602 Martin Rd, 715-568-2566, thenextplacebar. com), which serves 75 different burgers. *Bob's Processing* (2430 S Main St, 715-568-2887) has very popular beef sticks and hot dogs to take home. *Fat Boys Family Restaurant* (1312 Main St, 715-568-4464) is the place to get pizza.

BREWSTER BROS BREWING CO. & CHIPPEWA RIVER DISTILLERY

402 West River Street • Chippewa Falls, WI • 715-861-5100
brewsterbrosbrewing.com
Opened: March 16, 2016   **Brewmaster**: Robert Wilbur
Annual Production: 1,500 barrels   **Number of Beers**: 12 on tap

Staple Beers:

- » DARK TIMBER STOUT
- » GINGE RED ALE
- » MEL'S BBA AMBER ALE
- » RUMBLE BRIDGE CREAM ALE
- » WOODTICK PALE ALE

Rotating Beers:

- » FLYBY WED HOPPED IPA
- » HEFEWEIZEN
- » OKTOBERFEST
- » PORTERSVILLE PORTER
- » WEST RIVER LAGER

Most Popular Brew: Rumble Bridge

Tours? Yes, by chance or by appointment.

Samples: Yes, flights of four 6-oz pours.

Best Time to Go: Open Wed-Thu 4-10pm, Fri 3pm-12am, Sat 12pm-12am, Sun 12-7pm. Check website for seasonal hours. Closed Mon-Tue.

Where can you buy it? Here on tap and in growlers to go, and distributed in 6-pack bottles and on draft from Hudson to Green Bay and as far south as Madison.

Got food? Pretzels, snacks and fresh cheese curds, but also food friendly.

Special Offer: $1 off your first pint during your signature visit.

Directions: From US 53, take Exit 96 and head east into Chippewa Falls on Business WI 29/River Street for 1.7 miles. The brewery is on the left at the corner of River and Taylor Streets.

The Beer Buzz: Chippewa Falls has long been famous for an historic brewery, but now they're sharing the place with a new kid in town. Founded by a couple of mechanical engineers, Jim Stirn and Kurt Schneider, the brewery is also a distillery.

Jim and Kurt worked together years ago here in Chippewa Falls, and remained friends and hunting buddies ever since. Jim took up homebrewing in about 2000, finding pleasure in the process as much as the beer itself. Kurt once started a small business then sold it and had the itch to get back into working for himself. They started with the craft distillery idea, noting the recent growth in that industry, and added the brewery knowing it had similarities but also could generate revenue sooner. Kurt's grandfather owned a saloon downtown, and his father hauled beer out of his building back in the day – a fact unknown to Kurt when they bought this place.

They needed equipment and wanted to stay close to the design aspect so rather than just buying something, they created MSP Engineering with a third partner to design and build equipment for brewing and distilling. They then coordinated various suppliers and tradesmen to manufacture their own system. They first built a 3-vessel system and control set as a test system for homebrewing and developed the larger brew system for the brewery based on that design. They did the same with the distillery.

The varied tap handles have stories, and posters and packaging include photos of family and friends, including Arlyn Buchli, a breweriana expert and collector and a regular.

The building was a beer distributor in the '50s, and through the years, an auto parts store, a video rental and tanning salon (yes, at the same time), and now returns to its beer roots. The building was two buildings joined as one, and Kurt and Jim added a room with glass on three sides to show off the still. An outdoor beer garden and an upper deck offer river views. The brewing system occupies one half of the building visible through more windows. The tasting room has a bar, communal tables and tall tables, 3 TVs and a to-go fridge. Remodeling exposed the old tongue-and-groove ceiling with big steel beams, and the cement block walls have a lot of windows. Garage doors open in season. Robert Patrie operates the distilling side using local grains to make flavored vodkas, schnapps, gin, rum, rye, and cinnamon whiskey.

Free WiFi. Find them on Facebook.

Stumbling Distance: *Fill-Inn Station* (104 W Columbia St, 715-723-8282) is run by Kurt's cousin and has deep-fried cheese curds, 10 different burgers, pizza, and a Friday fish fry, prime rib Saturday. *Bresina's Carryout* (10 Jefferson Ave, 715-723-7869) is rated the best chicken and fish fry, but as the name suggests you need a place to eat it, so maybe grab some Brewster Bros beer and cross the street here to *Irvine Park* along the river for a picnic. *Mahli Thai Restaurant* (212 N Bridge St, 715-861-5333, mahlithaicuisine.com) gets high marks for their curry.

Jacob Leinenkugel Brewing

124 East Elm Street • Chippewa Falls, WI 54729 • 888-534-6437
leinies.com

Founded: 1867 **Brewmaster**: John Buhrow

Annual Production: 350,000+ bbls (estimated) **Number of Beers**: 10 (8 year round, 9 seasonal)

Staple Beers:
- » Berry Weiss
- » Creamy Dark
- » Honey Weiss
- » Leinienkugel's Light
- » Leinienkugel's Original Lager
- » Wisconsin Red Pale Ale
- » Sunset Wheat

Seasonal Beers:
- » Canoe Paddler (Kölsch)
- » Oktoberfest
- » Snowdrift Vanilla Porter

The Shandies:
- » Grapefruit Shandy
- » Harvest Patch Shandy
- » Orange Shandy
- » Summer Shandy (lemon)

Most Popular Brew: Summer Shandy

Brewmaster's Fave: Year round: Original Lager, Seasonal: Oktoberfest

Tours? Yes, every half hour or so, Sun-Wed 10am-6pm (last tour 4-4:30), Thu-Sat 10am-8pm (last tour 6-6:30). Tours cost $10 and include a free glass and either five 5-oz samples or two 12-oz beers. Go to the Leinie Lodge, not the brewery.

Samples? Yes, $10 gets you five 5-oz samples (and the tour if you want it).

Best Time to Go: The Leinie Lodge is open daily, Sun-Wed 10am-6pm, Thu-Sat 10am-8pm. Oktoberfest is a nice time to be here.

Where can you buy it? In all 50 states, but most widely distributed in the upper Midwest.

Got food? Pretzels, snacks, cheeses and sodas for purchase.

Special Offer: A free pint glass with any $10 purchase.

Directions: Follow Hwy 124 to the Elm St intersection. Turn onto East Elm Street and you'll see the Leinie Lodge on your left.

The Beer Buzz: This is a bit of a shrine for those of you who grew up knowing Leinie's as a local brewery. It's the seventh-oldest working brewery in the US and a *pils*-grimage here is indeed a must. In the 1840s, Matthias Leinenkugel brought his family from Prussia (now part of Germany) to settle in Sauk City where he started brewing. Is brewing genetic? Could be. His sons opened two more: one in Eau Claire (where an uncle already had one) and another in Baraboo. Another son Jacob wasn't about to be left out and moved north eventually finding the lumber center of Chippewa Falls. Apparently lumber workers like beer. Lots of it, in fact. And so it was that he and John Miller founded Spring Brewing Co. The oldest building here is a former malt house built in 1877. Why would that be built before a brewhouse, you may ask? In the beginning they brewed in the homes built in a line right out front. (A couple of those home were moved elsewhere in town years ago.) At that time they brewed as many as 400 barrels in a year. John Miller  left in 1884, and when they built a proper brewhouse in 1890, they were able to produce half of that... in a single day. (Today they brew upwards of 1200 barrels daily.) Jacob's name was added to the brewery's name, and not long after "Spring" was dropped. They continued to grow, survived Prohibition with Leino near beer and soda water, and until 1945, still delivered beer by horse and wagon. The name became household in Wisconsin.

Fast forward to 1988: Miller Brewing Co. (now MillerCoors), second largest brewer in the world, buys Leinie's. Purists clutch their chests, breaths are held, there is much gnashing of teeth. Somewhere in the distance a dog barks. But the brewery was not dismantled or swallowed up, and the old classic Leinie's has emerged bigger and better than before, producing some rather exceptional large market beers in a microbrew style. At the 2006 World Beer Cup, Sunset Wheat got bronze and Honey Weiss silver while Red Lager took gold in 2002. To keep up with sales, Leinie's operates 10th Street Brewery in Milwaukee. Honey Weiss is made with Wisconsin honey from Hauke Honey in Marshfield.

The Leinie Lodge, separated from the brewery itself by Duncan Creek, is where you go for the tours and tastings, and it contains a huge amount of merchandise as well as some exhibits of Leinie breweriana and history.

Facebook.com/Leinenkugels Twitter/Instagram @Leinenkugels

Stumbling Distance: One of the best rated eateries in town is *Chippewa Family Restaurant* (1701 Kennedy Rd, 715-723-4751, chippewarestaurant.com). *Bresina's Carryout* (10 Jefferson Ave, 715-723-7869) is rated the best chicken and fish fry, but as the name suggests you need a place to eat it. (Picnic in the park?) Leinie's hosts or gets involved with a lot of little fests and such, but one of the most unusual is the *Family Reunion*. On the Saturday of Father's Day weekend head out to meet members of the Leinenkugel family as they host a free get together featuring some live music, tours, and plenty of brats, beer, chips, beer, cookies, and of course beer. All free to over 6000 participants. The event lasts from noon to sunset and the first 100 guests get a little extra gift.

ALTERNATIVE USES FOR BEER CANS

So craft beer is starting to embrace the beer can. Besides recycling them, there are plenty of other ways to repurpose them. Consider these:

Party wear. Not sure what to wear to the next beer fest? How about a hat made out of cans and yarn? This will surely be hitting the runways in Paris (Paris, Wisconsin, population 1,473).

Davis Thuecks is sporting his grandpa's hat and shirt here. His friend, Robin Reese, apparently left his at home.

My great uncle John Lajcak had a knack for making furniture out of beer cans. A bit on the smallish size, but stylish.

If beer could fly...

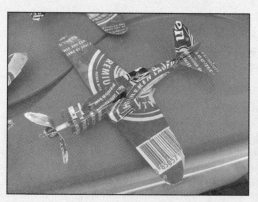

Remember Body on Tap shampoo? Me neither, but it was back in the 70s when it was believed beer would give your hair body. Back when the big curl was all the rage for the ladies, the steel cans made great rollers and the beer helped set the hair. A big thanks to Pat Breister and Sara Napiwocki down at Madison College for the re-enactment and Kristin Kizer, the brave volunteer. There was no permanent damage—other than possible emotional scarring.

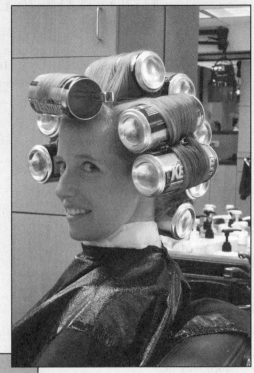

MoonRidge Brew Pub

501 Bridge St • Cornell, WI 54732 • 715-239-1341
moonridgebrewery.com

Opened: November 19, 2015   **Head Brewer:** Roger Miller
Annual Production: 100 barrels   **Number of Beers:** 7 on tap + guest beer

Staple Beers:

- » Below The Dam Oatmeal Stout
- » Fisher Honey Weizen
- » Haymeadow Irish Blonde Ale
- » Moonridge Brown Ale
- » Shaws Road Irish Draft
- » Stacker Cream Ale
- » Wayside American Amber

Most Popular Brew: Moonridge

Brewmaster's Fave: Moonridge

Tours? Yes, by chance, but it's small.

Samples: Yes, sample flights of four for $6.

Best Time to Go: Summer: Thu-Sun 12-10pm Winter: Thu-Fri 4-10pm, Sat 12-10pm.

Where can you buy it? Here on tap and in growlers to go.

Got food? Yes, housemade pizzas with interesting toppings and spent grain crust and beer sauce options.

Special Offer: A free flight of beer samples when you get your book signed.

Directions: WI-27 passes right through Cornell and actually becomes Bridge St for a few blocks. The brewpub is at the corner of Bridge and 5th St. *Cyclists:* The Old Abe State Trail crosses Bridge St four blocks from the brewpub.

The Beer Buzz: Owners Roger and Cindy Miller are from the area. Roger had home-brewed for years, and then on a trip to Maui he came across a nanobrewery brewing 25 gallons four times per day, and thought the same model would work in Cornell: "I should be able to keep Cornell happy."

The building looks a bit like a Wild West saloon with a lot of old wood siding and a porch. It had been a restaurant before the Millers took over and now Roger is looking to expand out the back and add a larger brewhouse. The dining aspect is popular with local families, and regulars pop in for a pint or growler. Order pizza at the kitchen window. Cribbage

and other games are on hand. The beer names are "secret" party spots all the kids knew growing up, and Moon Ridge is the most popular. Roger does a bit of barrel aging.

Free WiFi. On Facebook.

Stumbling Distance: *Brunet Island State Park* (23125 255th S, 715-239-6888) is a great campsite and situated on the Cornell Flowage (Chippewa River), ideal for paddling and fishing. **LaGrander Hillside Dairy** (W11299 Broek Rd, Stanley, 715-644-2275) is a half hour drive for fresh curds. *Yellowstone Cheese* in Cadott (24105 County MM, Cadott, 715-289-3800) is about 20 minutes due south.

VALKYRIE BREWING CO.
(FORMERLY VIKING BREWING CO.)

234 Dallas St. West, Dallas, WI 54733 • 715-837-1824
valkyriebrewery.com
Founded: 1994   **Brewmaster**: Randy and Ann Lee
Annual Production: 300 barrels   **Number of Beers**: 22+ annually, up to 16 on tap

Staple Beers:

- » BIG SWEDE (Swedish-style Imperial Stout)
- » DRAGON BLADE (American retro lager)
- » 4 BITTEN FRUIT (apple ale)
- » ODIN'S OATHKEEPER BLACK IPA
- » RUBEE RED (a Märzen style lager)
- » SUPERNOVA (Royal Australian IPA)
- » WAR HAMMER (coffee, oatmeal, milk porter)

Rotating Beers: (Most are seasonal batches and new ones come up once or twice a month.)

- » ABBY NORMAL (BELGIAN TRIPEL)
- » BERSERK BARLEYWINE
- » BLAZE ORANGE EXOTICALLY SPICED BEER
- » HOT CHOCOLATE (COCOA & CAYENNE)
- » INVADER DOPPELBOCK
- » LIME TWIST (WHEAT BEER)
- » NIGHT WOLF (SCHWARZBIER)
- » RAVEN QUEEN (BLACK WHEAT IPA WITH STAR ANISE)
- » VIENNA WOODS
- » VELVET GREEN (DRY IRISH STOUT)
- » WHISPERING EMBERS (OKTOBERFEST WITH BEECHWOOD-SMOKED MALT – SEPT)

Most Popular Brew: War Hammer

Brewmaster's Fave: Randy: Invader Doppelbock, Ann: Big Swede

Tours? Yes, free "deep" tours most Saturdays at 1PM (check website for when they are gone for Beer Shows) or by appointment.

Samples: Yes.

Best Time to Go: The tap room is open Fridays and Saturdays noon–8, add Thu in summer months. Taproom usually closed in Jan, and winter hour's

may be in effect in February. Check the website. Don't miss Oktoberfest, first Saturday of Oktober (see Beer Festivals).

Where can you buy it? In six-pack bottles (and occasional 22-oz bombers) in the four or five counties around them. Here in the Beer Cave you can build your own 6-, 9-packs or cases, plus growler fills in the taproom.

Got food? No, but there's free popcorn, the taproom is food friendly, and on Thursdays in summer, brats are served custom-made with their beer by Louie's Finer Meats in Cumberland.

Special Offer: A bottle of beer, sure, why not?

The Beer Buzz: Tiny Dallas makes a not-so-tiny mark on the beer map with this husband-and-wife operation. Housed in the basement of an old brick building on the main street, this was originally a Ford dealership selling Models T and A. (Was Ford a perv?) In the 30s it became a creamery and a handful of other things thereafter. Why did Randy open a brewery? "We were out of work at the time." Unemployment is the mother of invention. Or is it Randy's wife and co-brewer Ann? She comes up with a lot of the brew ideas and Randy makes the recipes. A stout with cocoa and cayenne? You better believe it. Dallas was dry until the early 60s, so heads turned when the brewery opened under its original name Viking Brewing and became one of the pioneers of microbrewing in the 90s in western Wisconsin. Randy sold the Viking name to an Icelandic brewery that wanted it worse than he did, and began brewing again as Valkyrie, a mythical Norse female who determines who lives and dies in battle. The tour lasts an hour and a half and is comprehensive, not just a show of what he's doing but also explanations of the different kinds of beers.

The brewery is in the basement but the taproom is upstairs in front. Inside is a bar in the corner next to the walk-in cooler Beer Cave for bottle sales. The walls are painted like castle stones and, along with the cool mural, were all painted by Ann, who also has many of her paintings for sale here as well. (Check out her work at evolvingcolors.com) Weapons and chain mail, most made by a local metalworker, hang on the wall, and you can see a giant pair of knockers on the double doors to the back room. The booths are reclaimed from an old Pizza Hut, and a homemade fire & water fountain symbolizes the Nordic Tree of Life, Yggdrasil. Games, such as cribbage and chess, are onsite if you come to linger. Be aware that Valkyrie brews unpasteurized beer. If you pick some up, take good care to keep it cool and out of the sun until you're ready to drink it!

Trivia note: Randy ran for state governor in 2002 as the BEER Party candidate. Hard to believe, but he didn't win. And now we are facing beer taxes. See where not voting gets you??

Stumbling Distance: This isn't far from lake country and nearby Chetek, and the surrounding area draws a lot of fishermen and outdoors types. Since Prohibition, Chicago travelers have come here for cabins. *Clicker's Restaurant and Bar* (210 W Dallas St, 715-837-1416) has the best eats in town and a Friday night fish fry. If you're into antiques, hit up *Old Farmer's Mercantile* (115 W Dallas St, 715-837-1919). Eyeball some local pottery and glass work at *Losse Clay Studio* (201 W Dallas St, 715-837-1109). 17 miles south is a good bed & breakfast: *Hay River House* (E4517 CR FF, Boyceville, 715-702-1809, hayriverhouse.com).

DURAND BREWING CO.

N6649 State Hwy 25 • Durand, WI 54736 • 715-672-3848
Web Site: see Facebook
Opening: Fall 2018   **Head Brewer:** Roger Hillestad
Annual Production: 200 bbls   **Number of Beers:** up to 6 on tap

Staple Beers:
- » KÖLSCH
- » PILSNER

Rotating Beers:
- » LEMON SHANDY
- » OKTOBERFEST

Most Popular Brew: Pilsner

Brewmaster's Fave: Kölsch

Tours? Yes, by chance or by appointment.

Samples: Yes, flights of four.

Best Time to Go: Open Sat 12-8pm to start. Check Facebook or call.

Where can you buy it? Only here on tap and in growlers and bottles to go.

Got food? Just a pizza oven. Food friendly, bring your own.

Special Offer: A free house beer or a free sticker when you get your book signed.

Directions: On US-10, which passes through the north end of Durand, head west 2 miles and turn right (north) on WI-25. Continue 1.2 miles and the brewery is on the left. *Cyclists:* Chippewa River State Trail comes from the north and connects to Main St, then US-10 to follow the same car directions.

The Beer Buzz: This brewery started in the front end of Roger Hillestand's oversized garage in town, with plans to build off of that -- until at the last minute he found this former welding shop on 8 acres of land just outside town. Roger Hillestad is a veteran and while stationed in Germany in the 80s, he got into Kölsch. Back in Wisconsin he shared his homebrews, and friends were only too happy to oblige. They encouraged him, and he already had a taproom in his garage for them to gather for brews and Packers games, so Roger finally decided to make it legit and get his permits. The original Durand Brewing Co. lasted until Prohibition, and Roger's logo has similarities to the original. He'll do some hoppy beers too, but as he puts it, "I prefer the taste of a good, crisp pilsner." Free WiFi.

Stumbling Distance: *RoosterTail Bar & Grill* (106 W Main St, 715-672-3640) has a Friday night fish fry. Family-owned since 1945, *Eau Galle Cheese* (N6765 WI-25, 715-283-4211) has your cheese fix nearby. Their asiago won 1st place in US competition. *Old Courthouse Museum & Jail* (315 W Madison St, 715-672-5423, oldpepincountycourthouse.org) is a 1874 wood-framed Greek Revival building on the National Register. *Chippewa River State Trail* – See "Biking For Beer."

THE BREWING PROJEKT

1807 Oxford Ave • Eau Claire, WI 54703 •   715-214-3728
thebrewingprojekt.com
Founded: 2015   **Brewmaster:** Ryan Myhre
Annual Production: 3,000 barrels   **Number of Beers:** 12 on tap

Staple Beers:
- » DARE MIGHTY THINGS
- » GUNPOWDER IPA
- » RESIST - MILKSHAKE IPA
- » SKULL DUGGERY IPA
- » TERMINAL DIPA
- » WISCOAST (wheat pale ale hybrid)

Rotating Beers:
- » DOUBLE GUNPOWDER IPA
- » MIDNIGHT OIL (cold press coffee stout)
- » THE STOLEN MILE (golden ale with basil, lemongrass, lemon zest)
- » WET HOPPED GUNPOWDER
- » SoWAH PROGRAM BEERS

Most Popular Brew: Gunpowder IPA

Brewmaster's Fave: Dare Mighty Things IPA

Tours? Yes, by appointment or by chance.

Samples: Yes, order a Pick 3—three 5-oz samples for about $4.

Best Time to Go: Open Wed–Thu 4-11pm, Fri 2pm-12am, Sat 12pm-12am, Sun 2-8pm.

Where can you buy it? Here on tap and to go in Crowlers. Growler fills are available but they don't sell the growlers themselves. Distributing 16-oz cans and some draft accounts as far east as Wausau, some in Madison and Milwaukee. Twin Cities

Got food? No, but food friendly, and possible food trucks.

Special Offer: Half off your first pint of house beer during your signature visit.

Directions: Business Highway 12 runs right through Eau Claire, crossing Chippewa River downtown on Madison Street Bridge. On the west side of the bridge, go north 500 feet on Oxford Ave/US 12 and the brewery is on the right before the curve at Platt St.

The Beer Buzz: The Brewing Projekt may be the finest example for how complicated and absurd old post-Prohibition laws still are. When founder (but not owner!) Will Glass, a Chippewa Falls native, got out of the Marine Corps, he went home again and worked a bit for Leinenkugel's before he and his wife decided to open Eau Claire's excellent craft beer bar, The Fire House back in 2009. By this time, Will had taken up homebrewing, so as the Firehouse became successful, he and his wife Rebecca figured the next step was to start brewing their own. This turned out to be way more difficult than they had imagined.

After Prohibition, laws went into effect that a person could not own a bar *and* a brewery. This became a long story of back and forth with the government, and for a time they had even considered getting a legal divorce so each of them could own one business. Even then they were told that Will would also have to give up legal claims on his children who were indirect joint in-

terests and thus still a no-no. Literally asking for your first born (and second and third). The solution was that his wife took over the bar 100% as a sole proprietor. Will's *father* owns the brewery. And Will? He works as an unpaid volunteer at his father's brewery because he can't legally take a paycheck here while his wife owns the bar. Oh, it gets better. Previous head brewer Eric Rykal's wife worked at a bar downtown. She had to quit so that Eric could work here. Time to change the laws, wouldn't you say? Eric spun off to start *Modicum Brewing*, while Ryan, who has brewed professionally in Texas and Washington, jumped on the chance to move back to his home state Wisconsin.

Things have gone quite well for the Projekt and they outgrew their digs at 2000 N. Oxford #3. Again with some public debate, a move across the street to an old brick industrial building was approved, and in 2018, they made the change. Expect bigger production, views of the Chippewa River from a deck, a bike trail along the water, a banquet hall, a window into the brewhouse, and more. Brewing runs the gamut here through ales and lagers, and all sorts of creative brews come and go. Their sour program will grow with the bigger space. Cribbage and cards are on hand.

Free WiFi. Facebook/thebrewingprojekt and Twitter @brewingprojekt Instagram @thebrewingprojekt

Stumbling Distance: Be sure to check out *The Fire House* (202 Gibson St, 715-514-0406, eauclairefirehouse.com), the best beer bar in town, with 40 rotating taps and 2 casks—and they even fill growlers. Short walk to *Lazy Monk Brewing* from here.

K Point Brewing

4212 Southtowne Drive • Eau Claire, WI 54701 • 715-834-1733
kpointbrewing.com
Opened: 2015   **Head Brewer**: Tom Breneman
Annual Production: 100 barrels **Number of Beers**: 9 on tap (some may be guest beers)

Staple Styles:

» American Pale Ale   » Helles
» Blood Orange Citra IPA   » Kölsch
» Coffee Stout   » Red Ale
» German Pils   » Saison
» Hefeweizen

Most Popular Brew: Coffee Stout

Brewer's Fave: American Pale Ale

Tours? By chance or by appointment.

Samples: Yes, four 5-oz. samplers for about $7.

Best Time to Go: Closed Mon-Tue. Open Wed–Fri 3-11pm, Sat 11am-11pm, Sun 11am-7pm.

Where can you buy it? Only here on tap and to go in growlers and Crowlers. Limited local self-distribution, often at *The Fire House* (202 Gibson St, eauclairebar.com) and *The Growler Guys.*

Got food? Yes, a changing menu featuring breakfast sandwiches, baked goods, tapas, and excellent house-roasted coffee. A wood-fired pizza food truck, Tutto Bene, parks outside occasionally.

Special Offer: One half-priced pint of K Point Beer during your signature visit.

Directions: From I-94 take Exit 68 and head north on WI 93 for 0.6 mile. Turn left on Damon St and an immediate left on Southtowne Dr and The Coffee Grounds is on your right. The brewery is inside or around back.

The Beer Buzz: Looks like a coffee shop, no? Eric and Julie Nelson started The Coffee Grounds, roasting beans in a mall back in 1990. It would become successful and grow, expand into a new location, and become a notable specialty shop that not only roasted and served great coffee, but also sold food, gourmet products, wines, and the finest selection of bottled craft beers in town. Eventually they outgrew the other location and opened up here. In 2015, Eric brought Lon Blaser and Tom Breneman, a couple of longtime homebrewers in. They started on a Sabco ½-barrel system but soon got a larger system as they moved into 2,100 square feet of space in the next room to increase production to about 150 barrels per year and set up a taproom. Tom took over the whole operation and the varieties of beers keep coming.

The taproom began as a stand alone counter in the center of The Coffee Grounds, but moved into a much larger space in back with taps and a fine assortment of spirits. Doors open to the outdoors in season making it a really lovely place to hang out and drink some beer. Watch for tastings, pairings and beer dinners.

Free WiFi. Facebook.com/KPointBeers

Stumbling Distance: *Manny's Cocina* (4207 Oakwood Hills Pkwy, 715-514-0818, mannyscocina. com) serves fine Mexican fare with an emphasis on the seafood of the Pacific coastal region. Book tours 24 hours in advance if you want to visit *Infinity Beverages Winery & Distillery* (3460 Mall Dr, 715-895-8020, infinitybeverages.com). *The Growler Guys* (2832 London Rd, 715-514-5140, thegrowlerguys.com) may have some K Point and other regional brews on draft and for fills.

LAZY MONK BREWERY

97 West Madison Street • Eau Claire, WI 54703 • 715-271-0848
lazymonkbrewing.com
Founded: May 2011   **Brewmaster:** Leos Frank
Annual Production: 460 barrels
Number of Beers: 14 on tap, including a few WI guest beers

Staple Beers:
- » BOHEMIAN PILSNER
- » BOHEMIAN DARK LAGER
- » LAZY DAY LAGER
- » MAD MONK IPA

Rotating Beers:
- » BALTIC PORTER
- » BERLINER WEISSE
- » BIER DE GARDE
- » DOPPELBOCK
- » IRISH RED
- » IRISH STOUT
- » MAI BOCK
- » MILK STOUT
- » OATMEAL STOUT
- » OKTOBERFEST
- » RUSSIAN IMPERIAL STOUT
- » RYE IPA
- » SCOTTISH ALE
- » SMOKED BOCK
- » VIENNA-STYLE LAGER

Most Popular Brew: Bohemian Pilsner

Brewmaster's Fave: Bohemian Pilsner

Tours? Yes, $10 includes 90-minute tour and tasting of four 5-oz samples. Must be 21 and older; check the website for current times.

Samples: Yes, a tasting flight of five 5oz. samples

Best Time to Go: Summer hours: Mon-Thu 2-10pm, Fri 2-11pm, Sat 12-11pm, Sun 12-10pm. Watch for many special events on their site and Facebook, and their Oktoberfest celebration.

Where can you buy it? Here on tap and in growlers to go. Distributed in Wisconsin in four-pack 16oz. cans as far away as La Crosse, Madison, Milwaukee, and Appleton.

Got food? Root beer and Spring Grove fountain sodas, hard lemonade, but no food. Food friendly, so bring your own, and watch for food trucks in summer and at events.

Special Offer: Not participating.

Directions: Business US 12 runs through downtown Eau Claire and crosses the Chippewa River on the Madison Street Bridge. The brewery is on the west side of the bridge, south side of Madison St near the corner of Madison St and Oxford Ave.

The Beer Buzz: Brewer/owner Leos Frank was born and raised in what was then Czechoslovakia (now central Slovakia). When he moved here, he couldn't find a beer he enjoyed and missed the brews of his culture. "It is a beer culture, it is part of life. Not too many people think they could make it, but they expect to have it." There were just a few microbreweries at that time just starting up. "I stopped drinking beer at one point. Until someone told me, 'Do you know you can make it at home?'" It all started as a hobby and became an obsession.

"I started with a 40 gallon kettle, the biggest I could find. Then 55. Not enough." Then he had a guy from Menomonie make him a 5.5-barrel kettle. That's how it all got started. "Then I got a stainless steel fermenter and really started feeling like a pro." The name makes reference to the tradition of the monks while adding a kick-back-and-relax attitude to it. Initially he distributed in growlers only, but popularity pushed him to 16-oz cans. The taproom, known as the Monk Cellar, became quite popular so Leos decided he'd expand. In 2015, Lazy Monk moved here, the former home of Charlson Building & Design, a 17,000-square-foot facility which now includes a 5,000-square-foot German/Czech-style Bier Hall with dark wood beams, family-style seating and a fireplace, as well as an outdoor beer garden/deck overlooking the Chippewa River. Watch for frequent events on their Facebook page, from a maypole on May Day to cribbage tournaments.

Leos makes some excellent traditional lagers, something a bit hard to find these days, but keeps a number of good ales on tap to satisfy any palate.

Free WiFi. Mug Club. On Facebook. Twitter @LazyMonkBrewing

Stumbling Distance: *Eau Claire Downtown Farmers Market* (300 Riverfront Terrace, 715-563-2644, ecdowntownfarmersmarket.com) is just across the bridge, as is the *Chippewa River State Trail* popular with cyclists. Pho, laab and curry get raves at *Egg Roll Plus Hmong Restaurant* (1611 Bellinger St, 715-832-6125). *The Brewing Projekt* is walkable from here. **Hotel:** *The Oxbow Hotel* (516 Galloway St, 715-839-0601, theoxbowhotel.com) hip hotel with phonographs in the rooms, an intimate live music venue and finer dining onsite at *The Lakely*.

Hop & Barrel Brewing Co.

310 2nd St. • Hudson, WI 54016 • 715-808-8390
hopandbarrelbrewing.com
Opened: December 16, 2017   **Head Brewer:** Chad Forner
Annual Production: 1,500 barrels   **Number of Beers:** 16 on tap

Beers:

LIGHT:
- » Beer Can Island Blonde
- » Minnesconsin Lager
- » Zorro Rojo Vienna Lager

HOPPY:
- » Chad's Pale Ale
- » Crooked Grin IPA
- » Hudson Fog
- » Hudson Haze
- » Wheaty McHop Face

DARK:
- » Dirty Scowl (dark ale)
- » Lactose Panda (milk stout)
- » Saint Black Lager

…plus nitro beers and a lot of barrel-aging

Most Popular Brew: Crooked Grin IPA

Brewmaster's Fave: Chad's Pale Ale

Tours? Yes, sign up online. $25 gets a tour, flight, sticker and pint glass.

Samples: Yes, 5-oz. tasters are $2-3 each and come in flights of four.

Best Time to Go: Open Sun-Thu 12-10pm, Fri-Sat 12-11pm. Fuckit Fridays offer beer discounts from 12-4pm.

Where can you buy it? Here on tap and in growlers, Crowlers, and six-pack cans to go.

Got food? Free popcorn, but food friendly and there's a binder of local menus.

Special Offer: A free pint when you get your book signed.

Directions: From I-94 take Exit 1 and turn north into Hudson on WI-35. Drive 0.7 mile and the brewery is on the right (opposite the river).

The Beer Buzz: In 2014, in some kind of momentary lapse of reason, the city council of Hudson passed a ban on breweries, wineries or distilleries in the downtown area. In 2017 they reversed that decision and by the end of the year, this, the first brewery, opened. The beers run the gamut, from light to hoppy to dark. All are very approachable and nearly all are sessionable with only a couple going above 6% abv. The brewery has a number of set styles or staple beers, but love to play with hops changes, fruited versions and barrel-aging. You can set yourself up with an entire flight of 16 beers.

We have Co-founders Brian Priefer and Justin Terbeest for this welcome brewery and tasting room. Justin got a homebrew kit from Northern Brewer and almost immediately went outside the lines and started making his own recipes. He's won 12 medals for homebrewing and has twice made it to the finals at the National Homebrew Competition. Brian is a certified BJCP beer judge and Cicerone Certified Beer Server and Certified Judge, and has worked at American Sky Beer, Lucid Brewing, and Inbound BrewCo. Brewer Chad brewed at Third Street Brewhouse and worked in quality control

at Cold Spring Brewing Co. in Minnesota. He holds a degree in Biology. His Chad's Pale Ale is a light pale ale series they dry hop at 4lb per barrel, originally with Mosaic but rotating through other hop varieties.

You can't miss the bright green of the taproom right on main street. Tall tables fashioned from barrels, a plank bar along the shop windows up front looking into the street (you can sort of see the river). A large back room is good for events, parking is on the street or the lot next door, and there's patio seating in season. For entertainment there are board games, cribbage, TVs, a couple arcade games, a jukebox and book exchange.

Free WiFi. ATM onsite. Mug Club. Facebook.com/hopandbarrelbrewing and Twitter @ hopandbarrelbc Instagram @hopandbarrel

Stumbling Distance: *Bricks Neapolitan Pizza* (407 2nd St #2, 715-377-7670, eatbricks.com) has great wood-fired oven pizza and some good salads as well. *Historic Casanova Liquor* (236 Coulee Rd, 715-386-2545, casanovaliquor.com) and *The Nova Wine Bar* (715-386-5333, thenovaofhudson.com) share the same space. The local-focused seasonal menu is slightly upscale American fare and the selection at the liquor store is impressive. They also do growler fills from 20 craft beer lines.

PITCHFORK BREWING

709 Rodeo Circle, Suite 104 • Hudson, WI 54016 • 715-245-3675
(NOTE: Spring 2019: moving to St Croix Meadows Complex in Hudson – watch the website.)
pitchforkbrewing.com
Founded: August 2013   **Brewmaster**: Mike Fredricksen
Annual Production: 600 barrels   **Number of Beers**: 10 on tap plus a firkin; 50+ beers per year

Staple Beers:
- » BARN DOOR BROWN
- » GERMAN PILSNER
- » MIDWEST PILSNER
- » THIRD STALL PALE ALE
- » Plus housemade root beer

Rotating Beers:
- » SUGAR SHACK MAPLE LAGER
- » VANILLA ROSE IMPERIAL PORTER
- » STOUTS, MAIBOCK, DOPPELBOCK
- » And loads of styles including local IPAs, English Porter, etc.

Most Popular Brew: One of the pilsner

Brewmaster's Fave: Barn Door Brown

Tours? Yes, detailed free tours at 2pm on Sundays (not during Packers games) and includes a couple of samples. Call ahead!

Samples: Yes, flights of five 5-oz pours for about $9.

Best Time to Go: Open Tue–Thu 3–8PM, Fri 3–10PM, Sat 12–10PM, Sun 11:30AM–7:30PM. Closed Mondays. Packer game days are popular. Watch for two festivals on site: Spring Fest in June and Harvest Fest/Birthday in August. Check the website. They also set up bus tours from the brewery to other area breweries.

Where can you buy it? Here on tap and in 25.4oz and 32oz Crowlers and growlers and limited release 22-oz bombers to go. Some growlers and bombers in area liquor stores and a few draft accounts as far as Eau Claire, south to Prescott.

Got food? Yes, Giovanni's Pizza and Milwaukee Pretzel Co. pretzels. *Paddy Ryan's* delivers their full menu to the brewery.

Special Offer: Buy your first Pitchfork beer, get a 10-ounce pour free when you get your book signed.

Directions: From I-94, take Exit 4 for US 12 going north about 0.3 mile. Turn left on Rodeo Dr, go 0.2 mile, and take a left on Rodeo Dr again. The brewery is in the line of shops on the right.

The Beer Buzz: Brewer Mike homebrewed with a buddy for 20 years and worked for 6 at Northern Brewer. He's a beer judge and started the local homebrew club. He's also a bit of a beer activist: in 2011 the Wisconsin Department of Revenue determined homebrewers couldn't take their beer out of the house, to friends, competitions, etc. Working with the Wisconsin Homebrewers Alliance, Mike rallied local officials and went to testify in Madison, and in April 2012, Senate Bill 395 passed and homebrew could be shared again and taken to competitions and exhibitions.

Sarah and Jason Edwards contacted Mike and wanted to start something, and his wife Jessie had been pushing him for years. They spent a year planning it and found a vacant space just off the interstate. They refurbished the place in an environmentally and agriculturally conscious fashion. The bar top is repurposed flooring, the tables were once doors, and the sconces are Kerr jars with chicken water bowls. Spent grain goes to a farmer and the brewing uses recirculated water. Two fermenters are dedicated to lagers. He uses whole-leaf hops, not pellets, and his alpha-acid hops are all local. He's not a fan of Yakima hops. Mike doesn't chill with glycol, but actually has different refrigerated spaces for specific temperatures. He has over 300 recipes so you can expect a lot of variation in the tap list.

The taproom has a couple of TVs (Packers games) and a few booths and tables in the storefront windows. He does an Irish Coffee Stout infused with Irish whiskey for Paddy Ryan's next door. That Vanilla Rose Imperial Porter (barrel-aged with vanilla beans) sells out in under an hour as does their barrel-aged barleywine Demeter's Choice.

Free WiFi. Growler's Club Card. Facebook/PitchforkBrewing and Twitter @ PitchforkBeer Instagram @PitchforkBrew

Stumbling Distance: *Stone Tap Gastropub* (517 2nd St, 715-808-8343, stonetaphudson.com) has some great food and the best tap list in town. *Casanova's Liquor Store* (236 Coulee Rd, 715-386-2545, casanovaliquor.com) has an excellent selection of craft beers including 20 taps for growler fills. *Paddy Ryan's* next door has pub grub.

CITY BREWERY

925 S. Third Street • La Crosse, WI 54601 • 608-785-4200
citybrewery.com
Founded: November 1999 (1858)   **Brewmaster**: Randy Hughes
Annual Production: 2,000,000 bbls (100% contract brewing)
Number of Beers: 40+

Brewmaster's Fave: "The one in my hand."

Tours? No public access, though there are some historical markers outside.

Samples? No.

Best Time to Go: Closed to the public, but great anytime for outdoor photos. See La Crosse's Oktoberfest in Festivals in the back of the book.

Got food? No.

Special Offer: Not participating.

Directions: Highways 14/61 go right through the city and the brewery is on it where it meets 3rd Street.

The Beer Buzz: This isn't any longer a place to tour or drink at, but it is a bit of history and a photo op: Look for the world's largest six-pack and you've come to the right place. Right across the street from there is a statue of King Gambrinus, one of the patron saints of beer. On Third and Mississippi St, this is the former G. Heileman Brewery, founded as a partnership in 1858 and officially G. Heileman's in 1890. Remember Old Style and Special Export? "Pure brewed from God's country; you can travel the world over and never find a better beer." In the late 19th century, after the death of her husband, Johanna Heileman was one of the first women presidents of a US corporation. In 1959, G. Heileman began buying up other breweries and became a bit of a giant producing 17 million barrels altogether. Bond Corporation of Australia bought G. Heileman in 1987 and then the brewery was passed about until it was sold to Pabst in 1999. All the breweries shut down and found different purposes except this facility which became City Brewery, owned partly by employees of the former company. The 1870 home of Gottlieb and Johanna Heileman is right across the street and holds the offices. The brewery sits on an artesian well from which it takes its water for brewing.

Brewmaster Randy was here 22 years with G. Heileman and all of City Brewery's years since. He studied biology at UW-La Crosse and went straight to the brewery to do lab work, ie. beer analysis. He's been brewmaster since 1995. Several beers have taken home awards including 2000 World Beer Cup Silver for City Lager/Light, La Crosse Lager/Light, silver for City Lager, La Crosse Lager, and Festbier at the 2004 World Beer Championships, and more silver for Winter Porter and Pale Ale at 2005 World Beer Championships. For a while City Brewery maintained ownership of the La Crosse brands, but since the sale of those, the brewery is doing contracted brews exclusively, and now has brewing facilities also in Latrobe, PA and Memphis, TN. Besides the big sixer, you can see some historical plaques here on the way to the other La Crosse breweries. And of course, say hi to King Gambrinus.

Stumbling Distance: *Kramers Bar & Grill* (1123 3rd St, 608-784-8541) next door is a good place to get a bite. Menu is mostly burgers and the like, plus deep-fried white cheddar cheese curds and beer-battered shrimp. If you are already road-tripping here, don't miss the *Great River Road* from Prescott to Prairie du Chien (by way of La Crosse). Signage is clear (a green pilot's wheel) and Hwy 133 goes all the way to Potosi (100 miles/2 hrs), home of *Potosi Brewery* and the *ABA National Brewery Museum*. The bluffs are beautiful and the drive is recommended by several national publications. *Grandad Bluff* is most popular for a sweeping view of the river valley and the city.

Pearl Street Brewery

1401 S Andrew Street • La Crosse, WI 54603 • 608-784-4832
pearlstreetbrewery.com
Founded: 1999   **Brewmaster**: Joe Katchever
Annual Production: 6,000+ bbls
Number of Beers: 16 on tap here; 20-25 in distribution each year

Staple Beers:
- » D.T.B. Brown Ale
- » El Hefe Bavarian Hefeweizen
- » Linalool IPA
- » Me, Myself and IPA
- » Java Lava Coffee Stout
- » Pearl Street Pale Ale
- » Rubber Mills Pils
- » That's What I'm Talkin''bout Organic Rolled Oat Stout!

Rotating Beers:
- » Appleweizen
- » Bedwetter Barleywine
- » Breakfast Beer
- » Dankenstein IIPA
- » Evil Doppleganger Dopplebock
- » Funk My Life (wine/oak-barrel-aged mixed fermentation beers)
- » Liederhosen Lager Oktoberfest
- » Raspberry Tambois (Belgian-style sour)
- » Rumpshaker IPA
- » Smokin' Hemp Porter

Seasonal Sour Series:
- » Winter Gose (with spruce tips & bergamot)
- » Pop Gose (lavender/hibiscus/cucumber)
- » 17-Up Lemon-Lime Gose
- » Fall Harvest Gose

...plus various barrel-aged and sours and funky beers on tap

Most Popular Brew: D.T.B.

Brewmaster's Fave: "I tend to drink the hoppier beers, but a good bock is a great thing!"

Tours? Yes, Friday tours at 5 & 6PM, Saturdays from 4PM–8PM on the hour, or call with your group or for a special event. Tours are about $8 and include a pint glass, a pint of beer and a coupon. Check the website to be sure.

Samples? Yes, a flight of 2-oz pours of 8 beers for about $7.

Best Time to Go: Tasting room open Tue–Thu 4–8PM, Fri 3–10PM, Sat noon–7PM. Cyclists: Free Wheelin' Wednesdays, a free pint when you bike in. Poses & Pints Yoga (see website). Watch for their Anniversary Party, the **Annual Winter Ball** in February, a Fri–Sat event with food and beer pairings with area chefs and restaurants, special beers only made for this weekend, plus live music, and beer releases every 1.5 hours.

Where can you buy it? Here on tap and to go in Pearl Street growlers only and four- and six-packs. Distributed throughout Wisconsin and parts of NE Iowa and SE Minnesota on draft, in four- and six-pack bottles, and some 22-oz bombers.

Got food? Just free pretzels at the bar, but La Crosse has lots of great restaurants that deliver right to the brewery.

Special Offer: A free pint when you get your book signed!

Directions: From I-90 take the Hwy 35/53 exit south to the first traffic light and go left on to George Street. After you've gone over the bridge over the train tracks, take a left at the 2nd set of traffic lights (Saint Andrew St) and go half a block down on the left to the four-story La Crosse Footwear building.

The Beer Buzz: Brewmaster Joe lived in Colorado and worked at several breweries there before journeying to La Crosse to found Pearl Street, which takes its name from its original location on Pearl Street downtown. Things were going well and he was putting out 12 different beers annually, but growth was inevitable. The new facility was up and running before renovations were even complete. They have much more space in this renovated boot factory from the early 1900s. It was once home to La Crosse Footwear which moved its operations to China in 2001 and left the factory empty. And as with most emptiness, beer just seems like the best solution for filling it. In 2015, they added several new fermenters to keep up with demand. Linalool IPA uses Northern Discovery hops, a wild variety found in 2007 growing in a guy's tree canopy.

The taproom opens right into the brewhouse and has a long curving concrete bar and a scattering of mismatched tables. A small stage hosts free live music most Thursdays and Fridays and a cooler stocks to-go beer. They have a nice little gift shop here as well. Foosball, ping pong and board games are provided for your entertainment.

Parking is on the gravel lot right outside the door or on the street. ***Do not park*** on the paved parking lot or you will be towed!

Free WiFi. ATM onsite. Facebook.com/pearlstreetbrewery Twitter and Instagram @ PearlStreetBrew

Stumbling Distance: The Mississippi is king here, and to take in a view of it and have some great eats, head down to *La Crosse Pettibone Boat Club* (2615 Schubert Pl, 608-784-7743, pettiboneboat-club.com, under the big blue bridge to Minnesota). Boaters can use the marina, and outside seating features a tiki bar. Famous for hand-dipped cheese curds, Pettibone serves anything from nice dinners to casual burgers. Open from May–Oct. And of course the biggest beer event in town is also one of the biggest in the state: *La Crosse Oktoberfest* (oktoberfestusa.com).

TOUR DE PEARL

If you like cycling for your beer, this awesome Pearl Street summer promotion is for you. Every summer the brewery puts on its Tour de Pearl. Your registration fee (about $20–25) gets you a tour badge/lanyard, t-shirt, bonus tour card, keychain, and promotional coupons and freebies from sponsors. La Crosse's Tour de Pearl runs from June–August. On your own time, pedal to each of the stages (40+) and order a pint of Pearl Street beer at each to get your tour card stamped. Completing a certain number of stages gets you an entry for a chance to win the grand prize (a sweet new bicycle). The end-of-tour party is held at the La Crosse Area Bicycle Festival (explorela-crosse.com) in La Crosse on the Saturday of Labor Day Weekend. Register online at pearlstreetbrewery.com/tour-de-pearl and follow Facebook.com/TourDePearl for organized rides.

---

608 BREWING CO.

83 Copeland Ave. • La Crosse, WI 54603
608brewingcompany.com
Opened: Summer 2018   **Head Brewer:** Phil Humphrey
Annual Production: 500 barrels   **Number of Beers:** 8-10 on tap

Beers:

- » A lighter beer
- » A few IPAs
- » Double IPA
- » Brown Ale
- » Milk Stout
- » Very into barrel aging and fruited sours

Brewmaster's Fave: IPAs

Tours? No.

Samples: Yes, sample flights of four 5-oz pours for about $6.

Best Time to Go: Open Wed-Thu 4-10pm, Fri 4-11pm, Sat 11am-11pm. Closed Sun-Tue.

Where can you buy it? Here on tap and in Crowlers to go (no growlers).

Got food? No, but food friendly and local food trucks on hand.

Special Offer: Half off your first pint of house beer when you get your book signed.

Directions: From I-90, take Exit 3 for US-53/WI-35, and head south on US-53/WI-35/Rose St for 1.9 miles. Stay on this for another 1.1 miles after it becomes Copeland Ave, and the brewery is on the right (west) side of the street.

The Beer Buzz: In case you hadn't figured, 608 is the area code in these parts. Brewer Phil went all in, quitting the day job to do this full-time with his wife Lorie and business partners Ryan and Danielle Beach from Oshkosh. Phil served in the Army National Guard with Danielle years ago, and the couples would run into each other at breweries. He'd been planning a brewery in his head for a long time and dropped the idea on Danielle and Ryan in the summer of 2017. They found this property, a former John Deere sort of place, already basically set up for a small brewery: garage door, cement floor for equipment with some drainage. Not complete, but a head start.

They brought in reclaimed barn wood, a concrete bartop, and put in tile behind the bar and polished concrete for the floors. They built their own beer hall tables and some high- and low-tops as well. Phil's brewing on a 7-barrel system from Stout Tanks. Live music is planned and board games are on hand. The location is on the parade route for Oktoberfest.

Free WiFi. Mug Club. Facebook.com/608brewingcompany and Twitter @608brewing Instagram @608brewco

Stumbling Distance: *Candlewood Suites* (56 Copeland Ave, 608-785-1110, ihg.com) is across the road and south another block or so. There's *The Sports Nut*, a good local tavern to watch the game with wings and bar food, and *Marges on Rose*, for homestyle breakfast and late lunch, both in the 800 block of Rose Street north of here. Otherwise head south into downtown for *Turtle Stack Brewery* and an abundance of eateries, or north and east 4 minutes from here to *Pearl Street Brewery*.

TURTLE STACK BREWERY

125 2ⁿᵈ Street South • La Crosse, WI 54601 • 608-519-2284
turtlestackbrewery.com
Opened: June 2015   **Brewmaster**: Brent Martinson
Annual Production: 300 barrels   **Number of Beers**: 9 on tap; 25 different beers each year

Beers:

- » BELGIAN BLONDE
- » BROWN ALE
- » CASCADE SMASH GOLDEN ALE
- » IPA

Rotating Beers:

- » BLACK LAGER
- » COCONUT BALTIC PORTER
- » FESTBIER
- » FOREIGN EXTRA STOUT
- » HEFEWEIZEN
- » IRISH RED
- » KÖLSCH
- » MAIBOCK

Most Popular Brew: Belgian Blonde

Brewmaster's Fave: "I have a hard time picking a beer"

Tours? Yes, by chance or by appointment. It can be done from a bar stool.

Samples: Yes, 4-oz pours for about $1.50 each.

Best Time to Go: Open Wed-Thu 4-9pm, Fri 2-11pm, Sat 12-11pm. Live music on Wednesdays.

Where can you buy it? Here on tap and growlers to go, plus area draft accounts.

Got food? Just snacks, but food friendly and local menus are on hand. Occasional food trucks park outside, more often in the summer. Plus Frostop Root Beer on tap.

Special Offer: $1 of your first pint when you get your book signed.

Directions: US 53 passes north–south through La Crosse and 2nd St runs parallel to the west. Take Main St or Pearl St toward the river from US 53 and the brewery is just north of the corner of Pearl and 2nd St.

The Beer Buzz: You know the way turtles climb on top of each other on logs and rocks while sunning themselves? That's a turtle stack. With the proximity of the Mississippi River and its own legion of stackable turtles, the name seemed appropriate for this most recent brewery to open in La Crosse. Then again it might be inspired by a certain children's story turtle who rhymes with Mertle.

Located in a 1880s building, in the city's historic architecture district, Turtle Stack is the creation of founder/brewer Brent Martinson. Hooked on homebrewing by a friend years ago, his hobby turned into a basement full of equipment. He already had a science background and started to believe beer was his future. Brent is originally from Fargo, ND but moved to La Crosse years ago. He left for Delafield to brew at Water Street Brewery for about 5 years but returned to La Crosse in 2013 to finally move forward on his own place. He eventually found this old building which had housed a printer for 60 years, a saloon, a mattress spring factory, and most recently, a clock shop. When they tore out the insides of the building, they found a 100-year-old wood floor underneath. Brent's small system allows him to keep switching things up on the taps, and that's exactly what he aims to do. Styles will range widely, though public response may determine some brews that end up on more often than others.

Free WiFi. No TVs. Music in the background. It's really about the beer and conversation.

Facebook/turtlestackbrewery Instagram @TurtleStackBrewery

Stumbling Distance: While not a brewery, *Bodega Brew Pub* (122 4th St S, 608-782-0677, bodegabrewpublax.com) nevertheless is an impressive craft beer bar, with hundreds from around the world plus good food. *La Crosse Distilling Co.* (129 Vine St, 970-231-2603) has a tasting room serving cocktails and some food. *Buzzard Billy's* (222 Pearl St, 608-796-2277, buzzardbillys.com) is around the corner for casual Cajun/Creole and beer. Right across the street from there is *The Cheddarhead Store* (608-784-8899), the original home of those foam cheesehead hats and a bunch of other Wisconsin products/apparel/souvenirs. **Hotel:** *The Charmant Hotel* (101 State St, 866-697-7300, thecharmanthotel.com) is a boutique hotel in a repurposed 1898 candy factory. Great place to crash and has a rooftop bar.

LUCETTE BREWING CO.

901 Hudson Road • Menomonie, WI 54751 • 715-231-6836
lucettebrewing.com
Founded: 2011   **Head Brewer:** Christian Thompson
Annual Production: 2,200 barrels   **Number of Beers:** 16 on tap

Staple Beers:

» THE FARMER'S DAUGHTER SPICED BLONDE ALE (coriander and grains of paradise)
» HIPS DON'T LIE BAVARIAN-STYLE WEISSBIER
» LUCETTE HARMONIA
» RIDE AGAIN AMERICAN PALE ALE
» SLOW HAND AMERICAN STOUT

Belgian Series:

» DOUBLE DAWN BELGIAN STYLE IMPERIAL GOLDEN ALE
» SHINING DAWN BELGIAN-STYLE GOLDEN ALE

Rotating Beers: (15 BBL Batch Series)

» COAL MINER'S DAUGHTER (Grisette)
» FRENCH CONNECTION (Biere de Garde)
» THE KURVE (Kölsch)
» RYE'D ON MAN (Rye Brown Session Ale)
» TERRY PORTER
» ...plus many more

Most Popular Brew: Farmer's Daughter

Brewer's Fave: Slow Hand

Tours? Not currently. Watch the website.

Samples: Yes, sample flights.

Best Time to Go: Open Mon-Tue 4-9pm with limited menu, Wed-Thu 4-10pm, Fri-Sat 11am-10pm, Sun 11am-9pm.

Where can you buy it? Here on tap and to go in growlers. Distributed mostly in western Wisconsin and the Twin Cities metro area on draft or in six-packs of 12- and 16-oz cans or 750 ml cork & cage bottles. They self-distribute to Madison as well.

Got food? Yes, wood-fired pizzas and calzones, salads, pretzel, breadsticks, bruschetta, plus some wines and ciders. GF and vegan available.

Special Offer: Not participating at this time.

Directions: From I-94 take Exit 41 for Hwy 25 and head south through downtown on Hwy 25. Go west on Hwy 29, across from the university, and follow it ¾ mile and you'll see Lucette in a white building on your left (south side).

Cyclists: This is right off the Red Cedar State Trail.

The Beer Buzz: Lucette is the name of Paul Bunyan's girlfriend (or so it was decided in a statue-naming contest in Minnesota) and big Paul is a legendary lumberjack popular around these parts where the lumber industry once boomed. From the road, this place could be mistaken for a farmhouse, painted white, a porch out front. Don't expect a big industrial brewery. They wanted to fit in with their surroundings. Co-founder Michael Wilson is very serious about the local aspect of beer and part of his business philosophy is making a difference not just for himself, but for the businesses that support him—thus the use of local ingredients as much as possible.

Mike is originally from Minnesota, and while studying at University of North Dakota he determined that he wanted to be involved with the craft brewing industry. He dabbled in homebrewing and learned he wasn't good at it, but that wouldn't deter him. He moved to Menomonie and got experience in distribution. He met his business partner Tim Schletty who had a retail background. The two had experience in two of the three aspects of a brewery; now they only needed the all-important brewer. They hired Jon Christiansen who brewed for them for a long time before departing to open his own brewery. In 2016 Christian Thompson came on as head brewer with experience at *Sand Creek Brewing* and Minnesota's Lift Bridge Brewing.

In 2015, the brewery tripled the size of the building to accommodate Lucette Wood-fired Eatery. The restaurant features a hand-cut stone oven from Naples for Neapolitan-style pizzas made with locally sourced ingredients. Patrons sit right in the middle of the brewery, not far from the canning line, for an open and visual beer and food experience.

Free WiFi. Facebook.com/LucetteBrewingCompany and
Twitter/Instagram @ lucettebrewing

Stumbling Distance: *Red Cedar State Trail* runs right past the brewery. If you're a biker, this is a nice ride. See Biking for Beer in the back of the book.

BREWERY NØNIC
(FORMERLY REAL DEAL BREWING)

621 4th St West • Menomonie, WI 54751
brewerynonic.com
Opening: Fall 2018　　**Brewmaster:** Ryan Verdon
Annual Production: 200 barrels　　**Number of Beers:** 10 taps (2 cask engines)

Beers:

» 4 year-round beers, plus seasonals
and one-offs

Brewer's Fave: English Mild Ale

Tours? Yes, by chance or by appointment.

Samples: Yes, sample flights of 4-oz pours.

Best Time to Go: Open Wed-Sun, check the website or Facebook for hours. Watch for seasonal hour changes and live music twice a month.

Where can you buy it? Here on tap or to go in Crowlers or your own growler.

Got food? Yes, some food trucks and local vendors, but also food friendly.

Special Offer: Buy your first pint and get 1 free when you get your book signed.

Directions: From I-94 take Exit 41 and head south on WI-35/Broadway St into Menomonie for 2 miles. Turn right on 1st Ave and then the next left on 2nd St. Continue 0.4 mile, turn right on Wilson and right again on 4th St and the brewery is the train station on the left.

Red Cedar State Trail runs through town and soon will be connected to this brewery via a path that takes the bridge north across the Red Cedar River. ** Biking for Beer

The Beer Buzz: *The Raw Deal* is a popular local shop that roasts their own coffee and serves a changing menu of organic and local dishes and desserts in a cozy, community-centric space. When they decided to brew some beer too, they brought Ryan on to form Real Deal Brewing. "No Crap on Tap. Period." Ryan eventually wanted to turn real deal into a bigger deal and this is the awesome result. (The Raw Deal is still there and you should check it out.)

Brewer Ryan is a graduate of the fortuitously beer-named UW-Stout right here in town, and during his student life he hung out at The Raw Deal doing his chemistry homework for a Food Science major. He started homebrewing with a kit from Northern Brewer, and when he took some time off from school, he worked at Rush River Brewing on the bottling line and doing odd jobs. In June 2014 he started brewing as Real Deal. In 2017 Ryan started kicking around the idea of getting his own brewery. The train station had been nothing more than a storage facility, but the community has always hoped someone would restore it and use it again. Dan Fedderly, co-owner of The Raw Deal had his eye on it, and finally the owners of the building agreed it was time to sell. He bought it and started restoration, planning to move The Raw Deal here, but Ryan had bigger plans and they offered to sell it on to him.

Ryan has a 5-barrel system and has no emphasis on style and plans to brew all over the spectrum, though he loves English ales. So you can expect bitters and milds, but a lot more with other yeast strains, including Belgians and lagers. He does occasional collaboration brews with Lucette Brewing and Zymurgy Brewing in town. The local homebrewers have a good relationship with him, and Beverage Artisan, a homebrew shop, is right across the street.

Free WiFi. Facebook.com/brewerynonic

Stumbling Distance: *Stacked Eatery* (617 Broadway St S, 715-309-4877, stacked-eatery.com) serves really nice food in an after-bar food style. *The Waterfront Bar & Grill* (512 Crescent St, 715-235-6541) has a reputable fish fry and a good tap list. If you enjoy disc golf, there are 4 courses in Menomonie. *Silver Dollar* (315 Main St E, 715-309-4440, silverdollar315.com) is another local bar & grill favorite.

NONIC PINT GLASS

I always associated this glass with a bulge in it with pubs in the UK. In fact, the design wasn't popular in England until after WWII. American Hugo Pick tried to patent his Nonik ("no-nick") glass in 1913, but similar designs had existed in the 19th century. His design's shallow bulge prevented sticking and crushing when stacking glasses, protected the rim from nicking, and offered a better grip for drinkers, but remained easy to clean.

Zymurgy Brewing Co.

624 Main St. East • Menomonie, WI 54751 • 715-309-2657
zymurgybrew.com
Opened: Summer 2018　　**Head Brewer:** Jon Christiansen
Annual Production: 250 barrels　　**Number of Beers:** 6-8 on tap, plus guest taps

Staple Beers:
- » German Weiss
- » Belgian Styles (three primary yeast strains, he lived there for 6 mos. In Belgium, Siebel Institute grad)

Rotating Beers:
- » Big English Style Beers
- » Russian Imperial Stout (barrel aging, especially sours)

Brewmaster's Fave: Russian Imperial Stouts and Barleywines

Tours? Yes, by chance or by appointment.

Samples: Yes, sample flights.

Best Time to Go: Open Tue-Sun. Check the Facebook page for hours.

Where can you buy it? Here on tap and in Crowlers and growlers to go.

Got food? Some food options, plus food trucks. Food friendly. Their own ginger beer and kombucha.

Special Offer: $2 off your first pint of house beer when you get your book signed.

Directions: From I-94 take Exit 41 and turn south on WI-25/Broadway St, continuing 2.3 miles. Turn left on Main St and drive 0.3 mile, being careful to take a slight right to stay on Main where Crescent St continues left, and the brewery is on the right.

The Beer Buzz: Menomonie already knows Jon from his work over at Lucette Brewing from 2010 to 2016. A Milwaukee native, he had brewed a couple years at Water Street in Delafield and in Vegas at Joseph James. He and his partner and girlfriend Chelsea Rickert wrote for a beer newspaper and worked at Oskar Blues in Colorado. A third partner, Zach Barker also worked at Lucette. When Jon decided he wanted to start his own brewery, he first looked at Milwaukee, but finally decided he likes Menomonie, so he stayed. Chelsea brings her own fermentation talents to the project with kombucha, sauerkraut, kimchee and the like. (But no wine or cider due to licensing.)

Until August of 2017, this was an old auto shop and the room is where they worked on cars. A car wash, attached in the 1980s, had the drains necessary for a brewhouse. But the shop area needed most of its concrete replaced. Two double glass doors open into the brewhouse. They have a parking lot in front of the building, and five garage doors, three of them of glass facing north toward the lake and two to the east for the brewery, a 7-barrel system.

They chose the name Zymurgy, the technical name for the study of fermentation in brewing, winemaking and distlilling, because there is an education element to their project. Jon is a BJCP-certified beer judge and Cicerone and hosts occasional beer classes. The taproom is pet-friendly and has a lounge feel – a good hangout spot. A stage hosts live music.

Free WiFi. Mug Club. Facebook/ and Twitter Instagram @ZymurgyBrewing

Stumbling Distance: The Farmer's Market is a block away in summer on Wed & Sat. *Waterfront Bar & Grill* (512 Crescent St, 715-235-6541) overlooks the water and has good food and a fish fry. *The Raw Deal* (603 Broadway St S, 715-231-3255, rawdeal-wi.com) is a café with great coffee, raw and vegan food, and craft beers.

BARLEY JOHN'S BREWING CO.

1280 Madison Avenue • New Richmond, WI 54017 • 715-246-4677
barleyjohnsbrewery.com
Opened: August 2015   **Brewers**: Nick Wilbricht, Kati Parker, Dennis Klegin
Annual Production: 4,000 barrels   **Number of Beers**: 16 taps; some guest taps

Staple Beers:

- » CONE GNOME IPA
- » LITTLE BARLEY SESSION ALE
- » OLD 8 PORTER
- » WILD BRUNETTE WILD RICE BROWN ALE

Rotating Beers:

- » MANGO GNOME DOUBLE PALE ALE
- » 6 KNOT IPA (STOCKYARD IPA at the brewpub in MN)
- » Maibock, Kölsch, Oktoberfest, Belgian styles, Doppelbock, Scotch Ale, and many more

Most Popular Brew: Wild Brunette

Brewmaster's Fave: Nick: Pilsner, Kati: Porter, Dennis: IPA

Tours? Yes, scheduled on Saturdays. About $5 for tour and a pint of beer. Check website for times.

Samples: Yes, four 5-oz pours for about $6.

Best Time to Go: Open Thu-Fri 4-10pm, Sat 12-10pm. Summer hours are longer, check the website. Open mic night 6-9pm on Thursdays.

Where can you buy it? Here on tap and in growlers to go, as well as kegs and cans. Four-packs of 16-oz cans and kegs distributed in WI and MN.

Got food? Yes, eclectic café style with sandwiches and small plates and appetizers, and no deep fryer.

Special Offer: A free 4-beer sampler flight with your book signature.

Directions: Coming into New Richmond from the south on WI 65, turn left on Richmond Way and go 0.6 mile. Turn right on Madison Ave, and of 0.4 mile to find the brewery on the right.

The Beer Buzz: John Moore and his wife Laura Subak have been running a highly successful brewpub in the Twin Cities area called Barley John's Brew Pub. Success compelled them to expand, but he'd have to buy a whole new brewhouse to increase capacity. Minnesota law prevents brewpubs (as opposed to production breweries) from distributing, and you can't own both. Someone told him he ought to go to beer-friendly Wisconsin, and New Richmond came up as a really nice community to work with. The City recommended a new build, but John was hesitant.

The law in MN says no owner of a brewpub in MN can have any ownership of a brewery *anywhere*. They consulted a lawyer, and it turns out the State of Minnesota considers a married couple as two separate entities. So Laura owns the brewpub now, and John owns the brewery. In Wisconsin this would be a problem (see *The Brewing Projekt's* story), but as they are married in Minnesota, they are in the clear. In the end they found they may have been able to do that separate ownership plan in Minnesota, but oh well, Wisconsin is happy to have them. The 30-barrel brewhouse occupies the great space in back. Kati is a longtime homebrewer and member of Pink Boots Society Minneapolis; she took her first professional brewing job here. Nick has a Chemisty degree from UW-La Crosse and has brewed with Tod Fyten, a figure in the Minnesota brewing scene. Dennis has homebrewed since 2011, and trained under Barley John's previous brewer Bob McKenzie who left to distill after many years of brewing.

The building, at the corner of Madison and Wisconsin, is almost 14,000 square feet. The taproom has a long bar of birch wood, seats 75, and has a fireplace in the corner. Hops grow on a trellis outside. There's a TV, some background music, Hammerschlagen, and you might find a cribbage board lying around. The outdoor beer garden has a firepit and they can make you a *Stachelbier*, a German tradition of lowering a hot poker into a beer and causing a caramelized head to foam up.

Free WiFi. Barley Beer Society (like Mug Club). Facebook.com/Barleyjohns and Twitter @ barleyjohnsbrew Instagram @BarleyJohnsBrewingCom

Stumbling Distance: Nearby *45th Parallel Distillery* (1570 Madison Ave, 715-246-0565, 45thparalleldistillery.com) does tours and tastings. **Hotels:** *Best Western Plus* (240 Paperjack Dr, 715-243-5600) is a nice place to crash and has an unusual saltwater pool.

Skeleton Crew Brew

570 Theater Rd. • Onalaska, WI 54650 • 715-570-9463
skeletoncrewbrew.com

Opened: Memorial Day Weekend, 2016   **Head Brewer:** Todd Wiedenhaft
Annual Production: 500 barrels   **Number of Beers:** 8 on tap

Staple Beers:

- » Anchors Away IPA
- » ARRRG Ale APA
- » Coconut Cream Ale
- » Hempen Halter – Honey Nut Brown Ale
- » Pillage & Plunder Black Porter
- » Red Beard Irish Red
- » Shiver Me Timbers – Oatmeal Stout

Rotating Beers:

- » Blunderbuss – Blueberry Hefe
- » Come About – Chocolate Milk Stout
- » Crow's Nest – Coconut Cream Ale
- » Eye Patch IPA – New England IPA
- » Hornswoggle – Pineapple Hefe
- » Nipperkin – Pumpkin Spice Hefe
- » Pieces of Eight – Bourbon Barrel Porter
- » Powder Monkey – Spicy Red Ale
- » Run A Rig – Raspberry Hefe
- » Scallywag – Coffee Stout

Most Popular Brew: Red Beard then Hempen Halter

Brewmaster's Fave: Red Beard

Tours? For wine tastings or by appointment.

Samples: Yes, Walk the Plank flights of four 4-oz pours for about $6. (Also, 3 free wine samples.)

Best Time to Go: Open Wed-Thu 4-9pm, Fri-Sat 12-10pm, Sun 12-5pm. Closed Mon-Tue.

Where can you buy it? Here on tap and in Crowlers to go. Wines are at Festival Foods.

Got food? Cheese and crackers, but carry-in is OK for the back room (not at the bar).

Special Offer: $1 off your first pint when you get your book signed.

Directions: From I-90 take Exit 5 and head south on WI-16 toward Onalaska. In less than a mile, turn right on Theater Rd and drive 0.2 mile. See a commercial strip of businesses on the left set back from the road and behind a parking lot. Turn left into this lot and the winery is at the far left (south) end of the building. (There's an entry to this lot from the Lester Ave side too.)

The Beer Buzz: Todd and Jennifer Wiedenhaft started Lost Island Winery in 2011. When they started hearing a lot of women saying that their husband/father/brother/son/ boyfriend would love this place if it only had beer, Todd, a homebrewer for 15+ years, took the idea to heart. The winery has a tropical/Caribbean theme going on – some touches of grass hut on the back bar and the awning outside work into a Tiki Hut look – so they decided to go "Pirates" with the beer. As the entire operation is just Todd and Jennifer, the term skeleton crew fit perfectly. They brewed 200 barrels their first full year and upgraded equipment so that they could triple production to keep up with demand. Mix the Coconut Cream Ale with the Chocolate Milk Stout to get an Almond Joy. Tiki Hut Brew Supplies is attached. Board games and a TV in the back room for games. The back patio also hosts live music.

No WiFi. Facebook.com/skeletoncrewbrew

Stumbling Distance: *Red Pines Bar & Grill* (W7305 County Rd Z, 608-779-2800, redpinesbarandgrill.com) or *Blue Moon Bar & Grill* (716 2nd Ave N, 608-781-6800, bluemoononalaska.com) has you covered for great food and Friday fish fry. And *Two Beagles Brewpub* is up that way as well.

TWO BEAGLES BREWPUB

910 2nd Ave N. • Onalaska, WI 54650 • 608-519-1921
twobeaglesbrewpub.com
Opened: May 2016   **Brewmaster:** Steve Peters
Annual Production: 250 barrels   **Number of Beers:** 8 on tap

Staple Beers:
- » LARRY KÖLSCH
- » IPAs

Rotating Beers:
- » BEAGLEFEST MÄRZEN
- » CARAMEL APPLE BOCK
- » DOUBLE IPA
- » FESTBIER
- » MILK STOUT
- » SOUR CHERRY WHEAT
- » WHEY BLACK BEAGLE
- » plus some barrel-aging

Most Popular Brew: Larry

Brewmaster's Fave: I'm a sucker for stouts.

Tours? Not really, but you can see the brewhouse behind the glass.

Samples: Yes, sample flights of four 5-oz pours for about $6.

Best Time to Go: Open Closed Mondays. Happy hour weekdays 3-6pm, 10-close. Occasional live music.

Where can you buy it? Here on tap and in growlers to go, plus some local draft accounts.

Got food? Yes, bar food (burgers, pizzas) meets supper club (fish fry, prime rib), highlighting local ingredients. Ellsworth cheese curds on the poutine. Pig wings: brined/cured/smoked ribs braised with *beer syrup* (that's a thing here!). Kids' menu.

Special Offer: Your first pint of house beer is free when you get your book signed.

Directions: From I-90 take Exit 3 and turn north on WI-35/Rose St. Stay on WI-35 for 2.2 miles and the brewpub is on the right (east) side, opposite the lake. Coming south on WI-35 from River Falls gets you here too, but meanders along the Mississippi first on the *Great River Road* (wigrr.com).

The Beer Buzz: Overlooking Lake Onalaska, the brewpub looks like a chalet, with high, peaked ceiling in the dining room area and a separate bar area with high-top tables. Owner/brewer Steve Peters started homebrewing in the 90s and took his first professional brewing job at City Brewery (the former G. Heileman brewery in La Crosse) in 2004 where he stayed for 10 years. He's helped build brewhouses in Denver, among other places. The building dates to the 1970s and was once Nob Hill Restaurant. Steve took over in 2015 and started renovations, renaming the place for his two dogs.

He works with a 7.5-barrel brewhouse producing some solid traditional beers and a good number of creative brews as well. 100 pounds of Honeycrisp apples went into the Caramel Apple Bock and Steve diced them all himself. Other than the two flagship brews, something new is always coming on. The food is not an afterthought and has some pretty inventive dishes. Beer syrup is made with sugar, maple and cinnamon and finds its way into a few items. Beer cocktails are also on the menu. 3 TVs pipe in sports, and the bar is popular for Badger games. Covered deck seating outside takes advantage of the hilltop lake views.

Free WiFi. ATM onsite. Facebook.com/TwoBeaglesBrewpub and Twitter/Instagram @2beaglebrewpub

Stumbling Distance: WI-35 makes up much of Wisconsin's 250-mile portion of the *Great River Road National Scenic Byway* (wigrr.com) which follows the Mississippi River. An excellent road trip, this connects brew towns Alma and La Crosse/Onalaska to Potosi, home of *Potosi Brewing*, the *National Brewery Museum* and the *Great River Road* visitor center.

Northwoods Brewpub and Grill

50819 West St • Osseo, WI 54758 • 715-597-1828
northwoodsbrewpub.com
Founded: 1997   **Brewmaster**: Tim Kelly and Eddie Rogers
Annual Production: 1,200 bbls   **Number of Beers**: 30 on tap; 40+ beers per year

Staple Beers:

» Birchwood Pale Ale
» Bumbl'n Bubba's Buzz'n Brew (honey golden ale)
» Floppin' Crappie (light caramel-colored ale with honey)
» Half Moon Gold
» Kelly's Stout
» Lil' Bandit Brown Ale
» Mouthy Muskie Light Ale
» Poplar Porter
» Prickly Pike's Pilsner
» Red Cedar Red Ale
» Rowdy Rye
» Walter's Premium Pilsener
» White Weasel Light Ale
» Whitetail Wheat

Rotating Beers:

» Buckshot Bock
» Bumbl'n Bubba's Lingonberry Light (an actual berry)
» Dunkelweizen
» Irish Stoat Ale
» Oktoberfest Lager
» Ripplin' Red Raspberry Wheat
» Wall IPA
» ...and some barrel-aging and the occasional sour beer

Most Popular Brew: Floppin' Crappie

Brewmaster's Fave: Lil' Bandit Brown

Tours? Yes, anytime.

Samples? Yes, a sampler with eight 4-oz beers for $9 and a free 8-oz beer with a brew tour.

Best Time to Go: Open Mon–Sat 7AM–close, Sun 8AM–close. Happy hour is 11–6 Mon–Fri. Popular with the college crowd on Friday and Saturday nights.

Where can you buy it? Here on tap and in growlers to go, and distributed in the Chippewa River Valley in six-pack bottles and cans.

Got food? Yes, they have a full menu, are big on burgers, open for breakfast and the typical Friday fish fry, deep-fry cheese curds. Free popcorn.

Special Offer: A free house beer or soda when you get your book signed.

Directions: The brewpub is on the frontage road on 53 just north of the I-94 interchange. Exit US-53 at Golf Rd and go west a short block to Oakwood Hills Parkway. Turn right (north) here and Oakwood Mall Drive is on your left.

The Beer Buzz: Jerry Bechard, a Wisconsin native, bought the famous pie mecca Norske Nook in 1990. But as a homebrewer, he couldn't ignore the call of beer, and in 1995 he decided he needed to make beer commercially and began Northwoods Brewing Co.

Brewmaster Tim grew up with Jerry, and Jerry wanted him to brew. So Tim went off to Siebel Institute to study, already knowing where he'd be working when he was done. Long ago the famous regional brew was Walter's Premium, and when the brewery found that this brand was dead, they revived it. They consulted with some lifelong Walter's drinkers until Tim dialed in the best guess of the original pilsner recipe. In 2016, the brewpub went even larger, moving to this former condensed milk and canning factory in Osseo.

The space is huge. Garage doors open to outdoor seating areas, and inside are high industrial ceilings and a load of tall tables, a lounge corner with a fireplace, and a large 3-sided bar with colored lights behind its glass blocks. TVs are everywhere as are some mounted bucks. A stage hosts live music, and darts, pinball and Giant Jenga are on hand. A 700-person event space is upstairs.

The interior aims at rustic for the Northwoods theme, and the pond-side beer garden and patio are great in the summer. Their Lil' Bandit Brown Ale won silver at the Great American Beer Festival in 2000 while Floppin' Crappie wowed the crowd and took a best beer title at Sturgis in 2004.

Free WiFi. ATM onsite. Facebook.com/northwoodsbrewpub

Stumbling Distance: *Norske Nook* (13804 W 7th St, 715-597-3069, norskenook.com) is a regional chain but the pie screams homemade. *Burly-N-Bucks* (13719 7th St, 715-597-2068) has good eats including a Friday fish fry. Hotel: *Super 8* (50663 Oak Grove Rd, 715-803-2628) or *Stoney Creek RV Resort* (50483 Oak Grove Rd, 715-597-2102) if you prefer to camp.

Rush River Brewing Co.

990 Antler Court • River Falls, WI 54022 • 715-426-2054
rushriverbeer.com
Founded: May 2004 **Brewmasters**: Dan Chang and Nick Anderson
Annual Production: undetermined **Number of Beers**: 14 on tap

Staple Beers:

» Bubblejack IPA
» Double Bubble Imperial IPA
» Lost Arrow Porter
» Minion IPA
» Small Axe Golden Ale
  (Hefeweizen with local wheat)
» The Unforgiven Amber Ale
  (dry-hopped)

Rotating Beers:

» Lyndale Brown Ale (Aug–Nov)
» Nevermore Chocolate Oatmeal
  Stout (winter)
» Über Alt (April–July)
» Winter Warmer (Oct–Jan)

Most Popular Brew: The Unforgiven Amber Ale

Brewmaster's Fave: Bubblejack IPA

Tours? Free tours with samples the second Saturday of each month at 1pm. Numbers are limited, and you must reserve a spot (use the website).

Samples? Yes.

Best Time to Go: Taproom open Thu–Sat 4-10pm.

Where can you buy it? Here on tap and in growlers to go, and distributed in six-pack and twelve-pack bottles and a few 750ml bottles. Their website shows their distribution in western Wisconsin, the Madison area, and eastern Minnesota (especially the Twin Cities).

Got food? Just pretzels and the occasional food truck, but food friendly, bring your own.

Special Offer: Not Participating.

The Beer Buzz: Dan and Nick were co-workers at a brewery in Seattle when they met. Nick's from Minneapolis and Dan hails from Milwaukee, so the logical place to set up shop was right in the middle, just inside the border of Wisconsin, as it turns out, in Maiden Rock. Dan put in some time at Summit Brewing Co. in St. Paul to perfect his art while Nick worked in retail to gain experience in that all-important aspect of the microbrewing world. Robbie Stair, a third partner, brought a site to the table—his farm on Lake Pepin. The twenty-barrel brewhouse, designed and built by the three owners, was a showcase of ingenuity. Then in March 2007, they packed up the farm, as it were, and moved into a new facility in River Falls. This change means more beer is a-flowing and bottles became available, but also we, the public, can now stop in for a tour.

The tasting area is right inside the brewery with picnic tables, foosball, darts, 2 TVs, cornhole, board games, and hammerschlagen. Garage doors open in summer. Free Wifi.

Stumbling Distance: *Steve's Pizza Palace* (110 N Main St, 715-425-8284, stevespizzarfwi.com) delivers and they also do pasta and gyros. Paddle or trout-fish the *Kinnickinnic River* (the "Kinni") (see my book *Paddling Wisconsin*). Near the brewery are good mountain biking trails at Whitetail Ridge.

SWINGING BRIDGE BREWING CO.

122 S. Main St. • River Falls, WI 54022 • 715-629-1464
swingingbridgebrewing.com

Opened: March 17, 2017   **Head Brewer:** Mike O'Hara
Annual Production: 300 barrels   **Number of Beers:** 16 on tap (8 guests)

Staple Beers:
- » CLEARY'S DRY IRISH STOUT
- » FOUR WINDS IPA

Rotating Beers:
- » ALT
- » BERLINER WEISSE
- » CALIFORNIA COMMON
- » IPAs
- » KÖLSCH
- » plus some barrel aging and sours

Most Popular Brew: Four Winds IPA

Brewmaster's Fave: Devotion Berliner Weisse

Tours? Yes, by chance or by appointment.

Samples: Yes, sample flights of four 5-oz pours for about $7.

Best Time to Go: Open Wed-Thu 3-10pm, Fri 3-11pm, Sat 11am-11pm, Sun 11am-9pm. Fridays release a new firkin.

Where can you buy it? Here on tap and in Crowlers, growlers, and Boston rounds to go. 3-4 special bottle releases per year. Some cans in DeVine Liquors, Dick's Fresh Market, and Whole Earth Coop.

Got food? Yes, giant pretzels, dips and soups, meat & cheese boards, some sandwiches. Local breads and meats, and honey from UW-River Falls bee program. House sodas and cold-brew coffee (from down the street) on nitro. Yet still food friendly – bring your own!

Special Offer: A free pint of house beer and a sticker when you get your book signed.

Directions: Coming down WI-35 from the north, take the Main St exit and it will take you right into downtown, with the brewery on the left. On River Falls' east side, WI-65/35 meets WI-29. Go west into town opposite direction of 29 East and it is Cascade Ave. Drive 0.7 mile, take the 1st exit at a traffic circle onto 6th St. Turn left on Walnut and go 0.4 mile to Main St. Turn right and it's there on the right.

The Beer Buzz: Beer brings people together and besides good drinking, the mission here has always been to be surrounded by community and be involved. And that community supports them: this is a CSB, a Community Supported Brewery. This membership and a Mug Club add stability to their business model. Founders Mike O'Hara and Dustin Dodge took a year to plan this and the brewery is active in charities and local events. The brewery is named for the bridge over Kinnickinnic Falls in Glen Park (worth going to see, by the way).

Brewer Mike founded the brewery with Dustin Dodge. Mike homebrewed for fun in 2009 but stepped up to assist at Pitchfork Brewing in Hudson before opening his own. He runs a 3.5-barrel system – with an unusual oil jacketed boiler from Minnetonka, the first of its kind when they started using it – and is focused on ales mostly to style but is willing to play a little. There is always something new on. They serve their Berliner Weisse with raspberry or woodruff syrup as is common in Germany. The brewery name is inlaid in the bar top which is built from wood reclaimed from an old house, and the walls show some really awesome stone work. Live music is once a month and 2 TVs might come on to show the big games. Board games and cribbage are on hand.

Free WiFi. CSB and Mug Club. Facebook.com/swingingbridgebrewing and Twitter @ SwingBridgeBrew Instagram @SwingingBridgeBrewing

Stumbling Distance: *Falcon Foods* (149 Food Science Addition, UW-River Falls, 715-425-3702) is a UW-River Falls campus store selling cheese, ice cream and meats produced by students. Only open Thu-Fri during the day, but worth it. *Steve's Pizza Palace* (110 N Main St, 715-425-8284, stevespizzarfwi.com) delivers and they also do pasta and gyros. Paddlers should check out the *Kinnickinnic River*, a fantastic and scenic run (see my book *Paddling Wisconsin*). **Hotel:** *Best Western Plus Campus Inn* is three blocks away and inside is *Junior's Restaurant & Tap House* (414 S Main St, 715-425-6630, juniorsrf.com) with cheese curds, wings, and a solid draft list.

BOBTOWN BREWHOUSE & GRILL

220 W Main St • Roberts, WI 54023 • 715-338-1046
bobtownbrewhouse.com

Opened: September 2016   **Head Brewer:** Katie Eells
Annual Production: 100 barrels   **Number of Beers:** 9-10 on tap

Staple Beers:

» CROOKED ROW AMERICAN PALE ALE
» LEAD OFF RUNNER CREAM ALE
» RALLY ALE KENTUCKY COMMON
» SCREAMIN' LAURIE AMERICAN BLONDE ALE
» WITHOUT A DOUBT OATMEAL STOUT

Rotating Beers:

» ALMOST FREE SESSION
» AND BOB'S YOUR UNCLE STRONG BRITISH BITTER
» ANNIE R U OK IPA
» BOBTOWN BLACK ALE
» BOBTOWN FRESH WET HOP ALE
» GET UP, GET DOWN AMERICAN BROWN ALE
» THE HASSELHOFF GERMAN
ALTBIER
» KRAFTWERK BELGIAN WITBIER
» OFF THE PATH PILSNER
» ON THE SLY RYE IPA
» PROMISES TO DELIVER COFFEE STOUT
» RING OF FIRE PEPPER PORTER
» SAISON SAISOFF BELGIAN SAISON
» (and so many more)

Most Popular Brew: Rally Ale Kentucky Common

Brewmaster's Fave: Lead Off Runner Cream Ale: The first beer she made that she thought was good enough to be produced commercially.

Tours? Not really.

Samples: Yes, flights of three 7-oz pours.

Best Time to Go: Open Mon-Thu 10:30am-12am, Fri-Sat 10:30am-2am, Sun 10:30am-11pm.

Where can you buy it? Here on tap and in Crowlers to go.

Got food? Yes, small plates such as hummus & pita, wings, burgers, soft pretzels. Free popcorn.

Special Offer: Not participating at this time.

Directions: From I-94 take Exit 10 for WI-65 and head north 1.4 miles. Turn right on Pine St, then a quick left on West Blvd. Continue 0.2 mile and it becomes Main St at the turn. Another 0.1 mile and the brewery is on the right.

The Beer Buzz: This unassuming small-town tavern added house beers to the menu not long after opening. Owner Mike Christenson has a background in corporate restaurant business. He ran the food side of a BW3 for several years, but was looking to get out and do his own thing. Back in high school he ran in the same circles as Brewer Katie.

Somewhere along the line a mutual friend passed him one of her homebrews and thus Mike found his brewer.

Katie had gotten the craft beer bug while working at Doc Powell's Brewing (long gone) in La Crosse. She started brewing after

college with the aim of having cheaper beer, but in fact, the effort got her hooked on the process. Working a part-time job at Northern Brewer Homebrew Supply in Minneapolis, she rubbed elbows with some talented brewers and really grew as a brewer herself. When Mike bought an old bar in Roberts and set up a brewhouse, Katie took her first job as head brewer. (She is also Lab Manager at Hop & Barrel in Hudson.)

There's a full bar with the grill right behind it and some tall table seating. The wood-paneled room has six TVs for some Green Bay Packers games and other sports viewing and live music a couple times per month, plus darts, a pool table, cribbage, board games and a couple gambling machines to entertain.

Free WiFi. ATM onsite. Facebook.com/bobtown.brewhouse

Stumbling Distance: Roberts is pretty small. *Sidetrack Saloon* (112 W Main St, 715-749-3891) is a good breakfast option, and *Roberts Café* (208 W Main St, 715-749-3133) is well liked for homestyle fresh-made fare. Hudson is 15 minutes west of here.

Trap Rock Brewing Co.

520 N. Blanding Woods Rd. • St. Croix Falls, WI 54024 • 651-269-6013
traprockbrewing.com
Opened: 2018   **Head Brewer:** Jason Kleschult
Annual Production: 200 barrels   **Number of Beers:** 12 on tap

Staple Beers:
- » Big Horn Pale Ale
- » Black Bear Stout
- » Monarch IPA
- » Red Stag Ale
- » Sconnie IPA
- » Whitetail Blonde Ale

Rotating Beers:
- » Fall Festival
- » X-Mas Ale
- » 25+ others

Most Popular Brew: Whitetail Blonde and Sconnie IPA

Brewmaster's Fave: Monarch IPA

Tours? Yes, by chance or by appointment.

Samples: Yes, sample flights of four 4-oz pours for about $8.

Best Time to Go: Open Thu-Sat 4-9pm, Sun 11am-9pm. Happy hour 5-7pm on Fri-Sat.

Where can you buy it? Here on tap and in Crowlers and growlers to go, plus local self-distribution.

Got food? Free popcorn plus regular food trucks or catering. Food friendly. Some local menus on hand for delivery.

Special Offer: A free pint of beer OR a discount on a Crowler/growler fill when you get your book signed.

Directions: From US-8 turn north on Industrial Parkway and take the first left on Pine St. Turn right on Blanding Woods Rd and the brewery is on the right.

Cyclists: The brewery is one block west of Gandy Dancer State Trail where it crosses Pine St.

The Beer Buzz: Brian Helm started with a homebrew kit back in the late 90s, and his other partners Jason Kleschult, Dan Campbell, Cad Van Dyke, and Todd Polipnick were part of a homebrewers club in North Branch, MN. Brian, originally from Granton, WI, had lived for a time in the Twin Cities, and when he moved to St. Croix Falls in 2014, he realized that the closest brewery was over 25 miles away. There was a need, the location was right and so was the time.

This two-story building in the town's industrial park was originally a manufacturing facility and over the years has made electrical heads for cassette players and solar-powered yardlights. The two rooms are now a brewhouse and a taproom with seating for 40. It bears a rustic look, with big electrical spools for seating, and slabs of oak for the bar top. Brewer Jason leads the crew and also is vintner at Wild Mountain Winery. Brian is a competitive runner and plans that the brewery will sponsor runs in the future. They worked with Cyclova Bike Club and shop (cyclova.com) and hosted an international fat tire race.

Expect board games, darts, and cornhole, plus the occasional movie night on the big screen. An outdoor patio is in planning.

Free WiFi. Dog friendly. Founders' (Mug) Club. Facebook.com/traprockbrewing

Stumbling Distance: Plenty to do here for outdoorsy types: camp, hike, or paddle the St. Croix River at *Interstate State Park* (1275 WI- 35, 715-483-3747, dnr.wi.gov). This is the western terminus for the *Ice Age National Scenic Trail* (iceagetrail.org). The brewery is also within blocks of the *Ice Age Trail, Gandy Dancer State Trail,* and the *Woolly Trail* for mountain bikes. *Dalles House* (720 S Vincent St, 715-483-3246, dalleshouse.com) is an historic supper club. If you are thinking grapes rather than grains, both *Dancing Dragonfly Winery* (2013 120th Ave, 715-483-9463, dancingdragonflywinery.com) and *Chateau St. Croix Winery* (1998 WI-87, 715-483-2556, chateaustcroix.com) are worthy visits. *Trollhaugen* in Dresser (2232 100th Ave, Dresser, 715-755-2955, trollhaugen.com) has 24 runs for skiing in winter but also ziplining and a challenge course in summer. Watch for *Music on The Overlook* (musicontheoverlook.com) Fridays in summer. *Wannigan Days* (wannigans.com) is a city festival weekend in July.

OLIPHANT BREWING

350 Main Street, Suite 2 • Somerset, WI 54025
oliphantbrewing.com
Founded: Spring 2013   **Brewmaster:** Matt Wallace and Trevor Wirtanen
Annual Production: 700ish bbls   **Number of Beers:** 12 always rotating taps

Beers: Nothing permanent—always rotating! But common returns:

- » ANT RAY COW PANTS
- » ANUTART WITH CHERRY
- » BROWN SUGAR BROWN BROWN
- » LAZERHAWKE HAZY IPA
- » MILKMAN MANBABY (milky weizen dunkel stout)

Tours? Maybe.

Samples: Yes, flights of 3.5-oz pours, 6 for $12, 12 for $20.

Best Time to Go: Open Wed-Thu 4-9pm, Fri 2-11pm, Sat 12–11pm, Sun 12–7pm; later hours in summer.

Where can you buy it? Here in pints and howlers, growlers and 32-oz "Crowlers" (on demand cans) to go. Self-distributed from the Twin Cities to Madison.

Got food? Fresh cheese curds, beef & cheese. Bring your own if you want.

Special Offer: Bring this book in and receive a pretty good high-five (maybe even a great one?). Also, if you get a permanent face tattoo of their logo, they'll give you free beer for life!

Directions: Take Hwy 64 west from New Richmond and take the Business 64 exit into Somerset. This becomes Main Street. You'll see Liquor Depot and the brewery is around back past a mural of a chameleon on the wall of the building.

The Beer Buzz: Some of their story is a bit suspect, but trouble is I can't figure out which parts. Best to quote them: Trevor and Matt "met in Nepal at the secret caves underneath Mt. Everest fighting the Secret Ninja of the would-be American Communists group 'El Luchadores.' Trevor was mortally wounded until he saw a toucan, smelled Fruit Loops, and was reborn. At that very instant, Matt fell asleep and dreamed of the Oliphant. The Oliphant approached Matt with his hot pink sucker-fins and commanded him to open a brewery and distillery in Somerset, Wisconsin, to spread the liquid consciousness of the Oliphant to the people."

Fortunately, Trevor and Matt had been brewing for a while prior to their mind-numbing experience with the Oliphant. Trevor started homebrewing on a whim with the help of a friend's equipment and instantly became a fervent supporter of fermentation in all aspects. Next thing Matt knew, Trevor was forcing him to participate in weekly brewing sessions at times in the morning when no one should be brewing. Although not the career path they originally planned on, (Trevor has a Master's Degree in Music Composition and Matt double majored in English and Anthropology) they felt like it was in everyone's best interest not to get on the wrong side of the Oliphant and to do what it told them to do. You know… for the citizens.

The brewery is in the back space of a shared building that once packaged 7-Up, and at another time, some guy was in here building armored vehicles, but something happened and he fled the country. Don't ask too many questions. They feature an ever-rotating tap list of beers. "We believe in having constant variety, and we feel that having only a few beers that we brew over and over is more akin to manufacturing  than crafting. We are brewers, not manufacturers, and we strive to create something that will keep our patrons excited and surprised." Jeremy Hughes does the chalkboard art for the beer menu. Taylor Berman is the creator of the giant chameleon. They've got cornhole and Giant Jenga, board games and comic books, or Free Wifi if you'd just prefer not to talk to anyone. Facebook.com/oliphantbrewing Twitter/Instagram @OliphantBrewing

Stumbling Distance: *Liquor Depot* (350 Main St, 715-247-5336) has a good assortment of Wisconsin products. *Pizza Planet* (253 Main St, 715-247-3399, pizzaplanetsomerset.com) serves carry out as well (hint, hint, taproom). 18 holes await at *Somerset Disc Golf Course* (390 Tower Rd, facebook.com/somersetdiscgolf). Your local cheese is made at *Bass Lake Cheese Factory* (598 Valley View Trail, 715- 247-5586, blcheese.com) and they also serve sandwiches, burgers and such. Go tubing down the Apple River with *Float Rite* (floatrite.com, 715-247-3453) but be sure not to take glass out on the water (that's what Crowlers are for).

FFATS BREWING CO.

18517 Blair St • Whitehall, WI 54773 • 715-538-3162
ffatsbrewingco.com
Opened: 2015   **Head Brewer:** Eric Staff
Annual Production: <300 barrels   **Number of Beers:** 14 on tap

Staple Beers:

- » AMISH SUPER HERO (blonde ale with lemon-lime)
- » BERSERKER (sahti)
- » DONKEY PUNCH (Kölsch inspired blonde)
- » FFAT N' HAZY
- » HAKA PALE ALE (NZ hops)

Rotating Beers:

- » AWKWARD NINJA (milkshake-style IPA)
- » DOG DAYS
- » FAT PUMPKIN LAGER
- » FIRE – Fruit Infused Rye Experiment
- » MOMMA BEAR HEFE
- » OCTOBERFEST
- » PALATE TRAUMA
- » SMOKED LAGER
- » UBPB (peanut butter porter)
- » VERDE BURRO (cucumber infused Kölsch)

Most Popular Brew: Donkey Punch

Brewmaster's Fave: UB Porter

Tours? Yes, by chance or by appointment.

Samples: Yes, sample flights of four 5-oz pours for about $6.

Best Time to Go: Open Thu-Sat 3-9pm, Sun noon-6pm. Closed Sundays in winter.

Where can you buy it? Here on tap and in Crowlers and growlers to go, plus maybe a couple draft accounts around town.

Got food? Free popcorn and Heggies pizzas.

Special Offer: A free regular tap beer when you get your book signed.

Directions: Whitehall is about 50 miles south of Eau Claire or an hour north of La Crosse on US-53 which passes right through town past the brewery at Main and Blair.

The Beer Buzz: Eric Staff and his wife Sarah founded FFATS Brewing Company in 2015. FFATS is just his last name backwards. Eric homebrewed for 7+ years and felt there was room in the ever-growing craft beer scene in little Whitehall, WI (pop 1,606). They purchased two adjacent buildings in downtown Whitehall and opened this nano-brewery producing 50-gallon batches. The brewery is a former garage building while the taproom is a brick building just behind the brewery on Blair St. He brought in a minority partner in 2017, Bryan Lee from Osseo with whom he worked in law enforcement for many years, and Bryan's wife Mary.

The small taproom shows reclaimed wood along the walls and bar, some communal tables, a large clock with windmill blades encircling it. Of the 14 taps, 7-8 are mainstays and the remainder rotating and guest taps plus a soda tap. You'll always find at least one beer on that is experimental. His Awkward Ninja is a good example: a milkshake-style IPA with blood orange and vanilla beans. They are still working out taproom hours and changing them seasonally. Two garage doors open for air and outdoor seating.

Free WiFi. Facebook.com/FfatsBrewingCo and Twitter @FFATSbrewingco Instagram @FFATSbrewing

Stumbling Distance: *Outright Affair* (36387 Main St, 715-538-9114) has sliders and artisan pizza (crab Rangoon pizza!). *Dog House Bar & Grill* (36356 Abrams St, 715-538-9121) does burgers and a good Philly steak. *Valasquez Tacos* is a local family's food truck worth tracking down. Cyclists should check out *Trempealeau Trails Bicycle Association* (TourDeTremp.com) which offers maps of a system of very nice pastoral road routes, three of which start out of Whitehall. **Hotel:** *Oak Park Inn* (18224 Ervin St, 715-538-4858, oakparkinn.com).

DAVE'S BREWFARM—A FARMHOUSE BREWERY

2470 Wilson Street • Wilson, WI 54027 • davesbrewfarm@gmail.com
davesbrewfarm.blogspot.com
Founded: March 2008   **Chief Yeast Wrangler**: Dave Anderson
Annual Production: 20 bbls **Number of Beers**: 8 taps at the farm, too many styles to list!

Rotating Beers:
- » AuBEXXX
- » BREWFARM SELECT
- » MATACABRAS
- » MOCHA DIABLO
- » SOB OMG (sour orange basil)
- » Anything goes here! You never know what to expect! Those 20 annual barrels come in 10-gallon batches.

Most Popular Brew: Mocha Diablo

Brewmaster's Fave: "You want me to pick my favorite child?!? Depends on the mood. I usually say the beer in my right hand."

Tours? Yes, they do free tours and have open taproom hours in the LaBrewatory, but they vary. Make an appointment or watch the blog or Facebook page.

Samples? "Oh yes, the best way to sell my beers!"

Best Time to Go: Taproom is open every other weekend more or less. Check the blog or the Facebook page to be certain.

Where can you buy it? For now, only in the taproom.

Got food? Just some frozen pizzas. He does heat them up first.

Special Offer: A 15% discount on a BrewFarm T-shirt.

Directions: Take Exit 28 off I-94, head north about 2.5 miles to 80th Ave. Take a right onto 80th to the "T" intersection. You can't miss the red barn board building with the wind generator on the 120-ft tower making power!

The Beer Buzz: Like many, Dave's brewing problem started with homebrewing in 1992, and progressed with him going to the Siebel Institute in 1996. By then he was too far gone and wanted to open his own brewery. He conceived of the "BrewFarm" in

1995. Dave wanted to brew beer and be out in the country in a farmhouse setting. He brewed for the short-lived Ambleside Brewery in Minneapolis and Paper City Brewery in Holyoke, MA, worked for a variety of beer distributors, worked both importing and exporting craft beer, and consulted with start-up breweries in places around the world, including Vietnam, Italy, and Israel. In the end he landed in Wilson, WI, to finally make the BrewFarm a reality. Dave started brewing here and an immediate demand compelled him to do some contract brewing offsite, producing cans and bottles. After a short while he decided that didn't feel right for him, so he cut the contract and now just brews at the farm. He's a one-man show, and this is quality not quantity.

Dave's beer is looking pretty green. You can see Jake, the 120-foot-tall 20kW wind generator that provides nearly all the power for Dave's brewery and home. (One blog entry shows his electric bill was 81-cents one month!) The beer name Matacabras comes from a Spanish term for a wind that "kills goats." But Wisconsin wind is a bit nicer; here on the wind-powered farm, it brews beer! Throw in some recycled dairy equipment repurposed for beer plus a solar thermal system in the works, and this is about as eco-friendly as a brewery can get. Drink some beer to protect the environment.

*At the time of writing, Dave was in a sort of transitional period. The brewery has been for sale, on and off the market a couple times as he decided what he's going to do next in this life. Someone may come in and buy the whole package and continue brewing here, or maybe not. Be sure to check the blog above or Facebook before trying to visit.

Stumbling Distance: There's not much out here, but if you are looking for a good place to eat, try *Peg's Pleasant View Inn* (3015 US Highway 12, Wilson, 715-772-4610).

ZONE 4

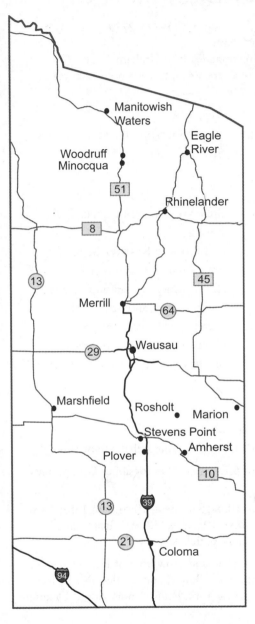

Amherst: Central Waters Brewery
Coloma: Mecan River Brewing Co.
Eagle River: Tribute Brewing Co.
Manitowish Waters: Some Nerve
  Brewing Co.
Marion: Pigeon River Brewing Co.
Marshfield: Blue Heron BrewPub
Merrill: Sawmill Brewing Co.
Minocqua: Minocqua Brewing Co.
Plover: O'so Brewing Co.
Rhinelander: Rhinelander Brewing
Co.
Rosholt: Kozy Yak Brewery
Rosholt: McZ's Brew Pub
Stevens Point: Stevens Point Brewery
Wausau: Bull Falls Brewery
Wausau: Great Dane Pub and Brewery
Wausau: Red Eye Brewery
Woodruff: Rocky Reef Brewing Co.

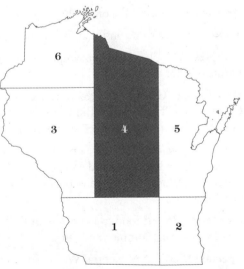

CENTRAL WATERS BREWING CO.

351 Allen Street • Amherst, WI 54406 • 715-824-2739
centralwaters.com
Founded: January 1998   **Brewmaster**: Paul Graham
Annual Production: 18,000 bbls **Number of Beers**: 24 on tap; 30+ beers each year

Staple Beers:

- » HHG APA
- » HONEY BLONDE
- » MUD PUPPY PORTER
- » OUISCONSING RED ALE

- » RIFT IPA
- » SATIN SOLITUDE IMPERIAL STOUT
- » SHINE ON ALE

Rotating Beers:

- » BREWHOUSE COFFEE STOUT
- » CAUGHT IN THE RAIN
- » DE KLEINE DOOD
- » ILLUMINATION DOUBLE IPA
- » OCTOBERFEST LAGER
- » PERUVIAN MORNING
- » RYE BARREL CHOCOLATE PORTER
- » SLÁINTE SCOTCH ALE
- » SPACE GHOST (Imperial Stout with ghost peppers)

- » SUMMARILLO INDIA-STYLE PALE LAGER
- » and BREWER RESERVE SERIES: bourbon barrel-aged brews (Barleywine, Cassian Sunset, Stout, Cherry Stout, and Scotch Ale) rum barrel-aged Coconut Porter, and CELLAR SESSIONS, barrel-aged brewery anniversary brews and more.

Most Popular Brew: Mudpuppy Porter

Brewmaster's Fave: The one in his hand.

Tours? Yes, free tours on Fri at 5PM, Sat at 3PM, but check the website to be sure.

Samples? Yes. Flagship beer sample platters of 6 five-oz. pours for about $9. Specialty flights of 6 for $15.

Best Time to Go: The Tap Room is open Fri 3–10PM, Sat 12PM–10PM, Sun 12PM–7PM. Open for retail sales Mon–Thu 8AM–5PM, Fri 8AM–10PM, Sat 12PM–10PM, Sun 12PM–7PM. Watch for their Anniversary Party every January; tickets go fast.

Where can you buy it? Here on tap and in Crowlers and growlers, bottles and kegs to go. Bottles and kegs around Wisconsin, Minnesota, Illinois, and bottles also in Iowa, Indiana, Michigan, Massachusetts, New Jersey, New York, Pennsylvania, South Dakota, and Vermont.

Got food? No, but food trucks often on Friday and Saturday from 4:30-8pm in the beer garden in spring, summer, and fall.

Special Offer: A free Central Waters sticker when you get your book signed.

Directions: From US Hwy 10 take the Cty Rd A Exit #240 and go north 0.7 mile. Turn left on Washington St, go 0.2 mile and turn left on Allen St. Go 0.3 mile and the brewery is on the right at the end of the road.

The Beer Buzz: Paul calls it a "hobby gone out of control." He was brewing in his dorm room when he was 18. Perfectly legal to buy the ingredients, but he wasn't allowed to drink his results. And I'm sure he didn't. Actually, at first, he really didn't—it was so bad, he said, he couldn't. He was just playing around but soon got the hang of it (as one can tell from the great beer here). Mike McElwain and Jerome Ebel opened the brewery first in a 1920s former Ford Dealership in Junction City in a small brick building with a flapping screen door that opened right out onto the highway through town. Paul called it a "glorified homebrew system," and he did the boils in a 300-gallon cheese starter tank with a commercial hot water heater element attached to the bottom. Converted dairy tanks functioned as fermenters, and the whole operation was built by hand. After 3 years Paul and Clint Schultz bought the brewery, and soon after Anello Mollica took Clint's place. Success led to expansion and Central Waters started a brewpub in Marshfield (now the independent Blue Heron) and moved the brewery into new digs in Amherst in 2006. The current brewing facility was the first green-powered brewery in the state (though no longer the only). Besides energy efficient lights and equipment and radiant-heat flooring, they have a bank of twenty-four solar collectors. In October 2011, they added 20,000-watt solar photovoltaic panels which provide 20% of their annual power needs. As they like to say at the brewery: "Making the world a better place, one beer at a time." Their Barleywine has gotten a couple of awards, and Bourbon-Barrel Barleywine and Bourbon Barrel Cherry Stout have both taken gold at Great American Beer Festival. Special releases are anxiously anticipated.

Facebook.com/CWBrewing Twitter/Instagram @CWbrewing

Stumbling Distance: *The Landmark* (102 S Main St, 715-824-2200) is an excellent breakfast/ lunch joint, but serves finer dining steak/seafood on Fri-Sat. Stay the night in Amherst at *Amherst Inn B&B* (303 S Main St, 888-211-3555, amherstinn.com) or *Artha Sustainable Living Center B&B* (9784 Cty Rd K, 715-824-3463, arthaonline.com). *Go paddling* on either the Waupaca River or the tubing-easy (but fun) Crystal River in nearby Waupaca (See my book *Paddling Wisconsin*).

MECAN RIVER BREWING CO.

113 E. Main St. • Coloma, WI 54930 • 608-369-0914
mecanriverbrewing.com

Opened: December 2017   **Head Brewer:** Bill Moll
Annual Production: 200 barrels   **Number of Beers:** 4-6 on tap

Staple Beers:
- » HONEY BLONDE
- » VANILLA CREAM ALE

Rotating Beers:
- » BELGIAN WIT
- » HEFEWEIZEN
- » BLUEBERRY ALE
- » PUMPKIN SPICE ALE
- » FARMHOUSE SAISON

Most Popular Brew: Vanilla Moon Porter

Brewmaster's Fave: Bill likes Hefe, Wendy prefers Saison

Tours? Yes, by chance or by appointment. It's small.

Samples: Yes, sample flights available.

Best Time to Go: Open Wed-Thu 4-9pm, Fri 4-10pm, Sat 1-10pm. Watch for expanded hours in summer. Occasionally closed for special events. Manic Mondays get women out of the house for a beer.

Where can you buy it? Here on tap and in growlers to go, and self-distributing to area breweries and bars.

Got food? Yes, house pizzas, Bavarian hot pretzels, housemade soups, Twig's sodas, Vines & Rushes wines from Ripon, WI.

Special Offer: A free pint of house beer when you get your book signed.

Directions: From I-39 take Exit 124 and turn east on WI-21 into Coloma. Drive 0.3 mile and turn right (south) on 1st St and drive one block. The brewery is on the right at the corner of 1st and Main.

The Beer Buzz: This brewery starts with a mid-life crisis and a couple of motorcycles. Founders Bill Moll, originally from Waukesha, and his wife Wendy, from the Green Bay area, moved to Coloma in 1999 where Bill became the tech director for the school district. Birthdays added up and the kids were leaving home, so they got cycles and motored around to waterfalls and brewpubs in the U.P. and the Great Lakes region. The best of what they saw stuck with them and now they're incorporating the best elements in their own place. David Knuth (see *Knuth Brewing*) shared his own trial and tribrewlations and pushed them on. Bill had homebrewed for over 12 years, and while stationed in Germany as a member of a WWII-bomb disposal team, he toured every brewery he could during his three years there, and learned how to brew German styles. The taproom opened first and served guest beers until the licensing was sorted closer to summer 2018.

Bill keeps a 3-barrel system inside this refurbished 1875 lumberyard. The tongue and groove wood is original, and wood on the walls is from a 1915 barn. They picked up the bar for a song at an auction – from the tavern where they first met. The taproom

shows windmill blades on the wall, some tall tables, a short bar, and some lounge seating. Entertainment is occasional live music, plus board games, puzzles and cribbage. There's a beer garden outside where the weigh station was for the nearby feed mill.

Free WiFi. Mug Club. On Facebook.

Stumbling Distance: *Coloma Hotel* (132 E Main St, 715-228-2401, colomahotel.com) offers budget rooms in an 1870s inn with a pub and bike rentals. *The Bread Bar* (157 Front St, 920-240-0352, thebreadbarcoloma.com) for coffee and morning cinnamon rolls. Roche-a-Cri State Park (1767 State Hwy 13, Friendship, 608-339-6881) is 20 minutes away with historical petroglyphs, camping and a massive rock outcrop. *The Ice Age Trail* (iceagetrail.org) and Mecan River (great for paddling) are close to the brewery (see my book *FalconGuides Paddling Wisconsin*).

TRIBUTE BREWING CO.

1106 Bluebird Road • Eagle River, Wisconsin 54521 • 715-480-2337
tributebrewing.com
Founded: February 2012   **Brewmaster:** Marc O'Brien
Annual Production: 800 bbl
Number of Beers: 6–7 of their own on tap, plus 5–6 guest beers

Staple Beers: (subject to change)
- » BAREFOOT CHARLIE IPA
- » BLUEBERRY TRAIN WHEAT ALE
- » GHOST LIGHTS AMBER LAGER (Vienna style)
- » OLD EAGLE PORTER
- » 28 LAKES LAGER (Dortmunder style)

Rotating Beers:
- » FINN'S IRISH RED ALE
- » FROSTWATCH CRANBERRY WHEAT ALE
- » MELE KALIKIMAKA COCONUT PORTER
- » SUMMER KAMP
- » SUMMER WIND
- » WHITE LEGS JALAPEÑO WHEAT ALE
- » … Anniversary beer early December

Most Popular Brew: Blueberry Train Wheat

Brewmaster's Fave: Barefoot Charlie IPA.

Tours? No.

Samples: Yes, a sampler tray of 6 of their beers for about $12-15.

Best Time to Go: The taproom is open Wed–Fri 3–9PM and Sat 1–9PM. Closed Sun–Tue.

Where can you buy it? Here on tap and in pre-filled growlers, and distributed in 4-packs of 16oz cans. Sold at *Trig's* in Eagle River, Minocqua & Rhinelander, *Stein's Lincoln Street Liquor* in Rhinelander, *O'Brien's Spirits* in Eagle River, *Save More Foods* in Minocqua,

Sentry Foods in St. Germain, *Three Cellars* in Oak Creek, and far south at *McFarland Liquors* and *The Cannery* in Sun Prairie.

Got food? Free peanuts and popcorn, or have pizza delivered. Food friendly.

Special Offer: $1 off your first pint of Tribute beer during your signature visit.

Directions: From downtown Eagle River head north on Highway 45 to Airport Road. Go left here and the next street is Bluebird Road. Go left again (south) and the brewery is on the right side.

The Beer Buzz: This isn't founder Bill Summers' first involvement with the craft beer scene. He and a few others originally started what is now Eagle River's Up North Beer Festival (eagleriver. org/featured/up-north-beerfest). After the short-lived Loaf & Stein brewpub came and went in the late 90s, there was really no craft beers for locals to enjoy. Bill did some research and visited a lot of places to see what sort of place might work for a brewpub. In the 1990s the trend was to buy an old brick building downtown somewhere (as South Shore in Ashland or Angry Minnow in Hayward) and refashion it into a pub. Then he saw brewers moving into industrial parks and metal buildings. In the end, Bill felt this model made a more casual atmosphere, made clients comfortable, and gave everyone more space. They were more talkative and laid back.

Bill found this building out near the highway and the airport and decided it was perfect. The former home to a log home design company and their woodcrafting shop, it had a good vibe. "Like going into a garage party, a keg in the corner." In fact, the brewery opens a garage door in nice weather for some good air. The style is all industrial: Barrels under the bar, cement floor, warehouse lighting, and galvanized metal utility panels along the walls. A couple of antennae towers frame the bar. You can also see Bill's collection of over 150 growlers. No pool tables or jukebox. What you'll get here is just a great place to hang out and talk craft beer or play cribbage, Uno and trivia games.

Brewer Marc is president of the L.U.S.H. Inc. homebrew club in the Northwoods and has won some awards for his homebrews. He and Bill were at a club meeting at Minocqua Brewing Co. a several years ago and tossed around the idea of going pro. And in 2012 that happened. Their beer is on tap at a lot of Northwoods bars and restaurants with a waiting list until they are able to increase production. Tribute names their beers as a "tribute" to local historical people, places or events. They added a canning line in 2017.

Stumbling Distance: Eagle River is on the Chain of Lakes, the largest inland fresh water chain of lakes in the world with 28 connected bodies of water. So boaters, anglers, and paddlers will find Nirvana here. Right next door is *Bortolotti's Cin Cin* (1114 N Bluebird Rd, 715-891-0775, bortscincin.com) a nice wine bar with tapas. Right across the street from the brewery is the *World Championship Snowmobile Derby Track* (derbytrack.com). *Leif's Café* (800 N Railroad St, 715-479-2766) is walking distance and is famous for breakfast and brunch. *Riverstone Restaurant & Tavern* (riverstonerestaurant.com, 219 Railroad St, 715-479-8467) has an eclectic dinner menu, a Friday fish fry, and very good wine and beer list. **Closest hotels:** *Days Inn* (844 N Railroad St, 715-479-5151) and *Best Western Derby Inn* (1800 US Highway 45 N, 715-479-1600).

CENTRAL WISCONSIN CRAFT COLLECTIVE

What started out as the Grain Circle Tour has since evolved into this collective of craft fermentation and distillation. This cluster of breweries plus a winery and distillery make for a nice little roadtrip in Central Wisconsin—and yes, you can bike it, if you prefer.

Leave the driving to someone else and book a private ride for your group:
Lamers (715-421-2400)
Xecutive Limousine (715-344-1153)
Courtesy Cab (715-342-8863)

The rails-to trails *Tomorrow River Trail* connects Plover to Amherst on a flat 14.8 mile ride. Biking the entire circle is about 55 miles.

For more information contact Stevens Point Area Convention & Visitor Bureau: 715-344-2556 | www.stevenspointarea.com.

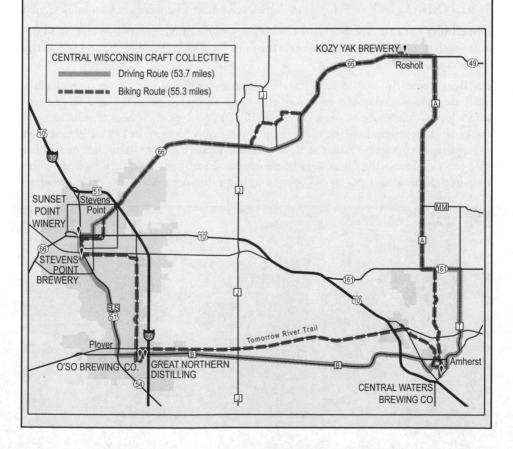

SOME NERVE BREWING CO.

5586 US-51 • Manitowish Waters, WI 54545 • 608-576-6040
somenervebrewingcompany.com
Opened: May 2018   **Head Brewers:** Bill and Jessica Ruef
Annual Production: 250 barrels   **Number of Beers:** 8 on tap

Probable Beers:

- » AMBER
- » BELGIAN
- » BLONDE or CREAM ALE
- » IPA
- » STOUT
- » TIM MCCRACKEN IRISH RED

Brewmaster's Fave: Irish Red

Tours? Yes, by chance.

Samples: Yes, sample flights.

Best Time to Go: Open Wed-Fri 5-9pm, Sat 1-9pm. Check the site to be sure.

Where can you buy it? Here on tap and in growlers to go.

Got food? Yes, fresh popcorn and some snacks. Food friendly, bring your own.

Special Offer: $2 off your first pint of Some Nerve beer when you get your book signed.

Directions: Located on US-51, the brewery lies south of Manitowish Waters (and 0.8 mile south of Little Bohemia Lodge) on the right (north/east) side of the highway at the intersection of Deer Path Road.

The Beer Buzz: Bill and Jessica's Excellent Adventure. I am not sure anyone else has purchased every version and edition of this book and worn them out and filled them with signatures as much as these two have. Bill has told me their beer travels with the book inspired them to have the nerve to open their own brewery. In 1999, Bill took over sausage-making from his father at Ruef's Meat Market in New Glarus, but he and his wife Jessica Murray-Ruef were avid homebrewers. Finally, in 2017, they took the jump. They sold the meat market (it's still open, stumbling distance from New Glarus Brewing)

and moved to the Northwoods to pursue the homebrewer's dream.

Originally a video arcade, then a pizza parlor, the space most recently housed an art gallery now converted to the art of brewing. The brewhouse and tap room occupy opposite sides of this building right along US 51, the pipeline to the Northwoods. No TVs, no jukebox, some games and maybe a book or two. It's a people place, good for conversation and hanging out.

They like to work through a variety styles, and while they brew a few hoppy things, this isn't an extreme hophead lineup. Expect some traditional styles but they aren't afraid to occasionally go off the map a touch—maybe a blonde with ginger, fruited beers—on occasion.

They built the bar and cooler themselves. Behind the bar is a large window that looks out to the forest.

Free WiFi. On Facebook.com/SomeNerveBrewing

Stumbling Distance: Hit the classic supper club *Little Bohemia* (142 U.S. 51, 715-543-8800, littlebohemialodge.com) just ¾ mile north, where Dillinger once had a shootout with the Feds. *Blue Bayou Inn* (5547 US-51, 715-543-2537, bluebayouinn.com) offers Cajun in the northlands. *Aberdeen Restaurant & Bar* (5325 Aberdeen Lodge Circle, 715-543-8700, aberdeendining.com) has dining (prime rib, blackened walleye) on the water. In nearby Boulder Junction, check out *Aqualand Ale House* (10450 Main St, Boulder Junction, 715-385-0380, aqualandalehouse.com) with 20 taps. **Hotels:** *The Pea Patch Motel & Saloon* (145 County Hwy W, 715-543-2455, thepeapatch.com) is a sort of fisherman/snowmobiler place. *Wittig's Point Resort* (9420 Fishtrap Lake Rd, Boulder Junction, 715-385-2464, wittigspoint.com) has cottages and a tavern.

Photograph Courtesy of Bill Ruef

PIGEON RIVER BREWING CO.

1103 N. Main St. • Marion, WI 54950 • 715-256-7721
pigeonriverbrewing.com
Founded: July 18, 2012   **Head Brewers:** Nate Knaack and Brett "Bub" Hintz
Annual Production: 1500 barrels   **Number of Beers**: 12 on tap (some guest taps)

Staple Beers:

- » BIG DROP SHANDY
- » BUXOM LASS SCOTTISH ALE
- » HOP OFFER IPA
- » TOWNIE (cream ale)
- » WET WILLY OATMEAL STOUT

Rotating Beers:

- » BELGIAN WHITE
- » BLUE JEWELS BLUEBERRY WHEAT
- » SALTY KNOT PRETZEL WHEAT
- » VANILLA JIMMY JAVA PORTER (aka The VaJJ)
- » Seasonals

Most Popular Brew: Big Drop Shandy

Brewer's Fave: Nate: Buxom Lass | Bub: He drinks anything.

Tours? Yes, if the brewers are there, you can ask.

Samples: Yes, a flight of all their beers 4.5-oz pours for about $6.

Best Time to Go: Open Wed–Fri 11am-9pm, Fri 11am-10pm, Sat 11am-9pm, Sun 11am-8pm. Closed Mon–Tue. Summer visitors can enjoy nearby campgrounds and outdoor recreation while winter visitors can take advantage of snow-mobile trails near the brewery.

Where can you buy it? Here on tap and in growlers to go. Draft accounts and bottles from Shawano to Fond du Lac and the Fox Cities.

Got food? Yes, a full kitchen with handcrafted pizza, craft burgers, wings, and appetizers (cheese curds). Friday fish fry.

Special Offer: One free pint when you get your book signed.

Directions: From US-45 running through Marion, turn south on Main St/WI-110 and the brewpub is on the right.

The Beer Buzz: Nate and Bub were childhood neighbors across the shores of the Pigeon River south of Marion. The pair of tuba players were sitting next to each other in band class one day when they stumbled across a magazine article about hop growing. This sparked an interest in homebrewing. Over the course of the next few years the boys experimented with homebrewing and perfected their recipes. In college, Nate served as president for the UW-Platteville Homebrew Club where he assisted with the micro-brewery in the student union.

Nate then married his high school sweetheart Kayla, a UW business graduate who has been instrumental in getting the administrative details of the whole project in order. "Without her we wouldn't be where we're at," says Nate. When the right place opened up for a brewpub in the fall of 2011, Nate and Kayla picked it up, planning to wait until they were ready for the next step. Two weeks later, O'so Brewing called; they were in the midst of a big move and upgrade and were looking to sell their old brew system. Things just kept falling into place. Kinda like an avalanche, all at once, until Pigeon River Brewing opened for business on July 18, 2012 in honor of the feast day of St. Arnold of Metz, patron saint of brewers.

Success kept coming and in 2016 they moved into this larger space (the same banquet hall where Nate and Kayla had celebrated their wedding reception) and added a bottling line. Dupont Cheese makes a beer cheese with their Scottish Ale and they sell it on site.

Facebook.com/PigeonRiverBrewingCo Twitter @PigeonRiverBrew Instagram @ pigeonriverbrewing

Stumbling Distance: As Nate puts it, Marion is "sitting at the gateway to the Northwoods" on Highway 45. An area special event that draws a big crowd is *Caroline Lions Colorama* (caroline-lionscolorama.com), the first weekend of October. *The Iola Old Car Show* (iolaoldcarshow.com), the largest in the Midwest, takes place on a long weekend in July in nearby Iola. Of other local interest is *Dupont Cheese Inc.* (dupontcheeseinc.com, N10140 Hwy 110, 800-895-2873) five miles south on 110 which makes some stellar cheeses.

BLUE HERON BREWPUB

108 W 9th Street • Marshfield, WI 54449 • 715-389-1868
blueheronbrewpub.com
Founded: 2005   **Head Brewer**: Ron Hulka
Annual Production: 300 bbls   **Number of Beers**: 10–12 on tap

Staple Beers:
- » HONEY BLONDE (made with local Hauke Honey)
- » HOP HEART IPA
- » TIGER'S EYE (English mild)

Rotating Beers: (a few possibilities)
- » AU NORD BIERE DE GARDE
- » HERON GO BRAGH-LESS STOUT
- » HUB CITY LAGER 2016
- » LOCH NESS STRONG SCOTCH ALE
- » OLD KNOTHEAD BARLEY WINE
- » RAUCH'EM SOCK'EM SMOKED ALE
- » SOUTHBOUND CHILI RYE ALE
- » SWEET BEAK AMARETTO WHEAT
- » TAPPER'S TRIPEL
- » WHITE FANG INDIAN GOLD ALE

Most Popular Brew: Honey Blonde

Brewmaster's Fave: Old Knothead Barley Wine

Tours? Yes, by appointment, usually Saturdays.

Samples? Yes, five 5-oz samples for $6.

Best Time to Go: Open Mon-Sat at 11am. Closed Sundays. Watch for pint of the day discount. Third Wednesdays host Science on Tap discussions.

Where can you buy it? On tap here and upstairs and in growlers to go.

Got food? Yes, full pub menu with pizza. Fried pickle slices are excellent. Upstairs since 2018 is The Oven Above the Pub (formerly 14th Street Restaurant) with a new wood-fired oven focus.

Special Offer: A free pint of house beer during your signature visit.

Directions: Coming into town on Business Hwy 13 (Central Ave), look for 9th St on the south side and the brewpub is on the corner on the west side across 9th from Holiday Inn.

The Beer Buzz: I was thrilled to death to know that my birth home was to have a brewpub. In 2005, Central Waters Brewery got together with Marshfield's finest restaurant and set up a brewpub/restaurant in this renovated brick creamery. The Parkin family built this dairy processing plant in 1941 and operated it until 1966. The ice cream here was tops and the family figured prominently in the so-called milk wars when grocers and dairy farmers formed the first cooperatives. The "Got milk?" people are part of that organization that John Parkin helped put together. Now you can still see some ice cream molds and some painted bricks on the wall which were used to match label colors on the ice creams. Check out the We Want Beer photo near the restrooms—anti-Prohibition marchers all decked out in suits and fedoras. Who said beer drinkers didn't have class?

Marshfield hadn't had its own beer since local mail-order cheese pioneer John Figi made an attempt to keep the Marshfield Brewery alive after its long run from 1889 to 1965. Figi Brewing Co. lasted less than two years. In 2008, the brewpub became independent of Central Waters Brewery and was renamed Blue Heron, and sister establishment West 14th Street Restaurant moved in upstairs. When the previous brewer left for Eugene, Oregon, Ron came from Rusty Truck Brewing in Oregon to replace him. In 2018, West 14th rebranded and overhauled its menu to become The Oven Above the Pub, a more casual eatery with 4 big-screen TVs for big games. A couple of TVs show sports, and a small merch corner by the door sells the pub's paraphernalia. Free WiFi. Facebook.com/blue.brewpub and Twitter @ BluHeronBrewPub

Stumbling Distance: At the Central Wisconsin Fairgrounds east on 14th Street you will find the *World's Largest Round Barn*. Come on, it's at least a photo op! *Lumberyard Bar & Grill* (1651 N Central Ave, 715-387-1920) has a good craft beer list. Just north of town off Cty Hwy E, *JuRustic Park* (jurustic.com, M222 Sugar Bush Ln, 715-387-1653) is a collection of large critters fashioned out of scrap metal. For fresh and cheap cheese curds and a great variety of other affordable cheeses (including aged varieties), don't miss *Nasonville Dairy* (nasonvilledairy.com, 10898 Hwy 10 West, 715-676-2177). The world's largest block of cheese? Well, at least the container for it. Head west on Hwy 10 to Neillsville and you can't miss this roadside attraction with a talking cow and the *Wisconsin Pavilion* from the 1964 World's Fair.

WHY CREAMERIES?

And gas stations?!? You may notice that some of the breweries occupy buildings with similar stories. More than a couple are renovated creameries from the early part of the twentieth century. Why such a common brewing site? Sloped tiled floors with drains in the middle—lots of filling and draining and mopping goes into the brewing process. Plus some of the old stainless steel dairy tanks are perfectly suited for brewing beer. Who knew? Basically any building that already has adequate drains for brewing is a bonus as refitting such a system into an old building can be quite an undertaking.

Sawmill Brewing Co.

1110 E. 10th St. • Merrill, WI 54452 • 715-722-0230
sawmillbrewing.net
Opened: March 2016   **Head Brewers:** Ben Osness and Chris Burger
Annual Production: 300 barrels   **Number of Beers:** 16 on tap (6-8 guest taps)

Staple Beers:
- » Boom Decker Becker IPA
- » Cant Hook Kölsch
- » Rip Saw Red Irish Ale
- » River Hog Oatmeal Stout

Rotating Beers:
- » Bourbon Hog
- » Don't Shoot Your Eye Out Stout
- » Oktoberfest
- » Pike Pole Pilsner
- » Saisons In The Sun
- » Stammholz German Alt
- » Trapper's Cabin Chocolate Porter
- » ...plus some fruited summer beers and barrel aging

Most Popular Brew: Cant Hook Kölsch

Brewmaster's Faves: The IPAs

Tours? Nothing official.

Samples: Yes, sample flights.

Best Time to Go: Open Mon-Thu 3:30-9pm, Fri-Sat 2-11pm, Sun 2-9pm.

Where can you buy it? Here on tap and in growlers to go, and a few draft accounts as far away as Stevens Point, Park Falls, and Eagle River.

Got food? Sort of. A kitchen for counter service is in planning, but for now there's the frequent food truck. They sell soda and house-brewed kombucha, and the taproom is food friendly if you bring your own.

Special Offer: Half off your first pint of house beer when you get your book signed.

Directions: Tricky. From US-51 take the northernmost Exit 211 for County Road K headed southwest into Merrill. Drive 1.9 miles and before you reach 9th St, you need to look to the right. A small sign and saw blade on a rock may catch your eye, but though the address says 10th St, there isn't a clear street there on your right. But through that parking lot you can see a drive that enters a large lot surrounded by tall pines with a two-story stone building at the end. If you find it on your first pass, give yourself a star for the day.

The Beer Buzz: Co-owners Stan Janowiak and Zach Kubichek have brought local beer back to Merrill for the first time in nearly 70 years. History put the name to this brewery. As Stan tells it, he was thinking, "What makes Merrill Merrill?" In fact, this was a boomtown of sawmills in its heyday. A room down at the local historical society museum (recommended) is called The Pinery, and here is where the inspiration struck.

This building previously housed the fire-fighting equipment for the Department of Natural Resources, and where you see sets of three tall windows in the original stone walls, there were once garage doors. But over time, modern equipment got bigger and bigger until this structure couldn't accommodate the vehicles. The DNR moved and the City took over the property. For a while it functioned as a sort of daycare center run by parks and recreation. Now it's adult daycare. (Ask Stan about the time he showed up with a tape measure and the kids were still there.)

Artifacts from the logging days adorn the walls. The wooden floor actually sits a foot or so above the concrete garage floor and is fashioned from some oak planks from upstairs and other reclaimed wood. In all, about 16 different species of trees contributed to the wood here. The Tornado of 2011 contributed all the white pine you see. The local guy who cut much of it up fashioned tables and the bar top for the brewery. A large elk head overlooks the drinkers. Look behind the bar for the wooden Lincoln Lager crate from this brewery's predecessor, Merrill's own Leidiger Brewing Co., which lasted from 1896 to 1948. The ceiling in the taproom reaches all the way up, making the second floor more of an open mezzanine with additional seating and a function room. Be sure to go upstairs and see the historical photos on the walls. The brew system, visible in a cramped space behind windows near the bar, was manufactured by QTS in Marshfield, Wisconsin. Fermenters are kept in the basement.

Beer names often relate to the logging industry, river hogs being the fellows who used pike poles and cant hooks to maneuver logs on the rivers. Boom Decker Becker is named for the ghost at the local school forest, which everyone knew growing up here.

Along the edge of the property is a stand of huge pines. In season, the outdoor beer area is like a state park campsite, with picnic tables and a fire ring under the big trees. Throw in some live music with your beer.

Free WiFi. Facebook.com/SawmillBrewing and Twitter @SawmillBrew

Stumbling Distance: People drive many miles to eat at the unassuming *China Inn* (3422 E Main St, 715-539-8118). *Council Grounds State Park* (N1895 Council Grounds Dr, 715-536-8773) sits on the Wisconsin River and has 55 family campsites and some short, casual hikes. History buffs, go see the *Merrill History & Culture Center* (100 E Third St, 715-536-5652, merrillhistory.org)

MINOCQUA BREWING COMPANY

238 Lake Shore Drive • Minocqua, WI 54548 • 715-356-2600
minocquabrewingcompany.com
Founded: 1997 / January 2006   **Brewmaster**: Ted Briggs
Annual Production: 600 bbls   **Number of Beers**: 7–8 at all times

Staple Beers:

- » BEAR NAKED BROWN ALE
- » LARGEMOUTH BLONDE
- » M.P.A. MINOCQUA PALE ALE
- » PUDGY POSSUM PORTER
- » ROADKILL RED ALE

Rotating Beers:

- » NEW SEASONALS ON THE BREW
- » WILD RICE BEER

Most Popular Brew: Red Ale or Pale Ale

Tours? No.

Samples? Yes, $14 for a paddle of seven 5-oz beers. ($2 for an eighth beer)

Best Time to Go: Open daily but watch for seasonal hours. Visit in summer when the town goes from Unincorporated to almost 200,000 people. Winter brings in snowmobilers. Beef-A-Rama shouldn't be missed! Watch for live entertainment on the weekends in the upstairs Divano Lounge.

Where can you buy it? On tap here and in growlers and howlers to go.

Got food? Yes! Expect a pub menu but with a gourmet twist. Beef and brie open-face sandwiches, sharp cheddar nuggets and calamari are popular. Try the wheat ale and smoked gouda soup or the wild rice veggie burger.

Special Offer: A free pint when you get your book signed!

Directions: Hwy 51 splits into two one-way streets, northbound and southbound, in the middle of town at Torpy Park. Take the southbound branch and the brewery is next to Torpy Park to the west.

The Beer Buzz: Like the mythological Phoenix rising literally from its own ashes, the MBC came back in 2006 and started brewing again after fire destroyed much of the guts of the building. In 2016 a bad storm dropped a tree on it. Still undeterred, they brew on. The White family passed the ownership torch to longtime fan Kirk Bangstad in 2016. Brewer Ted, originally from Michigan, has over 20 years of professional brewing experience throughout New Jersey, New York, Pennsylvania, as far south as Baton Rouge and out west in Wyoming. He designed and installed the system at Fermentorium in Cedarburg, and did some brewing at Fitger's in Duluth. He came to Minocqua to a do a little consulting, and Kirk and Co. convinced him to stay permanently. He tweaked all the beers and is adding more barrel aging, cask ales, and limited releases.

The brewpub/restaurant is located in a 1927 brick Masonic Temple. The upstairs Divano Lounge has become a nice source of good live music in the community bringing in big names from around the Midwest. Music tends toward folk, bluegrass, and originals. The lounge also functions as an event space or just a nice option for drinks while you're waiting for a table in the restaurant downstairs. There's always something going on in the summer around Minocqua and the MBC has a nice downtown location right on the water and next to a small shady park.

Facebook.com/MBCbrews Twitter @mbcbrews

Stumbling Distance: *The Cheese Board* (8524 Hwy 51, 877-230-1338, thecheeseboard.com) has a variety of Wisconsin cheeses and does gift boxes. *Otto's Beer & Brat Garden* (509 Oneida St, 715-356-6134) serves Sheboygan brats and over 80 different beers. The outdoor beer garden makes this a great summer hangout. Perhaps the quirkiest time to come here is for *Beef-A-Rama* (minocqua. org, 800-446-6784). First celebrated in 1964, the annual festival is the last Saturday in September. Friday night is a kickoff with polka music, then the next day 1500 lbs. of beef is roasted for the 10,000 or so that come out for the event. An arts and crafts fair is part of it, but the central moment is the Parade of Beef and sandwiches from the roasters along the sidewalks downtown.

O'SO BREWING COMPANY

2018-2019: 3028 Village Park • Plover, WI 54467 • 715-254-2163
(late 2019: County Road HH • Stevens Point, WI 54482)
osobrewing.com
Founded: 2007   **Brewers**: Marc Buttera and Team O'so
Annual Production: 10,000+ bbls
Number of Beers: 40 taps (¾ O'so and ¼ WI guest taps)

Staple Beers:
- » THE BIG O (American wheat w/ orange zest)
- » CONVENIENT DISTRACTION (Imperial Porter w/vanilla, coffee)
- » HOP DEBACLE
- » HOPDINGER (Pale Ale)
- » HOP WHOOPIN' (IPA)
- » INFECTIOUS GROOVE (kettle sour blonde)
- » NIGHT RAIN (Oatmeal Porter)
- » NITRO MILKSTACHE
- » RUSTY RED

Rotating Beers:
- » FRUITY MILKSHAKE IPA
- » HOP DEBAUCHERY
- » MARGROOVITA GROOVE (Gose-style w/Mexican sea salt, lime and orange peel, lactose)
- » O-TOBERFEST
- » O'SO EXTREME BEERS: a variety of wood cask-aged beers, especially well regarded sours ales and fruited beers (BLOOD OF THE CHERRY, DE PECHE A LA MODE, SCARLET LETTER, BRING ME THE DISCO KING)

Most Popular Brew: Night Rain

Brewmaster's Fave: Marc likes the stuff he's been putting in barrels.

Tours? Yes, Saturdays at 1 and 2pm. $5 includes a beer and a $2 donation to a different local charity each month.

Samples? A flight of as many samples as you want from the 40 taps.

Best Time to Go: The Tap House is open Mon-Fri 3-9pm, Sat 12-9pm, but check the website as things are changing. Watch for their anniversary party in November which is also a Toys for Tots event.

Where can you buy it? Here on tap and in growlers, six-packs, 750 ml bottles, and kegs to go. Distributed all over Wisconsin and Chicagoland. Some exclusive 750 ml bottles are only sold in the Tap House.

Got food? You can bring your own or order in; it's all cool.

Special Offer: 10% off of O'so merchandise when you get the book signed.

Directions: *Old Plover Location until late 2019:* From I-39/US-51, take Exit 153 at Cty Rd B/Plover Road heading west. Take the first left on Village Park Drive and you will go 1.5 blocks and see O'so across the big parking lot on your right. *NEW in late 2019:* From I-39/US-51, take Exit 156, and head east on County HH (McDill Ave) and the brewery is just past Crossroads Commons and Portage County Business Park. :

The Beer Buzz: Co-owner/brewer Marc Buttera started homebrewing in 1994. His first brew? Barleywine. Not a bad start, but he soon found there was no place to get supplies. So he and his wife Katina opened one: Point Brew Supply. "It was so tiny," says Katina, "customers had to wait in the hall for the previous customer to check out." The couple moved into a new location, opening a brewery adjoining the supply shop. They started on repurposed dairy equipment and used equipment from Central Waters and the now defunct Falls Brewery and Denmark Brewing. Growth was stupendous, and in 2011, O'so opened some much bigger digs just off the interstate in Plover with

the brew supply still next door. Marc and the O'so Team really moved into sour styles and soon had a stockpile of over 400 casks stored offsite. In 2019 they begin building a 35,000 square-ft facility in Stevens Point 4 miles north of the Plover location (see directions) and should be open by the end of 2019, with an even larger taproom, and all the barrels under one roof. They add food and an outdoor patio, and an orchard for the fruits they will brew with.

The name of the brewery comes from an old picture in a local restaurant with a delivery truck from O'so Beverage Co. and its claim: "O'so Good!" O'so is very into their local community, thus expect charitable events. You will see various sours on tap or in 750ml bottles at the liquor stores. O'so won its first Great American Beer Festival Award Gold Medal in 2015 for The Big O.

Free WiFi. Facebook.com/OsoBrewingCompany Twitter @osobrewing Instagram @ oso_brewing

Stumbling Distance: Next door is *Mikey's* (mikeysbarandgrill.com, 3018 Village Park Dr, 715-544-0157) serving good food and 40 beers on tap (anyone kicked out of O'so at 9 generally goes here). *Bamboo House* (ploverbamboohouse.com, 715-342-0988), also next door, is an Asian bistro, serving Chinese, Japanese and Southeast Asian fare. *Christian's Bistro* (3066 Village Park Dr, 715-344-3100, christiansbistro.com) finer dining with some deliciously creative menu items.

RHINELANDER BREWING CO.

43 South Brown St., Rhinelander, WI 54501 • 715-550-2337
rhinelanderbrewery.com
Founded: 1882   **Brewer:** Al Ewan
Number of Beers: 10 on tap **(7 in distribution)**

Beers:

- » RHINELANDER ORIGINAL
- » RHINELANDER EXPORT LAGER
- » RHINELANDER LIGHT
- » CHOCOLATE BUNNY STOUT
- » HODAG ALES
- » IMPERIAL JACK DOUBLE IPA
- » MYSTICAL JACK TRADITIONAL ALE
- » OKTOBERFEST
- » THUMPER AMERICAN IPA
- » UPTOWN GIRL

Most Popular Brew: Rhinelander Original

Tours? Yes, $12 gets you a tour, sample flight, and two beers and a glass to take home.

Best Time to Go: Taproom open Mon-Thu 10-5pm, Fri 10-9pm, Sat 1-9pm.

Where can you buy it? On tap and in growlers and howlers here in the taproom. Statewide in bottles.

Samples? Yes, flights of six 5oz pours.

Got food? Free popcorn, chips for sale, and food friendly.

Special Offer: A free 5oz. pour when you get your book signed.

Directions: From US-8 take Business US-8/Kemp St into town 0.7 mile, and turn left/ north on Sutliff Ave. Drive 0.6 mile, turn right on Davenport, the after 0.3 mile, turn right on Brown St. The brewery is on the left.

The Beer Buzz: That founding date is the real deal. Rhinelander beer has been around a long, long time. Founded by Otto Hilgermann and Henry Danner, it was once one of Wisconsin's dominant breweries. Prohibition stopped the beer flow but it picked right up again until 1967 when the brewery closed. But there were too many fans about, and

Joseph Huber Brewery in Monroe (now Minhas Craft Brewery) soon bought up the label and recipe and brought it back to the market. Have you ever heard of a "Shorty"? Rhinelander was the first to put out the squat little 7-ounce bottles of beer. Sort of a little pick-me-up I guess.

But the story doesn't end in Monroe. In 2009, Jyoti Auluck bought up the brands and assets and with intentions of building a brewery again back in Rhinelander. Finally, a taproom opened February 9, 2018 serving beers brewed in Monroe. But on March 24, 2018 an Irish Red Ale, brewed in Rhinelander on the two-barrel system here, was served over the bar.

Minhas continues to brew the distribution beers, but what you get here is now Rhinelander Brewing Co. beers brewed onsite and only available at the taproom. A collection of breweriana was donated to them. Al Ewan and two assistants brew the small-batch beers for the taproom. Brewer Al retired from manufacturing but the brewery contacted the local homebrewers club and put him back to work.

Facebook.com/RhinelanderBrewery

Stumbling Distance: *The Brick Restaurant & Spirits* (16 N Brown St, 715-369-2100, thebrickrhinelander.com) has good food and a nice tap list. *Rhinelander Logging Museum Complex* (rhinelanderchamber.com, Business Hwy 8, 715-369-5004) is free but only open Memorial Day to Labor Day. A logging camp replica and an old Soo Line depot are part of a fascinating look into the hodag-fearing, beer-drinking life of the loggers. *Hodag Country Festival* (hodag.com, 715-369-1300) is a long weekend event in mid-July that draws over 40,000 and features some big names in country music and plenty of space to camp. Tickets go on sale the November before! Fishing is big here including the *Saldo Hodag Muskie Challenge* with a $20K prize and the *Ice Fishing Jamboree* the second weekend in February. Contact the Chamber of Commerce for lots more information (rhinelanderchamber.com, 800-236-4346).

THE MYTHICAL HODAG, THE FEARSOME BEAST OF THE LUMBERJACKS

Kozy Yak Brewery

197 North Main Street • Rosholt, WI 54473 • 715-677-3082
kozyyak.com
Founded: August 2012   **Brewmaster**: Rich Kosiec
Annual Production: 60 barrels
Number of Beers: 4–6 on tap (4 flagships, 1 seasonal, 1 specialty)

Staple Beers:
- » Chicken Coop Cream Ale
- » Rosholt Red Beer

Rotating Beers:
- » Chocolate Milk Stout
- » Doubleday Northern Brown Ale
- » Ike "Steel Beach Picnic" IPA
- » Indy IPA
- » Minnow Ginger Ale
- » Night Ops (Top Gun with dark grains)
- » R³⁴ Porter Beauregard
- Southern Brown Ale
- » The Shot Revolutionary Porter
- » State of Confusion Strong Ale
- » Top Gun American Amber
- » Try Rye Again American Rye Ale
- » Yak "Lighter Than Normal Beer" Ale
- » Znoozen Saison

Most Popular Brew: Chicken Coop Cream Ale

Brewmaster's Fave: Bock

Tours? Well, it's kinda small to tour. But he'll show you if he's not busy.

Samples: Yes, flights of beer or wine.

Best Time to Go: When they're open. Seriously, though, often seasonally closed, and hours vary even in season so check Facebook or call. Rich serves his beer at the local church Friday fish fry in winter, closing up the tap room for most of winter.

Where can you buy it? Here on tap and to go in Grunters (growlers). Wine for sale by glass or bottle.

Got food? Yes, German-style malt beer pretzels, gourmet pizzas with Rich's housemade dough, plus their own wine for the non-beer people.

Special Offer: A free Kozy Yak coaster while supplies last.

Directions: WI 66 passes right through Rosholt just northeast of Stevens Point. At Main St, turn north and the brewery is on the left at the end of that first block.

The Beer Buzz: Population 489. Breweries 2. Not a bad per capita ratio, really. Owners Rich Kosiec and Rose Richmond started with grapes, not grains, planting a few vines and adding more until by 2007 they had a 6.5-acre vineyard. They decided to open Fresar Winery (fresarwinery.com) downtown where they might get some traffic. While shopping for yeast online, Rich saw a beer kit on clearance (with a bock recipe) and picked it up. He loved it and went to Point Brew Supply (O'so Brewing's shop in Plover) for more ingredients, and quickly moved from extracts to grains.

A son of Norwegian immigrants, J.G. Rosholt built a sawmill in these parts, and when he sold some land to the railroad in 1902, the line passed through here and the little town enjoyed a boom from the sale of timber and potatoes. By the 70s, however, those days were gone and people were leaving for work elsewhere. Rich and Rose are doing their best to keep a pulse going here, and wine seemed a place to a start. Fearing the wine would not be enough, Rich figured he should add beer as well. Easier said than done: A brewery needed no liquor license, but the winery did and it can't self-distribute. So they couldn't sell their wine in the taproom. They needed to change to a brewpub, but this meant they had to serve food. So, Rich converted a closet to a kitchen and got a pizza oven. What may have been a formality is now quite popular, and from time to time he sells so much pizza he goes through the day's dough. At least, finally, he could serve his wines and beers… except in bottles. To sell bottles, the Fed says this must be a brewery! So in the end, this is a winery (selling from another part of the house), and to the State of Wisconsin they are a brewpub. To the Federal government, this is a brewery. Everyone happy? Super.

The brewery and winery occupy an old house in bustling downtown Rosholt. A large deck out front overlooks Main Street. The taproom has a bar and seating area as well as a fireplace. PVC pipe functions as the bar rail and the tap handles are upside down carved wooden bottles. His 2-barrel system occupies one of the back rooms, and he still does a lot of homebrew-sized 5 gallon batches so he is constantly trying different things. Despite having 1–2 new beers each week, for a while he was creating unofficial label designs for each. You can see many of them around the place. The winery is a separate room of the building. Most of the wines are sweet, and there are several fruit varieties.

A teacher once mispronounced the family surname "Kosiak" and thus the brewery's name of Kozy Yak. Rich served on the U.S.S. Eisenhower and during the Iranian hostage crisis in 1980, they went 152 days without a port call, setting a record that would stand 15 years. The captain can authorize 2 drinks per sailor every 45 days without a port call, and during that time Rich says the beers flown in were ridiculously expensive. What's a guy to do? Ike IPA is also "Steel Beach Picnic," which is how they referred to a party on the flight deck. Yaks grunt when they are happy, thus not growlers, but refillable "grunters" for sale.

Facebook.com/KozyYakBrewery

Stumbling Distance: Great barbecue in Rosholt? Yep. *The Brick Pit House* (107 N Main St, 715-677-4740) is impressive. Another diminutive brewer lies right across the street: *McZ's Brew Pub.*

McZ's Brew Pub

178 N. Main St. • Rosholt, WI 54473 • 715-677-3287
facebook.com/mczsbrewpub
Opened: March 17, 2016   **Head Brewer:** Ben Schreiner
Annual Production: 80 barrels   **Number of Beers:** up to 6 on tap, plus guest beers

Staple Beers:
- Ancestral Waters Cream Ale
- Cornerstone Pale Ale
- Rua Irish Red Ale

Rotating Beers:
- Hefeweizen
- Kölsch
- Stout

Most Popular Brew: Cornerstone Pale Ale

Tours? Not really.

Samples: Yes.

Best Time to Go: Open Wed-Thus 4-9pm, Fri-Sat 4-11pm, but check the website! Longer hours likely in summer.

Where can you buy it? Here on tap and in growlers to go.

Got food? Yes, made from scratch: pizzas, paninis, flatbreads, salads and soups. No fryer. Some wines and sodas.

Special Offer: Two free sample size glasses of house beer when you get your book signed.

Directions: WI 66 passes right through Rosholt just northeast of Stevens Point. At Main St, turn north and the brewery is on the right just before the end of that first block.

The Beer Buzz: This little project has made Rosholt arguably the community with the most breweries per capita. (Not a lot of capita here). Thanks to Kate Zdroik. Sounds Polish, right? Well, ironically the other side of her family was McCourt, which sounds Irish, but was actually mostly German, and her Polish surname masks Irish roots. Indeed,

what's in a name? Rick Kosiec (Kozy Yak Brewing across the street) owned this former IGA building and originally had plans to expand his own little brew operation into it. Kate owns a farm market on 66 and had the idea to open an art studio with rentable space and tools for artists and maybe some art classes. Rich caught wind of the art idea and suggested his building. Kate liked it so much she bought it from him in late 2016. Now half the space is brewing art and the other half the art of brewing with a two-barrel system Rich sold her. Brewer Ben, who joined in 2018, is a member of Bull Falls Home Brew Club, and he has some awards for his homebrews. The cream ale's name, Ancestral Waters, is how Kate's late husband used to refer to the local Lake Helen where his father and his family lived. Rosholt founded by Polish and Norwegian immigrants, took a founder's surname, pronounced Ros-holt, but today it's Rosh-olt, and they've got local beer!

Free WiFi. On Facebook.

Stumbling Distance: *St. Adalbert Church* (3305 St Adalberts Rd, 715-677-4519, rosholtcatholic.org) has a Friday fish fry in the Lent season. *Rustic Raven Antiques* (187 N Main St, 715-677-6711) for "oddities & the unusual wine & gifts." From May-Oct, *Wisconsin Territories Farm Market* (10281 Hwy 66, 715-677-3030, wisconsinterritories.com) sells fresh produce, Wisconsin products, and the famed Babcock ice cream (from UW-Madison).

STEVENS POINT BREWERY

2617 Water St • Stevens Point, WI 54481 • 715-344-9310 / 800-369-4911
pointbeer.com

Founded: 1857   **Brewmaster:** Gabe Hopkins
Annual Production: 150,000 bbls   **Number of Beers:** 12 (also 5 gourmet soft drinks)

Staple Beers:
- » POINT BEYOND THE PALE IPA
- » POINT CLASSIC AMBER
- » POINT DROP DEAD BLONDE ALE
- » POINT MILKSHAKE PORTER

- » POINT ONYX BLACK ALE
- » POINT S.P.A. SESSION PALE ALE
- » POINT SPECIAL LAGER

Rotating Beers:
- » POINT BOCK
- » POINT BEACH PILOT STRAWBERRY WHEAT ALE
- » POINT COAST RADLER

- » POINT OKTOBERFEST
- » POINT SNOW PILOT PISTACHIO NUT BROWN ALE

Whole Hog Brewery: 6-HOP IMPERIAL IPA, COLD NIKITA RUSSIAN IMPERIAL STOUT, CUPPA ESPRESSO STOUT, DIXIE PEACH HEFEWEIZEN, JP'S CASPER WHITE STOUT, LORD JAMES SCOTCH ALE, PUMPKIN ALE

Ciderboys Hard Ciders: CRANBERRY ROAD, FIRST PRESS, GRAND MIMOSA, MAD BARK, PEACH COUNTY, PINEAPPLE HULA, RASPBERRY SMASH, STRAWBERRY MAGIC

Most Popular Brew: Point Special Lager

Brewmaster's Fave: Point S.P.A. Session Pale Ale

Tours? Yes, call ahead for tour times and reservations (800-369-4911)! Free gift at the end of the tour!

Samples? Yes, three 10-oz samples with the tour.

Best Time to Go: Any season! *Pointoberfest* in late September is an annual fundraiser promising plenty of Point beer, live music, and local food vendors.

Where can you buy it? Definitely Wisconsin, around the Midwest, and almost 30 states. Use the Beer Finder on Pointbeer.com and Cider Locator at Ciderboys.com

Got food? Nope.

Special Offer: Buy one get one free brewery tour at select times. Call first to inquire.

Directions: Look for Francis St off Business Hwy 51 just north of Forest Cemetery. Go west on Francis to Water St.

The Beer Buzz: This is the fifth oldest continuously running brewery in the US, and it was the site of my first *pils*-grimage back in 1988 when a retired brewery employee Bill ("Bilko") still did the tours. I clearly recall him jabbing me in the shoulder and saying, "And you know what *kreusening* is, dontcha?" I didn't. Partners Frank Wahle and George Ruder started making Point Special Lager back in the mid-1800s. They supplied the troops during the Civil War. Prohibition, of course, meant near-beer and soft drinks,

but the brewery survived those dry years and the Great Depression (notice the one started before the other) and came back with Point Bock. Mike Royko, a syndicated columnist from Chicago, declared Point Special the best beer in America in 1973, but for the longest time it remained a very local brew, and even in the 80s I still remember saying, "When you're out of Point, you're out of town." Finally, in the 90s Point crossed state lines and became available in Minnesota and Chicagoland. They do some contract brewing now too, and they brought back Augsburger. And like Leinie's, though a large regional brewery, they have moved beyond the standard American pilsners and offer various alternatives. Back in 2003 Point Special took the Gold at Great American Beer Festival beating Bud and Miller. In 2009 the brewery introduced a line of extreme beers with bold flavors and higher alcohol content called Whole Hog Limited Edition Brewmaster's Series. The brewery also purchased James Page brand beer in 2005 and began producing it for sale in the Minnesota market. The brewery has had six expansions in the last six years, investing nearly $7 million in upgrades and new equipment, bringing their capacity to 150,000 barrels!

Stumbling Distance: Hanging around town you should head to The Square—the historic downtown hosts a number of taverns (more than 10!) all serving the hometown brew. *Guu's on Main* (1140 Main St, 715-344-3200, guusonmaintavern.com) has an excellent beer menu plus good burgers and fish fry. The *Bottle Stop* (35 Park Ridge Dr, 715-341-7400) is an awesome liquor store with deep knowledge of Wisconsin craft beer! *Rusty's Backwater Saloon* (rustys.net, 1715 West River Dr, 715-341-2490), five miles southwest of Point off Cty P, is known for amazing Bloody Marys and also serves Cajun smelt, cheese curds, a variety of sandwiches and a fish fry. *SentryWorld* (sentryworld.com, 601 Michigan Ave North, 866-479-6753) is a Robert Trent Jones Jr.-designed par 72 golf course, a must for golfers. Colors are phenomenal here in fall. A twenty-minute drive away in Rudolph is *Wisconsin Dairy State Cheese Co.* (6860 State Rd 34, 715-435-3144, dairystatecheese. com) which offers free tours and fresh cheese curds and ice cream.

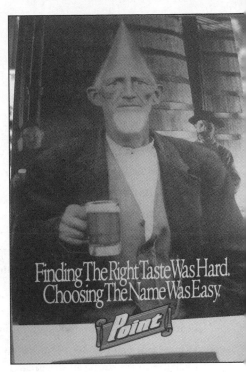

Finding The Right Taste Was Hard. Choosing The Name Was Easy.

BULL FALLS BREWERY

901 E Thomas Street • Wausau, WI 54403 • 715-842-2337
bullfallsbrewery.com
Founded: September 2007   **Brewmaster**: Michael Zamzow
Annual Production: 3,000 bbls   **Number of Beers**: 7 plus seasonals, 10-11 on tap

Staple Beers:
- » BAVARIAN-STYLE HEFEWEIZEN
- » BULL FALLS MARATHON LAGER
  (a revived regional Marathon City Brewery recipe)
- » FIVE STAR ALE (English Strong Ale)
- » HOLZHACKER LAGER (Munich-Style Lager)
- » MIDNIGHT STAR (German-style Schwarzbier)
- » NUT BROWN ALE
- » OATMEAL STOUT

Rotating Beers:

- » Bock Lager
- » Bourbon-Barrel Oatmeal Stout
- » Crossroads Coffee Lager (Costa Rican organic coffee)
- » Irish Red Ale
- » Legends Reserve (Dortmunder-style, brewed for Wisconsin Valley Fair)
- » Made In The Shade (ginseng with peach tea)
- » Oktoberfest
- » Prost-able Pils
- » Steinadler (Kölsch)
- » White Water Ale
- » ...plus various barrel-aged beers only on in the taproom

Most Popular Brew: Five Star Ale

Brewmaster's Fave: Midnight Star

Tours? Yes, every other Saturday at 1:30, limited to 20 people. Check the site for dates and sign up, or chance it and show up at 1:15. Groups of 15-25 can make an appointment. $6 includes the tour, a souvenir and a 14-oz Bull Falls beer.

Samples? Five 5-oz pours for $8

Best Time to Go: Open Mon-Thu 4–11pm, Fri-Sat 1pm–12am, Sat 1pm–12am, Sun 11am-7pm. Happy hour 1-5pm on Fri.

Where can you buy it? Here on tap and in growlers to go and four-pack 16-oz cans. Distribution is strong in the greater Wausau area but now statewide distribution has extended into major markets such as Green Bay, Oshkosh, Appleton, Milwaukee, Madison, La Crosse, Eau Claire and spaces in between. Also find them in the Twin Cities area in Minnesota.

Got food? Free shell-on peanuts and menus from some local places that deliver pizza and sandwiches. Food friendly.

Special Offer: Buy your first beer, get 1 free when you get your book signed.

Directions: From Hwy 51 take N Mountain Road (Cty Rd NN) east to River Dr at Lake Wausau. Then go north until Thomas St and go right to the end.

The Beer Buzz: Big Bull Falls, was the original name of Wausau during the lumber era when giant White Pine were prevalent in northern Wisconsin. The Bull Falls waterfalls

are located right in the city on the Wisconsin River which runs through town. That stretch of the river provides an Olympic-caliber course for whitewater kayaking and canoeing during the summer in Wausau. Bull Falls Brewery was named after the original city name: Big Bull Falls.

Let this be a warning to wives everywhere: "My wife got me a beer kit years ago," says Mike. A business associate informed him of commercial brewing equipment up in Eagle River, WI that had been sitting on the market for a while. He got a good deal on it and then stored it locally for five years. Mike and Don Zamzow bought the current brewery building in 2007 as well as a used 10-barrel system that was located in Stevens Point, Wisconsin. They sold the smaller 3-barrel Eagle River system to a place out in Peekskill, New York without ever having brewed a batch in it. In 2013, Bull Falls completed a 8,000-square-foot addition to the building bringing in a 30-barrel brewhouse, six 60-bbl fermenters and two 90-bbl fermenters, and canning and kegging lines.

When Mike and partners submitted a Bull Falls Brewery trademark, they received a challenge. "Yours is too close to ours and it will cause confusion in the market place." The offended company? Red Bull. A Red Bull attorney from California argued that someone might confuse Red Bull with the local microbrewery. One option was to go to Federal court to tell them they were ridiculous. Unfortunately, ridiculous people with money versus reasonable people without it... well, you know how THAT ends. After four years a three-page agreement was developed. Bull Falls can't use any bovine animals in their advertising. The words Bull and Falls cannot be separated. The colors blue and silver are not to be used in the fashion they do. And they are not allowed to brew root beer and call it Bull Falls Root Beer.

An interesting beer note: Mike's great uncle Walter A. Zamzow was treasurer of the now defunct Marathon City Brewing Company which closed in 1966. The brewery had been brewing beer for over 100 years. Mike had been searching for the recipe for Marathon Superfine Lager. The son of a worker who was involved with tearing down the old Marathon City Brewing Co. building had the log book from 1954 which his father had found during the demolition. Inside was a July 30, 1954 recipe for Marathon's beer. In 2009, Mike brought Marathon Super Fine Lager back and reintroduced the beer to the community as Bull Falls Marathon. The resurrected brew is available every year in Marathon, Wisconsin, on Labor Weekend at the Marathon Fund Days celebration, as well as at the Bull Falls brewery taproom. Like traveling back in time.

In a market that sometimes feels skewed to hoppy IPAs, Bull Falls Brewery is a refreshingly malt forward brewer offering traditional German and English styles with some interesting adaptations and new beers in between.

Country Fresh Meats (9902 Weston Ave, Weston) makes bratwurst with Bull Falls 5 Star Ale in it. Buy them there or here in the Bull Falls taproom.

Free WiFi. Facebook.com/bullfallsbrewery Twitter @Bull_Falls_Beer Instagram @ BullFallsBeer

Stumbling Distance: *Angelo's Pizza* (angelospizzawausau.com, 1206 N 6th St, 715-845-6225) is good for ordering in at the brewery tasting room. *City Grill* in the *Jefferson Street Inn* (jeffersonstreetinn.com, 203 Jefferson St, 715-848-2900) is also a good spot for eats. *Red Eye Brewing* isn't far away and also serves great food.

THE GREAT DANE PUB AND RESTAURANT

2305 Sherman Street • Wausau, WI 54401 • 715-845-3000
greatdanepub.com

Founded: 2009　**Brewmaster**: Rob LoBreglio　**Head Brewer**: Dan "Socks" Weber
Annual Production: 1,200 bbls　**Number of Beers**: 12

Staple Beers:

- » CROP CIRCLE WHEAT ALE
- » EMERALD ISLE STOUT
- » GEORGE RUDER'S GERMAN PILS
- » LANDMARK LITE ALE (pilsner)
- » OLD GLORY APA

- » SPEEDWAY IPA
- » STONE OF SCONE SCOTCH ALE
- » WOODEN SHIPS ESB
- » WOOLY MAMMOTH PORTER

Rotating Beers:

- » DUNKBRAU
- » IMPERIAL RED ALE
- » SAISON

- » SPRUCE TIP PORTER
- » ÜBER BOCK
- » ...and a rotating beer engine choice

Most Popular Brew: Stone of Scone Scotch Ale

Tours? By chance or appointment but always welcomed.

Samples? Yes, a sip to decide, or sampler platters of four beers for about $6.50 (add 2 more for $2.50).

Best Time to Go: Open Sun–Thu 11AM–12AM, Fri–Sat 11AM–2:30AM. Happy hour 4–6PM with free popcorn. Each day there's a Brewer's Choice pint on discount.

Where can you buy it? Here on tap and in growlers, pub kegs, half barrels (with 24-hour notice) to go. Some distribution in cans now as well. See their Madison/Fitchburg locations in Zone 1.

Got food? Yes, a full menu of soups, salads, burgers, and entrees. The bratburger (created on a dare) is an original with bacon on a pretzel bun. Beer, brat and cheese soup is Wisconsin in a bowl. Beer bread is standard, fish and chips available, and a load of other great dishes. Friday night pilsner-battered fish fry!

Special Offer: A free 10-oz beer

Directions: From Interstate 39/Highway 51 take Exit 191 heading east on Sherman Street. The Dane is right there on the right (south) side of the road just a stone's throw from the exit.

The Beer Buzz: Located just off the highway, and thus convenient to anyone heading past Wausau for the Northwoods, this place originally opened in 2000 as Hereford and Hops, a grill-your-own steakhouse with a rather nice brewpub. A few good brewers passed through and on to other gigs, and when the steakhouse didn't make it, the venerable Great Dane from Madison stepped in. The pub has plenty of parking, and inside you'll find the brewhouse behind glass and open to daylight from the other side. Circular booths in the main bar make a stylish lounge atmosphere while billiards, darts and the usual Dane shuffleboard give you something to do with your hands when you're not holding a beer. A beer garden with an outdoor bar was added in 2011 with room for 100. A fireplace takes the bite out of winter. Six TVs pipe in important games. If you have a wedding or work party, the Dane has private space for up to 300!

Stumbling Distance: *Milwaukee Burger Company* (2200 Stewart Ave, 715-298-9371, milwaukeeburgercompany.com) has 40 on tap. *Rib Mountain* is more of a hill, but we take what we can get here in the Midwest. At one billion years old, it is one of the oldest geological formations on the planet. And what do we do with it? Ski on it. *Granite Peak Ski Area* (www.skigranitepeak.com, 3605 N Mountain Rd, 715-845-2846) offers 72 runs as well as lodging and lessons. From Hwy 51 take Cty Hwy NN and the entrance is just over half a mile down. The state park here at the top charges a fee and offers camping, trails, and picnic areas. Exit 51 Cty Hwy N West. Turn right (west) at the first intersection (Park Dr) and go about 2.5 miles to the top. Get a close-up look at some whitewater with *Wausau Kayak Canoe Corporation* (www.wausauwhitewater.org, 1202 Elm St, 715-845-5664). They offer training courses for all levels, and if you prefer to stay dry come see one of three national and international competitions.

RED EYE BREWING COMPANY

612 Washington Street • Wausau, WI 54403 • 715-843-7334
redeyebrewing.com **Founded**: 2008   **Brewmaster**: Kevin Eichelberger
Annual Production: 432 bbls   **Number of Beers**: 10 on tap

Typical Beers:
- » BLOOM (Belgian wheat)
- » SCARLET 7 (Belgian-style dubbel with caramelized black mission figs)
- » THRUST! (American-style IPA)

A Rotating Dark Beer:
- » CHARLATAN IMPERIAL STOUT
- » MIND'S EYE RYE PORTER
- » VERUCA STOUT

Rotating Beers:
- » BELGIAN BLONDE WITH RASPBERRY
- » A CART RIDE TO MEXICO MAIBOCK
- » GERMAN PILS
- » LEMONGRASS RYE
- » MAN PANTS KÖLSCH
- » OKTOBERFEST
- » PUMPKIN ALE
- » SCHWARZBIER
- » SERENDIPITY DOUBLE IPA
- » VIENNA LAGER
- » TARTAN TODDY SCOTCH ALE
- » WISKANSAN TORNADO INDIA BROWN ALE

Most Popular Brew: Thrust

Brewmaster's Fave: He's partial to his lagers

Tours? No.

Samples? Yes, 4 tasters for $6, plus $1.65 each additional.

Best Time to Go: Open Mon-Sat 11am-close. Happy hour is Mon–Fri 4-6pm. Closed on Sundays.

Where can you buy it? Here on tap and in growlers and howlers to go, plus some draft accounts.

Got food? Yes, great artisan food. Try the wood-fired oven pizzas. The menu offers paninis, grass-fed beef burgers, wraps, soups, and salads as well as few signature entrees. For a gourmet take on Wisconsin's beer cheese soup, check out Red Eye Beer & Brie Bisque. An in-house smoker makes great ribs, chicken and more.

Special Offer: A free pint of beer during your signature visit.

Directions: From Hwy 51 take the Hwy 52 exit east which becomes Stewart Ave. Follow it across the Wisconsin River. It splits, and as you go right it becomes one-way. Follow it and it becomes First St, then Forest St. before it joins Grand Ave. Do not follow this to the right; rather stay left and turn onto 6th St and continue two blocks to Washington St and turn right.

The Beer Buzz: Kevin used to brew over at the now defunct Hereford and Hops (which reopened as The Great Dane here in Wausau). He is a creative brewer making some remarkable stuff and really likes Belgians (you may notice that two of the house beers are Belgian). He bought a brew system that had been sitting for four or five years for a good price and opened Red Eye. His promise: "Red Eye Brewing Company will never serve a beer that is not worthy of the most articulate beer drinker's palate."

He's also serious about his pizza. The oven came all the way from Italy. They ferment the dough overnight and hand toss it as it should be for an Italian pie. Most of the food is locally sourced, and every item on the menu is paired with one of the beers. A lot of people stop in frequently to fill their growlers, and Red Eye has become a social center for cyclists, especially after a day's ride.

Free WiFi. Facebook.com/RedEyeBrewing

Stumbling Distance: Next door is *Patina Coffeehouse* (610 Washington St, 715-298-0497, patina-coffeehouse.com) serving smoothies, café food and Milwaukee-roasted Colectivo coffee. You are just minutes from *Bull Falls Brewery*.

ROCKY REEF BREWING CO.

1101 1st Avenue • Woodruff, WI 54568 • 262-339-1230
rockyreefbrewing.com
Founded: 2015   **Brewmaster**: Tyler Smith
Annual Production: 350 barrels   **Number of Beers**: 15 on tap

Staple Beers:

- » A BIG RED HEN
- » HoWITzer
- » MUSKY BITE IPA
- » NEVER FAIL PALE ALE

- » THE OUTHOUSE (brown ale)
- » SOFT LANDING (dark ale)
- » STAYCATION (blonde ale)
- » UP NORT LAKEHOUSE SAISON

Rotating Beers:

- » CHOCOLATE PORTER
- » DUNKELWEIZEN
- » IMPERIAL STOUT

- » PINEAPPLE BLONDE
- » …plus seasonals, barrel-aged beers, and random one-offs

Most Popular Brew: Musky Bite IPA

Brewmaster's Fave: Musky Bite IPA

Tours? No, but you can see through the window.

Samples: Yes, flights of four 5-oz beers for about $8.

Best Time to Go: Open in summer Mon, Wed–Thu 4–9pm, Fri 4–10pm, Sat 12–10pm, Sun 12–6pm. Closed Tuesdays. Watch for possible seasonal changes. Anniversary party at the end of June.

Where can you buy it? Here on tap and to go in Crowlers, growlers, and 20oz. bombers, plus some local draft accounts and a couple in Milwaukee.

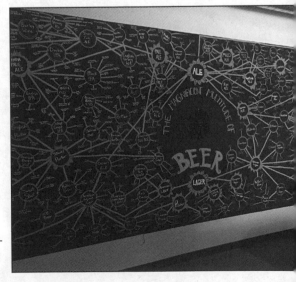

Got food? Occasional food vendors on site, but also food friendly.

Special Offer: A free sample glass (5 oz) of Rocky Reef beer during your signature visit.

Directions: Where US 51 and WI 47 cross in the center of Woodruff, go east (south) on WI 47 one block and it's on your right.

The Beer Buzz: Co-owners and co-brewers Tyler Smith and Christie Forrer had been homebrewing for a couple years when they decided to go part-time at their jobs as they laid the plans for a brewery in Milwaukee. When the time came to pull the trigger, they ended up here in the Northwoods. Christie's grandparents have a cottage in Boulder Junction, so she had been up here a lot throughout her life. In the summer of 2014, she and Tyler saw this place for sale. They liked the idea of a small town and so plans changed and they moved up here. The family cottage is on Rocky Reef Lane, so the name raises a glass to some great memories.

Tyler brews daily while Christie works as assistant brewer when she's not handling the rest of the operation. They are planning an unlimited rotation of styles and recipes, and they like to try new things, but a few favorites will end up being regular beers. They started on a half-barrel system, but as soon as they opened, they were already realizing they'd need to bump up their capacity, and in 2017 brought in a 10-barrel system.

The big metal-sided building houses their small brewing space and a taproom. They built the bar and 20 stools themselves. Two picnic tables and a ping pong table take up some space as well. Decoration is simple and a chalkboard lists the beers on tap, and the tap handles and flight paddles are designed to look like Northwoods street signs. The 2 TVs come on for sports, plus there are board games and shuffleboard. In summer they have a little outdoor beer garden.

Free WiFi. Find them on Facebook.com/rrbrewco and Instagram @ RockyReefBrewing

Stumbling Distance: *Monical's Pizza* (360 US-51, 715-358-9959, monicals.com) in Arbor Vitae does thin- and thick-crust pies for sit-down or takeout (bring one here)

Photographs Courtesy of Rocky Reef Brewing

ZONE 5

Algoma: Ahnapee Brewery
Appleton: Appleton Beer Factory
Appleton: Fox River Brewing Co.
Appleton: McFleshman's Brewing Co.
Appleton: Stone Arch Brewpub
Baileys Harbor: Door County Brewing Co. Taproom & Music Hall
Chilton: Rowland's Calumet Brewing Co.
De Pere: Legends Brewhouse and Eatery
Egg Harbor: Shipwrecked Brew Pub
Elkhart Lake: SwitchGear Brewing Co.
Green Bay: Badger State Brewing Co.
Green Bay: Copper State Brewing Co.
Green Bay: Hinterland Brewery
Green Bay: Legends Brewhouse & Eatery
Green Bay: Noble Roots Brewing Co.
Green Bay: Stillmank Brewing Co.
Green Bay: Titletown Brewing Co.
Green Bay (Allouez): Zambaldi Beer
Luxemburg: Thumb Knuckle Brewing Co.

Manitowoc: Courthouse Pub
Manitowoc: PetSkull Brewing Co.
Manitowoc: Sabbatical Brewing Co.
Marinette: Rail House
Neenah: Lion's Tail Brewing Co.
Omro: Omega Brewing Experience
Oshkosh: Bare Bones Brewing Co.
Oshkosh: Fifth Ward Brewing Co.
Oshkosh: Fox River Brewing Co.
Oshkosh: HighHolder Brewing Co.
Plymouth: Plymouth Brewing Co.
Ripon: Knuth Brewing Co.
Shawano: Stubborn Brothers Brewery
Sheboygan: Sheboygan Beer Co.
Sheboygan: 3 Sheeps Brewing Co.
Sturgeon Bay: Starboard Brewing Co.
Washington Island: Brews on the Rock

AHNAPEE BREWERY

105 Navarino St. • Algoma, WI 54201 • 920-785-0822
ahnapeebrewery.com
Founded: 2013   **Head Brewer**: Nick Calaway
Annual Production: 1500 barrels   **Number of Beers**: 8 on tap

Staple Beers:

- » LITTLE SOLDIER (American Amber Ale)
- » LONG GOODBYE (Bavarian Helles)
- » ROTATING IPA (always changing, always fresh)
- » TWO STALL (Chocolate Milk Stout)

Rotating Beers:

- » CAFÉ BLONDE (with coffee)
- » COLD TRUTH (cold-mashed stout)
- » FUN GUY- BROWN ALE (with mushrooms)
- » OKTOBERFEST

Most Popular Brew: Little Soldier

Brewer's Fave: Long Goodbye

Tours? Not yet.

Samples: Yes, $2 each.

Best Time to Go: Open year round. Hours vary seasonally, so check the website. May-Oct: Sun 12-6pm, Mon-Thu 12-9pm, Fri-Sat 12-10pm. Nov-Apr: Sun 12-6pm Mon-Thu 12-7pm, Fri-Sat 12-10pm.

Where can you buy it? On tap, growlers, 12oz bottles and 25oz limited release bottles in the taproom. Draft accounts and 12oz bottles in the surrounding counties.

Got food? Yes, flatbread pizzas, snack boards, and hot pretzels.

Special Offer: Not participating at this time.

Directions: WI 42 passes north–south through Algoma. Near the center of town just south of the Ahnapee River, go east 0.2 mile toward the lake on Navarino St and the brewery is on the left.

The Beer Buzz: A bit of history in the name. The name Ahnapee Brewing dates back to 1868. The original brewer, a Civil War veteran by the name of Henry Schmiling, is the

great-great-great-great uncle of Aric and Brad Schmiling who first opened this brewery in 2013. Their winery occupies the old brewery building next door which ceased beer production in 1886. Lagering tunnels underneath now hold wine instead of beer.

Nick had been homebrewing since he was 18, and worked at Titletown Brewing for a few years, but ironically, not as a brewer. Nevertheless, he was able to get feedback on homebrews and learn a bit on the side as he worked his way up from busser to general manager there. The Schmilings hired him as a production assistant and then general manager at the winery, and when the brewery idea moved forward, of course he took that on. He has since made it his own – literally. He purchased the brewery from the previous owners in 2017. He brews the beers offsite in a repurposed creamery nearby. At the 2015 Great American Beer Festival, Brewer Nick won a silver medal for Long Goodbye.

The taproom is housed in a converted two-stall garage down the block from the winery. Inside is a low L-shaped bar under a peaked corrugated-metal ceiling. A few tables sit along the wall, and a back room offers windows overlooking the Ahnapee River. In season, an outside deck lies beyond this with tall chairs and sort of bar-rail.

Be sure to also check out *von Stiehl Winery* (920-487-5208, vonstiehl.com) which makes 30 different varieties of grape and fruit wines and gets cherries from Door County and some of their grapes from their own Stony Creek Vineyard just outside of town. The winery is open year round, offering scheduled tours—daily from May through October, Saturdays from November through April.

Free WiFi. Facebook.com/ahnapeebrewery Twitter/Instagram @AhnapeeBrewery

Stumbling Distance: *Caffè Tlazo* (607 4th St, 920-487-7240, caffetlazo.com) is a marvelous little café in town with loads of teas, coffee, and a fresh, often organic menu for breakfast, lunch and dinner. *Skaliwags* (312 Clark St, 920-487-8092, skaliwags.com) offers finer dining with great seafood. Algoma is also a prime port for recreational fishing. Go angling for trout, salmon or steelhead on Lake Michigan. *Kinn's Sport Fishing* (60 Steele St, 800-446-8605, kinnskatch.com) next door is a good charter fishing service.

APPLETON BEER FACTORY

603 West College Avenue • Appleton, WI 54911 • 920-364-9931
appletonbeerfactory.com
Founded: December 2012   **Brewers:** Ben Fogle and Carl Pierce
Annual Production: 500 bbls   **Number of Beers:** up to 9 on tap

Staple Beers:
- » AMBER ALE
- » AMERICAN PALE ALE
- » BLACK ALE
- » BLONDE ALE
- » HEFEWEIZEN
- » STOUT

Rotating Beers:
- » BELGIAN TRIPEL
- » DOUBLE IPA
- » LIGHT LAGER
- » OKTOBERFEST
- » …and various experimental one-offs and a bit of barrel-aging.

Most Popular Brew: Blonde Ale or Hefeweizen

Brewmaster's Fave: "Mostly ales. Amber, Brown, Black, IPA, Hefe…"

Tours? Yes, by appointment for groups. A self-guided tour are available.

Samples: Yes, customizable flights of 4-oz beers.

Best Time to Go: Open Tue 4-close, Wed-Sun 11am-close. Kitchen closes 8pm Sun & Tue, 9pm Wed-Thu, 10pm Fri-Sat. Happy hour is 4–6pm Tue-Thu. Call in advance for reservations for large tables on weekends. Double check the hours online. Closed Mondays.

Where can you buy it? Here on tap and to go in Crowlers and growlers, plus draft accounts around town.

Got food? Yes. Jeff's wife Leah, the executive chef, developed a beer-centric menu, and there are some very notably delicious items here that are a bit uncommon. Their Reuben is the best you'll ever have, and there's a Friday fish fry.

Special Offer: Half off your first pint of house beer when you get your book signed!

Directions: Easy peasy: From US 41 just take College Avenue east into town. The "factory" will be on your right just after you cross the railroad tracks.

The Beer Buzz: I've had a few brewers say they are putting their own system together, meaning recycling some dairy equipment or other clever re-engineering, but when Jeff Fogle showed me his operation I was dumbfounded. He was literally building it. He was a pipe welder for Anheuser Busch and ended up in design management for them, working on multi-million dollar projects. So welding together some tanks from sheets of metal was just a tiny version of what he used to do.

The "factory" looks the part, set in a 1940s brick auto-parts building. The front bar/tasting room has polished concrete floors and warm wood ceilings, and the bar along the back

brick wall. Beyond that is a larger high-ceiling space where you can see the brew system around you and a stage for occasional live music. Another room up front provides more dining space. Recycled wood was used for the tables.

Jeff's son Ben, a mechanical engineer is in charge of the brewing. Jeff learned from his own father in 1983 and then passed the pleasure on to Ben in 2005. Rounding off Team Fogle is Ben's wife Mairi who handles marketing.

Free WiFi. Facebook.com/appletonbeerfactory Twitter @ABeerFactory Instagram @ AppletonBeerFactory

Stumbling Distance: If you need your Wisconsin cheese fix, head over to *Arthur Bay Cheese Co.* (237 E Calumet St, 920-733-1556) for the best selection in town. *Dairyland Brew Pub* (1216 E Wisconsin Ave, 920-903-9708, dairylandbrewpub.com) has 24 Wisconsin beers on tap, WI food including curds, Friday fish fry/Saturday prime rib, pizzas. Don't miss the awesome *Mile of Music* (mileofmusic.com), a four-day mostly free music festival in August hosted by 65+ venues, including *Appleton Beer Factory.* More free music happens every summer Thursday at Houdini Plaza on College Ave. Houdini fans should visit the *The History Museum at the Castle* (330 E College Ave, 920-735-9370, myhistorymuseum.org) with its exhibit dedicated to the escape artist/illusionist who called Appleton home. *McFleshman's Brewing Co.* is right across the back alley.

Fox River Brewing Co.

4301 W. Wisconsin Avenue • Appleton, WI 54911
(inside Fox River Mall) • 920-991-0000
foxriverbrewing.com
Founded: 1998   **Brewmaster**: Kevin Bowen
Annual Production: 1,600 bbls   **Number of Beers:** 9 on tap

Staple Beers:

- » 2 Dams Blonde Ale
- » Blü Bobber Blueberry Ale
- » Crooked Dock American Pale Ale
- » Marble Eye Scottish Ale
- » Reel It In Session IPA

Rotating Beers:

- » Defibrillator Doppelbock
- » Deep Dive Imperial Stout
- » Fox Light Kölsch
- » Foxtoberfest
- » German Pilsner
- » Maibock
- » Raspberry Wheat
- » Shakedown IPA
- » Slam Dunkel
- » Vixen's Vanilla Cream Ale
- » Winnebago Wheat Hefeweizen

Most Popular Brew: Blü Bobber

Brewer's Fave: The current seasonal beer!

Tours? On request, call ahead.

Samples? Yes, sample flights of four or eight 5-oz. beers.

Best Time to Go: Open Mon–Sat 11–10PM, Sun 11–8PM. Happy Hour runs Mon–Fri 3–6PM. Live music on occasion.

Where can you buy it? Here (and at their Oshkosh location) on tap plus growlers, quarter- and half-barrels and some local taverns serve it. Bottles and cans are distributed statewide.

Got food? Yes, the menu features a variety of steaks, seafood, pastas, sandwiches, and pizzas and much more on their full menu.

Special Offer: $2 pint on your first Fox River beer, additional pints regular price.

Directions: From Hwy 41 take the College Ave exit and go east to S Appleton St. Go right (south) and take a right on Water St before crossing the Fox River. It's inside the mall.

The Beer Buzz: Fox River Brewing Co. could be the highlight to a giant shopping mall trip for any true-brew connoisseur. This food court couldn't get any better—it boasts a brewery with a restaurant inside it! Kevin is working double duty, with this location and Oshkosh's Fox River Brew Co. (but each is brewed on site). This Fox River Mall location incorporates the waterfront theme of its sister brewery with an interior highlighting deep-water blues and a freshwater feel. There is an open kitchen, pizza oven, and an outdoor patio for the summer season. Serving lunch and dinner daily, their full menu offers steaks, pasta, seafood, pizzas, and sandwiches to accompany the handcraft beers. Kevin Bowen started at the restaurant in Oshkosh years ago and he began helping out in the brewery: cleaning kegs, filling bottles and such. After studying at Siebel Institute he worked for a few other brewhouses before returning to Fox River Brewing Co.

Free Wifi. Facebook.com/FoxRiverBrewingCompany Twitter @FoxRiverBrewing Instagram @frbcompany

Stumbling Distance: *OB's Brau Haus*, formerly *Old Bavarian Brewing Co.* (523 W College Ave, Appleton, 920-730-0202, obsbrauhaus.com), is a German lounge/eatery that has its recipes brewed at Fox River Brewing with German ingredients. Take in a ballgame at *Fox Cities Stadium* with the *Wisconsin Timber Rattlers*, a Midwest League affiliate of the Milwaukee Brewers. Fox River Brewing provides Snaketail Ale for the stadium. Look for *Fox River Brewing's* other location in Oshkosh.

McFleshman's Brewing Co.

115 S. State St. • Appleton, WI 54911 • 920-903-8002
mcfleshmans.com

Opened: 2018   **Head Brewer:** Bobby Fleshman
Annual Production: 500 barrels   **Number of Beers:** 16 on tap with some guest beers

Staple Beers:

- » Hildegard Czech Pilsner ("Hildy Pils")
- » Mild Angel Dark Mild
- » Pirates Cove Helles

- » The Public House Pint (dry stout)
- » Tall Mast IPA (English IPA)

Rotating Beers:

- » Oktoberfest
- » MSB (McFleshman's Special Bitter)

- » White Horse Porter

Brewmaster's Fave: Bocks

Tours? Yes, scheduled on website, and likely including Appleton Beer Factory across the alley.

Samples: Sips to help you choose but no flights.

Best Time to Go: Open Thu 4-10pm, Fri 4pm-12am, Sat 12pm-12am, Sun 12-6pm.

Where can you buy it? Here on tap and in growlers to go.

Got food? Occasional food trucks, snacks, local menus. Food friendly.

Special Offer: Half off your first pint of house beer when you get your book signed.

Directions: From US 41 just take College Avenue east into town. Cross the railroad tracks and turn right on State St. The brewery is on your right past the first alley.

The Beer Buzz: Brewer Bobby is a UC Davis grad and went on to work at several Oklahoma breweries after graduation, but finally moved here in 2013. He was offered a job at Hinterland Brewery just as Lawrence University offered him a professorship. He signed on as a physics professor, wanting to establish himself in the field of education as well as brewing. He still collaborates on projects with professors and students there. His wife Allison McCoy Fleshman hasn't quit her day job as a chemist at the university, but she is also heavily involved as a partner in the brewery. Several more partners followed them up from Oklahoma: Bobby's sister Cindi Jackman, lead brewer Shane Butner and taproom manager Layla Cowper.

Bobby is of German descent while Allison has Irish blood, so the name of the brewery reflects that combo—as do all the beers. All ales are cask ales and served on beer engines; Bobby uses decoction mashing, which German brewers will tell you gives their beers depth and superior malt character. The lagers are served from horizontal lagering tanks. The 10-hectoliter (8.5-barrel) brewhouse hails from Czech Republic and there's a Yorkshire square, a type of open fermentation vessel that was once used to brew the beers in Northern England. McFleshman's prefers to keep all the beers sessionable.

In 1918 this brick building housed Valley Dairy ("Val-Dair"), a bottler of milk. It closed when Prohibition ended (coincidence?) and Calumet Brewing moved in. Later on Blatz, Schlitz, and other brewers used this for distribution. McFleshmans is the ninth beer company to operate here. Initially they contract brewed with their friends across the alley, *Appleton Beer Factory*, and tours often visit both. A mezzanine overlooks the taproom and makes a great perch for bands too. Live music may also happen in the beer garden.

Free WiFi. Facebook.com/mcfleshmans and Twitter/Instagram @McFleshmans

Stumbling Distance: *Mai's Deli* (104 S Memorial Dr, 920-733-7900) serves great Thai food, and Mr. Taco (106 S State St, 920-915-4495, mrtacofoxvalley.com) is across the street. *Fox River House* (211 S Walnut St, 920-574-3950) is a great craft beer bar. On Saturday mornings in summer, part of College Ave nearby closes for the *Appleton Farm Market* (appletondowntown.org). In winter the market moves indoors. **Hotels:** *CopperLeaf Boutique Hotel & Spa* (300 W College Ave, 920-749-0303, copperleafhotel.com) and *Radisson Paper Valley* (333 W College Ave, 920-733-8000).

Stone Arch Brewpub

1004 S Olde Oneida Street • Appleton, WI 54915 • 920-731-3322
stonearchbrewpub.com
Founded: 2004   **Brewmaster**: Steve Lonsway
Annual Production: 3,200 bbls   **Number of Beers**: 14+ on tap

Staple Beers:

- » Coffee Brown Ale
- » English Six-Grain Ale (corn, barley, oats, rice, wheat, rye)
- » Houdini Honey Wheat
- » Marquette Pilsner
- » Pie-Eyed IPA
- » Scottish Ale
- » Sessions Pale Ale
- » Stone Arch Stout
- » Vanishing Vanilla Stout

Rotating Beers:

- » Adler Brau
- » Americana Pale Ale
- » Blindsided Barleywine gold medal
- » Blueberry Wheat
- » Caffeinator
- » Dark Ale
- » Dopplebock
- » ESB
- » First Snow Ale
- » Grand Cru
- » I.R.B.B.A.I.O.R.S.
- » Lemongrass Rye
- » Pumpkin Spice
- » Raspberry Porter
- » Stonetoberfest
- » ...and fruit beers in summer

Most Popular Brew: Scottish Ale

Brewmaster's Fave: Sessions APA

Tours? Yes, by appointment.

Samples? Yes, six or ten 4-oz samples for $10.

Best Time to Go: 11am–close daily, except for a few holidays. The beer garden is awesome in the summer and often features live music on Tuesdays and Saturdays.

Where can you buy it? Here on tap and in growlers, bottles, and kegs to go. On tap at numerous Fox River Valley pubs and distributed in six-packs in 20 counties in WI.

Got food? Yes, lunch and dinner. Bangers and mash, shepherd's pie, goulash, fish and chips, Scotch egg, deep-fried Wisconsin cheese curds, ale-steamed shrimp, cheese, sausage and beer for two, burgers, pizzas, and a Friday fish fry.

Special Offer: $1 off your first pint Stone Arch beer during your signature visit.

Directions: From Hwy 41 take the College Ave exit and go east 3 miles and turn right (south) on South Appleton St and it becomes Oneida. Go right, cross the bridge and take the second left (east) on S Olde Oneida. The brewery is on the right.

The Beer Buzz: Situated between the locks in a building called Between the Locks, this brewery carries on a long tradition on this site. In 1858 Anton Fischer, a German immigrant, founded the first brewery in Outagamie County and helped build the Fox River canal system. His Fischer Brewery was sold just a couple years later to Carl Meunch, a foreman from the Schlitz Brewery in Milwaukee. In 1884 the building lost a battle with fire and needed to be rebuilt. George Walter Brewing Co., the producer of Adler Brau, lasted until 1972. When the old building was converted into a little collection of stores and offices, Adler Brau Brewery and Restaurant tried to make a go if it as a microbrewery. In 2004, father and son partners Tom and Steve Lonsway took over the tradition. And one more thing: the building is haunted by "Charlie."

While studying science in college, Steve went to England for a semester and fell in love with beer history and beer itself and decided it had to be his career. "Beer is such a part of the culture there." And so it is here as well. He started *Homebrew Market* in 1993 (which sold ingredients and equipment for making beer, wine, and soda for 20 years). He attended the Siebel Institute in Chicago and then for six years did the brewing for both Fox River Brewing Co. locations until breaking out on his own. His brews have gotten some awards: Marquette Pilsner (Gold), Between the Locks (Silver) 2005, and others for Barleywine (Gold), Six-Grain, Stout, and Scottish Ale. Stone Arch Brewpub brews 3,000+ barrels each year, seven barrels at a time.

Stone Arch Brewpub started out as Stone Cellar Brewpub, but because of trademarks, they changed their name. Stone Their taproom has 24 tap lines focusing on their regular offerings, their Limited Releases, their Cellar Series and guests taps too! They also brew a special beer each year for the awesome August festival **Mile of Music—**Americana Pale Ale.

Stumbling Distance: *Skyline Comedy Café* is in the same building. Stop in at the *Outagamie Museum* (330 E College Ave, 920-733-8445, $5, open Tues–Sat 10–4, Sun 12–4, add Mon during summer) and see A.K.A. Houdini, an exhibit dedicated to the famous escape artist, an Appleton native (or so he claimed). *Simon's Specialty Cheese* (simonscheese.com, 2735 Freedom Rd, Little Chute, 920-788-6311, north on Hwy 41 exit Freedom Rd) has the fresh cheese curds as well as over 100 types of cheese (free samples), various fudge flavors (more samples), and a cheese mini-museum with a video about the cheese making process. *Octoberfest* (octoberfestonline.org) as well as *License to Cruise* (a classic car show) and *Applefest* are held downtown on College Ave in late September. "A mile of fun," as they call it. Do not miss *Mile of Music* (mileofmusic.com), an amazing event featuring over 200 artists, 65+ venues, and 800+ live performances every August.

Door County Brewing Co. Taproom & Music Hall

8099 Wisconsin 57 • Baileys Harbor, WI 54202 • 920-839-1515
doorcountymusichall.com
Founded: January 2013　**Music Hall Opened**: 2017
Brewmaster: Danny McMahon
Brand Sites: doorcountybrewingco.com, haciendabeerco.com
Annual Production: 3,500 barrels (DCBC) / 1,000 barrels (HBC)
Number of Beers: 12 on tap plus 1 nitro

DCBC Staple Beers:
- Bare Bottom Madness (oatmeal pale ale)
- Clawhammer Pilsner
- Little Sister Witbier
- Pallet Jack Cruiser Session IPA
- Polka King Porter
- Silurian Stout

DCBC Rotating Beers:
- Big Sister Witbier (with hibiscus)
- Punk Ass Cat IPA

Most Popular Brew: Little Sister.

Hacienda Beers:
- Closer Everywhere (juicy pale ale)
- Everything Eventually (double dry-hopped juicy pale ale)
- The Only Time Is Party Time (milk stout w/coffe, coconut)
- Velvet Bulldozer (imperial stout)
- Vertigogo (milk stout w/espresso, cinnamon)
- Whatever Feels Right (peach milkshake IPA)
- ...plus seasonal saisons in 750ml bottles, and more

Samples: Yes, flight paddles of five 5-oz pours.

Brewmaster's Fave: Bare Bottom Madness

Best Time to Go: Open Mon-Thu 1-9pm, Fri-Sat 11am-10:30pm, Sun 11am-9pm. Watch for winter hours when they may close a couple days or early. Live music most weekends, with some ticketed events. Music is varied but tends toward blue grass.

Where can you buy it? Here on tap and to go in growlers, howlers, and cans, plus draft and can distribution throughout Wisconsin, as well as the Twin Cities, St. Cloud, and Duluth areas. Hacienda Beer distributes in Milwaukee, Madison and Fox River Valley.

Got food? Milwaukee Pretzel Co. soft pretzels, Magnolia cheese boards, snacks, and food trucks in summer. Otherwise, food friendly, so bring your own.

Tours? Yes, scheduled on the website. For about $30 you get a 45-60 min. tour of both the production brewery and the nearby barrel-aging facility. Includes 2 beers, a glass and some swag.

Special Offer: Buy your first beer, get the second free when you get your book signed.

Directions: Take WI 57 into Baileys Harbor and its right in the center of town on the west side of the street (opposite the lake side).

The Beer Buzz: This fantastic music hall and taproom lies at the center of town, and if you thought Door County was seasonal, you're dead wrong. In the heart of winter live shows draw crowds on a Saturday night. This is a new build but the façade is designed to fit in with the town and the interior sports reclaimed barn wood and flooring, corrugated metal, chicken wire, and century-old brick to give this cathedral-ceilinged place a sort of barn feel. There's a fireplace and a stage in the corner and a beer garden with firepit outside. In back is a 15-barrel brewhouse, and a koelschip lies inside the little wooden building next door.

John McMahon co-founded the brewery with his son Danny, the head brewer. John's wife Angie is general manager, and their other son Ben manages the taproom and music bookings. John and Angie raised the boys here in Door County. Thus the name of the brewery. To keep up with distribution, they turned to contract brewing, but kept a brewery in a former feed store/grocery around the corner at 2434 County Rd F. Here they still keep barrel-aged brews, and 3 foeders (large wooden vats) in the basement for aging sours. But the taproom here closed when the music hall and taproom opened.

Danny went to school in Minneapolis and took up homebrewing as a hobby, but to step it up to pro, he attended the Siebel Institute. Door County has a rich history of Belgian immigrants—this was the largest population of Wallonians outside Wallonia (southern Belgium)—and Door County appropriately is into Belgian styles. Then in late 2017 they launched Hacienda Beer Co., or what we might call Danny's playground. While Door County is the family-friendly brand, with approachable beers, Hacienda is going exploring, with flavored stouts, adventures in IPA, milkshake IPA, and hazy IPA, and much more. Whereas DCBC has 6 flagship beers and 5-6 seasonals, HBC will top 20 beers each year.

Door County brew names have local stories: Little Sister and Big Sister are named after two islands on the Green Bay side of the peninsula. There actually was a Polka King: Freddie Kodanko, a local character who loved the oompah music, used to play 45s and LPs of it at area events while wearing a crown and cape. He liked his drink a bit much

and lost his driver license, so he ended up driving around on his red tractor, which didn't require one. Silurian Stout is not a geeky reference to Dr. Who, but rather a nod to a geological period between the Ordovician and Devonian Periods, 443.7 to 416.0 million years ago, when warm seas covered the area and laid down the materials that would become limestone and eventually the dolomite that underlies the peninsula. Thus, the fish fossil on the label. (A professor from the Field Museum in Chicago informed them their fish was from the wrong period, but who's gonna know that? A professor from the Field Museum, apparently.)

Free WiFi and board games. Parking on street or in back via School Lane. Facebook/ DoorCountyBrewingCo and Twitter @ DoCoBrewingCo and Instagram @ doorcobrewing

Stumbling Distance: *Blacksmith Inn on the Shore* (8152 WI-57, 800-769-8619, theblacksmithinn. com) is an outstanding bed & breakfast here in town. *AC Tap* (9322 WI 57, 920-839-2426) is a cash-only bar serving lunch and dinner and a reputable fish fry. Burgers, pizza and fish fry at *Cornerstone Pub* (8123 WI-57, 920-839-9001) are also nice. *Door County Trolley* (8030 Hwy 42, Egg Harbor, 920-868-1100, doorcountytrolley.com) runs a variety of tours in the area, from cherry themes to ghost tours in the fall. But don't miss their Wine, Spirits & Brew Tour. Pay a visit to the *Cana Island Lighthouse* (8800 E Cana Island Rd, dcmm.org) and see the light stations on a lovely walk through *The Ridges Sanctuary* (8270 WI 57, 920-839-2802, ridgessanctuary.org). Ten miles up the highway in Sister Bay, try *Bier Zot* (10677 Bayshore Dr, Sister Bay, 920-854-5070, Facebook.com/BierZot) a Belgian beer café with a long list of brews and Euro café fare.

Don't miss the *Door County Beer Festival* in mid-June here in Baileys Harbor! (doorcountybeer. com)

ROWLAND'S CALUMET BREWING
(ROLL INN BREW PUB)

25 N. Madison Street • Chilton, WI 53014 • 920-849-2534
rowlandsbrewery.com
Founded: September 1990, first beer on tap   **Brewmaster**: Patrick Rowland
Annual Production: 400 bbls   **Number of Beers**: 30 per year, 11 on tap

Staple Beers:
- » CALUMET AMBER
- » CALUMET DARK
- » CALUMET OKTOBERFEST
- » CALUMET RYE
- » FAT MAN'S NUT BROWN ALE

Rotating Beers:
- » BITTER BITCH BELGIUM ALE
- » BUCHOLZ ALT (formulated with Luther from Lakefront Brewery)
- » CALUMET BOCK
- » CALUMET ICE
- » CALUMET KOLSCH
- » CALUMET PILSNER (brewer's grandfather's recipe, a 1950 Coal miner from West Virginia)
- » CALUMET WHEAT
- » CONNOR JOHN'S SCOTCH ALE
- » DETENTION ALE
- » GUIDO'S GRAND IMPERIAL STOUT
- » HONEY LAGER
- » HUNTER'S CHOICE
- » KELLY'S IRISH RED LAGER
- » MADISON STREET LAGER (a pre-Prohibition pilsner)
- » MITTNACHT PILSNER (Schwarzbier)
- » MORTIMER'S ALE (English-style ale formulated with Kirby Nelson of Wisconsin Brewing)
- » TOTAL ECLIPSE

Most Popular Brew: A dead heat: Nut Brown or Oktoberfest

Brewmaster's Fave: "Whatever we have the most of—we make it exactly the way we like it."

Tours? Yes, by appointment.

Samples? Yes, $9 for eleven 3-oz beers and a root beer.

Best Time to Go: Open Tue–Thu 2PM–2AM, Fri–Sun 12PM–2:30AM. Closed Mondays, except holidays. Watch for the local street party in August, Crafty Applefest, or the brewery's famous Wisconsin Micro Brewers Beer Fest in May.

Where can you buy it? Growlers on site or area bars with draft accounts.

Got food? Pickled eggs and turkey gizzards? You make the call. "Eight or nine beers and it'll be the best food you ever had in your life." Also popcorn and Luige's frozen pizzas made in Belgium, WI.

Special Offer: A free 7-oz glass of the reason they're in business so long.

The Beer Buzz: Built around 1870, the building was Chilton's first firehouse and later city hall. At one time church services were held upstairs. John Diedrich made a tavern out of it in 1937, officially (though the back bar's mirror indicates 1926, so it may have been a speakeasy during Prohibition). Bob and Bonita Rowland opened the bar in '83. As the drinking age went from 18 to 19 and then to 21, Bob dealt with a lagging customer base and decided to take his homebrewing public. The Old Calumet Brewing Co. closed in 1942 when the Feds made an example of them for not paying beer taxes, and Bob saw it fit to adopt the name for what in 1990 was the 3rd smallest brewery in the US in the smallest city to have one. Madison Street Lager, a pre-Prohibition American-style lager, was formulated by Bob and Carl Strauss, the former head at Pabst for 40 years. Calumet Ice was the result of an equipment malfunction and the engineer sent out by the company to find the problem was Dan Carey, now the brewmaster at New Glarus Brewery. There's a handwritten note behind the bar from Kirby at Capital Brewery. As Bob once put it, "Brewers in Wisconsin are like cohorts in the same crime." Bob's son Patrick carries on this awesome family tradition. This is a true tavern, not to be missed, and laden with breweriana and some great stories. Small town prices are a bonus!

Stumbling Distance: *Vern's Cheese* (vernscheese.com, 312 W. Main St, 920-849-7717) has fresh curds on Tue and Thu evenings (or the following mornings) and various string cheeses besides a huge selection of other cheeses. *Ledge View Nature Center* (W2348 Short Rd, 920-849-7094, ledgeviewnaturecenter.org) is a 105-acre wooded park with a 60-ft observation tower and a couple miles of hiking trails. $6–7 scheduled tours are available for three natural caves here. Expect to get dirty and you might want to do this *before* you hit the brewpub. The park is free and open from dawn till dusk, but only till 4:30 at the office. Pick strawberries, buy honey or maple syrup, go on hay rides and explore a corn maze in fall at *Meuer Farm* (meuerfarm.com, N2564 Hwy 151, Chilton, 920-418-2676).

LOCAL INGREDIENTS—BRIESS MALT

Beer can only be as good as its ingredients. Garbage in, skunk beer out. So we are fortunate to have the Briess Malt and Ingredients Co. (briess.com), North America's leading producer of specialty malts, right here in Chilton, Wisconsin. Briess produces over 50 styles of malt—more than any other malting company in the world! Ignatius Briess started malting barley back in the 19th century in Moravia in what is now the Czech Republic. World Wars do little for business, and so grandson Eric brought the operation to the US in the 1930s. Great-grandson Roger saw that craft brewers could not buy in quantities as big as a box car and, sensing the coming trend toward hand-crafted microbrews, had the brilliant notion to start producing and bagging specialty malts in the 1970s. Specialized roasters were necessary to get the darker malts. Today they have 3 malt houses in Wisconsin, including this original one, plus one in Waterloo and the largest, a reactivated malthouse, in Manitowoc which doubled their capacity. (And there are two more there that could be brought back online when needed!) You'll find bags of Briess Malt in the back rooms of nearly all of the breweries in Wisconsin. Now *that's* some local beer.

Trivia note: Former Briess President Gordon Lane brews with his daughter at his own little brewery in Brookfield: Biloba Brewing.

LEGENDS BREWHOUSE & EATERY

875 Heritage Road • De Pere, WI 54115 • 920-336-8036
legendsdepere.com
Founded: 2001   **Brewmaster**: Ken Novak
Annual Production: 50 bbls   **Number of Beers**: 6 on tap

Staple Beers:
- » ACME AMBER
- » DUCK CREEK DUNKEL
- » FOUNDERS HONEY WEISS
- » LONGTAIL LIGHT

Rotating Beers:
- » CLAUDE ALLOUEZ IPA
- » CROCODILE LAGER
- » HALF MOON BRICK BELGIAN TRIPEL
- » HARVEST MOON OKTOBERFEST
- » IXTAPA BLONDE ALE
- » NICOLET NUT BROWN ALE
- » RUDOLPH'S RED-NOSE ALE
- » SCRAY'S HILL SCOTTISH ALE

Most Popular Brew: Acme Amber

Brewmaster's Fave: IPA

Tours? If Ken's out there, otherwise try to make an appointment.

Samples? Yes, $5 for six 2-oz beers.

Best Time to Go: Friday and Saturday nights, Packer game days, or after an event at St. Norbert College. Fridays the beers are on special. Sunday brunch is popular. Happy Hour is 2–6 PM Mon–Fri.

Where can you buy it? On-site growlers with super cheap refills.

Got food? Yes, pizzas, Friday fish fry (perch), beer cheese soup, wings, and ribs are notable.

Special Offer: Not participating.

Directions: Cross the Fox River heading east in De Pere and then go right (south) on S. Broadway. Where the road curves and Hwy 32 continues, go straight on Cty PP until you reach Heritage Road. Then go right (west).

The Beer Buzz: This used to be Splinters Sport Bar. The new owners remodeled a bit, and moved the bar to the side. Like the other locations, this has a sports bar theme. Read a bit about Ken at the Green Bay location listing. Sit outside on the deck during the summer. Free WiFi on site.

SHIPWRECKED BREW PUB

7791 Egg Harbor Rd, Egg Harbor 54209 • 920-868-2767
shipwreckedbrewpub.com
Founded: 1997   **Brewmaster**: Rich Zielke
Annual Production: 1,000 bbls   **Number of Beers**: 10 on tap

Staple Beers:

- » BAYSIDE BLONDE ALE
- » CAPTAIN'S COPPER ALE
- » DOOR COUNTY CHERRY WHEAT
- » INDIA PALE ALE
- » LIGHTHOUSE LIGHT
- » PENINSULA PORTER

Rotating Beers:

- » CARAMEL MILK STOUT
- » MAIBOCK
- » PUMPKIN PATCH PUMPKIN ALE
- » SPRUCE TIP ALE
- » SUMMER WHEAT

Most Popular Brew: Door County Cherry Wheat

Brewmaster's Fave: Captain's Copper Ale

Tours? No.

Samples? Yes, seven 3-oz samplers for about $8.

Best Time to Go: Open daily 11am-10pm in season, but only Fri-Sun 11-9pm from about Nov-Apr. Watch for Door County Beer Fest in June in Baileys Harbor.

Where can you buy it? On tap and in growlers to go and kegs on order. Six-pack bottles all over Wisconsin and in the Chicago and Twin Cities areas.

Got food? Yes, a pub menu including beer-boiled brats, pulled pork sandwiches, fried cheese curds, and salads.

Special Offer: Up to two $2 taps during your signature visit (for bookholder only).

Directions: Highway 42 passes right through town, and the pub is right on it at the bend in the road where Horseshoe Bay Dr connects from the west.

The Beer Buzz: Owned by the Pollmans of the Door Peninsula Winery (and Door County Distillery), this was the first brewpub in the ever-popular Door County. The brewpub was merely an idea for a good place to hang out and get a beer, and the food developed after that. The site dates back to the late 1800s when it attracted lumberjacks and sailors looking for a drink. Al Capone frequented the bar, and tunnels beneath it functioned as potential escape routes to other parts of the town. But in August 2017 Shipwrecked became fire-wrecked when an electrical fire brought it to the ground. By summer 2018, however, the building was rebuilt to the original appearance with expanded brewing and dining space, and without the previous upstairs guest rooms.

Shipwrecked also is known for its spirits—not whiskey and the like, but the ghostly kind. One of several frequently spotted apparitions is Jason, Capone's illegitimate son who hanged himself (perhaps with help) in the attic. Ask about the other haunts. We cannot confirm or deny that the ghosts have returned since the fire.

Brewer Rich brewed in Colorado for 12 years at Estes Park Brewery. He had been tending bar and moved over to the brewery side and just "kinda lucked into it." He moved to Door County in 2008 inheriting the recipes at Shipwrecked and adding some of his own such as the IPA. While he misses the mountains sometimes, he was landlocked in Colorado and loves the water and endless shoreline of Door County.

The bar is topped with metal like a truck's running boards, and the room is decorated with a sailing theme. Besides the bar there is a separate dining room and some second-floor seating and possible private party space, Windows look into the brewhouse. The patio out front is great for sunsets.

Free WiFi. Facebook.com/ShipwreckedBrewPub Twitter @ShipwreckedBrew

Stumbling Distance: *Door Peninsula Winery* (dcwine.com, 800-551-5049, 5806 Hwy 42) is ten minutes south in Carlsville. Tours are $3 and 50+ wines are on hand for free tasting. Also, attached to the winery is *Door County Distillery* (doorcountydistillery.com, 920-746-8463) which produces vodka, fruit-infused vodkas, brandies, gin, moonshine, rum, and whiskey. The distillery offers tastings, but you can taste them at the winery as well. Door County is famous for its cherries, and the season starts around mid-July. There are places to pick them or just stop at one of many roadside stands. Fish fries are less common than the fish boil, a tradition unique to Door County. *Pelletier's* (920-868-3313, Fish Creek, open May–Oct) is recommended for theirs. Whenever traveling up here during early spring, late fall and winter, it is advisable to call ahead to see what's open. Many places in Door County shut down during the off season. **Hotels:** *The Alpine* (7715 Horseshoe Bay Rd, 920-868-3000, alpineresort.com) and *The Landmark* (4929 Landmark Dr, 920-868-3205, thelandmarkresort.com) are walkable, as is *Lull-Abi Inn* (7928 WI-42, 920-868-3135, lullaby-inn. com).

TAKE AWAY: DOOR COUNTY DELICIOUS

Door County is synonymous with cherries. Various producers and shops sell cherries and cherry products throughout the peninsula (wisconsincherries.org). One good recommendation is *Schartner's Farm Market* (6476 WI Hwy 42, Egg Harbor, 920-743-8617); another is *Hyline Orchard Farm Market* (8240 WI Hwy 42, Fish Creek, 888-433-2087). But honestly, there are loads of them.

Schoolhouse Artisan Cheese (schoolhouseartisancheese.com) carries cheese from 30+ Wisconsin cheesemakers plus some specialty meats with locations in both Egg Harbor (7813 Highway 42, 920-868-2400) and at Ellison Bay (12042 Hwy 42, 920-854-6600) inside Savory Spoon Cooking School (Recommended! Savoryspoon. com)

Renard's Cheese & Deli (2189 County Rd DK, Sturgeon Bay, 920-825-7272, renard-scheese.com) is right off WI Highways 42/57 as you head north to Sturgeon Bay, and along with their fresh curds, they offer a load of other cheeses made inhouse or elsewhere. Tons of other products as well, including…

Salmon's Meat Products (107 4th St, Luxemburg, 920-845-2721, salmonsmeatproducts.com) Some of the best wieners you'll ever find plus brats, bacon, various sausages and more. Vince Lombardi went to these people for meats, and I pack a cooler for every trip to Green Bay/Door County to stock up. If you don't get to Luxemburg (but you should, for *Thumb Knuckle Brewery*), you can still find Salmon's in several select stores—but only in this NE corner of the state. (Pronounce the L; it's not like the fish.)

SwitchGear Brewing Co.

44D Gottfried St. • Elkhart Lake, WI 53020 • 920-781-5120
switchgearbrewing.com

Opened: May 2017   **Head Brewer:** Nick Kullmann
Annual Production: 360 barrels   **Number of Beers:** 9 on tap, 1 nitro, 10 guest taps

Staple Beers:

- » Boxcrusher Imperial IPA
- » Corner 5 Smash Pale Ale
- » Fat Cheeks Nut Brown Ale
- » Lead Foot Wee Heavy Scotch Ale

- » Pontoon Pounder Wheat
- » Resorter Red Ale

Rotating Beers:

- » Belgian Pale Ale
- » Jitterbug Coffee Porter
- » Kölsch

- » Oktoberfest
- » R&R Rye IPA

Most Popular Brew: Pontoon Pounder

Brewmaster's Fave: Boxcrusher

Tours? Yes, by chance or by appointment.

Samples: Yes, sample flights of three to six 7-oz pours for about $6.

Best Time to Go: Open Wed-Thu 4-9pm, Fri 4-11pm, Sat 11am-11pm. Watch for special events such as beer & yoga.

Where can you buy it? Here on tap and in growlers and Boston rounds to go, and a few draft accounts around town.

Got food? Free popcorn, various snacks for sale including cheese spread with their red ale in it, and food friendly. Juice boxes for the kids.

Special Offer: Buy your first house beer, get your second for half price when you get your book signed.

Directions: WI-67 passes right through Elkhart Lake. Turn west on Rhine St and follow it 0.3 mile and the brewery is in the big Feed Mill on the right.

The Beer Buzz: Situated inside the historic Feed Mill downtown, the brewery is located

at the historical start/finish line of the original Road America, a road race that has since moved to a proper racetrack here in Elkhart Lake. The electrical system-related name SwitchGear is meaningful on multiple levels. Brewer Nick is an electrician by trade

and the first location he looked at was the old village powerhouse, which Mathias Gottfried, a millionaire and brewer from Chicago, donated $15,000 to have built. But switching gears brings Road America to mind, not to mention the life change of opening a brewery.

For Nick, this is hobby-gone-out-of-control, having stared on an electric stove and working up to having 8 taps in his home. He and his wife brought in two other couples as partners. They built all the tables, chairs, the concrete bar with inlaid gears, plus that one table fashioned from a barn door. A mural of the original race course adorns the wall. Board games, cribbage, a guitar to pick up and play, and a couple TVs are here for entertainment.

Watch for half-barrel limited releases when Nick plays with one of the regular beers, adding fruits or spices, for example. Boxcrusher is named for when a friend had a half glass of it beyond the recommended one glass and proceeded to back his truck over his own mailbox.

Free WiFi. "I'm *Super* Special" Beer Club and "Participation Award" growler club. Facebook.com/switchgearbrewing

Stumbling Distance: *Off the Rail* (offtherailelkhartlake.com) is in the same feed mill and serves great sandwiches. *Paddock Club*

(61 S Lake St, 920-876-3288, paddockclubelkhartlake.com) and *Lake Street Café* (21 S Lake St, 920-876-2142) are excellent for dinner. *Road America* (N7390 Highway 67, Plymouth, 920-892-4576, roadamerica. com), one of the fastest racetracks, is the big attraction here, but for leisurely driving, check out *Kettle Moraine Scenic Drive* (dnr.wi.gov), a 115-mile winding route from Elkhart Lake to Whitewater Lake marked with green acorn signs. **Hotels:** This is a resort town, lots of places to stay. *The Osthoff Resort* (101 Osthoff Ave, 855-671-6870, osthoff.com) has an award-winning spa, cooking classes, and two restaurants, including *Lola's On the Lake*. *Jay Lee Inn* (444 S Lake St, 920-876-2910, jayleeinn.com) is a nice Victorian B&B.

BADGER STATE BREWING CO.

990 Tony Canadeo Run • Green Bay, WI 54304 • 920-634-5687
badgerstatebrewing.com
Founded: February 1, 2013   **Brewmaster**: Sam Yanda
Annual Production: 1,300 barrels   **Number of Beers**: 24 taps (8 guests)

Staple Beers:

- Bunyan Badger Brown Ale
- Buzzy Badger Coffee Ale
- Dubious Ruffian Chocolate Stout
- Green Chop Session IPA
- On Wisconsin Red Ale
- Peninsula Pils Craft Lager
- Walloon Witbier

Rotating Beers:

- CRN Delusion Cranberry Wheat
- Chile Gordo Jalapeño Porter
- Grassy Place Hazy IPA
- Honey Kölsch
- Mangotopia IPA
- Mashing Pumpkins Pumpkin Ale
- Mean Green New Zealand Hop IPA
- Porte Des Morts Maple Porter
- various IPAs and Stouts
- …plus frequent assorted pilot batches and barrel-aging.

Most Popular Brew: Green Chop IPA, Buzzy Badger Coffee Ale, On Wisconsin Red Ale year round. Walloon Witbier in summer.

Brewmaster's Fave: If forced to choose, one of the IPAs.

Tours? Public tours are typically scheduled on Saturdays, cost $10 including free beer and souvenir glassware, and can be signed up for via a link on their website.

Samples: Yes, 4-oz pours for $2 each or more for bigger beers.

Best Time to Go: Open Tue-Thu 1-10pm, Fri 1pm-12am, Sat-Sun 1-11pm. Open early on Sundays during Packers games.

Where can you buy it? Here in 4-, 10-, and 16-oz pours, plus growlers or Crowlers to go.

Distributed throughout Door County and Northeast WI down to Sheboygan/Oshkosh and west as far as Wausau for now, in four-packs of 16-oz cans and kegs.

Got food? No, but food friendly. Regular food trucks, especially for game days, summer Fridays, and catered events. Menus onsite for delivery, even from nearby restaurants that only deliver here.

Special Offer: A free 4-oz sample when you get your book signed.

Directions: From I-94 or from Ashland Ave/WI 32, turn onto Lombardi Ave and head toward Lambeau Field. Just east of the stadium, turn south on Holmgren Way. Turn left on Brett Favre Pass, follow it as it turns right, and then the next left is Tony Canadeo Run. The brewery is 300 feet along on the left beyond a big parking lot.

The Beer Buzz: Close enough to Lambeau to tailgate, Badger State Brewing was founded by Andrew Fabry whose family has a bit of Belgian blood in them. Andrew had a merry Christmas in 2011 when his brother bought him a brew kit. His friend Mike and Mike's cousin Sam had him over to learn a bit, and they brewed a batch in Sam's garage in 90+ degree July heat. The discomfort didn't dampen any enthusiasm.

When Andrew finished university in Madison, he headed back to Green Bay to stand at a crossroads: law school or beer. Tough choice, right? Disappointment in the local craft beer scene as compared to Madison's at the time, he sat down and wrote up a business plan. Andrew had worked for a distributor in high school and in bars in college, so he had experience in 2 of the 3 tiers of the beer industry but not the manufacturing side of it. Mike passed on the idea, and Sam remained silent on the matter until about a year later when frustration with his own job and Andrew's relentless efforts to convince him finally got him on board as head brewer.

They took over a vacant storage space in a much larger industrial building. Saranac and Hudson-Sharp occupy the other two spaces. They sold their first kegs in December 2013, and when they started selling growlers out the back door six months later, they knew they needed a taproom.

They had a lot of room to work with (and still do for brewery expansion), so the taproom is spacious with a large three-sided bar built of reclaimed pallet wood at center and abundant tables throughout the room. Two big TVs show sports (especially such games being played at the nearby stadium), music plays, and board games are on hand. There's even a gift shop. A glass utility door looks in on the brewhouse and opens for tours or larger crowds. Out a side door is a grassy area with a few picnic tables functioning as a beer garden. You can see the lights of Lambeau to the west of here. A factory sized parking lot serves the building.

The brewery logo includes a badger—the state's nickname that derives from the mining heritage, not the testy creature itself—and a pick and shovel, and barley on the sides.

Free WiFi. Facebook.com/BadgerStateBrewing and Twitter @ badgerstatebeer Instagram @BadgerStateBrewing

Stumbling Distance: *The Booyah Shed* (1800 S Ashland Ave, 920-371-6249) *Green Bay Distillery* (835 Mike McCarthy Way, Ashwaubenon, 920-393-4403, greenbaydistillery.com) has a full menu, WI beers, house-made vodkas, and TVs for the game. Filled with memorabilia from the all-star former quarterback, *Brett Favre's Steakhouse* (1004 Brett Favre Pass, 920-499-6874, brettfavressteakhouse.com) is next door and can deliver the goods to the taproom. **Hotel:** *Home2 Suites by Hilton* (810 Morris Ave, 920-227-5757) has simple, affordable suites a short walk from Lambeau and Badger State Brewing or *Hinterland Brewery*. Includes breakfast, sells craft beers from the fridge in the lobby.

BOOYAH!

No, not a rallying cry of satisfaction. This is something you may have never heard of outside of Wisconsin, or even just the northeast corner of it. Its origins are Walloonian, from Wallonia, a French-speaking area of Belgium. Many Belgians settled here in the Badger State. (Hello, Brussels, Wisconsin!) In 1906, a former lumberjack, Andrew Rentmeester, took a teaching job at the Finger Road School in Green Bay. He decided to have a fundraiser so he could get school supplies and books for the students. He put an ad in the *Green Bay Gazette* and told the clerk they'd be serving "bouillon." Rentmeester could pronounce French but he couldn't spell it. Thus when the clerk looked at him funny, he replied, and "b-o-o-y-a-h" went into print. And other fundraisers followed suit thereafter. Made from boiling chicken in a large cast-iron kettle over a wood fire, the clear soup took 1 or 2 days to cook. One might add potatoes, rutabaga, peas, carrots, cabbage, celery, but the original soup was likely fairly plain and practical. It's still a popular church picnic/fundraiser food and a rare restaurant may serve it. Check out *The Booyah Shed* (1800 Ashland Ave, 920-371-6249, facebook. com/TheBooyahShed) a food truck-turned-restaurant near Lambeau Field that serves it and other local comfort foods including fish fry. They often set up at *Badger State Brewing* or *Stillmank Brewing* and at the Wednesday *Broadway St Farmers Market* near downtown.

COPPER STATE BREWING CO.

313 Dousman St. • Green Bay, WI 54303 • 920-489-8575
copperstate.beer
Opened: June 1, 2017   **Head Brewer:** Jon Martens
Annual Production: 1,000 barrels   **Number of Beers:** 10-11 on tap

Staple Beers:

- » BARE BRICK IPA
- » KUPFER KÖLSCH
- » ONE CENT WHEAT
- » PLATINUM BLONDE COFFEE STOUT

- » RUGGED NORTH LAGER
- » SILENT CANARY DOUBLE IPA
- » SWIFT (AS MOLASSES) STOUT
- » UP NORT'ER NITRO PORTER

Rotating Beers:

- » FRUITED STOUT
- » OKTOBERFEST

- » …plus many pilot system beers

Most Popular Brew: Kupfer Kölsch

Tours? Yes, standard tours are first-come/first-served on Sat. at 1 and 3:30pm. $10 includes a beer. Clue-ery Brewery Scavenger Hunt tours are $20/person for groups of 2-10, while Ultimate Beer Geekery tours are $25 and led by the brewer with beers and a souvenir glass. Both are by appointment only

Samples: Yes, flights of four 5-oz. pours for $8, or six for $12.

Best Time to Go: Taproom open Mon-Thu 11am-11pm, Fri-Sat 11am-12am, closed Sundays. Coffee shop opens 6:30am weekdays, Sat 7am. No beer until 11am.

Where can you buy it? Here on tap and in Crowlers and growlers to go, plus draft accounts in Green Bay-Appleton area and Door County. Bottles/cans in planning.

Got food? Yes, full lunch and dinner menu and pub snacks. Copper Rock coffee shop opens for breakfast, 6:30-11am.

Special Offer: A free Copper State sticker when you get your book signed.

Directions: From US Highway 41 take Shawano Ave exit and go east to Ashland Ave. Go left (north) two blocks and take a right on Dousman St. The brewery is on the right after Broadway where you can enter the lot from Dousman, before the bridge over the Fox River.

The Beer Buzz: When they bought this building from Bill and Michelle Tressler of Hinterland Brewery, Bill Heiges and Gregg Mattek were already into brewing – coffee,

that is. Heiges has a successful shop Copper Rock Coffee Co. in Appleton. He'd open another coffee shop here but add another sort of brewing. Heiges brought in family to run the beer side of things. His sister Melissa and her husband Brewer Jon moved here from St. Paul to take it on. Melissa hails from Manitowoc while Jon grew up in Puerto Rico. Jon was not a homebrewer before this. His background is engineering and as a craftsman working with precision in woodworking and stained glass. He studied at Siebel Institute and did a 7-month apprenticeship with Hinterland – right here before they moved to their new digs next to Lambeau Field. So he trained on the system he would inherit. It took them two months to take over the space.

Hinterland first repurposed this former meat-packing building, and the hook receptacles can still be seen in the ceiling. The brick building is not exactly massive, yet a rather large brew system was magically packed into every available space with occasional structural alterations to accommodate large tanks. Before the badgers and lead mining, Wisconsin was a copper state. Visit the Neville Museum next door for more information about that! Jon focuses on sessionable beers, not the big abv variety.

Free WiFi. FermentNation loyalty club. Facebook.com/copperstatebrewing and Twitter @CopperStateBrew Instagram @CopperStateBrewing

Stumbling Distance: *Titletown Brewing Co.* is just across the street. Look both ways—you've been drinkin'. See Stumbling Around Downtown Green Bay.

HINTERLAND BREWERY
(GREEN BAY BREWING CO.)

1001 Lombardi Ave. • Green Bay 54304 • 920-438-8050
hinterlandbeer.com
Founded: 1995   **Brewmaster:** Joe Karls
Annual Production: 7,500 bbls   **Number of Beers:** 24 on tap, 10 guests

Staple Beers:
- » CITRA PALE ALE
- » EVER GREEN SESSION IPA
- » IPA
- » LUNA COFFEE STOUT
- » NITRO IPA
- » NITRO STOUT
- » PACKERLAND PILSNER

Rotating Beers:
- » BERLINER WEISSE
- » BODENBRECHER DOUBLE PILSNER
- » BOURBON-BARREL DOPPELBOCK
- » BOURBON-BARREL GRAND CRU
- » BOURBON-BARREL LUNATIC
- » DOOR COUNTY CHERRY WHEAT
- » LUNATIC IMPERIAL STOUT
- » MAPLE BOCK
- » OKTOBERFEST
- » SAISON BELGIAN FARMHOUSE ALE
- » STOVEPIPE BOURBON-BARREL IMPERIAL COFFEE STOUT
- » ...AND MORE!

Most Popular Brew: Packerland Pilsner

Brewmaster's Fave: "Depends on my mood and time of the year."

Tours? Yes, Saturdays at 1, 2 and 3pm. Cost is $10 and includes a pint glass and a beer. Check website and sign up there.

Samples? Yes, sample pours $1.50 per beer.

Best Time to Go: Open Mon-Sat 11am-close, Sun 10am-close. Kitchen closes 10pm (Sun 9pm). Hopping during Packers games (or big televised sporting events too).

Where can you buy it? Bottles and drafts of most brews are available in Green Bay, Milwaukee, Madison, Door County, and throughout the state of Wisconsin, Illinois, and the U.P.!

Got food? Yes, a seasonal, regularly changing menu of fresh produce, meats and seafood for entrees and shareable plates. Noodle bowls, burgers and sandwiches at

lunch; steaks and fine dining for dinner. Wood-fired oven focused meals including pizzas, as well as pasta selections. Late night menu during Packer home games. Reservations recommended during busy periods.

Special Offer: A glass of house beer when you get your book signed.

The Beer Buzz: This large production brewery, beer hall and restaurant within the Titletown District sits right across the street from Lambeau Field and steps from Lodge Kohler. Founder Bill Tressler studied journalism in college and started editing brewing magazines in the 90s. He also studied brewing at UC-Davis. So the logical next step, of course, was to open a brewery. Rahr Green Bay Brewing Co. was the longest running brewery in Green Bay, operating from 1858 to 1966, and Bill and his wife Michelle adopted Green Bay Brewing Co. as their corporation name as a nod to them. They found an old cheese factory outside town but after a fire there, moved to a former meat-packing plant at Broadway and Dousman.

They grew into a very tight space, creatively shifting around bigger and more equipment, until one day Bill received a call from a friend working for the Green Bay Packers organization. They heard he was looking for some space. They showed him the plans for the Titletown District, a development that now lies west of the stadium, and asked if he was interested. Of course, yes. It took five years to put together as the Packers bought out the land and laid the infrastructure. Finally, on April 12, 2017, Hinterland opened in this 24,000 sq ft. building.

The Beer Hall has two fireplaces and in summer garage doors open to the patio along the main corridor of the Titletown District. Play horseshoes and shuffleboard right outside the patio or in winter go to the sledding hill and ice skating rink. The upstairs features the High Gravity kitchen with random pop-up menu nights, at the whimsy of the chefs, no set schedule. Other times it's overflow seating for the big beer hall downstairs. The bar upstairs is always open. The plaza outside has a lot of events and Hinterland hosts live music on the patio in summer.

The beers have won many medals including silvers for the Pale Ale and IPA and a World Champion medal for Maple Bock. Joe has a pound of Luna Café (De Pere) coffee in each barrel of their popular Luna Stout (and I took some on *The Today Show* at Lambeau Field back in 2011 for Al Roker to try).

Free WiFi. Facebook.com/HinterlandBrewery Twitter/Instagram @hinterlandbeer

Stumbling Distance: *Lambeau Field* is just across the street. Look both ways—you've been drinkin'. Take a stadium tour or visit the *Green Bay Packers Hall of Fame* (packers.com). The stadium is the stuff of legends. Named after the year Curly Lambeau and George Whitney Calhoun organized the Green Bay Packers, *1919 Kitchen & Tap* is a gastropub with 40 beers on tap in the atrium at Lambeau Field. Next door is *Lodge Kohler* (1950 S Ridge Rd, 888-456-4537, lodgekohler.com) and on the other side of the stadium find *Badger State Brewing*. See also "Stumbling Around Downtown Green Bay." The Titletown District is not to be confused with *Titletown Brewery* another recommended brewery downtown across the street from the previous Hinterland location now occupied by *Copper State Brewing*.

STUMBLING AROUND DOWNTOWN GREEN BAY

Titletown and *Copper State* Breweries are right next to each other, and *Stillmank* is not far east. This puts a beer focal point right in the heart of downtown Green Bay, thus providing you some other cool things to do just stumbling distance away. Downtown is divided by the Fox River. Titletown and Copper State are on the **west side** at Dousman/Main St bridge. Both touch on Broadway. Once a sort of sketchy area, revitalization transformed it into a collection of great eateries, bars and shops, and on Wednesday evenings from Jun-Oct, On Broadway (onbroadway.org), a farmers market, closes off Broadway.

Highlights here include *Little Tokyo* (121 N Broadway, 920-433-9323, greenbaysushi. com) with sushi and other Japanese fare. Inside Titletown's brewery complex is *The Cannery Public Market* (320 N Broadway, 920-388-3333, thecannerymarket.com) with field-to-fork foods, fresh cheese curds being made before your eyes, a deli, beer and wine retail and many specialty products, primarily local in origin. Shop for home or sit and eat here with a selection of draft beers.

Before you cross the bridge, there is the *Neville Public Museum* (210 Museum Pl, 920-448-4460, nevillepublicmuseum.org) covering some Wisconsin history from the Ice Age to the 1940s, plus frequent traveling exhibits.

Just over the bridge on the **east side**, Washington Street runs parallel to the Fox River. Another farmers market closes this street as well Saturday mornings from May-Oct. One of Green Bay's best craft beer bars, *Ned Kelly's* (223 N Washington St, 920-433-9306, nedkellyspub.com) is here, as is craft-beer-friendly *Hagemeister Park* (325 N Washington St, 920-884-9909, hagemeisterpark.com). *The Libertine* (209 N Washington St, 920-544-6952, thelibertine209.com) is a cool, relaxed craft cocktail bar, extremely serious about mixology (enough to get the notice of *The New York Times* and other national outlets). No TVs or blaring music, just expertly mixed drinks and about 11 craft beers on tap.

Great burgers at a cheap price await at old-school *Al's Hamburger* (131 S Washington St, 920-437-5114). *Polito's* (201 N Washington St, 920-544-5086, politospizza.com) does pizza by the slice. For grapes rather than grains, visit *Captain's Walk Winery* (345 S Adams St, 920-431-9255, captainswalkwinery.com) The 1930 *Meyer Theatre* (117 S Washington St, 920-433-3343, meyertheatre.org) is the local concert/performance venue.

The City Walk portion of the *Packers Heritage Trail* (packersheritagetrail.com) is a self-guided walking tour chronicling the local legends of football with 17 commemorative plaques and some statues. The centerpiece is located at Washington and Cherry Streets. There are also Packing Plant and Lambeau-Lombardi sites outside downtown, and a *trolley tour* for the entire heritage trail (downtowngreenbay.com/tours) which covers the whole city. The tours line up with some Packers training camp dates, too (800-895-0071, candmpresents.com).

The Fox River Trail (dnr.wi.gov) runs right along the east bank in downtown and goes all the way south to Wrightstown.

Quality Inn & Suites Downtown (321 S Washington St, 920-437-8771) is walking distance to all of these places. St. Brendan's Inn (234 S Washington St, 920-884-8484, saintbrendansinn.com) also has rooms plus an Irish pub.

You cannot come to Green Bay and not at least see *Lambeau Field*, the legendary home of the Green Bay Packers. Tours are available (packers.com, 920-569-7512 (press 1)). *The Packer Hall of Fame* is another pilgrimage site for football fans right inside the stadium, and *1919 Kitchen & Tap* which serves excellent food and keeps 40 on tap. *Hinterland* and *Badger State* Breweries are right near the stadium. To get here from downtown, go west 3 blocks on Dousman to take a left (south) on Ashland. This will take you to Lombardi Avenue and you will turn right (west) and you're almost there. They live and die by football in this town. Bars will be hopping on game day; streets may be empty… until the game lets out anyway.

Don't miss **Green Bay Craft Beer Week** in May (gbcraftbeerweek.com) and Restaurant Week in July (gbrestaurantweek.com), a good time to explore the scene here.

For more downtown Green Bay goings-on, check downtowngreenbay.com

LEGENDS BREWHOUSE & EATERY

2840 Shawano Drive • Green Bay, WI 54313 • 920-662-1111
legendsgreenbay.com
Founded: 1998   **Brewmaster**: Ken Novak
Annual Production: 60 bbls   **Number of Beers**: 6 on tap

Staple Beers:

- » ACME AMBER
- » DUCK CREEK DUNKEL
- » FOUNDERS HONEY WEISS
- » LONGTAIL LIGHT

Rotating Beers:

- » CLAUDE ALLOUEZ IPA
- » CROCODILE LAGER
- » HALF MOON BRICK BELGIAN TRIPEL
- » HARVEST MOON OKTOBERFEST
- » IXTAPA BLONDE ALE
- » NICOLET NUT BROWN ALE
- » RUDOLPH'S RED-NOSE ALE
- » SCRAY'S HILL SCOTTISH ALE

Most Popular Brew: Duck Creek Dunkel

Brewmaster's Fave: Belgian Tripel "The best beer I've ever made!"

Tours? If Ken's out there, otherwise try to make an appointment.

Samples? Yes, $5 for six 2-oz beers.

Best Time to Go: Friday and Saturday nights, Packer game days. Fridays the beers are on special. Sunday brunch is popular. Happy Hour is 2–6 PM Mon–Fri.

Where can you buy it? Here on tap and in growlers on site.

Got food? Yes, Friday fish fry (perch), beer cheese soup, wings, and ribs are notable.

Special Offer: Not participating.

Directions: Head west on Shawano Ave (Hwy 29 West) off of 41 North, take Hwy 2 west to Riverdale Drive and turn right (north) and Legends is on the right, just past the *Village Green Golf Course*.

The Beer Buzz: Prior to this Legends, there was an old bar of the same name with an adjoining baseball field on this site. Thus, the name. The new building was completed in 1998, and the owners wanted a brewpub. Ken heard through a friend and got the job (nice friend!). Ken got his start homebrewing in 1993 with a kit he received as a gift, and he did his first beer on Christmas Day. He likes the hours and that no one tells him when he has to work or how to do it. The drawback, he says, "I work alone a lot. Not a lot of people to talk to."

Two large projection screen TVs are the flagships for a whole fleet of TVs piping in the day's sporting events. Sunday brunch is popular with folks staying around for noon kick-offs. Free WiFi is available and parking is off-street. They do their own root beer as well.

Stumbling Distance: Here it is, the local color you may have been scouring the pages for: *BOOYAH!* This is the regional hearty chicken-vegetable soup often made in mass quantities. *Rite View Family Dining* (2130 Velp Ave, 920-434-8981) makes 42-gallon batches. They also serve broasted chicken, Friday fish fry, cheese curds, and offer views of an old stone quarry and a yard full of peacocks. *Townline Pub & Grill* (2544 Lineville Rd, Suamico, 920-434-7943, town-line.com) has a lot of craft beer north of here.

NOBLE ROOTS BREWING CO.

2790 University Ave. • Green Bay WI 54311 • 920-489-2874
noblerootsbrewing.com
Opened: 2017   **Head Brewer:** Alex Falish
Annual Production: 250 barrels   **Number of Beers:** 7-9 on tap

Staple Beers:
- » BLONDE BELGIAN
- » EASTBOUND & BROWN
- » HAPSBURG PRETENDER
- » MACKINAC ISLAND AMBER
- » MIDNIGHT CONFECTION
- » NOBLE ROOTS IPA

Rotating Beers:
- » BLUEBERRY CREAM ALE
- » BOILS DOWN TO THIS (maple stout)
- » CARDINAL IPA
- » HIGH CLIMBER SESSION IPA
- » RED MORNING SKY IRISH RED ALE
- » ...plus GARAGE SERIES and kettle sours

Most Popular Brew: Blonde Belgian

Brewmaster's Fave: Cardinal IPA

Tours? Yes, quickest tour this side of the Mississippi.

Samples: Yes, sample flights of four 5-oz pours for about $8.

Best Time to Go: Open Thu-Fri 4-10pm, Sat 2-10pm.

Where can you buy it? Here on tap and in howlers and growlers to go with very limited onsite bottling, plus draft accounts in the Green Bay and Door County areas.

Got food? Just some free pretzels, but food friendly.

Special Offer: A free pint of house beer when you get your book signed.

Directions: From I-43 you want Exit 185 (Hwy 54/57) from either direction and follow the signs to get onto University Ave.

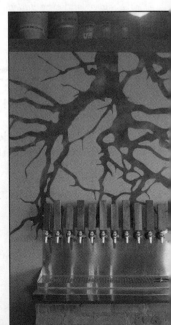

Merge onto Sturgeon Bay Rd (which becomes University) and take a left on University Ave at the first traffic lights (don't continue straight on University there). Go 0.8 mile (east on University) and the brewery is on the right. From downtown, Mason St heading north curves and become University (US-54/57) – be sure to turn right where University becomes Sturgeon Bay Rd.

The Beer Buzz: It's all in the name here. The roots part is about being Green Bay natives and about family: brother, father, sister, brother-in-law are all involved. Brewer Alex's father's roots are 100% Belgian, something some *might* associate with beer. Alex started homebrewing after a family trip to Europe and time studying in Germany. "Hobbies sometimes spiral out of control." The noble part refers to the traditional varieties of hops that were used to make early European beers – Hallertau, Saaz, Spalt, and Tettnang.

Originally a Sinclair gas station, and a slew of other things since, this corner brewery has a 7-barrel system and space for 50. The beer is reason enough to come, but it's also a very neighborhood type of place on the far east side of Green Bay. The glass garage door opens in summer when there's patio drinking.

The Garage Series beers are half-barrel batches on the old homebrew system and they hit the taps every 2-3 weeks with off-the-wall test batches. There's one big TV but it's only on for Packers or Badgers games. Board games are on hand. Cardinal IPA is inspired by Better Off Red from *Vintage Brewing* in Madison.

Free WiFi. Facebook.com/NobleRootsBrewing and Instagram @NobleRootsBrewing

Stumbling Distance: *Bay Beach Amusement Park* (1313 Bay Beach Rd, 920-448-3365,) since 1892, still no admission fee. 25-cent ride tickets, and a load of fun. *Black Sheep Pub & Grill* (2638 Bay Settlement Rd, 920-469-3200, blacksheeppubandgrill.com) for craft beer and curds, walleye, rib eye and other entrees, brick-oven pizzas and appetizers, and they do carry-out (and the brewery allows carry-in). *Mackinaws Grill & Spirits* (2925 Voyager Dr, 920-406-8000, mackinaws.com) has great comfort food in a log cabin setting with a good craft beer list (including Noble Roots). *Legend Larry's* (2035 University Ave, 920-435-7000, legendlarrys.com) has good wings and Noble Roots on tap. **See "Biking for Beer"** and the possibility of biking between here and *Stillmank Brewing* and even *Titletown*, *Copper State* and *Zambaldi* if you're ambitious.

STILLMANK BEER CO.

215 North Henry Street • Green Bay, WI 54302 • 920-785-2337
stillmankbrewing.com
Founded: April 1, 2014   **Brewmaster:** Brad Stillmank
Annual Production: 2,000 barrels   **Number of Beers:** 8 taps; 20 per year

Staple Beers:

» AWESOME SAUCE (apple cherry beer)
» PERKY PORTER

» TAILGATER (blonde ale)
» WISCO DISCO (unfiltered amber ale)

Rotating Beers:

» DOUBLE DISCO (Imperial ESB)
» OKTOBERFEST

» ...plus various barrel-aged beers

Most Popular Brew: Wisco Disco or Perky Porter

Brewmaster's Fave: Wisco Disco

Tours? Yes, every Saturday at 3pm. $10 gets yu 2 -12oz and a glass.

Samples: Yes, flights of four 5-oz pours for about $7.

Where can you buy it? Here on tap in 12- and 16-oz pours, and in Crowlers and growlers or cans to go. Distributed in 6-pack 12-oz cans and draft accounts in various places throughout Northeast Wisconsin.

Got food? No, only snacks, but food friendly.

Special Offer: $3 off one growler fill during your signature visit.

Directions: Going east from the Fox River on Main Street, turn left on Deckner, and left again on Henry St and the brewery is on your left.

Cyclists: Right off the Baird Creek Trail which connects to the East River Trail and via streets to the Fox River Trail. See "Biking for Beer" for more information.

The Beer Buzz: Milwaukee-native Brad Stillmank got his start as a homebrewer in the late 90s, throwing parties with his creations in college out in Colorado. The first batch was "good enough to keep me going. We were really surprised, actually, and emptied all the bottles over the weekend." In 2002 he started with keg washing and worked his way up to the brewhouse at Ska Brewery in Colorado but left in 2007 and moved to Green Bay with his wife to start a family. He brewed for a while for the now defunct Black Forest Dining and Spirits, but decided there is no greater joy than brewing it for yourself. He worked as a craft beer specialist for a distributor in De Pere for 8 years, brewing on the side. In 2014 he bought a building in April and brewed the first batch in August. The taproom opened two months later. The brewhouse was the indoor lumberyard of an old building supply store. The taproom was office cubicles and a showroom was torn down to open up a parking lot. The taproom has exposed ceiling beams, a bar at one end and a few picnic tables and tall tables. In season there is some outdoor seating as well.

Brad has certifications from the UC-Davis Institute of Brewing and Distilling and is a beer judge and a Certified Cicerone™ (sis-uh-ROHN), what you might call a beer

sommelier. Brad tries to use local ingredients. All his hops are from Wisconsin, his malt is from Briess (Chilton), his honey comes from Bellevue, and the coffee is roasted locally.

Stumbling Distance: *The Bar* (606 Lime Kiln Rd, 920-468-3566, meetatthebar.com) has great wings and craft beer and this is the original 1972 location. *Maricque's* (1517 University Ave, 920-432-9871, greenbayfishfry.com) is one of the best fish fries you'll ever have. *Titletown Brewing* and *Copper State Brewing* are 10 minutes from here, and *Noble Roots* too but in the other direction. See Stumbling Around Downtown Green Bay and Biking For Beer.

TITLETOWN BREWING CO.

200 Dousman Street • Green Bay, WI 54303 • 920-437-2337
titletownbrewing.com
Founded: 1996   **Brewmaster**: David Oldenburg
Annual Production: 5,500 bbls
Number of Beers: 6 year-round beer, about 25 new recipes/year plus one-offs
Tasting Room: 16 on tap, *Brewpub:* 14 on tap plus 2 casks

Staple Beers:

- » "400" HONEY ALE
- » CANADEO GOLD (Kölsch)
- » BOATHOUSE PILSNER
- » DARK HELMET SCHWARTZBIER
- » GREEN 19 IPA
- » JOHNNY "BLOOD" RED (Irish-style red ale)
- » ...ALSO SNO-CAP™ Root Beer

Rotating Beers: (the list is endless, but here are a few)

- » BRIDGE OUT STOUT
- » DOUSMAN STREET WHEAT
- » THE GREAT ZIZANI WILD RICE BROWN ALE
- » OKTOBERFEST
- » BELGIANS
- » AMBERS
- » PORTERS
- » BROWNS
- » DOUBLE IPAs
- » ...plus some barrel-aging, smoked beers, and occasional sours such as NED FLANDERS SOUR BROWN

Most Popular Brew: Green 19 IPA

Brewmaster's Fave: The beer in his glass.

Tours? Yes, scheduled on the website and for a nominal fee that includes some sampling.

Samples? Yes, sample flights for sale.

Best Time to Go: *Brewpub:* Open daily at 11AM. Hoppy hour 2–6PM. Join the Hoppy Campers Club. *Brewery Tap Room and/or Rooftap:* Closed Mondays. Tue–Fri 3–11PM, Sat-Sun 11AM–11PM. *Warning:* Tap room may close for private events, so double check the website.

Where can you buy it? On tap here in proper pints (20 oz) and in growlers and bottles to go, and draft accounts throughout the state, plus 6-pack bottles of their core beers (except "400") and some seasonals.

Got food? Brewpub: Yes, a great pub menu. Fish and chips, pizzas, artichoke dip, perch on Friday, deep-fried cheese curds, spicy beer cheese soup, the on-site baker makes beer breads. In fact, many of the entrees use beer in some way. The dinner entrees are excellent as well. Tap room: snacks and pizza. Rooftop: Different snacks, Taco Tuesday.

Special Offer: A free pint o' beer when you get your book signed.

Directions: From US Highway 41 take Shawano Ave exit and go east to Ashland Ave. Go left (north) two blocks and take a right on Dousman St. The brewpub is on the left just before the bridge over the Fox River. The brewery and taproom is across the street from the brewpub; you can't miss the giant smokestack with Titletown on it.

The Beer Buzz: Overlooking the Fox River, Titletown Brewery occupies a former train station that is listed in the National Register of Historic Places. Built in 1898, it was a stop for the Chicago & Northwestern railway. Prior to that, it was the Fort Howard Military Reservation. This was a center of the community when the "Peninsula 400" passenger service still ran. Three presidents rolled through on whistle-stops: Taft, Franklin Roosevelt and Eisenhower. The "400" ended service in 1971 and in '87 C&NW sold the tracks to Milwaukee to Fox River Valley Railroad. By 1994, after a couple more sales, it was just an empty building. That's when founder Brent Weycker, a fellow student union employee in college with yours truly, decided he would open a brewpub so that I would have something to write about 10 years later, and so we could all drink beer again just like we never, never did on the job. No, never. Well, hardly ever.

Brewmaster David earned a Bachelor's degree in... music. He started homebrewing in 2002 and then apprenticed here for many years. When the lead position opened up in 2006, he was a brew-in. He completed the Associate Program in Brewing Technology at the World Brewing Academy, and in 2015, was named Great American Beer Festival Large Brewpub Brewer of the Year. Not bad for a violinist. Nearly everything produced here is sold over the counter (except for just a few tap accounts). It's an impressive amount of beer, but then this is Green Bay. Railyard Alt got silver at 2008's Great American Beer Festival, Dark Helmet took bronze a year later, followed by a gold for Boathouse Pilsner in 2010. (For those of you visiting from another planet, Titletown is the nickname of Green Bay, in recognition of the many championships won by the beloved Packers.) In 2011, I personally shared a growler of David's Expect the Wurst (bratwurst ale) with Al Roker when they did the *Today Show* right on the turf at Lambeau Field. My 1:40 of fame.

In 2014, Titletown opened a much expanded production brewery with a state-of-the-art brewhouse, a bottling line, a tap room, event spaces, and rooftop drinking areas – the *Rooftap* (indoor and outdoor) for a brew with a view. A former vegetable cannery, the 160-year old building had been vacant since 2003, and its massive smokestack rises above with the name Titletown emblazoned on it. The brewery stands across the street and parking lot from the train station brewpub. The brewery tap room was once the boiling room for the vegetables, with kettles cut into the floor and the skylights above to let out the steam. It's a huge space with high ceilings, and during Packers games and other notable events, a screen is unrolled for projection TV. The long bar, with a foot rail from the old train at Bay Beach Amusement Park, runs along one wall with Art Deco design and blue lighting at night. One of the old kettle holes holds tempered glass so you can see through the floor (no skirts or kilts allowed). Two large garage doors open to Broadway St in season, and there is a front door and street parking here—though many park in back and enter through a hall from the side facing the former train station. Watch for the Beerbler, a true Wisconsin bubbler (drinking fountain) that shoots beer instead of water. They also have a mobile Beerbler for special events and fests. And there's beer for the kids too: root beer brewed with the original Grandma Gladys recipe from the old Sno-Cap drive-in restaurant on Velp Avenue.

That football player statue in front of the train station used to be at the Packers Hall of Fame. Titletown acquired it years ago and repainted it to be All-Star wide receiver and community hero Donald Driver. The city renamed the side street Donald Driver Way at that time.

Free WiFi. Facebook.com/titletownbrewing and Twitter @ titletownbeer Instagram @ titletownbrewing

Stumbling Distance: *The Cannery Public Market* (320 N Broadway, 920-388-3333, thecannerymarket.com) also occupies this building, with field-to-fork foods, cheese curds being made, a deli and lots of local products. *Copper State Brewing* is right across the street! Like the railroad theme going on here? Check out the *National Railroad Museum* (nationalrrmuseum.org, 2285 S. Broadway St, 920-437-7623) which has over 70 locomotives and cars, including Eisenhower's command train from WWII and the world's largest steam locomotive.

ZAMBALDI BREWING CO.

1649 S. Webster Ave. • Allouez (Green Bay), WI 54301
zambaldi.com
Opening: Early 2019 **Head Brewer:** David Malcolm
Annual Production: 500 barrels **Number of Beers:** 16 on tap

Staple Beers:
- » GOOD DOG PORTER
- » MEATBALL MAN AMBER ALE
- » YARD GAMES IPA

Rotating Beers:
- » PORTERS, STOUTS, AND BELGIANS
- » ...plus a whole range of styles

Brewmaster's Fave: Good Dog Porter

Tours? Yes, by chance for now, but scheduled in the future.

Samples: Yes, sample flights available.

Best Time to Go: Check website or Facebook for current hours.

Where can you buy it? Here on tap and in growlers and Crowlers to go, and in bottles in the Green Bay and Fox River Valley areas.

Got food? Limited snacks and such, but food friendly, bring your own.

Special Offer: $1 off your first pint of house beer when you get your book signed.

Directions: From WI-172 on the east side of the Fox River, take the US-57 Exit and follow signs for Webster Ave. Turn north on Webster, drive 1.4 miles and the brewery is on the right. *(WI-172 crosses under Green Bay, connecting I-41 on the west side and I-43 to the east.)*

Cyclists: Fox River State Trail runs along the river to the west but takes some creative road/sidewalk connection to get here. Exit trail either near St. Joseph across Riverside Dr or on Marine St into Monroe and south to Derby Lane to connect east to Webster Ave. *East River Trail* also passes within a mile of the brewery on the east side.

The Beer Buzz: Allouez gets its first brewery – even if the postal service may consider this Green Bay. David and Abigail Malcolm were born and raised in Green Bay and know very well that local culture is a bit weird about crossing the river and the township lines (Allouez, Ashwaubenon, De Pere, Howard, etc.) Allouez was once a sort of bedroom community to Green Bay, and it did not have its own brewery and neither did the SE corner of Green Bay just over that invisible line. As Allouez looks to be a place to stop rather than drive through, there are local efforts to create a sidewalk community and this brewery is a nice step in that direction with its sidewalk patio.

David got his professional start at *Titletown Brewery* in 2006. When Abby attended culinary school in California, he followed. Soon after she finished, he took a job at Big Sky Brewing in Montana where he stayed for two years before returning to Titletown for another four. In 2013 they started kicking around the idea of starting their own thing. David and Abigail have worked in the hospitality industry since their teens, and Abby's degree is in management. Perfect fit.

The brewery occupies 6,500 square feet in a new construction. The taproom is up front, and the brewhouse, a 20-barrel Wisconsin-made system from Quality Tank Solutions (QTS), lies beyond. Parents themselves, the owners made this kid-friendly, with a kids' area and changing tables in the restrooms. And the brewery name? A made-up word. Abby's maiden name is Zander and their last name is Malcolm so "**Z**ander **A**nd **M**alcolm" gets you to ZAM. Baldy is a reference to David's hair or lack thereof.

Free WiFi. Off-street parking. Facebook.com/ZambaldiBeer Twitter @ZambaldiBeer Insta @zambaldi_beer

Stumbling Distance: *Lorelei Inn* (1412 Webster Ave, 920-432-5921, lorelei-inn.com) great supper club with craft beers. Bike trails are close. History buffs should check out living history museum-park *Heritage Hill* (2640 S Webster Ave, 920-448-5150, heritagehillgb.org) or the 1837 Greek Revival *Hazelwood Mansion* (1008 S Monroe Ave, 920-437-1840, browncohistoricalsoc.org).

THUMB KNUCKLE BREWING CO.

E0208 Highway 54 • Luxemburg, WI 54217 • No Phone
thumbknuckle.beer
Opened: March 18, 2017   **Head Brewer:** Ed Thiry
Annual Production: 450-600 barrels   **Number of Beers:** up to 12 on tap

Staple Beers:

- » BELGIAN BEAUTY
- » BOATLOAD IPA
- » FARMERS TAN (Porter and Pale Ale)

- » GUNMETAL PORTER
- » HEYDER HELLES
- » RED BEARD FESTBIER

Rotating Beers:

- » BOCK
- » PECAN PEACH WHEAT

- » WHEAT
- » WINTER STOUT

Most Popular Brew: Belgian Beauty

Brewmaster's Fave: Helles

Tours? Yes, by chance or by appointment.

Samples: Yes, flights of four 5-oz pours.

Best Time to Go: Open Wed-Thu 4-8pm, Fri 4-10pm, Sat 12-10pm, Sun 12-6pm. Happy hour Wed-Thu 4-6pm. Closed Mon-Tue. Watch for Oktoberfest and Xmas market.

Where can you buy it? Here on tap and in growlers, sixth-, and quarter-barrels to go, and some draft accounts as far away as Neenah.

Got food? Free popcorn, Animal's frozen pizzas (Manitowoc, WI), soda. Food trucks on some Saturdays.

Special Offer: Buy your first house beer, get the second free when you get your book signed.

Directions: From WI-57 heading north toward Door County from Green Bay, exit onto WI-54 toward Algoma. Drive 6.4 miles and the brewery is on the left (north) side of the highway.

The Beer Buzz: Who knew you could get all the way to Luxemburg from Green Bay in under 20 minutes? Hello, Wisconsin! Thumb Knuckle comes from the common image of Wisconsin as a hand with Door County as the thumb, and right here, halfway between Algoma and Green Bay, is about where the joint of that thumb is.

Brewer Ed studied engineering at Miwaukee School of Engineering and went abroad for his junior year. He met a nice German woman, returned to finish at MSOE, then went back to Germay, got married, and stayed for about 8 years. He did a 1.5-year apprenticeship at the famous Weihenstephan Brewery, founded in 1040 by Benedictine monks in Freising outside Munich.

When it was time to come home, he brought his beer urged with him. He partnered up with his childhood friend Dain Treml, who brews with him. This building was always a tavern and originally an inn, part of a Belgian settlement. The foundation dates to the 1860s, while everything else burnt in the 1940s. The previous bar made some modifications, so now Ed and Dain are brewing in what was an indoor volleyball court.

Ed aquired and repurposed dairy tanks. He took a 3,000-gallon horizontal milk tank, cut off the insulation, stood it on its side, and put a burner under it. The taproom shows walls of corrugated metal and a wood-plank peaked ceiling. A few wooden cable spools make good round tables, and you can count on some board games, a TV, and regular live music. Ed may be the nicest guy you meet on your brew travels. In winter, see if he's serving *Stachelbier*. A German thing: take a very hot poker and carefully insert it into a pint of malt-forward beer. The head will foam up and caramelize, and it's sure to entertain the room.

Free WiFi. Knuckle Club. Facebook.com/ThumbKnuckleBrewingCo

Stumbling Distance: Vince Lombardi used to buy his sausage here: *Salmon's Meats* (107 4th St, 920-845-2721, salmonsmeatproducts.com) makes excellent hot dogs and much more. Try the seasoned ground beef (locals eat it raw with onion and rye toast). *Burdick's Bar & Grill* (525 Main St, 920-845-2807) for fish fry. Family-owned *Theys Orchards* (E0974 WI-54, 920-362-5884) for apples, cider and much more. Stock up on Wisconsin's *other* famous product at *Ron's Wisconsin Cheese* (124 Main St, 920-845-5330, ronscheese.com).

COURTHOUSE PUB

1001 S 8ᵗʰ Street • Manitowoc, WI 54220 • 920-686-1166
courthousepub.com
Founded: 2001   **Head Brewer**: Brock Weyer
Annual Production: 300 bbls   **Number of Beers**: 6 on tap

Beers: (Beers change often, rarely repeat)

- » ADAMS STREET ALE
- » AMERICAN AMBER ALE
- » BLACK PEPPERED LAGER
- » CANADIAN LIGHT
- » DARK JUSTICE IPA
- » EXECUTIONER IMPERIAL STOUT
- » IMPERIAL RED ALE
- » MÄRZEN
- » MEXICAN LIGHT
- » MUNICH HELLES

- » THE PRECEDENCE IMPERIAL PALE ALE
- » PUB PORTER
- » SCOTTISH ALE
- » SING-THAI
- » TRIPPEL JON
- » UNFILTERED WEISS
- » WILLINGER WHEAT
- » ...plus some barrel aging in wine barrels

Brewmaster's Fave: Double West Coast IPA

Tours? Not really.

Samples? Yes, five beer samplers and a root beer for about $6.

Best Time to Go: Open Mon-Thu 11am-8:30pm, Fri-Sat 11am-9pm. Closed Sundays.

Where can you buy it? Only here on tap and in growlers to go.

Got food? Yes, serious food for both lunch and dinner. Ultra contemporary menu with small plates and a sustainable, as local and fresh as possible, no freezer items. Pork saltimbocca, steaks, and fresh seafood flown in three times a week.

Special Offer: A free pint of house beer when you bring in this book to be signed!

Directions: Take Exit 149 east off of I-43. Then travel east on 151/10/Calumet Avenue (turns into Washington St) until 8th. Street. The pub is on the southeast corner of 8th and Washington Street in Downtown Manitowoc.

The Beer Buzz: This site was originally home to F. Willinger's Beer Hall, and an old black and white photo behind the bar shows the former beer joint. The pub was rebuilt to the hall's likeness. Once there were five breweries in Manitowoc, but by the mid-70s, there was not a one. Founder John Jagemann wanted to bring back a little of that tradition and so the pub was born. After 16 years, John retired, and Ryan Morris and Brock Meyer – both of whom have worked here – took over as co-owners. Beer is not the only libation here. Since 2002, the restaurant has maintained a Wine Spectator Award of Excellence. Follow the website's blog to find out about upcoming live music. The beers are brewed in 4-barrel batches, and when they run out, it's on to the next brew. This means a lot of variety in a short period of time.

Free WiFi. Outdoor seating. Facebook.com/CourthousePubWI and Twitter @ CourthousePub Instagram @CourthousePubWI

Stumbling Distance: Look for the big cow and you'll find *Cedar Crest Ice Cream Parlor* (2000 S 10th, 800-877-8341, cedarcresticecream.com). Award winning stuff. Stop in at the *Wisconsin Maritime Museum* (866-724-2356, wisconsinmaritime.org) and tour the submarine U.S.S. Cobia. Twenty-eight subs were built here in Manitowoc during WWII. *Tippy's Bar, Grill & Miniature Bowling* (1713 East St, 920-553-8479) in Two Rivers (pronounced "T'rivers" by locals) serves smelt six days a week! (A small fish which is netted and then fried—and eaten—whole. It's a Wisconsin thing.) The Manitowoc VFW or Eagle's Hall are rumored to have the best fish fries, but there are tons of them here. Get your cheese fix at *Pine River Dairy* (10115 English Lake Rd, 920-758-2233, pineriverdairy.com) south of 151 on Range Line Rd (since 1877). Over 250 varieties!

GATEWAY TO WISCONSIN II

From mid-May to mid-October, the S.S. Badger (ssbadger.com, 800-841-4243), a coal-powered car ferry, makes the four-hour crossing of the big lake to Manitowoc from Ludington, Michigan.

PETSKULL BREWING CO.

220 N. 9th St. • Manitowoc, WI 54220 • 920-717-0237
petskullbrewing.com
Opened: 2017   **Head Brewer:** Paul Hoffman
Annual Production: 250 barrels   **Number of Beers:** 10 on tap

Staple Beers:
- » FREAKY 220 DOUBLE IPA
- » JAKE'S MALT LEMONADE
- » SCHNITZKY GERMAN HEFEWEIZEN

Rotating Beers:
- » DEBOCKL WEIZENBOCK
- » THE FIELD CREAM ALE
- » NORTHSIDE CHOCOLATE OATMEAL PORTER
- » PETSKULL PILOT PALE ALE
- » PORTLY FELLOW CHERRY VANILLA PORTER
- » UNGIRTHED SCOTCH ALE
- » …and many more

Most Popular Brew: Schnitzky

Brewmaster's Fave: Freaky 220 Double IPA

Tours? No.

Samples: Yes, flights of 2 to 10 five-ounce pours for about $2 per beer.

Best Time to Go: Open Thu 4-8pm, Fri 3-9pm, Sat 2-9pm. Hours expand in summer, so check the Facebook page.

Where can you buy it? Here on tap and in growlers to go, plus a few local draft accounts.

Got food? No, but food friendly. Free popcorn and pretzels.

Special Offer: A free pint when you get your book signed.

Directions: Coming in on US-10 drive 3.5 miles east of I-43 and turn south (right) on 9th St. Drive 1 mile and it's on the right. Coming in on US-151, follow it 3.1 miles and turn left (north) on US-10/8th St. Cross the bridge, turn left on York St, and take the next right on 9th and the brewery is on the left.

The Beer Buzz: A pet skull is "Any domesticated or tamed skull that is kept as a companion and cared for affectionately." You know there has to be a story behind this. There is, and it goes back to 1993 when one of owner/brewer Paul's friends had a goat skull on the center of his table. Paul jokingly referred to it as a Pet Skull, which he thought was a pretty cool phrase. He told himself: I will use that someday for something. A few years ago that friend visited and didn't remember that story until Paul reminded him. A couple weeks later that goat skull arrived in the mail. It's hanging in the taproom.

Paul started homebrewing in about 2006, and when he traveled he always loved visiting different taprooms. Manitowoc didn't have one, and he thought, "Why not give something crazy a try?" He then turned this former car shop (and a number of retail stores) into a place to hang out and drink beer. Just a bar and some tables, no darts or pool, but some board games. The focus is beer, conversation, and camaraderie. And a pet skull.

Free WiFi. Facebook.com/PetSkullBrewing and Twitter @PetSkullBrewing Instagram @PetSkullBrewingCompany

Stumbling Distance: Visit *Wisconsin Maritime Museum* (75 Maritime Dr, 920-684-0218, wisconsinmaritime.org) and go inside a submarine. In summer there's a pub on the roof overlooking the lake where you can have PetSkull on tap. *Ryan's On York* (712 York St, 920-905-0700, ryansonyork.com) is gastropub far like you've never seen. Bulgogi sandwich? Bangkok fries? So much awesome here, with a great craft beer selection. *Maretti's Deli* (823 Buffalo St, 920-684-9151) for stellar sandwiches. *Shooter Malone's* (901 Buffalo St, 920-682-4116, shootermalones.com) for solid bar & grill. *Pizza Garden* (1602 N 30th St, 920-682-6151, pizzagardenmanitowoc.com) delivers to the taproom. Fine dining and house brews at *Courthouse Pub* and more craft brewing at *Sabbatical Brewing*. **Hotel:** *Baymont Inn & Suites* (101 Maritime Dr, 920-482-2097, wyndhamhotels.com)

SABBATICAL BREWING CO.

Manitowoc, WI • Phone: TBD
.sabbaticalbeer.com
Opening: 2019 **Head Brewer:** Will Schneider
Annual Production: 600 bbls **Number of Beers:** 12-16 plus guest taps

Staple Beers:
- » GLORIA – WIT BIER
- » HEAVY TIPP'AH – WISCONSING HOPPED PALE ALE
- » MORNING COMMUTE – COFFEE MILK STOUT
- » PORCH PACK – AMERICAN PALE ALE
- » STHU (SHUT THE HELL UP) – NEIPA

Rotating Beers:

- » Lush Lake Vibes Series (Blonde Ale with alternating hops and fruits)
- » Pinch Hitter Series (ales from their homebrew days)
- » Spirit Woods Series (barrel-aged ales)

Most Popular Brew: Morning Commute

Brewmaster's Fave: Morning Commute

Tours? TBD

Samples: 5oz pours for $2-3.

Best Time to Go: TBD, but from breakfast to dinner. Morning and weekly daytime hours.

Where can you buy it? Here in tap or in cans to go.

Got food? Yes, a sweet and savory menu intended to pair well with the beers, plus a kids' menu to make this a family-friendly spot.

Special Offer: A free sample flight of four when you get your book signed.

The Beer Buzz: Since 2009, owners Will and Cassie Schneider have operated a youth mentoring organization with after-school and summer programs for kids and young adults with special needs and mental health diagnoses as well as some community based supportive home care settings. We have varying services throughout Manitowoc, Sheboygan and Winnebago Counties. It's a truly rewarding field, but also an emotionally draining one. Sabbatical means 'a rest from work, or a break' and operating the brewery as well gives them and their customers "one more reason to break for beer."

Brewer Will's gateway to the brewing addiction was Big Hitter Brewing, a small home-brew group. They started with extracts but quickly graduated to all grain brewing, soon sharing beers with friends and competitions, and even serving at their own wedding reception out East. Cassie has family in New Hampshire, and their frequent visits there eventually revolved around craft beer. As parents of three kids, they appreciated the family friendly environment at many of the breweries and sought to incorporate this in their own endeavor. They discovered **Barley to Barrel** (see Index), a 10-week brewery incubator program in Milwaukee. This highly valuable knowledge, plus a trip to Denver, Colorado for GABF, gave them the inspiration to move forward. They are starting with a 5-barrel Psycho Brew system from Franklin Street Brewing Company in Manchester, IA.

Expect large community tables, counter-service type food, games, and music served up on a record player (remember those?). Watch Facebook for limited beer releases and collaborative events with the city and other local businesses. Free WiFi, charging stations, and the daytime hours make this a good temporary office and work space—with beer as a bonus and a coffeehouse vibe.

Facebook.com/sabbaticalbrewing Twitter/Instagram: @SabbaticalBeer

Stumbling Distance: Don't miss *PetSkull Brewing*, *Courthouse Pub* and *Ryan's on York*, all within a reasonable walking distance downtown. For wraps, paninis and quesadillas on the quick, try *Wrap It Up* (830 S 8th St, 920-242-6445, wrapitupmanitowoc.com).

RAIL HOUSE RESTAURANT & BREWPUB

Founded: 1995   **Brewmaster**: Kris Konyn
2029 Old Peshtigo Court • Marinette, WI 54143 • 715-732-4646
railhousebrewpub.com

Annual Production: 300 bbls
Number of Beers: 16 on tap

Staple Beers:

- » BELGIAN DUBBEL
- » BIG MAC IPA
- » BLONDE ALE
- » BLUEBERRY DRAFT
- » BOCK
- » BOURBON OAK CASK ALE
- » BREWER'S BEST PILSENER
- » CARAMEL CREAM
- » HONEY WEISS (Honey from Crivitz, WI)

- » IMPERIAL PILSENER
- » IRISH RED ALE
- » NUTTY BROWN ALE
- » OATMEAL STOUT
- » SCOTTISH ALE
- » SILVER CREAM PILSENER

Rotating Beers:

- » OKTOBERFEST
- » ZUMMER FEST

Most Popular Brew: Silver Cream

Brewmaster's Fave: Nutty Brown

Tours? Not really.

Samples? Yes, large sample car (15) of 4-oz samples for about $12, four for $4.

Best Time to Go: Open Mon-Thu 11am–10pm, Fri-Sat 11am-11pm, Sun 11am-9pm. Happy hour Mon-Thu 3-6pm, Fri 1-5pm, Sat 1-4pm. M&M Fishermen Club Brown Trout Derby is in late July and Menominee Water Front Festival is the first long weekend in August.

Where can you buy it? Here on tap in pints and 10oz pours, and to go in growlers.

Got food? Yes, the menu offers a big variety including Italian (the muffuletta sandwich is highly recommended) and Mexican. Pizzas, beer-battered shrimp, Wisconsin beer and cheese soup, and a big Friday night fish fry. House root beer.

Special Offer: A free house beer during your signature visit.

Directions: The pub is on the right side of US41 as you come into Marinette from the south. Turn right (east) at Cleveland Ave and take the next 2 rights. There are large signs to direct you with the Rail House and Country Inn hotel on them.

The Beer Buzz: The pub was originally in a smaller building on the same lot, and in 1997 it reopened in the new facility. The Silver Cream Pilsner is a bit of nostalgia. It is a reproduction of the turn-of-the-century beer once produced by Menominee-Marinette Brewing Co. (just over the border in the Michigan sister city). The back bar here is a fantastic wood-carved affair all the way from Bavaria. Its original Wisconsin residence was a saloon in Blackwell. Two projection screen TVs are on hand for the big games, and an outdoor covered patio is the place to be in summer.

Kris began homebrewing in college using a couple of plastic pails and a big stainless kettle borrowed from his fraternity house kitchen. At first he used malt extracts and experimented with mini mashes and colder fermenting lagers. (He went to school in the cold U.P. climate of Houghton, MI after all.) One year after graduation he was having a beer with a friend in a brewpub and found himself in a brewing conversation with the owner. The conversation was in fact a cleverly disguised job interview. The next day Kris was offered the brewer position. His first batch of Scottish-style Ale was kegged a month later confirming they had the right guy for the job. Kris loves to try new beers and keeps up on the latest news and ideas in brewing in technical and scientific publications, beer reviews, magazines and homebrewing blogs and books.

Free WiFi. Facebook.com/railhousebrewpub

Stumbling Distance: South of town is *Seguin's Cheese* (W1968 US 41, 800-338-7919, seguin-scheese.com) offering a vast assortment of Wisconsin's other finest product and a variety of other local yummies (mustards, jams, sauces). They even ship it. Cheese curds and aged cheddar—can you ask for much else? For you outdoorsy types, grab a growler from the brewpub and check out one of the 14 cascades that make *Marinette County* the "Waterfalls Capital of Wisconsin" (marinettecounty.com, 800-236-6681). More info on Marinette is found in a chapter from my book *Backroads & Byways of Wisconsin*. **Hotel:** *Country Inn & Suites* (2020 Old Peshtigo Ct, 715-732-3400) is right across the street.

CASK-CONDITIONED ALES

Cask comes from the Spanish word for "bark" like tree bark (cáscara). The little wooden barrel holds the beer in the same way bark surrounds a tree trunk I suppose. This is Old School beer storage (think of the original IPAs on their way to India to be drunk right out of the container) and the beer is unfiltered and unpasteurized.

Cask-conditioned ale goes through its secondary fermentation right in the cask or firkin from which it is poured. The yeast is still active and so still conditioning the brew. In many cases, the cask is right behind the bar, tilted on a shelf so the beer is delivered by gravity, without added carbon dioxide. Cask ale will only last a few days if air is going in to replace that draining beer. Some casks have CO_2 breathers that allow a bit of gas in but not enough to cause more carbonation. By definition, the cask-conditioning can be going on in any tank downstairs as long as it is a secondary fermentation, but the little wooden firkins behind the bar are a rare treat of authenticity.

LION'S TAIL BREWING CO.

116 S. Commercial St. • Neenah, WI 54956 • 920-215-6443
lionstailbrewing.com

Opened: 2015   **Head Brewer:** Alex Wenzel
Annual Production: 500 barrels   **Number of Beers:** 12 on tap, plus 6 guests

Staple Beers:
- » BOUNDARY WATERS
- » JUICE CLOUD NE IPA
- » KULA WHEAT GOLDEN ALE (With Pineapple)

Rotating Beers:
- » CPA – CUSTOM PALE ALE
- » DEVIL'S GOLD BELGIAN ALE
- » IMPERIAL MAPLE PORTER
- » "KRISTIN" CHOCOLATE CHERRY BOCK
- » MO' JUICE, MO' CLOUD
- » MILE OF MUNICH DUNKEL
- » #90 RED – VIENNA LAGER
- » OKTOBERFEST
- » ROYALE NOIR (French saison honey aged in pinot noir barrels)

Most Popular Brew: Juice Cloud

Brewmaster's Fave: Juice Cloud

Tours? Yes, by chance or by appointment.

Samples: Yes, sample flights of four 5-oz pours for $9-14

Best Time to Go: Open Mon-Thu 3-10pm, Fri 2pm-12am, Sat 12-12. Closed Sunday.

Where can you buy it? Here on tap and in growlers to go.

Got food? Yes, cheese plates, spiced nuts, chips, and free popcorn, plus wine, soda and bottled water. Broken Tree Pizza and The Ground Round deliver here. Also, food friendly.

Special Offer: Not participating at this time.

Directions: From US-41 take Exit 132 and go east on Main St 1.6 miles, staying on as it turns into Wisconsin Ave at a curve. Turn right on Commercial St and the brewery at the next corner on the left.

The Beer Buzz: Inspired by taprooms they visited on beer travels in Michigan, founders/owners Alex and Kristin Wenzel decided there was a need for more of them in the Fox River Valley. While Oshkosh and Appleton had a few, Neenah had nothing. A space opened up in a 1908 building downtown, and plans moved to reality. Previously this was the Equitable Reserve Association Building, home to an insurance company, now it insures Neenah and you have beer.

Alex graduated from UW-Stevens Point with a degree in Chemical Engineering, and took up homebrewing as a hobby. In preparation for the leap to professional brewing, he studied at Siebel Institute. He operates a 10-barrel brewhouse here. The brewery logo draws upon the Bohemian lion, something he has had tattooed on his arm for years. In the spirit of brewers sticking together, *Appleton Beer Factory* helped him have batches of his beer ready for opening day.

The taproom features a long bar in one room and more tables in a second room beyond. There are board games and cribbage, but no TVs for sports and such.

Free WiFi. Keg Club. Facebook.com/LionsTailBrewing and Twitter @LionsTailBrew

Stumbling Distance: *Copperstill Bourbon Bar* (211 E Wisconsin Ave, 920-486-1951) has a wide assortment of exactly what you think. Wood-fired pies at *Broken Tree Pizza* (124 W Wisconsin Ave #170, 920-720-2275, brokentreepizza.com).

OMEGA BREWING EXPERIENCE

115 E. Main St. • Omro, WI 54963
920-376-1884
Web Site: On Facebook
Opened: 2018   **Head Brewer:** Steve Zink
Annual Production: <250 barrels   **Number of Beers:** 12 on tap

Staple Beers:
- » ABBY ALE (Belgian Dubbel)
- » AMEREAU (French Saison)
- » GOLDEN HOUR (American Cream Ale)
- » LEAVE IT TO CLEAVER (Red Ale)
- » OMEGA PALE ALE
- » THIGH HI (IIPA)

Rotating Beers:
- » DARK SIDE IMPERIAL STOUT
- » HARVEST SAISON
- » OMEGA DRY STOUT
- » OMEGA PORTER
- » OMEGA WHEAT ALE
- » OZ KÖLSCH
- » SMASH SERIES
- » TEMPTATION PALE OAT ALE

Most Popular Brew: Amereau and Golden Hour

Brewmaster's Fave: Omega Pale Ale

Tours? Yes, by chance, but you can see it all from the bar stool.

Samples: Yes, sample 5-oz pours for $1.50-$3.

Best Time to Go: Open Fri-Sat 5-9pm and special events.

Where can you buy it? Here on tap and in growlers to go.

Got food? No, but food friendly, and menus on hand to order in.

Special Offer: $2 off your first house beer when you get your book signed.

Directions: 15 minutes west of Oshkosh. WI-21 passes right through Omro and follows Main St. The brewery is half a block east of Main and Webster on the north side of the street.

The Beer Buzz: Owner/brewer Steve homebrewed for over 25 years, getting more and more serious in the last decade when his sons and son-in-law took an interest. Classic hobby gone out of control. The 1927 building originally held a butcher shop and was also a restaurant and art gallery over the years. The simple, one-story brick and block building sits along the Fox River in downtown Omro, and is listed on the historic registry. The façade was recently improved while maintaining the historic appearance and the interior was completely renovated from 2016-2018. Plans are for a deck addition off the back of the building that will overlook the Fox River and the River Walk Park area.

Free WiFi. Facebook.com

Stumbling Distance: *Los Amigos Family Restaurant & Cantina* (103 E Main St, 920-685-6778, losamigosomro.com) next door has good Mexican and serves breakfast. Bike or walk the *Historic Walking Tour* (futureomro.org) that passes up to 50 local historical sites. Self-guided tours from under 1 to 3 miles in length. *Stearns, Scott* and *Fred Miller Parks* lie on the Fox River if you plan to *paddle* or fish. **Hotel:** *Reed Hill B&B* (627 E Main St, 920-379-6129, reedhillbandb.com) is walking distance.

BARE BONES BREWING CO.

4362 County Road S • Oshkosh, WI 54904 • 920-744-8045
barebonesbrewery.us
Opened: 2015   **Brewmaster**: Jody Cleveland
Annual Production: 600 barrels   **Number of Beers**: 14 taps

Beers:

- » AMBER
- » BRAVER HUND ALTBIER
- » CLIFFORD
- » DOG DAZE IPA
- » DOUBLE DOG DAZE
- » HARV DOG SWIFTYS IRISH RED
- » HURRICANE DAN RYE IPA
- » PAWESOME PILSNER
- » PUPPY LOVE AMERICAN WHEAT
- » SERGEANT STUBBY NUT BROWN
- » WICKED BADASS BLACK APA
- » American, German, and English styles and some mixes among them plus some sour beers and cask ales
- »

Most Popular Brew: Dog Daze, Pawesome Pils & Hurricane Dan

Brewmaster's Fave: Sours and Belgians if he had to pick.

Tours? Yes, watch for schedules online or take your chances. **Oshkosh Brewery Tours** (715-297-5021, oshkoshbars.com) runs 2 buses on Saturdays hitting *Fox River, Bare Bones, Fifth Ward* and *HighHolder* breweries for tours for a very reasonable price.

Samples: Yes, sample flights of 6 for about $12

Best Time to Go: Summer: Open Wed-Thu 3-9pm, Fri 12-9pm, Sat 11-9pm, Sun 11-7pm. Closed Mon–Tue, but that may change. Winter slightly earlier closing times. Check the website or Facebook for current hours.

Where can you buy it? Here on tap and in growlers and howlers to go, plus Festival Foods, Woodmans, and many draft accounts in the Lake Winnebago/Fond Du Lac area.

Got food? Yes, local frozen pizzas and cheese curds, and food trucks. Food-friendly, and there are menus from local places that will deliver.

Special Offer: A free pint of Bare Bones beer when you get your book signed.

Directions: From US 45 take the exit for County Road T west toward CR S/Ryf Rd. Turn right on CR S heading north 0.4 mile and the brewery is on the right.

Cyclists: This is just off the Wiouwash State Trail.

The Beer Buzz: Located in a sort of red pole shed just outside of Oshkosh, this brewery shares the space with Puro Clean next door. Both are owned by the husband and wife team of Dan and Patti Dringoli. Dan's a homebrewer, and when he went to the S.O.B. (Society of Oshkosh Brewers) about his idea to start a brewery, he met Lyle Hari, Jr. who was planning a one-barrel operation himself. Dan had a 15-barrel system and they agreed it'd be a good idea to collaborate.

Dan originally picked up a 2-gallon kit, then a bigger one, and so forth, brewing without knowing any other homebrewers for five years. Ten years from the stovetop to the brewhouse. Dan's other business needed a bigger space, and when he went looking, he found this empty lot at the edge of the bike trail. He built this building for both businesses. Jody Cleveland, a Menasha native, started with a Mr. Beer kit from Fleet Farm, trying to recreate Dixie Brewing Company's Crimson Voodoo, a brew never made again after Hurricane Katrina. That initial mission led him to eventually work as assistant brewer here and at Fox River Brewing before stepping up to the lead position.

The taproom is in front on the right, with a bar and some pub tables, and a dart board. No TVs, just a flat-screen menu for the beers. Beers rotate a lot and some are one-offs. Sergeant Stubby is named for a dog that served 18 months on the Western Front with the US 102nd Infantry Regiment in World War I.

Free WiFi. Mug Club. Facebook.com/barebonesbrew

Stumbling Distance: For a Wisconsin supper club experience, head over to *Jimmie's Whitehouse Inn* (5776 Main St, Butte Des Morts, 920-582-7211, jimmieswhitehouseinn.com), or *Butte des Morts Supper Club* (5756 Main St, Butte Des Morts, 920-582-0665, buttedesmortssupperclub. com).

Fifth Ward Brewing Co.

Opened: 2017   **Brewers:** Ian Wenger and Zach Clark
1009 S Main St. • Oshkosh, WI 54902 • 920-479-1876
fifthwardbrewing.com
Opened: 2017   **Brewers:** Ian Wenger and Zach Clark
Annual Production: 300 barrels   **Number of Beers:** 22 on tap (several guest beers)

Staple Beers:
- BURL BROWN (Cinnamon Molasses)
- COMB & CROCUS (Honey Saffron Wheat Ale)
- 842 PALE (Dry-Hopped APA)

Rotating Beers:
- DOPPELBOCK
- DOUBLE OAT SEVEN (Oatmeal Ipa)
- FORMAN'S BASEMENT RED ALE
- HADES' SECRET CHOCOLATE MINT PORTER
- TWO MAN JOB (Imperial Oatmeal Stout)
- VANILLA RASPBERRY CREAM ALE
- VIENNA LAGER
- ...To Name A Few, And Many Pilot Batches Plus Some Future Barrel-Aging And Sours

Most Popular Brew: Burl Brown

Tours? Yes, scheduled on Saturdays. **Oshkosh Brewery Tours** (715-297-5021, oshkoshbars.com) runs 2 buses on Saturdays hitting *Fox River, Bare Bones, Fifth Ward* and *HighHolder* breweries for tours for a very reasonable price.

Samples: Yes, sample flights of four 5-oz pours for about $6.

Best Time to Go: Open Wed-Thu 3-10pm, Fri-Sat 12pm-12am. Closed Sun-Tue. Check Facebook for Sundays during sporting events and shortened winter hours.

Where can you buy it? Here on tap and in growlers to go, plus draft and bottles in the Fox River Valley area.

Got food? Free popcorn. Soda but no booze. Food friendly.

Special Offer: Buy your first house beer, get a second free when you get your book signed.

Directions: From I-41 take Exit 117 and head east into Oshkosh on 9th Ave for 2.2 miles. Turn right on Main St, drive 1.5 blocks, and the brewery is on the right.

The Beer Buzz: Housed in a former vending machine service center, Fifth Ward brings two homebrewers and a couple business partners together in central Oshkosh right across from the sports arena. The original Fifth Ward Brewery operated from 1856 to 1882, so the name is a nod to history though this goes far beyond the old-school lagers of yesteryear. Ian Wenger and Zach Clark began brewing on UW-Oshkosh campus in 2012, and while the homebrew system still exists, they've added a brewhouse and eight 14-barrel fermenters from Wisconsin's own Quality Tank Solutions.

Ian has a culinary training background. The honey saffron wheat ale recipe was based on an ice cream made in culinary training. The taproom is a bright space with high-top tables and a long tile-fronted bar. A beer garden is planned for out back. Off-street parking.

Free WiFi. ATM onsite. Loyalty Club. Facebook/FifthWardBrewingCo and Twitter @ FifthWardBeer Instagram @FifthWardBrewing

Tip: Local beer historian Lee Reiherzer (oshkoshbeer.blogspot.com) can tell you more about the long tradition of brewing in Oshkosh and the surrounding counties.

Stumbling Distance: For Thai and other Asian dishes try *Tasty Thai* (1027 S Main St, 920-292-8888, tastythaiwi.com) down the street. *Pete's Garage Bar* (1514 Oregon St, 920-235-9897, petesgaragebar.com) serves up cheap and delicious bar food. Watch for music and sporting events at *Menominee Nation Arena* (1212 S Main St, 920-744-2039, menomineenationarena.com) across the street and south a block, home to the *Wisconsin Herd* (wisconsin.gleague.nba.com), a G league affiliate of the Milwaukee Bucks basketball team.

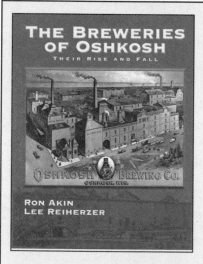

OSHKOSH BREWING HISTORY

Oshkosh's brewing history goes back a lot further than Fox River Brewing Co. and the various other craft breweries now blossoming in the area. Since the 1840s, the city has been home to more than a dozen breweries and a robust beer culture that continues to thrive. You history and breweriana buffs out there should check out a book about that old profession (I mean brewing). Co-written by Ron Akin, a retired University professor and breweriana collector, and Lee Reiherzer, a beer columnist and blogger, this is a lively account of beer and breweries in "Sawdust City," with over 400 illustrations. Check out the Oshkosh Beer website and order yourself a copy. Lee is your best source of history about beer in the area. Keep an eye out for other books and presentations from him. oshkoshbeer@gmail.com, oshkoshbeer.blogspot.com

Fox River Brewing Co.

1501 Arboretum Drive • Oshkosh, WI 54901 • 920-232-2337
foxriverbrewing.com
Founded: December 15, 1995   **Brewmaster**: Kevin Bowen
Annual Production: 1,400 bbls   **Number of Beers:** 13 on tap (9 on the patio)

Staple Beers:

- » 2 Dams Blonde Ale
- » Blü Bobber Blueberry Ale
- » Crooked Dock American Pale
- Ale
- » Marble Eye Scottish Ale
- » Reel It In Session IPA

Rotating Beers:

- » Defilbrillator Doppelbock
- » Deep Dive Imperial Stout
- » Fox Light Kölsch
- » Foxtoberfest
- » German Pilsner
- » Maibock
- » Raspberry Wheat
- » Shakedown IPA Slam Dunkel
- » Vixen's Vanilla Cream Ale
- » Winnebago Wheat Hefeweizen

Most Popular Brew: Blü Bobber

Brewer's Fave: The current seasonal beer!

Tours? On request, call ahead. **Oshkosh Brewery Tours** (715-297-5021, oshkoshbars. com) runs 2 buses on Saturdays hitting *Fox River*, *Bare Bones*, *Fifth Ward* and *HighHolder* breweries for tours for a very reasonable price.

Samples? Yes, sample flights of four or eight 5-oz. beers.

Best Time to Go: Open Mon–Sat 11–10PM, Sun 11–8PM. Happy Hour runs Mon–Fri 3–6PM. Live music on occasion.

Where can you buy it? Here (and at their Appleton location) on tap plus growlers, quarter- and half-barrels and some local taverns serve it. Bottles and cans are distributed statewide.

Got food? Yes! The menu features a variety of steaks, seafood, pastas, sandwiches and pizzas and much more on their full menu.

Special Offer: $2 pint on your first Fox River beer, additional pints regular price.

Directions: In Oshkosh, cross the Fox River heading east on Congress (Hwy 21) and it's the first street on the left. You'll see it from the bridge.

The Beer Buzz: Fox River Brewing has

always been the beer portion of Fratello's Restaurants but has dropped that name and now both locations are Fox River Brewing. On the banks of the Fox River, this trendy restaurant is one of the most happening spots in town. This restaurant has a view like no other and offers a family-friendly atmosphere with a separate taproom. There are forty slips for boaters, and the patio outside has a large tiki bar with 9 taps. It's a great time in the summer (rumor has it my cousin once danced on a table here—she denies it to the last). Cross the river heading east on Congress (Hwy 21), and it's the first street on the left. You'll see it from the bridge. Kevin Bowen worked at the restaurant years ago and started at Fox River Brewing Co. in an undeclared apprenticeship working from the bottom up: cleaning kegs, filling bottles, and such. After attending Siebel Institute to study the art and science of brewing, he worked for a few other brewhouses before returning to FRB. He's nabbed silver for his Kölsch in 2010 at the World Beer Cup as well as for his Abbey Normal Belgian Dubbel aged in a brandy barrel in 2012. In fact, he has started doing more barrel-aged beers and bringing new brews into the lineup. Foxtoberfest comes on mid-Sept–Oct while Red Baron Altbier comes on tap during the EAA Fly In. If you like baseball, catch a Timber Rattlers game in Appleton and drink Fox River's Snaketail Ale at the stadium, or watch the Dock Spiders in Fond du Lac while sipping Dock Spiders Pale Ale.

Free Wifi. Facebook.com/FoxRiverBrewingCompany Twitter @FoxRiverBrewing Instagram @frbcompany

Stumbling Distance: *EAA* (Experimental Aircraft Association) (eaa.org) has a museum (just off Hwy 41 adjacent to Wittman Airport, 920-426-4818) with over 250 historic planes, five theatres, and a flight motion simulator. Don't miss the largest aviation event in the world. The *AirVenture*, when hundreds of experimental and homemade aircraft come to the week-long "Fly In" in late July, is like nothing you've ever seen. *Hughes Homemade Chocolate Shop* (1823 Doty St, 920-231-7232)— look for the open sign on the porch, walk up the driveway and to the side door, and head directly downstairs. If there is a line (which there always is) you'll have to wait on the steps. No displays or candy counters or fancy colors—just clean white boxes of chocolates that get unbelievable raves by choco-junkies. Call first—they are often closed and keep erratic hours. Best around holiday seasons. Look for *Fox River Brewing* in Fox River Mall in Appleton (4301 Wisconsin, Appleton, 920-991-0000)

HIGHHOLDER BREWING CO.

2211 T2 Oregon St. • Oshkosh, WI 54902 • 920-744-5122
(O'Marro's "Taproom" is 2211 T Oregon St.)
highholderbrewing.com
Opened: February 2018   **Head Brewer:** Mike Schlosser
Annual Production: 20-30 barrels
Number of Beers: 2-3 HighHolder brews on tap (+300 others!)

Possible Beers:

- » BLOODY 6TH IRISH RED ALE
- » THE BORDERLANDS ALT
- » HELLES
- » HOI-HOLDEN HEFEWEIZEN
- » THE INKY VANILLA MILK STOUT
- » KÖLSCH
- » OKTOBERFEST
- » ORANGE CREAM ALE
- » POKE THE BEAR PORTER
- » SUMMERTIME STOUT SERIES
- » …Traditional German Ales And Lagers

Most Popular Brew: The Inky Stout

Brewmaster's Fave: The Borderlands Alt

Tours? Yes, by appointment or **Oshkosh Brewery Tours** (715-297-5021, oshkoshbars. com) runs 2 buses on Saturdays hitting *Fox River*, *Bare Bones*, *Fifth Ward* and *HighHolder* breweries for tours for a very reasonable price.

Samples: Yes, samples available.

Best Time to Go: O'Marro's Public House open daily 2-close, Sat 5-close, Sun 10am-3pm. Brewery open randomly in the afternoons. Send a Facebook message to see if Mike plans to be there.

Where can you buy it? Here on tap and in growlers to go, with a wee bit that makes it to area bars.

Got food? Yes, housemade pizzas, and Sunday Service: eggs, comfort food for hangovers.

Special Offer: $1 off your first pint of HH beer when you get your book signed.

Directions: From I-41 take Exit 116 for WI-44 and head east into Oshkosh about 0.7 mile. At 20th Ave turn right and drive 1.6 miles. Turn right on Oregon St and continue 0.2 mile, and the brewery is on the right.

The Beer Buzz: While hitchhiking in Colorado back in 1992, Mike Schlosser came into a pub in Crested Butte that had a small brewing system. Prior to that he had only known all the flavors of the 70s, so his first craft brew left him flabbergasted. The bar stopped charging him just to let him drink so they could laugh at his reactions. "When I get back to Wisconsin, I'm gonna brew this," he said.

Mike Schlosser and Shawn O'Marro go way back. Shawn says Mike used to karate kick beer cans off Shawn's head. In 2009 they thought to open a nanobrewery, and even bought a Brew-Magic by Sabco system. But that was too small, so they sold it and the idea went to the back burner again—until 2018. The trouble is Shawn owns the distinguished Irish-themed O'Marro's Public House, and as Eau Claire's *Brewing*

Projekt infamously found out, current law prohibits ownership crossing the lines between breweries, distributors and retailers (bars in this case). So, sadly, Shawn is "not a partner and he does not work here" so just ignore the volunteer behind the bar. Mike brews in 2211 T2 Oregon St. in back and sells Shawn the beer to put on tap up front in 2211 T. Mike goes out the back door with a dolly and comes in the front door with the beer. Barrels kick in less than a week typically, so something new is nearly always on.

Mike had planned to name this Sawdust City Brewing Co., Oshkosh's nickname during its sawmill heyday, and registered it in about 2008 as an LLC. But the registration expired and someone in Canada snatched it. Mike could have lawyered up and got it back, but didn't love the name enough and went with another very local name. In the mid-1800s, a lot of German immigrants arrived in the area, and they spoke a dialect from Bavaria and the Bohemian Forest, the borderlands. When asked in passing where they were going and what they were doing, local women in that community would respond "hoi-holden," meaning "collecting hay." These immigrants stuck together and settled south of the Fox River in the "Bloody Sixth" District. The immigrants who came before them sought to belittle them and called them Highholders. But from this community came much of the beer culture. The first president of Oshkosh's Peoples Brewing Co. was a Highholder. The term's use lasted as late as WWII but by then cultures had mixed and intermarried and so it faded away.

Free WiFi. Live music, board games, cribbage, Hammerschlagen, bag toss.

Stumbling Distance: *Artie and Ed's Drive-in* (2413 S Main St, 920-231-5455, ardyandeds.com) is a classic with carhops on skates. The Experimental Aircraft Association's *EAA Aviation Museum* (3000 Poberezny Rd, 920-426-4800, eaa.org) has a fascinating collection of over 200 historical planes, and in July you should consider attending the *EAA AirVenture*, a weeklong fly-in/airshow that brings people and planes from all over the world. *Hops & Props* (eaa.org/hopsprops) is their fine food and beer festival usually held in March right inside the museum. VIP tickets include dinner.

PLYMOUTH BREWING CO.

222 East Main Street • Plymouth, WI 53073 • 920-400-1722
plymouthbrewingcompany.com
Opened: April 20, 2011   **Brewmaster**: Joe Fillion
Annual Production: 110 barrels
Number of Beers: 14 taps (5 plus guest taps); 43 beers per year

Beers:

- » HUBCITY HEFE
- » LONG DAY AMERICAN IPA
- » NUTT HILL NUT BROWN
- » SILBER BLACK PHANTOM BIKE
- » STAFFORD OATMEAL STOUT (with French Vanilla Almond Coffee)
- » ... plus many more and some barrel aging

Most Popular Brew: Stafford Oatmeal Stout

Brewmaster's Fave: Silver Black Phantom Bike

Tours? Not really. Casually by chance.

Samples: Yes, sample flights available.

Best Time to Go: Wed-Thu 5-10pm, Fri-Sat 5-11pm.

Where can you buy it? Here in pints and half-pints, and in growlers and howlers to go.

Got food? Free pretzel sticks and food friendly. Delivery menus are on hand.

Special Offer: $1 off your first pint of Plymouth brew during your signature visit.

Directions: From WI 23 across Plymouth's north side, take WI 67 south about 1.3 miles and stay straight on Milwaukee St. Turn left on Mill St and go 0.2 mile and the brewery is on the left.

The Beer Buzz: Plymouth Brewing Co. actually used to exist, from 1887-1937, managing to survive Prohibition but then failing shortly after it ended. Joe named his own operation the same and has a collection of breweriana, some of it from that original brewery. The building here dates back to 1923 when it opened as a women's dress shop. Joe built the bar himself, had all the plumbing and electric redone, and kept the old wood floor. Tall tables with beer labels under the glass tops stand along the wall of this narrow and deep shop.

Back in the 90s, Brewer Joe got a homebrew kit, and a year later he was brewing four times a week. It took him a while, like over a decade, but in 2009 he started thinking… why not a brewery? He operates a one-barrel system here and brews a wide variety throughout the year.

Free WiFi. Facebook/Plymouth-Brewing-Company and Twitter @ PlymouthBrewing

Stumbling Distance: Racing fans (or racing curious) should not miss *Road America* (N7390 WI 67, 920-892-4576, roadamerica.com), a popular racetrack with a long history, 10 minutes north. *52 Stafford* (52 S Stafford St, 920-893-0552, 52stafford.com) is an Irish-style inn (think B&B) and pub in town.

STUBBORN BROTHERS BREWING CO.

220 S. Main St. • Shawano, WI 54166 • 715-903-6118
stubbornbros.com
Opening: *Early 2019*   **Head Brewers:** Erik and Aaron Gilling
Annual Production: 1,500 barrels   **Number of Beers:** 22 on tap

Staple Beers:

BROWN ALE

FARMHOUSE ALE

IPA

LEMON WHEAT

MILK STOUT

PALE ALE

PILSNER

RASPBERRY WHEAT

Rotating Beers:

Monthly seasonals for Mug Club

Brewmaster's Fave: Aaron: Brown Ale; Erik: Pale Ale

Tours? Yes, scheduled on website, about $10 and includes beer.

Samples: Yes, flights of six 4-oz pours for about $10-12.

Best Time to Go: Open Tue-Wed 11am-10pm Thu-Sat 11am-12am, Sun 11am-10pm. Closed Mondays. Happy hour for Mug Club members.

Where can you buy it? Here on tap and in growlers and Crowlers to go.

Got food? Yes, full menu of American pub fare, including Friday night fish fry. Full bar.

Special Offer: You can drink "Mug Club-only beers" without being a member during your signature visit.

Directions: From WI-29 take Exit 225 and head north into Shawano on WI-22, which becomes Main St, for 1.7 miles. Look for the marquee on the right.

Cyclists: Mountain Bay State Trail crosses Main Street 4.5 blocks south of here.

The Beer Buzz: Brothers Erik and Aaron Gilling went to school for physical therapy at Marquette University but within 24 hours of graduation they were on a plane to Colorado where they would attend brewing school. They returned to Wisconsin to open a brewery. Their hometown was Marion, but *Pigeon River Brewing* was already there. In a search for an underserved community, they found Shawano.

The magnificent old Farmers Brewing Co. building still stands there but a site inspection revealed it would be difficult to work with – massive thick concrete walls uncooperative for renovations. But the old Crescent Pitcher Show, a local cinema looked attractive. They had no idea it was historic. Built in 1914-1915, it hosted Vaudeville acts with full orchestra and silent movies, before going full-time talkie cinema until 2010 when it went into foreclosure when it was unable to upgrade to digital. They bought the building and raised a lot of the money themselves for this project, and the City of Shawano, focused on revitalizing the downtown area, gave them incentives for the restoration. They reopened the banquet hall upstairs, which hadn't operated in 70 years. They recovered the stage and original tin ceiling and hardwood floor and other details. A campaign to save the marquee brought people together as well.

They brew 7- to 15-barrel batches at a time. Weekends see live music on the restored stage. 8 of the beers on tap are available to the public, but 14 are only for mug club members. Don't be dismayed: Mug club is $10/year and includes your first beer and makes you eligible for happy hour prices – and 14 more beers. Outside games and firepits in the beer garden.

Free WiFi. Mug Club. Facebook.com/StubbornBrothersBrewery and Twitter @ StubbornBros Instagram @StubbornBeer

Stumbling Distance: A local 1951 bottling company, *Twig's Beverage*, would eventually bottle and distribute Sun Drop soda-pop (which would help keep me awake through college). They now have their own line of gourmet sodas and operate *Sun Drop University Museum* (920 South Franklin St, 715-526-5031, twigsbeverage.net). Tours are possible with a week's advance notice. You'll find Twig's sodas around Wisconsin. *Luigi's Pizza & Pasta* (607 S Main St, 715-524-4791, luigisshawano.com) does regular, pan and stuffed pizzas. Paddling on the *Wolf River* here is a nice easy float (see my book *Paddling Wisconsin*) and see *Mountain Bay State Trail* in "Biking for Beer" in the back of the book. **Hotels:** *Quality Inn & Suites* (104 Airport Rd, 715-526-2044) or *Boarders Inn & Suites* (7393 River Bend Rd, 715-524-9090).

KNUTH BREWING CO.

221 Watson St. • Ripon, WI 54971 • 920-748-5188
knuthbrewingcompany.com
Opened: April 2015   **Brewers:** David Knuth and Ryan Avery
Annual Production: 600 barrels   **Number of Beers:** 10 on tap

Staple Beers:

- » AMERICAN PALE ALE
- » BLUE EYED BLONDE ALE
- » COFFEE STOUT
- » KNUTH HONEY WHEAT
- » RED HOUSE ALE
- » WORKER'S MILD BROWN ALE

Rotating Beers:

- » CITRA SPICE IPA
- » HEFE"WIFE"ZEN
- » MAIBOCK
- » MY SOPHIA BELGIAN TRIPEL
- » ...Plus Some Barrel-Aging

Most Popular Brew: Red House

Brewmaster's Fave: American Pale Ale

Tours? Not really.

Samples: Yes, flights of six 5-oz pours for about $9.

Best Time to Go: Open Tue-Thu 11am-9pm, Fri-Sat 11am-10pm. Closed Sun-Mon.

Where can you buy it? Here on tap and in growlers, howlers and six-packs to go, plus some area draft accounts.

Got food? Yes, pizzas, soups and sandwiches, prime rib on Saturdays, plus cakes, cookies, coffee and wine.

Special Offer: Buy your first house beer, get one free when you get your book signed.

Directions: WI-23 passes right through the middle of Ripon, much of the time following Fond Du Lac St. Whether you are coming from the west or the east, stay on Fond du Lac St where it departs from WI-23 and follow it to Watson St and then turn right. The brewery is on the east side of the street.

The Beer Buzz: German immigrant John Haas partnered in Ripon City Beer Brewery in about 1860 and upon his death in 1907 his son took it over and named it Haas Brewery. He died of influenza months before Prohibition took effect. After that disaster, it came back as Ripon Brewing but only lasted from 1933-1937. So Ripon was brewery-less until David Knuth fixed that.

Owner/brewer David has a background in the restaurant biz, something he studied in college, and the first thing he opened here was the pizzeria as he waited for his brewer's permit. The two sides used to be separate buildings and back in 1914 this place showed silent movies and the other housed a general store. David runs a half-barrel system so new beers come quickly, but among the regulars you can expect there's typically an IPA in there as well. In 2018 they started bottling in the basement.

The old wood floors and a pressed tin ceiling still show, and church pews along the wall line up with facing tables. At the bar you can also get espresso drinks and delightful dessert items from a deli cooler. There are board games, cribbage, and a TV above the bar that might show some sports, plus there's live music on Saturday nights.

David homebrewed five years before opening this and he doesn't aim to do anything too extreme stylewise. "We didn't get too crazy. Just good quality ingredients. I just like good tasting beer." Patrons appear to agree.

Free WiFi. Facebook.com/knuthbrewingcompany

Stumbling Distance: *J's BBQ* (333 Watson St, 920-748-2232, jsbbqripon.com) has Knuth on tap. *Pastimes Pub & Grille* (120 Scott St, 920-748-8222, pastimes.homestead.com) has a good fish fry and much more. *Vines & Rushes Winery* (410 County Rd E, 920-748-3296, vinesandrushes.com) operates on what is also a strawberry farm. They have a wood-fired pizza oven, too. **Hotel:** *Comfort Suites at Royal Ridges* (2 Westgate Dr, 920-748-5500) will do in town, otherwise *Heidel House Resort & Spa* (643 Illinois Ave, Green Lake, 920-294-3344, heidelhouse.com) is 15 minutes away in Green Lake.

SHEBOYGAN BEER CO.
(8TH STREET ALE HAUS)

1132 N. 8th St. • Sheboygan, WI 53081 • 920-208-7540
8thstreetalehaus.com
Opened: Pub 2010 | Brewery 2012   **Head Brewer:** Eric Hansen
Annual Production: 150 barrels
Number of Beers: 30 on tap (7-8 house beers, plus 1 cask)

Staple Beers:

- » AUTUMN MOONBEAN AMBER
- » FOUNTAIN PARK PALE ALE
- » FRESHWATER SURFSIDER (Kölsch)
- » HARD ROLL HEFE
- » KADUNE NE IPA

Rotating Beers:

- » CHERRY OAKED PORTER
- » ENGLISH MILD
- » OKTOBERFEST
- » ST. CLAIR QUAD
- » TWO EXES LAGER
- » …plus many more

Most Popular Brew: Hard Roll Hefe or Kadune

Brewmaster's Fave: FFMPH Double IPA

Tours? Not really.

Samples: Yes, flights of as many as you want. Write down 8 on a sheet.

Best Time to Go: Open Mon 11am-12am, Tue-Thu 4pm-12am, Fri 11am-1am, Sat 10am-1am, Sun 10am-12am. Happy hour runs weekdays 4-6pm. Badgers and Packers games are popular here.

Where can you buy it? Here on tap and in growlers to go.

Got food? Yes, a full menu. Kitchen closes at 10pm but pretzels and chips & salsa run late. Over 100 bottled beers on offer.

Special Offer: A free Haus beer when you get your book signed.

Directions: From I-43 take Exit 126 for WI-23 and follow it 2.9 miles into Sheboygan (it becomes Erie Ave). Turn left on 8th St and it's two blocks down on the left at the next corner of St Clair Ave.

The Beer Buzz: With the many tap lines and a large collection of bottles, 8th Street Ale Haus is quite a craft beer bar that so happens to also brew its own. Set in a main street type of building that previously housed a church, the business first opened as a pub and restaurant, but drew the Sheboygan Sudzzers, the local homebrewers club who brought in small batches. Two years in, owners Randy Oskey and Kurt Jensen added the brewery element, and Randy brought in his homebrewing equipment initially to make 5-gallon batches. They have since expanded to a 10-barrel system to keep up with the demand.

In addition to the beer selection, expect good pub fare, plenty of dining room seating and a long bar. Several TVs, darts and a pool table entertain. Mural of the Bavarian Neuschwanstein Castle adorns the wall. Good whiskey selection. In 2018 they rebranded their beers to Sheboygan Beer Co. and opened a separate taproom next door.

Free WiFi. ATM onsite. Facebook.com/sheboyganalehaus Twitter @8th_St_Ale_Haus Instagram @8thstreetalehaus

Stumbling Distance: *Il Ritrovo* (515 S 8th St, 920-803-7516, ilritrovopizza.com) serves certified true Napoli-style pies – Verace Pizza Napoletana – plus house pastas and more. The deli attached is a foodie dream, and *Trattoria Stefano* (522 S 8th St, 920-452-8455, trattoriastefano.com) across the street has the same owner and is the fine dining version. Superb all around.

3 SHEEPS BREWING

1837 North Ave • Sheboygan, WI 53083 • 920-395-3583
3sheepsbrewing.com
Founded: February 2012   **Brewmaster:** Grant Pauly
Annual Production: 4,000+ bbls   **Number of Beers:** 17 taps + 5 nitro lines

Staple Beers:

- » CASHMERE HAMMER NITRO STOUT
- » FIRST KISS IPA
- » REALLY COOL WATERSLIDES IPA
- » REBEL KENT AMBER ALE

Rotating Beers:

- » HAPPY SUMMER IPA NITRABERRY (Nitro Tart Wheat Ale With Blackberries)
- » BARREL-AGED SMALL BATCHES:
- » MANGOES ON MY MIND
- » PAID TIME OFF (Imperial Black Wheat)
- » ROLL OUT THE BARREL
- » ÜBER JOE (Nitro Tart Wheat Ale With Blackberries)
- » NOBLE TONGUE SERIES (22-Oz Bombers)
- » HOEDOWN!
- » HOPPY SPICE
- » MIDNIGHT BOURBON
- » OAKEY DOKEY

Most Popular Brew: Really Cool Waterslides IPA

Brewmaster's Fave: "I'm a hop head: the IPA"

Tours? Yes, Fridays at 6pm, Saturdays at 3pm (or groups by appt). $10 tour gets you 4 samplers, a commemorative glass, a free beer coupon for a local establisment.

Samples: Yes, flights of 6 three-oz pours.

Best Time to Go: Open Mon-Thu 4-10pm, Fri 3-11pm, Sat 11am-11pm, Sun 11am-7pm. Watch for Yoga & Beer (1st Tue) and trivia nights (Wed.)

Where can you buy it? Here on tap and in howlers and growlers to go. Distribution in 6-pack bottles and 22-oz bombers throughout Wisconsin and in the Twin Cities and Chicagoland areas.

Got food? Just pre-packaged chips and local popcorn, but food friendly.

Special Offer: 15% off any apparel purchase during your signature visit at the brewery.

The Beer Buzz: "So many great breweries in Sheboygan have been forgotten," says Brewer Grant. True the brewing history goes way back to 1847 with Gutsch Brewing Co., a year before Wisconsin's statehood. After Prohibition knocked Gutsch out, the still-familiar Kingsbury took over in 1933 brewing until

1974. Heileman had already bought them in 1963, so one could still go "swinging with the King" even after that brewery closed its doors. In fact, 3 Sheeps took over the old Hops Haven on Huron Ave and in less than 5 years developed an impressive reputation and following and so outgrew the small space. In 2016 they moved into a $3 million repurposing of a Coca Cola bottling plant.

Grant started homebrewing in 2005 when his wife bought him a brew kit, but once he started counting yeast cells, he figured this was getting serious. He studied at the Siebel Institute, and made the leap when Hops Haven closed. The IPA name comes from a t-shirt Grant once saw that showed a little boy at a crossroads forced to choose: Fame, Fortune, Success? or REALLY COOL WATERSLIDES! It perfectly expresses Grant's choice to leave the financial security of a job he was not passionate about to take the risk on something he really enjoyed.

The brewery is in one big warehouse building and the taproom is across the lot in another. Inside the big space are communal tables, a three-sided concrete bar, and an area reserved for barrel-aging beers. There's a game room with shuffleboard, and a stage for live music. Huge garage doors open in summer plus there's a beer garden out back. Plenty of parking in the lot.

Free WiFi. ATM onsite. Mug Club-Warehouse Club. Facebook.com/3sheeps Twitter/ Instagram @3sheepsbrewing

Stumbling Distance: Sheboygan is known for a Wisconsin classic: brats (bratwurst, not rotten children). While Johnsonville has gotten national fame, devotees direct you to the local butcher *Miesfeld's Triangle Market* (4811 Venture Dr, 920-565-6328, miesfelds.com) a family-owned fixture since 1941. *Charcoal Inn* (1313 S 8th St, 920-458-6988) has a charcoal grill (big surprise) for brats and burgers. *Schulz's Restaurant* (1644 Calumet Dr, 920-452-1880) is a good place for a bratwurst sandwich. Check out *Brat Days* (sheboyganjaycees.com) in August—1000s of brat eaters, live music and a brat eating contest with serious competitors from around the world. By the way, brats are "fried" in Sheboygan. A "grill out" or "cook out" is referred to as a "fry out." **Hotel:** Some heavy beers in the line-up here, stay the night at *Blue Harbor Resort* (725 Blue Harbor Dr, 866-701-2583, blueharborresort.com), which also hosts *Blue Harbor Craft Beer Festival* in September with 3 Sheeps.

STARBOARD BREWING CO.

151 North 3rd Ave. • Sturgeon Bay, WI 54235 • 920-818-1062
starboardbrewing.com
Founded: October 2014   **Brewmaster**: Patrick Surfus
Annual Production: 120 barrels
Number of Beers: 11 on tap; nearly 140 beers per year

Previous Beers:

- » ABBIE GALE'S SINGEL
- » ADMIRAL BULLY'S IPA
- » AMERICAN AMBER ALE
- » BLARNEY STONE IRISH RED
- » BOWSPRIT WIT
- » CITRA SMASH
- » THE DEMER'S CHARM BELGIAN DARK STRONG ALE
- » DOWNTOWN BROWN
- » EDINBURGH ALE
- » ERWOOD ESB
- » FIVE MINUTE FIX IPA
- » FUGGLESTOUT
- » IMP IPA
- » NO APOLLOGIES DOUBLE IPA
- » RYETOUS ALE
- » WEIZEN DUNKEL

Most Popular Brew: The IPAs or seasonals

Brewmaster's Fave: Changes like the menu

Tours? Not really.

Samples: Yes, flights of four 5-oz pours for about $8 or $2 per taster.

Best Time to Go: In season: Open Wed–Thu 3-9pm, Fri–Sat 12–9pm, Sun 12pm–6pm. Watch for winter hours to be shortened. Open Tuesdays in summer as well.

Where can you buy it? Only here on tap or in growlers to go.

Got food? Small plates such as cheeses, smoked salmon, or chips and dips, and some flatbread pizzas. Food friendly, bring your own.

Special Offer: A free serving of kettle chips when you get your book signed.

Directions: From the south on WI 42/57, take the exit for Business 42/57 and follow it through town, crossing the Sturgeon Bay Bridge. Turn left on 3rd Ave and the brewery is on the left. From the north on WI 42/57, turn right on County Rd B/Michigan St. Go 1.4 miles and turn right on 3rd Ave.

The Beer Buzz: Patrick's mother bought him a Mr. Beer Kit for Christmas in 2005. He brewed a batch and it was awful. That didn't deter him, and he brewed a few more extract batches before jumping into all grain brewing. Two years before Starboard opened, Patrick was toying with a business plan, still not taking the idea too seriously. When Ahnapee Brewing opened in Algoma, he and his wife found themselves driving there every weekend. They realized there must be a call for it in Sturgeon Bay too. Ahnapee had a 2-barrel system at that time, and so Patrick was confident he could make it work with a one-barrel. This nano-brewery model affects the tap list. Rather than developing a few mainstays and keeping them on tap, he figured he could experiment a lot more, keep developing new recipes, and give his patrons reasons to come back soon and often for something different. He even has a request board from which he picks one idea a month and brews it. There is some predictability to the tap list: he has six tap targets, so there will nearly always be at least one of each—amber/brown, IPA, pale ale, stout/porter, wheat, and something truly unique, often outside of any single category. Patrick named his Belgian dark strong ale after the Demer, a river in Belgium. Thus far this is the only beer that has been brewed twice, and this repeat occurred when he asked his drinkers to vote on a beer they'd like to see back on tap. It's not just one of the favorites of the brewer.

Sturgeon Bay is famous for shipbuilding and also straddles a ship canal that connects the namesake bay on the Green Bay side of the peninsula to Lake Michigan. Thus, the nautical term for the brewery name. Brace yourself for boat puns and sailing themes.

The taproom is a light and airy space without any frills. The bar top is repurposed bowling lane wood. There's no TV, no WiFi, but maybe a bit of background music, so it's a great place for a social gathering. Door County Folk Alliance comes in and plays some Irish music once a month. Parking is on the street.

Facebook.com/starboardbrewing

Stumbling Distance: *Bluefront Café* (86 W Maple St, 920-743-9218, thebluefrontcafe.com) has delicious, reasonably priced food, great sandwiches and craft beers. *Nightingale Supper Club* (1541 Egg Harbor Rd, 920-743-5593) has the old school décor and menu, with a Friday night fish fry and prime rib on Thursdays. *Sonny's Pizzeria* (129 N Madison Ave, 920-743-2300, sonnyspizzeria. com) offers Chicago-style pies and more pub food with a view over the water. Watch for *Steel Bridge Songfest* (steelbridgesongfest.org) in June when venues all over town open up for visiting musicians, with a ticketed event at the main stage at the quirky *Holiday Music Motel* (30 N 1st Ave, 920-743-5571, holidaymusichotel.com). Jackson Browne has played here before, a friend of organizer, musician, and motel owner pat mAcdonald (of "The Future's So Bright, I Gotta Wear Shades" fame).

BREWS ON THE ROCK

2006 Lobdell Point Rd. • Washington Island, WI 54246
920-370-0045
brewsontherock.com
Opening: Spring 2019   **Head Brewer:** Erika Gonzalez
Annual Production: 1,200 barrels   **Number of Beers:** 6 on tap (2 guests)

Beers:

- » BELGIAN STYLES
- » BITTERS ALE
- » DARK BEERS IN WINTER
- » LAVENDER SAISON
- » MEXICAN LAGER

Brewmaster's Fave: Lavender Saison

Tours? Yes, scheduled in summer only.

Samples: Yes, sample flights available.

Best Time to Go: Open daily in spring and summer. Limited hours fall and winter, closed in a couple winter months, probably Jan-Feb.

Where can you buy it? Here on tap and in growlers and Crowlers to go. (Plus their custom-made beers available at the partner local businesses only.)

Got food? No, but food friendly.

Special Offer: Buy your first house beer, get one free when you get your book signed.

Directions: Follow WI-42 to the tip of the Door County peninsula (it is the famous wavy road of fall-color photos) where you can take the Washington Island Ferry (car/bike/foot; 920-847-2546, wisferry.com). From the pier on Washington Island, follow Lobdell Point Rd 1.7 miles north and the brewery is on the left. If you don't bring a car/bike, there is a local taxi (Island Shuttle, 920-535-0617) and at some point the brewery may have a shuttle service.)

The Beer Buzz: This is the only brewery in the book that requires a ferry to get there. Locals call Washington Island "The Rock" as it is a large limestone and granite piece of the Niagara Escarpment, a geological formation that curves from New York, through Canada, all the way to Wisconsin and Illinois.

Latino owned and operated, the brewery was founded by siblings Alex and Diego Anderson and "Head Honcho," Erika Gonzalez. Erika has 20 years in the restaurant/culinary industry, and used to be a jack-of-all-trades at Next Door Brewing where she found her way into brewing as an assistant. She then brewed at Capital Brewing in Middleton and Stone Arch in Appleton before Alex and Diego convinced her to move back to Washington Island. (Erika's family moved here in 1997 when she was in college.) Both Erika and Diego attended the Craft Beer and Brewing Program at Madison College. Alex, a graphic designer, handles all the marketing.

The brewery was originally a gas station and the pump out front still operates (credit card only). So you can fill your tank and your growler in one stop. Don't expect flagship beers; they want to explore continually. Part of their model is to brew tailor-made beers in partnership with local businesses. Fruits and herbs from Gathering Grounds Farm end up in several brews. They brew an ale with Angostura bitters for Nelsen's Hall, famous for serving shots of said bitters (a rite of passage on the island). Fragrant Isle Lavender Farm is the source of the flowers that go into the saison. Enjoy the rustic taproom or the grassy space out front. There's at least one TV for Packers games, and occasional live music.

Free WiFi. Facebook.com/brewsontherock and Twitter/Instagram @brewsontherock

Stumbling Distance: Get your customary shot of bitters at *Nelsen's Hall Bitters Pub* (1201 Main Rd, 920-847-2496). *Island Pizza* (264 Lobdell Point Rd, 920-847-3222) delivers. *Albatross Drive-in* (777 Main Rd, 920-847-2203, albatrossdrivein.com) has served great burgers and ice cream since 1977. *Rock Island State Park* (920-847-2235) is reachable by passenger ferry at the other end of the island. A long hike, rustic camping, a lighthouse and an impressive historical stone boathouse make it worth your time. **Hotels:** *Viking Village Motel* (736 Main Rd, 920-847-2551, vikingvillagemotel.com) and *Dor Cross Inn* (1922 Lobdell Point Rd, 920-847-2126, dorcrosinn.com) are both short walks from the brewery.

ZONE 6

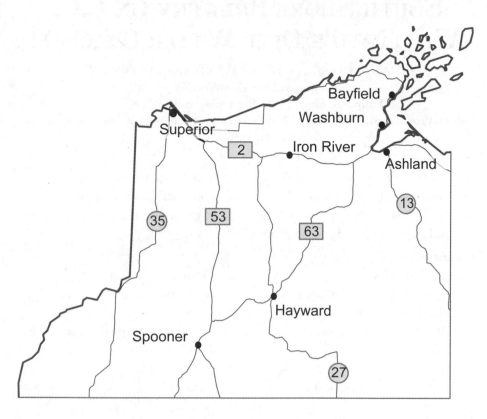

Ashland: South Shore Brewery
Bayfield: Adventure Club Brewing
Hayward: Angry Minnow Restaurant and Brewery
Iron River: White Winter Winery
Spooner: Round Man Brewing Co.
Superior: Earth Rider Brewery
Superior: The Thirsty Pagan
Washburn: South Shore Brewery

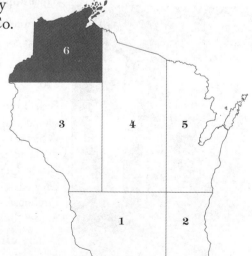

SOUTH SHORE BREWERY (IN L.C. WILMARTH'S DEEP WATER GRILLE)

808 West Main Street • Ashland, WI 54806 • 715-682-9199
www.southshorebrewery.com
Founded: May 1995   **Brewmaster**: Bo Bélanger
Annual Production: 1,000 bbls   **Number of Beers**: 8 on tap, 20+ beers throughout the year

Staple Beers:
- » INLAND SEA PILSNER
- » NORTHERN LIGHTS CREAM ALE
- » NUT BROWN ALE (it's English-style and they've got the darts and crusty bread to go with it)
- » RHOADES' SCHOLAR STOUT
- » WISCONSIN PALE ALE

Rotating Beers:
- » AMERICAN PALE ALE
- » APPLEFEST ALE (with local cider direct from the orchard)
- » BELGIAN-STYLES SAISON AND TRIPEL
- » BITTER BLONDE
- » BOURBON-BARREL COFFEE-MINT STOUT
- » BRACKET
- » ESB
- » HONEY DOUBLE MAIBOCK
- » IRISH MILK STOUT
- » MAIBOCK
- » PORTER
- » PUMPKIN BEER (with maple syrup)
- » RED LAGER
- » SCHWARZBIER
- » STREET CORNER 40 MALT LIQUOR
- » SUMAC WIT
- » WHEAT DOPPELBOCK
- » …Special beers for special events

Most Popular Brew: Nut Brown Ale

Brewmaster's Fave: Inland Sea Pilsner

Tours? Not here, see their Washburn brewery.

Samples? Yes, four 5-oz. pours for $6 or eight for $10.

Best Time to Go: Open daily 11AM–close (food served until 10PM). Watch for local festivals: Whistlestop Marathon, Blues and Brews (second weekend in Oct), Applefest in Bayfield (first weekend in Oct), Bay Days in Ashland (mid-July), Red Clay Classic (WISSOTA-sanctioned stock-car race), Firehouse 40 Bike Race, Fat Tire Bike Race, Book Across the Bay, etc.

Where can you buy it? On tap and in growlers to

go on site, and bottles distributed throughout much of Wisconsin, western Upper Peninsula Michigan, North Shore of Minnesota, and Duluth Metro area.

Got food? Yes, salads, sandwiches, and entrees. Walleye fish fry on Fridays and fresh Lake Superior whitefish. Beer cheese soup, ham, mushroom and wild rice soup, pale ale onion soup, and a stout BBQ sauce put the brews in the kitchen. They use malt flour or wort reduction on desserts. The adjoining dining room The Alley serves pizza.

Special Offer: 10% off South Shore Brewery merchandise during your signature visit.

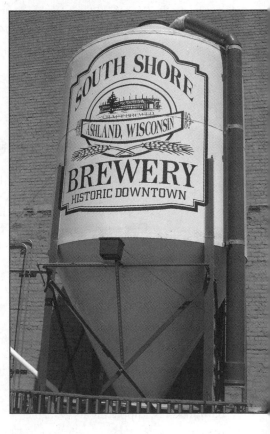

The Beer Buzz: Ashland Brewery made a run from 1886 to 1892, and Ashland Brewing Co. served the city from 1901 to 1937, and it wasn't until South Shore opened up in a renovated railway station that local brew returned to Chequamegon Bay. Originally, the brewery operated with the Railyard Pub in the historic Soo Line Depot downtown. But fire and buildings don't mix, and when they did anyway, the brewery relocated to join Deep Water Grille in one of three Main Street buildings built by Lewis Cass Wilmarth (1833–1907), Ashland's fourth mayor. The brownstone accents and footings are all locally mined, and the cornerstone dates the structure at 1895. The restaurant is the best in town, and it doesn't hurt to have fresh beer on tap. The bar shows some antique stained glass and serves free popcorn. Brewmaster Bo likes to push the envelope a bit on some things. (See the peppermint in that coffee stout!) All of the base malt used in South Shore's beers is grown right there in the Chequamegon Bay / Bayfield Peninsula area and 65% of their hops are from Wisconsin—that's some impressively local beer. Bo collaborates with Iron River mead maker Jon Hamilton at White Winter Winery to make bracket, a sort of cross between mead and ale and precursor to modern beers. Bo's Nut Brown Ale is so popular he says he could get by on that brew alone. With all the continued success, South Shore's growth shouldn't come as a surprise: in 2015 they opened a production facility with limited tasting room hours across the bay in Washburn. With that shift of burden to the new location, you can expect a lot more play in the brewhouse here.

Attached to Deep Water Grille is The Alley, a pizza joint with a lot of TVs for sports. Come for the pizza buffet Thu 4–9PM.

Stumbling Distance: *Frankie's Pizza* (1315 Lake Shore Dr E, 715-682-9980) is the great greasy variety you can't get enough of (does carry out). *Ashland Baking Company* (ashlandbakingco.com,

212 Chapple Ave, 715-682-6010) is an artisan bakery bringing a bit of Europe to the Northwoods. Don't miss *Whistlestop Marathon and Festival* (whistlestopmarathon.com, 800-284-9484). Great blues concerts, a Lake Superior fish boil, pasta feed, beer, and running events the second full weekend in October. *Applefest* (bayfield.org) is the weekend before up in Bayfield and South Shore hauls out the specialty Applefest Ale for it. 60,000 people turn out for this massive celebration of Wisconsin apples. A rare roadside attraction might be the so-called *"Plywood Palace"* out in nearby Moquah, an odd little tavern that looks like it was nailed together by some fellas that already had a few; it's on the snowmobile/ATV trail. *Big Top Chautauqua* (bigtop.org, 888-244-8368) is an outdoor music/theatre venue that runs all summer up in Bayfield. *Stage North* (stagenorth.com, 123 W Omaha St, 715-373-1194) in Washburn runs music and theater events year round.

ADVENTURE CLUB BREWING

35265 S. County Rd. J • Bayfield, WI 54814
Phone: NONE YET
adventureclubbrewing.com
Opening: Spring 2019　　**Head Brewer:** Matthew Gerdts
Annual Production: 100 barrels　　**Number of Beers:** 12 on tap (some guest taps)

Beers:

» APA

» BLONDE ALE

Rotating Beers:

» IMPERIAL STOUT

» SAISON

» Barrel-aged, seasonal sours

» He's a big fan of variety

Brewmaster's Fave: Cherry-honey-rosehip saison

Tours? Yes, by chance or by appointment.

Samples: Yes, sample flights available.

Best Time to Go: Open mid-afternoon most days until maybe 10pm, but with limited days and hours during winter. Check Facebook/website.

Where can you buy it? Here on tap and in growlers and Crowlers to go, and special-occasion bombers.

Got food? Limited snacks, but food friendly – bring your own.

Special Offer: Your first house beer for $1 when you get your book signed.

Directions: Follow US-13 north for 18 miles from where it parts from US-2 at the roundabout west of Ashland. Turn left on County Road J and it's on the left.

The Beer Buzz: Brewer Matthew worked at Brew & Grow supply shop in Madison for five years and washed kegs at *Next Door Brewing* before working his way to head brewer at Madison's *One Barrel Brewery*. His uncle and aunt, John and Mary Thiel had been in Bayfield 25 years. They had several acres south of Bayfield and in 2018 built this building as *Howl Clothing & Adventure* (howlinbayfield.com), a shop for adventure gear and apparel, and mountain bike sales, rental, and repair. What's missing but beer? They invited their nephew Matthew in to start a nano-brewery and here he operates a two-barrel system. The focus is on the beer, no TVs, and with the big outdoor space, they have more than just a beer garden. There are mountain bike trails on the property (to try out bikes for sale) and Matthew hopes to add some disc golf baskets as well.

Free WiFi. Mug Club. Facebook.com/adventureclubbrewing

Instagram @adventureclubbrewing   Twitter @AdvntrClbBrew

Stumbling Distance: *Blue Vista Farm* (34045 S Co Hwy J, 715-779-5400, bluevistafarm.com) has pick-your-own organic blueberries and apples, plus raspberries and various preserves. More of a swim than a stumble, but *Tom's Burned Down Café* (274 Chebomnicon Rd, La Pointe, 715-747-6100) on Madeline Island is worth the ferry trip out of Bayfield. Plenty of good restaurants in Bayfield, and abundant outdoor recreation including *Apostle Islands National Lakeshore* kayaking (see my book *Paddling Wisconsin*). *Bayfield Apple Festival* first weekend in October (bayfield.org). **Hotel:** *Woodside Cottages of Bayfield* (84790 State Hwy 13, 715-779-5600, woodsidecottages.com) is just across US-13. *Old Rittenhouse Inn & Restaurant* (301 Rittenhouse Ave, 715-779-5111, rittenhouseinn.com) is a pretty fabulous B&B in town.

ANGRY MINNOW RESTAURANT & BREWERY

10440 Florida Avenue • Hayward, WI 54843 • 715-934-3055
angryminnow.com
Founded: September 2004   **Brewmaster**: Jason Rasmussen
Annual Production: 670 bbls   **Number of Beers**: 6–7 on tap, 12–14 per year

Staple Beers:

- » HONEY WHEAT
- » MINNOW LITE
- » OAKY'S OATMEAL STOUT (nitro)
- » RIVER PIG AMERICAN PALE ALE

Rotating Beers:

- » BELGIAN BLONDE
- » CHARLIE'S RYE IPA
- » DOPPELBOCK
- » HEFEWEIZEN
- » IMPERIAL IPA
- » LAST NOTCH WHEAT
- » McSTUKIE'S SCOTCH ALE
- » MINNOW PILS
- » OKTOBERFEST
- » SAISON OLIVIA
- » VIENNA LAGER
- » ... and a couple Belgians around winter

Most Popular Brew: River Pig Pale Ale

Brewmaster's Fave: Rye IPA, River Pig Pale Ale, Stouts in winter

Tours? Yes, by appointment or by chance.

Samples? Yes, $10 for six 6-oz samples.

Best Time to Go: Closed Sundays. Taproom is open Mon–Sat 11AM–close. Call for seasonal hours! Muskiefest is the third week in June each year and the Birkebeiner is in late February.

Where can you buy it? Pints and growlers at the bar and kegs and cans from as far north as Bayfield all the way south to Chippewa Falls.

Got food? Yes. The menu featuring everything from sandwiches to full meals changes regularly. The emphasis is on locally sourced ingredients. Burgers are popular. Fresh whitefish and perch come from Lake Superior, and crayfish are on the menu. Deep-fried cheese curds are still here, and Friday features the traditional fish fry (walleye, perch, and whitefish). Look for the Lake Superior whitefish sandwich.

Special Offer: A free pint and half off an appetizer when you get your book signed!

Directions: Look for Florida Ave to intersect with Hwy 63 just four blocks south of the junction with Hwy 27.

The Beer Buzz: Lumber put Hayward on the map back in the nineteenth century, and

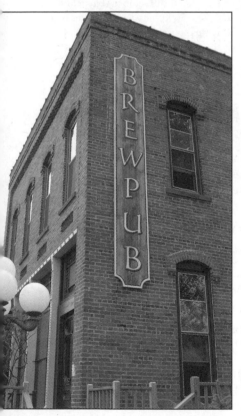

the Angry Minnow has inherited a bit of its legacy. The restaurant and brewery occupy a restored 1889 brick building that once served as the offices for Northwest Lumber Co. Exposed brick, hardwood floors, tasteful lighting, and a good menu are notable enough. Like anything, add some great beer and it's all a little bit better. Brewmaster Jason got his start at the Great Dane in Madison as an apprentice and then returned to his hometown to show the results. Spent grain is used in pretzels and bread. The name was a twist on the local icon, the massive and elusive muskellunge (that's muskie to you and me). Hayward has the record for the largest one caught. So the pub went with the little guy on the hook who does all the work of catching the big fish. Appropriate for the brewpubs that are the little guys in the beer industry and yet really doing the most impressive work. The bar offers free Wi-Fi. Facebook.com/AngryMinnowBrewPub

Stumbling Distance: OK, no one goes to Hayward—angler pro or not—without stopping in to see the giant muskie (over 4 stories tall!) at the *National Fresh Water Fishing Hall of Fame* (www.freshwater-fishing.org, 10360 Hall of Fame Dr, 715-634-4440). Go, and at *least* take a photo. The museum itself lives up to its icon in the fiberglass giant fish menagerie outside—400 fish mounts, classic motors, lures and equipment. *West's Dairy* (westshaywarddairy.com, corner of 2nd and Dakota, 715-634-2244) has been around since the 1920s and serves excellent homemade ice cream, malts, sundaes, and some sandwiches. Grab a coffee and some Wi-Fi here too.

White Winter Winery

68323A Lea Street • Iron River, WI 54847 • 800-697-2006
whitewinter.com
Founded: 1996   **Mead Maker**: Jon Hamilton
Annual Production: 5500 cases
Number of Beers: 2 plus a lot of meads, ciders and five distillates

Beers:

> » Premium Oak Brackett (aged with oak chips)
> » Traditional Brackett

Mead and Distillates:

> » A wide variety of meads and a port-like fortified mead (delicious)
> » Apple Mist (honey and cider on applewood)
> » 3 varieties of Eau de Vie (Blueberry, Raspberry, Strawberry)
> » Shadow Mist (black current and honey on oak)
> » Apple Brandy

Tours? Yes.

Samples? 3 samples for $5, 7 for $10, 15 for $20 (and you keep the glass if you get 7 or 15)

Best Time to Go: Open Mon–Sat 10–6, Sun 11–4, but hours change seasonally, so call first or check the site. Summer Festival (mid-June), Saturday before the 4th of July is Makers' Fair, Blueberry Festival (late July) in Iron River, and Oktoberfest. Sundays in the summer often host live music. Don't miss the Labor Day Weekend Sunday "Emergency Pig-out" with live music, pig roast, and more—to benefit local emergency responders.

Where can you buy it? Bottles and pouch-o'-mead on site, and in liquor stores throughout Wisconsin and Minnesota. Pouch-o'-mead (a mylar bag, not glass) is great for canoeing and other outdoor activities. I've dragged it behind my canoe.

Got food? Great fresh popcorn, baguette and cheese trays featuring locally baked bread and Wisconsin cheese.

Special Offer: 10% off any White Winter meads, bracketts or hard ciders or other products made on site.

Directions: At the west end of Iron River along the north side of US Hwy 2, look for the winery set back from the road across a parking lot.

The Beer Buzz: Jon comes from a long line of beekeepers, and though his family lived in the Minneapolis area, his father kept an empty hive out in the backyard while Jon was growing up. Jon knew of mead since middle school when he would do his term papers on honey and bees. When he was older, he decided making this ancient fermented honey concoction was easier than sneaking into the liquor store. Just off US 2 at the west end of town, his winery offers a great variety of meads and ciders all made from local ingredients, but he also has a couple types of bottled brackett. This is the missing link in the evolution of beer, you might say. Fermented honey (mead) is believed to be the happy hour drink of choice with the longest history, and the Scandinavians came up with brackett which is a cross between mead and ale by adding malted barley to the recipe. Brewmaster Bo over at South Shore Brewery in nearby Ashland helps out with this one since a winery must otherwise get another license to brew beers. Mead is associated with Winter Solstice celebrations (daylight hours start getting longer after December 21, and you are hopeful winter might actually end in May this year instead of June). The winery name comes from the legend of Old Man Winter, who is a resident in these parts for all but those two weeks of road construction in summer. Just kidding. Sort of.

Jon got his distiller's license in 2014 and is now making five varieties of *Eau de Vie*. Meaning "water of life" in French, it is a colorless brandy not aged in barrels so that the fruit essence remains. *Eau de Vie* is good as a digestif, easing your big stuffed belly after a hearty Wisconsin meal. Oak-rested varieties of *Eau de Vie* are also available, as is an apple brandy, and there's more to come.

Stumbling Distance: Pick up some fresh brats and meat sticks from *Jim's Meat Market* (68455 District Ave, 715-372-8566, jimsmeat.com). For some excellent diner fare with some very creative twists (baked puffy pancakes, baked omelets), head over to *Delta Diner* (deltadiner.net, 715-372-6666), southeast of Iron River on Cty Hwy H. You can't miss it—it's one of those classic shiny, aluminum-sided 1940s Silk City diners, restored and parked in the middle of the Northwoods. There are local bottled beers on hand, and dishes are also made with many local ingredients. Pick up some of Jalapeño Nina's Spicy Pickled Garlic while you're there too. *Oulu Glass* (ouluglass.com, 1695 W Colby Rd, Brule, 888-685-8969) eight miles west of Iron River features the amazing blown-glass work of the Jim and Sue Vojacek family from May 1 to January 5. Free demonstrations in November and December. Herbster, a town to the north, has sponsored an annual *smelt fry* every April since 1956, and it is a delicious taste of local culture. There are also many other area festivals—check with the Iron River Chamber of Commerce (iracc.com, 800-345-0716) for specific event dates.

Round Man Brewing Co.

234 Walnut St. • Spooner, WI 54801 • 715-939-1800
roundmanbrewing.com
Opening: Fall 2018   **Head Brewer:** Brian Sunderland
Annual Production: 300 barrels   **Number of Beers:** up to 18 on tap

Possible Beers:

- » Chocolate Peanut Butter Stout
- » Cream Ale
- » IPAs
- » Pale Ale
- » Pilsner

Brewmaster's Fave: He's an IPA fan

Tours? Yes, by chance or by appointment.

Samples: Yes, flights available.

Best Time to Go: Open Mon-Thu 11am-10pm, Fri-Sat 11am-12am, Sun 10am-8pm. Happy hour weekdays.

Where can you buy it? Here on tap and in growlers to go, and a few area draft accounts.

Got food? Yes, Northwoods-inspired finer cuisine from culinary-school-trained chef Chris Ray. Steaks, seafood, artisan burgers, fish fry. Full bar.

Special Offer: Your first pint of house beer free when you get your book signed.

Directions: US-63 passes right through town as River St. If coming from the south, turn left (from the north turn right) on Walnut and the brewery is mid-block on the right.

Cyclists: Wild River State Trail passes through town a few blocks from here.

The Beer Buzz: It's a family affair. Jeff and Sue Churchill had the idea. Their son Spencer graduated with a political science degree in spring 2017 and planned to go to law school. He came to Spooner for a month to spend time with his family, and his parents asked him: Why be a lawyer? To make money, sure, but is it going to make you happy? Probably not, he admitted. How about find something incredible but you'll probably never get rich? After a bit of soul searching he pushed law school aside and agreed to manage the brewery. He and his sister Xan (Alexandra) Nelson own *The Dock Coffee* (thedockcoffee. com) two doors down, serving breakfast and lunch food, plus wine, beer, and ice cream. His brother Blain is an artist who takes part as well. (Side note: "Spencer" was Winston Churchill's mother's maiden name, and Spencer's parents are fans.)

Renovations started in January 2018. The 1902 building originally housed a funeral home and in the mid-1930s when the entire block burnt down, the rebuilt structure continued as such. But the owner figured if you can build a coffin you can build a couch, and over the years the post-life furniture was phased out in preference for living rooms. The Churchills redesigned the whole thing, with exposed beams, concrete and brick for an industrial look, and added a concrete bar and a brewhouse behind glass for public viewing.

Brewer Brian, a longtime area homebrewer, came recommended to the Churchills by a friend and was on board early in the planning stages. While the owners are hopheads and love IPAs, they do not plan to be a niche brewery, but rather brew both ales and lagers for a wide variety of styles. The name Round Man is a bit of ribbing about Jeff.

Free WiFi. Mug Club. Angle parking out front. Facebook.com/roundmanbrewing

Stumbling Distance: See "Biking for Beer" in the back of the book: *Wild River State Trail* (dnr. wi.gov, 715-635-4490) is a 104-mile crushed gravel ride from Superior to Rice Lake. Set in the 1902 train depot, the *Railroad Memories Museum* (424 N. Front St, 715-635-3325, spoonerrrmuseum.net) is a fascinating stop. (Also on the bike trail.) **Hotels:** *Northwest Lodging* (N4848 Hwy 253, 715-635-3535, northwestlodging.net) or *Best Western Spooner Riverplace* (101 W Maple St, 715-635-9770).

EARTH RIDER BREWING CO.

Cedar Lounge Address: 1715 N 3rd St • Superior, WI 54880
715-394-7391 • earthrider.beer / cedarlounge.beer
Opened: 2017   **Head Brewer**: Allyson Rolf
Annual Production: 2500 barrels
Number of Beers: 10-16 on tap with some guest taps

Staple Beers:

- » CARIBOU LAKE IPA
- » NORTH TOWER STOUT
- » PRECIOUS MATERIAL HELLES
- » SUPERIOR PALE ALE

Rotating Beers: Lots of them! Rotation is frequent, often a new beer every couple of weeks or so.

- » ALLOUEZ AMBER ALE
- » APRICRUSH TART (KETTLE-SOURED WHEAT, ROTATING FRUITS)
- » EARTH RIVER DULUTH COFFEE PALE ALE
- » ROYAL BOHEMIAN PILSNER
- » TWIN PORTER
- » VALHALLA WINTER WARMER
- » ...PLUS VARIOUS SOURS

Most Popular Brew: Superior Pale Ale

Brewmaster's Fave: Royale Bohemian pilsner and her Tart Series

Tours? Yes, Saturdays at 1pm. One-hour tours start from the Cedar Lounge and include samples and a souvenir glass for $6. Also, The Duluth Experience offers tours that stop here (218-464-6337, theduluthexperience.com)

Samples? Yes, sample flights of four 5-oz pours.

Best Time to Go: Open Mon-Thu 11am-11pm, Fri-Sat 11 am-12am, Sun 11am-9pm. Happy hour Mon-Thu 3pm-6pm.

Where can you buy it? Here on tap and in Growlers and cans to go (but will fill growlers). Cans in the Twin Ports area, a few places in Ashland and Cable, WI.

Got food? Yes, Heggies Pizza, Yker Acres Craft Beer Pork Sticks, and other bar snacks. Beer cocktails also.

Special Offer: A free can coozie and a bumper sticker when you get your book signed..

Directions: Coming into Superior on US-53/2nd St, take the exit for US-35 South/ Superior Business District and follow it to where it joins 3rd St.

The Beer Buzz: Tim Nelson, one of the former partners at distinguished Fitger's Brewpub across the bridge, founded the Northland's newest brewery. Nelson came to Wisconsin for better market opportunity, a bit more brewing room in Superior. Having the support of city government was a bonus. Due to Minnesota state laws, Nelson couldn't package his beer for 20 years as a brewpub owner and envied the opportunities in Wisconsin. Driving by Cedar Lounge and saw a For Sale by Owner sign and he noted it had empty lot space nearby for new construction. But as it turned out, the Leamon Mercantile building across the lot became available and they chose to lease that instead.

Five generations of beer distributors had operated there and the coolers and floor drains ere already there, and only needed to be updated. The brewery stands alone on its block, one street east from the Cedar Lounge, which also has its own block at the bend in Hwy 35.

From 1898-1967, Northern Brewing Co. supplied Superior's brews and in 1912 built the Cedar Lounge building as a tied-house. Today it functions as the official Earth Rider tap room though it also serves other guest beers. Brewer Allyson made a name for herself at Thirsty Pagan before joining this project.

Free WiFi. Facebook.com/EarthRiderBeer and Twitter/Instagram @EarthRiderBeer @CedarLoungeBeer

Stumbling Distance: *Anchor Bar* (413 Tower Ave, 715-394-9747, anchorbarandgrill.com) has their beer and other craft brews plus the best burgers in town. *The Hammond Steak House* (402 N 5th St, 715-392-3269, hammondsteakhouse.com) is your best bet for steak and seafood in town.

Thirsty Pagan Brewing

1623 Broadway • Superior, WI 54880 • 715-394-2500
thirstypaganbrewing.com
Founded: 1996　　**Brewmaster**: In transition!
Annual Production: 600+ barrels　　**Number of Beers**: 16 on tap plus a beer engine

Staple Beers:

» Burntwood Black Ale (named after a local river; cool points if you can name which one!)
» Derailed Ale (classic American Pale Ale)
» Indian Pagan Ale (IPA)
» Lawn Chair Light Lager
» North Coast Amber Ale
» Trouble Maker Tripel
» Velo Saison

Rotating Beers: Lots of them! Depends on the season, doesn't it? Check the website.

Most Popular Brew: Indian Pagan Ale

Owner's Fave: Burntwood Black Ale

Tours? Informal ones by chance or by appointment.

Samples? Yes, 3-oz pours in a house flight (up to 9 house beers) or seasonal flight (up to 9 beers) for about $12.25.

Best Time to Go: Open daily 11AM–10PM. Live music every night.

Where can you buy it? Only here and to go in growlers.

Got food? Yes, the best pizza in town and various appetizers and a kids' menu.

Special Offer: A free 10-oz glass of prune juice! No, I'm kidding—it's a beer.

Directions: Follow Hammond Ave south from the interchange with Hwy 53/I-535. Continue driving south, and one block past the first stop light, take Broadway to the right (west). Or US Hwy 2 from the west becomes Belknap St. Take this to Ogden Ave and turn right (north) to Broadway where you will see the brewery on the corner of Ogden Ave and Broadway.

The Beer Buzz: In 1999, brewer Rick Sauer moved his Twin Ports Brewing to this 1910 creamery building on the corner of Broadway St and Ogden Ave. It's an unassuming place, still tiled like the creamery and all the feel of a northern town tavern. Steve Knauss took over and changed the name to Thirsty Pagan in 2006. Before this place, Superior hadn't had its own beer since Northern Brewing Co. emptied its tanks for the last time in the late '60s. They're serious about their beer here, but loads of fun to drink it with. The bar has expanded a bit adding space for forty more patrons. The restaurant side of the brewpub can seat larger parties. A great beer garden awaits out back.

Guest brewers and collaborations are common. The brewery added a 7-barrel system in 2014, but still uses the previous 2-barrel system which is a fun and flexible system that they can really use to engage with a lot of people and do a lot of beer styles.

Free WiFi. Cribbage and cards. No TVs.

Stumbling Distance: Dive into a dive at the *Anchor Bar* (413 Tower Ave, 715-394-9747, anchor-barandgrill.com) five blocks away. Burgeoning (yes, I really just used that word) with ship-themed paraphernalia, this cozy local tavern has many kinds of burgers—some weighing in at a pound—that are excellent, cheap, and inventive (*cashew* burger??). Take a growler of Burntwood Black Ale and get some fresh air at *Wisconsin Point* (Moccasin Mike Road), the world's largest freshwater spit (a sand bar with trees) with a lighthouse, Native American burial grounds, driftwood, agates, and many species of birds. History buffs shouldn't miss the *Richard I. Bong World War II Heritage Center* (www.bongheritagecenter.org, 305 Harbor View Parkway, 888-816-9944) where the ace of aces namesake is commemorated along with all the veterans of that war in an informative and sharply designed museum. A restored Lockheed P-38 Lightning fighter plane—the type of plane Bong used in his record 40 enemy kills—is on site.

SOUTH SHORE BREWERY

532 West Bayfield Street (WI 13) • Washburn, WI 54891
No phone (see Ashland)
southshorebrewery.com
Opened: 2015   **Brewmaster**: Bo Bélanger
Annual Production: 3,400 barrels   **Number of Beers**: 8 taps

Staple Beers:

- » INLAND SEA PILSNER
- » NORTHERN LIGHTS CREAM ALE
- » NUT BROWN ALE
- » RHOADES' SCHOLAR STOUT
- » WISCONSIN PALE ALE

Rotating Beers:

- » AMERICAN PALE ALE
- » APPLEFEST ALE (with local cider direct from the orchard)
- » BELGIAN-STYLES SAISON AND TRIPEL
- » BITTER BLONDE
- » BOURBON-BARREL COFFEE-MINT STOUT
- » BRACKET
- » ESB
- » HONEY DOUBLE MAIBOCK
- » IRISH MILK STOUT
- » MAIBOCK
- » PORTER
- » PUMPKIN BEER (with maple syrup)
- » RED LAGER
- » SCHWARZBIER
- » STREET CORNER 40 MALT LIQUOR
- » SUMAC WIT
- » WHEAT DOPPELBOCK
- » …many more experimental batches at this location

Most Popular Brew: Nut Brown Ale

Brewmaster's Fave: Inland Sea Pilsner

Tours? Yes, on Saturdays; check the schedule on the website.

Samples? Yes, four 5-oz. pours for $6 or eight for $10.

Best Time to Go: Tasting room is open Tue 4-9pm (game and vinyl night), Fri 4-9pm, Sat 2-9pm. Come for Brownstone Days at the end of July. (Washburn Homecoming is every 5 years on that weekend.) Every night is vinyl night.

Where can you buy it? Here on tap and in growlers and six-packs to go. Bottles distributed throughout much of Wisconsin, western Upper Peninsula Michigan, North Shore of Minnesota, and Duluth Metro area.

Got food? Free salted peanuts. Otherwise, there are area to-go menus from local restaurants, and the tasting room is food friendly.

Special Offer: Buy your first beer, get 1 free during your signature visit.

Directions: From Ashland, WI 13 passes north right through Washburn as Bayfield St. Where the road bends in downtown, watch for the brewery on the left side (not the lake side) of the street.

The Beer Buzz: See South Shore Brewery in Ashland for the full history here, but this is what happens when your beer gets popular and you run out of room to brew it: you open a separate production brewery. Brewer Bo did just that up the lakeshore a short way from where he got his start. Set in a former bowling alley, this 15-barrel brewhouse with 30-barrel fermenters produces more than triple of what is produced out of the basement at their loca-

tion in Ashland. The tasting room, set in a 1920s bar building attached to the old bowling alley, has limited hours, but it's worth finding your way here. Don't expect WiFi and TVs, but there may be some vinyl playing in the background, board games, and a shuffleboard table made from an old bowling lane. Otherwise, this is all about the beer.

Stumbling Distance: *Washburn Cultural Center* (1 E Bayfield St, 715-373-5591, washburnculturalcenter.com) has a regional historical museum where you can see my grandfather in one of the old Du Pont dynamite makers photos. *Coco Artisan Breads* (146 W Bayfield St, 715-373-2253, coconorth.com) is way more than a bakery, with soups, sandwiches, and pasties plus coffee. *Stage North* (stagenorth.com, 123 W Omaha St, 715-373-1194) runs music and theater events year round. Summer blueberry pickers should visit *Blue Vista Farm* (34045 S Co Hwy J, Bayfield, 715-779-5400, bluevistafarm.com) and *Highland Valley Farms* (87080 Valley Rd, Bayfield, 715-779-5446, bayfieldblues.com). *Applefest* (bayfield.org) is a three-day weekend in October up in Bayfield and South Shore hauls out the specialty Applefest Ale for it. 60,000+ people turn out for this massive celebration of Wisconsin apples. *Big Top Chautauqua* (bigtop.org, 888-244-8368) is an outdoor music/theater venue that runs all summer up in Bayfield. Don't miss the *South Shore Brewery* location in Ashland which is connected to *Deep Water Grille*.

BEER FESTIVALS

Ah, there is nothing quite like a beer fest. Brat tents, music, and copious amounts of great beer. Variety is the spice of life, and a good brew festival allows you to travel through a whole lot of breweries that would have required a much longer trip.

This is only a general guideline. New beer fests pop up all the time. Specific dates change from year to year as do ticket prices. Also, some festivals sell out the same day tickets go on sale, months in advance, so plan ahead!

JANUARY

Ice Cold Beer Festival takes place around mid-January to mid-February in Minocqua, WI. Tickets for the Wisconsin Brewers Guild event are cheaper in advance. Along with the beer from 45+ breweries, sample some gourmet cheeses and other fine foods. (wibrewersguild.com).

Isthmus Beer & Cheese Fest is in Madison on a Saturday in January. Over 30+ brewers pair beers with about 2 dozen artisanal cheesemakers' best stuff. Bigger every year. (isthmusbeercheese.com).

FEBRUARY

Milwaukee Ale House Mid-Winter Brewfest is on a Sunday in February (ale-house.com) at Milwaukee Ale House and benefits the MACC Fund (Midwest Athletes Against Childhood Cancer).

Fond du Lac Brewfest got its start in 2010. This event aims to be annual and breaks up a bit of winter blues with four hours of beer pouring from Wisconsin brewers, live music, and food. Tickets are cheaper in advance or cost around $50 (facebook.com/FDLBrewfest).

Food and Froth is Milwaukee Public Museum's fundraising fest, offering samples of Midwest and import beers, plus great local food. Tickets are about $70 (cheaper for museum members) and $100 for VIP. (mpm.edu/plan-visit, click Calendar).

MARCH

Hops & Props brings in over 250 beers on a Saturday evening in early March. The event benefits the EAA AirVenture Museum in Oshkosh. VIP tickets also available. (800-236-1025, eaa.org).

Madison on Tap brings out 70+ brewers for a few hours on a Saturday in early March. VIP tickets available. (americaontap.com)

APRIL

Dells Rare Barrel Affair (wibrewersguild.com/dells-rare-barrel-affair) is a barrel-beer fan's dream. Organized by the Wisconsin Brewers Guild it's held in mid-April in Wisconsin Dells. Tickets are about $50.

Superior Gitchee Gumee Brewfest (ggbrewfest.com) is in early April. A $25 ticket gets you access to over 120 beers from 30 brewers.

The Dairy State Cheese and Beer Festival (kenoshabeerfest.com) benefits the Boys and Girls Clubs of Kenosha. Watch for it in mid- to late-April at The Brat Stop right off I-94 outside Kenosha.

Milwaukee Beer Week (milwaukeebeerweek.com) is a late April series of events around the Brew City which features a passport so you can keep track of where you've been and need to go. These can also win you prizes.

Between the Bluffs Beer Wine Cheese Festival (beerwinecheese.explorelacrosse.com) hosts 3,500 and takes place in La Crosse around the end of April. Tickets are around $45, with VIP options as well.

MAY

Great Taste of the Midwest tickets usually go on sale May 1. The 6,000 tickets sell out in a couple hours (see August).

American Craft Beer Week is a nationwide event typically in May, and many communities follow suit or host a similar event the week before or after the national one:

Green Bay Craft Beer Week takes place in May (gbcraftbeerweek.com)

Kenosha Craft Beer Week takes place in May (kenoshacraftbeerweek.com).

Madison Craft Beer Week is a 10-day (2 weekend) series of events around the city typically starting around the first week of May (or late April) before the national event. Beer walks, parties, food/beer pairings, films, lectures—you name it! (madbeerweek.com).

Wisconsin Micro Beer Fest in Chilton has been running since 1992 when late founder and brewer Bob Rowland of Calumet Brewing Co. started a small event that quickly became the second largest of its kind in the state. Held in late May (Sunday before Memorial Day weekend), it features over 100 beers from more than 20 Wisconsin brewers. Sample these while enjoying good food and live music. Tickets go on sale at the end of March and sell out early. Held at the Calumet County Fair Grounds, Chestnut and Francis Streets, Chilton. Contact Rowland's Calumet Brewpub at 920-849-2534.

JUNE

Kohler Festival of Beer is a three-day fest usually held in late May/early June and hosting craft brewers from around the country. Check akohlerexperience.com under Events for more information.

Milwaukee Beer Barons World of Beer Fest is in early June (beerbarons.org) and features over 250 beers from over 90 brewers. The Beer Barons also host a Monster Mash Homebrew Competition.

Door County Beer Festival on a Saturday afternoon in mid-June brings craft beer and local food together with live music, seminars, and more in Bailey's Harbor. Tickets are $35–40, plus a bit more for limited VIP tix. (doorcountybeer.com).

Great Northern Beer Festival is held in Eagle River the second Saturday in June

CRAFT BEER WEEK

The Brewers Association honors American Craft Beer Week (craftbeer.com) nationwide in the month of May. While anyone anywhere can tip back a few beers this week, several communities in Wisconsin have organized local craft beer weeks, coordinating a calendar of events that range from beer tastings and pairing dinners to lectures and presentations about beer and brewing-related topics for the general public and for hardcore beer geeks.

Kenosha Craft Beer Week

kenoshacraftbeerweek.com

In tandem with the national craft beer week, the city hosts events at about a dozen bars and restaurants, while the three breweries—Public Craft Brewing, R'Noggin Brewery, Rustic Road Brewing—are heavily involved.

Madison Craft Beer Week

madbeerweek.com

Spans two weekends and includes so many venues and events that it merits its own mobile-friendly website complete with personalized calendar to help you sort it all and share your itinerary with friends. This 10-day event, organized to include all area distributors, brings in brewers from all over for tap takeovers, beer dinners, presentations, and tastings. As of 2018 it was already up to 110+ venues and 400+ events.

Milwaukee Beer Week

milwaukeebeerweek.com

Held in April rather than competing with the national event, the Milwaukee Beer Week is organized by Beechwood Distributors, and spotlights the 20+ breweries they represent for a series of tap takeovers.

Green Bay Craft Beer Week

gbcraftbeerweek.com

Green Bay had their first craft beer week in 2015, paralleling the dates of the national event. A booklet was available with the schedule of events which involved the four big breweries—Titletown, Hinterland, Stillmank, Copper State, Noble Roots and Badger State—plus many craft beer bars and notable restaurants. Establishments in De Pere joined the activities as well.

(greatnorthernbeerfestival.com). Tickets typically sell out early. 30+ brewers turn up for this—many from Wisconsin but also several foreigners (from Minnesota and Michigan and the like)—and it grows a bit each year.

Rotary Brewfest is hosted by the Ketchum/Sun Valley Rotary Club and takes place mid-June. Sample beers, wines, craft liquor, and help charitable causes. Tickets are about $20. (rotarybrewfest.com).

Wisconsin Beer Lovers Festival in Glendale is hosted by the Wisconsin Brewers Guild in mid-June and features Wisconsin-only brews and their brewers, plus local chefs with foods to pair beers with. (wisconsinbeerloversfest.com).

JULY

Bacon, Brew & BBQ Fest (bbbfest.com) brings a holy trinity together for a fest with 40 brewers, nearly as many restaurants and caterers, plus bands on 2 stages. Held on a Saturday in mid-July in Sun Prairie.

Oshkosh Brews & Blues (oshkoshjaycees.org/bnb.htm) takes place around the second Saturday of July at the Leach Amphitheater in Oshkosh and proceeds go to local charitable causes.

Milwaukee Firkin Craft Beer Festival highlights cask-conditioned beers from over 50 breweries. Held on a Saturday in mid- to late July, tickets about $50 or $80 with VIP option. (milwaukeefirkin.com).

German Fest is a huge ethnic party at Maier Park in Milwaukee at the end of July. (germanfest.com).

Lac du Flambeau Lions Club Brewfest is held at the end of July on a Saturday in Minocqua. Over a decade old, the fest brings nearly 50 brewers together with food and live music to boot. $35–40 tickets, either ordered or at the gate. (lacduflambeaubrewfest. com)

Milwaukee Brewfest takes place in late July and features over 200 craft brews, live music, Wisconsin food for sale and sample, exhibits, games, and even the crowning of the Brewfest Queen. A great time right down by the lakeshore (milwaukeebrewfest. com, 414-321-5000).

AUGUST

Great Taste of the Midwest is sort of the big kahuna of beer fests and the second longest running craft brew festival in North America. Over 500 beers from over 150 brewers! All 6,000 tickets typically sell out in a couple hours and go on sale around May 1. The event itself is the second Saturday in August. Contact the Madison Homebrewers & Tasters Guild at mhtg.org. Tickets only in advance!

The Firemen's Catfish Festival in Potosi, home of the National Brewery Museum, serves up some the town's original beer for a massive fish fry. Also features music, truck and tractor pulls, a euchre tournament, fireworks and dance. Call 608-763-2261 for more info.

West Bend Germanfest in late August (downtownwestbend.com) features two stages of continuous music, authentic food, dancing, Sheepshead tournaments and daily raffles. Friday hosts a Fish Fry.

SEPTEMBER

The Fiery Foods and Beer Festival is from the same geniuses who brought you Bacon, Brew & BBQ, and takes place in Sun Prairie at Angell Park in mid-September. fireicefest. com

Great Lakes Brew Fest is in the middle of September, third Saturday generally, several great hours in the afternoon with the beer of over 60 brewers represented and unlimited sampling right on the shore of Lake Michigan. Lots of food is served and various forms of entertainment are provided. It gets bigger and better every year. Festival Park in Racine. About $50 plus a VIP option for more (greatlakesbrewfest.com).

Wisconsin Oktoberfest (wisconsinbeerloversfest.com) Held in Wausau on a Saturday in late September this is another Wisconsin Brewers Guild event with over 35 breweries and as many food vendors.

Chippewa Falls Oktoberfest (visitchippewafallswi.com) Northern Wisconsin State Fairgrounds (Hwy 124/Jefferson Ave), three days in the middle of September ($8 daily or weekend rates). Lots of song, dance, sauerkraut eating contests and Leinie's beer. Good family event.

Thirsty Troll Brewfest is around the second Saturday of September in Grundahl Park, 301 Blue Mounds St, Mt Horeb (trollway.com).

Egg Harbor Ale Fest brings 40+ brewers together on a Saturday in September, with live music, VIP early entry and a trolley shuttle for local lodging. (eggharboralefest.com)

Blue Harbor Craft Beer Festival (facebook.com/BlueHarborFest) is hosted by Blue Harbor Resort in Sheboygan in partnership with 3 Sheeps Brewing in late September.

Appleton's Octoberfest is late in September and draws over 100,000 people. octoberfestonline.org.

La Crosse Oktoberfest (oktoberfestusa.com) starts the last weekend of September (or first of October) and lasts four days.

Quivey's Grove BeerFest is at 6261 Nesbitt Rd, Fitchburg, 608-273-4900, quiveysgrove. com and takes place at the end of September or in early October. This beer fest features 45 breweries, 100 beers, and great food.

Weissgerber's Gasthaus Oktoberfest at 2720 N. Grandview Blvd., Waukesha 262-544-6960 in late September.

OCTOBER

Dallas Oktoberfest (no not Texas!) First Saturday in October. Very family friendly event, not your usual drunkfest. Live music, arts and craft fair, car show, various fun and/ or funny events, and a 7am Fire Department Pancake Breakfast. Valkyrie Brewing Co. makes its home here. Not huge, but worth the trip! "You never know who else will be there. Or how dangerous it may become." valkyriebrewery.com, 715-837-1824.

New Glarus Oktoberfest is in Village Park, New Glarus the last weekend in September or the first full weekend in October. New Glarus Brewery hosts a beer tasting and there is lots of live music, food, and entertainment including kids' games (swisstown.com, 800-527-6838).

Sand Creek Brewing Oktoberfest (sandcreekbrewing.com, 715-284-7553) 320 Pierce St, Black River Falls, the first Saturday in October right on site in a huge tent with crafts and music all day and night.

Northeast Wisconsin Beer Festival brings in 30+ brewers in mid-October. It's indoors since this could either be beautiful weather or the eternal winter depending on the year. There is wine, food and music on hand. (craftbeerfestivalgb.com, stonecellar.com).

Wisconsin Dells is home to **Dells On Tap** in October (a weekend around the 20th), part of Autumn Harvest Fest, a family friendly festival with a craft fair, farmer's market, hayrides and more (wisdells.com).

NOVEMBER

Janesville Kiwanis Fall Fest of Ale occurs in November (fallfestofale.com) with beer, food and music and benefit local charities.

DECEMBER

I got nothing here. Get yourself a growler or a few six-packs of craft brew from the local brewer or liquor store and have some friends over for the holidays. Don't forget your lederhosen. Prost!

OKTOBERFEST

Oktoberfest was originally a wedding celebration. Prince Ludwig of Bavaria married Princess Therese in 1810. They hosted a horse race outside Munich and 40,000 people came to watch. The event celebrated the marriage (I imagine it was open bar) but also was a sort of harvest fest, a religious thanks for the crops and such. Each year, parades bring together floats and bands, and of course BEER. Munich may be the home of the festival, but Wisconsin provides a nice variety of them, most notably in La Crosse. And the namesake beer, which is traditionally aged from spring until this event, is often available at non-October times as well. Check with your local brewer!

Beer, Boats, Buses And Bikes

BOOZE CRUISES

Sort of the malt and hops version of the Love Boat, or Gilligan's Island without the hole in the hull. Or the big storm. Or the Professor. Or Ginger. OK, *nothing* like Gilligan's Island. Here are a few boat rides with beer:

Madison

Drink local craft beer and dine on *Ian's Pizza* on this boat cruise around Madison's lakes with great views of the Capital, the University, and one of the finest cities in the country. Check tour calendar online. Reservations are required. Betty Lou Cruises (bettyloucruises.com, 608-246-3138).

Milwaukee

Get on the **Brew City Queen II** or **Milwaukee Maiden II** and set sail along the Milwaukee River for a booze cruises. Be aware that they no longer offer tours that stop at local breweries. Check tour times and which boat you are on when you make your reservation. Tickets are around $30 and typically include food and drink. For information or reservations, call Riverwalk Boats (Dock: Pere Marquette Park, 950 N. Old World 3rd St, 414-283-9999, riverwalkboats.com).

Edelweiss Milwaukee River Cruise Line hosts various themed cruises including a **Beer and Cheese Cruise** and a **Beer and Brat Cruise**. Cruise along the Milwaukee River and Lake Michigan shoreline while drinking local beer and eating (local) Usinger brats. (edelweissboats.com, 414-276-7447)

You can actually *paddle* along the Milwaukee River to visit *Lakefront, Rock Bottom*, and *Milwaukee Ale House*.

GET ON THE BUS

Think of this as the ultimate designated driver option—you and a busload of other beer enthusiasts being carted around, beer in hand, to various beer destinations. Brewery tours, beer bars, sporting events with beer. Think of this as the ultimate designated driver option—you and a busload of other beer enthusiasts being carted around, beer in hand, to various beer destinations. Brewery tours, beer bars, sporting events with beer.

Zone 2

Milwaukee

Fun Beer Tours Milwaukee brings history and beer together. Paul Hepp, the owner and guide, talks you through the "Beer Capital of the World" by bus or on foot. They also offer themed pub crawls and scavenger hunts. (414-202-3611, FunBeerToursMKE.com)

Heritage Brewery Tours is dedicated providing fun brewing tours (public and private) with a historic context regarding the rich brewing heritage of Milwaukee and the rest of Wisconsin. Email dave@wisconsinbreweriana.com or go to heritagebrewerytours.com or the Heritage Brewery Tours Facebook page.

As the name suggests, **Milwaukee Food & City Tours** (414-255-0534, milwaukeefoodtours.com) isn't *only* taking you to breweries. But it does take you to breweries.

Check out their many different public tours or book a private one.

Untapped Tours is a locally owned and guided bus-tour operation that offers a 3.5-hour brewery tour through **Milwaukee**, hitting *Company Brewing*, *Lakefront Brewery*, *Black Husky* and *Gathering Place*. A City Tour hits *Lakefront Brewery* and *Clock Shadow Creamery* for cheese, while rolling past historical attractions in between. (414-698-8058, untappedtours.com)

Zone 3
Eau Claire
West Central Wisconsin Brewery Tour is run by **Bus Bros. Tour Co.** (715-533-9396, busbrostourco.com) based out of Eau Claire and covering a good number of regional breweries and wineries.

Zone 5
Green Bay
Veteran-owned **Another Way Entertainment** (920-217-2317 anotherwayentertainment.com) tours **Green Bay area** breweries and wineries and gives a percentage of their profits to support veterans.
Oshkosh
Oshkosh Brewery Tours (715-297-5021, oshkoshbars.com) runs 2 buses on Saturdays hitting *Fox River*, *Bare Bones*, *Fifth Ward* and *HighHolder* breweries for tours for a very reasonable price.

Zone 6
Superior/Duluth
The Duluth Experience (211 E 2nd St, Duluth, MN, 218-464-6337, theduluthexperience.com) is obviously a Minnesota thing, but they are awesome and do bus across the border to involve **Superior** breweries.

BIKING FOR BEER!

Wisconsin has a large network of bike trails, many of them former railway corridors, and what better way to end a ride than with a locally made beer? Here are some options for where to ride and where to take a break.

Where required, bicyclists ages sixteen and older must purchase a **State Trail Pass** which costs $5/day or $25/year (dnr.wi.gov). Often they can be purchased at self-pay stations along state trails.

Zone 1

The **Glacial Drumlin Trail** (920-648-8774) starts in Cottage Grove heading east and passes south of **Lake Mills**, home to *Tyranena Brewing Co.* and *Sunshine Brewing* and ends in Waukesha. Ambitious bikers may veer off the trail at **Delafield** for *Delafield Brewhaus* and *Water Street Lake Country*. Trail pass required. (Another trail, the Lake Country Recreation Trail, connects Waukesha and Delafield.) You may also ride bike-friendly roads west from the Glacial Drumlin trailhead to reach the *Great Dane* Eastside pub at 876 Jupiter Dr., **Madison**.

The **"400" State Trail** (608-337-4775, 608-524-2850) starts in **Reedsburg**, home to *Corner Pub*, and heads north where it connects to the Hillsboro, Omaha and Elroy–

Sparta trails. Reedsburg is 16 miles from **Wisconsin Dells** where you'll find *Wisconsin Dells Brewing Co.* and *Port Huron Brewing Co.* Trail pass required.

Madison has over 100 miles of trails in and around the city and special lanes in some streets just for bikes. With the high number of breweries in the city and the adjoining cities of **Fitchburg** and **Middleton**, you have a lot of options here. **Capital City Trail** winds around Lake Monona and passes within three blocks of the *Great Dane* off the Capitol Square, a half block on Brearly from *Giant Jones Brewing*, right past *Working Draft Beer* on Wilson, and *One Barrel Brewing* and *Next Door Brewing* on Atwood and, and within one block of the *Great Dane* Fitchburg location.

Military Ridge State Trail (608-437-7393) will take you from **Madison** (home of several brewers), through **Verona** (right past *Hop Haus Brewing* and not far from *Wisconsin Brewing Co.* and *Boulder Brewpub*) and **Mount Horeb** (*The Grumpy Troll*). The trail ends at Dodgeville and provides trails to Blue Mounds and Governor Dodge state parks. Trail pass required.

Cheese Country Recreation Trail (608-776-4830) connects **Mineral Point** (*Brewery Creek*) to **Monroe** (*Minhas Craft Brewery* and *Bullquarian Brewhouse*) and **Darlington** (*City Service Brewery*).

Badger State Trail (608-527-2335) stretches from **Madison** to Freeport, Illinois, via **Monroe** (*Minhas Craft Brewery* and *Bullquarian Brewhouse*) and within a few miles of **New Glarus** (*New Glarus Brewery*) down the **Sugar River Trail**. Trail pass required.

Sugar River State Trail (608-527-2334) starts in **New Glarus**, home of *New Glarus Brewery*, of course. Trail pass required.

Great Sauk State Trail (608-355-4800) is under development but currently passes behind *Vintage Brewing Sauk Prairie* in **Sauk City**, soon to be connected to Devil's Lake State Park and more.

Zone 2

Ozaukee Interurban Trail (interurbantrail.us, 800-237-2874) is a paved trail connecting **Port Washington** (*Inventors Brewpub*) to historic **Cedarburg**, home of *Rebellion Brewing* and *Fermentorium*. The trail crosses Washington Ave in downtown just a couple blocks from the Cedarburg Mill, Rebellion's home.

Oak Leaf Trail (800-231-0903) in **Milwaukee** is an asphalt trail right through Brew City and yet somewhat peaceful and secluded as it passes along the river. You'd have to venture into the streets to get to breweries though. *Gathering Place Brewing* is close. (Also see *Glacial Drumlin Trail* in Zone 1.)

Zone 3

La Crosse River State Trail (608-337-4775, 608-269-4123) connects the **Elroy–Sparta Trail** to the **Great River State Trail** and **La Crosse** is home to *City Brewery, 608 Brewing, Turtle Stack Brewing* and *Pearl Street Brewery*. Trail pass required. Be sure to check out *Pearl Street Brewery's* summer Tour de Pearl for a great way to pedal for pints and win something.

Old Abe State Trail (715-726 7880) passes through **Cornell** near *MoonRidge Brew*

Pub and ends in **Chippewa Falls**, home of *Leinenkugel's* and *Brewster Bros Brewing Co.* The trail ends right at the brewery. Say no more! Trail pass required.

Lucette Brewing Co. lies right alongside the **Red Cedar State Trail** (715-232-1242) in **Menomonie** and is connected to *Nonic Brewing* and *Zymurgy Brewing* farther into town. The Red Cedar heads south 14 miles to connect to the **Chippewa River State Trail** which could then get you to **Eau Claire** for *Lazy Monk Brewery*, *The Brewing Projekt*, and *K Point Brewing* or even *Durand Brewing* farther south. Trail pass required.

The **Chippewa River** and **Old Abe State Trails** connect so that **Eau Claire, Chippewa Falls, Menomonie, Cornell** and **Durand** are all connected by a rails-to-trails bike system.

Stower Seven Lakes State Trail runs 14 miles from **Amery** (*Amery Ale Works*) to Dresser, a stone's throw from Interstate State Park on county roads. Heading east of **Amery** is **Cattail State Trail**, 18 miles to Almena! Trail pass required.

Zone 4

Bearskin State Trail (715-453-1263) starts south from (or ends north to?) **Minocqua**, home of *Minocqua Brewing Co.* Trail pass required.

See also **Mountain Bay Trail** in Zone 5. By the way, *Red Eye Brewing* in **Wausau** has a great number of cyclist fans who stop by after their rides each day. Brewer Kevin Eichelberger is also an avid pedaler.

Tomorrow River State Trail (715-346-1433, co.portage.wi.us/parks) connects *O'so Brewing Co.* in Plover/Stevens Point with *Central Waters Brewing Co.* in Amherst. See also the Central Wisconsin Craft Collective (cwcraftcollective.com) for a circle tour that adds *Kozy Yak Brewery & McZ's Brewpub, Stevens Point Brewery, Sunset Point Winery* and *Great Northern Distilling*.

Zone 5

Green Bay has a good biking network. **Fox River State Trail** (foxrivertrail.com) starts in downtown across Dousman Street Bridge from *Titletown Brewery* and *Copper State Brewing*. Ride south from here and get close to *Zambaldi Brewing* in Green Bay/Allouez. Or connect into **East River Trail** (also passes within a mile of *Zambaldi*) and cross the East River on a trail bridge to Baird Creek Trail, which crosses Henry St 500 ft north of *Stillmank Brewing*, and continues east to its end at Baird Creek Rd only 1.6 miles from *Noble Roots Brewing* and with wide paved off-street paths along University Ave.

Mountain Bay Trail (mountain-baytrail.org) connects **Wausau** in Zone 4 to **Green Bay** via **Shawano**. This means *Red Eye Brewing, Bull Falls Brewery* and *The Great Dane Pub and Brewery* are connected to *Titletown, Copper State, Hinterland, Badger State, Stillmank, Noble Roots* and *Legends* in **Green Bay**. And *Stubborn Brothers Brewing* in **Shawano** is right off the trail.

Wiouwash State Trail (dnr.wi.gov) passes right in front of *Bare Bones Brewing* in **Oshkosh**.

Zone 6

Osaugie Trail (800-942-5313) starts in **Superior**, home of *Thirsty Pagan* and *Earth Rider Brewery* and heads east. This connects to the **Tri-County Corridor Trail** (715-

372-5959) which passes through **Iron River** near *White Winter Winery* and connects to **Ashland** (61 miles), home of *South Shore Brewery*. This one is pretty rough though for a biker. Mountain bike? ATV?

Wild River State Trail (dnr.wi.gov, 715-635-4490) is a 104-mile crushed gravel rails-to-trails ride starting south of **Superior** (*Thirsty Pagan* and *Earth Rider Brewery*) through **Spooner** (*Round Man Brewing*) to **Rice Lake** (possible future *Agonis Brewing*).

For up-to-date information and other state trails go to wiparks.net and click on Find a trail.

ROAD TRIPS FOR BEER

Maybe you've gotten signatures at all the Wisconsin breweries in this book. Or perhaps you have a cousin in Minnesota or a friend in Michigan. If you are fan of craft beer, you've got a lot more ground to cover in two more Midwestern states. As in Wisconsin, Kevin Revolinski takes you on a pils-grimage to find the locally made brews and the people who make them.

Michigan's Best Beer Guide and *Minnesota's Best Beer Guide* are available in bookstores and online, or check out Revolinski's website TheMadTraveler.com

Got a bookstore or a gift shop and think you might want to stock the latest beer guides? Contact Thunder Bay Press in West Branch, Michigan. thunderbaypressmichigan.com

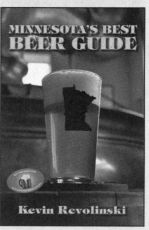

Homebrewers Associations

A.L.E. Club, Appleton Libation Enthusiasts
General club meetings are the third Thursday of
even-numbered months at Stone Cellar Brewpub
1004 South Olde Oneida Street • Appleton
www.thealeclub.org

Beer Barons of Milwaukee
Meets fourth Wednesday 7:30PM, $5.00/meeting fee
10448 W. Forest Home • Hales Corners
www.beerbarons.org

Belle City Homebrewers & Vintners
www.bellecitybrew.org

Bull Falls Home Brewers of Central WI
Meets second Thursday of the month
www.bullfalls-homebrewers.org

Central Wisconsin Draught Board
Meets the second Tuesday each month.
facebook.com/CWDraughtBoard

Chippewa Valley Better Beer Brewers
www.cvbetterbrewers.org

Green Bay Rackers
www.rackers.org

Kenosha Bidal Society
kenoshabidal.com

**LUSH, Inc., Lazy Unmotivated Society of
Homebrewers (Northwoods)**
Meets second Thursday of each month
Eagle River / Minocqua area
northwoodslushinc@gmail.com

Madison Homebrewers & Tasters Guild
Meets two Wednesdays a month.
www.mhtg.org

Manty Malters
Meets the first Thursday of every month.
www.mantymalters.org

**MASH, Marshfield Area Society of
Homebrewers**
Meets the first Thursday of the month
www.mash54449.org
marshfieldhomebrewers@gmail.com

Menomonie Homebrewers Club
Meets the first Monday of the month
www.mhbrewers.com | info@mhbrewers.com

Milwaukee Beer Society
Beer appreciation club
milwaukeebeersociety.com

SOB's, Society of Oshkosh Brewers
Meets third Wednesday of the month.
www.realsob.org

UWP Homebrewing Club
University of Wisconsin Platteville
uwplatt.collegiatelink.net/organization/
homebrewingclub

Homebrew Shops

Brew & Grow
2246 Bluemound Rd Ste B | Waukesha
262-717-0666 | brewandgrow.com
1525 Williamson St | Madison
608-226-8910 | brewandgrow.com

Farmhouse Brewing Supply
3000 Milton Ave Suite 109 | Janesville
608-305-HOPS | farmhousebrewingsupply.com

The Frugal Homebrewer
238 W. Broadway | Waukesha
262-544-0894 | www.frugalhomebrewer.com

Grape Grain and Bean
816 S 8th Street | Manitowoc
920-682-8828 | www.grapegrainandbean.com

Hop to It
234 Wisconsin Avenue | Racine
262-633-8239 | www.dpwigley.com

House of Homebrew
415 Dousman Street | Green Bay
920-435-1007 | www.houseofhomebrew.com

Point Brew Supply
1816 Post Road | Plover
715-342-9535 | www.pointbrewsupply.com

Purple Foot
3167 S. 92nd Street | Milwaukee
414-654-2211 | www.purplefootusa.com

Smokin' Brew
9 S Wisconsin Street | Elkhorn
262-729-3001 | shop.smokinbrew.com

Wine & Hop Shop
1931 Monroe Street | Madison
608-257-0099 | www.wineandhop.com

GLOSSARY OF BEERS

Ale — Short answer: beer from top-fermenting yeast, fermented at warmer temperatures. Long answer: see Ales vs. Lagers in the History of Beer Section.

Altbier means "old" beer—as in a traditional recipe, not a brew that's gone bad. It's a bitter, copper-colored ale.

Amber is that funny rock-like stuff that prehistoric bugs got trapped in and now makes great hippie jewelry or that pretty girl you were sweet on in middle school. But here I think they're just talking about the color of a type of American ale that uses American hops for a bitter, malty and hoppy flavor.

American IPA is generally a term used for an IPA recipe made with American ingredients, especially the hops.

APA (American Pale Ale) is a pale ale using American hops. The hops flavor, aroma and bitterness are pronounced.

Barley wine is like precious gold wherever it's brewed. This ale jumps off the shelves or out of the tap. It is strong, sweet, a bit aged, and those who know are waiting to pounce on it.

Berliner weisse is a wheat ale made a bit tart or sour with lactic acid bacteria.

Bitter is part of the family of pale ales, cousin perhaps to the IPA. Like folks in a small Wisconsin town, all beer is related in some way, I guess. This brew has a wider range of strength, flavor and color than the IPA. See "ESB." You'll be back.

Blonde or Golden Ale is a lighter form of pale ale usually made with pilsner malt. It's a popular Belgian style and gentlemen prefer them.

Bock is a strong lager darkened a bit and brewed in the winter to be drunk in spring. Monks drank it during the Lenten fasting period because it had substance to it, you know, like liquid bread? The name comes from the medieval German village of Einbeck. So, no, it does not mean Bottom of the Keg or Beer of Copious Kraeusening. (*What IS kraeusening anyway?*) Bock means goat in German. Thus the goats on so many of the labels and the popularity of headbutting at fraternity bock parties. Brewmaster Jamie in the Dells calls it the "chili of beers."

Brackett (also called braggot) is the first form of ale and a sort of beer and mead hybrid. It was first brewed with honey and hops and later with honey and malt—with or without hops added.

Brettanomyces or "Brett" does not refer to the Green Bay Packers' Hall of Fame quarterback, but rather the genus name of a group of yeasts used to make sour beers such as lambics, wild fermented Flanders red ales, and *oud bruins*.

Cask ale or cask-conditioned ale: see **Real Ale**

Cream Ale is a smooth and clean, light-colored American ale similar to a pale lager. Cleaner flavor than your usual ale.

Doppelbock see "Bock" and read it twice. Seriously, just a bock with a stronger punch to it though not necessarily double.

Double IPA (Red, Pilsner, etc.) or **Imperial** beers are higher in alcohol content, although the word-mincers will point out that Imperial only applies to stouts based on their relationship with the Russian empire.

Dunkelweiss is a dark wheat beer, a German style. "Dunkel" means dark.

Eisbock if you say it outloud is probably easier to guess. No, it's not beer on the rocks. Take a bock, freeze it, take the ice out, and you have a higher alcohol content bock. Weizen eisbock then is a wheat version of this beer and it's delicious. Technically this is distillation by freezing.

ESB (Extra Special Bitter) see "Bitter" and add some more alcohol. Isn't that what makes beer special?

Foeder (pronounced FOOD-er) is a large wooden vat, commonly used by winemakers aging wine, but now often also employed by brewers who are aging sour beers.

Gose is an unfiltered 50% malted wheat beer style still found in Leipzig, Germany. Some lactic acid and the addition of ground coriander seeds and salt make an unusual sour beer.

Gueze is a blended beer made by combining a young 1-year-old lambic with an older one of 2 or 3 years.

Gruit or **Grut** is a mixture of herbs that beer makers used to use before hops came into favor. It added bitterness and in some cases preservative qualities, and the unique blends offered a variety of flavors for beers. Some brewers might do unhopped beers and use things like juniper berries, chamomile, heather or other things that sound like lawn clippings.

Hazy IPA is a recently accepted style, though some detracting brewers/drinkers still aren't too keen on it. Often referred to as New England IPA, it is unfiltered and "juicy," with fruity/citrusy notes and low bitterness. Hops go in late in the boil and early during fermentation to get those flavors.

Hefeweizen (German Wheat Beer) is *supposed* to be cloudy—it's unfiltered. Don't make that face, drink it. That's where all the vitamins are and stuff. See also "Weisse" et al. It's recommended not to drink beers directly from the bottle, but to use a proper glass, but especially in this case. Germans even write that on the bottle sometimes in case you forget.

Imperial Stout see "Stout." The Brits originally made this for the Russian imperial court. It had to cross water as cold as International Falls so the high alcohol content kept it from freezing. Expect roasted, chocolate, and burnt malt flavors and a strong left hook. Also called **Russian Imperial Stout**.

IPA (India Pale Ale) is what the Brits used to send to India. The long journey spoiled porters and stouts, and so this recipe calls for lots of hops. Did you read that part yet? About hops as a preservative? You can't just skip parts of the book. I'll catch you. And there will be a quiz. Don't say I didn't warn you.

Irish-style Stout is a dry version of stout, typically served under nitro for the creamy special effect. However, it's very dark and thus too difficult to dye green on St. Patty's Day. (Just don't.)

Kettle Sour is a beer made sour in the brew kettle, not later in a barrel.

Kölsch is just an excuse to use those little dot things—"What is an umlaut?" for those of you looking to score on *Jeopardy*—and a difficult-to-pronounce-correctly-and-still-retain-your-dignity name for a light, subtley fruity, warm- and top-fermented beer that originated in Köln, or Cologne... the city in Germany; please don't drink your aftershave no matter how nice it smells. Traditionally served in 200ml "stange" glasses and ferried about in a *Kranz* (wreath) by servers.

Lager — Short answer: beer with bottom-fermenting yeast, fermented colder than ale. Long answer: see Ales vs. Lagers in the History of Beer Section.

Lambic — Let's just call this the Wild One. It's a Belgian ale with a bit of unmalted wheat and it uses naturally occurring yeast, the kind that's just floating around out there. The brew is tart and may have a fruit element added such as raspberries or cherries.

Low alcohol — See "Near Bear."

Maibock is not your bock and if you touch my bock, there's gonna be trouble. This is the lightest of the bocks and is traditionally brewed to be drunk in May, but we're not always hung up on tradition and it is often around whenever you want it.

Märzen takes its name from March, the month in which this lager is typically brewed so it can age in time for Oktoberfest when it magically becomes Oktoberfest beer.

Mead is honey fermented in water. It ain't beer but it's good. And there's plenty of honey in Wisconsin to make it. The word "honeymoon" comes from a tradition of gifting a newlywed couple a month's worth of mead to get things off to a smooth start. From this you can guess why we say "the honeymoon's over" with such lament.

Meerts (pronounced 'mertz') is a low-alcohol sour beer made from the second runnings of a lambic and served after only a few months in the barrels. *Funk Factory Geuzeria* in Madison may be the only place you find it!

Milkshake IPA is another recent trend, a thick mouth-feel beer typically with lactose (milk sugar) in a hazy IPA. Often brewers will go one step further and flavor it with fruits or spices.

Near Beer — Let's just pretend we didn't hear this and move on, shall we?

New England IPA or NE IPA — See "Hazy IPA."

(Nut) Brown Ale uses brown roasted malt, and a bit of hops brings some bitterness. Brown ales can be a bit malty sweet or a bit hoppy; the style varies even from London to Newcastle (malty, almost nutty) where the term originated. Originally it was simply a description of the color (of porters, stout), but it has evolved to be a style. In America they tend to be a bit hoppier and stronger. *Does not contain nuts and is not processed in a facility that uses nuts.*

Oktoberfest is Märzen after the 6–7 month wait as it ages a bit.

Pilsner is a style that comes from Plzen, a Czech version of Milwaukee. Dry and hoppy, this golden lager is hugely popular and most of the mass-produced versions fail to imitate the Czech originals. Best to try a handcrafted version at your local—or someone else's local—brewpub. Also a term I use to describe residents of Moquah, Wisconsin, which is also the Township of Pilsen where my grandparents lived. Interestingly, the first pilsner was brewed in Plzen in 1842 by Josef Groll, a brewer hired from Bavaria. The pale malt, the Saaz hops, bottom-fermenting yeast (lager), and the super soft water of Plzen created a very different brew from the (until then) top fermenting ales of Bohemia, and it quickly became a sensation.

Porter is not only a Wisconsin brewer (Tom at Lake Louie) but also a fine, dark ale made with roasted malt and bitter with hops. Baltic Porter (a bit stronger to be shipped across the Baltic Sea) and Robust Porter (may be stronger, more aggressive with the hops).

Rauchbier is beer made with smoked barley malt. It may be an acquired taste, but if you like bacon… Back in the day, when open fires were sometimes used to dry malt, most beers likely had some smokiness to them. Beginning in the 1600s, the use of kilns eliminated this effect. This intentional style is associated with Bamberg, Germany, where it is still done.

Real ale is another way of referring to **cask ale**. It is unfiltered and unpasteurized and completes its secondary fermentation in the cask it is served from, without the use of carbon dioxide or nitrogen pressure "pushing" it through a serving line. They are either hand-pulled (on a hand pump or "beer engine") or gravity fed.

Rye beer substitutes some malted rye for some of the malted barley. Remember in that "American Pie" song, the old men "drinking whiskey and rye?" Yeah, that's something else. This gives a distinct slight spiciness to the beer.

Sahti is an old Finnish style of beer, herbal in its ingredients, typically employing juniper berries but not always hops.

Saison is French for "season" (those people have a different word for everything it seems) and this beer was intended for farm workers at the end of summer. It's Belgian in origin and the yeast used ferments at a higher ale temperature. It's generally cloudy and often has something like orange zest or coriander in it. While it was originally a low-alcohol brew so the workers could keep working, many American revivals of the style are packing a bit of a punch.

Saké — This is more of a trivia note than anything. It's not wine or rice wine; it's actually a Japanese rice beer, technically, as it is a fermented grain.

Schwarzbier is the way they say "black beer" in Germany. This lager is black as midnight thanks to the dark roasted malt and has a full, chocolatey or coffee flavor much like a stout or porter.

Scotch Ale or Scottish-style Ale is generally maltier than other ales and sometimes more potent. The FDA insists it be labeled "Scottish-style" as it is not actually from Scotland if brewed here in Wisconsin. Fair enough.

Smash is a slang term for "single malt and single hop" referring to the brew recipe.

Sour Beer is not a specific style but a description of the flavor. Not all are created equally. Flanders Red, Oud Bruin, Gose, Geuze, Berliner Weisse, barrel-aged sour vs. kettle sour – any variety of beer that uses wild yeasts and bacteria to get a brew that makes you pucker a bit. Beer can become unintentionally and unpleasantly sour when bacteria infect it. This is different; it's intentional and when done traditionally, it can be kinda risky to other nearby brewing, so steps must be taken to keep unintended infections from happening.

Stachelbier is a German practice of taking a very hot poker and inserting it into a mug of beer in winter. It creates quite a show with steam and extra head while caramelizing it a touch and warming the beer only a wee bit. *Thumb Knuckle Brewing* and *Barley John's Brewing* like to offer this.

Stout is made with dark roasted barley and lots of hops, and it is a black ale most smooth. It can be bitter, dry, or even sweet when it's brewed with milk sugar (lactose). On occasion brewers add oatmeal for a smoother and sweeter ale and you have to start wondering if there is something to that saying, "Beer, it's not just for breakfast anymore." Imperial Stout is a strong variation on the recipe first done up by the English exporting to the Russians in the 1800s. The real fun of it is when it is on a nitrogen tap. Look that up!

Tripel is an unfiltered Belgian ale that has a very high alcohol content. The combination of hops and large amounts of malt and candy sugar give a bittersweet taste to this powerhouse. Many brewpubs will only allow you to drink one or two glasses to make sure you can still find the door when you leave.

Wheat Beer is beer made with wheat. You didn't really just look this up, did you? Dude.

Witbier, Weisse, Weizen, Wisenheimer — three of these words are simply different ways of saying white wheat beer that originated in Belgium. They are sometimes flavored with orange peel and coriander and are mildly to majorly sweet. The fourth word describes the kind of guy that would write that Wheat Beer definition.

MEASURE FOR MEASURE

A **growler** is a half-gallon (64-oz.) jug, refillable at your local brewpub. Many brewers sell them to you full for a few dollars more than the refill.

A **howler** or **grumbler** or **squealer** is a term coined variously for a container that is 32 oz. or half a growler.

A **Boston round** is the same as a howler but round without a handle.

A **Crowler** is a 32-oz can fillable on demand at the taproom like a growler.

A **bomber** is a 22-oz bottle.

One **US barrel** (1 bbl) is two kegs or 31 gallons or 248 pints, so you better start early.

A **keg**, sometimes casually and inaccurately referred to as a barrel, holds 15.5 gallons—this is the legendary half-barrel of the college party fame

A **Cornelius keg** is a pub keg, similar to one of those soda syrup canisters and holds 5 gallons.

A **US pint** = 16 oz = a proper US beer. (Also defined as 1/8 of a gallon)

A **can** = 12 oz or 16 oz typically, unless you are from Australia.

A **UK or Imperial pint** = 20 oz (lucky chumps) and there are laws protecting the drinker from improperly filled pints! Look for that little white line on the pint glass.

**Ah, but wait. Imperial pints are 20 *Imperial* ounces, which are different from the American ounces. The imperial fluid ounce is 28.4130625 ml while the US fluid ounce (as opposed to the dry ounce) is 29.5735295625 ml exactly, about 4% larger than the imperial unit. And if that isn't clear, be aware that the US *also* defines a fluid ounce as exactly 30 milliliters for the purposes of labeling nutrition information.

A **firkin** is a small cask or barrel, usually the equivalent of a ¼ barrel or about 9 gallons (34 liters)

A **buttload** is a real thing. In winespeak, a butt was a large cask with the volume of four standard wine barrels, just about 480 liters. In US gallons, that would be about 126. So just over 4 barrels of beer would truly be a buttload of beer.

Getting confused yet? I gave up at "pint" and drank one. And don't even get me started on the whole metric vs. Imperial gallon vs. US gallon vs. 10-gallon hat conundrum.

BIBLIOGRAPHY

Akin, Ron and Reiherzer, Lee. *The Breweries of Oshkosh – Their Rise and Fall*, 2012.

Apps, Jerold. *Breweries of Wisconsin*, 2nd Ed., University of Wisconsin Press, 2005.

Glover, Brian. *The Beer Companion: An Essential Guide to Classic Beers from Around the World*, Lorenz, 1999.

Harper, Timothy and Oliver, Garrett. *The Good Beer Book: Brewing and Drinking Quality Ales and Lagers*, Berkley Books, 1997.

Kroll, Wayne. *Wisconsin's Frontier Farm Breweries*, self-published.

Smith, Gregg. *Beer: A History of Suds and Civilization from Mesopotamia to Microbreweries*, Avon Books, 1995.

Swierczynski, Duane. *The Big Book o' Beer: Everything You Ever Wanted to Know About the Greatest Beverage on Earth*, Quirk Books, 2004.

Yenne, Bill. *The American Brewery*, MBI, 2003.

INDEX

Numbers

A

B

SIGNATURES

1840 Brewing Co. (Milwaukee)

_____ Date _____

2nd Street Brewery (Milwaukee)

_____ Date _____

3 Sheeps Brewing (Sheboygan)

_____ Date _____

10th Street Brewery (Milwaukee)

_____ Date _____

608 Brewing Co. (La Crosse)

_____ Date _____

841 Brewhouse (Whitewater)

_____ Date _____

Adventure Club Brewing (Bayfield)

_____ Date _____

Ahnapee Brewing Co. (Algoma)

_____ Date _____

Ale Asylum (Madison)

_____ Date _____

ALT Brew (Madison)

_____ Date _____

Amery Aleworks (Amery)

_____ Date _____

Angry Minnow Restaurant and Brewery (Hayward)

_____ Date _____

Appleton Beer Factory (Appleton)

_____ Date _____

Badger State Brewing Co. (Green Bay)

_____ Date _____

Bare Bones Brewing (Oshkosh)

_____ Date _____

Barley John's Brewing (New Richmond)

_____ Date _____

Bavarian Bierhaus (Glendale)

_____ Date _____

Big Head Brewing Co. (Wauwatosa)

_____ Date _____

Biloba Brewing Co. (Brookfield)

_____ Date _____

Black Husky Brewing Co. (Milwaukee)

_____ Date _____

Bloomer Brewing Co. (Bloomer)

_____ Date _____

Blue Heron Brewpub (Marshfield)

_____ Date _____

Bobtown Brewhouse (Roberts)

_____ Date _____

Boulder BrewPub (Verona)

_____ Date _____

Brewery Creek Brewpub (Mineral Point)

_____ Date _____

brewery nønic (Menomonie)

_____ Date _____

Brewfinity Brewing Co. (Oconomowoc)

_____ Date _____

The Brewing Projekt (Eau Claire)

_____ Date _____

Brews on the Rock (Washington Island)

_____ Date _____

Brewster Bros. Brewing Co. (Chippewa Falls)

_____ Date _____

Broken Bat Brewing Co. (Milwaukee)

_____ Date _____

Bull Falls Brewery (Wausau)

_____ Date _____

Bullquarian Brewhouse (Monroe)

_____ Date _____

Capital Brewery (Middleton)

_____ Date _____

Central Waters Brewing Co. (Amherst)

_____ Date _____

Cercis Brewing Co. (Columbus)

_____ Date _____

City Brewery (La Crosse)

_____ Date _____

City Lights Brewing Co. (Milwaukee)

_____ Date _____

City Service Brewing (Darlington)

_____ Date _____

Company Brewing (Milwaukee)

_____ Date _____

Component Brewing Co. (Milwaukee)

_____ Date _____

Copper State Brewing Co. (Green Bay)

_____ Date _____

Corner Pub (Reedsburg)

_____ Date _____

Courthouse Pub (Manitowoc)

_____ Date _____

D14 Brewery & Pub (Milwaukee)

_____ Date _____

Dave's BrewFarm (Wilson)

_____ Date _____

Dead Bird Brewing Co. (Milwaukee)

_____ Date _____

Delafield Brewhaus (Delafield)

_____ Date _____

Delta Beer (Madison)

_____ Date _____

Door County Brewing Co. (Baileys Harbor)

_____ Date _____

Driftless Brewing Co. (Soldiers Grove)

_____ Date _____

Durand Brewing Co. (Durand)

_____ Date _____

Eagle Park Brewing Co. (Milwaukee)

_____ Date _____

Earth Rider Brewery (Superior)

_____ Date _____

East Troy Brewing Co. (East Troy)

_____ Date _____

Enlightened Brewing Co. (Milwaukee)

_____ Date _____

Esser's Cross Plains Brewery (Cross Plains)

_____ Date _____

Explorium Brew Pub (Milwaukee)

_____ Date _____

Fermentorium Barrel House (Wauwatosa)

_____ Date _____

Fermentorium Brewery & Tasting Room (Cedarburg)

_____ Date _____

FFATS Brewing Co. (Whitehall)

_____ Date _____

Fifth Ward Brewing Co. (Oshkosh)

_____ Date _____

Fox River Brewing Co. (Appleton)

_____ Date _____

Fox River Brewing Co. (Oshkosh)

_____ Date _____

Full MileBeer Co. & Kitchen (Sun Prarie)

_____ Date _____

Funk Factory Geuzeria (Madison)

_____ Date _____

Gathering Place Brewing Co. (Milwaukee)

_____ Date _____

Geneva Lake Brewing Co. (Lake Geneva)

_____ Date _____

Giant Jones Brewing Co. (Madison)

_____ Date _____

Good City Brewing Co. (Milwaukee)

_____ Date _____

Good City Brewing Taproom (Milwaukee)

_____ Date _____

Gray Brewing Co. (Janesville)

_____ Date _____

Great Dane Pub and Brewery (Fitchburg)

_____ Date _____

Great Dane Pub and Brewery (Hilldale)

_____ Date _____

Great Dane Pub and Brewery (Madison)

_____ Date _____

Great Dane Pub and Restaurant (Wausau)

_____ Date _____

Grumpy Troll Brew Pub (Mount Horeb)

_____ Date _____

Hacienda Beer Co. (Baileys Harbor)

_____ Date _____

HighHolder Brewing Co. (Oshkosh)

_____ Date _____

Hillsboro Brewing Co. (Hillsboro)

_____ Date _____

Hinterland Brewery (Green Bay)

_____ Date _____

Hop & Barrel Brewing (Hudson)

_____ Date _____

The Hop Garden Tap Room (Paoli)

_____ Date _____

Hop Haus Brewing Co. (Verona)

_____ Date _____

Hubbleton Brewing Co. (Waterloo)

_____ Date _____

Inventors Brewing Co. (Port Washington)

_____ Date _____

Jacob Leinenkugel Brewing (Chippewa Falls)

_____ Date _____

K Point Brewing (Eau Claire)

_____ Date _____

Karben4 Brewing (Madison)

_____ Date _____

Knuth Brewing (Ripon)

_____ Date _____

Kozy Yak Brewery (Rosholt)

_____ Date _____

Lakefront Brewery (Milwaukee)

_____ Date _____

Lake Louie Brewing (Arena)

_____ Date _____

Lazy Monk Brewery (Eau Claire)

_____ Date _____

Legends Brewhouse & Eatery (De Pere)

_____ Date _____

Legends Brewhouse & Eatery (Green Bay)

_____ Date _____

Lion's Tail Brewing Co. (Neenah)

_____ Date _____

Littleport Brewing Co. (Racine)

_____ Date _____

Lone Girl Brewpub (Waunakee)

_____ Date _____

Lucette Brewing Co. (Menomonie)

_____ Date _____

Lucky's 1313 Brewing (Madison)

_____ Date _____

McFleshman's Brewing Co. (Appleton)

_____ Date _____

McZ's Brew Pub (Rosholt)

_____ Date _____

Mecan River Brewing Co. (Coloma)

_____ Date _____

Melms Brewing Co. (Hartland)

_____ Date _____

Mel's Micro Brewing and Pubbery (Richland Center)

_____ Date _____

Miller Brewing Co. (Milwaukee)

_____ Date _____

Milwaukee Ale House (Milwaukee)

_____ Date _____

Milwaukee Brewing Co. / 2nd Street Brewery (Milwaukee)

_____ Date _____

Milwaukee Brewing Co. / 9th Street Brewery (Milwaukee)

_____ Date _____

Minhas Craft Brewery (Monroe)

_____ Date _____

Minocqua Brewing Company (Minocqua)
_____ Date _____

MobCraft Beer (Milwaukee)
_____ Date _____

Modicum Brewing Co. (Altoona)
_____ Date _____

MoonRidge Brew Pub (Cornell)
_____ Date _____

New Barons Brewing Cooperative (Milwaukee)
_____ Date _____

New Glarus Brewing Co. (New Glarus)
_____ Date _____

Next Door Brewing (Madison)
_____ Date _____

Noble Roots Brewing Co. (Green Bay)
_____ Date _____

Northwoods Brewpub and Grill (Osseo)
_____ Date _____

Octopi Brewing Co. (Waunakee)
_____ Date _____

Oliphant Brewing (Somerset)
_____ Date _____

Omega Brewing Experience (Omro)
_____ Date _____

One Barrel Brewing (Madison)
_____ Date _____

O'so Brewing Company (Plover)
_____ Date _____

Pabst Milwaukee Brewing Co. (Milwaukee)
_____ Date _____

Parched Eagle Brewpub (Westport)
_____ Date _____

Pearl Street Brewery (La Crosse)

_____ Date _____

Pecatonica Brewing Co. (Gratiot)

_____ Date _____

PetSkull Brewing Co. (Manitowoc)

_____ Date _____

Pigeon River Brewing Co. (Marion)

_____ Date _____

Pitchfork Brewing (Hudson)

_____ Date _____

Plymouth Brewing Co. (Plymouth)

_____ Date _____

Port Huron Brewing Co. (Wisconsin Dells)

_____ Date _____

Potosi Brewing Company (Potosi)

_____ Date _____

Public Craft Brewing Co. (Kenosha)

_____ Date _____

Racine Brewing Co. (Racine)

_____ Date _____

Rail House Restaurant & Brewpub (Marinette)

_____ Date _____

Raised Grain Brewing Co. (Waukesha)

_____ Date _____

Rebellion Brewing Co. (Cedarburg)

_____ Date _____

Red Eye Brewing Company (Wausau)

_____ Date _____

Rhinelander Brewing Co. (Rhinelander)

_____ Date _____

Riverside Brewery & Restaurant (West Bend)

_____ Date _____

R'Noggin Brewery (Kenosha)

_____ Date _____

Rock Bottom Restaurant & Brewery (Milwaukee)

_____ Date _____

Rock County Brewing Co. (Janesville)

_____ Date _____

Rockhound Brewing Co. (Madison)

_____ Date _____

Rocky Reef Brewing Co. (Woodruff)

_____ Date _____

Round Man Brewing Co. (Spooner)

_____ Date _____

Rowland's Calumet Brewing (Chilton)

_____ Date _____

Rush River Brewing Co. (River Falls)

_____ Date _____

Rustic Road Brewing Co. (Kenosha)

_____ Date _____

Sabbatical Brewing Co. (Manitowoc)

_____ Date _____

Sand Creek Brewing Co. (Black River Falls)

_____ Date _____

Sawmill Brewing Co. (Merrill)

_____ Date _____

Second Salem Brewing Co. (Whitewater)

_____ Date _____

Sheboygan Beer Co. (Sheboygan)

_____ Date _____

Shipwrecked Brew Pub (Egg Harbor)

_____ Date _____

Skeleton Crew Brew (Onalaska)

_____ Date _____

Some Nerve Brewing Co. (Manitowish Waters)
_____ Date _____

South Shore Brewery (Ashland)
_____ Date _____

South Shore Brewery (Washburn)
_____ Date _____

Sprecher Brewing Co. (Glendale-Milwaukee)
_____ Date _____

St. Francis Brewery and Restaurant (St. Francis)
_____ Date _____

Starboard Brewing Co. (Sturgeon Bay)
_____ Date _____

Stevens Point Brewery (Stevens Point)
_____ Date _____

Stillmank Beer Co. (Green Bay)
_____ Date _____

Stock House Brewing Co. (Wauwatosa)
_____ Date _____

Stone Arch Brewpub (Appleton)
_____ Date _____

Stubborn Brothers Brewery (Shawano)
_____ Date _____

Sunshine Brewing Co. (Lake Mills)
_____ Date _____

Swinging Bridge Brewing Co. (River Falls)
_____ Date _____

SwitchGear Brewing Co. (Elkhart Lake)
_____ Date _____

Third Space Brewing Co. (Milwaukee)
_____ Date _____

Thirsty Pagan Brewing (Superior)
_____ Date _____

Thumb Knuckle Brewing Co. (Luxemburg)

_____ Date _____

Titletown Brewing Co. (Green Bay)

_____ Date _____

Trap Rock Brewing Co. (St. Croix Falls)

_____ Date _____

Tribute Brewing Co. (Eagle River)

_____ Date _____

Turtle Stack Brewery (La Crosse)

_____ Date _____

Two Beagles Brewpub (Onalaska)

_____ Date _____

Tyranena Brewing Co. (Lake Mills)

_____ Date _____

Union Corners Brewery (Madison)

_____ Date _____

Urban Harvest Brewing (Milwaukee)

_____ Date _____

Valkyrie Brewing Co. (Dallas)

_____ Date _____

Vennture Brew Co. (Milwaukee)

_____ Date _____

Viking Brew Pub (Stoughton)

_____ Date _____

Vintage Brewing Co. (Madison)

_____ Date _____

Vintage Brewing Co. (Sauk Prairie)

_____ Date _____

Water Street Brewery (Milwaukee)

_____ Date _____

Water Street Grafton Brewery (Grafton)

_____ Date _____

Water Street Lake Country Brewery (Delafield)

_____ Date _____

Water Street Oak Creek Brewery (Oak Creek)

_____ Date _____

Westallion Brewing Co. (West Allis)

_____ Date _____

White Winter Winery (Iron River)

_____ Date _____

Wisconsin Brewing Co. (Verona)

_____ Date _____

Wisconsin Dells Brewing Co. (Wisconsin Dells)

_____ Date _____

Working Draft Beer (Madison)

_____ Date _____

Zambaldi Beer (Green Bay-Allouez)

_____ Date _____

Zymurgy Brewing Co. (Menomonie)

_____ Date _____

About the Author

Kevin Revolinski is an amateur beer snob and born-again ale drinker with a writing habit. A Wisconsin native, he has written for a variety of publications including *The New York Times*, *Chicago Tribune*, *Wisconsin State Journal* and many postcards to his grandmother. He's appeared on The Today Show and Wisconsin Public Radio talking about beer. His other travel books include *Minnesota's Best Beer Guide*, *Michigan's Best Beer Guide*, *Paddling Wisconsin*, *Best in Tent Camping Wisconsin*, *Best Hikes Near Milwaukee*, *Backroads and Byways of Wisconsin*, *60 Hikes Within 60 Miles of Madison*, *Camping Michigan*, and *The Yogurt Man Cometh: Tales of an American Teacher in Turkey*. Check out his website and blog, The Mad Traveler at www.theMadTraveler.com and revtravel.com. He also contributes to the beer travel site www.Pilsgrimage.com. Look for him at your local brewpub. (It's more likely he's at one of his own local brewpubs in Madison though.)

PHOTOGRAPH COURTESY OF TOM RISTAU

About the Photographer

Preamtip Satasuk is originally from Bangkok, Thailand. Her work has appeared in *Chicago Tribune* and various guidebooks. She maintains a bilingual food and travel blog at TipsFoodAndTravel.com.